8th Edition

P9-CNB-281

Keeping Your School Safe & Secure:
A Practical Guide

Topics Include:

- Student Searches
- Transportation
- Cell Phones
- Athletics

- Bullying
- Infectious Diseases
- Weapons
- Mental Health

- Drugs and Alcohol
- Allergies
- Crisis Management
- Intruders

Center for
Education & Employment Law

CEEL

Center for Education & Employment Law
P.O. Box 3008
Malvern, Pennsylvania 19355

> "This publication is designed to provide accurate and authoritative information in regard to
> the subject matter covered. It is sold with the understanding that the publisher is not engaged
> in rendering legal, accounting or other professional service. If legal advice or other expert
> assistance is required, the services of a competent professional person should be sought."—
> *from a Declaration of Principles jointly adopted by a Committee of the American Bar
> Association and a Committee of Publishers and Associations.*

ISBN 978-1-933043-85-2

Published 2014   by: Center for Education & Employment Law

Library of Congress Control Number: 2008937927

Cover Design by Patricia Jacoby

Other Titles Published By
Center for Education & Employment Law:

Deskbook Encyclopedia of American School Law
Higher Education Law in America
Legal Update for Teachers: The Complete Principal's Guide
Private School Law in America
Students with Disabilities and Special Education
Deskbook Encyclopedia of Public Employment Law
Deskbook Encyclopedia of Employment Law

TABLE OF CONTENTS

CHAPTER ONE
Access and Building Security

TABLE OF CONTENTS

CHAPTER TWO
Emergency Preparedness and Response

CHAPTER THREE
School Safety and Liability

TABLE OF CONTENTS

CHAPTER FOUR
Campus Law Enforcement

CHAPTER FIVE
Employment

CHAPTER SIX
Extracurricular Activities

CHAPTER SEVEN
Health Issues

CHAPTER EIGHT
Statutes and Regulations

CHAPTER NINE
Forms

TABLE OF CONTENTS

TABLE OF CONTENTS

TABLE OF CONTENTS

INTRODUCTION

We are excited to introduce this updated edition of *Keeping Your School Safe & Secure: A Practical Guide*. Designed for the busy education professional, this easy-to-use resource presents a unique combination of materials designed to help administrative professionals formulate and implement a comprehensive plan to keep schools a safe place to learn. Case summaries, source materials, forms, checklists and practical guidance are organized into chapters by subject area for easy reference. A comprehensive index and case tables make it easy to quickly find the information you need.

Now more than ever, school security and related issues predominate the education landscape. Rely on *Keeping Your School Safe & Secure: A Practical Guide* with confidence as a valuable tool to avoid legal liability and protect the health and safety of your students.

ABOUT THE EDITORS

Curt J. Brown is the editorial director of the Center for Education & Employment Law. Prior to assuming his present position, he gained extensive experience in business-to-business publishing, including management of well-known publications such as *What's Working in Human Resources, What's New in Benefits & Compensation, Keep Up to Date with Payroll, Supervisors Legal Update,* and *Facility Manager's Alert.* Mr. Brown graduated from Villanova School of Law and graduated magna cum laude from Bloomsburg University with a B.S. in Business Administration. He is admitted to the Pennsylvania bar.

James A. Roth is the editor of *Legal Notes for Education* and *Special Education Law Update.* He is a co-author of *Students with Disabilities and Special Education Law* and an adjunct program assistant professor at St. Mary's University in Minnesota. Mr. Roth is a graduate of the University of Minnesota and William Mitchell College of Law. He is admitted to the Minnesota bar.

Thomas D'Agostino is a managing editor at the Center for Education & Employment Law and is the editor of *Higher Education Legal Alert.* He graduated from the Duquesne University School of Law and received his undergraduate degree from Ramapo College of New Jersey. He is a past member of the American Bar Association's Section of Individual Rights and Responsibilities as well as the Pennsylvania Bar Association's Legal Services to Persons with Disabilities Committee. Mr. D'Agostino is admitted to the Pennsylvania bar.

Elizabeth A. Wheeler is editor of the monthly newsletter *Private Education Law Report* and the *Private School Law in America* deskbook. She's also a contributing editor for the newsletters *Higher Education Legal Alert* and *School Safety and Security Alert.* A graduate of Macalester College and Capital University Law School, she's a member of the Massachusetts bar. Before joining the Center for Education and Employment Law, she was a legal editor for a South Boston publisher, where she edited employment law and education law newsletters.

Carol Warner is the editor of *EducationTechNews.com* and two monthly newsletters: *School Safety & Security Alert* and *Legal Update for Teachers.* She is also a contributing editor for *HigherEdMorning.com* and *Higher Education Legal Alert.* Before joining the Center for Education & Employment Law, she was an editor for two employment law newsletters: *What's Working in Human Resources* and *What's New in Benefits & Compensation.* Ms. Warner is a graduate of The New York Institute of Technology and holds a Bachelor of Arts in English with an emphasis in professional writing.

HOW TO USE YOUR GUIDE BOOK

We have designed *Keeping Your School Safe & Secure: A Practical Guide* in an accessible format for both attorneys and non-attorneys to use as a research and reference tool toward prevention of legal problems.

Research Tool

As a research tool, our guide book allows you to conduct your research on two different levels – by topics or cases.

Topic Research

♦ If you have a general interest in a particular **topic** area, our **table of contents** provides descriptive chapter headings containing detailed subheadings from each chapter.

➢ For your convenience, we also include the chapter table of contents at the beginning of each chapter.

Example:
For information on MRSA infection, the table of contents indicates that a discussion of this topic begins in Chapter Seven on page 320:

HOW TO USE YOUR GUIDE BOOK

♦ If you have a specific interest in a particular **issue**, our comprehensive **index** collects all of the relevant page references to particular issues.

Example:

For information on entranceway security, the index provides references to all of the text dealing with building security instead of only the text dealing with entranceways:

Building security, 2-40
    Coordinating with first responders, 17-18
    Doors, 9-10
➤ Entranceways, 11-14
        Biometrics, 14
        Card readers, 13
        Closed-circuit television (CCTV), 12
        Metal detectors, 11-12
        PIN codes, 14
        Security personnel/greeters, 13
    Eye-scanning systems, 14
    Fingerprinting, 14-15
    Legal decisions, 20-40

Case Research

♦ If you know the **name** of a particular case, our **table of cases** will allow you to quickly reference the location of the case.

Example:

If someone mentioned a case named *Daniels v. City of New York,* looking in the table of cases, which has been arranged alphabetically, the case would be located under the "D" section.

D

D.C. v. Harvard-Westlake School, 127
D.C. v. R.R., 128
Dailey v. Los Angeles Unified School Dist., 104
Daniel v. Hancock County School Dist., 260
➤ Daniels v. City of New York, 21, 61
Danso v. Univ. of Connecticut, 124

✓ Each of the cases summarized in the guide book also contains the case citation, which will allow you to access the full text of the case if you would like to learn more about it. *See How to Read a Case Citation, p. 525.*

♦ If your interest lies in cases from a **particular state**, our **table of cases by state** will identify the cases from your state and direct you to their page numbers.

Example:
    If cases from California are of interest, the table of cases by state, arranged alphabetically, lists all of the case summaries contained in the guide book from California.

➡ **CALIFORNIA**

A.J. v. Victor Elementary School Dist., 120, 275
American Nurses Ass'n v. Torlakson, 301
Avila v. Citrus Community College Dist., 251
Broney v. California Comm'n on Teacher Credentialing, 281
C.A. v. William S. Hart Union High School Dist., 104
C.B. v. City of Sonora, 177
Castaneda v. Inglewood Unified School Dist., 205

✓ Remember, the judicial system has two court systems – state and federal court – which generally function independently from each other. *See The Judicial System, p. 521.* We have included the federal court cases in the table of cases by state according to the state in which the court resides. However, federal court decisions often impact other federal courts within that particular circuit. Therefore, it may be helpful to review cases from all of the states contained in a particular circuit.

    We hope you benefit from the use of *Keeping Your School Safe & Secure: A Practical Guide.* If you have any questions about how to use the guide book, please contact Thomas D'Agostino at tdagostino@pbp.com.

TABLE OF CASES

TABLE OF CASES

TABLE OF CASES

TABLE OF CASES

TABLE OF CASES

TABLE OF CASES BY STATE

TABLE OF CASES BY STATE

TABLE OF CASES BY STATE

TABLE OF CASES BY STATE

CHAPTER ONE

Access and Building Security

I. INTRODUCTION

An important key to maintaining school safety and security is controlling access to school facilities. A variety of tools are available to help schools ensure that access to school facilities is gained only by authorized personnel. A one-size-fits-all approach to controlling school access is inappropriate. Although some issues relating to school access are common to most schools, an individualized assessment must be undertaken to determine which specific security steps are best-suited for your particular facility.

Several factors should be taken into consideration when determining how best to ensure safe access to school facilities. These include:

- the grades that the school serves
- the layout of the school campus
- the enrollment level
- the location of the school (e.g., urban vs. suburban or rural), and
- the crime level in the neighborhood where the school is located.

II. ENVIRONMENTAL DESIGN

It is important to note the value of incorporating environmental design elements that ensure school safety and security to the maximum extent possible. While this is a benefit that can be most fully utilized by incorporating environmental design principles into new facilities at the design stage, some of these design elements can also be incorporated into existing school campuses. In addition, expansion and reconstruction plans create a valuable opportunity to increase school safety by incorporating environmental design elements that take school safety into account. In all of these cases, the likelihood of crime can be reduced via an effective use of the school's physical environment.

A. Crime Prevention Through Environmental Design

An approach to increasing safety called Crime Prevention Through Environmental Design (CPTED) recognizes the important role that the design of the built environment can play in reducing the risk of criminal activity. CPTED is not intended to replace traditional crime prevention approaches. Instead, it should be thought of as a complementary tool that can be incorporated into an overall comprehensive plan to make schools safer.

The CPTED approach incorporates several concepts that are applied to increase the security level of the studied facility. The approach has been used to provide an increased measure of security at facilities such as government buildings, commercial complexes and parks. Although not originally developed specifically with schools in mind, the approach is particularly useful in school settings, partly because application of its principles can substantially increase the safety of school premises while preserving a welcoming environment and avoiding a prison-like atmosphere. CPTED is also relatively cost-effective.

CPTED has a strong record of success. The Broward County, Florida school district experienced a dramatic reduction in crime after implementing CPTED, and some state legislatures have mandated its use in schools.

The CPTED approach involves several discrete components, including natural surveillance, natural access control, and territoriality.

1. Natural Surveillance

The natural surveillance component of CPTED seeks to maximize the safety advantage that is gained when the environment's physical features keep obstacles to surveillance to a minimum and enable authorities to observe the facility's entire physical environment without undue interference and without a need to resort to advanced technological measures. Essentially, this component seeks to maximize the ability of authorities to observe the environment, in general, and especially higher-risk areas, such as parking lots and building entrances. Several potential barriers impede the ability to maximize surveillance capabilities, such as solid walls, overgrown shrubbery, and inadequate lighting.

2. Natural Access Control

Natural access control, a second important component of CPTED, refers to the benefit obtained by taking steps to design the facility's physical environment in a way that deters criminal activity by creating a perception of risk to potential offenders. This is accomplished, for example, by constructing the physical environment so that visitors are guided through the physical space of the facility by means of clear routing, signage, and other steering features.

3. Territorial Reinforcement

A third component of CPTED is territorial reinforcement. This component seeks to create an environment that encourages authorized users of the space to develop a sense of territoriality or ownership over the space. When users develop this sense of territoriality, potential offenders are discouraged from engaging in criminal activity. An example of a design feature that encourages territoriality is clear border definition.

Professional resources are available to aid schools in conducting a CPTED analysis. School personnel also can perform a CPTED analysis by undertaking a comprehensive study of criminal behavior and other misconduct that occurs on campus. Such a study can identify and categorize the types of problems that take place and ascertain whether patterns exist with respect to time and/or location. Ideally a comprehensive study will yield information that can be used to change the physical environment in a way that reduces the incidence of criminal behavior or other improper conduct.

4. Case Study: Effective Use of CPTED

The Broward County, Florida school district was one of the first in the country to effectively utilize CPTED concepts in the school environment. After completing an evaluation, the district applied a number of CPTED strategies. Based on the assessment, the district considered changes relating to vehicle access and border definition. It also considered relocating parking lots and replacing restroom entrance doors with open mazes. In addition, it evaluated strategies relating to the maintenance of landscaping and the effective use of lighting and color in and around school facilities. The district's use of CPTED techniques resulted in a significant reduction in school-related crime.

B. Specific Environmental Elements

The following are examples of ways in which schools can help prevent crime in the school environment by controlling specific environmental elements in ways that increase the security of entrance areas.

1. Entrances

A basic key to maintaining a safe school environment is controlling access to the school campus. The school campus should be designed (or redesigned) so that students and visitors must pass through a particular designated entrance or entrances. The school's main entrance should be the school entrance that is closest to the school's main parking lot. It should be clearly marked and in the front of the school near the administrative areas of the building. By locating the main entrance in this manner, visitors will be steered toward it and not to another less prominent entry point. In addition, main entry points should be located in areas of high visibility so people entering and exiting can be observed easily by school personnel. Glazing of windows and doors enhances the ability to conduct effective surveillance. Windows should be kept free of announcements and other postings that impede the ability to conduct effective surveillance of the entrance area. It is preferable for both the entrance area and the parking area to be observable from the school's administrative area. The entrance should be wide enough to minimize pedestrian traffic congestion during peak periods. For many schools, an opening of at least 20 feet will be required to enable smooth ingress and egress.

Minimizing the number of entry points is a critical key to maintaining building security. Providing just one entry point is not a feasible option for most schools and, in fact, can be counterproductive to the overall effort to maintain safety. Decisions relating to the number of entrance points that should be provided in addition to the main entrance must be made with reference to each school's particular characteristics, keeping in mind that it is desirable to maintain a number of entry points that allows for manageable ingress and egress without unnecessarily creating the added risk that each additional entrance point potentially represents. Secondary entrances are an area of particular concern, and they require special attention because they are often a problem area. Secondary entrances should be placed in visible locations and should be monitored. They should be subject to all the security controls that apply at the main entrance point.

☑ CHECKLIST – *Entrances*

☐ The main entrance is located close to the school's main parking lot.
☐ The main entrance is marked by clear and adequate signage.
☐ The main entrance and parking lot can be easily monitored
   by administrative personnel from inside the school building.
☐ Windows and doors near the main entrance include glazing.
☐ Windows are kept free of postings and other impediments
   to visibility.
☐ The entrance is wide enough to accommodate pedestrian traffic
   at peak times.
☐ The number of entrances is kept to a minimum.
☐ Signage steers visitors to a particular entrance.
☐ Secondary entrances are monitored.

2. Traffic Control/Parking

School parking areas require extra attention because they frequently are locations where vandalism and other crimes take place.

Access to the school and its parking areas should be controlled by limiting the number of entrance and exit points to campus. The number of access points to parking areas should be limited. This reduces the likelihood that the parking area will be perceived as a public space. Vandal-proof lighting in parking areas should be provided, and the use of gates to limit or prevent access to parking areas during low-use times should be considered.

Controlling the flow of both vehicular and pedestrian traffic is of critical importance. Vehicular and pedestrian traffic should be routed in a manner that separates the two and minimizes congestion while also enabling easy observation. Where feasible, traffic lanes of ingress and egress should be separated by a landscaped median. In addition, automobile traffic should be separated from bus traffic once entry to the school campus is gained. Bus parking should be configured so that buses can maneuver the lot without needing to back up to park or turn. It is preferable to avoid long and straight stretches of roadway on the campus. Avoiding long straight stretches helps to keep down the speed of vehicles and reduce the risk of injury to pedestrians. Where appropriate, traffic-control devices, such as speed bumps, can help reduce the probability of vehicles traveling at excessive speeds on the school campus.

Visitor parking should be designated as such via proper signage, and signage should further define authorized uses within the parking area. The ability of students to gain access to parking areas at times other than arrival time and dismissal time should be restricted. In addition, parking areas and vehicular routes should be observable from a point or points within the building's interior that include administrative areas and/or classrooms.

It is necessary to maintain proper access routes for emergency service personnel. Service and delivery routes should be separated from other traffic routes.

☑ CHECKLIST – *Traffic Control/Parking*

☐ Vehicular routes and parking areas can be observed from administrative areas and/or classrooms inside the school.

☐ Access to parking areas is restricted to a limited number of entrances.

☐ Automobile traffic is separated from bus traffic by barriers and/or routing.

☐ Pedestrian traffic is separated from motor vehicle traffic by barriers and/or routing.

☐ Undesignated spaces within parking areas are minimized.

☐ Traffic control devices are used to control speeds as needed.

☐ Long, straight stretches of roadway are minimized.

☐ The parking area includes signage that sets out the authorized use of the assigned space.

☐ The parking area has vandal-resistant lighting.

3. Signage and Sightlines

Signage serves the dual role of helping to control access and providing notice of prohibited behavior.

The campus should include clear signage that directs all visitors to the school's main office, where they can be screened to make sure they have a legitimate reason to be on the campus. Preferably, the main entrance should be visible from both the administration area and main point of vehicular access.

Maintaining open sightlines is another important key to campus security. Building placement, landscaping, the placement of signage and lighting should all take into account the need to maintain open sightlines. This is especially true in higher-risk areas of the school campus, such as parking lots, pickup/drop-off points, bus stops, hallways and stairwells. These higher-risk areas can be identified by analyzing the school's incident history.

Borders within the school's campus should be clearly defined.

☑ CHECKLIST – *Signage*

- ☐ There is a sign or marquee that identifies the school by name and is visible from a point beyond the school's physical borders.
- ☐ Signs include large lettering.
- ☐ Signs are well lit.
- ☐ Directional signage is used as needed to control traffic flow.
- ☐ Signage directs visitors to a main point of entry.
- ☐ Signage does not create a place to hide.
- ☐ Signage does not block lines of sight.
- ☐ Signage indicates restricted areas.
- ☐ Signage indicates bus-loading and drop-off zones.

4. Preventing Roof Access

A number of steps can be taken to reduce the likelihood of unauthorized access to the roof of a campus building. Access to rooftop areas should be available only from inside the building, preferably from a locked point. Placement of landscaping and trees should not enable access to the roof of any building.

Covered walkways should be designed in a manner that does not create opportunities for unauthorized access to a building's roof or other upper-level area. In addition, if the campus includes columns that potentially could be scaled to gain unauthorized access to a roof or upper-level area, the columns should be made from smooth building materials. Alternatively, a slippery finish or coating should be applied to the columns. Campus walls and other architectural features should be designed in a manner that does not allow for footholds or handholds to create an ability to gain unauthorized roof access. Niches in exterior walls should be avoided or eliminated, as these can create hiding places for unauthorized and dangerous materials.

5. Landscaping

As previously noted, landscaping should take into account the need to maintain open sightlines and to deny unauthorized access to rooftop areas. There are additional important points to keep in mind regarding the important role that landscaping can play in maintaining building security. It generally is advantageous to delineate space throughout the school campus both internally and externally. Delineating space as a defined area with a particular purpose helps to remove any perception that the space is available and open. It also makes it easier to assign security responsibilities for specific areas within a school's campus. One way to delineate space in the outside areas of a school campus is through the effective use of landscaping.

Landscaping can be used to define the outer boundaries of school property without the use of fences. Where fences are used, landscaping can be added to help create a more welcoming look while maintaining the security that the fences provide.

It is important to make sure landscaping is maintained so that it does not create hiding places. Shrubbery should be trimmed to a height of less than two feet. Tree canopies should be kept at a minimum height of eight feet, and hedges should be kept low enough to avoid serving as a hiding space. Controlling the growth of landscaping plants is also important to enabling clear lines of sight. Landscaping also can serve as a way to direct and control traffic, giving direction to vehicles and pedestrians, or limiting access to particular areas.

☑ CHECKLIST – *Landscaping*

- ☐ The school's landscape design does not create hiding places.
- ☐ The school's landscape design maintains open sightlines.
- ☐ The school's landscaping is well maintained and is not overgrown.
- ☐ The school's landscaping does not block lighting.
- ☐ Shrubbery is kept at a maximum height of less than two feet.
- ☐ Tree canopies are trimmed to a minimum height of eight feet.

III. TRAINING AND EDUCATION

School staff, students and parents all play an important role in preventing criminal activity that results from unauthorized access. Staff should be trained to intercept strangers and to report them to administration if they do not feel safe approaching a stranger on campus. Students should be instructed not to open doors or otherwise enable access by strangers. Students also should be instructed that they are not to assist other students in circumventing prescribed access procedures or routes. Parents should be provided with detailed information regarding the access control strategies the school utilizes. Parents need to understand the importance of following the school's rules and procedures governing access to school facilities.

It is helpful to take inventory of particular skills or expertise staff members possess that would be useful in the event of an emergency, such as experience in firefighting, or search and rescue. Such individuals can be added to the school's crisis team. For examples of forms that can be used to conduct a staff skills inventory and to create a crisis team member list, see Form I-1 and Form I-2 in Chapter Nine.

The Pennsylvania Department of Education has set out school safety recommendations that encourage school staff and students to be watchful for and to report suspicious activities, including the following:

- an unusual interest in entry points, security points and/or access controls
- an interest in gaining site plans, bus routes, attendance lists or other sensitive information
- an unusual degree of interest in personnel or vehicles approaching or leaving facilities or parking areas
- observation of security drills and procedures
- prolonged surveillance by people appearing to be vendors or others not usually seen in the area, and
- an unexplained presence of people in areas where they should not be.

IV. DOORS AND WINDOWS

A. Doors

Exterior doors should be designed to prevent unauthorized building access. The National Clearinghouse for Educational Facilities offers a checklist that lists a number of desirable attributes for exterior school doors, including the following:

- Doors should have a minimal degree of exposed hardware and should be installed using non-removable pins.
- Although exit-only doors do not need outside locks and handles, access should be possible in some manner in an emergency, such as by using a proximity card.
- Doors should be made from steel, aluminum alloy, or solid-core hardwood. If constructed of glass, doors should be fully framed and equipped with tempered glass that is breakage-resistant.
- To prevent doors from being pried open, door frames should be installed without excess flexibility.
- Exterior locks should be mounted flush to the door surface and should not rely on protruding lock devices such as a key-in-knob device.
- Exterior swinging doors should be equipped with a deadbolt lock that is at least one inch with a one-inch throw bolt and hardened steel insert, as well as a free-turning glass or steel-tempered guard, and double-cylinder locks if glass is located within 40 inches of the locking mechanism.
- Panic bar latches should be protected by pick plates.
- Panic push bars should be equipped with tamper-proof deadbolt

locks and a metal plate covering the gap between the doors.

- Strike plates should be securely fastened to door frames.
- If the door is key-controlled, it can be equipped with contacts so it can be tied into a central monitoring and control system.
- Double doors should be equipped with heavy-duty, multiple-point long flush bolts.
- If a door is particularly vulnerable to unauthorized use, consider installing door alarms or delayed opening devices, or using sensors or cameras to monitor it from a central location.

Exterior doors should permit a view of the outside via narrow windows, sidelights, fish-eye viewers or cameras, while preventing intruders from opening any door from the inside by breaking a window or sidelight.

If schools fail to implement the listed safety measures, injuries can occur. Here's an example: An Oregon middle school student was walking into school on a rainy day when she suddenly slipped. Her foot slammed into and shattered the glass door. The broken glass severed her Achilles tendon and left her permanently injured.

A common and potentially devastating problem is that of students who open locked doors for outsiders seeking entry to the interior of a school building. Oftentimes, students do so thinking they are being helpful and polite. School administrators need to make students understand how important it is to follow the strict rule against opening outside doors for people seeking entry. But how? Mark Baker, a school superintendent in Indiana, developed a plan to get the message across to students without scaring them. Baker ensured that students received frequent reminders about the rule, including during assemblies, in homeroom, by way of morning announcements, and from special advisers such as guidance counselors.

Even the most secure exterior doors won't be very effective if staffers or others on the inside open them for unauthorized visitors. To address this danger, the principal of a New Jersey school aimed a school surveillance camera at a locked door and had two outsiders – a college-age man and a young mother – knock on the door every 10 minutes for an hour. The camera caught images of students and faculty opening the door. The principal then used the video as "teachable moments," thus reducing the frequency with which the doors were opened to outsiders.

In response to the tragic mass shooting at Sandy Hook Elementary School in December of 2012, Connecticut Gov. Dannel Malloy created a 16-member public safety panel called the Sandy Hook Advisory Commission. In March of 2013, the commission issued an interim report that included a number of specific recommendations relating to school doors. The panel recommended that all K-12 classrooms be equipped with doors that can be locked from the inside by the teacher. It also recommended that all exterior doors in K-12 schools be equipped with hardware that can implement a full perimeter lockdown.

Some devices are designed to create an additional layer of security by making it more difficult for an intruder to breach a locked interior door. One such tool is called a "Bearacade." The Bearacade is a door control system that creates another layer of protection between students and would-be attackers. The device can be installed on doors without leaving the classroom. It slides on the bottom of the door and secures the classroom with a 1/4" stainless steel pin. Reflective markings on the outer portion of the device let authorities know that the device is in use, and its makers say it can withstand up to 4,000 pounds of external pressure.

A similar device is called "The Sleeve." The Sleeve is a 12-gauge steel case that fits around an interior door's closer arm, securing it from the inside. The closer arm is installed at the top, in the inside of classroom doors. The device covers the closer arm, preventing it from being opened from the outside. It can withstand more that 550 foot-pounds of pressure.

B. Windows

School administrators who want to provide staff and students with the advantages afforded by natural lighting should do so with an awareness of the security risks that windows can create, especially with respect to unauthorized entry.

Placement of windows plays a key role in minimizing unauthorized entry. Ideally windows are placed where they enable easy surveillance of school grounds, and especially higher-risk areas. For example, it is important to include windows that enable staff to monitor the school's main entrance. These windows should be kept free of announcements or other postings that create an obstacle to effective surveillance.

Windows that are operable (that is, ones that can be opened and closed) should have locks that can secure them in a closed position. Window film can be used to reinforce window glass and hold it in place should it be subjected to impact. Second-floor windows should be inaccessible from the outside. Ideally, each room should include at least one designated window that can be used to escape in the event of an emergency.

Basement windows are an area of particular concern and should be protected by window well covers or grills.

V. SPECIFIC MEASURES AT ENTRANCEWAYS

Specific security measures implemented at entrance areas will depend on factors such as budget and incidence history. These measures are not undertaken singly but are part of a comprehensive overall security plan.

A. Metal Detectors

The use of metal detectors at school entrance points is an extreme measure that can help prevent unauthorized access but is often subject to criticism. Walk-through metal detectors can be utilized in conjunction with handheld detectors, which can be used to investigate further when an individual triggers the walk-through detector. Use of a walk-through detector requires a significant investment of space. The detector itself will typically fill a space approximately three-feet wide and two-feet deep. Of course, the staging area is much larger. It must allow enough room to provide a comfortable environment for those waiting to pass through. Space also is needed for people who are being scanned to place items in a pass-through container and to turn around and pass through a second time, if needed. Care must be taken to locate the system in an area where it will not be subjected to potential sources of interference, such as nearby electromagnetic equipment or even plumbing in the walls.

Opponents say metal detector use is overly intrusive and creates an atmosphere of fear. Because metal detectors cannot distinguish between items that are prohibited (such as a knife) and items that are not (such as a set of keys), trained personnel are needed to operate and monitor them. This need, in combination with the cost of the detectors, the cost of hiring trained personnel to man them, and the fact that the layout of many schools makes it difficult to efficiently implement a metal-detection system, makes the use of metal detectors impractical for many schools. But metal detectors can also be an effective tool for reducing the likelihood of an unauthorized intrusion.

B. Closed-Circuit Television (CCTV)

Closed-circuit television technology can deter unauthorized access and help prevent crime throughout the school campus. A CCTV system intended to prevent access by intruders must be designed with reference to, and in coordination with, conditions that exist at the school with respect to external lighting and landscaping conditions. When cameras are placed at external locations, steps should be taken to minimize the likelihood of compromises to performance that can arise due to vandalism and exposure to outdoor elements. These systems typically monitor entrance points and parking areas, recording images that can be preserved electronically. Decisions relating to placement are made with reference to the level of risk associated with particular areas. Although full-time monitoring of CCTV cameras is not financially feasible for many schools, CCTV creates a record of any suspicious or illegal activity and can serve as an effective deterrent.

Case in point: In Wisconsin, a school's CCTV system recorded a student spraying a sticky substance on the steps of his high school as a senior prank. But the prank stopped being funny after two people were hurt after slipping and falling on the steps. The student was charged with two counts of recklessly endangering safety and was subjected to up to 20 years in jail and a $50,000 fine.

Many school administrators have seen the benefits of security cameras, and in a November 2010 release the National Center for Education Statistics and Bureau of Justice Statistics reported that the percentage of public schools using security cameras increased from 19% to 55% between the 1999-2000 school year and the 2007-08 school year. But despite the benefits, some students and parents express concerns that surveillance cameras may violate students' privacy rights. Calming concerns is a crucial step. One of the most effective ways to get parents and students on board is to develop a written policy outlining how and where security cameras will be used. Consider including the following information in the policy:

- list specific areas in school that will be monitored by the cameras
- list areas of the school where cameras will not be used, such as bathroom stalls and locker rooms, and
- say whether recordings from cameras will be produced as well as how long they will be kept and who has access to the recordings.

C. Security Personnel/Greeters

The use of security guards and/or greeters is a low-tech but effective tool for preventing unauthorized access to a school's campus. Located at entrance points, security guards can check identifications and respond immediately to suspicious activities. Greeters, who are often parent volunteers, can serve a similar function at entrance points. Grandparents, caregivers, and retired community members also serve as good sources of greeters. The greeter's role is not to directly intervene to stop criminal activity. Instead, greeters can determine whether a visitor has a legitimate reason to be on the school's grounds and can direct the visitor to a specific location where he can complete applicable sign-in procedures. Ideally, greeters should also receive training relating to the school's evacuation plans and emergency procedures. Students should not be used as greeters.

D. Card Readers

Access-control card systems can be used to help keep track of who is entering a school facility. When this technology is used, an identification card is encoded and recognized by a card reader. When the reader recognizes the card, access is gained, such as by lifting a mechanical arm to permit access to a parking area. This system carries the advantage of not requiring live personnel to operate. But there are drawbacks. Cards can be passed from one person to another person, and more than one individual or vehicle may be able to enter at the same time using just one authorized card.

1. Case Study: Use of 'Smart Cards'

Cards can also be used to regulate the movement of students inside the school. At New Jersey's Dumont High School, for example, students are given "smart cards" that allow administrators to control specific areas the students can access. For example, access to a gym can be limited to sports team members. The cards also permit administrators to track the use of bathrooms and computers. In addition, they can be used to pay for meals and to take books from the school's library.

E. Use of PIN Codes

Access can also be limited by requiring individuals to enter a personal identification number (PIN) code into a keypad in order to gain entrance to a designated area of the school. The use of PIN codes is more effective as a security measure when it is combined with the use of identification cards and card readers. Their use includes potential drawbacks, including a vulnerability to vandalism and the ability of authorized users to permit entry by unauthorized personnel.

F. Biometrics

Biometric devices permit access only upon identification of a particular physical trait associated uniquely with the authorized user. Examples include fingerprint readers, systems that verify identity by measuring the size and shape of the entering individual's hand, and technology that reads retinal impressions. This technology works in essence by collecting data relating to a specific individual's physical or behavioral characteristics and comparing it to data that already is on file. These devices carry the advantage of allowing authorized users to enter without having to remember any type of identification card. Because they rely on unique individual characteristics, they also carry the advantage of being more reliable than identifiers such as identification cards. Although biometric devices are more commonly used in applications that require the highest level of security, such as prisons and international border points, they may become more prevalent in school applications as technologies improve.

1. Case Study: Eye-Scanning System

A 2006 evaluative study of an eye-scanning system used in three New Jersey elementary schools highlighted the advantages and shortcomings of relying on this particular type of biometric technology as an access security measure in the school setting. Teachers and staff, and more than 700 school parents, had their eye images scanned into a computer system. To gain access to the school, they were required to have a camera on school grounds scan images of their irises. Five cameras were placed in exterior locations, and another six were placed in interior locations. The study found that the system provided an accurate identification and unlocked the door 78% of the time. Another 6% of attempted entries were properly denied because the individuals' eye scans were not in the computer. But 16% of the time, there were problems with scanning due to outdoor lighting conditions or a failure of the individual to line up his eyes properly with the camera. Despite the shortcomings, parents and staff indicated a perceived increase in school security.

2. Case Study: Fingerprinting

One of the nation's largest providers of child care and early educational services has installed biometric security systems at all of its corporate locations. Tutor Time, which has more than 100 locations nationwide and serves more than 28,000 students, began requiring fingerprint information and a PIN number from individuals seeking access to its facilities. The organization does not maintain a database of actual fingerprints. Instead, fingerprints are scanned into a system and converted into a series of numbers to produce something similar to a bar code. The "bar code" is then matched with a specific authorized user.

VI. LIGHTING

Proper illumination of entry areas and parking areas is a key to preventing unauthorized access to facilities. Because light fixtures are vulnerable to vandalism, they should be mounted as high as possible and covered with a material or housing that prevents breakage of lenses. Lighting fixtures can be controlled by clocks or by photocells that turn them off at dawn and on at dusk, although a manual override feature should be included. Lighting controls and switches must be protected, and the accessibility of electrical panels must be restricted.

Lights should be placed so as to minimize glare and the creation of shadows. Ideally, the lighting near entrance points should cast a pattern of light horizontally rather than vertically. Flush-mounted or recessed light fixtures should be used when possible. Because light-colored surfaces reflect light more efficiently than dark-colored surfaces, the presence of light-colored surfaces at entry points will increase the overall level of entry-point security. Maintaining a fixed schedule for maintenance of all outdoor lighting, including lighting at entrance points, is another important safety key. Decisions relating to the provision of lighting must be made with reference to the need of lighting to work effectively with other security measures that may be in place, such as the use of closed-circuit television.

☑ CHECKLIST – Lighting

☐ There is a regular schedule of maintenance for outside lights.

☐ Special attention is paid to adequacy of lighting at entrance points and other high-risk points of potential intrusion.

☐ Light lenses are protected by an impact-resistant material.

☐ Lighting fixtures do not provide handholds that can be used to climb into the building.

☐ Exterior lighting minimizes glare and shadows.

VII. CONTROLLING ACCESS BY VISITORS

A detailed procedure for controlling access to the school by authorized visitors is essential. Visitors should be steered to a main entrance by clear appropriate signage and by the layout of the school's exterior. Ideally, they will be intercepted by a greeter or security officer outside the school building before they can proceed to sign in at a main office, where school personnel can verify that they are at the school for a legitimate purpose. A similar measure was implemented in the Burke County School District in Waynesboro, Georgia. School visitors there are identified and cleared with the help of a camera outside of the building. Once inside, visitors complete the check-in process and receive an identification badge.

Schools should strongly consider implementing a requirement that visitors produce photo identification to verify identity. Visitor badges, which must be located outside the reach of visitors in a secure area, should be dated and issued once authorization for the visit is confirmed. The date, time, name, purpose, and intended destination of the visitor should be recorded in a log that each visitor should sign. School personnel should accompany visitors to the specific area of the visit. An important but sometimes overlooked feature of a visitor access policy is the incorporation of a "checkout" procedure whereby the visitor surrenders his pass or badge before leaving and the time of the visitor's departure is noted in the school's log. The log should be checked periodically during the day to determine whether any visitor appears to be remaining at the school for an inordinate amount of time.

A relatively extreme measure is to ban unannounced parent visits. The step was taken by Nathan Parker, the superintendent of the Summit Public Schools in New Jersey. Saying the move would improve safety, Parker told parents that unannounced school visits were being banned, regardless of the reason for the visit. For a sample authorization to release a student, see Form I-3 in Chapter Nine.

A. Case Study: Visitor Screening

More and more schools are adding another layer of protection to visitor screening policies by checking the identities of visitors against lists of sexual predators. Typically, the prospective visitor's driver's license is swiped through a computer that searches for a match against lists of offenders. Some systems also allow administrators to search for a match against lists of court orders that restrict parental custody of students. The Charter School for Applied Technologies, located in Tonawanda, New York, has utilized the tool. When a license does not show a match against the lists, the school issues a pass that includes the visitor's photograph. In the event of a match, school officials are notified immediately by phone and email.

Schools considering implementation of a background check system should be aware of a new associated threat: lawsuits challenging the legality of the systems under the Constitution.

A couple filed a suit against a Texas school district, claiming its background check system violated their rights to freely associate with their children. They also added a claim of unreasonable search and seizure.

The couple cited concerns about identity theft. They didn't like the idea of a private company collecting their personal information. One of the plaintiffs asked the school to check her status against a database maintained by the Justice Department. She said the school denied her request. The school district's director of police and public safety said before the suit was filed, there had been no complaints about the system.

☑ CHECKLIST – *Visitor Policy*

- ☐ School entrance points include signage that steers visitors to an office location.
- ☐ Sign-in areas are adequately staffed.
- ☐ Visitors must produce photo identification.
- ☐ Visitors are required to wear dated visitor passes or badges once authorization is confirmed.
- ☐ Visitors are escorted to their specific visit location.
- ☐ Visitor identification passes and badges are kept in a secure area.
- ☐ Visitors are required to sign a log indicating date, time, and intended destination.
- ☐ Visitor identification passes and badges are collected from visitors upon exit.
- ☐ Time of building exit is recorded in a log.

For steps key personnel should take in response to a school intruder, see Form II-12 in Chapter Nine. Information about specific steps to take in situations involving a weapon, and in potentially violent situations in general, can be found on Form I-4 and Form I-5 in Chapter Nine. For resources for victims and families in child abduction cases, go to the federal Office of Juvenile Justice and Delinquency Prevention's Web page, located at *http://www.ojjdp.gov*.

VIII. COORDINATING WITH FIRST RESPONDERS

Coordinating with first responders, such as police, fire and EMS personnel, is key to maintaining building security. In September 2007, the Attorney General of Pennsylvania introduced a tool schools can use to improve coordination between schools and first responders in the event that security at a school's entrance is breached and an emergency response is required. The Attorney General's Office created a School Safety Project CD-ROM. Based on a program that was developed by a local school district within the state, the CD-ROM helps schools create building safety plans that first responders can access on websites in an emergency. The CD-ROM helps districts create a secure website that includes information relating to many aspects of the facility, such as floor plans, photographs of school grounds, and a contact list of school administrators. The program on which the Attorney General's guide is based was developed by the Susquenita School District at a cost of approximately $1,000. First responders can access a password-protected website and view floor plans, school access roads, and photographs of classrooms and corridors. They can even access a real-time view of classrooms and offices, as the website includes images taken from school security cameras. This feature enables first responders to gain an inside view of the school building before entering.

IX. EFFECTIVE LOW-TECHNOLOGY ALTERNATIVES

Ideally, technological measures designed to protect entry points should be combined with less technical, but effective strategies and techniques to decrease the risk of criminal behavior. The U.S. Department of Justice's Office of Justice Programs has compiled the following list of low-technology but effective tools for deterring unauthorized entry to school facilities. Some of these measures are discussed elsewhere in this chapter. Utilizing the combination of them that best fits a particular school's needs can have the effect of increasing entry-point security.

- Post signs warning that unauthorized trespassers are subject to arrest.
- Post signs indicating that all vehicles on campus are subject to search.
- Provide a guard to check identifications at the main entrance to the school.
- Provide authorized vehicles with parking stickers so that unauthorized vehicles can be more easily identified and removed.
- Require student uniforms so that outsiders can be easily identified.
- Implement a school policy that bars hats, shirts that include messages related to alcohol, drugs, violence or gangs and exposed tattoos.
- Provide greeters at all open entrances.
- Provide a minimal number of entrances.
- Implement a policy under which students walking around the school campus during class time are challenged for a pass and are potentially subjected to search.
- Close off the main student parking lot during the day.
- Provide fencing that defines school property and discourages casual intruders.
- Confiscate the student ID of students who are suspended or expelled and make their photographs available to security staff.

Here's an instance that proves low-tech preventive measures are effective ways to keep students safe: A swift, coordinated response to warning signs enabled school officials and law enforcement authorities to thwart a shooting plot at a Pennsylvania high school. Local police had been informed that guns had been stolen from the home of a 15-year-old student. When school officials realized the student fit the profile of a potential shooter – a white teenage loner with few friends – they took action quickly.

School officials began to check students' backpacks and lockers. They also talked to students who knew the possible suspect. The superintendent notified school board members about what was going on, and the faculty met with its emergency response team.

The student's plan to go on a shooting rampage near the start of the new year unraveled when one of his friends told a teacher that he knew the location of the missing guns. The teacher immediately reported the information to school officials, and police recovered the guns. The student was arrested – before causing any harm.

X. CASE STUDY: INSTALLATION OF FACILITY MANAGEMENT SYSTEMS

The Harrison County School District Two, located near Colorado Springs, Colorado, serves more than 11,000 students and has 23 schools. In 2002, the district decided to upgrade its security systems at all of its schools, which included elementary schools, middle schools, high schools, alternative schools and charter schools. After soliciting several proposals, the district decided to install a security system that included closed-caption television, digital video recording, and card access control.

A vendor installed card readers on perimeter doors of schools, and all staff members were issued combination identification badges and access cards. All exterior building locks were re-keyed, and key distribution was limited. A digital video recording unit was installed at every district school. All front lobbies were outfitted with cameras. Surveillance was added for exteriors and some interior areas. Digital video recorders replaced VCRs, and some secondary buildings were outfitted with pan-tilt-zoom cameras.

A policy was implemented whereby all perimeter school doors, except the ones at front lobby entrances, remained locked at all times. Cameras began recording all activity at lobby entrances at all times, with monitors enabling school staff to observe those areas. Each school's security system was linked to a central location, where monitors at all the school facilities could be viewed at all times. The installed system also enabled administrators and security personnel to view video from a remote location by using a Web browser.

The system was installed in a way that enabled it to interface with the district's pre-existing burglar alarm system. This alarm system alerted the district's private security company whenever an alarm was triggered after hours.

In cases of a security breach, the system enables personnel to export video clips to a CD-ROM for delivery to local law enforcement authorities. The system includes an authentication process which verifies that stored video has not been altered.

A lockdown capability is also included. Staff can activate a button in the front office that locks perimeter doors and deactivates card readers. When a school is placed in lockdown, entry can occur only via the front door after staff has had the opportunity to view the person or persons seeking access, and chooses to permit access by manually unlocking the door.

The system also provides wireless personal panic control devices that are distributed to key personnel. These devices can be activated to signal a need for assistance from any location on the school grounds. When activated, the devices cause a white strobe light to turn on in the school's front office and send emails and pages to members of a designated response team.

The district reported great success with the new system. Soon after installation was completed, an individual who entered three different school buildings during a lunch hour, and stole cash and credit cards from teachers' purses, was caught on tape. The system also reduced fighting and vandalism.

XI. LEGAL DECISIONS

A. Intruders

◆ A seventeen-year-old non-student intruder sexually assaulted an elementary school student in a school bathroom. Approximately 14 years later, the student sued the school district and claimed a violation of her equal protection rights. **The court rejected her claim because she did not show that the district discriminated against her** and that the district treated her worse than students who were not in her protected group. *McGuire v. Northwest Area School Dist.*, No. 3:11-CV-1022, 2011 WL 5444084 (M.D. Pa. 11/8/11).

◆ An intruder entered an elementary school through its main entrance. A teacher asked him if he needed help, but he ignored her. She then went to the office to see if he had signed in. Two other teachers also saw the intruder in the hallway. When one of them questioned him, he said he needed to use a restroom. The teacher pointed out a restroom and told the intruder he needed to return to the office after using it. The teachers then lost sight of the intruder, who entered another restroom and sexually assaulted a five-year-old student. The student's mother filed a negligence claim against the school district. A trial court ruled against her on the basis that the intruder's assault of the student was not foreseeable. An appeals court reversed, finding that the question of whether the assault was foreseeable was a question of fact. **Reasonable minds could differ as to whether the district's response to the presence of the intruder constituted a breach**

of its duty of care and as to whether the assault was a foreseeable consequence of the district's failure to initially note the intruder's entry into the building and to monitor the situation more closely. *A.W. v. Lancaster County School Dist. 0001*, 784 N.W.2d 907 (Neb. 2010).

◆ A non-student entered the premises of a high school and requested a visitor's pass. When his request was denied, he became angry. School employees escorted the man from the school building, but they did not make sure he left the school's premises. The man then re-entered the school and stabbed a former schoolmate in a school hallway. The schoolmate and her parents sued the school, its principal and others, claiming the attack occurred as a result of their negligence. A trial court granted a defense motion for summary judgment, and an appeals court upheld the trial court's ruling. The appeals court explained that the defendants owed a duty of reasonable supervision to the student who was attacked. However, **they could not be liable for negligence because the attack was not reasonably foreseeable and preventable**. The attacker did not go to the school looking for the student he attacked, and he did not even know she was a student there. There was no evidence that the defendants had any warning indicating the attacker would come into the building and stab a student. The stabbing occurred suddenly and without warning, and the defendants' failure to prevent it was not negligent. *Boudreaux v. St. Tammany Parish School Board*, No. 2007 CA 0889, 2007 WL 4480703 (La. Ct. App. 12/21/07).

◆ While teaching a volleyball class, a teacher noticed two young men come into the gym. She recognized one as a student at the school, but she did not recognize the second man. When the teacher walked toward the men and blew her whistle, the unknown man struck her in the left temple. The man left but returned a short time later and punched her in the back of the head, causing her to lose consciousness. She suffered serious injuries. **The teacher sued the city, claiming it was negligent as a landlord of the high school when it allowed the attacker to gain unauthorized access.** She also claimed the city breached a special duty to protect her from harm and breached a contract with a teachers' union by failing to properly implement a school safety plan. The court granted the city's motion for summary judgment. Because the city was acting as a public government entity and not as a landlord when it undertook efforts to provide security at the school, it was immune to the teacher's claim of negligence. The court also rejected the teacher's claim that the city breached a special duty it owed to her when it allegedly failed to implement a school safety plan and protect its teachers. Neither the maintenance of a comprehensive security system nor school officials' representations that they "take security seriously" created a special duty. Finally, the court rejected the contract claim because the city could not be held liable to individual teachers for any alleged contract breach between it and the teacher's union. *Daniels v. City of New York*, No. 04-CV-7612 (CM), 2007 WL 2040581 (S.D.N.Y. 6/26/07).

◆   A deranged convicted felon entered a school building holding a picture of a young girl. The school principal confronted the intruder, who then left. The school subsequently instituted a new access control policy. An individual was stationed in the school's lobby to screen people entering the school, and people entering the school were instructed to sign in at the principal's office. The policy further required staff to monitor visitors through a floor-to-ceiling window in the principal's office. Approximately one year following the incident involving the intruder, a different intruder gained unauthorized access to the school. **The intruder walked between 100 and 150 feet into the school before stopping in a school hallway and attacking a 10-year-old student with a hammer. The attack caused serious injury.** The student's parents sued the school's principal, the county school superintendent, the board of education and others, alleging they were negligent in failing to develop a school safety plan as required by state law and allowing the attack to occur. A trial court granted the defendants' motion for summary judgment, and an appeals court affirmed the trial court's ruling. The school had prepared and put into place a school safety plan before the attack on the student took place. Because the school safety plan was in place before the attack occurred, the defendants were entitled to official immunity on the negligence claims raised against them. The ruling of the trial court was affirmed. *Leake v. Murphy*, 644 S.E.2d 328 (Ga. Ct. App. 2007).

◆   A father drove his 12-year-old son to a high school that the 12-year-old and his brother attended. The father waited outside while the boy entered the school to find his brother, who was participating in a school event. The 12-year-old was sexually assaulted in the school by a convicted sex felon who had gained unauthorized access. The incident took place on a Saturday, when school was not in session. The parent sued the school, its president and its principal, **claiming they were negligent in leaving the school doors unlocked and unattended during school-sponsored activities**. The court upheld a ruling against the parent, finding that he failed to show the defendants owed him a duty of care. There is generally no duty to protect others from the criminal acts of third parties. Although a duty may be found to exist when there is a special relationship between the defendant and the plaintiff, potentially including the relationship between a school and a student, a special relationship giving rise to a duty did not exist in this case. School was not in session, and the 12-year-old was not participating in any school-sponsored event at the time of the assault. In addition, the parent did not show the assault was foreseeable. *Roe v. Univ. of Detroit Jesuit High School and Academy*, No. 264269, 2006 WL 475285 (Mich. Ct. App. 2/28/06).

◆   A high school student sued a board of education, a high school and others after she was raped in a school bathroom by a non-student intruder. **The student alleged that the defendants wrongfully failed to provide security guards in the area of the alleged attack and near the exterior doors of the building.** The student claimed students frequently opened exterior doors of the school to allow other students to enter from the outside. The board of education, high school and private security firm appealed a trial court's decision to deny their motions for summary judgment. The appeals court reversed the trial court's ruling. The alleged security deficiencies arose from the allocation of security resources, which was a governmental function. Because decisions relating to the allocation of school security resources are in the nature of a governmental function, the district and high school could not be held liable unless they had a special relationship with the student that created a special duty to protect her. No special duty existed here, as there was no direct contact between the student and the school defendants before the alleged attack. Also, the school defendants did not have notice of prior sexual assaults at the school and had no reason to anticipate an intruder would enter and commit a violent crime against a student. Finally, the claim against the private security firm failed because the school defendants controlled the security guards at the school. The lower court's ruling was reversed. *Doe v. Town of Hempstead Board of Educ.*, 795 N.Y.S.2d 322 (N.Y. App. Div. 2005).

◆   A substitute teacher sued a board of education after she was attacked by a school intruder, claiming the board negligently failed to provide adequate security. The court reversed a trial court's decision to deny summary judgment to the board. **Because the provision of security against attacks by school intruders is a governmental function, there is no liability unless there is a special duty to protect.** In this case, there was no special duty to protect the substitute teacher. The implementation of security measures did not create a special duty, and the board made no special promise of protection to the substitute teacher. The trial court's decision was reversed. *Bain v. New York City Board of Educ.*, 702 N.Y.S.2d 334 (N.Y. App. Div. 2000).

◆   A high school secretary noticed a neatly dressed man carrying what appeared to be flower boxes near a school entrance. The secretary asked the man if she could help him. He uttered an incoherent response, thanked her, and moved along. A short time later, the man was observed by an individual who worked at the school as a water safety instructor. At the time, the man was standing between a swimming pool and bleachers. **The layout of the school building made it easy to become disoriented, and it was not unusual for male visitors to become disoriented and walk through the girls' locker room.** The water safety instructor, who also believed the man was delivering flowers, concluded that he had reached the area by walking through the girls' locker room. She began to walk toward him to ask why he was in the building. While doing so, she met a school custodian who had also seen the man exit from the girls' locker room into a lobby area. When the custodian saw the man, he commented that it was odd to see someone coming out of the girls' locker room. The man again uttered an incoherent remark and moved on. About an hour after the secretary first saw the man, she observed him again near a school entrance. This time, the man was talking to a student. She did not confront him, even though she later admitted that he did not belong in that location because it was not the school's main entrance. A short time later, the man sexually assaulted a student in the locker room. The student's parents sued the school district, claiming it failed to provide adequate supervision and security. A lower court granted immunity to the individual school employees but not to the school district, and the school district appealed. The appeals court affirmed, finding that the school district was not entitled to immunity on the parents' claims. **The employees engaged in discretionary acts which deserved the protection of official immunity. However, this immunity did not extend to the school district. If it did, the district would be rewarded for failing to develop and implement a basic security policy.** The lower court's ruling was affirmed. *S.W. v. Spring Lake Park School Dist. No. 16*, 592 N.W.2d 870 (Minn. Ct. App. 1999).

◆ A teacher was killed when a local resident with a history of mental illness entered her day care center through an unlocked rear entrance and shot her. The center was operated out of a wing of a local high school. The rear entrance was open because it was being used by construction contractors. The teacher's husband sued the school district and owner of the day care center, claiming they created the danger that resulted in the teacher's death by unlocking the back entrance. A trial court ruled against him, and he appealed. The appeals court affirmed the ruling against the teacher's husband. The state generally has no obligation to protect citizens from the violent acts of private individuals. Although an exception applies when the state creates a danger that causes harm, the exception was not applicable. **The district could not have foreseen that allowing construction workers to use the back entrance would result in the shooting, and it did not willfully or deliberately disregard a foreseeable danger.** *Morse v. Lower Merion School Dist.*, 132 F.3d 902 (3d Cir. 1997).

◆ While providing instruction in her classroom, a teacher was confronted by four intruders. One of the intruders accused the teacher of having physically abused a student. The intruder then assaulted the teacher with a metal chair, causing back injuries. **The teacher sued the board of education, claiming it was negligent because it failed to monitor and control the people who entered the school.** The teacher also claimed that the school negligently failed to provide proper security and created a dangerous condition. In addition, she claimed the board breached a union contract that required school principals to develop safety plans. The court granted the board's motion for summary judgment. The board was immune to the negligence claim because the provision of security was a governmental function rather than a proprietary function. The court rejected the teacher's claim that the school assumed a special duty to protect her and thus was not immune to the negligence claims against it. The teacher alleged that this special duty arose when the school's principal told her not to worry because she was "in a good school." She also alleged that a special duty arose based on the collective bargaining agreement between the teachers' union and the board. The court held that neither the principal's statement nor a collective bargaining agreement provision requiring principals to develop safety plans created a special duty. Therefore, the teacher's negligence claims failed and summary judgment was awarded to the board. *Genao v. Board of Educ. of the City of New York*, 888 F.Supp. 501 (S.D.N.Y. 1995).

◆   While leaving her high school following her last class for the day, a student inadvertently bumped shoulders with another student. The second student told the first that "she was going to kill her." The first student then met her sister, who also attended the school, in another area of the school. She attempted to report the incident at a security office, but she received no response when she knocked at the door. She and her sister were then assaulted as they tried to leave the school. **The second student struck one of the sisters in the head and elbow with a hammer, and the second student's brother, who was not a student at the school, stabbed the other.** The sisters sued the city's board of education and others, claiming negligent supervision. A jury returned a verdict of $50,000 for one of the sisters and $750,000 for the other. A lower court set aside the verdict and dismissed the complaint, finding the evidence did not prove negligent supervision. On appeal, the court reinstated the verdict, finding the jury could permissibly find that the board failed to provide adequate supervision. *Mirand v. City of New York*, 190 A.D.2d 282 (N.Y. App. Div. 1993).

◆   A teacher selected one of her fourth-grade students to supervise a classroom of second-graders while their teacher went to retrieve supplies from another part of the building. While the teacher was away, the fourth-grader was lured from the second-grade classroom by an intruder. The intruder exited the school with the student by proceeding through an unlocked rear door and through an open gate of a security fence. He then forced her into a wooded area, where he raped her. The student's mother sued the school district, claiming negligence. A jury found in her favor and awarded nearly $251,000 in damages. The district appealed, arguing that it could not be held liable in negligence because the actions of the intruder were not foreseeable. The appeals court rejected the argument and upheld the jury's verdict. There was enough evidence for the jury to find that school officials were on notice that students were in danger of being assaulted by intruders. The school was located in a statistically high crime area, and there had been sexual assaults and other violent crime in the surrounding area. In addition, school security was deficient in several ways. **The gate on a security fence at the rear of the school was left open and unlocked, and a set of doors at the back of the school did not close and lock properly due to an alignment problem. Doors at the front of the school did not close properly, and an intercom system was not functioning properly at**

the time of the assault. Further, unaccompanied and unknown adult males were permitted to roam school hallways. All of these things raised a factual issue of foreseeability that was properly submitted to the jury. The trial court's judgment was affirmed. *District of Columbia v. Doe*, 524 A.2d 30 (D.C. Ct. App. 1987).

B. Search and Seizure

◆   A student at a California high school informed campus security officers that she had witnessed a classmate shoot someone on a public bus. School administrators instructed a campus security officer to find the student. The officer often saw the student hanging around another student's locker. That locker was searched, but no weapons were found in it. The locker next to it was also searched, and that search revealed a sawed-off shotgun. Other officers located the alleged shooter, who had a gun in his backpack. In criminal proceedings, the student who had the shotgun asked the court to suppress the evidence of the shotgun. He claimed the search violated his Fourth Amendment rights. The court rejected the claim, finding that **the decision to search the locker with the shotgun was reasonable under the circumstances.** *In re J.D.*, 225 Cal.App.4th 709 (Cal. Ct. App. 2014).

◆   Police in Florida received a tip that a student might have a gun at school. After the tip was passed along to the school, an assistant principal and two security guards brought the student to a conference room and opened his book bag. **A loaded handgun was in the book bag.** At his criminal trial, the student argued that the search was unreasonable because it was based on an anonymous tip. The court rejected his argument. It found the search was justified because an extraordinary danger was present and because students at school are entitled to less privacy than free adults in other settings. *K.P. v. State*, 129 So.3d 1121 (Fla. Dist. Ct. App. 2013).

◆   An elementary school's assistant principal noticed a commotion at a cafeteria table. Students told her that someone had dropped money and a student had gone under the table to get it. A $20 bill was reported missing. The assistant principal took the student to an office. With a custodian acting as a witness, the assistant principal had the student turn his pockets inside out and strip to his underwear. She then ran her finger inside his waistband and lifted his undershirt. She did not find the missing money, **which was later located on the floor of the cafeteria**. The student's parents sued, claiming the search violated the Fourth Amendment. A magistrate judge recommended against dismissing the suit, finding that the parents had stated a claim that the search was unconstitutionally intrusive under the circumstances. *Cox v. Sampson County Board of Educ.*, No. 7:12-CV-00344-FL (E.D.N.C. 9/9/13).

◆   A high school student reported that a classmate was driving in an unsafe manner in the school parking lot. The assistant principal called the classmate to the office, where he detected an odor of cigarette smoke. Pursuant to school policy, the assistant principal and the school resource officer searched the classmate's car. They found brass knuckles and a glass pipe that was coated with marijuana residue. In criminal proceedings, the classmate sought to suppress the evidence, arguing that the search of the car violated his rights under the Fourth Amendment. He said that since he was old enough to use tobacco legally, the odor did not justify the search. The court rejected his claim, because **even though he was old enough to use tobacco the use of it on school grounds was a violation of school policy.** *State v. Voss*, 267 P.3d 735 (Idaho Ct. App. 2011).

◆ Under a high school's written policy, students who left campus and returned on the same day could be searched. Pursuant to the policy, a student who left school and returned during the same day was searched. When he was told to empty his pockets, he pulled out a bag containing 44 tablets of ecstasy. The student later claimed that the search violated his Fourth Amendment rights. He asked the judge in a juvenile proceeding to suppress the evidence uncovered by the search. The judge denied the request, and the student appealed. The appeals court upheld the judge's ruling. It decided that the school did not violate the student's Fourth Amendment rights. The search was conducted pursuant to a written policy, and the policy applied to all students. Also, **the policy was justified by legitimate safety concerns, and the search was not overly intrusive.** *People v. Sean A.*, 120 Cal.Rptr.3d 72 (Cal. Ct. App. 2010).

◆ An alternative learning center, which was attended by students who had been removed from other school campuses due to disciplinary problems, subjected all students entering the center to a search. **The search, which was conducted every day, required students to pass through a metal detector, be patted down, remove their shoes for inspection, and empty their pockets.** All students and parents attended an orientation session that included a description of the search policy. During a search, an examining officer found a marijuana cigarette inside the shoe of a student. At a trial held to determine whether he should be adjudicated delinquent, the student filed a motion to suppress the evidence. The motion was denied, and the student was adjudicated delinquent. He appealed, renewing his argument that the evidence should have been suppressed because it was discovered as a result of an unlawful search. The court rejected the student's argument and affirmed the lower court's decision. Even though the search was not conducted based on individualized suspicion, it was justified by the school's need to maintain a safe learning environment in a high-risk setting. Public school students are subject to a greater degree of supervision than adults, and the state had a compelling interest in maintaining safe schools. In addition, the uniform nature of the searches guarded against an abuse of discretion by administrators. The search was an administrative search that intruded on the privacy of students only to the extent necessary to satisfy the state's interest in maintaining safety. The lower court's ruling was affirmed. *In re O.E.*, No. 03-02-00516-CV, 2003 WL 22669014 (Tex. Ct. App. 11/13/03).

◆   A public high school in Philadelphia periodically subjected all students to a point-of-entry search for weapons. When the searches were conducted, students were required to stand in line and empty their pockets while their backpacks, coats and other personal effects were searched. Students were also scanned by a handheld metal detector. During one such search, a student removed a Swiss army-type knife from his pocket. He was arrested for bringing a weapon onto school property and was adjudicated delinquent after a juvenile hearing. After a court affirmed the disposition, the student appealed again. On appeal, he renewed his argument that the evidence should have been suppressed because the search was made without any individualized reasonable suspicion. The court rejected the argument and affirmed the lower court's decision. **The search was justified because it affected a limited privacy interest and was minimally intrusive.** In addition, the student population and parents were notified of the purpose of the search and the manner in which it was conducted via a school policy and procedure manual, mailings, and notices that were posted throughout the school. The purpose of the search – to keep weapons out of public schools – was compelling. Therefore, the search did not violate the student's constitutional rights. *Ex rel. F.B.*, 726 A.2d 361 (Pa. 1999).

◆   A high school subjected students to random searches for weapons using a handheld metal detector. It provided students and their parents with notice of this practice before it was instituted. On one day, the school decided to search all students who entered the attendance office without hall passes or who were late. A knife was found in the pocket of one of the students who was searched, and she was charged with the crime of bringing a knife onto school grounds. The trial court denied her motion to suppress the evidence and sustained the petition against her. She appealed, challenging the denial of her motion to suppress the evidence. The appeals court affirmed the lower court's decision. **Special needs administrative searches can be conducted without individualized suspicion so long as the government need is great, the privacy intrusion is limited in nature, and it would be unworkable to require a more rigorous standard of suspicion.** In this case, the searches were minimally intrusive, and it would be unworkable to institute a system that relied more on suspicion. Therefore, the search did not violate the student's rights under the Fourth Amendment. *People v. Latasha W.*, 70 Cal.Rptr.2d 886 (Cal. Ct. App. 1998).

◆   To keep weapons out, a public high school set up metal detectors that students passed through shortly after they entered. A student entered the school and turned around to leave when he saw other students lined up to pass through a metal detector. When he was stopped by a police officer and told he would be required to go through the detector, he raised his shirt to reveal a pistol and said "someone put this gun on me." The student was arrested, and he filed a motion to suppress the evidence. The trial court sustained the motion, finding that **the student could have turned around for innocent reasons that were unrelated to the metal detector**. The state appealed, but the reviewing court affirmed the lower court's decision. A person is seized when his freedom of movement is restrained, and the student's detention constituted an illegal seizure. Although the state argued that the officer was performing an administrative search, the cases it relied on to support its argument did not prevent people from choosing not to pass through a checkpoint. In addition, the officer did not have a reasonable suspicion to believe the search would turn up incriminating evidence. Instead, the decision to order the student to pass through the detector was based on a hunch. The order suppressing the evidence was affirmed. *People v. Parker*, 672 N.E.2d 813 (Ill. App. Ct. 1996).

◆   The parent of a student who was fatally shot at his high school sued the city, the board of education and others. The parent claimed the city and board negligently allowed people who were armed and dangerous to gain unauthorized access to the school and failed to use metal detectors on the day of the shooting. The parent further claimed that by placing metal detectors at the school, the city and board voluntarily assumed a duty to provide special protection against criminal acts by third persons. She separately claimed that the city and board owed a special duty to the student because he was in their control and because they were uniquely aware that he was at risk. A lower court ruled against the parent, and she appealed. The appeals court affirmed the lower court's ruling. The city's decision to use metal detectors at the school did not negate the immunity it enjoyed under a tort immunity statute. Nor did a special duty exception to immunity apply, because the parent did not show that a special relationship existed between the city and the student. For similar reasons, the decision favoring the board was affirmed. **The decision to use metal detectors did not make the board an insurer against all criminal activity.** In addition, there was no showing that the decision not to use the metal detectors every day increased the incidence of crime at the school. The lower court's ruling was affirmed. *Lawson v. City of Chicago*, 662 N.E.2d 1377 (Ill. App. Ct. 1996).

◆   As he entered his public high school in Philadelphia, a student was instructed by a school employee to remove his coat and place his book bag on a table to be searched. The employee then scanned the student with a metal detector and patted him down. All entering students were subjected to the same scan and pat-down procedure that day. When the employee felt a bulge resembling a knife in the student's coat, he searched the coat and found a box cutter in one of its pockets. The student was later arrested and charged with possession of a weapon on school property. At the criminal trial, his motion to suppress the physical evidence was denied, and he was convicted and placed on probation. He appealed, claiming the physical evidence should have been suppressed because he had been subjected to an unlawful search and seizure. **The student claimed the search and seizure were unlawful because there was no reasonable suspicion or probable cause to believe he had violated any law or school regulation.** The court held that the search did not violate the student's constitutional rights. Administrative searches are permitted even in the absence of individualized suspicion when they are conducted as part of a general regulatory scheme to ensure public safety. The search was reasonably related to the school's interest in promoting student safety, and it was justified because of the high rate of violence that was present in the Philadelphia public schools. All students were subjected to the search, and the uniform procedure that was followed assured that officials would not improperly exercise discretion with respect to the searches. The order adjudicating the student delinquent was affirmed. *Ex rel. S.S.,* 680 A.2d 1172 (Pa. Super. Ct. 1996).

◆ A school chancellor adopted guidelines for searching students as they entered public high schools, and several schools were selected for periodic scanning. At the start of the school year, students at the selected schools were told they would be subjected to a search at some point. The students were not told ahead of time precisely when the searches would take place. Although all entering students were potentially subject to being searched, the guidelines allowed personnel to limit the search, such as by searching every second or third student. Any student chosen to be searched was asked to place bags and parcels on a table, and to remove any metal objects from pockets. Students were then scanned with a metal detector. When a bag or parcel activated the detector, students were asked to open the bag or parcel. If a body scan activated the detector, students were again asked to remove metal objects. Students were taken to a private area if a second body scan activated the detector again. They were then asked a third time to remove metal objects before being subjected to a pat-down search. A student who was subjected to a search under the guidelines was arrested after a metal detector activated on her bag and a knife was discovered inside. She filed a motion to suppress the evidence, arguing it was discovered in violation of the Fourth Amendment. The court denied the motion. **The search was permissible because the need to maintain school safety outweighed the minimally intrusive nature of the searches.** In addition, the searches were permissible even though the guidelines did not include any provision requiring administrators to gain the consent of students before conducting a search. Children are required to attend school, and a consent element "would be all but impossible to administer." The motion was denied. *People v. Dukes,* 580 N.Y.S.2d 850 (N.Y. Crim. Ct. 1992).

C. Release of Students

◆ A father dropped his son off at school. Later that day, a woman identifying herself as the boy's mother called the school. She claimed that the boy had an appointment and that her boyfriend would pick him up. The boyfriend was not on a list of people who could pick up the child, and the school allowed the man to leave with the child. The child was then taken to Mexico, where his mother lived. The father sued, and **a jury awarded $2 million to him and $850,000 to the child**. It also added $3,500 in punitive damages. *Ramirez v. Escondido Unified School Dist.* (S.D. Cal. 2013).

◆   The guardians of a nine-year-old female student filled out a school form that listed the adults who had permission to remove the child from the school. Six times, the school released the child to a man who said he was the student's father. **The school did not ask the man for identification, and on several occasions he sexually abused her and then returned her to school.** The student's parents sued the school district and other defendants, claiming a violation of the student's due process rights under the federal Constitution. A district court granted a defense motion to dismiss, and a federal appeals court affirmed. The district did not create or knowingly increase the danger to the student, so there was no constitutional violation. *Doe v. Covington County School Dist.*, 675 F.3d 849 (5th Cir. 2012).

◆   A man entered a high school and told a front-office employee that he was the uncle of a student at the school. The man told the employee he was at the school to pick up the student and take her to an appointment. School policy called for the staffer to ask the man for picture identification and to verify that the adult was listed in the student's file as a person who was authorized to remove her from school. However, **the staffer did not ask for picture identification or check the student's file, which would have revealed that only the student's parents were authorized to remove her from school**. The student was released to the man, who took her to a house and molested her. When the student's mother sued the staffer for negligence, a trial judge ruled for the staffer. However, an appeals court reversed. It said that although public school employees in the state can't be sued for negligently performing discretionary acts, the student-checkout policy made her acts "ministerial." Therefore, the staffer could be sued. However, a jury was needed to decide whether the molestation of the student was a reasonably forseeable consequence of the staffer's failure to adhere to the policy. *Cotton v. Smith*, 714 S.E.2d 55 (Ga. Ct. App. 2011).

◆   A custodian at a high school repeatedly sexually molested a student at the school. The custodian would remove the student from class with written permission he obtained from the school's main office. Then, the custodian would proceed to sexually abuse the student. The abuse was discovered when school surveillance video showed the custodian taking the student into a custodial closet. The custodian was criminally charged, and he was incarcerated. The student's parents sued the local board of education, alleging claims under the federal Constitution. The federal constitutional claims were based on the board's alleged failure to ensure students were free from sexual assaults, its alleged deprivation of educational services and its alleged failure to supervise a safe and open environment for educational services. **The parents claimed their son was sexually molested as a result of the board's policy of granting permission to the custodian to repeatedly remove the student from class.** The complaint also asserted a federal statutory claim and state tort and constitutional claims. The board of education filed a motion to dismiss. The court refused to dismiss the claims the parents raised under the Fourteenth Amendment. The law recognizes liability for sexual molestation, and it also recognizes a property interest in educational benefits that are temporarily denied. Further, the law recognizes that in some circumstances the state has an affirmative duty to care for and protect particular individuals. In this case, it would be premature to dismiss the parents' claim that the board failed in its duty to protect the student. The state law tort claims were barred by immunity, and the claim under the state constitution was dismissed because there was an adequate state remedy. Finally, the court dismissed claims of breach of contract and violation of the Americans with Disabilities Act. *Cooper v. Brunswick County Board of Educ.*, No. 7:08-CV-48-BO, 2009 WL 1491447 (E.D.N.C. 5/26/09).

◆   A mother enrolled her six-year-old daughter at a school. At the time of enrollment, the mother informed the school secretary that the mother's estranged husband had abducted the child in the past and was not to have any contact with her. The secretary did not note the warning on the child's registration form, and it was not entered into the school's computer system.

School procedures required the school receptionist to check a student's registration card before releasing any child in order to make sure the person picking up the child was authorized to do so. If a particular child's registration card did not list the person attempting to pick up the child from school, the receptionist was to consult a school administrative official.

During school one day, the receptionist received a call and a fax from someone who posed as the child's mother. The impostor instructed the receptionist to release the child to the estranged husband. The receptionist looked for the child's registration card but could not locate it. She then released the child to the estranged husband. The school reprimanded the receptionist for failing to comply with school procedures by failing to consult with an administrator before releasing the child.

The child's mother sued the school principal and the receptionist. The trial court concluded that the principal and the receptionist were immune from liability under state law. The mother appealed, but only as to the ruling regarding the receptionist. The appeals court explained that public officials are generally immune from damages caused by their performance of discretionary functions. However, they are not entitled to immunity if harm is caused by their negligent performance of ministerial acts. In this case, the receptionist was performing a ministerial act when she released the student. **The policy regarding the release of students did not allow for the exercise of any discretion on her part.** She had been specifically instructed that she was to consult an administrator if she received a fax request to release a child from school. Because the receptionist's conduct did not involve the use of discretion, she was not entitled to immunity. The lower court's ruling in favor of the receptionist was reversed. *Smith v. McDowell*, 666 S.E.2d 94 (Ga. 2008).

◆ A high school teacher brought a 14-year-old special education student to the assistant principal's office, stating that she had found the student walking in the school's hallways. The student provided the telephone number of a man she said was her uncle. **School policy barred the release of students to anyone other than a parent, legal guardian, police authority, or a person designated in writing by a parent. Nonetheless, the assistant principal allowed the student to call the man she identified as her uncle to arrange for her to be picked up from school.** He then left the student alone in the lobby of the school's main office without assigning anyone to supervise her. The man identified by the student as her uncle picked her up from school and allegedly sexually abused her at his home. The student's mother sued the vice principal and the school district, asserting due process and state-law claims. A magistrate judge granted summary judgment in favor of the assistant principal, finding that he was immune from suit. The mother appealed. The appeals court affirmed the decision in favor of the assistant principal. The assistant principal was entitled to qualified immunity on the student's federal claims because the student did not adequately allege a violation of substantive due process. The assistant principal was not obligated to protect the student due to a special relationship. The student could not prove her claim that the assistant principal had a duty to protect her because he created the danger that led to her alleged harm. The assistant principal did not restrain the student in a way that created a constitutional obligation to protect her. In addition, he did not act with deliberate indifference. The student's state-law claims failed as well, because the assistant principal's actions did not result in the student's alleged injury. The decision of the lower court was affirmed. *Doe v. San Antonio Independent School Dist.*, 197 Fed.Appx. 296 (5th Cir. 2006).

◆ The father of two children sought a divorce from his wife. The wife obtained a temporary restraining order splitting custody of the children. A school policy allowed students to leave with their parents if the approval of the principal was first obtained. The date and time of student departure and return was to be recorded with the reason for leaving school. The father became upset when he came to school and learned his mother-in-law had taken the children to their mother. The mother told staff not to release the children to their father, but a staff member said that would require a court order. The next day, the father came to the school for both children. The reasons he gave for signing them out were "keeping promise by mother" for the daughter and "pay back" for the son. Police later arrived at the father's house to find it ablaze. The father brandished a knife, and the police killed him. The children's bodies were found inside the house. The mother sued the school board in a state court for negligence.

The court held for the board, and the mother appealed. The state court of appeals held that schools, teachers, and school administrators have a duty to exercise ordinary care for student safety. The board was not liable for negligently violating its own sign-out policy. There was no evidence that staff knew about a dispute until the mother called the day before the murders. Without a court order, a school has no legal duty to follow the instruction of one parent not to release a child to the other parent. The court affirmed judgment on a claim based on the father's violent nature. However, failure to read his reasons for signing out the children was evidence of breach of the duty to exercise ordinary care. **The court rejected the board's claim that it had no legal duty to examine a parent's reason for signing out a child.** The reasons the father gave for signing out the children might cause a reasonable person to suspect he intended to cause them harm. The state Governmental Tort Liability Act did not protect the board, since the decision to release the children did not involve planning. The decision was reversed, and the case was remanded. *Haney v. Bradley County Board of Educ.*, 160 S.W.3d 886 (Tenn. Ct. App. 2004).

D. Other Cases

◆ A high school student's mother said she told school officials that a schoolmate was getting violent with her son. The student said that while he was standing outside a school office, the schoolmate and the schoolmate's father physically attacked him. He sued the school district officials, alleging a violation of his substantive due process right to be free from harm. The court ruled against him, finding that "the failure to create greater security barriers for entry to a public school" did not support a substantive due process claim. **School officials generally do not have a constitutional duty to protect students from attacks by third parties.** Though an exception to this rule would apply if the district created the danger that caused the injury, the district did not create the danger in this case. *Campbell v. Brentwood Union Free School Dist.*, No. CV 12-1582(LDW), 2012 WL 5564405 (E.D.N.Y. 11/13/12).

◆ A high school student was seriously injured in her school's parking lot when the car she was sitting in was rear-ended by a student who was driving another vehicle. The injured student's parents sued the school district for negligence, claiming it was liable for failing to ensure safe driving conditions in the lot. **The court ruled for the district, finding it was immune to the claim raised against it** because an element of judgment was involved with respect to regulation of school parking lot traffic and because the judgment involved economic concerns and public policy. *J.S. v. Lamarr County School Dist.*, No. 2011-CA-00260-COA, 2012 WL 2895914 (Miss. Ct. App. 7/17/12).

◆ A high school student's father objected to a school's plan to have students use "Smart IDs," which include a radio frequency chip that help track students. The father rejected the district's offer to let the child use an ID without the chip. **The student and her father sued, claiming a violation of their religious rights.** They alleged that they would be "condemn[ed] to hell" if they allowed tracking of the girl at school. The court rejected the father's request to order the district let the girl stay at school without the ID while the case proceeded. It said the father was not likely to win the case. The offer of a chip-free ID resolved any religious rights breach. *A.H. v. Northside Independent School Dist.*, No. SA-12-CA-113-OG, 2013 WL 85604 (W.D. Tex. 1/8/13).

◆ A school's entrance doors had glass panes. A seventh-grader pushed on the glass and it shattered, cutting him. He and his mother sued, claiming the school had maintained a dangerous and defective condition. The court denied the school district's motion for judgment without a trial. Though safety glass wasn't required when the school was built and no current law required retrofitting, the district was in the habit of replacing broken glass with Plexiglass. Therefore, **a question existed as to whether the district knew it was dangerous to leave glass in the doors**. A trial was needed. *Karathanasis v. Union Free School Dist.*, No. 56217/2011, 2013 WL 3828389 (N.Y. Sup. Ct. 7/24/13).

◆ A ninth-grader was expelled for having a knife at school. He was allowed back on the condition that he would not again violate any major rule, but he subsequently threatened one student and punched another. He also wrote a threatening message on his backpack. His readmission was finally rescinded after he became irate at a meeting and the principal concluded he had violated a rule barring intimidation and harassment. After his expulsion, he continued visiting the school to pick up friends and use the weight room. When a teacher told him to leave, he punched a locker and was banned from campus. He was cited for trespassing after he ignored the ban. He sued, claiming the district wrongfully failed to provide him with notice and a hearing before instituting the ban. He lost, because once he was expelled from the school he had the same right as any other member of the general public to access it. At that point, **he had no constitutional right to access the campus**. *Hannemann v. Southern Door County School Dist.*, 673 F.3d 746 (7th Cir. 2012).

◆ Parents of students divorced, and the father was granted physical custody. Following the divorce, the mother needed the father's permission to see the children. The father informed the children's school that he did not want the mother to visit the children at school. When the school denied the mother access, she sued and claimed a violation of her constitutional right to control the education of her children. The court rejected her claim. **Parents do not have a constitutional right to make decisions relating to**

how a school is run. The school's actions did not prevent the mother from raising her children as she saw fit. *Schmidt v. Des Moines Public Schools*, 655 F.3d 811 (8th Cir. 2011).

◆ A woman drove to a high school to drop off her son at a field house that was located on the high school's grounds. As she was leaving, she drove her vehicle into a free-swinging metal gate. The gate penetrated the vehicle and injured the woman. She and her husband sued a school resource officer, alleging he violated a duty to secure the gate, report its broken latch to authorities, and have the gate equipped with a working latch. Under state law, the school resource officer could be sued if the acts of inspecting the gate and reporting/repairing any damage to it were discretionary. If the acts were ministerial and did not involve the exercise of discretion, the school resource officer was entitled to immunity unless he acted with malice or intent to injure. **The court ruled that the school resource officer was entitled to immunity.** The parties agreed that he did not act with malice or intent to injure, and there was no formal policy or procedure that created a ministerial duty on the part of the school resource officer to inspect the gate. *Scott v. Waits*, 703 S.E.2d 419 (Ga. Ct. App. 2010).

◆ A school district regulation required all visitors to present state-issued photo identification before entering secure areas of the school where students were present. Pursuant to the regulation, information on the visitor's identification document was photographed and checked against lists of registered sex offenders. The parent of elementary school students visited their school but refused to allow school officials to scan her driver's license or input her information manually. As a result, the parent was not permitted to access areas of the school that she wished to visit. Instead, she met with her children's teachers in a conference room. The parent subsequently was similarly blocked from accessing particular areas of the school when she visited to attend a musical, a volleyball game and a Thanksgiving lunch. The parent sued the district, claiming violations of her constitutional rights to speech, assembly, association, freedom from unreasonable search of seizure, privacy, procedural due process and substantive due process. She also asserted claims under state law. A trial court ruled against her, and a federal appeals court affirmed. **The parent did not have a fundamental right to access the secure areas of the school, and she was not denied the ability to make fundamental decisions about her children's education.** Further, the regulation was narrowly tailored to achieve the compelling state interest in determining whether a potential visitor to the school was a registered sex offender. *Meadows v. Lake Travis Independent School Dist.*, 397 Fed. Appx. 1 (5th Cir. 2010).

◆ A high school student was suspended for three days for packing snow into the gas cap of a schoolmate's car. The student's father went to the school and acted in a loud and threatening manner. The father left at the request of the vice principal, but he said he planned to complain to the superintendent and local media. He also reportedly told the vice principal he "better look for another job." The father was later arrested for creating a disturbance at the school, but the charge against him was eventually dismissed. The father and student filed a lawsuit. The student claimed he was suspended without due process, and the father accused the police of malicious prosecution. The court rejected the claims. The student's due process rights were not violated because the vice principal spoke to the student about the incident three times and allowed him to tell his side of the story. And **the father's claim of malicious prosecution failed because witness reports supported the conclusion that the police had ample cause to arrest him for creating a disturbance at school**. *Scrocca v. Alton Police Dep't*, No. 1:08-cv-0042-JL, 2009 WL 2246753 (D.N.H. 7/28/09).

◆ A 17-year-old high school student was killed in his school's parking lot when a vehicle driven by another student struck him. The administrator of the student's estate sued the school district and a security company employed by the school district, claiming negligent supervision of the parking lot where the accident happened. **The court held that the district was not liable because it did not have specific notice or knowledge of a particular danger at a particular time.** Therefore, the district could not have reasonably anticipated the occurrence of the accident. Also, the security company could not be held liable for the student's death because there was no evidence that it failed to perform its contractual duties under its contract with the school district. Even if it failed to supervise its security guards at the school, such a breach could not be deemed a proximate cause of the accident. *Ravner v. Autun*, 876 N.Y.S.2d 453 (N.Y. App. Div. 2009).

◆ A parent entered a school gymnasium to pick up his stepson. He left the gymnasium by going through double doors that led to a commons area. One of the doors came off a closing mechanism and fell on the parent's head. When the parent sued for negligence, a trial court ruled in favor of the district. It found a state tort claims act recreational use exception to liability was applicable. Under the exception, a claim could not be brought if injury occurred while the property was being used for recreational purposes. After a state appeals court affirmed the trial court's decision, appeal reached the state's highest court. The parent argued that the recreational use exception was inapplicable because the injury occurred in a commons area and not in the gymnasium. The lower court had found the school commons was a "transitional area" from outside the school into the gymnasium. The lower court found the commons was an appendage to the gymnasium and was therefore a part of a "recognized recreational use area." **The state's high court explained that the legislative purpose of the tort claims act was to immunize government entities so as to encourage them to build recreational facilities without fear of lawsuits.** To be immune, the school district had to show the parent was claiming only ordinary negligence and that the injuries resulted from the use of a "qualifying property," meaning a property that was "public" and was intended to be used for recreational purposes. Although the commons was not used exclusively for recreational purposes, the court found it was "an integral part of the use of the gymnasium." The commons was used to sell tickets and concessions during events, and it was not "incidentally connected" to the gymnasium. The commons was necessarily connected to the gymnasium as a principal means of access and for purchasing tickets and concessions. The parent's use of the commons at the time of the injury was consistent with the plan of the building. **Extending immunity in this case was consistent with legislative intent. A school would be discouraged from opening a gymnasium for recreational use if liability was permitted in an area that was integral to its recreational usage.** Even though the primary use of the commons may have been non-recreational, its use was integrally tied to the gymnasium when it was being used for recreational purposes. Therefore, the school district was immune from liability under the recreational use exception. *Poston v. Unified School Dist. No. 387, Altoona-Midway, Wilson County*, 189 P.3d 517 (Kan. 2008).

◆   After a fire alarm sounded at a high school, a guidance counselor was severely injured when a student pushed open a door. The guidance counselor sued several defendants, including the city where the school was located. He relied on the theory that the swinging double doors were negligently designed. A jury issued a verdict in his favor, and the defendants appealed. The appeals court negated the jury's verdict and issued a ruling in favor of the defendants. It explained that the issue in the case was whether the building design complied with safety standards that were in place when the school was constructed. The guidance counselor's expert testified that the design of the double doors was unsafe because it placed people going through the left door into the path of the door on the right. The expert also testified that the lack of a restricting mechanism allowed the doors to be opened too quickly. The court explained that the expert's testimony did not establish that the design of the doors violated the building code that was applicable when the school was built in 1970. **Rather, expert testimony offered by the defense showed that the doors complied with the building code that was in effect at the time of construction. In addition, the guidance counselor did not show the design of the doors was unsafe in light of the design standards that applied when the school was built.** The guidance counselor did not prove his claim of negligent design. Therefore, the judgment entered on the jury's verdict was reversed. *Hotaling v. City of New York*, 866 N.Y.S.2d 117 (N.Y. App. Div. 2008).

◆   A school parent volunteered at the school where her children were enrolled. On a day when she was at the school to volunteer, another parent asked her to check on the other parent's child at the school. The volunteer parent said she signed a volunteer sign-in sheet and then went to the classroom of the other parent's daughter. She said a teacher's aide nodded her approval to enter the classroom, and the volunteer parent visited with the girl and a paraprofessional for about two minutes. The volunteer parent then left the building before returning at lunch time to perform volunteer duties. During lunch, the other parent asked the volunteer parent to check on the other parent's daughter again. On her way out of the building that day, the volunteer parent looked in the window of the girl's class. She did not stop to go in because the door was closed. **The same day, the school sent the volunteer parent a letter banning her from the school for five weeks.** It claimed the volunteer parent had violated a state law that banned "interfering with peaceful conduct of activities." The volunteer parent objected to the ban. After a hearing, the length of the ban was reduced. The volunteer parent sued the school district, claiming a violation of her due process interest in the care, custody and control of her children. She also asserted other claims, including a claim of emotional distress. The court granted the school's dismissal motion. It noted that **public education is committed to the control of school authorities, and parents do not have a right to total control over every aspect of their children's education**. Instead, school authorities have broad discretion when it comes to operating their schools, and the school permissibly limited the volunteer parent's access to its premises. *Mayberry v. Independent School Dist. No. 1 of Tulsa County, Oklahoma,* No. 08-CV-416-GKF-PJC, 2008 WL 5070703 (N.D. Okla. 11/21/08).

◆   A school parent, who was the president of the Parent Teacher Student Organization (PTSO) at her son's elementary school, criticized the school's performance and safety policies. The school's principal said the parent threatened administrators and teachers and violated visitation policies. He banned her from school, prevented her from distributing flyers and cancelled a PTSO meeting. The parent sued the principal and other school officials, **claiming the actions taken against her violated the First Amendment because they were designed to prevent her from criticizing the school**. She claimed the defendants' actions were a retaliatory response to her criticisms. The court denied cross-motions for summary judgment, finding factual issues were present. There was conflicting evidence about whether the principal took adverse action against the parent for a permissible reason. Also, it was not clear whether the school had created a public forum for speech. Therefore, it was too soon to issue a definitive ruling on the First Amendment claim. *Williamson v. Newark Public Schools*, No. 05-CV-4008 (WJM), 2008 WL 1944849 (D.N.J. 5/1/08).

◆   A parent who was visiting a school got into a confrontation with a school employee. A school safety agent witnessed the confrontation and attempted to separate the parent and the school employee. The school safety agent advised the school employee to walk away from the confrontation. The school employee walked to a staircase to return to her classroom. Moments later, the parent followed her into the stairwell and attacked her. The school employee sued the board of education to recover for her injuries. A trial court denied the board's motion for summary judgment, but the appeals court reversed. **The appeals court held that the school employee did not show that the school safety agent had assumed an affirmative duty to act to prevent the attack.** The school employee did not show that the school agent was aware that the parent posed a threat of violence. Therefore, the board was not liable for the school employee's injuries. *France v. New York City Board of Educ.*, 834 N.Y.S.2d 193 (N.Y. App. Div. 2007).

♦   The parent of a high school student complained to the school's principal after the student broke his leg during a school football practice. The parent claimed that the student received no medical attention from any of the coaches present at the practice. Two years later, the parent complained to the principal again after the student was inserted into a football game even though he was feeling ill. A short time after he made the complaint, the principal barred the parent from entering any school district property except to drop off and pick up his son. The principal also circulated a memo stating that he physically feared the parent and that the parent was "the most out-of-control parent [the principal] had witnessed in 31 years of education." The parent later sued the school district, claiming it violated his constitutional rights by barring him from school property. The court granted the district's motion to dismiss the claim. The court was unable to locate any authority for the proposition that the parent had a constitutional right to enter school property. To the contrary, **school officials have a right to assure that parents conduct themselves properly while they are on school property**. The parent did not show that the decision to bar him from school property violated his constitutional rights. *Van Deelen v. Shawnee Mission Unified School Dist. #512*, 316 F.Supp.2d 1052 (D. Kan. 2004).

CHAPTER TWO

Emergency Preparedness and Response

I. INTRODUCTION

From Columbine to Sandy Hook, from Superstorm Sandy to the severe cold, ice and snowfall of the 2013-14 winter, today's schools have to plan for the unthinkable because the unthinkable keeps happening.

That's exactly why you go to so much trouble to think things through in advance, have training exercises and incorporate the lessons learned from your and other school's crises.

You don't want to be caught short when glass is shattering around you, or the halls are filled with smoke, or you've just been notified a serious storm is heading your way – and suddenly the power goes out in the building. If a crisis hits, you want to already know what to do next.

Legally, school emergency operations plans are governed by state law and local regulations.

Federal law typically factors in as the same compliance always expected of your school. For just a few obvious examples, schools can't assign students to shelter-in-place rooms based on race, ignore the special needs of those with disabilities, or post confidential student records to the school's Facebook page just to make sure the records survive the crisis.

Apart from your usual compliance issues, school emergency operations plans aren't legally mandated on the federal level.

That said, the federal government takes the matter so seriously that it has issued guidance to schools and districts: the *Guide for Developing High-Quality School Emergency Operations Plan*, a collaboration by the departments of Education, Health and Human Services, Homeland Security and Justice along with the Federal Bureau of Investigation and the Federal Emergency Management Agency.

The guide is available online at *rems.ed.gov*.

In this chapter we'll look at the federal guidance as well as other best practices for school emergency operations plans. We'll also look at two issues raised by real-life school disasters: school intruders and tornado safe rooms.

We'll conclude with court decisions in which students, parents and school employees brought lawsuits connected to school crisis planning or a school's response to an emergency.

II. SCHOOL EMERGENCY OPERATIONS PLANS

A. Federal Guidance

1. Overview

The developers of the *Guide for Developing High-Quality School Emergency Operations Plan* understand your school is almost certain to already have an emergency operations plan in place.

The way they envision you using the guidance is not to tear up your current plan and start over from scratch but to perform needed tweaks by comparing your existing M.O. to the info and procedures suggested in the guide. (Again, the guide is available online at *rems.ed.gov*.)

The main focus of the guidance is on planning, but that's intended to be seen in the context of the five mission areas announced in the March 2011 Presidential Policy Directive 8. Applied to school emergencies, they're:

- **Prevention** of threatened or actual school emergencies
- **Protection** of students, teachers, visitors, school networks and property
- **Mitigation** of threatened or actual harm at school
- **Response** that establishes a safe and secure school environment, saves life and property there, and facilitates the transition to:
- **Recovery**, which means a restoration of the learning environment

2. Your Planning Team

Having set the example by having six federal agencies team up to produce the *Guide*, the guidance emphasizes the importance of collaboration in school safety planning.

It suggests your "core planning team" should include not only administrators but also:

- teachers
- school psychologists and nurses
- facilities and transportation managers
- food personnel
- representatives of students, parents, persons with disabilities, racial minorities, and religious minorities, and
- first responders, such as: police officers, SROs, fire officials, EMTs, and also public health and mental health practitioners.

3. The Feds' Standard for 'High Quality'

The guidance also contains benchmarks to help you assess the quality of your plan.

As a basic matter, your plan has to comply with the state laws and local requirements that pertain to school emergency operations plans.

Beyond that, the guidance says plans are:

- **adequate** if they effectively address critical courses of action
- **feasible** if tasks can be accomplished with the available resources, and
- **acceptable** if they get tasks done on time and within budget and the plan complies with the law.

The guide calls a plan **complete** if it:

- "Incorporates all courses of action to be accomplished for all selected threats and hazards and identified functions"
- "Integrates the needs of the whole school community"
- "Provides a complete picture of what should happen, when, and at whose direction"
- "Estimates time for achieving objectives, with safety remaining as the utmost priority"
- "Identifies success criteria and a desired end state" – and
- "Conforms with planning principles outlined in this guide."

4. Useful Features

Perhaps the most helpful features in the new guidance relate to compliance with federal law in the context of a school crisis.

The guide contains an overview of the Family Education Rights and Privacy Act (FERPA) that helps to clarify FERPA concerns that schools have found confusing in the past.

The guide also contains info on the Health Insurance Portability and Accountability Act of 1966 to help you with matters of confidential health records.

There is also information about how to make sure your plan complies with the Americans with Disabilities Act.

As we discuss later in this chapter, the new guidance also contains a helpful "Active School Shooters" section.

Now let's move on to best practices.

B. Plan Considerations

1. Basic Plan Elements

There is no one-size-fits-all approach to crisis management plans.

Each school has a unique school community with unique needs, and schools in different parts of the country face different risks. For example, if your school is in an earthquake-prone area, you'll want to check out FEMA's Earthquake Preparedness Checklist in Chapter Nine (Form II-19).

Even schools in the same area can face very different challenges if one is in a big city and the other's in a quiet suburb.

Importantly, each state has different laws that its schools must follow.

All of this means that for a crisis management plan to be truly effective, it must be tailored to your school's specific needs.

That said, some things are true of all plans. For example, each one has to comply with its state and local laws.

Also, every crisis management plan should be considered a work in progress. That's because the day-to-day realities at school are constantly changing.

One important preparedness step is to assign crisis duties to personnel – but staff come and go. You may lose (or gain) a CPR expert. But it's important to keep that in mind in case a pregnancy leave, a resignation, or a new hire means you need to change up key go-to responsibilities.

Students also come and go, shifting the established needs of your community. That can mean different disabilities to make sure are accommodated or new languages to cover to make effective communication with students and their parents possible.

Also, lessons learned from a previous incident can mean that the plan should be tweaked to take advantage of real-life experience.

☑ CHECKLIST – *Basic Plan Elements*

☐ complies with state and local laws
☐ is periodically reviewed and updated as needed
☐ includes provisions relating to students with disabilities
☐ addresses potential language barriers, and
☐ is updated based on real-life experiences
  when appropriate.

2. Students Not on Campus

Have you planned for the possibility that some students and staff might not be on campus when a crisis occurs – but you still have responsibility for them? For example, a class might be on a field trip or a team might be in transit to an away game.

Concerns to address here include:

• establishing communication protocols ahead of time – not just between the school and the away-group, but also between the school and the student's parents

• making sure staff always have emergency supplies before they leave campus – which might include water, energy bars, first aid supplies, a flashlight and a reliable communication device, and

• anything else that seems appropriate given the circumstances of the away trip and the risks the travelers are likely to encounter along the way.

It's also important to remember to take before- and after-school programs and events into account in emergency plans. Do you and your staff know what to do if an event occurs while clubs are meeting or when there's a packed house in the auditorium for the annual talent show?

3. Communicating With Parents

Are you sure you can access contact info as needed in an emergency?

It's a good idea to keep contact info in multiple places – both online and in hard copies that are laminated or kept in reliably waterproof containers.

Also, having compiled this info in the first place, you'll want to make sure to make it someone's responsibility to update it regularly.

Another important consideration is letting parents know where and how to get information about an ongoing incident.

One thing you may want to let families know in advance is that they should not come to campus during an emergency as they and their cars could physically block ambulances, fire trucks and emergency personnel.

Does it make sense to use social media to communicate with parents during an emergency? If so, you'll want to consider how to go about that, whose responsibility to make it, and how best to get the word out to families.

Even if you're planning to be all over social media, you'll probably want to provide as many other sources as you realistically can. Many parents have smartphones and access to the Internet, but it's nothing like 100%.

Alternative ways for parents to get information about an incident in progress include calling a pre-arranged phone number to hear a recorded message that will be updated as often as possible under the circumstances. You may also be able to direct them to a local TV or radio station that has agreed to broadcast info about your school in case of an emergency.

See Chapter Nine for a Reunification After a Crisis checklist (Form II-20).

4. Emergency Supplies

Do you store emergency supplies at school in case of an emergency?

There are many approaches for schools that do, but they all tend to fall under two categories: either the school gathers all the emergency supplies, or the school gathers some of the supplies while parents and students or some other party supplies the rest.

Under one model plan, for example, parents are instructed to pack up specified drinks and snacks and a few other items (such as a laminated copy of the student's emergency card, a reassuring message and photo from the family, pocket-sized tissues and a small book or game) in a gallon zip-lock bag placed inside a 50-gallon plastic snap-top container and then bring it to school for storage.

The American Red Cross reports that some schools make it a practice to donate their emergency stockpiles of food to a charity at the end of each school year.

In addition to food and water, emergency supplies typically include first aid gear, radios and flashlights.

5. Evacuation and Lockdown

Evacuation and lockdown plans are basic – but that's because they're so important. It's never a bad idea to take another look at yours.

Evacuation requires pre-determined routes and on-site assembly sites (to evacuate from) and off-campus assembly sites (to evacuate to). You need several of each as the first choices might be unreachable or unusable due to the emergency.

Schools generally expect to evacuate staff and students by using school buses, but the roads may be impassable or buses may be unavailable. Therefore, alternate ways to remove students from danger should be discussed.

The evacuation provisions in model plans stress the importance of making sure students remain accounted for by:
- keeping classes together during the evacuation so that teachers can continue to keep track of their own students, and
- having teachers take roll both immediately before the evacuation and as soon as they arrive at the evacuation destination.

Keep in mind that authorities may ask that a school be evacuated during a broader crisis. On September 11th, for example, Stuyvesant High School was near ground zero, but that was not why it was evacuated – the FBI wanted to use the school building as a command center.

Lockdowns are needed when the danger is outside the school and the best chance of keeping students safe is to secure them inside. The school's outside doors are locked, and students and teachers remain in classrooms. If possible, classroom doors are also locked and windows may need to be covered. An example of a sample notice to parents regarding a school lockdown drill is provided in Chapter Nine (Form II-2).

6. Sheltering-in-Place

Sheltering-in-place is a response to the more specific danger of needing to minimize students' exposure to contaminants in the environment – a chemical accident, for example. Sheltering-in rooms should have as few windows as possible. Basic necessities, such as food, water and bedding, should be stored there in advance, along with emergency supplies, such as flashlights and radios, as well as first aid supplies and medicine.

For sheltering-in-place, the American Red Cross suggests an interior room that's located above the ground floor and has no windows. This is because some dangerous chemicals are heavier than air. Even with precautions, heavy chemicals could seep into basement rooms. As an extra safety measure, provide people a wet cloth to keep over their noses and mouths.

The Red Cross also says all HVAC and fans should be turned off and all vents and cracks around doors should be sealed with duct tape. If only a room with windows is available, it should be covered with plastic and sealed over completely with duct tape. Checklists showing specific steps to take in the event of a gas leak or hazardous spill are provided on Form II-3 and Form II-4 in Chapter Nine.

7. Planning for Your Staff in a Crisis

Virtually every crisis presents twists no one could have imagined – and therefore no one could have planned for. That's one reason training staff on the plan is so important. Having the basics down makes it a lot likelier staff will be able to intelligently adapt the original plan to cover unexpected events.

Sometimes the unexpected element is people's reactions. No one knows what they'll be like under pressure until they actually experience it. Also, people are different – and so are their responses to a crisis. Some people may find themselves cool-headed and decisive, while others might have to fight the tendency to panic or freeze. Training can help tilt the scale toward cool-headed decisiveness.

Another thing that can help is having easy-to-read-and-understand checklists on hand. Many plans call for them – and some call for them to be laminated to make them not only more durable but also more legible, since you can wipe off a laminated surface.

Simple, straightforward checklists that contain basic action plans and also relevant contact info can help get frozen people up and going again and on to the next step.

Even if you trust everyone to stay calm, focused and move quickly, it's a good idea to have simple reminders that can be easily scanned and followed. Examples of a crisis team member list and a list of emergency telephone numbers are provided in Chapter Nine on Form I-2 and Form II-6.

Here's something else to keep in mind and possibly include in the plan: One common mistake experts have cited is schools waiting too long to call in emergency services and alert its own crisis team.

The best bet is to go ahead and call for help and alert the team even if there's a chance the situation might be resolved by the time help arrives. If that turns out to be the case, that's actually a good thing. And if there's any risk of injury or loss of life or property, it's best to err on the side of safety.

8. Planning for After the Crisis

Experience has shown that there are several predictable recovery needs that many schools experience after an emergency is over.

Because they're predictable, they can be planned for and addressed in the crisis plan. They include:

- helping students, families and staff cope with trauma
- repairing any physical damage to the facility
- addressing insurance requirements, and
- dealing with the media.

Perhaps the most predictable recovery need in the wake of a crisis at school is that students, families and school staff are likely to need help coping with the emotional fall-out that accompanies living through a disaster. One way to support staff is by utilizing a thank-you letter such as the one provided on Form II-10 in Chapter Nine.

You may want to get before-the-fact advice from experts in whatever field is needed. And don't forget in planning for coping with the after-effects of trauma that you may have your own onsite experts. School counselors have the added advantage of already having a relationship with many of the people who might be needing help.

Schools that go to off-campus professionals for preliminary advice for the plan might use the advice-gathering process as a kind of audition to determine if the expert might also be a good person to bring back to help the school if the worst happens.

Another predictable recovery need concerns the brick and mortar of the school building. Even apart from additional safety considerations – such as leaking roofs that could lead to slip-and-fall accidents or falling rubble that could cause injuries – the physical damage left after a disaster can be a potent reminder of a traumatic experience. Apart from other pressing reasons, making repairs can be an important psychological way to start moving beyond the event.

One thing you can do to prepare for property damage is make sure you have plenty of "before" pictures. Still photos work, and so do videos. If you can manage it, aerial photos are also a good idea if FEMA is likely to be involved. You'll probably also want to make sure some kind of camera is on hand to take "after" photos of property damage as well.

It can also be a good idea to find out in advance exactly what other kind of insurance requirements the school is likely to have to comply with in case it has to make claims on any policies.

Another predictable recovery-stage need is for a spokesperson or spokespeople to deal with the media. Many schools already have staff and established procedures in place for this.

Finally, the plan should call for debriefing sessions with school staff and emergency personnel after any actual crisis so the school can incorporate lessons learned from the incident into the plan.

C. Special Considerations

The Governmental Accountability Office (GAO) is the agency that acts as the investigative arm of Congress.

The GAO made a 2007 study of school planning and preparedness and found that the overwhelming norm among schools was an emergency operations plan that addressed multiple specific scenarios.

It found virtually all plans addressed bombs or bomb threats, hostage situations, and the natural disasters likely for the locality. Those bases are pretty thoroughly covered in the majority of school crisis management plans. For a bomb threat report form, see Form II-11 in Chapter Nine. Schools should also be prepared to follow-up on environmental risks, such as chemical spills. To respond to a chemical spill, see Form II-15, a parental consent form, in Chapter Nine.

The GAO also found that city-based school districts were more likely than rural school districts to plan crisis responses for terrorism (86% as opposed to 70%) and much more likely to plan for incidents involving radiation (60% compared to 29%) or anthrax (57% of urban districts versus 26% or rural districts).

In addition to those findings, the GAO study also identified four areas in which many plans weren't following recommended practices by:
- including procedures to ensure the safety of special needs students
- including a plan to continue teaching students in case the school closed due to a pandemic or other emergency
- conducting school drills and exercises, and
- training with first responders and community partners.

This section will focus on the topics that many schools and districts may still need information in addressing.

1. Special Needs Students' Safety

Just as a good crisis management plan is tailored to address the crises a school is likely to face, a good plan for students with disabilities is drafted to take into account the special needs of the students the school actually has in its own community.

The GAO found that 28% of school districts with plans had not included specific provisions for students with disabilities. Of those that had, the provisions were not in writing.

The GAO's report focused on the following recommended practices concerning special needs students:

- keeping track of where special needs students are located throughout the school day
- identifying the staff assigned to evacuate or shelter with these students, and
- providing any devices needed to transport them to evacuation areas.

Educators told the GAO that districts devise their own procedures for keeping special needs students safe in a crisis because disability groups don't agree on the best practices.

One reason for this might be that while all students are unique, students with disabilities tend to be the most unique of all. Some need motorized wheelchairs to cross a room, while others need specialized laptops to communicate. Still others – Down syndrome or autistic children, for example – have cognitive limitations that may require a teacher with real experience of what works with a particular student in order to get him or her on the evacuation bus or keep the child from panicking during lockdown or sheltering-in. And while first responders can tell at a glance if a student has Down syndrome, the same isn't true if a student is autistic.

The CDC puts the average number of children with an autism spectrum disorder at one in every 50 children. The number of children diagnosed with an autism spectrum disorder is increasing – increasing the need for crisis planning to specifically address these students.

Info provided by The Autism Society for paramedics and ER staff warns of typical reactions that could be especially problematic in a crisis.

Children with autism may over-react to loud noise and bright lights – running away or turning aggressive if confronted by a siren accompanied by flashing lights, for example. They also may not understand the significance of first responders' badges or uniforms, not follow directions, refuse to make eye contact, get inappropriately close, fail to respond to requests for information or else respond in confusing ways: saying "Yes!" to every question or using gestures instead of language.

The unique problems posed by autistic children during emergencies have led several groups to create specialized training for first responders in dealing with this population – something you may want to discuss when you liaise with your own first responders for planning or practice drills.

For more on first responder training on dealing with individuals with autism, go to *autismalert.org*. The Autism Safety Project also provides helpful crisis-related info at *autismspeaks.org/family-services/autism-safety-project/helping-children-respond-disaster*.

Autistic students and other special needs students often need extra help under normal circumstances, and this need for extra help can be greatly increased during a crisis. As the National Organization on Disability has said, perhaps the most effective tactic for special needs individuals to survive an emergency is to have strong relationships with nondisabled people.

Disabilities are categorized differently by different groups, but there are some special needs experiences that may be common enough to take account of for crisis management planning. For example:

- People who need wheelchairs, crutches or other mobility devices are going to need special help if an emergency disables elevators or leaves piles of rubble blocking paths – especially if a speedy exit is required.
- Individuals who are blind are likely to be badly disoriented by loud, overwhelming noises – like sirens. Extremely loud noises drown out the ambient sounds that normally give blind people cues about who and what is in their immediate environment and what is happening there.
- People with cognitive or developmental disabilities like ADHD, Down syndrome and Tourette's are likely to have trouble following instructions.

☑ CHECKLIST – *Special Needs Planning*

☐ Establish a pre-set location to which special needs students can be escorted so they can be rescued.

☐ Consult with emergency responders about their own protocols for dealing with special needs individuals – and adopting them if appropriate.

☐ Alert emergency responders to the presence of any special needs students likely to need additional help, such as the mobility-impaired.

☐ Obtain devices – such as specialized, light-weight chairs – to help evacuate students with severe mobility problems.

☐ Train staff to use any specialized devices deemed necessary to evacuate these students, and play it safe by assigning more people to operate them than are actually needed.

☐ Provide (or train) a sign-language interpreter if needed.

☐ Provide written instructions in Braille if needed.

☐ Make sheltering-in arrangements for service animals. Although pets aren't permitted in shelters, federal regulations allow service animals –

although they can be excluded if they threaten others' lives or safety or if they become a nuisance. That said, anyone with known allergies to animals should be assigned to a different room.

☐ Store pet foods, medicines, plastic bags and disposable gloves for service animals along with other emergency supplies – and earmark water for them.

☐ Store backup devices of any vital special-needs device.

☐ Store spare or alternative power sources for the devices.

☐ Store needed medicine along with emergency supplies.

☐ Provide cards for special needs students to wear to alert first responders of their condition and the limitations it causes them. For example, a card for a person with a cognitive disability might state that this person has trouble understanding language, so patience and a simple vocabulary are needed.

A form that can be used to build a list of students and staff who require special assistance for evacuation can be found at Form II-13 in Chapter Nine. The American Academy of Pediatrics and the American College of Emergency Physicians have created a form designed to present a brief but accurate record of special needs students to help ensure they receive proper care during an emergency. It can be downloaded at *www.aap.org/advocacy/ blankform.pdf*.

2. Planning for a Pandemic

Another area of crisis planning that the GAO identified as neglected was planning for a pandemic flu event and how to continue to educate students in case of the extended school closure likely to accompany it.

Flu pandemics are caused by a highly contagious flu virus so new that people have built up little or no immunity to it. A virus-specific vaccine may not be available until six months after the virus is identified, and this lack of natural and vaccine-related immunity heightens the chance people will become seriously ill or die.

This risk is already significant, as the regular seasonal flu strains kill approximately 36,000 Americans and send another 200,000 to the hospital. As a comparison, the 1918 pandemic killed 500,000 Americans.

The fatality numbers aren't always so dramatic. The 1957-58 pandemic caused 70,000 fatalities. The 1968-69 pandemic caused only 34,000.

When it came to crisis management planning for pandemic flu, the GAO found only 52% of urban schools and 36% of rural schools had plans in place. That was before the wake-up call of the 2009-10 H1N1 pandemic – which researchers estimate killed 2,634 more people than would have died if it had been a regular flu season.

Thanks to widespread public outreach, most schools have taken onboard the recommendations from the U.S. Department of Health and Human Services (HHS) and the Centers for Disease Control and Prevention (CDC).

They suggest pandemic flu planning could include education campaigns

to prevent spread of the virus by:
- frequent hand washing
- sneezing and coughing only into either a tissue which is then immediately disposed of, or against the upper arm if a tissue isn't available, and
- encouraging everyone in the school community to stay home at the first sign of illness.

Guidance from *flu.gov* and the CDC forms the basis for the following checklist.

☑ CHECKLIST – *Flu Virus Avoidance*

☐ Focus on protecting high-risk students and staff, such as anyone who's pregnant or has asthma or diabetes

☐ Establish a plan to cover key personnel if they're out sick

☐ Work out ways to make it harder for the virus to spread – such as by holding class outside when feasible, regularly washing much-handled surfaces (like door knobs and computer equipment) with the usual cleaning supplies and moving student desks farther apart

☐ Cut any program that might encourage staff or students to come to school when sick – for example, prizes for good attendance

☐ Set up a special room to care for anyone who's sick until they can be sent home

☐ Have a supply of gloves and masks on hand for those who care for them

Based on experiences schools had with the H1N1 virus, it also might be a good idea to get a supply of disposable thermometers. A fever is associated with the flu, and some schools dealing with H1N1 outbreaks had several students displaying flu symptoms at once.

You should also be aware that some students displaying flu symptoms may be in your care longer than you expect. In fact, some schools had a serious problem with parents sending sick children to school during the spring 2009 outbreak. That's probably not too surprising, given the economic pressures many parents face plus the difficulty of finding child-care. In any event, realities being what they are, this may be something you want to anticipate and plan for.

The CDC also advises schools to contact and work with local health authorities in anticipation of a pandemic.

The GAO identified these procedures for educating students when the school is closed:
- electronic or human telephone trees to convey academic information
- web-based instruction
- mailed lessons and assignments, and

- classes broadcast over local TV or radio stations.

Depending on the availability of electricity during a crisis and the level of Internet access among your school community, you may want to consider some kind of web-based delivery of education.

Alternative-education plans are extremely important because experts can anticipate circumstances in which schools could be closed for longer than a year – although a more conservative estimate is that pandemic-related school closures could last from a few weeks up to three months.

The spring of 2009 saw schools closed to protect public health by limiting the spread of the virus. These closures weren't long, but future closures could be – not just to limit spread of a virus but because there might be so few teachers available due to illness that there aren't enough to supervise the students.

Much more info on school planning is available at *flu.gov*.

3. Training

Based on its survey of school districts, the GAO estimated that 27% of districts had never trained with first responders on implementing the school's crisis management plan and that approximately three-quarters of all districts were not training at least once a year with each of the following three resources: law enforcement, firefighters and emergency medical services.

Hopefully the numbers are better now.

The danger of not conducting this participatory training is that it can lead to confusion over who's doing what during an actual event.

Training, on the other hand, can provide responders basic and necessary information, such as how to get into the school, where to turn on (or off) utilities, and how to find their way around. It can speed up response time and may save lives if, for example, medics told to report to the gym already know where the gym is.

For a sample list to be used to compile phone numbers of first responders and other emergency response personnel, see Form II-6 in Chapter Nine.

a. Training With First Responders

It is important to keep in mind that law enforcement, firefighters and emergency medical services have their own protocols. By training with them, schools can learn whether any protocols conflict or are otherwise counterproductive. Also, first responders have a level of training and experience that most school staffs lack. This is a valuable resource. Schools should take advantage of it.

Training with first responders can also clarify whether you're likely to have communication problems. FEMA suggests always using plain language to make sure everyone understands what is needed. It may be obvious to someone very familiar with the campus that "Ken-one" is short for No. 1 Kendall Street and means the auditorium, but it won't be obvious to Officer Rodriguez who just moved here from two states away.

Plain language is a good idea even when it comes to communicating effectively with staff inside the school. A first-time substitute teacher will have no idea that the "Code Purple" announcement over the intercom means she's supposed to lock her classroom door and tell students to lie flat on the floor.

Training with first responders can also help schools make sure in advance that their technology will work with emergency responders' equipment so that they can communicate in a crisis. Incompatible equipment can lead to the school and responders failing to connect or even jamming each other's gear and shutting down communication entirely.

Eight of the 27 districts that the GAO interviewed in researching its 2007 study said that their one-way radios and other equipment didn't work with the first responders' equipment. School officials in Iowa told the GAO that their district had a special problem in that it shared a radio frequency with only some of the first responders, not all of them.

It's vital to fix such disconnects *before* an emergency.

b. Training With Community Partners

While the police, the fire department and emergency medical services spring immediately to most school staffs' minds, not as many think of working with public health professionals and benefiting from the training and expertise they can provide. These community partners can be especially helpful in the event of a biological and radiation emergency.

In addition to other help, public health professionals can help schools plan the best response to biological and radiation events. They can provide expert guidance on specific hazards as well as such info as when sheltering-in-place is called for and how to care for children who may have been outside when an event occurred.

Biological weapons ultimately make people very ill, but the initial symptoms can fall within the normal range of everyday complaints. Therefore, one of the greatest risks of a biological attack is that it will not be recognized as such until after there has been a significant loss of life. The more quickly a biological attack is recognized, the more casualties can be prevented by distributing the available vaccines and antidotes.

In the case of anthrax, for example, the initial signs of the gastrointestinal form of the disease look a lot like food poisoning. The preliminary symptoms of the inhalation form of anthrax could easily be mistaken for a cold or the flu. Symptoms could appear within a month after contact with the bacterium, but they can take longer than a month to appear.

There is a vaccine to prevent anthrax. Even after it's contracted, a 60-day course of antibiotics can sometimes provide a cure.

Schools can help reduce the lag time between seeing symptoms and recognizing a biological attack – and thus save lives – by assigning a staff member to monitor diseases at school and look for patterns. It also helps to have staff who:

- can distinguish between normal illnesses and anomalies caused by biological weapons
- keep in close touch with the public health department, and
- know how and where to report unusual symptoms.

In terms of crisis management planning for an actual incident, a supplement to the Report of the National Advisory Committee on Children and Terrorism suggests:

- training staff in Blood Borne Pathogen Standards
- training staff to use personal protective gear and respirators and conduct a decontamination
- having one accessible switch to perform an emergency shutdown of the HVAC system in order to keep anything airborne from spreading, and
- having a procedure in place to let parents know about the illness and the best way to treat it.

As with pandemics, a biological attack might require schools to close – with all that this implies – in order to avoid the spread of disease.

The CDC's website has an A-Z listing of bioterrorism agents posted at *emergency.cdc.gov/bioterrorism.* This listing includes information about how the diseases are contracted, the symptoms, and if vaccines or cures are available.

With respect to radiation, ideally schools would be prepared to administer potassium iodide in case of radiation exposure within two hours of a "dirty bomb" explosion or a catastrophic incident at a nuclear plant.

A radiation event could require either sheltering-in-place or an evacuation. Public health professionals can help schools to determine when each of these options is the most appropriate choice.

D. Issues Raised by Real-Life Crises

1. School Intruders

Twenty first-graders and six school staff members were killed by an armed intruder at the Sandy Hook Elementary School in Newtown, Connecticut, in December 2012.

The school had a security system in place, but the gunman, a disturbed 20-year-old, shot his way into the building.

What happened was horrific – but safety experts say it could have been even worse if teachers hadn't followed lockdown procedures and if police hadn't arrived quickly. The gunman killed himself as they approached.

The Sandy Hook tragedy prompted a national discussion about whether school personnel should be armed and whether schools should be required to have active shooter drills.

States went on to pass laws saying yes to each.

According to the Council of State Governments Justice Center's report "Arming Teachers and K-12 School Staff," 33 states considered such laws, but only seven passed them – Alabama, Arkansas, Kansas, Oklahoma, South Dakota, Tennessee and Texas.

However, *USA Today* has reported that 21 additional states allow adult gun owners to carry guns in schools.

As for active shooter drills in schools, states with laws requiring the drills include Arkansas, Illinois, Louisiana, Missouri, New Jersey, Oklahoma and Tennessee. The Alabama State Board of Education also requires active shooter drills in the state's schools.

The feds' *Guide for Developing High-Quality School Emergency Operations Plans* comes out in favor of active shooter drills but urges schools to tailor them to the students' ages. The guide includes an "Active Shooter Situations" section that provides a lot of useful information. Again, the guide is available online at *rems.ed.gov.*

For specific steps key personnel should take in the event that an intruder gains unauthorized access, see Form II-12 in Chapter Nine.

Though no one wants to think about violence happening on their campus, it's something every school needs to plan for – and there are some excellent online resources available:

- The International Association of Chiefs of Police has put together *The Guide for Preventing and Responding to School Violence.* You can access it at: *www.ojp.usdoj.gov/BJA/pdf/IACP_School_Violence.pdf.*
- No. 32 in the Problem-Oriented Guides for Police: *Bomb Threats in Schools.* You can access it at: *www.cops.usdoj.gov/Publications/e061120371_POP_BombThreatsi nSchools.pdf.*
- You can also sign up for free online training sponsored by the Department of Homeland Security on "Understanding and Planning for School Bomb Incidents." It's provided by the Energetic Materials Research and Testing Center of New Mexico Tech and can be accessed at: *emrtc.nmt.edu/training/upsbi.php.*

2. Tornado Safe Rooms

In May, 2013, a massive tornado in Moore, Oklahoma, destroyed two elementary schools and killed seven second- and third-graders.

This opened up widespread debate on whether tornado safe rooms should be required in schools.

According to info provided by FEMA: "A safe room is a hardened structure specifically designed to meet FEMA criteria and provide 'near absolute protection' in extreme weather events, including tornadoes and hurricanes."

On the pro side of the debate, requiring safe rooms in schools – especially in states where severe storms are common – could save lifes. On the con side, the cost would be astronomical. One school safe room can cost as much as $1 million.

Currently, there are few mandates requiring schools to have safe rooms. Alabama law requires new schools to have safe rooms, and a few school districts have also decided to find a way to make safe rooms happen – but those are the exceptions.

That may change. What happened in Moore has prompted more states and school boards to seriously consider if safe rooms should be added to the list of requirements for schools.

For more info, check out the video *The ABCs of School Safe Rooms* at *fema.gov/medialibrary/media_records/8506*.

You may also want to check out FEMA's Safe Room Funding page at *fema.gov/safe-room-funding*.

III. LEGAL DECISIONS

A. Intruder- and Student-Attack Cases

Students and teachers have tried to hold schools responsible for injuries caused by students or school intruders by arguing that the school's crisis planning somehow created a duty to ensure their safety.

When the claim is brought as an alleged constitutional violation, courts virtually never find "the state" (here, a public school or the police) legally responsible for the violent acts of private individuals.

There are two very narrow exceptions, not recognized by every jurisdiction. The first is the state-created danger (or enhanced danger) doctrine. The second is the special relationship doctrine.

Under the **state-created danger doctrine**, the state can be held responsible for a person's injury if the state did something that either created the danger that caused the injury or significantly increased it.

Under the second exception, the **special relationship doctrine**, an injured party can prevail by showing that the government took actions that created a legal duty to protect him or her. (The special relationship doctrine can also create liability under states' personal injury laws.)

The decision in a case filed after the Columbine shootings clearly illustrates the operation of the legal framework described above.

The Colorado federal court dismissed most of the injury lawsuits brought by students and teachers in the wake of the Columbine shootings, finding the state was not legally responsible for private individuals' violent acts. But the court refused to dismiss the following case, finding both the state-created danger and special-relationship exceptions applied.

◆   The police created a legal duty to protect a Columbine teacher who bled to death after medical attention was delayed for four hours. **The police interfered with the teacher's ability to save himself and took actions that increased his danger of bleeding to death.**
A teacher was standing outside a cafeteria packed with early lunch

period students when he saw two students approaching with guns. The teacher went into the cafeteria and shouted for the other students to run. He lagged behind until the last of the students escaped up a stairway. As he was urging the last ones up the stairs, one of the gunmen shot him twice in the back. The teacher managed to shepherd approximately 50 students into an upstairs classroom before he collapsed.

The teacher had spotted the gunmen at approximately 11:35 a.m. and was shot about five minutes later. Perhaps half an hour after that, rooftop police sharpshooters with high-powered binoculars saw the gunmen commit suicide in the library.

Although the officers in command knew about the suicides almost immediately, they incorrectly characterized the state of affairs inside the school as a "hostage situation" and followed "hostage situation" procedure by allowing no one in or out of the building – including the firefighters and SWAT team that wanted to rescue the teacher and the emergency medical staff that wanted to provide him onsite care.

Inside the classroom, another teacher and several students applied makeshift compresses to staunch the injured teacher's bleeding. By 12:30 p.m., at least two people had made 911 calls – which were relayed to the responding officers – to report how seriously the teacher had been injured and to tell emergency responders exactly where to find him. They also hung a large sign in the window reading: "1 BLEEDING TO DEATH."

An uninjured teacher spent the afternoon keeping 911 operators informed of the deterioration of the injured teacher's condition. Starting at around noon and continuing for more than three hours, the 911 operators kept relaying the police's message that help was "on the way" and would arrive soon, and that no one should leave the classroom to seek medical help.

At around 2:00 p.m., a 911 operator alerted the police that the people in the classroom were threatening to throw chairs through the windows to attract help for the injured teacher. Although the police knew the gunmen were dead, they told the operator to say this plan was more likely to draw the gunmen than medical help. About half an hour later, an uninjured teacher tried to leave the school to find a medic, but a SWAT team member, acting under police orders, forcibly pushed him back inside.

Once rescue personnel did enter the building, the injured teacher was the last wounded person they reached – even though he was the only person identified as someone who could be saved by emergency medical treatment and they had been told exactly where to find him. A SWAT team finally reached him at 4:00 p.m. By that time, his originally survivable injuries had become fatal. He died.

The deceased teacher's personal representative sued the board of county commissioners, the sheriff's department and several individual officials, alleging deprivation of life in violation of the deceased teacher's right to due process. The United States District Court for the District of Colorado denied the government defendants' request to dismiss the suit.

The district court explained that the U.S. Supreme Court held in 1989 that the Fourteenth Amendment's Due Process Clause does not impose a duty on a state to protect individuals from private acts of violence. Its purpose is "to protect the people from the State, not to ensure that the State protects them from each other." *DeShaney v. Winnebago County Dep't of Social Services*, 489 U.S. 189, 109 S.Ct. 998, 103 L.Ed.2d 249 (1989).

However, the district court continued, the Tenth U.S. Circuit Court of Appeals – which has jurisdiction over Colorado – had adopted two exceptions to this rule, both of which applied here. The special relationship doctrine applied because the government created a duty to protect this teacher by interfering with his ability to save himself, falsely assuring those caring for him that help was coming soon and ordering them not to seek other aid. **The state-created danger exception also applied because the police took actions that increased the teacher's danger of bleeding to death** by keeping him from the medical treatment that could have saved his life. Because these exceptions applied, the court refused to dismiss the case. *Sanders v. Board of County Commissioners of County of Jefferson, Colorado*, 192 F.Supp.2d 1094 (D. Colo. 2001).

As the following cases show, courts have not been persuaded by arguments that schools should be held legally responsible for injuries caused by a student or a school intruder because the schools had – or didn't have – a crisis plan.

It's also worth noting that the federal *Guide for Developing High-Quality School Emergency Operations Plans* makes a point of specifying up front that it is meant as "informal guidance" and doesn't create legal duties or rights.

Instead, to hold the schools liable, courts have insisted the injured parties must establish that either the special relationship doctrine or the state-created danger exception applies.

◆ A gym teacher hospitalized after an intruder's attack couldn't sue the city for her injuries. **The city didn't create a special relationship with her by putting safety measures in place or breach a duty of protection to her by not complying with its own school safety plan.**

A strange man appeared in the gym during class. He struck the teacher and then left. The teacher sent a student to alert a security guard about the intruder, but the student came back to say he couldn't find a guard. The intruder returned unnoticed and hit the teacher from behind, knocking her unconscious. Her injuries included a fractured skull, a fractured rib and hemorrhaging around her left temple.

The teacher sued the city for personal injury, but the court granted the city summary judgment.

New York law almost always found the city immune to personal injury suits based on the operation of a school's security system. The only exception was if the injured party could prove a special relationship that created a duty of protection. The teacher couldn't.

She claimed the school assumed a special duty to protect her because it implemented safety measures, such as metal detectors, door locks, panic bars, video surveillance, patrols by school aides and safety agents, and security telephones in the classrooms.

But the rule in New York was that police protection was owed to the community at large, not to specific individuals.

The teacher needed to show someone with the authority to make promises on the city's behalf created a special relationship with her by promising the city would keep her safe. Instead, she admitted the safety training she received from city employees was for all teachers, not just her. *Daniels v. City of New York*, No. 04-CV-7612(CM), 2007 WL 2040581 (S.D.N.Y. 2007).

◆ A student at a high school with escalating violence and chronic security shortages couldn't hold the school district responsible for injuries he suffered in another student's attack.

A tenth-grader was punched in the eye by a student in a school stairwell. The other student was aiming at someone else, who ducked. The injured student had a fractured facial bone and traumatic hyphema of the eye. He spent six days in the hospital.

Violence at the high school had gotten worse over the previous four years. The principal described the school as "out of control" with fights, fires and other serious issues.

The student said there should have been a surveillance camera in the stairwell. Also, the school was short four security officers that and had not had full security staffing in 83 of the 85 previous days.

The student sued the school district, alleging it violated his Fourteenth Amendment right to bodily integrity and safety. The court granted the school district summary judgment. The student appealed to the Third U.S. Circuit Court of Appeals, but it affirmed judgment for the school district.

The student couldn't hold the school district responsible for his injury because the district didn't create the danger he faced.

The general atmosphere of violence at the school made it foreseeable any student might be attacked by another student, but the court didn't find the attack was a direct result of the district's actions.

The student also didn't show a surveillance camera in the stairwell would have prevented the attack or that security staff shortages increased the danger he'd be injured. Even if all the guards had been there that day, there was no guarantee one would have been in the stairwell at the time of the attack. *Mohammed v. School Dist. of Philadelphia*, 196 Fed.Appx. 79 (3d Cir. 2006).

◆ A teachers' union contract and an official circular creating a school security plan didn't create a special relationship that let a teacher hold the state responsible for his injuries from an attack in a school hallway.

A teacher was assaulted in the hall outside his classroom. He sued the school board, alleging his union contract and the state's official circular adopting and implementing a school security plan created a duty for the school to protect him.

A jury found in the teacher's favor but the trial court set the verdict aside, finding the teacher's union contract and **the state's adoption of a school security plan didn't create a special relationship** between school authorities and the teacher. Without a special relationship, he couldn't hold them liable for not protecting him from third-party violence on school property. The teacher appealed, but the appellate court affirmed. *Krakower v. City of New York*, 217 A.D.2d 441 (N.Y. App. Div. 1995).

B. Negligence Claims

In the cases below, students and parents had mixed success in convincing a court to find their schools were negligent for not following a security plan.

◆   An Indiana appeals court found a middle school principal's school safety plan didn't qualify for immunity under state law, so it refused to dismiss personal injury suits filed by two students who were injured in a school shooting.

Michael Phelps was at the middle school four years, as he had to repeat a grade. In those years he racked up 50 discipline referrals. Seven were for harassing, threatening and physically assaulting other students.

Phelps was suspended after classmates reported he'd said he wanted to "just blow up the school." The principal initiated expulsion proceedings, but his mother forestalled them by withdrawing Phelps from school.

Phelps had been friends with classmate C.J. – but then they both dated N.A. She chose Phelps, and C.J. enraged Phelps by making insulting remarks about N.A. Just before Phelps left the school, a teacher overheard the boys arguing. Phelps also threatened C.J. at a school game, which C.J.'s girlfriend, A.M., reported to teachers.

About a week later, A.M., was on a bus with N.A. She overheard N.A. telling Phelps over the phone that C.J. had made fun of her again. After ending the call, N.A. told A.M. that C.J. was "doomed."

A week after that, Phelps' Facebook page status said, "Today is the day" and "Don't use your mind, use your nine."

Phelps was banned from the middle school campus, but he arrived there around 7:00 a.m.

The principal had developed a safety plan for the school. The surveillance cameras at the school entrances were working properly, and the five school employees monitoring students knew Phelps and knew he wasn't allowed on campus. Despite this, none of the monitors realized he was there, although several students did. N.A. warned C.J. just before Phelps approached him. C.J. texted the news to his mother, who texted him back to go to the office. He didn't.

When Phelps arrived, C.J. told him he didn't want to fight. Phelps said,

"[T]oo bad," and shot C.J. twice in the stomach. The bullet casings hit another student's hand, injuring him. Both boys survived. They and their mothers sued the district for personal injury.

The district argued the principal's school safety plan made it immune to the suit. The trial court found it didn't, and an appeals court affirmed. The state's law provides immunity for loss that results from the "performance of a discretionary function" by "public officials." The principal's plan didn't meet this standard for two reasons.

First, the claimed negligence wasn't in the arguably discretionary function of formulating the plan but in the way staff implemented it. Second, earlier decisions had established principals are administrators rather than "public officials." As the district wasn't immune to the suit, the trial court refused to dismiss it, and the appeals court affirmed. *M.S.D. of Martinsville v. Jackson*, 9 N.E.3d 230 (Ind. Ct. App. 2014).

◆ Finding state education department regulations had "the force and effect of law," the Delaware Supreme Court OK'd a negligence per se claim based on an alleged breach of rules concerning suicidal students.

The Delaware Department of Education's (DOE's) Regulation 621 required school districts to have written emergency plans that followed the DOE's Emergency Preparedness Guidelines.

A "Quick Referral Reference" posted on the DOE's website said schools with a suicidal student should contact the student's parents or guardian immediately.

To comply with the guidelines. the school district adopted the policy: "Crisis Intervention Procedures for Suicide Threats." Third on its list of six protocols was: "Contact Parent[.]"

After 16-year-old Roger Ellerbe's friend told a teacher and then a school counselor that Ellerbe was suicidal and had attempted suicide two days earlier, the counselor called Ellerbe into the office.

The counselor was working under a contract with the district. She didn't know the district had a protocol for dealing with suicidal students.

She spent four hours with Ellerbe and sent him back to class when she decided his crisis had ended. She sent an email to teachers, counselors and an assistant principal to tell them about the incident. She didn't call the boy's grandmother, his guardian.

That night, Ellerbe hanged himself at home.

Ellerbe's family sued the district for wrongful death. This claim required them to show the district was negligent. Finding they couldn't, the trial court granted the district judgment without a trial.

The family appealed to the state's highest court. It reversed, finding the case could go forward because the family stated a valid claim of negligence per se.

In Delaware, violating a statute or ordinance enacted for the safety of others constituted negligence per se. **The family claimed the district violated a school policy, but the court found it had "the force and effect of law."** As the family could make a valid negligence claim, their wrongful death claim could go forward. *Rogers v. Christina School Dist.*, 73 A.3d 1 (Del. 2013).

◆ A trial was needed for a student's personal injury suit because factors – including the school's failure to follow its security plan – indicated a New York district may have breached its duty to supervise students.

The district was aware of escalating aggression between two students.

First, a teacher had to restrain seventh-grader Ashley Bivens from physically attacking ninth-grader Tajoura Walley. A week later, the students got into a physical fight on a school bus, and a volleyball coach had to break it up. The next day, Bivens and Walley started a fight as soon as they got to school. Teachers had to separate them, and both girls were suspended.

The day their suspensions ended, Bivens went straight from the school bus to Walley's locker and stabbed Walley in the leg with a knife.

Walley sued the district, alleging it breached its duty to supervise them. She argued their escalating dispute put the district on notice that another incident could occur when they returned to school from their suspensions for fighting. She also **argued the school had failed to follow its security plan** by not:

- providing counseling, and
- having teachers stand outside their classrooms at the start of the school day to prevent problems.

The district agreed it breached its duty to supervise, but asked for judgment without a trial as its negligence wasn't the proximate cause of Walley's injury. It argued Bivens' attack was so sudden and spontaneous no amount of supervision could have prevented it.

The judge agreed and granted the district judgment. But Walley appealed, and the appellate court reversed.

As a prior New York decision held, the test for proximate cause was "whether under all the circumstances the chain of events that followed the negligent act or omission was a normal or foreseeable consequence of the situation created by the school's negligence." If it wasn't foreseeable, the school couldn't be held liable for it. But if that wasn't clear, a jury was needed – and that was the case here. *Walley v. Bivens*, 81 A.D.3d 1286 (N.Y. App. Div. 2011).

◆ The Nebraska Supreme Court rejected a mother's argument that the state education department's regulations for school safety plans created a legal duty that could be violated if a school district didn't follow the regs.

An intruder entered an elementary school's unlocked door and ignored a sign telling all visitors to check in at the office.

Two teachers spotted him and reported him to the office.

Meanwhile, five-year-old C.B. came back from the bathroom to tell his teacher "a bad man" was in there. C.B. later said the man pulled down his pants and performed oral sex on him.

The district's "Safety and Security Plan" and the school's "Emergency

Procedures and Security" guidelines called for dealing with an intruder by talking to the person and then deciding whether to lock down the school and call 911.

The administrator went inside the restroom and found the man sitting in a stall. After C.B.'s teacher told the administrator what C.B. said, the administrator locked down the school and called 911. Police arrived and arrested the intruder.

C.B.'s mother sued, alleging the district was negligent because its security system was ineffective. The trial court granted the district summary judgment. It found the assault on C.B. wasn't foreseeable and the district had made a *prima facie* showing that its security plan was adequate.

On appeal, the Nebraska Supreme Court sent the case back for a trial to decide if the attack was foreseeable – but **rejected the mother's argument the school should be held liable because its safety plan allegedly didn't follow the state education department's regulations**.

The regulations set the standard for school security plans but didn't create an extra legal duty that went beyond the district's existing duty to act with reasonable care to protect students from a sexual assault. *A.W. v. Lancaster County School Dist. 0001*, 280 Neb. 205 (Neb. 2010).

◆   The district's state-law-required transportation safety plan (TSP) may have triggered a legal duty to stop a six-year-old from getting off a school bus before it left to drive the children home.

Eric M. was a first-grader. His parents signed him up for the school bus, but sometimes drove to school and picked him up instead. Whether he took the bus or drove home with a parent changed from day to day.

About a month into the school year, Eric got on the bus but then told the bus driver he was getting off because he'd just seen his father's car. The bus driver grabbed Eric's arm to stop him and asked if he was sure. Eric said he was – but he was mistaken.

After Eric couldn't find his father, he started to walk with other students. He was struck by a car while crossing a busy street.

Eric sued the district for personal injury, alleging it breached its duty of care when it "negligently permitted, allowed, and let [him] wander away from school." The court dismissed his claim. He appealed, and the appellate court reversed.

California law required districts that provided transportation to prepare a TSP that set out procedures for school personnel to follow "to ensure the safe transport of pupils." The procedures for grades preK-8 were supposed to include "boarding and exiting a schoolbus[.]" Based on this and provisions giving drivers and school personnel responsibility for supervising students, the court found the district had undertaken a duty of care toward students.

The court decided a trial was needed to determine if the duty of immediate and direct supervision of pupils was breached here. *Eric M. v. Cajon Valley Union School Dist.*, 174 Cal.App.4th 285 (Cal. Ct. App. 2009).

C. Claims Based on State Requirements

◆   California laws require public schools to have school safety plans. The plans must include anti-harassment and anti-discrimination policies.

An appeals court found the father of a boy who was allegedly bullied for being disabled and Hispanic could seek to enforce those laws against a school district his son no longer attended.

Hector F.'s seventh-grade son Brian was eligible for special education based on emotional disabilities including bipolar disorder. English wasn't Brian's first language, and he was in the school's only bilingual classroom.

Hector went to administrators after seeing Brian had large bruises and scratches. Brian went on to file reports with the school to say other students were physically and verbally abusing him, including with ethnic slurs.

The principal's proposed solution was to move Brian out of the bilingual classroom. His parents rejected this proposal.

Hector and Brian sued the school district. **The father claimed the district hadn't adopted state-required safety plans.** He also alleged the district wasted taxpayer money by responding to harassment complaints in a way that discriminated against Hispanics and the disabled. He wanted a "writ of mandate" to enforce the laws. After Brian moved on to a high school in another school district, a trial court decided Hector couldn't seek this remedy – but an appeals court found he could.

Generally, the state allows writs of mandate only to "beneficially interested" persons, but Hector fell within a public interest exception. The appeals court wrote that the laws "articulate a well identified public interest in maintaining a system of taxpayer funded public education which is free of the destructive influence of discrimination, harassment and bullying." Here, the writ was intended to enforce a public duty. The court found Hector had a right to seek enforcement of the law both as a taxpayer and a member of the public. *Hector F. v. El Centro Elementary School Dist.,* 227 Cal.App.4th 331 (Cal. Ct. App. 2014).

In 2007, Georgia courts heard three appeals involving the interplay between the state's requirement that schools have crisis management plans and lawsuits brought by students who were seriously injured at school. In two cases, the school was sued because it didn't have a plan in place. In the third, the school was sued, although it did have a plan in place. In each case, the court found the school was immune to the student's lawsuit.

◆   A student who was nearly raped at school couldn't sue the members of the school board for negligence based on the board's failure to implement a school safety plan at her school because the board had state immunity to this claim.

A female student was sexually molested at school by a male student who also tried to rape her. Despite a state law requiring schools to have safety plans, there was no such plan in place at her school.

The student brought a Title IX claim against the school board. She also sued the individual board members, alleging they were negligent for failing to implement a school safety plan. The board members objected to her lawsuit, arguing they couldn't be held negligent because they had no individual legal duty to create the safety plan.

In Georgia, state employees were immune to lawsuits alleging negligence only if the duty they allegedly failed to perform was discretionary rather than ministerial. Discretionary duties called for greater personal authority and judgment, whereas ministerial duties were more like those performed pursuant to orders.

Because the *Murphy v. Bajjani* case (reported below) had determined Georgia school boards and superintendents had a discretionary duty when it came to preparing school safety plans, this court agreed with the board members that the student could not sue them for negligence based on their failure to develop a school safety plan. As a result, the court invited the board members to ask the court to grant it summary judgment. *Snethen v. Board of Public Educ. for the City of Savannah*, No. 406CV259, 2007 WL 2345247 (S.D. Ga. 2007).

◆ The Georgia Supreme Court held that a student severely injured by another student at school couldn't sue school administrators or members of the school board for negligence based on their failure to create a school safety plan as required by state law. Georgia law granted them immunity to negligence claims unless they acted with actual malice or intent to cause injury – which they did not.

In June 2007, the Supreme Court of Georgia reversed a lower court's judgment in favor of a high school student who was seriously injured at school by another student. The lower court determined the individuals sued by the student – including his principal, vice principal and members of the school board – were responsible for the student's injuries because the school hadn't created a school safety plan as required by Georgia state law. The law called for schools to devise a plan to respond to the following potential emergencies: natural disasters, hazardous material or radiological accidents, terrorism and violence.

The state supreme court reversed the judgment for the student and dismissed the case against the school defendants because it determined **these public employees had qualified immunity under the state's constitution with respect to safety plans**. This meant that they could not be sued for negligence unless they had acted maliciously or with intent to injure.

This decision hinged on which kind of duty the safety-plan law created: ministerial or discretionary. The court determined that drafting safety plans was a discretionary act (an exercise of educated, personal judgment) as opposed to a ministerial act (something more akin to following established procedures). Ministerial acts weren't covered by qualified immunity for negligence, but discretionary acts were.

The court dismissed the case against the school defendants because it found that creating a school safety plan was a discretionary act and the school defendants hadn't acted with actual malice or intent to cause injury. This meant they were immune to the student's claims. *Murphy v. Bajjani*, 647 S.E.2d 54 (Ga. 2007). A Georgia appellate court adopted the supreme court's judgment in another proceeding based on the same incident. *Bajjani v. Gwinnett County School Dist.*, 651 S.E.2d 366 (Ga. Ct. App. 2008).

◆ **A county board of education, its individual members, the superintendent and a school's principal and staff were entitled to official immunity because there was a valid safety plan in place at the school when a psychologically disturbed stranger gained unauthorized entry to it and attacked a 10-year-old with a hammer**.

Georgia law requires schools to create safety plans. This school provided evidence that it did have a safety plan in place before the intruder attacked the 10-year-old, but the child's parents argued that the plan wasn't valid because it had been developed by the Georgia Emergency Management Agency (GEMA) and other third parties instead of the school itself. But the Georgia Court of Appeals found that the law specifically sanctioned input from approved third parties and that it required GEMA to provide public schools training and technical assistance, which included safe school planning and model school safety plans.

This case pre-dated the state's supreme court decision that settled the law by finding creation of a school safety plan was a discretionary duty instead of a ministerial duty. But it also held the duty was discretionary and therefore shielded school officials from negligence charges. *Leake v. Murphy*, 644 S.E.2d 328 (Ga. Ct. App. 2007).

D. Evacuating Students With Disabilities

◆ A student with a disability couldn't sue the school board for disability discrimination based on school personnel's failure to properly execute the emergency evacuation plan for children with disabilities.

A middle school student had a form of dwarfism that limited her strength and mobility. She operated a computer with voice recognition software so that she didn't have to type. She also had a motorized wheelchair and a full-time aide.

In 1996, her school was evacuated because of a bomb threat. For just over an hour, this student and another student with disabilities were left alone in the building under adult supervision. No bomb was discovered.

Her parents filed a complaint with the state department of education, alleging the school board discriminated against her based on her disability by not evacuating her from the building during the bomb threat. After mediation, the parents agreed to drop their complaint in exchange for the school board's agreement to adopt a new emergency preparedness plan for students with disabilities.

This plan called for sending students with disabilities to one of several "safe rooms" during school emergencies. Each safe room was assigned a responsible adult (plus an alternate) and was equipped with a special flag to alert emergency responders of their presence and also a cell phone. In case evacuation was necessary, the plan called for emergency personnel to rescue the students from the safe rooms.

The school instituted the plan based on advice from local fire and police officials and then explained it to staff and students. It also held a successful practice drill. But two months later, the school had an unscheduled fire drill and the student was left alone for two minutes until the student's math teacher – not assigned as a responsible adult for that room – stopped by to make sure the student was OK. The math teacher stayed with the student for the rest of the fire drill.

The student's parents sued the school board, alleging disability discrimination in violation of Section 504 of the Rehabilitation Act and Title II of the Americans with Disabilities Act based on the bomb-threat and fire-drill incidents.

The court granted the school board summary judgment. The parents appealed, but the Fourth U.S. Circuit Court of Appeals affirmed judgment for the school. The parents couldn't sue concerning the bomb-threat incident because the parents definitively resolved that dispute with the school board when they agreed to drop the complaint in return for institution of the new safety plan.

Based on only the fire-drill incident, the parents couldn't show the school board excluded the student from safe evacuation procedures during an emergency. The school had developed a plan, based on expert advice, specifically aimed at safely evacuating children with disabilities. It had equipped its safe rooms and run a successful drill. **Although the student was left alone for two minutes in a safe room, the imperfect execution of an otherwise reasonable evacuation plan did not constitute disability discrimination.** *Shirey v. City of Alexandria School Board*, 229 F.3d 1143 (4th Cir. 2000).

E. Cases Involving Staff

◆   A New York appellate court affirmed a ruling that a board of education acted in bad faith by replacing a union position with a virtually identical – but nonunion – position.

After a school district abolished its Director of Emergency Planning position, the union of the person who lost the job sued the district's board of education.

The union accused the board of acting in bad faith, claiming it replaced the emergency planning position with a nearly identical one called Homeland Security Coordinator – which union members couldn't hold because it was civil-service exempt.

Both positions required a comprehensive understanding of emergency management and involved responsibilities relating to

emergency preparedness, including implementing safety plans and organizing training programs.

The board argued it was entitled to abolish a position at any time – but prior New York decisions had held "a position may not be abolished as a subterfuge to avoid the statutory protection afforded to civil servants." The court found that was the case here and held the board acted in bad faith. The board appealed, but the appellate court affirmed. *Gallagher v. Board of Educ. for Buffalo City School Dist.*, 81 A.D.3d 1408 (N.Y. App. Div. 2011).

◆ The Ninth U.S. Circuit Court of Appeals reversed a lower court's decision that a school district's former security specialist couldn't make a First Amendment retaliation claim.

Robert Posey's high school security specialist position included liaising with police, enforcing truancy policies, searching students and investigating student misconduct – until the new principal relieved him of those duties. After that, he mainly monitored the parking lot, grounds and hallways. The principal asked him to update the school's emergency plan – but later reassigned the job, finding "Mr. Posey was not in full charge of those issues."

Posey met with the principal to say he was worried about the way discipline and safety issues were being handled. The principal didn't respond directly, and Posey became increasingly worried.

Posey had a friendly relationship with the district's chief administrative officer (CAO). About a year after his meeting with the principal, Posey gave the CAO a long letter about school safety issues, he hoped writing it would prompt the district to "correct the problems before somebody gets seriously hurt." In it, he detailed concerns about the administration's:

• lack of responsiveness to safety problems
• inadequate staff training
• failure to properly document safety violations
• ineffective truancy and sexual-harassment policy enforcement, and
• inadequate fire safety and school evacuation planning.

Posey substantiated each concern with specific examples. The letter was copied to the superintendent and two school administrators.

At the end of the year, Posey was told the district was combining his and two other employees' job duties to create a new "preventative specialist" position. Posey applied for it but wasn't hired.

He filed a grievance, and the school district found he'd been retaliated against because of his letter – but the district's governing board overrode that determination and refused to rehire Posey.

Posey sued the district, alleging it violated his First Amendment rights by firing and then not rehiring him in retaliation for raising safety concerns. But the court granted the district summary judgment. The Supreme Court decision *Garcetti v. Ceballos*, 547 U.S. 410 (2006), had held public employees don't have free speech rights in statements made concerning their official duties. The court determined Posey's letter wasn't protected speech because it concerned his official duties.

On appeal, the Ninth Circuit reversed. It found the safety concerns Posey raised were matters of public concern, protected speech under *Garcetti*, and disagreed that Posey's remarks concerned his official duties. It returned the case to the lower court for further proceedings. *Posey v. Lake Pend Oreille School Dist. No. 84*, 546 F.3d 1121 (9th Cir. 2008).

◆ A security officer who was attacked by a student couldn't hold the school district legally responsible for his injuries. The district hadn't promised him special protection, as it couldn't have predicted the student would attack him and her act was too fast and unexpected for anyone on the scene to have prevented it.

Two girls were fighting in the hall of their high school, and a security officer came over to break it up. But while he was physically restraining one of the girls against the lockers, he was attacked from behind and injured.

He sued the school district for personal injury, but the district asked for summary judgment. It argued the security officer couldn't hold the district liable for personal injury for two reasons: **the district didn't owe him a special duty, and the attack happened so quickly and unexpectedly that the school couldn't have prevented it**. The court agreed and granted the district judgment.

To show the district owed him a special duty of protection, the security officer had to demonstrate the district made a special promise to protect him on an individual basis – not simply to provide him the same protection it offered the public at large. He couldn't.

He also couldn't show the school district could have predicted, based on the student's past behavior, that she was likely to attack him. Because he couldn't, he couldn't hold the district legally responsible for the attack. It was an impulsive, unanticipated act that happened so fast that even the best supervision couldn't have prevented it. *Stinson v. Roosevelt U.F.S.D.*, 851 N.Y.S.2d 66 (N.Y. Sup. Ct. 2007).

Stinson appealed, but the court dismissed his appeal.

The appellate court clarified that the district owed a duty to students to adequately supervise them to prevent foreseeable injuries to other students. But since this duty was based on the fact that the school was acting *in loco parentis* (a kind of parental responsibility), this duty didn't extend to adults on its premises.

Since the district had established it owed Stinson no legal duty, it was entitled to judgment as a matter of law. The appellate court affirmed the lower court's judgment and dismissed Stinson's appeal. *Stinson v. Roosevelt U.F.S.D.*, 877 N.Y.S.2d 400 (N.Y. App. Div. 2009).

◆ A teacher, who was arrested and prosecuted for making a phone call threatening to shoot staff and bomb the school, couldn't sue the district or police after she was acquitted because her arrest and prosecution were supported by probable cause.

The teacher had received two written warnings about her job

performance, and students and parents had complained about her. The principal offered her the option of resigning, and she accepted. Eleven days later, the teacher had a physical fight at school with a female student and the principal told her to stay home on paid leave until he investigated. Two days later, someone identifying herself as the teacher called the school and told a secretary she was going to shoot everyone on the administrative staff and blow up the school.

After unsuccessfully trying to reach the teacher at home, the principal called a police officer assigned to a nearby school. The principal turned the investigation over to the officer before focusing on evacuating the school.

The secretary who had spoken to the caller told the officer she had recognized the voice as belonging to the teacher. The officer arrested the teacher for aggravated harassment.

The district issued a press release stating that "a female voice identifying herself as [... the teacher] threatened to blow up the school and shoot office staff. [... The principal] immediately notified the police and implemented the school security plan. The school was locked down and the case was turned over to the police."

The former teacher was acquitted. Among other parties, she then sued the district, the principal and the officer who arrested her, raising claims including libel, malicious prosecution, false arrest and a violation of her civil rights.

The court dismissed the former teacher's lawsuit. **Concerning the libel charge, the court found that the district's press release contained no false statements.** Although it identified her by name, the release stated only that someone claiming to be the former teacher had called the school and made threats. This accurately described what had happened. As for the other charges, the police had probable cause to arrest the former teacher based on the secretary's report of the call and her identification of the voice as belonging to the former teacher. *Rizzo v. Edison, Inc.*, 419 F.Supp.2d 338 (W.D.N.Y. 2005). The judgment was affirmed on appeal to the Second U.S. Circuit Court of Appeals. *Rizzo v. Edison, Inc.*, 172 Fed.Appx. 391 (2d Cir. 2006).

CHAPTER THREE

School Safety and Liability

I. BULLYING AND HAZING

Although state legislatures and the U.S. Department of Education have responded vigorously to bullying among K-12 students, anti-bullying laws and regulations have for the most part not created private causes of action leading to school liability. Liability in bullying cases is typically determined under traditional negligence and constitutional law principles. In negligence cases, a school district or board of education may be held liable for student-on-student violence only if it had "specific, prior knowledge of the danger that caused the injury."

An exception was made by the Court of Appeal of California in *Hector F. v. El Centro Elementary School Dist.*, 227 Cal.App.4th 331,173 Cal.Rptr.3d 413 (Cal. Ct. App. 2014). The court held a parent had standing as both a citizen and taxpayer to enforce a comprehensive law requiring safety plans in all schools. It found a "manifest public interest in enforcing the antibullying statutes" and no countervailing reasons not to enforce them.

A. School Violence

1. Legislative Responses

Oklahoma's School Protection Act imposes civil and criminal penalties on students who attempt to harm education employees or volunteers. Under a 2014 law, students in grades 6-12 who try to physically harm an education employee or volunteer at a school are subject to an out-of-school suspension. School employees who are injured due to an assault or battery in the performance of their duties are entitled to a leave of absence without loss of their leave benefits. Penalties under the act are in addition to and do not amend state Government Tort Claims Act remedies. Additional provisions of the School Protection Act prohibit people from making false accusations of criminal activity against education employees to law enforcement officers or school district officials. Adults who violate the false reporting provision are subject to misdemeanor convictions and fines, while those under 18 are subject to juvenile court proceedings. Fifty-Fourth Oklahoma Legislature, First Extraordinary Session 2013, Ch. 7 (H.B. 1009). Oklahoma Statutes Title 70, Sections 6-149.1, 6-149.2, 6-149.3, 6-149.4, 6-149.5, 6-149.6, 6-149.7, 6-149.8, 6-149.9.

A 2014 amendment to **Michigan**'s Student Safety Act established a 24-hour hotline for reporting harm or criminal activity directed at students, school employees and schools. Under the act, the state attorney general's department was required to establish a program for receiving reports and information from the public regarding potential self-harm and potential harm or criminal acts directed at students, school employees or schools. The act required a hotline for receiving reports and information that is available 24 hours per day, 365 days a year. The program will provide for a means to review information submitted through the hotline. Such information, including analysis of a potential threat, is to be directed to school officials and law enforcement officials. Under the act, the state attorney general's department must ensure appropriate training for program personnel in crisis management, including recognition of mental illness and emotional disturbance. Training must be provided regarding resources available in the community for providing mental health treatment and other services. Reports to the hotline will be considered reports to a law enforcement agency and will be subject to the act's confidentiality provisions. Ninety-Seventh Michigan Legislature, Regular Session, Public Act No. 183, S.B. No. 374. Michigan Compiled Laws, Sections 752.911 through 752.918.

An amended **Illinois** law requires each school board in the state to adopt a policy that declares teen dating violence unacceptable and prohibited. A district policy must state that each student has the right to a safe learning environment. Board policies must incorporate age-appropriate education about teen dating violence into training programs for students in grades 7-12 and school employees. District policies must establish procedures for employee responses to incidents of teen dating violence taking place at schools, on school grounds, at school-sponsored activities, or in school vehicles. Policies are to identify by job title the school officials who are responsible for receiving reports related to teen dating violence. Ninety-Eighth Illinois General Assembly, P.A. 98-190, H.B. 3379. Illinois Statutes Section 105-110/3.10.

New York's Dignity for All Students Act declares the state's policy to afford public school students an environment free of discrimination and harassment. Under the act, no student can be discriminated against on the basis of race, color, weight, national origin, ethnic group, religion, religious practice, disability, sexual orientation, gender or sex by school employees or students on school property or at school functions. The act defines "harassment" as "conduct, verbal threats, intimidation or abuse" based on one's "actual or perceived race, color, weight, national origin, ethnic group, religion, religious practice, disability, sexual orientation gender or sex."

"Harassment" includes the creation of a hostile environment by conduct or verbal threats, intimidation or abuse that unreasonably and substantially interferes with a student's educational performance, opportunities or benefits, or mental, emotional or physical well-being. Harassment may include conduct, threats, abuse or intimidation that reasonably causes students to fear for their own safety. School boards must create policies and guidelines to create a school environment free from bias and harassment. The amendment includes reporting requirements and guidelines for nondiscriminatory instructional and counseling methods, and it requires the state to provide model policies and other assistance to school districts.

Ohio law prohibits harassment, intimidation and bullying of students and expressly provides for the suspension of any student responsible for such conduct by an "electronic act." By law, school policies must include a statement extending the prohibition to school buses and expressly providing for the possibility of suspension of a student who is found responsible for harassment, intimidation or bullying by an "electronic act." The term "electronic act" is defined in the amended law as an act committed through the use of a cell phone, computer, pager, personal communication device or other electronic communication device. Ohio school policies must include a means by which a person may anonymously report an incident of harassment or bullying. Policies must include a statement prohibiting students from deliberately making false reports of harassment, intimidation or bullying, and a disciplinary procedure for any student responsible for deliberately making a false report of that nature. The act is named for Jessica Logan, who committed suicide shortly after she reported cyberbullying and harassment by her peers. Ohio 2012 Session Laws, File 74, H.B. No. 116, Ohio Revised Code Sections 3313.666, 3313.667, 3319.073, 3333.31.

New Jersey's "Anti-Bullying Bill of Rights Act" requires prompt reporting and investigating of harassment, intimidation or bullying at school. A school safety team is to be formed in each school and is intended to foster and maintain a positive school climate and receive complaints. Each school is to appoint a school anti-bullying specialist, who is to lead school investigations. School districts will be required to have anti-bullying coordinators. School employees must immediately report incidents of harassment, intimidation or bullying to appropriate school officials.

Administrators who receive reports of harassment, intimidation or bullying and fail to take action may be subject to discipline. School administrators will receive complete training on the prevention of harassment, intimidation and bullying, and superintendents will be required to report all acts of harassment, intimidation and bullying to their boards. Reports will include the nature of the bullying, names of investigators and the type of student discipline imposed. School report cards will include data identifying the number and type of reports of harassment, intimidation or bullying. Schools will be graded on their efforts to identify harassment, intimidation and bullying, and to address these types of misconduct. An amendment requiring student suspension or expulsion is included in the act.

2. Negligence

Courts have found no liability for harm that is "sudden" or "without warning" and have held that schools and staff members are not liable for injuries that are unforeseeable. Schools are not considered the "insurers of student safety," and state immunity laws offer school districts and their employees immunity unless there is some intentional misconduct, deliberate indifference or other gross departure from professional standards.

For example, **New York courts have held there is no school liability for injuries caused by sudden, impulsive acts that are not preceded by prior misconduct**. In *Mirand v. City of New York*, 84 N.Y. 44, 637 N.E.2d 263 (N.Y. 1994), the state's highest court held a school is liable for student-on-student violence only if it had "specific, prior knowledge of the danger that caused the injury." A student's acts must have been foreseeable by the district to impose liability. If an assault occurs so suddenly that it could not be prevented by any amount of supervision, there is no school liability. Prior unrelated incidents of student discipline do not put a school on notice of a specific threat of danger requiring supervision. While schools have a duty to supervise students, "this duty does not make schools insurers of the safety of their students, for they cannot be reasonably expected to continuously supervise and control all movements and activities of students."

◆   In contrast to the court's decision in *Hector F. v. El Centro Elementary School Dist.*, 227 Cal.App.4th 331,173 Cal.Rptr.3d 413 (Cal. Ct. App. 2014), this chapter, a Connecticut court held there is **no private cause of action** to enforce the state's anti-bullying statute.

The case was filed by the parents of a student who claimed she was bullied extensively by a classmate, leading to an attack that seriously injured her. In reviewing the parents' 24-count complaint, the court held they could not base a negligence claim on lack of compliance with the anti-bullying law. No statutory language provided for private enforcement, and a review of legislative history did not reveal any such intent. As a result, the parents' claim had to be dismissed. *Mazzo v. Town of Fairfield Board of Educ.*, No. CV 126031781S, 2013 WL 4872203 (Conn. Super. Ct. 8/20/13).

◆   Soon after a student's family moved from Georgia to New Jersey, she encountered problems in her classroom. During her fourth-grade year, her mother reported that classmates had spit on the student, hit her, kicked her and confronted her physically. The school called meetings at which the parents and students discussed the reports and appropriate behavior. More incidents were reported the next year. Most reports came from the mother, and the school could not verify many of them. The student said she felt the misconduct was directed toward her mother's obesity and her aunt's disability. She was placed in a new school but had difficulty with her peers there. An escort plan was formulated to ensure the student's safety and to separate her from girls who were making her feel uncomfortable. Near this time, the family spent time in a shelter and began counseling sessions. The student was diagnosed with adjustment disorder, enuresis and trichotillomania. Her mother sued the school board, superintendent and others in a federal court for violations of the Constitution and the New Jersey Law Against Discrimination (LAD). In pretrial activity, the court explained that the state Anti-Bullying Act required each school district to adopt a policy prohibiting harassment, intimidation or bullying. **Although the act required schools to have procedures for investigating such reports, the law created no private cause of action** and did not create or alter any state law tort liability. A number of incidents were investigated by a school anti-bullying specialist, but no evidence or witnesses were found. As for the LAD claim, the court found no reasonable jury could find there had been bullying based on gender. The family had reported bullying by both male and female students, and nothing indicated the bullying was due to the student's sex. Although the mother asserted discrimination on the basis of being from the South, the court held this did not support a claim for national origin discrimination. As there was no evidence of discrimination based on a protected status, the court dismissed the LAD claim. School officials were entitled to qualified immunity. The court held for the board and officials. *Thomas v. East Orange Board of Educ.*, Civ. No. 2:12-01446 (WJM), 2014 WL 495133 (D.N.J. 2/6/14).

◆ An Illinois student said peers subjected him to verbal and physical abuse at school for an extended time. He said he was punched and pushed by other students and that he told school officials many times about bullying. After the student claimed to have been beaten up outside his classroom by peers, he sued the school district in a state court for negligence, asserting it failed to provide him with a safe environment. The court dismissed the case, finding the district had immunity under the Illinois Local Governmental and Governmental Tort Immunity Act. Appeal went before the Appellate Court of Illinois. It noted the trial court's finding that dealing with student bullying was a discretionary decision for which the Tort Immunity Act provided absolute immunity. The court explained that the act protected local entities and employees from liability arising from government operations. Immunity was a legislative choice to prevent the diversion of public funds from their intended purposes to pay out claims. A public employee in a policy-making position or exercising discretion was not liable for any injury resulting from an act or omission in determining policy. The court held this meant there was an absolute grant of immunity from liability for public entities. Under prior state cases, a principal had broad discretion in handling bullying cases and was entitled to discretionary immunity under the Tort Immunity Act.

A bullying policy could provide a school district with discretion to determine whether bullying had occurred, what consequences would result and any remedial actions. Since a school's handling of bullying incidents fit within the definition of a "discretionary act" under the Tort Immunity Act, the court held for the school district. *Malinksi v. Grayslake Community High School Dist. 127*, No. 2012-CA-002178-MR, 2014 WL 1004199 (Ill. App. Ct. 2/14/14).

◆ An Illinois parent claimed three classmates bullied her daughter from kindergarten through grade four. She asked the principal to reassign her child to a different classroom. The parent later said the principal declined the request. Later in the school year, the parent met with the district superintendent and principal to discuss the bullying problem. She also sought to arrange a meeting that would include parents of the other girls and police. After an incident in which the student said the girls trapped her in a school lavatory and threatened her, the parent called the police. She again called the principal, who promised appropriate disciplinary action. A second police report was made after the student said one of the girls again threatened her in a lavatory. An investigating officer spoke to the parents of the other girls, who stated they had never been told previously that their children were bullying the student. After the parent was denied a meeting with police, school administrators and a teacher, the parent sued the school district and administrators in a state court for negligence. The case was dismissed, and the parent appealed to the Appellate Court of Illinois.

On appeal, the court explained that government employees may qualify for immunity under the Illinois Tort Immunity Act if their jobs require determination of policy or the exercise of discretion. Under the parent's theory, the district's anti-bullying policy required administrators to respond to reported bullying without any exercise of discretion. But the court explained that **school administrators balance competing interests when handling bullying cases**. As maintaining the anti-bullying policy called for the broad exercise of discretion, the court held immunity was correctly granted under the Tort Immunity Act. While expressing sympathy for the parent's claims, the court held the administrators were entitled to immunity from any liability. It affirmed the lower court's judgment. *Hascall v. Williams*, 996 N.E.2d 1168 (Ill. App. Ct. 2013).

◆   While in a high school hallway, a Washington student was fatally shot by a student with disabilities. The victim's family sued the school district in a state court, arguing the disabled student's behavior and medical records indicated he was a risk to others. It was asserted that the district negligently failed to maintain a safe environment. In trial court proceedings, evidence was produced that the disabled student had paranoid schizophrenia and tried to commit suicide two years before the shooting. His doctors noted he heard voices at the time of the shooting and claimed to get into fights with people he did not know. After hospitalization, the disabled student underwent 11 months of outpatient mental health care and received anti-psychotic medication. Since his condition had been found to be stable on medication, the outpatient services were terminated. There was no evidence that the disabled student had previously committed any assaults. In pretrial activity, the court rejected the estate's theories of liability. After the court denied the estate's request to reconsider dismissal, the estate appealed.

On appeal, the Court of Appeals of Washington held that **school districts must exercise reasonable care when supervising students. But the duty to exercise reasonable care extends only to foreseeable risks of harm.** Although the court agreed with the estate that foreseeability is normally a jury question, it found nothing in school or medical records indicating the disabled student presented a risk of harm to anyone at school. Since there was no indication that he might try to harm someone, the court found the shooting was not foreseeable to the district. The court found the estate's arguments ignored state and federal antidiscrimination laws and school district obligations to serve the disabled student. As the district did not have evidence that he would act violently, the court affirmed the judgment for the school district. *Kok v. Tacoma School Dist. No. 10*, No. 44517-4-II, 2013 WL 5761203 (Wash. Ct. App. 10/22/13).

◆   A 14-year-old Iowa student was considered vulnerable and functioned at a third-grade level. She was rarely without direct supervision, and her teachers usually took precautions beyond what school policy required. A special education teacher saw her spending time with a 19-year-old special education student. Although she saw them touching and kissing, she assumed they had an age-appropriate relationship. On a day when the student's mother allowed the student to ride the bus home from school with a friend, the student skipped her last class. She then left school with the friend, met the 19-year-old student and went to still another student's house.

The 19-year-old then took the student to the garage and raped her. After the mother learned of the rape, she sued the school district in a state court for negligence. After a jury trial, the court denied motions by the district. The jury returned a verdict of $500,000 for the student, reducing it by 30% based on her own fault. When the case reached the Supreme Court of Iowa, it held the scope of liability was for a jury to decide. Generally, tort law limits liability to the physical harm resulting from the risks that make an actor's conduct a tort in the first place. Questions about the scope of liability were fact-intensive. As there was no "bright-line rule" to resolve such questions, the court held the issue was left to the judgment and common sense of the jury. In the court's opinion, there was sufficient evidence in this case to generate a jury question on the issue of whether the student's injuries were among the potential harms that made the school district's conduct a tort. The court rejected the district's argument that **the off-campus location of the assault and the fact that it took place after school hours disposed of the case**. As a result, the court held for the student. *Mitchell v. Cedar Rapids Community School Dist.*, 832 N.W.2d 689 (Iowa 2013).

◆   A federal district court dismissed an action by a deceased student's family against a Utah school district that sought to hold school officials liable for his suicide death based on failure to address harassment and bullying. Although the family claimed school administrators knew of the harassment and bullying and failed to act, the court found the family did not file an action until more than a year after his death. **A state-law notice of claim requirement thus barred the action.** *Hancock v. North Sanpete School Dist.*, No. 2:12-cv-00072, 2012 WL 3060118 (D. Utah 7/25/12).

◆   A Tennessee student claimed a classmate began threatening and harassing him. He complained about the bullying to an assistant school principal and the principal, and his father also reported it to teachers and school officials. But the next school year, the bully paid a friend $5 to hurt the student. The attack was carried out at school, and the student was severely beaten. In a state court action against the bully, friend, their parents and the board of education, the court found the board 25% at fault for the student's injuries. It found the bully, his friend and their parents jointly and severally liable for the remaining 75% of fault. But the court held the board had state-law immunity. As a result, the board was dismissed from the case and the judgment was modified to hold the bully, his friend and their parents liable for a damage award in excess of $50,000. On appeal, the Court of Appeals of Tennessee explained that state law immunized the conduct of government employees who performed discretionary functions. Policy-making and planning-level acts were thus entitled to immunity.

The court agreed with the student that school officials did not follow the board's disciplinary procedures and policies. It held the relevant policy arose from a state law against school bullying. Implementing a policy is operational, not discretionary, so immunity was removed. Administrators did not follow the board policy on bullying and harassment. No complaint manager was assigned to investigate, and school disciplinary guidelines were not followed. As the trial court held, **the school was on notice of possible injury to the student**. All the defending parties played a role in the harm, so the court held them equally liable. *Moore v. Houston County Board of Educ.*, 358 S.W.3d 612 (Tenn. Ct. App. 2011), appeal denied 1/13/12.

◆   A West Virginia high school student created a MySpace.com web page that ridiculed a classmate. She opened the page to about 100 MySpace "friends," and some of them added vulgar criticisms of the classmate. The classmate filed a harassment complaint with the school, which found the student had created a "hate website" in violation of a school policy against harassment, bullying and intimidation. She was suspended for five days and excluded from school social activities for 90 days. In a federal court, the student sued the school district for speech rights and due process violations. After the court held for the district, the student appealed. In upholding the discipline, the court found that bullying is a major concern in schools, leading to student depression and even thoughts of suicide. **The court held "schools have a duty to protect their students from harassment and bullying in the school environment."** It was foreseeable that the student's conduct would reach the school via computers or other devices. The nexus between the speech and school pedagogical interests justified discipline. The court found the speech was materially and substantially disruptive, and it held speech originating outside of school "but directed at persons in school and received by and acted on by them was in fact in-school speech." *Kowalski v. Berkeley County Schools*, 652 F.3d 565 (4th Cir. 2011).

◆   Two female students in Idaho reported that two males were planning a Columbine-style attack at school. The principal confronted one of the male students, who said he was "going to have a school shooting" on a specified date. The two male students were warned about their threatening conduct, and they agreed not to make further statements. But one month later, the students were accused of threatening to shoot guns at a school dance. Two years after these incidents, one of the male students wrote threatening notes that were viewed by his locker partner. Although the threats were brought to the attention of the school resource officer and a vice principal, they were "dismissed." The same month as the notes were found, the student and a male accomplice murdered a female student at the house of her friend. When her parents sued the school district in a state trial court, it was found that **the district owed no duty to protect the student off school grounds and after school hours**. On appeal, the Supreme Court of Idaho affirmed the judgment. Nothing in the record convinced the court that the district knew that one of the male students would commit a murder based on information received about him some 30 months earlier. As the murder was not foreseeable, the district had no duty to prevent it. *Stoddart v. Pocatello School Dist. #25*, 239 P.3d 784 (Idaho 2010).

◆   After being beaten in an off-campus incident, a California student sued his school district in a state court for negligence. The district defended on grounds of immunity based on discretion. It also argued it could not be held liable for an injury that took place off school grounds after school hours. The case was dismissed, and the student appealed to the Court of Appeal of California. It considered the case under Section 44808 of the state education code, which declares that **school districts are generally not liable for the conduct or safety of any public school student at any time when the student is not on school property**. According to the Court of Appeal, "school districts and their employees have never been considered insurers of the physical safety of their students, but rather are placed under a general duty to supervise the conduct of children on school grounds during school sessions, school activities, recesses and lunch periods." When the state legislature enacted Section 44808, it endorsed the principle that school districts are not legally responsible for accidents to students on their way to and from school. Neither school districts nor their employees are liable for the conduct or safety of any student when not on school property, unless there is a specific undertaking by a school district or a sponsored activity.

This general principle was in conflict with this language in Section 44808: "otherwise specifically assumed such responsibility or liability or has failed to exercise reasonable care." The court held that "what occurs after school on nonschool property when the student is not under the supervision of the school does not result in the school's liability." Since the student had insufficient facts for a claim against the district, the judgment was affirmed. *Cortinez v. South Pasadena Unified School Dist.*, No. B214772, 2010 WL 2352046 (Cal. Ct. App. 6/14/10) (Unpublished).

◆   A Michigan elementary school student claimed some classmates assaulted him at school twice within a few days. He said that he reported the first incident to the principal's secretary two days after it happened, but the secretary failed to notify the principal about the student's report. The student's parent sued the school district and principal for negligence and gross negligence. Appeal reached the Court of Appeals of Michigan. The court explained that operation of a school system is a governmental function. For this reason, the school district had immunity from tort liability for any negligence or gross negligence. Government employees also enjoy immunity from tort liability if the injury is caused while they act in the course of their employment, or in the reasonable belief they are doing so.

On the other hand, a governmental employee is not immune from tort liability if an injury is caused by the employee's gross negligence. **"Gross negligence" is conduct so reckless that it demonstrates a substantial lack of concern for whether injury will result.** As the student failed to present evidence that the principal knew or should have known of the first fight, the court found no reasonable person could find her negligent or grossly negligent for failure to investigate. The lower court judgment was affirmed. *Reynolds v. Detroit Public Schools*, No. 276369, 2008 WL 2389492 (Mich. Ct. App. 6/12/08).

3. Constitutional Claims

Federal constitutional liability for school entities is sharply limited by *DeShaney v. Winnebago County Dep't of Social Services*, 489 U.S. 189 (1989). In *Deshaney*, the U.S. Supreme Court held there must be a "special relationship" between a state agency and a victim of private violence for a constitutional duty to exist. Since federal courts have yet to find that public school students have any special relationship with school officials, schools have not been held liable for acts of bullying committed by private persons.

While no federal law prohibits bullying, the federal government has targeted peer bullying by holding bullying prevention summits and joining other federal agencies in the Federal Partners in Bullying Prevention Steering Committee. A "Dear Colleague" letter by the U.S. Department of Education's Office for Civil Rights details federal expectations for school districts to confront bullies in their schools. The letter is posted at *http://www2.ed.gov/about/offices/list/ocr/letters/colleague-201010.html.*

◆ A North Carolina high school senior attacked a freshman with a box cutter in a school hallway, injuring her face, neck and scalp. A teacher/coach intervened almost immediately. After the attack, the senior pled guilty to assault and no contest to a weapons possession charge. She received a suspended sentence and was placed on supervised probation.

After an investigation, the principal suspended the freshman for 10 days. She attended a half-day school schedule for the rest of the school year. Meanwhile, the senior was suspended for the rest of the school year. In a state court lawsuit, the freshman's parent claimed the school board violated her child's right to the opportunity for an education free from psychological abuse and harm. After a hearing, the court dismissed both the negligence and constitutional claims on the basis of state law immunity. On appeal, the Court of Appeals of North Carolina noted the state supreme court has held that no state constitutional claim could be made other than for matters directly related to public school educational opportunities. **Public school students had no constitutional right to recover damages from an education board for injuries resulting from a negligent failure to supervise public school employees.** Similarly, the court held there was no right under the state constitution for a student to recover damages from a board of education for injuries resulting from a negligent failure to remain aware of and supervise the conduct of other public school students. While the court held the student was permitted to raise a constitutional claim, it held for the board, finding no actions by the board affecting the nature, extent and quality of the educational opportunities made available to public school students. *Mack v. Board of Educ. of Public Schools of Robeson County*, 748 S.E.2d 774 (N.C. Ct. App. 2013).

◆   Pennsylvania parents said their children were bullied and injured at their middle school. They said that despite notice, the school district did not respond. In fact, the parents claimed school officials criticized and belittled them to deflect their responsibility to stop the misconduct. The parents sued the school district and officials in a federal court, asserting constitutional violations and a number of state law claims. The court dismissed the case, and appeal reached the Third Circuit. First, the court dispensed with a claim that officials had retaliated against the families. The court held allegations of inaction were insufficient to maintain a constitutional claim.

As the parents did not plead any retaliatory action by the school district, the trial court correctly dismissed the First Amendment claim. Their claims based on violation of due process rights were also properly dismissed. The families did not assert any affirmative acts by the school district but only argued that it did not act to prevent bullying by the classmates. To recover for a constitutional violation, **any deprivation of rights must be attributable to a state actor and not a private actor such as a bully**. As the actions at issue were attributed to students and not the district, the court found no due process violation. *Monn v. Gettysburg Area School Dist.*, 553 Fed.Appx. 120 (3d Cir. 2014).

◆   An Oklahoma student who was often ill and absent from school said others ridiculed and threatened her. A psychotherapist diagnosed her with depression, and her mother homeschooled her for several weeks. When she returned to public school, her mother gave the school nurse ibuprofen and Aleve to administer for headaches. During the school year, the mother claimed that nurses denied her child medication or delayed giving it when it was needed. Incidents of bullying by peers increased, and the family's house was vandalized. Some Internet postings were claimed to be cyberbullying. The school issued detentions and counseled the students about some misconduct. But the mother felt they should have been suspended, and she eventually removed her child from school due to depression and a suicide attempt. The family moved so the student could attend a new school.

The parent sued the district and officials – including the superintendent and principal – in a federal court. In pretrial activity, the court dismissed the claims against the district and state tort claims against the school employees. According to the parent, school staff members had a constitutional duty to protect the student based on a "special relationship." She claimed the actions by school staff to deny or delay her access to medication prevented her from caring for herself, rendering her vulnerable. The court found no legal authority for a claim that public school students have a special relationship with their teachers or other school employees. Staff members did not create a danger or increase the student's vulnerability, so no constitutional claims could be made against them. **State actors are liable only for their own acts, not those of third parties.** In any event, qualified immunity protected the staff members. *Reyna v. Independent School Dist. No. 1, Oklahoma County, Oklahoma*, Nos. CIV–09–1223–D, CJ–2009–9583, 2012 WL 1023526 (W.D. Okla. 3/27/12).

◆ After a Texas middle school student committed suicide, his mother claimed he was the victim of constant bullying by other students at school. She sued the school district in a federal court, asserting that no one protected him from harm at his school. In pretrial activity, the court refused to dismiss claims filed under Title IX of the Education Amendments of 1972 and the Due Process Clause of the Fourteenth Amendment. A few weeks later, the U.S. Court of Appeals, Fifth Circuit, decided *Doe v. Covington County School Board*, 675 F.3d 849 (5th Cir. 2012). Upon reviewing *Doe*, the court agreed with the district that reconsideration of a judgment was appropriate. **As a general matter, a state's failure to protect an individual against private violence does not constitute a due process violation.**

According to the court, a "special relationship" exists only when the state has taken the person into its custody and held her there against her will. The relationship exists in three situations, none of which involve public schools. While the mother argued that the school district's failure to enforce its anti-bullying policies violated her son's due process rights, the court held *Doe* barred such a ruling in the absence of a special relationship. An alternative argument, based on the school's "culture that condoned bullying" which increased the danger posed to the child during the school day, also failed. *Estate of Brown v. Cypress Fairbanks Independent School Dist.*, 863. F.Supp.2d 632 (S.D. Tex. 2012).

◆ An action by the parents of a student who committed suicide because of bullying at his school was dismissed as untimely and without merit by a federal district court. According to the parents, their son was regularly bullied and harassed at school as a 17-year-old senior. They claimed the school and a particular teacher did nothing to intervene. The court agreed with the school board that the action was untimely filed. **It also found the school district had no constitutional duty to take affirmative action to protect the student from bullying or to prevent his suicide.** In addition, the court held the lack of a school policy against bullying and failure to train employees also created no liability in this case. *Mohat v. Mentor Exempted Village School Dist. Board of Educ.*, No. 1:09 CV 688, 2011 WL 2174671 (N.D. Ohio 6/1/11).

◆   A North Carolina student was suspended for the second semester of her sophomore year for fighting. She was not offered alternative education. After a hearing, a school panel upheld the superintendent's decision to suspend her without services. In a state court lawsuit, the student asserted violation of her right to a sound basic education under the North Carolina constitution. Appeal reached the Supreme Court of North Carolina. It held state law vested school administrators with authority to issue long-term suspensions to students who willfully violated school conduct policies. But the law required education boards to establish alternative learning programs.

According to the court, state law provided a comprehensive scheme that granted students a right to an alternative education "when feasible and appropriate" during long-term suspensions. **There was no constitutional right to an alternative education, but there was a constitutional right for a suspended student to know the reason for exclusion from school.** In reaching this conclusion, the court accepted the student's claim that prior rulings on state educational funding applied to her case. The funding cases established that "equal access to participation in our public school system is a fundamental right, guaranteed by our state constitution and protected by considerations of procedural due process." While students had a right to a sound basic education under the state constitution, the court held school administrators had to articulate an important or significant reason for denying a student access to an alternative education. In this case, administrators did not articulate a reason for denying the student access to alternative education. Since she had a right to education guaranteed by the North Carolina Constitution, the court reversed the judgment and returned the case to the lower courts so the education board could have an opportunity to explain why alternative education had been denied. *King v. Beaufort County Board of Educ.*, 704 S.E.2d 259 (N.C. 2010).

B. Threatening and Bullying Speech

Students accused of bullying often assert that school discipline based on their speech and other conduct would violate a First Amendment right to free speech. In making this argument, they typically rely on *Tinker v. Des Moines Independent Community School Dist.*, 393 U.S. 503 (1969). Under *Tinker*, student speech may be regulated by school officials only if they could reasonably forecast substantial disruption or material interference with school activities, or if the speech would infringe upon the rights of others.

◆   A Tennessee student and classmate argued with each other. They liked the same boy. After the classmate called a friend to let her know she was with the boy, the student tweeted to the friend that she would help the friend shoot the classmate in the face. She then tweeted additional statements mentioning harm to the classmate. Although the student said she did not mean anything by her tweets and that she even added monkey faces to one of them, the classmate's mother took the tweets seriously. When the tweets were reported to the school, the student was assigned to 45 days in an alternative school. The student's mother requested a disciplinary hearing. This led to a reduction in the discipline to 10 days. In a federal court, the student asserted violation of her speech rights. The court held schools may prohibit vulgar, lewd, indecent or offensive speech, and may censor school-sponsored student speech in a manner consistent with pedagogical concerns.

In cases allowing school regulation of student speech for online off-campus speech, courts have approved discipline based on a reasonable showing of a risk of disruption. But the court found the tweets in this case had little to do with the school. They were not made at school or during school hours. No school computers were used, and the messages were not directed toward the school setting. Significantly, the court found no disruption of school activities or impact on the school environment. Since the school officials were unable to show they were entitled to pretrial judgment regarding the First Amendment claim, the court held the student could proceed with it. But the court dismissed the due process claim. As she was suspended for 10 days, the school was only required to offer her minimal due process procedures. The court dismissed other federal claims filed by the family and refused to accept their state law claims. *Nixon v. Hardin County Board of Educ.*, 988 F.Supp.2d 826 (W.D. Tenn. 2013).

◆ From off-campus locations, a Nevada student sent friends a series of increasingly violent and threatening instant messages. He invoked the image of the Virginia Tech massacre, boasting he could "get 50+ people / and not one bullet would be wasted." Friends grew concerned when he sent messages about a school shooting to take place on April 20. This is Hitler's date of birth and the date of the Columbine shootings. Some of the student's friends told a coach about the threats, and the principal was notified. Police interviewed the friends and viewed the online messages. They questioned the student in the principal's office. After a hearing, the school board voted to expel the student for 90 days. He sued the board for constitutional rights violations. A federal court held for the board, and the student appealed.

The U.S. Court of Appeals, Ninth Circuit, held that courts had to balance the speech rights of students against the need to provide a safe school environment. In doing so, the courts were "not to react in favor of either." The idea was to strike an appropriate balance between safety and speech rights. In this case, the court held school officials did not violate the student's rights. The nature of the threats was "alarming and explosive." For this reason, the court held **officials did not have to wait for an actual disruption to materialize before acting**. As it was reasonable for the officials to interpret the student's messages as a safety risk and a substantial disruption, there was no speech rights violation. The court held the student had adequate warning from a student handbook that he faced discipline for making threatening statements. There was no due process violation, and the judgment for the school district was affirmed. *Wynar v. Jefferson County Board of School Commissioners*, 728 F.3d 1062 (9th Cir. 2013).

◆   A Nevada student-athlete made off-campus tweets about his coaches. According to the student, his Twitter account settings made his tweets private. School administrators gained access to the account from a third party and initiated discipline against him for cyberbullying. An appeal panel reassigned the student to another high school. In a federal court, the student and his father sought a preliminary order to return him to the school he had formerly attended. In assessing the speech rights claim, the court examined the tweets, which repeatedly referenced coaches and administrators in a disparaging and profane manner. One of the tweets stated that a coach should be repeatedly sodomized. Others implied similar conduct. According to the court, **only the tweet that explicitly referred to sodomy was considered obscene and unprotected**. It held other tweets reviling the coaching staff had stated a preliminary case for a speech rights violation, and it refused to dismiss this claim. Although the student contended he had a privacy interest in his tweets that was constitutionally protected, the court held he had no reasonable expectation of privacy in them. The court dismissed his equal protection and due process claims as meritless. Finding no validity to a federal race discrimination claim and tort claims, the court dismissed them. But it refused to dismiss claims for defamation and conspiracy. These claims, as well as the First Amendment claim, would require further consideration. *Roasio v. Clark County School Dist.*, No. 2:13-CV-362 JCM (PAL), 2013 WL 3679375 (D. Nev. 7/3/13).

A 2014 **New Jersey** amendment required each school district to incorporate instruction on the responsible use of social media into their technology education curriculums for students in grades 6-8. Effective immediately, the new requirement becomes a part of each school district's implementation of the state Core Curriculum Content Standards in Technology. Instruction required by the legislation shall provide students with information on: (1) the purpose and acceptable use of social media platforms; (2) social media behavior that ensures cyber safety, cyber security, and cyber ethics; and (3) potential negative consequences of failing to use various social media platforms responsibly, including cyberbullying. Two-Hundred Fifteenth New Jersey Legislature, 2d Annual Session, Ch. 257, Assembly No. 3292. Title 18a, New Jersey Statutes Section 35.4.27.

Minnesota amended its laws in 2014 to make bullying or cyberbullying forms of "prohibited conduct." The law requires school districts to adopt written policies to prevent and prohibit student bullying. A district that does not adopt and implement a local policy will have to comply with a state model bullying policy. School district policies must establish research-based, developmentally appropriate best practices to address and deter bullying. Policies are to emphasize remedial responses to bullying reports and must be included in student handbooks with school policies.

Provisions of the law allow schools to address the skills and proficiencies of students with individualized education programs or Section 504 plans to address skills and proficiencies for avoiding prohibited conduct. The law specifies that it does not establish a private right of action or limit rights available under other civil or criminal laws, including the state Human Rights Act and speech provisions of the Constitution. Eighty-Eighth Minnesota Legislature, 2014 Regular Session, Ch. 160, H.F. No. 826. Minnesota Statutes Sections 121A.031, 121A.0311, 124D.10, 127A.052.

Connecticut legislators amended the state's school climate law in 2014 to provide for parental notification when a bullying incident is being investigated and to invite parents of students involved in bullying incidents to attend school meetings to prevent further bullying. Safe school climate plans must require each school's safe school climate specialist to promptly notify the parents of students involved in a bullying incident that an investigation has commenced. Safe school climate plans must further require that each school invite the parents or guardians of a student who commits any verified act of bullying to a meeting to discuss specific interventions by the school to prevent further acts of bullying. The law authorizes prevention and intervention strategies that may include culturally competent, school-based curriculums focusing on social-emotional learning, self-awareness and self-regulation. Interventions with a bullied child under the act may include referrals to a school counselor, psychologist or other appropriate social or mental health service, and periodic follow-up. Connecticut General Assembly, 2014 February Regular Session, P.A. No. 14-172, S.B. No. 106. Connecticut Statutes Section 10-222d.

California legislators enacted a law in 2014 to include off-campus communications by telephones or electronic devices for the purpose of school discipline. "Electronic act" includes the creation and transmission of a communication by a telephone or other electronic device, or a wireless communication device, computer, or pager, whether the communication originated on or off school grounds. California 2013-14 Regular Session, Ch. 700, A.B. No. 256. California Education Code Section 48900.

◆ Pennsylvania sisters claimed they were repeatedly threatened, assaulted and racially intimidated by another student and her friend at their high school, by phone and the Internet. Eventually, the other student was put on probation and ordered to have no contact with one sister. She was adjudicated delinquent, and no-contact orders from the juvenile court were provided to the school. Despite the court orders, the other student boarded the sisters' bus and threatened one sister. That evening, she elbowed the other sister in the throat at a school football game. After the incidents were reported, officials told the sisters they could not guarantee their safety. Officials asked the parents to consider moving the sisters to another school, and they soon did so. In a federal court, the sisters sued the school district and assistant principal, claiming due process violations. It dismissed the case, and the sisters appealed to the U.S. Court of Appeals, Third Circuit.

On appeal, the court held **the Due Process Clause did not create an affirmative duty by a state to protect a person from other persons**. A narrow exception applied if a "special relationship" existed between a state and a person who is taken into custody against his or her will. But this exception had only been applied to prisoners or involuntarily committed individuals. A public school's authority over a child during the school day did not create the type of physical custody to create a "special relationship." Neither state compulsory school attendance laws nor the doctrine of *in loco parentis* created "custody" for the special relationship exception. The court noted that every other federal appeals court to have considered the question (in a precedential opinion) had rejected the notion that a special relationship exists between public schools and their students. Even though the specific threat in this case was "a violent bully subject to two restraining orders," the court found no special relationship that imposed a constitutional duty on the school district. Nor did knowledge of the risks created by the other student's presence create a duty. While the school's response might have been as "inadequate as it was unfair," the court held the school did not authorize the other student to bully the sisters. As the Supreme Court has declared, "the Constitution does not provide judicial remedies for every ill." There was also no reason to apply the "state-created danger" theory of constitutional liability in this case. There was no affirmative act by the school district that would create liability under the state-created danger theory. Finding no constitutional duty to prevent the bullying in this case, the court held for the school district. *Morrow v. Balaski*, 719 F.3d 160 (3d Cir. 2013).

◆   A New York student said his peers subjected him to severe anti-Semitic bullying. He wrote an essay for his English Class titled "Anti-Semitism." In the essay, the student described incidents at his school in which others called him "hey Jew," or said "God bless Jew" when he sneezed. He wrote that a peer had asked "What's the difference between a Jew and a pizza? A pizza doesn't scream when it goes in the oven." Although a teacher read and edited the essay, she did not contact the student's parents or report it to school administrators. Late in the school year, the parents learned of the extent of the harassment and sought to obtain protection for their son and to educate other students about the dangers of harassment and bullying. Although they said school administrators told them a message of tolerance would be given to students and that this topic would be discussed in social studies classes, it never happened. Claiming the harassment continued, the student decided not to return to the high school. His parents sued the district, superintendent and principal in a federal court for constitutional violations.

In the court's opinion, **the student asserted enough facts to state an equal protection claim against the school district**. There was evidence that the administrators received the names of some of the harassers when the parents met with them. Because school officials had disciplinary oversight to deal with students, the court found their inaction could be seen as "clearly unreasonable" in light of the known circumstances. For this reason, the court refused to dismiss the federal equal protection claim. Although public schools were not subject to liability under the state human rights law, the student could pursue a claim under the state civil rights law in further proceedings. *G.D.S. v. Northport Union Free School Dist.*, 915 F.Supp.2d 268 (E.D.N.Y. 2012).

In *Doninger v. Niehoff*, 527 F.3d 41 (2d Cir. 2008), the U.S. Court of Appeals, Second Circuit, held that school officials have a duty to prevent school disruption. The question was not whether there had been actual disruption, but whether it could be forecast. *Doninger* is one of a number of recent federal court decisions holding that school officials do not have to wait for an "actual disruption" to occur before acting to prevent student violence. **While student speech may implicate the First Amendment, threats of violence have never been considered "protected speech" that warrant First Amendment protection.**

◆   A New York fifth-grader responded to a science assignment by writing "Blow up the school with the teachers in it" on his paper. He was suspended for one day in-school and for five days out-of-school, as the principal found the picture had frightened a girl in the class. Although the student claimed he was just kidding, the school board upheld the discipline. A federal court dismissed the family's First Amendment violations lawsuit, and his parents appealed to the U.S. Court of Appeals, First Circuit. It observed that the threat had been drawn in crayon and that no prior events indicated the student was a danger. More proceedings were needed to determine whether the student had caused a foreseeable risk of material and substantial disruption. When the case returned to the district court, evidence of prior incidents was introduced about the student. He had previously drawn a picture of a person firing a gun and wrote "one day I shot 4 people each of them got four blows + they were dead." And in fourth grade, the student wrote a story about "a big wind that destroyed every school in America." Based on this evidence, the court held for the school district. When the case returned to the Second Circuit, it held that student rights are not coextensive with the rights of adults in other settings. Student speech may be curtailed by administrators if "the speech will materially and substantially interfere with the requirements of appropriate discipline." Significantly, the court held "this test does not require school administrators to prove that actual disruption occurred or that substantial disruption was inevitable."

In fact, an "actual disruption standard would be absurd." In view of the complete record, the court found school officials could reasonably foresee that the drawing submitted by the student could create substantial school disruption. **Administrators needed to react quickly and decisively to address threats of violence in schools.** As for the parent' claim that the punishment was excessive, the court found that was for school officials to determine. *Cuff v. Valley Cent. School Dist.*, 677 F.3d 109 (2d Cir. 2012).

◆   After a Texas school district prohibited Confederate flag displays on school grounds, the number of reported race incidents decreased. Two students carried purses to school with large images of a Confederate flag. After they unsuccessfully appealed the school policy through an internal school administrative procedure, they sued the principal and the school board in a federal district court. The court held for the school officials.

On appeal, the U.S. Court of Appeals, Fifth Circuit, held school officials reasonably concluded that the ban on displays of the Confederate flag at school was imposed to prevent substantial and material disruption. The decision was based on the historical atmosphere of racial hostility at the school, some of which involved Confederate flags. The court rejected an assertion that the "material disruption standard" from *Tinker v. Des Moines Independent Community School Dist.*, above, requires a "direct connection" between the prohibited student speech and anticipated disruption. Instead, the court held **Tinker permits limits on student speech if facts lead them to forecast substantial disruption or material interference with school activities.** In this case, school officials reasonably anticipated that the Confederate flag displays would cause substantial disruption or material interference with the school. Significantly, the court held "*Tinker* permits school officials to act based on the potential for disruption." The judgment was affirmed. *A.M. v. Cash*, 585 F.3d 214 (5th Cir. 2009).

C. Hazing

Hazing was traditionally seen at higher education institutions, but some incidents have occurred in secondary schools. A plaintiff in a hazing case must show that the school was aware of the hazing before liability may be imposed on the school. Ordinary negligence principles may apply, but school liability may also depend on state law definitions.

Kathleen Conn, Ph.D., J.D., LL.M., Associate Professor for the Division of Education and Human Services at Neumann University says schools should take the following steps to address athletic team hazing:

• Increase bus and locker room supervision
• Have a district anti-hazing policy at the high school and middle school levels
• Recognize sexualized hazing as sexual violence and address it as such, and
• Ensure coaches do not approve, participate in or turn a blind eye to hazing.

◆ According to an Ohio state court complaint filed by parents of a student with Down syndrome, their child was sexually assaulted due to "an extreme lack of teacher oversight" in her classroom. They claimed the school knew that one of her attackers had a history of psychological issues relating to abuse and assault. According to the complaint, teachers were reckless in placing students in the class and in monitoring class activities. It was alleged that staff did not even notice when students disappeared from class.

A state trial court held for the school district and employees. On appeal, the Court of Appeals of Ohio held the attackers' conduct was not "hazing" under state law. Although the parents claimed the trial court had improperly dismissed claims under a state anti-hazing statute, the court found no error. **"Hazing" applied to an initiation into a student organization.** A prior Ohio case restricted the term "student organization" to voluntary membership in a group and not an entire student body. The part of the lower court decision regarding the hazing statute was affirmed. School districts were protected by a general grant of immunity by state law, unless an exception applied. But a claim that the student was sexually assaulted under circumstances of recklessness and "an extreme lack of teacher oversight" was sufficient to establish potential liability by school employees, and the trial court should not have dismissed the claim. *E.F. v. Oberlin City School Dist.*, No. 09CA009640, 2010 WL 1227703 (Ohio Ct. App. 3/31/10).

◆   Several Washington high school seniors arranged for an off-campus beer party at a remote location without adult supervision. They purchased six kegs of beer, which was enough for about a gallon for each of the 100 attendees. Three seniors confronted a high school junior at the party because he was the only underclassman there. One of the seniors hit the junior on the forehead with a heavy beer mug. Although the wound appeared minor, the junior collapsed and fell into a coma four months later. After surviving for four years in a persistent vegetative state, the junior died. His estate filed a state court action against senior class members who purchased the beer, the students who confronted the junior at the party, and the beer distributor that made the beer kegs available. The case reached the Court of Appeal of Washington, where the estate asserted a criminal assault. The court found the conduct in this case was outside the "field of danger traditionally covered by the duty not to furnish intoxicating liquor to an obviously intoxicated person."
   Without some notice of harm, a criminal assault was not a foreseeable result of providing too much alcohol to students. No evidence indicated that the party planners or those who furnished beer knew that the assailants had any violent tendencies. Liability applied to the assailants, not those who provided the beer. Without specific knowledge by officials of any violent tendencies of intoxicated persons, there was no school liability. *Cameron v. Murray*, 214 P.3d 150 (Wash. Ct. App. 2009).

◆   A New York school athletic director (AD) complained to the school board and district superintendent that the high school football coach improperly supervised students and encouraged them to use a dangerous muscle enhancer. A parent of one team member wrote to the school board president that she heard stories of severe misconduct in the locker room, including shoving a bottle up a student's rectum. During a subsequent school investigation, a 14-year-old freshman football player told the AD that some teammates had rubbed their genitals in his face, a form of hazing called "tea-bagging." The district changed its supervision protocols in football locker rooms. It also sought involvement by the state police and advised parents that unspecified sexual harassment and/or hazing had been discovered. The AD sent the superintendent a letter repeating his criticisms of the football coach. He further expressed concern about the district's handling of the tea-bagging investigation. A number of students and teachers were arrested, and the entire high school football coaching staff was suspended. The school board met in an executive session and reached "informal consensus" to abolish the AD position from the district budget.

After being demoted to a social studies teaching position at a lower salary, the AD sued the board and administrators in a federal district court for retaliation and related claims. The court held for the school board, finding no causal connection between the AD's speech and the elimination of his position. On appeal, the U.S. Court of Appeals, Second Circuit, stated **"the First Amendment protects any matter of political, social or other concern to the community."** The AD's speech arose from an incident of obvious public concern – the sexual assault of a student on school property. The fact that the letter was private did not make its content a purely private grievance. Having a personal stake in the speech did not destroy any public concern the speech contained. The court held a reasonable jury could reject the board's argument that the AD's position would have been eliminated even if not for his protected speech. *Cioffi v. Averill Park Cent. School Dist. Board of Educ.*, 444 F.3d 158 (2d Cir. 2006).

◆   An Ohio student claimed two older students invited him to a "jazz band meeting" early in a school year. He followed them into a lavatory, where he was punched and kicked by a group of students. The student said he received numerous bruises and neck and back injuries, and was threatened with more beatings. He sued the board and school officials in a state court, asserting the school board and administration knew of and tolerated a "Freshman Beating Day." The court held for the board and administrators, and the student appealed. State law authorized civil actions against student organizations, schools and school employees, if the school knew or should have known of hazing and made no reasonable attempt to prevent it. The Court of Appeals of Ohio held "student organization" meant a specific organization, not an entire student body. The "jazz band meeting" reference did not make the beating an initiation into a student organization. "Initiation" implied voluntary membership and consent by the victim to be hazed. The student did not agree to be beaten and would probably not have entered the lavatory had he known it was planned. **The court held that even if the school officials were aware of and tolerated "Freshman Friday," the beating did not constitute "hazing" under state law.** *Duitch v. Canton City Schools*, 157 Ohio App.3d 80, 809 N.E.2d 62 (Ohio Ct. App. 2004).

II. THREATS AND VIOLENCE

A. Students

◆   A Mississippi student had an ongoing conflict with another girl about a boy. At school, she received a threatening text message from the other girl's mother. Police were called, and both students were interviewed. Within a few weeks, the mother of the other girl drove in front of the student's car on a street near the high school. She and her daughter then attacked and injured the student. In a state court, the student's family asserted claims under the Mississippi Tort Claims Act. It was claimed that the district breached a duty of supervision to avoid assaults and to provide a safe school. The court denied the school board's request for immunity, and appeal went before the Supreme Court of Mississippi. It explained that to prevail in a negligence case, a party has to establish there was a duty owed by the defending party. State law created a duty to use ordinary care to minimize foreseeable risks. The lower court had misplaced its reliance on this provision to deny immunity to the board. State law required school staff to maintain and control discipline over students while they were at school. But the incident occurred off school grounds and after the students had been dismissed.

The street in front of the school was not "school property" under state law, as the student urged. **State law did not impose a duty on schools to provide a safe environment to students who had been dismissed from school and were off school property.** This claim had been properly dismissed. The student argued that the school handbook created a duty by the school to notify law enforcement of threats. But the court found the handbook was not in the record and had not been reviewed by the trial court. As a result, this claim was returned to the trial court for more consideration. *Moss Point School Dist. v. Stennis*, 132 So.3d 1047 (Miss. 2014).

◆ A Florida student reported being attacked by another student with a history of school discipline, bullying, fighting and class disruption. She said the attacker was in possession of a blade prior to the attack and should have been serving an in-school suspension (ISS) on the day of the attack. As a result of the incident, the student suffered a broken leg. In a state court action against the board, the family of the injured student submitted four theories of negligence. One was the theory that the board was negligent for not placing the attacking student in ISS on the scheduled day. A jury agreed with this theory and with the theory that the board negligently supervised the attacker just before the assault took place. On appeal, the board argued the trial court committed an error by excluding testimony by a third party that a racial slur may have prompted the incident. But the court noted no student, administrator, teacher or other student heard a slur. It found any such evidence "amounted to no more than improperly stacked inferences."

Next, the court held the board was foreclosed from arguing that the jury should not have been able to hold it liable for failing to place the attacker in ISS under sovereign immunity principles. The court held the board could not now challenge the jury's alternative basis for liability – that negligent supervision of the attacker resulted in harm to the student. The court found the board's current argument was different from its initial defenses that it had no duty to the student and enjoyed sovereign immunity. As **negligent supervision was an accepted basis for school liability**, and the court found "plentiful evidence" to support the verdict, it held for the student. *Duval County School Board v. Buchanan*, 131 So.3d 821 (Fla. Dist. Ct. App. 2014).

◆   While in his high school's student center, a New York student told some of his classmates and a teacher that he was "going to just blow this place up." After discussing the statements, school administrators were unsure about the seriousness of the risk, and they called the student's parents and the police. The student was suspended for five days and charged with insubordinate, disorderly, violent, disruptive conduct and violation of the school code. Following a manifestation determination at which no connection was found between the student's behavior and his disability, the school board held a hearing and recommended suspension for 25 more days.

After the district superintendent and board adopted the recommended discipline, the student appealed. The state commissioner of education approved the board's action, and appeal reached the New York Supreme Court, Appellate Division. The court explained that the relevant inquiry was whether his conduct might reasonably have led school authorities to forecast substantial disruption of or material interference with school activities. In this case, the student had declared to several others that he was going to blow up the school. In the court's opinion, these **statements on school property made it reasonably foreseeable that there would be a substantial disruption**. Although the administrators were not sure whether the threat was serious or not, the court found this irrelevant. The statement prompted a call to the police. In addition, the student had compounded the threat of substantial disruption by making his declaration to classmates who might try to copy or escalate the threat. Since school officials could reasonably conclude that the student's statements would substantially disrupt the school, their decision to suspend him did not violate his speech rights. The commissioner's decision upholding the suspension was affirmed. *Saad-El-Din v. Steiner*, 953 N.Y.S.2d 326 (N.Y. App. Div. 2012).

◆   A Mississippi student with a mental disability was placed in a regular classroom for part of each school day. According to a classmate, the student had a "documented history of emotional outbursts and misbehavior." She said that on two occasions, the student threatened her. She said that on the second occasion, he grabbed her, held her head against a wall and rubbed a cleaning wipe into her eye. In a federal court, the classmate's mother said school officials violated her child's due process rights by failing to immediately remove the student from the classroom when they learned of his violent propensities. The court held for the school district, and appeal reached the Fifth Circuit. In *Doe v. Covington County School Dist.*, 675 F.3d 849 (5th Cir. 2012), this chapter, the Fifth Circuit refused to adopt the state-created danger theory in a case involving a school's failure to protect a child from being signed out from her school by an unauthorized adult. In affirming the judgment for the school district and officials, the court noted language from *Doe* declaring that **to create any opportunity for school liability, "the school must be aware of an immediate danger to a specific**

and identifiable student." The court found the classmate was only one of many who "faced a generalized risk resulting from the school's attempt to integrate a mentally disabled child into a normal school environment." It affirmed the judgment for school officials. *Dixon v. Alcorn County School Dist.*, 499 Fed.Appx. 364 (5th Cir. 2012).

◆   A Michigan law specifies that if a student in grade six or above assaults another student, the school board "shall suspend or expel the pupil from the school district for up to 180 school days." A school board had a policy to enforce this provision. After a student assaulted a classmate, a school investigation determined his actions were intentional and not a manifestation of his disability. He was suspended for 180 days. After the school board upheld the discipline, the case reached the Court of Appeals of Michigan. **The court described the assault as an "extreme bullying incident."** It explained that school officials have wide discretion in creating rules to maintain order. Adequate notice of a 180-day suspension was provided based on the state law and school board policies. Moreover, the handbook allowed adjustment of the term of a suspension based on the circumstances. Since there was no arbitrary or capricious conduct by the board, the court affirmed the discipline. *Stansky v. Gwinn Area Community Schools*, No. 305287, 2012 WL 5290301 (Mich. Ct. App. 10/25/12).

◆   An Illinois student with autism kicked, punched and bit his teacher. He was suspended, but not expelled. When the student reached grade three, the teacher asked to be reassigned, but the principal declined her request. An IEP team recommended transferring him to a therapeutic day school. But the parents and their attorney resisted, and the student was again placed in a supported general education setting for grade four. He had a behavioral support plan and a solitary room or "office" where he could go when his behavior became a problem. Late in the school year, the teacher encountered him in an agitated state. She said he picked up a chair and swung it at her.

As a result, the teacher hit her head on a white board and her neck on a chalk ledge. She later filed a claim for workers' compensation benefits. The student was suspended and placed in an alternative school after the incident. The teacher then sued the school district and school administrators in a federal court. The case reached the U.S. Court of Appeals, Seventh Circuit, which noted that many cases have held the Due Process Clause of the Fourteenth Amendment generally does not impose a duty on a state to protect individuals from harm by students and other private parties. Only state action that "shocks the conscience" may give rise to a due process violation. No conduct that was shocking to the conscience was found in this case. In a 1986 case, the court held the **"due process clause does not assure safe working conditions for public employees."** While the administrators' actions "may well have been short-sighted, flawed, negligent, and tortious," there was no constitutional violation. *Jackson v. Indian Prairie School Dist. 204*, 653 F.3d 647 (7th Cir. 2011).

◆   After being expelled from their high school for fighting two other students, two South Carolina brothers appealed to the district superintendent and the school board. When the decisions were upheld, they did not appeal to a court. Nearly two years later, the family sued the school district in the state court system, claiming due process violations. The court held for the district, finding the students' decision not to appeal their expulsions to a court was a failure to exhaust administrative remedies. The state court of appeals reversed the decision. Appeal reached the Supreme Court of South Carolina, which found the students received all the process they were due.

Under *Goss v. Lopez*, 419 U.S. 565 (1975), **a public school student facing a short-term suspension only needs to receive notice of the charges being brought and an opportunity to explain his or her side of the story**. As expulsion is a more serious disciplinary action than a short-term suspension, the South Carolina court found an accused student deserves greater procedures and protections when facing expulsion. Section 59-63-240 of the state code specifies that parents must be notified in writing of the time and place for a hearing in expulsion cases. At a hearing, parents have statutory rights to have counsel present and to present evidence and question witnesses. In this case, the family chose not to have counsel at the initial hearing and did not exercise the right to present evidence or question witnesses. Finding the state law protections were constitutionally sufficient, the court reinstated the trial court's decision. *Stinney v. Sumter School Dist. 17*, 391 S.C. 547, 707 S.E.2d 397 (S.C. 2011).

◆   During a physical education class, an Ohio student was threatened by a girl and responded "I'm sick and tired of you threatening me. If you're going to beat me up, then just do it already." On this basis, the school suspended both girls for three days. An Ohio court modified the decision. It held the student's behavior did not amount to a threat of physical harm and was not an "assault" in violation of the relevant student handbook provision. As a result, the penalty was reduced to a Saturday detention. On appeal, the state court of appeals agreed with the lower court that the student did not commit an "assault." According to the court, the relevant handbook provision "first and foremost requires an unlawful threat to injure another person." But it held the student never made any threat. Despite a school associate principal's position that the student committed an assault by "offering to fight with somebody," the court found she had only told the other girl to stop threatening her. Since **none of the student's statements was an "assault,"** it was not error to modify her suspension. *Cisek v. Nordonia Hills Board of Educ.*, Case No. CV 2009 10 7363, 2011 WL 806518 (Ohio Ct. App. 3/9/11).

◆   North Carolina school staff members tried to break up a fight between two students in the cafeteria. One of the students admitted hitting a teacher about 20 seconds after being separated from the other student. An assistant principal interviewed the students, staff members and witnesses. Police also conducted an investigation. The student was charged as a juvenile with assault on a school employee and disorderly conduct, and the other student was charged as an adult with a misdemeanor. The school board suspended the student for 10 days for violating four school board policies, including one providing for a long-term suspension for assaulting a school employee.

After the suspension was imposed under North Carolina law, the student received a number of hearings where he was represented by an attorney, and the long-term suspension was upheld. Appeal reached the Court of Appeals of North Carolina. It appeared to the court that the student had an opportunity to learn the nature of his offense and respond to the charges. He received two hearings, which included an "exhaustive fact-finding inquiry" by the school board. While the student asserted self-defense, he had admitted a delay of 20 seconds from the end of the fight to the time he hit the teacher. No witnesses supported his claim of self-defense. State law required imposing a long-term suspension for violating the policy against assaulting school employees. **Protecting school employees is a goal of school discipline, so the court upheld the suspension.** *Watson-Green v. Wake County Board of Educ.*, 700 S.E.2d 249 (N.C. Ct. App. 2010).

◆ A North Carolina school decided a ninth-grader should attend an alternative school pending a risk assessment based on threats to harm himself and others. A school counselor recommended a psychological evaluation of the student, but the parents resisted. An in-school suspension (ISS) was imposed after classmates said the student tried to cut or stab himself and threatened violence. He remained in ISS for the rest of the school year and was assigned to an alternative learning center (ALC) pending completion of a risk assessment. A panel found the assignment to the ALC was not disciplinary in nature. It found a reasonable basis to believe the student was a danger to himself or others and upheld the decision to place him in the ALC until he underwent a risk assessment. He sued the board in a state court for constitutional violations, but the court affirmed the ALC assignment. On appeal, the state court of appeals held **students who were recommended for alternative or ALC placements as an alternative to suspension were entitled to a hearing before the district superintendent**. The student had been suspended for refusal to submit to a risk assessment, and the court found the ALC assignment for the same behavior was an "alternative to suspension" as described in a district policy. Since an ALC assignment would be reflected in the student's cumulative record, the court held he was entitled to a hearing. It reversed the judgment. *Rone v. Winston-Salem/Forsyth County Board of Educ.*, 701 S.E.2d 284 (N.C. Ct. App. 2010).

◆ Two female students in Idaho reported that two males were planning a Columbine-style attack at school. The principal confronted one of the male students, who said he was "going to have a school shooting" on a specified date. The two male students were warned about their threatening conduct, and they agreed not to make further statements. But one month later, the students were accused of threatening to shoot guns at a school dance. Two years after these incidents, one of the male students wrote threatening notes that were viewed by his locker partner. Although the threats were brought to the attention of the school resource officer and a vice principal, they were "dismissed." The same month as the notes were found, the student and a male accomplice murdered a female student at the house of her friend. When her parents sued the school district in a state trial court, it was found that the district owed no duty to protect the student off school grounds and after school hours. On appeal, the Supreme Court of Idaho affirmed the judgment. Nothing in the record convinced the court that the district knew that one of the male students would commit a murder based on information received about him some 30 months earlier. **As the murder was not foreseeable, the district had no duty to prevent it.** *Stoddart v. Pocatello School Dist. #25*, 239 P.3d 784 (Idaho 2010).

◆ Section 380.1311a(1) of Michigan Compiled Laws requires the permanent expulsion of a student in grade six or above for a physical assault at school against a school employee, volunteer or contractor. If an assault is reported to the school, the school board is required by law to "expel the pupil from the school district permanently." Four teachers claimed that pupils in grade six or higher physically assaulted them in their classrooms and that the assaults were reported to a school administrator. Instead of expelling the students, the school district only suspended them. The teachers and their association filed an action in the state court system against the school board under Section 380.1311a(1). The court held it had no authority to supervise a school district's exercise of discretion, and the state court of appeals affirmed the decision. Appeal reached the Supreme Court of Michigan, which first held the teachers had legal standing to pursue the case. They were likely to suffer an injury that other members of the public did not face. **The legislative history of Section 380.1311 revealed an intent to create a safe school environment and a more effective workplace for teachers.** As a result, the lower court decisions for the board were reversed. *Lansing Schools Educ. Ass'n MEA/NEA v. Lansing Board of Educ.*, 487 Mich. 387, 792 N.W.2d 686 (Mich. 2010).

◆ A New York City special education teacher initiated a Type Three referral to remove an aggressive student from her class, and she contemplated quitting because of his behavior. Her supervisors told her to "hang in there" because referral could take up to 60 days. Forty-one days after initiating the referral, the student attacked another child and the teacher intervened, sustaining injuries. She sued the city for negligence, alleging that a "special relationship" supported her claim. A jury awarded her over $512,000, and appeal reached the state's highest court. According to the New York Court of Appeals, no special relationship existed between the teacher and the board that would create a cause of action for negligence.

Even if the court gave the teacher a favorable take on the evidence, it found no rational basis for a jury to find that she "justifiably relied on assurances by the Board of Education." **Her supervisor's vaguely worded statements would not have lulled her into a false sense of security or caused her to rely on the school board.** As there was no special relationship between the teacher and board, the court reversed the judgment. *Dinardo v. City of New York*, 13 N.Y.3d 872, 893 N.Y.S.2d 818 (N.Y. 2009).

◆   A Montana student turned in a list of resolutions with violent themes for a school typing assignment. His teacher told administrators about the list, and the family was called in for meetings. No subsequent action was taken. About 17 months later, the student intentionally ran over a jogger near the high school. Before doing so, he told a passenger in the car that he planned to run over the jogger and commit necrophilia with her corpse. In a state court action against the school district, the jogger claimed the district negligently handled the student after learning of his resolution list. A Montana district court disagreed, finding no "special relationship" between the district and the student or the jogger that would create a district duty to protect the jogger. On appeal, the Supreme Court of Montana rejected the jogger's argument that there was no requirement of a special relationship in this case. Instead, it held the jogger was not a "foreseeable plaintiff."

In ruling for the school district, the court held foreseeability is of primary importance in establishing the existence of a legal duty of care. **If a reasonably prudent person cannot foresee any danger of direct injury, there is no duty, and thus no negligence.** It was not foreseeable that 17 months after writing the resolution list, the student would deliberately run over a jogger, after school hours and off school grounds. The list had no specific threats, and some statements were sufficiently ridiculous or random to support the characterization that it was a teenager's misguided attempt at black humor. There was no error by the lower court in finding the principal was entitled to immunity, and the judgment was affirmed. *Emanuel v. Great Falls School Dist.*, 351 Mont. 56, 209 P.3d 244 (Mont. 2009).

B. School Employees

In *Lambert v. Escambia County Board of Educ.*, below, an Alabama court rejected a school employee's Second Amendment argument based on an asserted right to bear arms. Citing *Dist. of Columbia v. Heller*, 554 U.S. 570 (2008), the court held Second Amendment cases did not "cast doubt on longstanding prohibitions" created by laws forbidding the carrying of arms in sensitive places such as schools and government buildings.

◆   An Alabama high school band director with 38 years of good service was dismissed after a school custodian found a loaded gun with an extra ammunition clip in his locked office. At the time, the director was with the band on an out-of-town trip. At a later hearing before the board of education, the superintendent voiced concerns for school safety and consistency with zero-tolerance policies. Although the director emphasized his clean record as an educator and serviceman, the board voted to dismiss him for violating its weapons-free policy. A hearing officer then found the Alabama Students First Act of 2011 required deference to the board's decision and prevented him from modifying a board order. On appeal, **the Alabama Court of Civil Appeals found the policy was sufficiently clear to put the director on notice that firearms were not to be brought to school**. The director knew of the zero-tolerance policy regarding weapons on campus and that having a loaded firearm on campus violated the weapons-free campus policy. The director's argument based on a Second Amendment right to bear arms was foreclosed by Supreme Court authority. There was no merit to a claim based on a Fourth Amendment theory that there had been a search of his office. As there was no error by the hearing officer, the decision to terminate the director's employment was upheld. *Lambert v. Escambia County Board of Educ.*, No. 2120350, 2013 WL 5583739 (Ala. Civ. Ct. App. 10/11/13).

◆   A New Jersey teacher accused of touching two middle school students was unable to proceed with a federal malicious prosecution case after his criminal charges were dismissed. Following a student's report, the teacher was suspended, arrested and kept in police custody. After the charges were dismissed, he sued police and school officials. When the case reached the U.S. Court of Appeals, Third Circuit, it agreed with the trial court that **the officials took action based on probable cause of child endangerment by the teacher**. This was sufficient to dispose of his claims against the officials. *Schirmer v. Penkethman*, 553 Fed.Appx. 268 (3d Cir. 2014).

◆   Maryland's highest court agreed with criminal prosecutors that intimate (but not sexually explicit) letters from a paraeducator to an eight-year-old student supported the paraeducator's sexual abuse conviction. The Court of Appeals of Maryland held there was sexual abuse despite the lack of sexual contact. In a prior case, the court had held **child sexual abuse includes failure to act to prevent molestation or exploitation when it is reasonably possible to do so**. Another Maryland case had found exploitation when a person in custody of a child took advantage of the child or unjustly used the child for his own benefit. Based on the totality of the letters and evidence that the two had hugged and held hands, the court found the child was exploited under the Maryland Child Sexual Abuse Statute.

In affirming a prison sentence of 13 years, the court rejected numerous arguments by the paraeducator and found sufficient evidence to support the conviction. It held "sexual abuse" was not limited to specified acts of incest, rape, sexual offense, sodomy and other practices listed in the statute. The court found the statute was not impermissibly vague and held the broad statutory language struck a careful compromise between the need for specificity and the desire of legislators to craft a law to "target the ever-shifting manner in which some people will target and abuse children." *Walker v. State of Maryland*, 432 Md. 587, 69 A.3d 1066 (Md. 2013).

◆   Three Colorado students who were subjected to inappropriate conduct by a former teacher at their high school lost their appeal against their school district and administration. The students claimed the teacher sent them explicit texts, sought nude pictures and solicited sexual relations with them. While the court allowed claims against the teacher to proceed, it held the case could not proceed against the district or administrators who did not know of the teacher's conduct. **A single state law claim for failure to report child abuse was allowed to proceed against a school security guard and coach who knew of an incident of sexual conduct between the teacher and one student.** In a brief order, the U.S. Court of Appeals, Tenth Circuit, affirmed the judgment. *Doe v. Boulder Valley School Dist. No. RE-2*, 523 Fed.Appx. 514 (10th Cir. 2013).

◆   A Massachusetts teacher argued with her principal. She then found a substitute and left the building. She went to a hospital and told a psychiatrist that she had "the urge to kill" the principal. To comply with a state law, the remark was reported to police. When the school learned of this, the teacher was placed on leave. A court order was then obtained to bar her from the school. The school committee discharged the teacher for insubordination, conduct unbecoming a teacher and incapacity. An arbitrator found she had not engaged in conduct warranting termination under state law. A state court affirmed the award, and the case reached the state court of appeals. There, the school committee argued the arbitrator had substituted his judgment for that of the committee and did not consider the best interests of the students. But the court found that after the argument with the principal, the teacher did not attack or threaten her. She found a substitute and sought treatment. Her statements to the psychiatrist were made in the context of trying to seek treatment. **The court held she "plainly intended to threaten no one."** As the court found no reason to question the arbitrator's conclusions, it affirmed the award. *School Committee of Boston v. Underwood*, 82 Mass.App.Ct. 1113, 874 N.E.2d 656 (Table), 2012 WL 4033770 (Mass. App. Ct. 9/14/12).

◆   A Kentucky teacher sent many inappropriate letters to a colleague, then threatened her with "increasing danger." After investigating, the school principal reprimanded the teacher and authorized his transfer to another school. The teacher signed a memorandum (MOU) requiring him to stop communicating with the colleague. Three years later, he emailed the colleague about a meeting of the Louisville Area Chemistry Alliance (LACA). The principal reprimanded him for violating the MOU. The reprimand instructed him to have no more communication with the colleague and permanently barred him from LACA meetings. In a federal court, the teacher sued the school board and officials for constitutional violations. The court held for the board and officials, but the U.S. Court of Appeals, Sixth Circuit, reversed the ban on attending LACA meetings. It affirmed the rest of the judgment for the board and officials.

In later proceedings, the lower court entered an order preventing the board from barring the teacher from LACA meetings. But it dismissed the claims against school officials. The teacher appealed to the Sixth Circuit, which held his association with the LACA was protected by the First Amendment, and that the district's ban was overly broad. As the board had "no tenable explanation for such a sweeping and everlasting prohibition," the board was properly denied judgment. In developing a reprimand, the principal and a district human resources director did not follow any simple procedure or standard policy. **Since they had used their discretion, the court held qualified immunity applied.** The principal and director were not final policymakers, and so could not create school board liability. *Baar v. Jefferson County Board of Educ.*, 476 Fed.Appx. 621 (6th Cir. 2012).

◆   A California student claimed a school counselor engaged him in sexual conduct. He filed a state court negligence action against the school district, counselor and others that reached the state supreme court. It held that although districts and their employees are not "insurers of the physical safety of students, California law has long imposed on school authorities a duty to supervise at all times the conduct of the children on the school grounds and to enforce those rules and regulations necessary to their protection." Lack of supervision or ineffective supervision may constitute a "lack of ordinary care" in cases alleging lack of student supervision, and a district is liable for injuries caused by such negligence.

   Previous California decisions had found that a school district and its employees have a "special relationship" with students. In *Dailey v. Los Angeles Unified School Dist.*, 2 Cal.3d 741, 87 Cal.Rptr. 376 (1970), the court established that school personnel may be individually held liable for the negligent failure to protect students. Rejecting the district's arguments, the court held administrators have the responsibility of taking reasonable measures to guard students against harassment or abuse from foreseeable sources, including teachers or counselors. Administrators could be held liable for employee misconduct based on a "special relationship" theory. But even if an administrator was liable, the court found the greater share of fault would likely lie with the counselor herself. The case was returned to the lower courts for further consideration. *C.A. v. William S. Hart Union High School Dist.*, 138 Cal.Rptr.3d 1, 270 P.3d 699 (Cal. 2012).

◆   A Kentucky teacher injured her head in a bicycling accident and had post-concussive syndrome, memory and attention problems, outbursts of anger and other symptoms. She confronted students playing basketball outside her school, and a parent later accused her of threatening to kill them. After an investigation, the teacher was fired for conduct unbecoming a teacher. The Kentucky Education Professional Standards Board then revoked the teacher's teaching certificate for 10 years. Based on the basketball incident, the teacher was also convicted of terroristic threatening. A state court fined the teacher $4,500 and ordered her to refrain from abusive conduct with the victims. She appealed the license revocation to a state court, which held the terroristic threats justified revocation. The state court of appeals affirmed the judgment. **State law permitted the revocation, suspension or refusal to renew or issue a teaching certificate for reasons including physical or mental incapacity** preventing a teacher from performing duties with "reasonable skill, competence or safety." *Macy v. Kentucky Educ. Professional Standards Board*, Nos. 2008-CA-002234-MR, 2008-CA-002293-MR, 2010 WL 743668 (Ky. Ct. App. 3/5/10).

C. Parents

In *Doe v. Virginia Dep't of State Police*, below, the U.S. Court of Appeals, Sixth Circuit, rejected a parent's argument that a state law sex offender requirement violated her constitutional rights. In doing so, the court relied on *Connecticut Dep't of Public Safety v. Doe*, 538 U.S. 1 (2003). In that case, the U.S. Supreme Court held a state's decision to publish registry information on sex offenders was not a denial of due process, even if the offender could prove he was not currently dangerous.

◆ A Virginia parent was convicted of carnal knowledge of a minor in 1993. As required by law, she registered on the state Sex Offender and Crimes Against Minors Registry. A 2008 amendment to state law reclassified the parent's crime as a "sexually violent offense." As there was no procedure for sexually violent offenders to remove their names from the registry, she would "now remain on the registry for life." Sexually violent offenders could not go on school property or daycare centers, so she was barred from churches offering on-site daycare. The parent challenged the law in a federal court, which denied her petition.

Appeal reached the U.S. Court of Appeals, Fourth Circuit, which held that since the parent had not yet petitioned a state court or her school board for access, any injury was hypothetical. As for her constitutional claims, the court held failure to follow the law's procedures made the effect of the law unclear. Since the parent had been reclassified by the state police superintendent as a sexually violent offender and placed on the state registry, she had standing to pursue a claim against him. But this proved to be irrelevant, as the court found *Connecticut Dep't of Public Safety v. Doe*, 538 U.S. 1 (2003), foreclosed the claim. In that case, the U.S. Supreme Court held **a state's decision to publish registry information on sex offenders was not a denial of due process, even if the offender could prove he or she was not currently dangerous**. As a result, the court affirmed the judgment against the parent. *Doe v. Virginia Dep't of State Police*, 713 F.3d 745 (4th Cir. 2013).

◆ A Mississippi parent argued with a middle school principal about a student disciplinary matter. Tensions escalated, and when the principal told the parent to leave his office, he called him a "coward." The principal called the police, and the parent was charged with creating a public disturbance. Police escorted him to a court, and a judge barred him from appearing on county school property. Later, the charges were dropped. In a federal court action against the school district and principal, the parent asserted First Amendment violations and unlawful seizure in violation of the Fourth Amendment. The court refused to dismiss many of the claims prior to a trial. In holding that the parent could pursue a speech claim against the principal, the court found that criticism of public officials "lies at the very core of that speech protected by the First Amendment." It found the parent had been "seized" within the meaning of the Fourth Amendment when the police told him of a warrant and requested that he come to the police station. Although the court found the principal would have to defend his actions in further proceedings, it held **a government entity may not be held liable for constitutional rights violations unless the violation was due to an official policy**. As a result, the court held the claims against the school district could not proceed. *Cash v. Lee County School Dist.*, No. 1:11-CV-00154-SA-DAS, 2012 WL 6737540 (N.D. Miss. 12/28/12).

◆   A Michigan teacher claimed a parent became upset during a disciplinary hearing and hit her in the stomach before leaving with his son. She was pregnant at the time, and a student witness heard her scream. The teacher reported the incident to police, and the parent was prosecuted on a charge of assault with intent to do great bodily harm. A jury found the parent not guilty of the criminal charge, and he sued the teacher and school district in a state court for malicious prosecution, infliction of emotional distress and defamation. After the court dismissed the action, the parent appealed.

The Court of Appeals of Michigan noted that the parent had been criminally charged by the county prosecutor, not the teacher. **There is an important state policy of encouraging citizens to report possible crimes.** According to the court, a person who has no active role in initiating a criminal prosecution cannot be held liable for malicious prosecution. The teacher was not accused of lying to authorities, and she did not institute the charges. As she made a full and fair disclosure of the incident and the prosecutor recommended the action, no malicious prosecution claim against her could succeed. **A person needs only reasonable grounds of suspicion of a person's guilt to file a report with authorities.** And the prosecutor had conducted an independent investigation of the incident based on the teacher's account, which was corroborated by a student witness. Governmental immunity protected the school district, the teacher and another staff member from liability in this case. Since information available to the prosecutor would cause a reasonable person to believe the parent was guilty and there was no evidence of false testimony by the teacher, the court affirmed the judgment. *Bradley v. Detroit Public Schools*, No. 292749, 2011 WL 255274 (Mich. Ct. App. 1/27/11).

◆   A Chicago third-grader had conflicts with another girl at school. The other girl's mother and a companion threatened the student's mother at her home. The school principal set up a meeting between the families. Near the end of a school day, the other girl's parent and an adult cousin fought the student's mother and grandmother in a school office. The principal called police and swore out criminal complaints for disorderly conduct against all four adults. Criminal charges were dismissed, and the principal later said he had made a mistake and should have only had two of the women arrested. The parent and grandparent sued the board of education in the federal court system. The U.S. Court of Appeals, Seventh Circuit, noted the issue was not whether a parent or grandparent had actually committed disorderly conduct. **It was only necessary to show a reasonable person in the principal's position had probable cause to believe there was disorderly conduct.** The principal entered a chaotic situation and could easily have viewed the mother to be an equal participant in the fight. Each of the family's civil rights claims failed. *Stokes v. Board of Educ. of City of Chicago*, 599 F.3d 617 (7th Cir. 2010).

◆   After a sex offender entered a Texas school and exposed himself to a child, the district implemented a regulation requiring every visitor to produce a state-issued photo identification as a condition of entering secure areas where students were present. Under the regulation, pictures were taken of visitor identification cards but no other information was taken. The system enabled schools to check visitor names and birth dates to determine if they were listed on national registered sex-offender databases. A parent refused to allow her child's school to either scan her driver's license or permit manual entry of her information. As a result, she was denied access to areas of the school. She and her husband sued, challenging the policy as a violation of their constitutional rights. A federal court held for the district, and the Fifth Circuit affirmed. **The regulation addressed a compelling state interest and was not overly intrusive.** The system took only the minimal information needed to determine sex offender status. *Meadows v. Lake Travis Independent School Dist.*, 397 Fed.Appx. 1 (5th Cir. 2010).

◆   A Louisiana father gave his children's middle school documentation that he had their sole "provisional custody." He claimed that they could only be released to him. School policy allowed only the persons listed on a check out form to sign a student out of school. When the children's mother appeared at their school prior to a holiday break, the principal telephoned the father. He stated that under no circumstances could they be released to her, and that he would come to the school. But when the father arrived at school 20 minutes later, the principal had already released the children to the mother. The father sued the school board, principal and insurer. After the case was dismissed, the state court of appeal held that the father's claims for out-of-pocket expenses could proceed if the school officials owed him a duty to refrain from allowing the mother to check the children out of school. **Schools have a "duty to make the appropriate supervisory decisions concerning a student's departure from campus during regular school hours."** As the father asserted violation of the policy on checking out students, and claimed the sole authority to do so, the principal had violated the policy and her duty to the children and father. *Peters v. Allen Parish School Board*, 996 So.2d 1230 (La. Ct. App. 2008).

◆ California parents had a 20-year history of intervention by children and family services authorities and were subject to a dependency court proceeding for charges of physical abuse, neglect and failure to prevent sexual abuse. The parents were uncooperative with authorities, and the mother once attempted to hide her children from them. After two children were declared dependent due to the abuse and neglect of their siblings, their attorney sought an order that they be sent to a public or private school, rather than educated at home. The request was made to allow the children to be in regular contact with mandatory reporters. A state superior court refused the request, and the case reached the California Court of Appeal. It found that homeschooling arose as an issue in the case because one child, who had been homeschooled by the mother, wanted to attend public school. The children and families agency claimed the child was dependent because her parents' refusal to send her to public school placed her at risk of serious emotional damage. The petition alleged the children should attend a public or private school for their safety, so that they would have regular contact with mandatory reporters. The superior court had incorrectly found there was an absolute parental right to homeschool children. Instead, **the constitutional liberty interest of parents to direct the education of their children had to yield to the state interest in child protection and safety**.

The court noted this was a dependency case, in which the children had already been found dependent due to abuse and neglect of a sibling. "The parents in dependency have been judicially determined not to be fit," wrote the court. Without contact with mandated reporters at school, the court found the children's safety might not be guaranteed. By allowing them to attend school, they could remain in a home placement, while educators would provide them "an extra layer of protection." The court returned the case to the superior court for reconsideration. *Jonathan L. v. Superior Court*, 165 Cal.App.4th 1074, 81 Cal.Rptr.3d 517 (Cal. Ct. App. 2008).

◆ A Tennessee couple began divorce proceedings. The wife told school staff not to release the children to their father, but a staff member told her that would require a court order. The husband signed the children out of school early the next day, giving as a reason: "keeping promise by mother" for the daughter and "pay back" for the son. A staff member read the reasons for early dismissal on the sign-out sheet after the father left, and she told the principal. Police were called. They arrived at the father's house to find it ablaze. The father brandished a knife, and the police shot him to death. The children's bodies were found inside the house. Later, the mother sued the school board for negligence in the state court system. A trial court held for the board, and the mother appealed. The state court of appeals held that the board was not liable for negligently violating its own sign-out policy.

There was no evidence that staff knew of a dispute until the mother called the day before the murders. The trial court had correctly held that a **school has no legal duty to follow the instruction of one parent not to release a child to the other parent without a court order to this effect**. But failure to read the father's reasons for signing out the children was evidence of breach of the duty to exercise ordinary care for safety. The court rejected a claim that the board had no duty to examine the reason for signing out a child. The trial court was to further consider this claim. *Haney v. Bradley County Board of Educ.*, 160 S.W.3d 886 (Tenn. Ct. App. 2004).

◆   An Ohio student with autism and pervasive disability disorder exhibited violent, disruptive behavior in kindergarten and first grade. His second-grade individualized education program (IEP) placed him in regular classes with a full-time aide. Early in the year, the student disrupted his class during a math test, flew into a rage and repeatedly struck his teacher. She took him to the hallway and restrained him, but when she released him, he kicked her in the face and neck. The teacher sued the student's parents and the school district in a state court. The court found nothing in the student's behavioral history indicated he would cause injuries of the kind alleged by the teacher.

The Court of Appeals of Ohio held that parents may be held liable for the wrongful conduct of their children when the injury is a foreseeable consequence of their negligence. Ohio courts have recognized that **parents may be held liable for failing to exercise reasonable control over a child, despite knowledge that injury to another person is a probable consequence**. The student frequently hit and kicked students, teachers and aides, lashing out when frustrated in his classes or when touched or bumped by classmates. Merely advocating for the placement of the student in regular education settings could not make the parents liable. However, there was evidence that the parents' "aggressive participation and pressure at the IEP meetings was a major factor in the IEP team's final decision." The court reversed the judgment for the parents, but held the trial court had correctly held the district was entitled to sovereign immunity under state law. *Coolidge v. Riegle*, No. 5-02-59, 2004 WL 170319 (Ohio Ct. App. 2004).

◆   In a case involving harassment of school staff by a non-custodial Virginia parent, the U.S. Court of Appeals, Fourth Circuit, held "school officials have the authority and responsibility for assuring that parents and third parties conduct themselves appropriately while on school property." It added that while the specific contours of their authority and responsibility were defined by state law, school **"officials should never be intimidated into compromising the safety of those who utilize school property."** The right of the parent to communicate on school grounds was not limitless, and he had received ample opportunity to communicate his message before he was barred from school. *Lovern v. Edwards*, 190 F.3d 648 (4th Cir. 1999).

D. Others

♦ **A federal court upheld significant parts of New York's SAFE Act, which was enacted in response to the 2012 Newtown, Connecticut shootings.** It upheld the act's regulation of "assault weapons" and large-capacity gun magazines, finding it furthered the interest in public safety and did not violate the Second Amendment. The court upheld a requirement for ammunition sales to take place "face-to-face" to prevent Internet sales. It also upheld the act's ban on military-style gun features. But the state did not justify a prohibition on the possession of gun magazines with more than seven rounds of ammunition. Also struck down was the act's reference to muzzle "breaks" and the regulation of semiautomatic pistols that were a "version of an automatic rifle, shotgun or firearm." The court held the act's definitions for these terms were unconstitutionally vague. *New York State Rifle and Pistol Ass'n v. Cuomo*, 990 F.Supp.2d 349 (W.D.N.Y. 2013).

♦ A Virginia court convicted a man of taking indecent liberties with a child in his custody. Upon his release from a brief period of imprisonment, he registered as a sex offender and completed his term of probation. After a hearing, a state court considered the man's application to go onto school property to observe his stepson's activities, and to pick him up, drop him off and go to school conferences. The court granted him conditional rights to be on school property and terminated his duty to re-register every 90 days as a sex offender. The Commonwealth of Virginia, city school board and its superintendent of schools appealed to the Supreme Court of Virginia.

According to the Commonwealth, Virginia Code Section 18.2-370(B) granted school boards authority to determine whether to allow a convicted sex offender to enter onto school property. After noting that Section 18.2-370.5 prohibited convicted violent sex offenders from entering public school grounds in most circumstances, the court held the law gave circuit, juvenile and domestic relations courts the authority to remove this statutory ban. It held "decisions regarding the safety and welfare of students are manifestly a part of the supervisory authority granted the school boards under Article VIII." Allowing the offender a right to enter school property related to the education of his stepson, and not the public safety. Instead, the Commonwealth correctly argued that a court had supervision over a violent sex offender on probation or a suspended sentence. **Once a court lifted the statutory ban on sex offenders from entering school property, the school board would be permitted to exercise its supervisory authority under the state constitution.** The court reversed the judgment and returned the case to the circuit court for it to decide whether and under what circumstances the statutory ban from school property on the offender might be lifted. *Comwlth. v. Doe*, 278 Va. 223, 682 S.E.2d 906 (Va. 2009).

♦ A 2007 legislative amendment placed private contractor employees under the scope of Florida Statutes Section 1012.467. This required criminal background screening for non-instructional contractors. Those who were found to have been convicted of child abuse and certain other charges were disqualified from access to public school grounds when students were present. The statute defined the term "convicted" to include a no contest plea. An employee of a private contractor underwent a level-two criminal background screen as required by the new law and was notified that he would no longer have access to school property due to a 1996 no contest plea to a child abuse charge. As he had to work on school property when students were present in order to perform his job duties, the contractor fired him. A state court enjoined the board from barring him from school property. The board appealed to a state district court of appeal.

On appeal, the employee argued the 2007 amendment would retroactively convert his plea to a conviction. The court held the statute changed the nature of a no contest plea. It held a "substantive, vested right" is in turn an "immediate right of present enjoyment, or a fixed right of future enjoyment," and not a mere expectation. In this case, the trial court had improperly referred to the employee's loss of a job and his "right" to come on school property. **The school board never terminated the relationship or demanded that the contractor fire him, and he had no vested right to go on school grounds.** Since the employee failed to show the school board had divested him of any right of present enjoyment or a present fixed right of future enjoyment, the court reversed the judgment of the trial court. *School Board of Miami-Dade County, Florida v. Carralero*, 992 So.2d 353 (Fla. Dist. Ct. App. 2008).

III. STALKING AND HARASSMENT

A. Gender

1. Harassment

In the mid-1980s, courts began recognizing sexual harassment as a form of sex discrimination that violates federal law. Sexual harassment and assault may create school liability for failing to comply with Title IX of the Education Amendments of 1972, the Equal Protection Clause of the Fourteenth Amendment, and other federal laws. Failure to prevent sexual harassment and assault also gives rise to state law tort claims.

To avoid liability under Title IX, educators are best advised to comply with the basic regulatory requirements of federal law. Schools must publish a notice of non-discrimination, and name the particular laws involved. They should explain what kind of conduct these laws prohibit, state that the school will enforce them and describe what the penalty will be.

A number of legal commentators have observed that many victims of peer bullying and harassment do not know how or where to report such misconduct. Schools must appoint a Title IX coordinator and conspicuously post information on how and where to report misconduct. The nationally known law firm of Hogan Lovells has devised the following checklist for helping to prevent student harassment claims.

☑ CHECKLIST – *Harassment Prevention*

- ☐ Foster an atmosphere of mutual respect among faculty, staff and students.
- ☐ Have clear policies on prohibited conduct.
- ☐ Set clear boundaries of acceptable behavior for students and employees.
- ☐ Make sure teachers, staff, students and parents are aware of policies and expectations.
- ☐ Make clear who is available to **welcome** concerns and complaints about such issues.
- ☐ Encourage staff and students to speak up about inappropriate behavior whenever it occurs.
- ☐ Intervene early to monitor and correct potentially problematic behaviors: sexual or gender-based teasing; inappropriate jokes about sex; "casual" comments of a sexual nature; or any unwelcome touching.

Thorough investigation of harassment reports is another key to avoiding school liability in Title IX cases. Here are Hogan Lovells' suggestions:

☑ CHECKLIST – *Harassment Investigation*

- ☐ Develop a timeline for the investigation to ensure that it is completed properly.
- ☐ Develop a plan for the investigation.
- ☐ Determine the type of harassment that may be present.
- ☐ Determine what facts are necessary to show the type of harassment.
- ☐ Determine potential witnesses that need to be interviewed.
- ☐ Determine what, if any, documents need to be reviewed.
- ☐ Draft possible questions for each interview.
- ☐ Conduct interview of complainant and witnesses.
- ☐ Consider using a team approach.
- ☐ Use open-ended questions.
- ☐ Ask the complainant and/or parents what they would like done.
- ☐ Ask questions that establish a foundation for the incidents, such as who was there, where each incident took place and when each incident took place.
- ☐ Tell the witness that the investigation is ongoing and that no decision will be made until all witnesses and relevant information have been

considered.

☐ Ask questions that elicit facts – not perceptions.

☐ Ask if there are any other witnesses.

☐ Take notes.

☐ Analyze all relevant information.

☐ Communicate the results, but be careful of privacy rights.

The checklist information above is copyrighted by Hogan Lovells (formerly Hogan & Hartson) and the National School Boards Association (NSBA). See *http://www.nsba.org/* and *http://www.hoganlovells.com/*.

2. Peer Harassment Case Law

Title IX prohibits sex discrimination by recipients of federal funding. In *Davis v. Monroe County Board of Educ.*, this chapter, the Supreme Court first held schools could be liable under Title IX for student-on-student harassment. To prevail in a Title IX action, students must show (1) sexual harassment by peers; (2) deliberate indifference by school officials with "actual knowledge" of the harassment; and (3) harassment so severe, pervasive and objectively offensive it deprived the student of access to educational opportunities. A teacher's knowledge of peer harassment is sufficient to create "actual knowledge" that may trigger district liability.

In *Fitzgerald v. Barnstable School Committee*, this chapter, the Supreme Court held Title IX does not bar gender discrimination claims against schools under 42 U.S.C. § 1983. Section 1983 is a post-Civil War statute that creates no rights, but is a vehicle to enforce rights created by other federal laws and the Constitution. Because the *Fitzgerald* case has the potential to expand school liability in peer sexual harassment cases, educators must be willing to investigate all harassment claims and intervene promptly in a manner that is reasonably calculated to remedy misconduct.

◆ An Indiana high school basketball team manager said four senior team members harassed him constantly in the school locker room. By his account, the seniors taunted him with sexual comments, "flashed" him and grabbed his genitals. He said they "gooched him," a term used for anal penetration with fingers, either directly or through clothing. After two or three gooching incidents, the student began wearing two layers of shorts to school. He claimed a senior pushed him over and simulated a sexual assault.

During a school bus trip, the student claimed some seniors called him to the back of the bus, held him down and anally penetrated him. Others then blocked his return to the front of the bus. A parent reported the incident a few weeks later, and some of the seniors were expelled. In a federal court, the student asserted Title IX violations and other claims. The court found a same-sex harassment claim may survive under Title IX based on gender stereotyping. Although the court held there had been severe and objectively offensive harassment that denied the student educational opportunities, it found the school acted almost immediately upon learning about the bus incident. **Actual notice of harassment was required for school liability to exist under Title IX.** The student claimed that the coaches and school must have known about the sexual assaults because they had been occurring in the basketball program for years. He said they were common knowledge in the community. But the court dismissed the Title IX claim as unsupported by admissible evidence. While the court found no merit to the student's constitutional claims, it agreed to consider his state tort law claims in further proceedings. *Davis v. Carmel Clay Schools*, No. 1:11-cv-00771-SEB-MJD, 2013 WL 5487340 (S.D. Ind. 9/30/13).

◆   A California shop teacher lent a metal shop key to a student. According to the student's former girlfriend, the student sexually assaulted her at knifepoint in the shop. She sued the student, his parents, the school district and the shop teacher in a state court. Among the claims was negligent supervision. A state superior court held for the district and shop teacher, and the former girlfriend appealed. She claimed the teacher knew the student sometimes brought a "multitool" with screwdrivers, pliers and a knife to school. The court found the student used the multitool for farm chores and did not use it during the assault. According to the former girlfriend, he had been caught with a knife on campus before but had not been disciplined. The district noted there had not been a sexual assault on the campus for over 25 years. The teacher had known the student since infancy and had a relationship of trust with him. There was also evidence that it was common for teachers at the school to give students keys.

School records indicated no prior assaults by the student, and he had no history of behavior issues or mental disability. The multitool played no part in the incident, and the student had concealed it at school. **As nothing indicated to the school district or the teacher that the student would sexually assault anyone at school, the court upheld findings by the lower court that the assault was unforeseeable.** It held for the district. *Sheaffer v. Scott Valley Union School Dist.*, No. C069156, 2012 WL 6059248 (Cal. Ct. App. 12/6/12).

◆   Members of a Michigan middle school basketball team engaged in locker room horseplay that escalated during the course of the season. Eighth-graders on the team victimized seventh-grade team members in "games" with sexually violent overtones. One involved "turning off all the lights in the locker room, then 'humping and gyrating on the seventh graders.'" Eventually, some eighth-graders grabbed a seventh-grader, forced him to the floor, "pulled his pants down and anally penetrated him with a marker." The incidents were not met with a speedy response by school administrators, and the seventh-graders soon stopped going to the school. In a federal court, the seventh-graders sued the board of education for sexual harassment and assault by the eighth-graders. A jury returned twin $100,000 verdicts for the seventh-graders on their Title IX claims. Appeal reached the U.S. Court of

Appeals, Sixth Circuit. It held **a jury could have reasonably viewed the marker incident as "not just horseplay gone awry, but rather as a serious incident of sexual assault."** A jury could have reasonably expected the school would impose more punishment than 11-day school suspensions and a month of team suspension on the eighth-graders. *Mathis v. Wayne County Board of Educ.*, 496 Fed.Appx. 513 (6th Cir. 2012).

◆ A Connecticut student reported frequent bullying and harassment by a classmate. During the student's sophomore year, he said there were times when the bullying and harassment would stop when a male vice principal "clamped down on them." But the student claimed that the classmate continued saying anti-gay epithets. When the student complained to the male vice principal, he was told that the school resource officer would be "on alert" for trouble. The classmate was then suspended for two days.

After the classmate returned to school, he followed the student out of the cafeteria and assaulted him in a school hallway. In a state court negligence action against the classmate, vice principals, board of education and others, the student asserted there was a duty by the officials and government entities to protect him from known bullying. The court rejected a claim by the school's female vice principal that she had no duty to protect the student. It found both vice principals were responsible for monitoring the student body. A school policy required staff to "be particularly alert to possible situations, circumstances or events which might include bullying." **The ultimate test for the existence of a duty to use care was found in the foreseeability that harm might result if reasonable care was not exercised.** Although the court agreed with the board that the acts involved in this case were discretionary, it denied their claim to immunity. It found there were genuine issues of fact involving the question of whether the student was an "identifiable victim" and whether he faced imminent harm. As a result, the court denied the school board's motion for pretrial judgment. *Straiton v. New Milford Board of Educ.*, No. DBD CV 10 6003255S, 2012 WL 1218160 (Conn. Super. Ct. 3/13/12).

◆ A Massachusetts kindergarten student told her parents that a third-grader on her school bus bullied her into lifting her skirt. The parents reported this to the principal, but the third-grader repeatedly denied the report, and the school could not corroborate the student's account. After she said the boy made her pull down her underpants and spread her legs, the school called the police, who found insufficient evidence for criminal charges. Finding insufficient evidence for school discipline, the principal suggested transferring the kindergartner to a different bus or leaving rows of empty seats between students of different ages. The parents suggested moving the third-grader or placing a monitor on the bus.

The superintendent denied the requests. After the parents reported that the student had experienced more encounters with the third-grader at school, she began staying home. The family sued the school committee under 42 U.S.C. §

1983, claiming a violation of Title IX. A federal court and the First Circuit held that Title IX's private remedy precluded using 42 U.S.C. § 1983 to advance Title IX claims. The U.S. Supreme Court reversed the judgment. It held that Title IX was not meant to be the exclusive mechanism for addressing gender bias in the schools. Nor was it meant to be a substitute for parallel Section 1983 lawsuits as a means of enforcing constitutional rights. According to the Supreme Court, **Section 1983 is available as a remedy to enforce Equal Protection claims for gender discrimination in schools.** *Fitzgerald v. Barnstable School Committee,* 555 U.S. 246, 129 S.Ct. 788, 172 L.Ed.2d 582 (2009).

◆   In *Davis v. Monroe County Board of Educ.,* the U.S. Supreme Court first held that school districts may be held liable for peer harassment under Title IX of the Education Amendments of 1972. **In order for school liability to exist, there must have been deliberate indifference by school officials to known acts of peer sexual harassment, where the school's response is clearly unreasonable under the circumstances.** A recipient of federal funds may be liable for student-on-student sexual harassment where the funding recipient is deliberately indifferent to known sexual harassment and the harasser is under the recipient's disciplinary authority. Significantly, a teacher has disciplinary authority over classrooms, and a teacher's failure to report sexual harassment may lead to school liability.

To create Title IX liability, the Court held the harassment must be so severe, pervasive and objectively offensive that it deprives the victim of access to educational opportunities or benefits. In this case, the Court held the harassment alleged by the student was sufficiently severe enough to avoid pretrial dismissal. *Davis v. Monroe County Board of Educ.,* 526 U.S. 629, 119 S.Ct. 1661, 143 L.Ed.2d 839 (1999).

◆   A California school district operated a free after-school program on a school playground. Between 200 and 300 children participated, with two adults typically present to supervise them. One day, only one supervisor was present to watch over 113 participants. A second-grade girl was led by an older girl to an unlocked shed on campus that was off-limits to program participants. The older girl forced a boy to have sexual contact with the second-grader. Both the boy and the second-grader later said the girl held them against their wills and threatened to hit them. The second-grader's mother sued the school district for negligent supervision, claiming the district and employees knew for some time that some of the children had been kissing and engaging in other inappropriate activity. The case reached the state court of appeal, which noted that the after-school program was voluntary. A question remained regarding whether the absence of a supervisor from her post contributed to the injury. As a result, the case required more fact-finding. **If the supervisor allowed dangerous conduct to go on, liability could be imposed.** *J.H. v. Los Angeles Unified School Dist.,* 183 Cal.App.4th 123, 107 Cal.Rptr.3d 182 (Cal. Ct. App. 2010).

◆   An Illinois kindergartner reported a male classmate jumped on her back during a recess period near the start of the school year. He continued to exhibit inappropriate behavior, including repeatedly unzipping his pants. The school assigned the classmate to detention and sent him to the school psychologist's office. Several female students then reported the classmate had been jumping on them and kissing them during recess. Later in the year, the principal suspended the classmate for two days and reassigned him to a new classroom, lunch and recess period. But he was later returned to the same lunch and recess periods, and the student's mother said he continued to bother her. The school district granted the parents' request to transfer her to a different school, and they sued the district for sexual harassment under Title IX. A federal district court awarded the district summary judgment.

The parents appealed to the Seventh Circuit, which applied the *Davis* deliberate indifference standard. As noted in *Davis*, **young students are still learning how to act appropriately, and they "regularly interact in a manner that would be unacceptable among adults."** For this reason, **"simple acts of teasing and name calling among children" do not create Title IX liability**. The kindergartner was unable to report conduct other than "vague and unspecific" allegations that the classmate "bothered her by doing nasty stuff." This did not provide the court with necessary details to evaluate its severity and pervasiveness. There was evidence kindergartners were unaware of the sexual nature of the conduct. The kindergartner was not denied access to an education, as neither her grades nor her attendance suffered. The court affirmed the judgment, because the district's response to the harassment was not deliberately indifferent. *Gabrielle M. v. Park Forest-Chicago Heights School Dist. 163*, 315 F.3d 817 (7th Cir. 2003).

3. Harassment by School Employees

A 2014 amendment to **Iowa** law allowed the state board of educational examiners to disqualify an applicant for a license or to revoke a license under listed circumstances. Under the amended law, the board has authority to adopt rules declaring that a licensee engages in unprofessional and unethical conduct that may result in disciplinary action by committing or soliciting sex from a student. Potential discipline will also apply to licensees who solicit, encourage, or consummate a romantic relationship with a person who was formerly a student within a 90-day period prior to the conduct. Eighty-Fifth Iowa General Assembly, Second Regular Session, H.F. 2389. Section 272.2, Iowa Code 2014.

New Jersey legislators amended state law in 2014 by requiring each school district to adopt a written policy concerning electronic communications between school employees and students enrolled in the district. The policy shall include, at a minimum, provisions designed to prevent improper communications between school employees and students made via email, cellular phones, social networking websites, and other Internet-based social media. "Electronic communication" in the amendment means a communication transmitted by an electronic device, including telephones, cellular phones, computers, computer networks, personal data assistants or pagers. Two-Hundred-Sixteenth New Jersey Legislature, First Annual Session, Ch. 2, Senate No. 441. Title 18a, New Jersey Statutes, Section 36-40.

◆   A 26-year-old Wisconsin teacher brought a 14-year-old student to her apartment. She later admitted kissing him for 15 to 20 minutes, while he asserted there was also some additional touching. When the student's mother discovered some text messages they had sent, she transferred him to a private school. The teacher was fired and pleaded guilty to fourth-degree sexual assault charges. The mother then sued the school district in a federal district court under Title IX. The court held for the district, and the family appealed to the U.S. Court of Appeals, Seventh Circuit. It explained the liability standard for sexual harassment by school staff members was announced in *Gebser v. Lago Vista Independent School Dist.*, this chapter. **Seventh Circuit case law required proof of "actual knowledge of misconduct, not just actual knowledge of the risk of misconduct"** in order to impose Title IX liability. In this case, the teacher had denied the encounter with the student when the principal questioned her. Later, the district superintendent continued investigating. As soon as the mother made a report, the school took prompt action. Suspicions of an improper relationship between the student and teacher did not make the true nature of the relationship "obvious" or a "known risk." In holding for the board, the court noted "judges must be sensitive to the effect on education of heavy-handed judicial intrusion into school disciplinary issues." It dismissed the federal claims and a state court claim as well. *Doe v. St. Francis School Dist.*, 694 F.3d 869 (7th Cir. 2012).

◆   A Georgia teacher called, emailed and wrote to an eighth-grade student. His parents met with the school principal at least twice and reported the continuing communications. But they told the principal they "did not think anything was going on" between the two. It was later learned that the teacher had performed oral sex on the student at least five times during the summer before his eighth-grade year. She pled guilty to criminal child molestation charges and was sentenced to prison. The parents sued the school district in a federal court for violating Title IX. The court found no evidence that the principal knew of sexual harassment by the teacher and held for the district. On appeal, the U.S. Court of Appeals, Eleventh Circuit, stated that the principal was a person with authority to take corrective measure in response to actual notice of sexual harassment under Title IX.

In a previous case, the court had found that lesser forms of harassment may provide actual notice of sexually violent conduct. But in this case, the court found it clear that **the principal was never put on notice of a single act of sexual harassment by the teacher**. The court rejected the parents' claim that reports of repeated texting and other contacts put school officials on notice of harassment. It appeared to the court that the principal knew the teacher's conduct was "inappropriate, devoid of professionalism, and reeked of immaturity." But in the court's estimation, her known conduct was not of a sexual nature and could not have put the principal on notice of sexual harassment, defeating the Title IX claim. *J.F.K. v. Troup County School Dist.*, 678 F.3d 1254 (11th Cir. 2012).

◆ A North Dakota high school student claimed a custodial supervisor sexually harassed and touched her while she worked for a school district, and twice put her in a "chokehold." However, she did not inform any school official about either incident. Some time later, the student claimed the supervisor told her to "bend over," while he was behind her, then pushed her by the neck. The student told her mother about the third incident, and the mother reported it to the building principal. According to the mother, the principal only responded "well, that's just how Gary is, rough." Although a district policy designated the building principal as the person to receive sexual harassment reports, the principal instructed the mother to report to the district superintendent. She did not make a report. Later, the student said the supervisor put his hands in her pants and pulled her toward him. This time, the mother made a report to the district superintendent. In response, the superintendent ordered the supervisor to have no contact with the student and to participate in an improvement plan.

Two years later, the student sued the district in a state court for negligence, assault and battery. A two-year state statute of limitations barred the assault and battery claims, and the court dismissed them. It found the supervisor's conduct was not foreseeable and held the negligent supervision and retention claims were barred by the state Workforce Safety and Insurance Act. On appeal, the Supreme Court of North Dakota held that while employee actions against employers are typically barred by the exclusive remedy provisions of the act, certain exceptions are included in the law. In this case, the student did not seek workers' compensation benefits for her injuries. According to the court, the essence of her action was not to recover for her physical injuries, but for non-physical injuries. It held the district did not show the student suffered any injury that was compensable under the workers' compensation act, so the act did not bar recovery in this case. **The court found sufficient evidence of negligent supervision for the student to proceed with that claim, as the district had failed to address the supervisor's misconduct after it was reported.** *Richard v. Washburn Public Schools*, 809 N.W.2d 288 (N.D. 2011).

◆ A California teacher formed close relationships with three third-graders and eventually developed a "husband-wife" relationship with one of their parents. He was a frequent visitor to her home and began staying overnight there. Near this time, the teacher cultivated relationships with two other third-graders and their single mothers. The mothers and a grandparent gave their boys permission to go to the teacher's house and spend the night there. The teacher molested each of the boys and continued doing so until it was reported to the grandmother. Following the teacher's arrest, he pled guilty to criminal charges of sexual abuse. None of the acts of molestation occurred at school. In a state court action, the families sued the teacher, school administrators and school district, asserting negligence and failure to report sexual abuse in violation of the state penal code. Following a trial, a jury voted against the families on all theories of recovery.

On appeal, the Court of Appeal of California noted that because of the grandmother's consent to the teacher's relationship with the boys, the principal did not further investigate the matter. It was speculation that any investigation of this information would have led to an earlier discovery of the teacher's abuses. In the court's view, any earlier reporting of overnight stays would likely have led to further shielding of the misconduct by the grandmother. As a result, the court upheld the rejection of a proposed jury instruction to consider conduct by employees not named in the complaint. There was also no merit to the families' claim that district training of staff on pedophile behavior would have led staff members to promptly recognize the teacher's "grooming" behavior prior to his abuse. **Federal guidance from the U.S. Department of Education's Office for Civil Rights (OCR) concerning sexual harassment of students by school employees had been properly rejected as the standard of conduct for liability.** No Title IX claim was made in this case, and any such claim would have failed because no school official knew of the teacher's molestations. As a result, the judgment was affirmed. *A.J. v. Victor Elementary School Dist.*, No. E049404, 2011 WL 1005009 (Cal. Ct. App. 3/22/11) (Unpublished).

◆ An Illinois student told her mother that a Junior Reserve Officer Training Corps (JROTC) instructor improperly touched her. After the instructor admitted wrongdoing, he was charged criminally and he resigned. In a federal district court sexual harassment action, the student included an equal protection claim under 42 U.S.C. § 1983. She also brought a claim under Title IX against the district. Judgment was entered for the school district, and the student appealed. The U.S. Court of Appeals, Seventh Circuit, found the dismissal of the Section 1983 claim for equal protection violations was based on a theory of supervisory liability. It noted the U.S. Supreme Court held Title IX did not bar concurrent Section 1983 claims against school officials in *Fitzgerald v. Barnstable School Committee*, below. But as the Section 1983 claim was based on supervisory liability, the court held **the lack of any knowledge of the instructor's misconduct by either the school district or the JROTC supervisor was fatal to the claim**. No school official knew of any sexual abuse of the student until the day she reported it. The court found remarks attributed to the JROTC supervisor were insufficient to pursue Section 1983 claims. As a result, they had been properly dismissed. As there was no legal support for the student's Title IX theory, the judgment for the district and supervisor was affirmed. *Trentadue v. Redmon*, 619 F.3d 648 (7th Cir. 2010).

◆   A Kentucky teacher sexually harassed a student and then began texting him and making inappropriate remarks. The student did not report the misconduct, even after the teacher exposed himself in a locker room. He complied with the teacher's request to text him nude photos. The student's girlfriend found the photos on the student's phone, and he attempted suicide. After learning of this, the school principal called the police and then suspended the teacher, who was soon fired. The student sued the teacher, principal, board of education and district superintendent in a federal court for negligence. He argued school officials negligently hired the teacher because they knew he had resigned from another school system after being accused of sodomy. But the court noted he was acquitted of these charges.

State law immunity protected officials who exercised discretionary functions, such as hiring decisions and supervision of employees. A background check relied upon by the board did not reveal the teacher had a criminal record. **The court noted the student had taken care to conceal events and made no complaints to anyone.** His negligent hiring claim failed for several reasons, including lack of any breach of duty by the principal and superintendent to further investigate the teacher, and qualified immunity for performing discretionary functions. There was no notice of harm to the school until the suicide attempt. **No school official was aware of the teacher's texts or the requests for nude photos.** As the student did not show it was reasonably foreseeable that he would be victimized or would attempt suicide, the court held for the school officials. *Cole v. Shadoan*, 782 F.Supp.2d 428 (E.D. Ky. 2011).

◆   In 1998, the U.S. Supreme Court examined the liability of school districts for sexual harassment of students by teachers and other staff under Title IX. The case has become one of the most important legal precedents for courts attempting to analyze school liability based on harassment of students by staff members. The case involved a Texas student who had a sexual relationship with a teacher. The Court rejected the liability standard advocated by the student and by the U.S. government, which resembled *respondeat superior* liability under Title VII.

Title IX contains an administrative enforcement mechanism that assumes actual notice has been provided to officials prior to the imposition of enforcement remedies. **An award of damages would be inappropriate in a Title IX case unless an official with the authority to address the discrimination failed to act despite actual knowledge of it, in a manner amounting to deliberate indifference to discrimination.** Here, there was insufficient evidence that a school official should have known about the relationship to impose Title IX liability. Accordingly, the school district could not be held liable for the teacher's misconduct. *Gebser v. Lago Vista Independent School Dist.*, 524 U.S. 274, 118 S.Ct. 1989, 141 L.Ed.2d 277 (1998).

4. Non-Student Harassment and Assault Cases

◆ A Mississippi adult was able to sign a young child out of school by falsely indicating he was her parent six different times. He then sexually molested her and returned her to school. After the child's parents learned of this, they sued the school district in a federal court. Among their claims was that the school's check-out policy violated the Constitution by allowing employees to release a child without first verifying the signer's identity or authority to sign out the child. A federal court held constitutional liability was foreclosed under *DeShaney v. Winnebago County Dep't of Social Services*, 489 U.S. 189 (1989).

Appeal reached the Fifth Circuit, where a three-judge panel held for the family. But a majority of judges of the Fifth Circuit voted to rehear the case and found a constitutional claim could proceed only if the district had a duty to protect the student from a private party. This required a special relationship between the student and district. But state compulsory attendance laws did not create a special relationship between schools and their students. The court held **public schools have no special relationship with students that would require protection from harm by private actors such as the adult in this case**. The parents raised other arguments, but the court rejected them. It held the student's young age was not a relevant factor under the special relationship analysis. Carelessness by school employees did not mean they knew that the adult was unauthorized to sign out the child. And the parents did not claim the district was deliberately indifferent to a known danger. The court held for the district. *Doe v. Covington County School Dist.*, 675 F.3d 849 (5th Cir. 2012).

◆ A Nebraska elementary school policy required visitors to check in at the main office. An intruder entered and was confronted by a teacher. She asked him if she could help him, but he ignored her. Two other teachers also noticed him, and one directed him to a restroom. Although she told him to report to the office after he was finished, he instead went to another restroom where he sexually assaulted a five-year-old student. The student's mother sued the school district in a state court for negligence. After finding the district's security plan was adequate, the held for the district. Appeal reached the Supreme Court of Nebraska, which stated that under prior law, the foreseeability of a particular injury was part of the inquiry into whether an entity had a legal duty to the injured party. But the court found that approach required a court to decide legal questions "uniquely rooted in the facts and circumstances of a particular case." In any negligence case, the legal duty of a party was to conform to the standard of conduct. By contrast, foreseeability questions depended upon the unique facts of each case.

The court held foreseeability is not part of the analysis of duty, as this transforms a factual inquiry into a legal issue. It also expands the authority of judges at the expense of juries. The court found this improper, as **foreseeability questions involve common sense, common experience, and the application of community standards and behavioral norms**.

These areas have long been understood to be within the province of a jury, and not a judge. Under the court's decision, a jury would have to determine, based on the facts of each case, whether or not the evidence established a breach of duty. **School districts owe their students a duty of reasonable care, as the duty of teachers to supervise and protect their students is well-established.** But the question of whether the assault in this case was reasonably foreseeable involved a fact-specific inquiry for a jury to determine. As the teachers had permitted the intruder to evade them, reasonable minds could differ as to whether the assault was foreseeable. It had thus been improper for the lower court to award pretrial judgment to the school district. The court returned the case to the lower court for further proceedings. *A.W. v. Lancaster County School Dist. 0001*, 784 N.W.2d 907 (Neb. 2010).

◆ A Texas State University student was leaving a campus library one night at around 11:00 p.m. when an unknown person sexually assaulted her at knifepoint. She said the attacker dragged her under a dark stairwell of a campus building. The student sued Texas State and others, in a state district court, alleging it was negligent. She asserted the security on campus was inadequate because Texas State employees had "negligently implemented the campus safety policies." Texas State also was negligent, the student said, in its use or misuse of the lighting in the area where she was attacked and its use of security boxes on campus. The student contended she got hurt because Texas State did not use ordinary care to keep the campus safe, properly lit, and free from criminal trespassers. Furthermore, she said, the university failed to inspect the property for dangerous conditions or to warn the student of any such defect. The district court granted a motion to dismiss, and the student appealed to the Court of Appeals of Texas.

The court explained that under the Texas Tort Claims Act, state entities can waive governmental immunity only under limited circumstances. Section 101.021(2) of the act provides a state governmental unit is liable for personal injury if, as a private person, it would be liable according to Texas law. **The student failed to establish immunity was waived because she did not show a connection between the alleged defect and her injuries. The court found the actions of the student's attacker, not the allegedly defective lights, were what caused her to be harmed.** It rejected the student's argument that governmental immunity was waived. As the negligent implementation of a security policy does not waive governmental immunity, the judgment was affirmed. *Dimas v. Texas State Univ. System*, 201 S.W.3d 260 (Tex. Ct. App. 2006).

5. Stalking

◆ A Connecticut university student contacted a female student in a chat room. He made several attempts to date her, but she rejected his advances. Despite the rejections, the student continued to pursue her, appearing uninvited at her dormitory room and presenting her with gifts. The student then sent an email to a professor expressing an "excessive interest" in the female classmate. The professor was disturbed by the email, and reported the student to a community standards specialist at the university. After interviewing the student, the classmate and the professor, the specialist instructed the student he was to have no further contact with the classmate.

About a month later, the student offered to pay the classmate's friend to spy on her. A disciplinary hearing was held by the university, after which an administrative hearing officer concluded the student had stalked the classmate. The officer suspended the student from the university for a period of 15 months. The student filed an unsuccessful internal appeal, then sued the university in state court requesting reinstatement as a full-time student. The court denied the student's request. He would be entitled to the requested injunction only if he could show the suspension proceeding failed to meet due process requirements. The student failed to make this showing. **He could not prove a violation of any substantive due process right, because there is no fundamental right to attend college.** Nor was there any violation of the student's procedural due process rights. He received notice of the charges against him, and neither the form nor content of the notice prejudiced his ability to defend the charges. Because the student failed to show he was denied due process with respect to the university's procedures, the court denied his request for a preliminary injunction. *Danso v. Univ. of Connecticut*, 919 A.2d 1100 (Conn. Super. Ct. 2007).

◆ A Western Kentucky University student died three days after she was assaulted, raped and set on fire in her dormitory room. Two men who were not residents of the dorm were later charged in the case. The student's estate filed negligence claims in a state court against the university, a foundation that operated the dormitory, and university officials. The court dismissed the case, and the state court of appeals affirmed the decision to dismiss the claims against the university and the officials. However it reversed the decision to dismiss the claims filed against the foundation. The parties appealed to the Supreme Court of Kentucky.

The supreme court explained that governmental immunity extends to state agencies that perform governmental functions, but does not extend to agencies which are not created to perform a governmental function. Officials of state agencies can also be entitled to immunity if the agency itself is immune to suit. Applying these principles, the court held the university was immune to the claims raised. It rejected the argument that the university's operation of the dorm was a proprietary rather than a discretionary function. **The university operated the dorm as part of its statutory duty to provide college instruction. As such, its operation of the dorm was not proprietary, and it was entitled to immunity.** Because the claims against the university were barred by immunity, the claims against the officials in their official capacities were also barred. The foundation was entitled to immunity because it acted as an alter ego of the university and derived immunity status through it. The decision to grant immunity to the university and officials was affirmed, and its decision to deny immunity to the foundation was reversed. *Autry v. Western Kentucky Univ.*, 219 S.W.3d 713 (Ky. 2007).

◆ A New York college student was assaulted at knifepoint in her dorm room. At the time of the attack, the college had a security policy that required all outer doors to its residential halls be locked 24 hours a day. An exception was that during office hours, a "breezeway" entrance remained open to allow students to enter from the open quadrangle created by the four other student dorms. The policy also required those visiting a dorm to register with personnel stationed at resident hall lobby desks. Despite the policies, students held and even propped open doors to the resident halls so people could enter without registering. The student sued the college in a federal district court, alleging it was negligent. The court dismissed the complaint, and the student appealed. The U.S. Court of Appeals, Second Circuit, disagreed with the district court's conclusion that the attack was unforeseeable because of the low history of on-campus crime. In each of the previous five years, there had been significant events and a security reporting firm reported there were other undocumented assaults on campus. **A jury could readily have found the college administration had been alerted to the presence of more crime than it publicly reported.** The district court's analysis of foreseeability was flawed, because it assumed that only actual prior crimes could put the college on notice of the risk of future crimes. The security firm had repeatedly raised security concerns with the college. **While the attack was foreseeable, the district court reasonably found that the student did not establish a causal connection between negligence by the college and the attack.** Because the attacker was never caught or identified, she did not prove he was a resident of the dorm. While New York law did not require the student to identify her assailant, she had to provide some evidence that he was an intruder. As she failed to do so, the judgment for the college was affirmed. *Williams v. Utica College of Syracuse Univ.*, 453 F.3d 112 (2d Cir. 2006).

◆ A Massachusetts high school student sodomized a six-year-old and was charged with various felonies. His school principal obtained a police report describing the student's description of the incident as "a joke." The principal suspended the student, finding he posed a threat to the safety, security and welfare of students at the high school. School officials notified the student's parents by letter of the disciplinary action, and they appealed to the superintendent of schools. After a hearing, the superintendent upheld the suspension and the parents sought a preliminary order from a state superior court. The court denied the request for preliminary relief but later reversed the suspension, finding the superintendent's action was an abuse of discretion.

According to the court, Massachusetts General Laws Chapter 71, § 37H 1/2 requires more than criminal charges alone to justify a student suspension. On appeal, the Massachusetts Supreme Judicial Court observed that Section 37H 1/2 authorizes the suspension of students who have been charged with felonies. School administrators must provide students written notice and a hearing before any suspension takes effect. As the trial court had found, a felony charge against a student is an insufficient basis for suspension. **There must be a finding that the student's continued presence in school would have a substantial detrimental effect** on the general welfare of the school. **The superintendent's decision was within his discretion because it was fully supported by the evidence.** The principal was permitted to draw inferences from the nature of the crime and the student's lack of remorse. Given the seriousness of the charges, the principal reasonably concluded there was a danger the student would attempt similar behavior at school. The principal met the procedural requirements of Section 37H 1/2. As the superintendent acted within his discretion by suspending the student, the court reversed and remanded the case. *Doe v. Superintendent of Schools of Stoughton*, 437 Mass. 1, 767 N.E.2d 1054 (Mass. 2002).

B. Sexual Orientation

In *Romer v. Evans*, 517 U.S. 620 (1996), the U.S. Supreme Court held that sexual orientation discrimination violates the Establishment Clause. In *Oncale v. Sundowner Offshore Services, Inc.*, 523 U.S. 75 (1998), the Court held same-sex harassment may violate Title VII of the Civil Rights Act of 1964. In addition many state human rights acts establish sexual orientation as a protected class of persons. But the U.S. Court of Appeals, Eighth Circuit, has held that bullying or harassment that is not based on a student's gender does not create liability under Title IX. Instead, it held that under Title IX, the "acts of discrimination" must be "on the basis of sex."

In *Donovan v. Poway Unified School Dist.*, a California court observed that school administrators are better situated than courts to address peer sexual harassment. Administrators can take affirmative steps to combat racism, sexism and other forms of bias which courts cannot. And administrative actions are typically resolved more quickly than lawsuits.

◆   Two Illinois students wore shirts to school saying "My Day of Silence, Straight Alliance" on the front, and "Be Happy, Not Gay" on the back. A school official crossed out "Not Gay" based on a school rule forbidding derogatory comments referring to race, ethnicity, religion, gender, sexual orientation or disability. The students sued school officials in a federal district court, asserting First Amendment violations. The court denied their request for a preliminary order allowing them to wear the T-shirts, and they appealed. The U.S. Court of Appeals, Seventh Circuit, found the school was not trying to ban student discussion of public issues. It only sought to prohibit derogatory comments about sensitive personal characteristics. **The court found it foreseeable that the high school environment would deteriorate if negative comments were made by students on either side of the debate.** It held the students were not entitled to a preliminary order suspending the school rule.

However, the slogan was only a play on words that was not derogatory or demeaning. Since the message was not targeted toward anyone and was "only tepidly negative," the students could wear the shirts on a preliminary basis.

After the case returned to the district court, a preliminary order was issued permitting the students to wear the shirts. A permanent order was entered for the students, and they were awarded $25 each for infringement of their constitutional rights. The case returned to the Seventh Circuit, which agreed with the students that any evidence of harassment of homosexual students at the school was negligible. It found "a handful of incidents years before the T-shirt was first worn" to be insufficient evidence of school disruption to justify banning the slogan. **Federal court precedents make it clear that speech cannot be stifled just because it offends others.** So the fact that homosexual students and their sympathizers harassed one of the shirt-wearing students was not a permissible ground for banning the shirts. Opposition by others to the shirts in this case "did not give rise to substantial disruption." The court found the damages awarded were justified and did not "exaggerate the harm" to either student. The judgment in their favor was affirmed. *Zamecnik v. Indian Prairie School Dist. # 204*, 636 F.3d 874 (7th Cir. 2011).

◆ A California student attended a private school. Death threats and insults based on sexual orientation were posted to his website, and classmates were eventually implicated in posting them. The student's father called the police, and the family then moved to another part of California. The private school newspaper reported the hate speech and revealed the family's new address. The student filed a state court action against the school for negligence, violation of state hate crimes laws and related claims. The case was dismissed and arbitrated under an agreement in the private school contract. **An arbitrator held the school was not liable for the student postings, even though some of them had been made from school computers.** The arbitrator had ordered the parents to pay the school's arbitration costs and attorneys' fees. The state court of appeal reversed the award of fees and costs of over $521,000. It held agreements which attempt to exempt parties from violations of law are against public policy and cannot be enforced. *D.C. v. Harvard-Westlake School*, 176 Cal.App.4th 836, 98 Cal.Rptr.3d 300 (Cal. Ct. App. 2009).

In a separate action, the student sued a former classmate who posted violent messages on his website. One message stated "I want to rip out your fucking heart and feed it to you," and "I've wanted to kill you. If I ever see you I'm going to pound your head with an ice pick." The student asserted claims under California's hate crimes laws, as well as defamation and intentional infliction of emotional distress. To avoid these claims, the classmate asserted his comments were of public interest and protected by the First Amendment. The court denied a motion to strike the claims under the state strategic lawsuit against public participation (anti-SLAPP) statute. On appeal, the Court of Appeal of California held the student's complaint was not subject to the anti-SLAPP statute. The classmate did not show the message was protected and **even assuming the message was a joke, the court found it did not concern a public issue under the statute**. *D.C. v. R.R.*, 182 Cal.App.4th 1190, 106 Cal.Rptr.3d 399 (Cal. Ct. App. 2010).

◆   An Arkansas student was widely ridiculed by classmates. He reported pushing, shoving, name-calling, and being falsely called a homosexual. He withdrew from school in tenth grade and sued the school district in a federal court for sexual harassment in violation of Title IX. At trial, school officials and classmates claimed the misconduct did not violate Title IX because it was not gender-based. A jury was told that to win, the student had to show he was harassed "on the basis of sex" in a manner so severe, pervasive, and objectively offensive that it deprived him of access to educational benefits or opportunities. He further had to show that the district knew of the harassment but was deliberately indifferent to it. The jury held for the officials, and the student appealed. On appeal, the Eighth Circuit Court of Appeals held the jury instructions reflected Title IX's "on the basis of sex" requirement and correctly summarized Supreme Court precedents.

The court rejected the student's argument that it would be enough under Title IX that peers called him names and spread rumors to "debase his masculinity." In *Davis v. Monroe County Board of Educ.*, this chapter, the Supreme Court held that **to be actionable, harassment must be gender-oriented conduct amounting to more than "simple acts of teasing and name-calling."** There was no authority supporting the student's claim that the use of sex-based language in rumors or name-calling proved sex-based discrimination. As a result, the court held for the school officials. *Wolfe v. Fayetteville, Arkansas School Dist.*, 648 F.3d 860 (8th Cir. 2011).

◆   Two California students claimed they were subjected to so much severe verbal and physical anti-gay harassment that they had to leave school. They kept logs of anti-gay peer harassment and gave them to school administrators. After getting little response, the students completed their high school careers in home-study programs. They sued the school district, principal, assistant principal and district superintendent. A jury found that the district violated the Education Code and that the principal and assistant principal violated the male student's rights under the Equal Protection Clause. According to the jury, the principal violated the female student's equal protection rights. The verdict awarded the male student $175,000 in damages and the female student $125,000. They also received attorneys' fees of over $427,000. The Court of Appeal of California found the students had made out a successful claim for "deliberate indifference" to known anti-gay harassment. This satisfied the stringent Title IX standard. In finding for the students on their equal protection claims, the jury had found that **administrators had actual notice of harassment but were deliberately indifferent to it**. As the principal was an appropriate person to act on behalf of the school district to address peer sexual orientation harassment, and there was evidence that the administrators took no meaningful action to stop the harassment, the judgment for the students was upheld. *Donovan v. Poway Unified School Dist.*, 167 Cal.App.4th 567, 84 Cal.Rptr.3d 285 (Cal. Ct. App. 2008).

◆   A New Jersey student claimed he was repeatedly and severely taunted by classmates who directed homosexual epithets at him beginning in grade four. He endured slurs in the halls and was struck while in the school cafeteria, when 10 to 15 students surrounded and taunted him. The assistant principal did not punish or reprimand the students. During the student's eighth-grade year, his mother claimed a school guidance counselor simply urged her son to "toughen up and turn the other cheek." The principal later agreed to let the student leave classes to report problems directly to him, and the school began to discipline perpetrators. Verbal abuse persisted, but to a lesser degree. When the student entered high school, the harassment resurfaced. To avoid derision on school buses, he decided to walk home from school. He reported being followed by others as he walked home.

Other students punched the student and knocked him down, and he had to miss school. The students were suspended for 10 days, and one pled guilty to assault charges. The student never returned to the high school, and his mother filed a harassment complaint with the state Division on Civil Rights. The student won $50,000 in emotional distress damages, and his mother won $10,000 for emotional distress. The district was fined $10,000 and ordered to pay attorneys' fees. On appeal, **the Supreme Court of New Jersey recognized a cause of action against school districts for student-on-student harassment based on perceived sexual orientation**. Liability would be imposed for peer harassment only if a district failed to reasonably address harassment and the district knew or should have known about it. The case was returned to the lower courts. *L.W. v. Toms River Regional Schools Board of Educ.*, 189 N.J. 381, 915 A.2d 535 (N.J. 2007).

C. Race and National Origin

Title VI of the Civil Rights Act of 1964 prohibits race discrimination in any program that receives federal funds. Title VI is based on the principles of the Equal Protection Clause, and many discrimination complaints allege violations of Title VI, the Equal Protection Clause, and analogous state law provisions. Courts require proof of intentional discrimination in Title VI cases. School officials may be held liable for violating Title VI if they are deliberately indifferent to clearly established student rights. As in other harassment cases, the courts frequently analyze race-based student-to-student harassment under the liability standard described in *Davis v. Monroe County Board of Educ.*, this chapter.

◆   A high school in northern California had a history of gang and race-related violence. In 2009, the school recognized Cinco de Mayo in a "spirit of cultural appreciation." But the event prompted threats among students of different ethnic backgrounds. Some students hung a makeshift U.S. flag and chanted "USA." During the 2009 incident, a school assistant principal (AP) had to intervene when a student threatened others who had raised the U.S. flag. A student who had worn U.S. flag clothing to school on Cinco de Mayo in 2009 was among several students who again sought to display the flag on Cinco de Mayo 2010. In response to rumors of a confrontation between students of different ethnic backgrounds, the AP told the student he should turn the shirt inside out or risk his own safety. The student first said he would risk it, but he later agreed to go home instead. The student and another student who went home with an excused absence joined their parents in a federal court action against the school district, principal and AP.

After all the claims were dismissed, the families appealed only the judgment for the AP. The court found recent federal appeals court cases, some of which involved displays of the Confederate flag, have held that schools may prohibit speech that might reasonably lead school officials to forecast substantial disruption of (or material interference with) school activities. **Many federal cases have held school officials need not wait for actual disruption before acting. "In fact, they have a duty to prevent the occurrence of disturbances."** The administrators in this case were faced with a threat of school disruption and impending violence, and the court found the AP was entitled to judgment on the speech rights claim. Since the lower court had correctly held for the AP, the court affirmed the judgment. *Dariano v. Morgan Hill Unified School Dist.*, 745 F.3d 354 (9th Cir. 2014).

◆ A part-white, part-Latino student moved to an overwhelmingly white New York school district. Students began threatening him and repeatedly calling him "nigger." During the rest of the student's high school career, he continued to report incidents of racial harassment and taunting, some of which involved physical contact, death threats and a reference to lynching. The family attorney, and later the local human rights commission and the local NAACP affiliate, suggested a "shadow" to accompany the student while he was at school. These entities also sought to implement racial sensitivity programs in the district. Although these services were offered for free, the district declined them. A district compliance officer, who was supposed to investigate Title IX violations, did not respond to complaints. The student's mother made the choice to allow him to accept a special education diploma rather than to attend school further.

The student sued the school district in a federal court for race discrimination. A jury found the district violated Title VI and awarded the student $1.25 million. After the court reduced the damages to $1 million, appeal went to the U.S. Court of Appeals, Second Circuit. Applying *Davis v. Monroe County Board of Educ.*, this chapter, the court held **official action was "deliberately indifferent" under either Title IX or Title VI if it was "clearly unreasonable in light of the known circumstances."** A reasonable juror could find the harassment met Title VI liability standards, as it was "severe, pervasive, and objectively offensive." Peers "taunted, harassed, menaced and physically assaulted" the student, called him "nigger" nearly every day, and threatened him with death. Staff members reported many incidents to the principal, and the mother contacted school administrators 30 to 50 times. Other reports were lodged by the human rights commission, the NAACP, and the police. While the school district was not required to eliminate all the harassment, it ignored many signals that more action was necessary. The decision for the student was affirmed. *Zeno v. Pine Plains Cent. School Dist.*, 702 F.3d 655 (2d Cir. 2012).

◆ Missouri twin high school students created a website with racist, bullying speech. School administrators linked the twins to the site and suspended them for 10 days. After two hearings, the district suspended the twins for 180 days, allowing them to enroll in a public academy. The twins sued the school district in a federal court and sought a preliminary order to lift the suspensions. At a hearing, they said the postings were satirical, not serious, and they denied being racists. School witnesses claimed the website caused substantial disruption at the school. Numerous attempts were made at school to access the site and teachers said that their students were distracted or upset. Media representatives had come to the school, and two teachers stated that the incident ranked among the most disruptive events of their careers. Although the court issued the order sought by the twins, it found the website had caused considerable disturbance and disruption. In addition, the court found the site was "targeted at" the school. Appeal went before the U.S. Court of Appeals, Eighth Circuit. It held that in prior federal court decisions, *Tinker v. Des Moines Independent Community School Dist.*, **this chapter, had been applied to off-campus student speech** when it was reasonably foreseeable that the speech would reach the school community and cause a substantial disruption. As the postings had caused substantial school disruption, the court reversed the lower court's contrary order for the students. *S.J.W. v. Lee's Summit R-7 School Dist.*, 696 F.3d 771 (8th Cir. 2012).

◆ A Minnesota high school student council encouraged students to dress according to various themes during homecoming week. Some students wore oversized jerseys, sagging pants, "doo-rags" and other items that an African-American student found racially offensive. According to the student, officials did not respond when a similar display was staged the next year, until state and federal government officials intervened. She sued school officials in a federal court for negligence and race discrimination under state and federal laws. School officials moved to dismiss the claims, including one filed under Title VI. The court noted that in Title IX cases, courts have found schools may be held liable for peer sexual harassment. Since Congress had modeled Title IX after Title VI, the court found it appropriate to look to Title IX for guidance. **Several federal circuit courts have recognized Title VI claims based on a school district's intentional failure to address a racially hostile environment.** Since Title VI supported a lawsuit against a school district for intentional discrimination, the court allowed the student's case to proceed. *Pruitt v. Anderson*, Civil No. 11-2143 (DSD/JJK), 2011 WL 6141084 (D. Minn. 12/29/11).

◆ A Tennessee school district policy banned Confederate flag items, based on a history of racial conflicts in district schools, some of them involving Confederate flags. A student wore a shirt and belt buckle to school with Confederate flag images and refused to comply with the dress code after several warnings, resulting in a suspension. He sued the school district, its board and school officials in a federal court. The court held for school officials, and appeal reached the Sixth Circuit. Quoting its decision in *Barr v. LaFon*, 538 F.3d 554 (6th Cir. 2008), the court held "*Tinker* does not require disruption to have actually occurred." Courts are to evaluate the circumstances "to determine whether the school's forecast of substantial disruption was reasonable." As explained in *Barr*, **school officials need not tolerate student speech that is inconsistent with their educational mission**. In view of the record of problems at district high schools which involved Confederate flags, the court held officials reasonably forecast that flag displays would be disruptive. Unlike the display of an anti-war armband in *Tinker*, these **flag displays communicated "a message of hatred toward members of the student body" and thus presented a situation involving "substantial disorder or invasion of the rights of others."** It was reasonable to conclude that future flag displays would likely lead to unrest. Since school officials could reasonably forecast substantial disruption if they allowed Confederate flag items, the court affirmed the judgment. *Defoe v. Spiva*, 625 F.3d 324 (6th Cir. 2010).

D. Disability

According to the U.S. Department of Education, Office for Civil Rights (OCR), complaints about disability harassment and bullying represent the fastest growing group of complaints within the agency's oversight. This includes compliance with federal laws prohibiting race, gender, national origin and disability discrimination. Some courts have based school district liability for peer-based disability discrimination on theories of negligence and constitutional violations, as well as the Individuals with Disabilities Education Act (IDEA). Many courts have simply applied the liability standard from *Davis v. Monroe County Board of Educ.*, this chapter, to peer harassment cases based on disability.

◆ A California parent claimed his son was repeatedly abused, beaten and kicked by peers because of his disabilities and his non-native English speaker status. The parents made two written incident reports detailing attacks on their son and identifying the assailants. But they claimed school officials did not act and suggested only that he change classrooms to avoid the perpetrators. In a California superior court, the father sought a special order against the school district. In pretrial activity, the father asserted that the district had failed to adopt or implement a comprehensive safety plan that met the requirements of California Education Code Section 32282.

The court dismissed the case, holding the parent did not have standing to pursue it. On appeal, the Court of Appeal of California held the case involved a well-identified public interest in maintaining a school system that was free of the destructive influence of discrimination, harassment and bullying. State legislators had enacted a scheme of interrelated statutes to protect students from discrimination and harassment based on race, gender, sexual orientation or disability. California public schools had an affirmative duty to combat racism, sexism and other forms of bias. A code provision required school districts to have comprehensive school safety plans. For these reasons, the court held the father had standing to pursue the case both as a parent and a state taxpayer. There was a "manifest public interest in enforcing the antibullying statutes and no urgent competing interests which outweighed that public interest." *Hector F. v. El Centro Elementary School Dist.*, 227 Cal.App.4th 331,173 Cal.Rptr.3d 413 (Cal. Ct. App. 2014).

◆   The family of a Georgia high school student with Asperger's syndrome could not recover damages from his school district after he committed suicide. According to the family, the student was repeatedly bullied at school in the months before he died. A federal court held that in hindsight, the school should have done more to address disability harassment. **But it held the family did not meet the high standard of liability for "deliberate indifference"** under the U.S. Constitution and federal laws including Rehabilitation Act Section 504. On appeal, the U.S. Court of Appeals, Eleventh Circuit, noted that "deliberate indifference is an exacting standard" under which administrators are held liable only if their response (or lack of one) is found "clearly unreasonable in light of the known circumstances." As this standard was not met, the court held for the school district. *Long v. Murray County School Dist.*, 522 Fed.Appx. 576 (11th Cir. 2013).

◆   A Pennsylvania student with bipolar disorder began having mood changes during grade eight. She had an excessive desire to sleep and trouble maintaining relationships with her school peers. She became self-destructive, cut herself, and attempted suicide. When the student entered high school, her boyfriend told classmates about her condition. One of these classmates was a cousin of the student, who began calling her names and threatening her. After beginning her junior and senior years in her regular high school, the student again had problems with other students, and she left school for homebound instruction. She sued her former district and school officials in a federal court for disability discrimination. In the court's view, the student did not qualify for protection under federal disability laws. It held that "the genesis of the harassment was conflicts about boys." On appeal, the U.S. Court of Appeals, Third Circuit, held that proof of a bias claim under federal disability law requires a student to establish she has a disability, is "otherwise qualified" to participate in a school's program, and was discriminated against based on a disability. While the student's bipolar disorder was a mental or physical impairment, the court held **she did not demonstrate that her limitations substantially limited her ability to interact with others, care for herself, concentrate on school work or sleep**. No information was provided regarding the frequency, severity or permanency of the student's symptoms. This prevented the court from finding that she was significantly restricted in a major life activity. For this reason, she was not considered an individual with a disability under federal law definitions. Since the lower court had correctly found the student was not substantially limited in a major life activity, the court affirmed the judgment for the school district. *Weidow v. Scranton School Dist.*, 460 Fed.Appx. 181 (3d Cir. 2012).

◆ A Michigan special education student believed a classmate was his girlfriend. He shoved her into a locker because he saw her talking to another boy and later demanded that she perform oral sex on him. At a school basketball game, the student made obscene gestures at the classmate and her stepfather told him to stay away from her. The stepfather wrote to administrators about the incident and the prior attempt to solicit sex. In response, the school formed a 30-day plan to constantly supervise the student. Seven weeks after the supervisory period passed, the student sexually assaulted the classmate at school. Later, the school board voted to expel him. In a federal court action, the classmate said the student's history of misconduct put school officials on notice of a risk of harm. But she did not assert that any prior misconduct included sexual harassment, and the court held for the school district and officials. On appeal, the U.S. Court of Appeals, Sixth Circuit, held harassment must take place in a context subject to a school's control in order to impose liability. Victims of peer harassment lack rights to make particular remedial demands. The court held the incidents in this case did not amount to severe, pervasive and objectively offensive conduct. **The classmate could not rely on incidents involving other victims to meet the "severe and pervasive" part of the Title IX liability analysis.** When the school district learned of the harassment, it imposed a supervision plan. The district's response to the assault was "prompt, reasonable, and not deliberately indifferent." Constant supervision of the student was not required. No authority supported the argument that activity at other schools or off campus was relevant to a Title IX claim, as the district had no control over it. As the district was not deliberately indifferent to peer harassment, the court held in its favor. *Pahssen v. Merrill Community School Dist.*, 668 F.3d 356 (6th Cir. 2012).

◆ Parents of a Maryland child with autism claimed their child was attacked at school by a male student and suffered black eyes and a swollen lip. It was claimed that the same student had previously attacked the child. The parents claimed they told school officials and a teacher about the perpetrating student, but that he was allowed to sit in close proximity to their child shortly after the attack. At some point after the incident, the parents said their child was placed in a lower grade, taken off the academic "graduation" track and not afforded an opportunity to be educated in the least restrictive environment. The complaint did not say why or when the child's placement was changed. A federal district court held that the family's failure to request an administrative due process hearing was fatal to their claims under the IDEA and Section 504. A claim for monetary damages did not make the administrative process futile. **Tort-like damages are inconsistent with the IDEA's statutory scheme, which exists to assure the provision of a free appropriate public education** (FAPE).

The Section 504 claim for disability discrimination was also subject to the exhaustion requirement, since it was linked to an IDEA claim. An additional reason for failure of the Section 504 claim was that the parents failed to allege any disability discrimination. While they asserted a constitutional violation based on denial of FAPE, the court found such claims had been barred in the Fourth Circuit since 1998. Essentially, the constitutional claim amounted to a restatement of the IDEA claim. In the court's view, the parents' conspiracy claim could not prevail because of a complete lack of evidence of a conspiracy. A conspiracy among members of the same entity was impossible. As the court found no facts to support the claims, it dismissed them. *Wright v. Carroll County Board of Educ.*, Civ. No.11-cv-3103, 2012 WL 1901380 (D. Md. 5/24/12).

◆ New York parents claimed teachers and school administrators did not intervene when classmates subjected their autistic child to daily name-calling, abusive language and violent conduct. A teacher was alleged to be present during some of the incidents. In a federal court complaint against the school district and several teachers, administrators and staff members, the student claimed peers called him a "fucking retard," "asshole," "faggot" and "bitch." According to the parents, nobody took effective measures to deter the harassment or discipline the harassers. In pretrial activity, the court refused to dismiss the disability harassment claims. It used the standard of liability from sexual harassment cases under Title IX and *Davis v. Monroe County Board of Educ.*, this chapter. Since the student claimed he was regularly harassed and bullied and that officials took no meaningful action, **the court held he could pursue the harassment-based Section 504 claims**. Although he cited many incidents in which sexual questions and terms were involved, the court found no evidence of anti-male bias, and it dismissed claims for gender-based harassment under Title IX and the Equal Protection Clause. But the student could pursue claims against the district for negligent hiring and negligent supervision, violation of the state civil rights act, and discrimination under Section 504. *Preston v. Hilton Cent. School Dist.*, 876 F.Supp.2d 235 (W.D.N.Y. 2012).

◆ New York parents claimed their learning disabled child's school principal avoided discussing an ongoing bullying problem. They said they complained to the school about bullying almost daily throughout an entire school year. When no meeting was scheduled to discuss bullying, they requested an impartial hearing. An impartial hearing officer (IHO) heard testimony by two aides and a substitute who reported significant classroom ostracism and teasing of the student. One aide characterized the conduct of peers as "constant negative interaction" and intentionally staying away from her and pushing her away "for fun." She said teachers would get upset with her instead of addressing peer misconduct. A federal district court later noted that no incident reports were generated about the conduct of classmates. An aide claimed she told teachers about the bullying, but "it was ignored." She also stated that when she tried to discuss an incident with the principal "she was turned away" and told there was no time for a meeting. The parents claimed they sent the school letters expressing concern about bullying. After the IHO held for the New York City Department of Education, a state review officer affirmed the decision.

On appeal, a federal court noted that **45 states have laws regarding bullying and harassment in schools**. It found that when a school is "not supportive or is negative, bullying thrives." **Bullying rates were higher when teachers downplayed it.** Some states have recognized that students with learning disabilities are at a greater risk for bullying than non-disabled peers, and that "IEPs should take this into account." Massachusetts required IEP teams to address social skills and proficiencies to avoid and respond to bullying. The court applied the "deliberate indifference" approach from *Davis v. Monroe County Board of Educ.*, this chapter. It held **"a school must take prompt and appropriate action" in response to bullying incidents**. Schools have to investigate reports, and if harassment occurred, "the school must take appropriate steps to prevent it in the future." A school's duty exists regardless of whether the conduct was covered in an anti-bullying policy and regardless of whether a student has complained. The court held "Title IX, IDEA and Section 504 of the Rehabilitation Act place upon schools the affirmative duty to address bullying and harassment." It found the IHO erred in finding bullying was irrelevant to the student's IEP. The case was returned to the IHO. *T.K. and S.K. v. Dep't of Educ. of City of New York*, 779 F.Supp.2d 289 (E.D.N.Y. 2011).

◆ A New York student had an individualized education program (IEP) and behavior problems. He had been removed from his parents' home at age three for neglect and possible abuse, then hospitalized for severe aggression, but he had no record of sexual aggression. During a two-year stay in a psychiatric center, the student continued to have behavior problems. Upon being released, he was placed in a community residence and began attending school under an IEP. A case coordinator noted the student had been free of physical aggression since his admission to a community residence and was having positive peer interactions. But an IEP summary review noted his prior conduct included exposing himself and masturbating in public. After being placed with foster parents, the student entered another year of public school under an IEP. In March of the same school year, a kindergartner's parent complained to a school bus driver that the student had called the kindergartner "his girlfriend." She asked that the two be separated. Some time later, the student exposed himself to the kindergartner and forced her to touch him while they were sitting on the bus. The mother sued the school district. The case reached the Court of Appeals of New York, the state's highest court. The court explained that it is well-settled that schools have a duty to adequately supervise students.

School districts are liable for foreseeable injuries that are caused by the absence of adequate supervision. On the other hand, **unanticipated acts by third parties, such as the student in this case, do not create school liability unless the school had some notice of prior similar conduct**. According to the court, the sexual assault in this case was not foreseeable. While the student had a history of severe behavioral issues, there had been no manifestation of them for over two years. Since his hospitalization, each of his programs noted he had not displayed aggression. Significantly, the court found the student's history did not include sexually aggressive behavior. The mother failed to name him in her first report to the bus driver. As the student's past conduct did not indicate sexually aggressive behavior that would give the school district specific knowledge or notice of similar conduct, a judgment for the district was affirmed. *Brandy B. v. Eden Cent. School Dist.*, 15 N.Y.3d 297 (N.Y. 2010).

IV. USE OF TECHNOLOGY

A. Internet and Cyberbullying

◆ Three Colorado students who were subjected to inappropriate conduct by a former teacher at their high school were denied an appeal to review their claims against their school district and administration. According to their federal court complaint, the teacher sent the students explicit texts, sought nude pictures and tried to solicit sexual relations with them. **While the court allowed claims against the teacher to proceed, it held the case could not proceed against the district or administrators**, who did not know about the teacher's conduct. A single state law claim for failure to report child abuse was allowed to proceed against a school security guard and coach who knew about an incident of sexual conduct between the teacher and one student. In a brief order, the U.S. Court of Appeals, Tenth Circuit, affirmed the judgment. *Doe v. Boulder Valley School Dist. No. RE-2*, 523 Fed.Appx. 514 (10th Cir. 2013).

New York's "Cybercrime Youth Rescue Act" law created an education reform program for individuals charged in family or criminal court with cyberbullying or the sending (or receipt of obscenity or nudity), when the sender and receiver were both under the age of 20 and not more than five years apart in age. The act specifies up to eight hours of instruction for eligible persons concerning the legal consequences and potential penalties for sharing sexually suggestive materials, explicit materials or abusive materials. A court may direct an individual to attend and complete an education reform program as a condition for dismissal of a non-felony criminal act. A family court may require an individual to attend and complete an education reform program in order to receive a conditional case discharge. Instruction under the education reform program includes the potential connection between bullying and cyberbullying and juveniles sharing sexually suggestive, explicit or abusive materials.

Instruction will also cover the non-legal consequences of sharing sexually suggestive materials, explicit materials or abusive materials, such as effects on relationships, loss of educational and employment opportunities, and the potential for being barred or removed from school programs and extracurricular activities. Additional instruction under the reform program will describe the unique characteristics of cyberspace and the Internet, "including the potential ability of an infinite audience to utilize the Internet to search for and replicate materials," and the unforeseen consequences of sharing sexually suggestive, explicit or abusive materials. Two-Hundred Thirty-Fourth New York Legislature, Ch. 535, A. 8170-B. N.Y. Social Services Law Section 45-1, Penal Law Section 60.37, Family Court Law Sections 315.3, 353.1, 735.

California legislators added language to further specify what will be deemed bullying under existing provisions of law, including written communications and posts on social networking sites. Under the amended law, a "post on a social network" will include a "burn page." The amended law also includes creating a credible impersonation of a pupil and creating a false profile. In addition to Internet communications, "electronic act" includes a message, text, sound or image that is posted on a social network Internet website. A "burn page" is one intended to have one or more harmful effects listed under current bullying definitions, including the placing of a student in fear of harm. A new definition of a "credible impersonation" of a student applies to a knowing impersonation of a student for the purpose of bullying that student. California Legislature 2012, Chapter 157, A.B. No. 1732, Education Code Section 48900.

◆ Jessica Logan committed suicide in 2008, shortly after graduating from an Ohio high school. Her family attributed her suicide to her anguish over the "sexting" of a nude photo of her among other high school students. In a federal action, it was asserted that high school students were circulating the nude photo with their cell phones. When the student reported the activity to a counselor, the counselor referred her to the high school resource officer. The resource officer agreed to speak to the other students, and he asked them to delete the photo from their cell phones. Later, Jessica appeared on a television broadcast about sexting. She claimed the harassment increased after the broadcast. She committed suicide. Her parents sued her school district, school officials, the resource officer and his municipal employer in a federal court. The school district argued that it could not be held liable because neither the student nor anyone acting on her behalf made a sexual harassment report. The court held **there is no constitutional duty of government actors to protect individuals against private parties such as the harassing students in this case**. As there was no evidence that the resource officer acted unreasonably, he was entitled to qualified immunity. There was also no viable claim against his municipal employer for failing to train or supervise him. *Logan v. Sycamore Community School Board of Educ.*, 780 F.Supp.2d 594 (S.D. Ohio 2011).

In a later order, the court found other courts have **held appropriate persons for reporting under Title IX of the Education Amendments of 1972 "do not need to be aware of the exact details of a plaintiff's experience to have notice, as long as they 'reasonably could have responded with remedial measures.'"** Since evidence indicated that school officials knew of the harassment, the mother could proceed with her Title IX claim. *Logan v. Sycamore Community School Board of Educ.*, No. 1:09-CV-00885 (S.D. Ohio 6/5/12). After the court's order of June 5, 2012, the lawsuit was settled for $220,000, including attorneys' fees.

◆ A Mississippi student admitted having a key logger program demonstration disk, and after an investigation, he was suspended for possessing software that damaged the school computer system. The student's mother was a school employee. After the superintendent recommended placing the student in an alternative school for 45 days, he learned that personal data on teachers might have been compromised when the student used his mother's computer. She was reassigned and soon discharged. The student and his mother sued the school district for speech and due process violations, and related claims. After a federal court held for the district, the family appealed. The U.S. Court of Appeals, Fifth Circuit, stated that a state's extension of the right to an education is protected by the Fourteenth Amendment and cannot be withheld absent fair procedures. **A student's transfer to an alternative education program does not deny access to public education, and such an assignment does not violate the Fourteenth Amendment.** The student and his parents had opportunities to meet with school officials, and he had "multiple opportunities" to tell his side of the story. As the court found he received notice and a chance to explain himself, no due process rights were violated. Finding no merit to the mother's First Amendment claims, the court held for the school district. *Harris v. Pontotoc County School Dist.*, 635 F.3d 685 (5th Cir. 2011).

◆ A New Hampshire principal and teacher received sexually explicit messages and reported them to the police. Both messages were traced to a student who attended their school. She admitted opening an email account on a computer at home, then sending both messages. After a hearing, the board voted to suspend the student for 34 days for violating several student handbook rules. These included the board's use policy for school computer systems, the behavior and discipline code and the anti-harassment policy.

Appeal went to the state education board, and a hearing officer upheld the suspension. On appeal to the Supreme Court of New Hampshire, the parents argued the 34-day suspension violated state law and the rules of the state board. They also claimed the district violated its own rules for long-term suspensions. The court rejected the parents' claims regarding state law and state board rules violations. **State law authorized suspensions of up to 10 days for gross misconduct or for neglect or refusal to conform to reasonable school rules.** A school board could expel a student for a variety of enumerated reasons. State and local boards had authority to create rules and policies regarding student conduct and discipline. But the court held the family had correctly argued that a suspension of 34 days was improper due to the school board's failure to comply with the limits of its own school policy. As the policy limited long-term suspensions to between 11 and 20 school days, the court affirmed the part of the judgment pertaining to the claimed state law violations, but vacated the part of the decision that would have permitted a suspension of over 20 days. *Appeal of Keelin B.*, 162. N.H. 38, 27 A.3d 689 (N.H. 2011).

◆ A New York student received three emails from a male classmate's school email account. One was profane and disparaged her appearance, and the others sought sexual relations. Although the student promptly reported the emails to the school administration, the classmate denied sending them and claimed other students had his email password. The classmate's account was later disabled, but the sender of the emails was never conclusively identified. Believing that the school district's investigation was inadequate, the student sued the school district in a federal district court for violating Title IX and other federal laws. The court held that no reasonable jury could find the student met the liability standard under Title IX for peer sexual harassment established in *Davis v. Monroe County School Board*, this chapter. The student appealed to the U.S. Court of Appeals, Second Circuit, which explained that to prevail on a Title IX claim, she had to show the district acted with deliberate indifference. As the district court held, the student did not meet these requirements. While the emails were offensive, they did not create liability under Title IX. **Since three offensive emails in a 10-day time period did not demonstrate "severe and pervasive harassment," the Title IX claim had been properly resolved in favor of the school district.** The student's equal protection claim based on the district's allegedly more aggressive investigation and pursuit of a prior incident of race-based misconduct did not persuade the court, and the judgment was affirmed. *R.S. v. Board of Educ. of the Hastings-on-Hudson Union Free School Dist.*, 371 Fed.Appx. 231 (2d Cir. 2010).

◆ A Missouri student sent instant messages during non-school hours from a home computer to a friend, saying he was depressed and wanted to take guns to school, kill other students and then kill himself. The school principal learned of this and called the police. Juvenile proceedings were brought against the student. An assistant principal suspended him, and the school board voted to exclude him for the rest of the year. When the student reached the age of majority, he sued the school district and school officials, seeking to clear the discipline from his record. A federal district court held the record did not show his messages substantially disrupted the school. But as the student had received a hearing, due process was satisfied.

Months later, the court reviewed the school district's request for pretrial judgment and found this was a "school speech case," even though it involved messages sent on private computers during non-school hours. The court found the student's instant messages were "true threats" that were not due First Amendment protection. It explained, **"in this digital age, a reasonable person could foresee the transmittal of internet communications."** According to the court, the student's state of mind and access to weapons made his threats believable. He expressed the wish to kill at least five classmates and told the confidant that he had a .357 magnum pistol. Since a reasonable person would take these messages as "true threats," officials "acted entirely within their permissible authority in imposing sanctions." There was no merit to the student's claim that his speech did not disrupt the school. A single claim for administrative review of the student's discipline was preserved for review by a state court. *Mardis v. Hannibal Public School Dist. #60*, 684 F.Supp.2d 1114 (E.D. Mo. 2010).

B. Cell Phones and Other Electronic Communication

Michigan legislators enacted the Internet Privacy Protection Act, which will prohibit employers and educational institutions from requiring their employees, students and applicants to supply their passwords or otherwise allowing access to personal Internet accounts. The act prohibits employers and educational institutions from seeking access information such as user names, passwords, login or other security information for personal Internet accounts. The act does not prohibit educational institutions from seeking student access information for electronic communications devices paid for by the educational institution, or on accounts or services provided by the educational institution either obtained by virtue of the student's admission to the educational institution, or which are used by the student for educational purposes. The act does not prohibit educational institutions from viewing, accessing, or utilizing information about students or applicants that can be obtained without any required access information or which are in the public domain. Employers may not discharge, discipline, fail to hire or penalize employees or job applicants for failing to grant access to or refusing to disclose information allowing access to personal Internet accounts. But employers are not prohibited from disclosing access information for accounts or services provided by the employer, used for the employer's business purposes or obtained via the employment relationship.

Ninety-Sixth Michigan Legislature, Public Act No. 478, H.B. No. 5523. Michigan Statutes Sections 37.271 – 37.278.

◆   An investigation of sexting by students was begun in Tunkhannock, Pennsylvania schools after officials found photos of nude and semi-nude female students on cell phones. Officials learned that male students had been trading the images over their cell phones. The district attorney investigated and made a public statement to the media that possession of inappropriate images of minors could justify criminal prosecution for possession or distribution of child pornography. Teens suspected of "sexting" were then presented with a choice of either attending an education program or facing child pornography charges. As part of the education program, female students were asked to write a report explaining "why you are here," "what you did," "why it was wrong," and related issues. Several parents brought a federal court action to halt the proceeding. They said the threat of prosecution came in retaliation for their refusal to attend the education program. The court granted them preliminary relief, and appeal went before the U.S. Court of Appeals, Third Circuit.

The court noted that parents have a due process right to raise their children without undue state interference. **The government cannot coerce parents to accept official ideas of morality and gender roles.** While the district attorney could offer the education program voluntarily, he could not coerce attendance by threatening prosecution. It appeared that the district attorney's motive in bringing the prosecution was retaliatory and was not a good-faith effort to enforce the law. Ruling that a decision not to attend the program was constitutionally protected, the court upheld the preliminary order. *Miller v. Mitchell*, 598 F.3d 139 (3d Cir. 2010).

◆   An Arkansas coach texted frequently with female students. He agreed to stop it after parents complained, but continued making suggestive comments. A student told the superintendent that her ninth-grade cousin "might have a crush" on the coach, and often left classes to visit him in the gym. The student told the ninth-grader's mother of these suspicions, and she approached the principal to discuss it. The cousin offered more information and identified staff members who allegedly knew of inappropriate conduct. According to the mother, the principal promised to investigate. Soon the coach was accused of texting "OMG you look good today" to a student. Due to this report and other concerns, the district made preparations to nonrenew the coach's contract. When students reported details of sexual contact between the coach and ninth-grader, the coach was arrested. He was eventually prosecuted and sentenced to 10 years in prison.

A federal court dismissed the students' claims against the district and most of the officials, but the principal was denied immunity. On appeal, the U.S. Court of Appeals, Eighth Circuit, found the principal could be liable for constitutional violations if she knew of the coach's conduct but failed to take remedial action in a manner that caused injury. The court held **the**

coach's texts did not provide the principal with "actual notice of sexual abuse." Inappropriate comments alone did not alert her to a possible sexual relationship. School administrators investigated each report they received, and at the relevant time they lacked any evidence of improper contact. The court held "a student's familiar behavior with a teacher or even an 'excessive amount of time' spent with a teacher, without more, does not automatically give rise to a reasonable inference of sexual abuse." It reversed the order denying immunity to the principal and held the district was not liable under Title IX. *Doe v. Flaherty*, 623 F.3d 577 (8th Cir. 2010).

♦   Maryland law officers charged a 26-year-old teacher with sex crimes after a 17-year-old student at his high school reported their sexually oriented text, telephone and instant message communications. The teacher had emailed the student sexually explicit pictures of himself. She came to his classroom, where he exposed his penis to her. A few weeks later, the student reported the teacher's conduct, and police persuaded her to place a one-party consent call to him. In the course of the call, the teacher admitted exposing himself. Police then obtained a search warrant for his residence, vehicle, cell phone and computers. A state court denied his motion to suppress evidence found through the warrant. A jury found him guilty of sexual abuse of a minor, indecent exposure and telephone misuse. The teacher appealed to the Court of Special Appeals of Maryland, which held that the search warrant application identified reasonable grounds to believe that evidence of crime could be found in his house. **Enough evidence was present to reasonably infer that the teacher used home computers to communicate with students** and that this evidence remained in the house. As a result, the court affirmed the judgment. *Ellis v. State of Maryland*, 185 Md.App. 522, 971 A.2d 379 (Md. Ct. Spec. App. 2009).

♦   New York City school rules forbade students from bringing cell phones into public schools without authorization from principals. A state court held that any enforcement system focusing on the use, rather than possession, of cell phones would require teachers to observe and enforce the ban. Teachers would become involved in confronting students and punishment decisions. For that reason, the board had a rational basis for a complete ban. The involvement of teachers in enforcing the cell phone ban would take time from their teaching mission and increase the perception of teachers as adversaries to students. Each principal could address specific situations by allowing students to carry cell phones when there was a special need for it. The court rejected claims by parents who asserted a right to be able to communicate with their children at school. It held that "the department has a rational interest in having its teachers and staff devote their time to educating students and not waging a 'war' against cell phones." **The use of cell phones for cheating, sexual harassment, prank calls and intimidation was a threat to order in the schools.** *Price v. New York City Board of Educ.*, 51 A.D.3d 277, 855 N.Y.S.2d 530 (N.Y. App. Div. 2008).

◆   A Tennessee teacher seized a student's cell phone when it began to ring in a classroom. A student code provision prohibited cell phones and other devices on school property during school hours. Violations were to be reported to the principal, and the phone or device was to be confiscated for 30 days. The student's parent went to the school to retrieve the phone, but the principal refused to return it. The vice principal then assigned the student a day of in-school suspension. The parents sued the school board, principal and vice principal in a federal district court for constitutional rights violations. When the case reached the U.S. Court of Appeals, Sixth Circuit, it held an in-school suspension could deprive a student of educational opportunities in the same way an out-of-school suspension would. But in this case, the student was allowed to do her school work. Other courts have held in-school suspensions do not implicate a student's property interest in public education. The court held for the board, finding that **"in-school suspension does not exclude the student from school and consequently a student's property interest in public education is not implicated."** *Laney v. Farley*, 501 F.3d 577 (6th Cir. 2007).

◆   A Delaware student used his cell phone at a school assembly, in violation of the school code. He refused to surrender his phone to a staff member, and the principal asked him four times to hand it over. The principal tried to escort the student from the assembly. The student struggled, pushed the principal and stepped on his foot. After being removed, he continued to use his cell phone. The student remained disruptive in the school office and told the principal "you can't touch me," and "just wait till I call my mom. She'll sue you." The police arrived at the school and took the student into custody. The school board expelled the student and assigned him to an alternative school. The state board of education affirmed the action, and the student appealed to a state court.

The court held the state board could overturn a local board decision only if it was contrary to state law or state regulations, was not supported by substantial evidence, or was arbitrary and capricious. **The court found sufficient evidence that the student pushed the principal and stepped on his foot,** in violation of the school code. Expulsion with referral to an alternative program was not disproportionate to the misconduct. The court affirmed the decision. *Jordan v. Smyrna School Dist. Board of Educ.*, No. 05A-02-004, 2006 WL 1149149 (Del. Super. Ct. 2006).

C. Surveillance

☑ CHECKLIST – *Practice Tips For School Video Surveillance*

Sara C. Clark, Deputy Director of Legal Services for the Ohio School Boards Association, has the following suggestions for school surveillance:

☐ Install surveillance cameras only in locations where people would not have a reasonable expectation of privacy, such as hallways, lunch rooms and parking lots.

☐ Notify staff, parents, students and others in the community that surveillance cameras are present and in use.

☐ Post signs in the areas where cameras are in use. Include a notice in staff and student handbooks.

☐ Narrowly limit the time and scope of taping.

☐ Establish procedures for maintaining and viewing records.

The checklist is copyrighted by the National School Boards Association.

◆ A Texas school district announced a pilot program requiring students to wear ID badges with radio frequency identification chips to track their whereabouts on campus. Badges would also be used as multi-purpose "smart cards" to check out library books, buy food at the cafeteria and buy tickets for school events. A student's parent claimed the chip was "the mark of the beast" and declared that tracking his daughter at school would "condemn us to hell." A district administrator offered to let the student wear an ID card without a tracking chip. But the parent rejected this and other efforts by the district to compromise and filed a lawsuit. When the case came before a federal court, it noted the parent's conflicting statements and found he had been "pushing for dissolution of the entire … pilot program."

The court rejected a religious free exercise challenge, finding the policy was neutral and generally applicable to all students. The rule served many purposes that had nothing to do with religion. **The court found the district had a legitimate need to easily identify students for safety, security, attendance and state-funding reasons.** A smart ID badge rule was a rational way to meet that need. The student could not show that wearing an ID badge without a tracking chip substantially burdened the free exercise of her religion. She had worn a badge with no tracking chip for years in other district schools. While the family asserted speech, equal protection, and due process claims, and added a claim for violation of the Texas Religious Freedom and Restoration Act, the court rejected the claims and dismissed the action. *A.H. v. Northside Independent School Dist.*, 916 F.Supp.2d 757 (W.D. Tex. 2013).

◆ A Pennsylvania student discovered webcam photos and screenshots of himself on a school laptop. The school district agreed to disable the security tracking software on the laptop, but the student and others pursued a federal district court case. The court prohibited the district and its agents from remotely activating webcams on laptop computers issued to students. Under the court order, the school district could not remotely capture screenshots of laptops, except for maintenance, repairs or trouble-shooting. The district could use an alternate means to track lost, stolen or missing laptops.

A global positioning system or other anti-theft device that did not permit the activation of webcams or capture screenshots was permitted. The order prevented the district from accessing any student-created files on laptops, such as emails, instant messages, Internet use logs and web-browsing histories. Under the court order, the district was required to adopt official policies governing the use, distribution and maintenance of student laptops. It was further required to issue regulations for student privacy on laptops and to train staff on the oversight and enforcement of the policies. Under the order, the district would have to provide students and parents an opportunity to view images already taken from webcams. Such images were to be destroyed when the process was completed. *Robbins v. Lower Merion School Dist.*, No. 10-665, 2010 WL 1976869 (E.D. Pa. 5/14/10).

◆   Parents of disabled Illinois students claimed a special education teacher and classroom aide verbally and physically abused their children. They claimed their children were screamed at, degraded, force-fed, pushed, slapped and abandoned in a time-out room or a lavatory. An investigation forced the resignation of the teacher and aide, but the parents raised new concerns. To help prevent future abuse incidents, the school board proposed installing security cameras with both audio and video in classrooms. A group of teachers sued the board under the Illinois Eavesdropping Act and the Fourth Amendment. A federal court held a "search" occurs when an expectation of privacy that society would consider reasonable is infringed upon. **Teachers had no reasonable expectation of privacy in a classroom,** and the court found nothing private about the communications taking place there. It held instead that a "classroom in a public school is not the private property of any teacher." *Plock v. Board of Educ. of Freeport School Dist. No. 145*, 545 F.Supp.2d 755 (N.D. Ill. 2007).

After the federal case was dismissed, a state court held "eavesdropping" occurred when a person knowingly and intentionally used a device to hear or record a conversation, or when a conversation was intercepted, retained or transcribed without the consent of all parties. A "conversation" was defined as "any oral communication between two or more persons." This definition applied regardless of whether one or more of the parties intended a communication to be "private under circumstances justifying that expectation." **The court found this broad language defeated the board's claim that teaching did not constitute a "conversation" as defined in the Act.** As the Act defined "conversation" to include any oral communication, the trial court had ruled correctly for the teachers. *Plock v. Board of Educ. of Freeport School Dist. No. 145*, 920 N.E.2d 1087 (Ill. App. Ct. 2009).

◆   Based on a review of surveillance camera video, some Washington school employees identified a former student as the person who broke into a junior high school and damaged it. After police arrested him and charged him with criminal conduct related to the break-in, a fingerprint analysis showed he was not the offender. By the time the fingerprint analysis exonerated him, the former student had spent 19 days in jail. He sued the school district in a state court for malicious prosecution. It found the district could not be liable, as it did not initiate the prosecution. On appeal, the Court of Appeals of Washington found malicious prosecution actions are not favored. It is in society's best interest to take steps to arrest offenders. **According to the court, a citizen acting in good faith should not face damages if the accused party is not ultimately convicted.** The court held the former student did not prove a malicious prosecution claim. He had to show more "evil intent." The conclusory statement that school staff "had it in for him" did not show hostility or ill will. As a result, the judgment for the school district was affirmed. *Hubbard v. Eastmont School Dist. No. 206*, 152 Wash. App. 1040 (Wash. Ct. App. 2009).

◆ A surveillance video camera on a school bus videotaped a fight by two Washington elementary students. The school district denied a request by the parents of one of the students for a copy of the tape. The district claimed the videotape was exempt from public disclosure under the state Public Disclosure Act (PDA). The parents sued the district in a state superior court, which agreed with the district's decision not to disclose the tape. The state Court of Appeals affirmed the judgment, and the parents appealed. The Supreme Court of Washington noted that the videotape was a "public record" and that the district was an "agency" under the PDA. So the district had to disclose the videotape unless an exemption applied. The court held the PDA's student file exemption contemplated the protection of materials in a public student's permanent file, such as "grades, standardized test results, assessments, psychological or physical evaluations, class schedule, address, telephone number, social security number, and other similar records." **The videotape differed significantly from the type of records maintained in student files.** The district could not change the videotape's inherent character by placing it in a student file or using it as the basis for discipline. As the videotape could not be legally withheld as a student file document, the court reversed the judgment. *Lindeman v. Kelso School Dist. No. 458*, 162 Wash.2d 196, 172 P.3d 329 (Wash. 2007).

V. TRANSPORTATION

This section has cases about potential liability in transportation cases. For steps key personnel should take in the event of a bus accident, see Form III-1 in Chapter Nine. For a sample parent letter to be sent in the event of a bus accident, see Form III-2 in Chapter Nine. A school board's duty to students stems from its physical control over them. See *Pratt v. Robinson*, 39 N.Y.2d 554, 385 N.Y.S.2d 749, 349 N.E.2d 849 (N.Y. 1976).

◆ New York's highest court held a school district was not liable in a lawsuit filed by a special education student who was injured while waiting for her bus. The student was a 12-year-old sixth-grader with attention deficit disorder, attention deficit hyperactivity disorder and a mild mental disability. Although she lived within walking distance of her school, her individualized education program (IEP) called for bus transportation due to concerns about her safety. The IEP did not call for a monitor or escort to wait with her at bus stops. On the day of the accident, the driver forgot to stop at the student's house. The bus monitor told him he forgot to make the stop, and he drove some distance before turning around to pick her up.

Although the driver later stated that he intended to turn around again and pick the student up at her regular stop, she instead crossed the road to try to catch the bus. She was then struck by another vehicle and seriously injured. In a state court negligence action, the court held the student's status as a special needs child imposed an expanded duty on the district. Appeal reached the New York Court of Appeals, which held **a school had no duty to prevent injury to a student released from a bus in a safe and anticipated manner**. But it held a school breached a duty if it released a child without supervision into a foreseeably hazardous setting it helped to create. The court disagreed with the parent's claim that the injury took place "during the act of busing, broadly construed." Evidence showed the student had walked onto the highway and was not in the district's custody when she was struck. Finally, the court found no special duty was owed to the student by virtue of her IEP or "the special busing services" afforded her in the IEP. In fact, the IEP only directed the district to transport her to and from school. Rejecting the parent's other arguments, the court held for the school district. *Williams v. Weatherstone*, 22 N.Y.3d 384 (N.Y. 2014).

◆ West Virginia's Supreme Court upheld the dismissal of a school bus driver who left her bus running to use the lavatory while students were onboard. In a brief memorandum, the court noted **the driver violated a state law against leaving a bus while it was still running**. The driver admitted she did not have to leave the bus running despite her urgent need to use the lavatory. *Hale v. Board of Educ. of Lewis County, West Virginia*, No. 13–0469, 2014 WL 350892 (W.Va. 1/31/14).

◆ An 11-year-old Arizona charter school student was struck and injured by a truck in the crosswalk of a busy intersection as she rode her bicycle home from school. The intersection had traffic lights and crosswalks but no crossing guards. The student's parents sued the school for negligence in a state court. In pretrial activity, the court held the school had no duty to protect the student as she traveled to or from its campus. The parents appealed to the Court of Appeals of Arizona, which stated that **as a general rule, an educational institution had no duty to supervise students going to or from their homes**. Arizona law recognized that if a school voluntarily offered protection at a street crossing, a duty of care was then imposed on that conduct. Although a school may create a duty for itself by an affirmative act, the court found no such act in this case. It held the school did not owe the student any duty of care to protect her while she went home.

Instead, the court found the student had left the school's custody at the relevant time. Since the charter school did not have custody of the student at the time, the court held it had no protective obligation to her and lacked any student-school relationship when she was hit. Rejecting all the parents' other arguments, the court held for the charter school. *Monroe v. Basis School, Inc.*, 234 Ariz. 155, 318 P.3d 871 (Ariz. Ct. App. 2014).

◆ Washington school officials were not liable for injuries to a middle school student who was hurt when a car hit her as she crossed a street in front of a neighboring elementary school. On the day of the incident, the supervising adult monitor dismissed the school safety patrol at 3:00 p.m. Seven minutes later, the student was struck in the elementary school crosswalk by a private vehicle. The driver admitted he had failed to keep a proper lookout and "just spaced." In a state court lawsuit, the student's guardian filed a personal injury action against the driver and the school district. She claimed negligent supervision, failure to have safe policies and procedures, failure to properly train and supervise adult monitors, and having no safety patrol in place only a few minutes after school dismissal.

When the case reached the Washington Court of Appeals, the guardian argued the district had a common law duty to station patrols or monitors at designated crosswalks. But the court found no support for this allegation, as the case involved a middle school student crossing a street in front of an elementary school. State laws and regulations authorizing school patrols had "suggested procedures" and did not address the time a patrol should be on duty. **The court rejected the guardian's argument that the district had a duty to supervise the crosswalk at the time of the injury.** The accident occurred after the school day ended and the school patrol had been dismissed. As a result, the court held for the school district. *Brady v. Reinert*, 175 Wash.App. 1074 (Wash. Ct. App. 2013).

◆ An Indiana high school student was struck and injured by a school bus as he bicycled to school. According to records of the bus transportation service that served the student's school district, the driver left the bus terminal about 10 minutes late on the morning of the collision. In a state court, the student's family sued the driver and transportation service for negligence. The student argued the contract between the school district and transportation service "called for money back guarantees when a driver is late," making the contract relevant to his theory that the driver was running late and was negligent. At the close of the trial, the student's attorneys asked the jury to return a $35 million verdict. Instead, the jury awarded the student $5.2 million, reduced by the amount of his own negligence, which was found to be 25%. On appeal, the state court of appeals found no merit to the bus service's claim that there had been unfair trial tactics or an unfair trial.

The court also rejected arguments that the trial court made incorrect rulings of evidence. The service failed to specify why evidence of the contract and insurance was prejudicial to its case. The driver admitted that she could be penalized for lateness. The court rejected a claim that the verdict was the result of a "runaway jury." **The reduction for comparative negligence indicated the jury had exercised discretion.** Since there was evidence to support the $3.9 million damage award, the court left it intact. *Reed v. Bethel*, 2 N.E.3d 98 (Ind. Ct. App. 2014).

◆   A Louisiana high school student was struck and killed by a school bus as she fought with another student near their school. In a state court action for negligence, the student's mother said school employees did not supervise students, failed to timely respond to the fight and did not adequately staff the area. Eight school board employees avoided liability by asserting that no cause of action existed against them under Louisiana Statutes Section 17:439(A). This section precluded claims against school employees based on "any statement made or action taken" within the course and scope of an employee's duties and within specific guidelines for employee behavior set by a school board. As for the bus driver, the trial court held there could be no direct claim against him under Section 17:439(D). Appeal reached the Supreme Court of Louisiana. It held that persons are liable for acts of omission and acts of commission under Civil Code Article 2315. The court reversed the decision regarding school employees other than the drivers. A determination had to be made regarding whether their statements or actions were covered under Section 17:439(A). A lower court had correctly held the driver was subject to a direct action to the extent of his insurance or self-insurance. **The case was returned to the court of appeal to consider whether employee statements or actions were "within the course and scope" of their duties** and whether they were within specific guidelines for employee behavior established by the board. *Credit v. Richland Parish School Board*, 85 So.3d 669 (La. 2012).

◆   A Florida parent who claimed her child was inappropriately touched by another student on a school bus did not state sufficiently definite facts to pursue a lawsuit against her school board and principal. A federal district court dismissed the parent's claims under the U.S. Constitution for failing to state a claim. It also dismissed her state law claims but allowed her to pursue them in the state court system. The parent then appealed to the U.S. Court of Appeals, Eleventh Circuit. On appeal, the court found no error by the trial court in granting a motion by the school board for a more definite statement. Her original complaint was vague and ambiguous.

The court affirmed the lower court's ruling that she did not state a claim with regard to alleged lying, harassment and bias. The parent contradicted her claim that school officials failed to address her report that a male student had improperly touched her daughter by admitting that school officials had taken action after her report. A vice principal had met with the male student and prohibited all males from sitting with females on the school bus. A report had been made to the state child protection agency. **Schools do not generally have the required level of control over students to have a**

constitutional duty to protect them from third parties. As the parent identified no district policy or custom that deprived her daughter of her federal rights, the court affirmed the judgment for the board. *Porter v. Duval County School Board*, 406 Fed.Appx. 460 (11th Cir. 2010).

◆   A nine-year-old North Carolina student was seated on a school bus next to another student who was poking holes in paper with a pencil. The driver told the other student to put the pencil away and told the student to turn around in the seat and stay out of the aisle. When the bus went over a dip in the road, the driver heard a scream. The student's left eye was punctured by the other student's pencil, causing a serious injury. In a State Tort Claims Act proceeding before the North Carolina Industrial Commission, the student's parents claimed the bus driver's failure to supervise the other student was the cause of the eye injury. The commission found the student's injuries resulted from the driver's negligence and awarded the student $150,000 in damages. The state court of appeals upheld the award. **Evidence supported the commission's finding that the driver had a duty of care to enforce school safety policies but failed to do so.** And this failure was the legal cause of the student's eye injury. *Lucas v. Rockingham County Schools*, 692 S.E.2d 890 (N.C. Ct. App. 2010).

◆   An Ohio kindergartner was left on a school bus during her first day of school. According to the parents, the bus driver drove away from the child's stop even though one parent was waiting there and became hysterical. They stated that the driver did not inspect the bus at the conclusion of her route and the child later awoke alone in a dark school bus garage. In the parents' state court action for personal injury, the district sought dismissal based on sovereign immunity. It argued that any injury to the student did not occur as the result of the "operation" of a school bus. After the court denied the motion, the district appealed. The state court of appeals explained that in *Doe v. Marlington Local School Dist. Board of Educ.*, this chapter, the Ohio Supreme Court held **a state law exception to immunity for negligent operation of a motor vehicle pertained only to negligence in driving or otherwise causing a vehicle to be moved**. In this case, the driver was operating the bus, not supervising the conduct of any students. Since the evidence supported the lower court's decision, the court affirmed the judgment. *Swain v. Cleveland Metropolitan School Dist.*, No. 94553, 2010 WL 3722280 (Ohio Ct. App. 9/23/10).

◆   A Florida middle school student was killed while crossing a street to get to her bus stop. She was using the stop because of problems she had with other students at the stop on her side of the road. Her school counselor told her to use the stop across the street. Her family sued the board in a state court. Appeal reached the state court of appeal. It found that if a student was harmed before reaching a designated bus stop (or after leaving one), the student was outside the board's duty of care. **Florida regulations placed**

the burden on parents to ensure the safe travel of students to and from home, when they were not in school custody. Since the student was under the exclusive control of her parents while she walked to the bus stop, the school district had no duty to ensure her safe arrival. The court affirmed the judgment for the board. *Francis v. School Board of Palm Beach County*, 29 So.3d 441 (Fla. Dist. Ct. App. 2010).

◆   A disabled Ohio student rode a bus with three middle school boys with special needs. An aide on the afternoon route saw a male student with his hand up the student's dress. They were immediately separated. When questioned, the female student said the male student had sexually molested her each day on the afternoon route. The parents claimed that the assaulting student had serious behavior problems and exhibited physical and verbal aggression. They sued the school board and officials in the state court system, asserting negligence and related claims. The case reached the Supreme Court of Ohio, which noted that state law barred immunity for injuries arising from the "operation of any motor vehicle," but did not define the term "operation." According to the family, the term meant all the essential functions that a driver is trained or required to do by law, not just driving. A dictionary definition of "operate" is to "control or direct the functioning of." This suggested that the term is limited to driving the vehicle itself. **The court held the exception to immunity for negligent operation of a motor vehicle applied only to negligence in driving the vehicle.** It held for the school board. *Doe v. Marlington Local School Dist. Board of Educ.*, 122 Ohio St.3d 124, 907 N.E.2d 706 (Ohio 2009).

◆   A six-year-old California student took the bus irregularly, due to his parents' schedules. About a month after starting school, he got on his bus, but soon told the driver that he saw his father's car. The driver grabbed him by the arm and asked if he was sure, and he said he was. When the student left the bus, he could not find his father and began walking with other students. He was later struck by a car as he tried to cross a busy street. In a state court, the family sued the school district, bus driver and car driver for personal injuries. The case reached the Court of Appeal of California, which recited the general rule in the state that "a school district owes a duty of care to its students because a special relationship exists between the students and the district." Once a district agreed to provide transportation for its students, it had a duty to exercise reasonable care. It rejected the district's claim that "transportation" occurred only while a bus was moving.

The district had undertaken a duty of care to its students after dismissal. During bus loading, students were still on school premises, and under school supervision. The fact that the injury took place later and off-campus did not decide the case. The lower court should have considered whether there was a duty of supervision, and whether the duty was breached. **Once the child was on the bus, the district had a duty to exercise ordinary care over him.** The case was returned to the lower court to consider questions such as the foreseeability *Eric M. v. Cajon Valley Union School Dist.*, 174 Cal.App.4th 285, 95 Cal.Rptr.3d 428 (Cal. Ct. App. 2009).

◆ A nine-year-old New Jersey student was left quadriplegic after being struck by a car several blocks from school and about two hours after school dismissal. His family sued the car driver, the school principal and the board of education. They asserted that the district and principal breached their duty of reasonable supervision during dismissal. The complaint claimed the parents did not have advance notice on the day of the accident that it was an early-dismissal day. The family settled its claims against the car driver. But a state trial court then held that the board's duty did not apply to an accident that occurred two hours after dismissal and several blocks from school.

When the case reached the Supreme Court of New Jersey, it explained that dangers to students continued at dismissal time because they were susceptible to numerous risks. It was foreseeable that young students leaving school grounds without parental supervision were vulnerable. **A school's duty to exercise reasonable care for students was integral to the state's public education system. "Dismissal is part of the school day."** The school's duty of supervision did not disappear when the school bell rang. The duty required school districts to create a reasonable dismissal supervision policy, provide notice to parents, and to comply with the policy and with parental requests concerning the dismissal of students from school. The court returned the case to the trial court for further proceedings. *Jerkins v. Anderson*, 191 N.J. 285, 922 A.2d 1279 (N.J. 2007).

VI. STUDENT SAFETY

In *Estate of C.A. v. Castro*, this chapter, the U.S. Court of Appeals, Fifth Circuit, rejected arguments to recognize the "state-created danger" theory under the Due Process Clause of the Fourteenth Amendment. It followed its decision in *Doe v. Covington County School Dist.*, 675 F.3d 849 (5th Cir. 2012), this chapter. But federal courts in Pennsylvania and Oklahoma have allowed students and their families to pursue state-created danger claims.

◆ Indiana's highest court held a principal's four-hour delay in reporting the rape of a student in a school lavatory triggered liability for a misdemeanor. During the delay, the court found the principal was neither reporting nor investigating the rape. It found he was instead "ignoring the issue." He spent two hours interviewing candidates for an open position. After the superintendent told the principal to contact the appropriate child protection agency, he did so. The perpetrator admitted the rape and made a guilty plea, and the investigation shifted to the principal. The state charged the principal with failure to report the incident. He was tried and convicted.

The principal's 120-day jail sentence was suspended to probation with community service and a $100 fine. He filed a lawsuit that reached the state supreme court. It found the state had proven **the principal had reason to believe the student was a victim of child abuse or neglect**. The student was a rape victim, and by virtue of her prior designation as a ward of the county, she was "a person who needed care, treatment or rehabilitation" that was unlikely to be provided or accepted without the coercive intervention of a court. The principal knowingly failed to make an immediate report to a child protection agency or police. While he argued "immediate" was a vague term allowing up to 24 hours to make a report, the court disagreed. It had no sympathy for the principal's four-hour delay, noting he had dropped the matter for a routine interview. The principal admitted to investigators that he had not read relevant reporting policies. He and his staff held the mistaken view that an allegation of a rape by another minor could not be child abuse. The court commented that the principal was not entitled to take time to "assess and reflect" about a report, as he did not need a high level of certainty to do so. There was sufficient evidence for him to believe the student was a rape victim. Mandated reporters had to identify and report the facts within their knowledge. As a result, the principal's conviction and sentence were upheld. *Smith v. State of Indiana*, 8 N.E.3d 668 (Ind. 2014).

◆   New Jersey's Supreme Court held a school principal was not liable for injuries to a pedestrian who cut across public school grounds on a Saturday and was attacked by a dog. According to the pedestrian, the dog had previously slipped out of its leash and accosted other passersby. She said the principal had called animal protection officials at least one other time when a dog was loose while school was in session. In the pedestrian's state court action, she advanced claims against the school district, principal, dog owner and the owner of the property where the dog had been leashed. After the claims against the dog owner and property owner were dismissed for failure to prosecute them, the court rejected arguments by the pedestrian that the principal and school district had a duty to prevent future attacks. She said the dog was a known danger on school property. The court held for the school district and principal, but a state appellate division court disagreed.

On appeal, the pedestrian argued the principal was on notice of the risk of an attack because he had received a report that the dog had attacked two others nine days before her injury. He had also reported dogs to the animal control unit of the police when dogs were observed at school during school hours. According to the pedestrian, the school district should also be held liable in this case because the principal knew that a vicious dog created a dangerous condition on school grounds. The court explained that proving a negligence claim depends upon the finding of a duty of care that the party being sued owes to the party bringing the lawsuit. Once a duty is found to exist, liability follows if there is a breach of the duty that causes injury and damages. In this case, **neither the principal nor the school board had any control over the dog or the activities on neighboring property**. Once the school day ended, the principal could not monitor school grounds. There was also no relationship between the school and the pedestrian. Finally, the court found no public interest in imposing a duty on school personnel to protect persons with no relationship to a school from attacks by neighborhood dogs. Since there was no duty of care to protect the pedestrian in this case, the court held for the principal and school district. *Robinson v. Vivirito*, 217 N.J. 199, 86 A.3d 119 (N.J. 2014).

◆   An Oklahoma student drank alcohol and became intoxicated before his prom. The superintendent instructed two other students to take the student home in his vehicle. He did not call the parents or the police, nor did he assess whether the students assigned to drive had also been drinking. After the students left campus, the student took the wheel and dropped off the others at their homes. He then called and texted others, expressing his anger and threatening to outrun the police. The student was then killed in a one-vehicle crash. His parents sued the school district and superintendent for constitutional rights violations and negligence. The court noted the U.S. Court of Appeals, Tenth Circuit, has recognized a "state-created danger" theory of constitutional liability that may be based on reckless or intentional conduct by state actors that "shocks the conscience."

In this case, the court held the parents asserted facts that could support a state-created danger claim against the superintendent. They had also asserted conduct by the superintendent that could be seen as "shocking to the conscience." A meaningful analysis of the factors for liability would have to be made to assess whether his conduct, as alleged by the parents, met this high standard. **Although the superintendent sought immunity from liability, the court found he should have been on notice that allowing a student to go home intoxicated without calling his parents first would violate his rights.** The parents could also pursue claims against the district. *Kerns v. Independent School Dist. No. 31 of Ottawa County*, 984 F.Supp.2d 1144 (N.D. Okla. 2013).

◆   Michigan school officials could not be held liable for the death of a high school student and injuries to three others after a shooting at a Detroit high school. The shooting occurred at a school with a long history of violence and gang activity. School officials had merged the high school with a neighboring school. It was later asserted by the families of the victims that the merger increased a risk of violence due to gang rivalries. In a federal district court, the families of the victims sued the shooter and his accomplices for assault and battery. They added claims against the school district, high school principal and security officers for gross negligence, constitutional violations and public nuisance. The court entered judgments totalling $8 million in damages against each of the shooters for assault and battery. But it dismissed the school system from the case. Before the U.S. Court of Appeals, Sixth Circuit, the families claimed the merger of the high schools resulted in a state-created danger of increased violence due to the known gang presence. **The court explained that there is no constitutional requirement for the government to protect life, liberty and property of**

citizens against private actors such as the shooters in this case. To create liability, an affirmative government act must present a special danger to an individual whom the government has placed at risk.

The court found that "failure to act is not an affirmative act under the state-created danger theory." It must be shown that government actions placed the victim specifically at risk. In the court's view, neither the merging of the high schools nor the breaking up of the fight prior to the shootings satisfied the "affirmative act element of the state-created danger claim." As the tort claims were barred by state law immunity, the court held for the school district and employees. *Walker v. Detroit Public School Dist.*, 535 Fed.Appx. 461 (6th Cir. 2013).

◆ The U.S. Court of Appeals, Fifth Circuit, held a Texas school district and administrators were not liable to the estate of a student who drowned in a school pool. The parents sued the school district, principal and other officials in a federal court, asserting constitutional rights violations based on a state-created danger theory. The court held for the school district and officials, and the parents appealed to the Fifth Circuit. On appeal, the parents argued their son's death occurred despite the school's knowledge of an obvious danger of unsupervised use of the swimming pool. The court noted that the parents' claims arose under the Due Process Clause of the Fourteenth Amendment. Although they urged liability under the "state-created danger theory," the court explained that it had already refused to recognize the theory. State actors such as the school officials in this case were entitled to qualified immunity so long as their conduct did not violate clearly established constitutional rights of which a reasonable person would have known. In this case, **the family was unable to identify a constitutional violation because the state-created danger theory was invalid.** Even had they shown a constitutional violation, the court held they would still be unable to show such a right was clearly established at the relevant time. *Estate of C.A. v. Castro*, 547 Fed.Appx. 621 (5th Cir. 2013).

◆ An 11-year-old New York student fell from a banister at school while unsupervised and suffered serious injuries. When his parents sued the district for negligence, it asserted that he had assumed the risk of harm by engaging in horseplay when he slid down the banister. The case reached the Court of Appeals of New York, which found that assumption of risk is typically raised in cases involving athletic and recreational activities. Allowing the defense here would have unfortunate consequences and could not be used to nullify the district's duty. If assumption of risk was allowed, students would be deemed to consent in advance to the risks of their own misconduct. Children often act impulsively and without good judgment. This does not mean they consent to assume the resulting danger. **If the student's injury was attributable to his own conduct, this could be handled by allocating comparative fault.** The court returned the case to a lower court for more proceedings. *Trupia v. Lake George Cent. School Dist.*, 927 N.E.2d 547 (N.Y. 2010).

◆   A Texas student missed his school bus twice during his first week of kindergarten. Later in the month, school officials required him to a sign a disciplinary form due to bus misbehavior, even though he could not read and no parent was present. After an investigation by the school district and subsequent hearings, the district's board denied the parent's grievance. On appeal, a state administrative law judge held the Texas education commissioner had no authority to hear federal law questions and that the parent did not claim violations of state law. A state trial court affirmed the commissioner's order, and appeal reached the Court of Appeals of Texas. It noted the commissioner's power to review school board actions was limited to actions or decisions by a school board that violated the school laws of the state or a provision of an employment contract. The court found the parent did not show any violation of Chapter 26 of the Texas Education Code.

The parent did not show the district neglected to adopt a grievance process for parental complaints. At most, he showed an inaccurate investigation of his son's bus incidents and failure to accurately follow its local grievance policy. **The court found no merit to the parent's claim that the commissioner had power over claims regarding the creation of an unsafe learning environment.** A state code provision regarding safe and disciplined school campus environments contained only "a mission statement." Because federal claims arising under the Paul D. Coverdell Teacher Protection Act and the Family Educational Rights and Privacy Act were outside the commissioner's authority, the case had been properly dismissed. *Maiden v. Texas Educ. Agency*, No. 03-09-00681-CV, 2011 WL 1744963 (Tex. Ct. App. 5/6/11).

◆   A New York child was hurt when she fell off a slide on a school playground. The playground used no ground cover and was grass and dirt. Other playgrounds operated by the city and school district had protective ground cover to reduce the chance of injuries. The child's parent filed a personal injury action in a state court against the school district and city. After the trial court denied pretrial dismissal, a state appellate division court reversed the judgment. On appeal, the New York Court of Appeals held the parent's expert had only calculated the force of the child when she landed on the ground, relying on prior tests in which he had used rubber mats. By contrast, U.S. Consumer Product Safety Commission guidelines were based on the use of various different ground covers. **The expert witness did not provide a scientific or mathematical foundation to substantiate his opinion that the type of ground cover did not cause injury in this case.** He did not address the shock-absorbing capacity of pea stone that the district used at its other playgrounds. As a result, the court reinstated the claims. *Butler v. City of Gloversville*, 12 N.Y.3d 902 (N.Y. 2009).

◆   A New Hampshire student with learning disabilities was having problems at his middle school. During his seventh-grade year, a teacher's aide overheard him say he "wanted to blow his brains out." A guidance counselor called the student's mother and had the student sign a contract for safety, but she took no other action. Several weeks later, the mother claimed that a special education teacher made a false and knowing attempt to impose discipline on her son. The next day, the student was reported to the vice principal and suspended. After the suspension, the student returned home and hanged himself. The mother sued the school administrative unit, a teacher and the guidance counselor for negligence, infliction of emotional distress and wrongful death. A state trial court dismissed the case, and later the Supreme Court of New Hampshire affirmed this decision. It rejected the mother's claim that the counselor and administrative unit had a special duty to prevent the suicide and that the counselor voluntarily assumed a duty to prevent it. **There was no intentional or malicious conduct in this case that might create a duty to prevent the suicide.** *Mikell v. School Administrative Unit #33*, 972 A.2d 1050 (N.H. 2009).

◆   A Wisconsin high school student admitted writing a note that said a bomb was in a school locker. As a result of the note, the school was evacuated and students were moved to off-campus sites for over four hours. A state court placed him on probation after he pled no contest to causing a bomb scare under a state criminal statute. In addition to ordering the student to perform 100 hours of community service, the court ordered him to pay the school district restitution of over $18,000. The student appealed the order to pay restitution to the Court of Appeals of Wisconsin. It noted most of the amount represented salaries and benefits of teachers and staff who had been working but had to evacuate the school due to his threatening note. **State law permitted a court to order "special damages" that could be recovered in a civil action as part of a criminal restitution order.** The court held the determination of restitution is within a court's discretion. In this case, the school district was the property owner and was entitled to restitution for a direct loss. The payment of teachers and staff who had to vacate the building amounted to "special damages" that could properly form the basis of an order for restitution. As the restitution was found reasonable, the judgment was affirmed. *State of Wisconsin v. Vanbeek*, 316 Wis.2d 527, 765 N.W.2d 834 (Wis. Ct. App. 2009).

CHAPTER FOUR

Campus Law Enforcement

I. SEARCH AND SEIZURE

A. The *New Jersey v. T.L.O.* Standard

The Fourth Amendment to the U.S. Constitution protects individuals from unreasonable searches and seizures. The Fourth Amendment states:

"The right of the people to be secure in their persons, houses, papers and effects, against unreasonable searches and seizures, shall not be violated, and no Warrants shall issue, but upon probable cause, supported by Oath or affirmation, and particularly describing the place to be searched, and the persons or things to be seized."

Underlying all search and seizure cases in the criminal context is the "exclusionary rule," which allows a suspect to exclude from consideration any evidence that is seized in violation of the Fourth Amendment.

Since unlawfully seized evidence is considered "the fruit of a poisonous tree," it is excluded from evidence in a criminal or juvenile case and may result in dismissal of the case. These considerations are not always present in school searches, where student discipline, not criminal prosecution, is the potential sanction, and school safety is the primary consideration. The Fourth Amendment's warrant and probable cause standard does not typically apply to school officials who search students suspected of violating a law or school rules. Instead, the courts apply a "reasonableness" standard, by which the legality of a school search depends upon its reasonableness under all the circumstances. The test was established by the U.S. Supreme Court in *New Jersey v. T.L.O.*, below.

School searches are deemed "administrative searches" as they do not result in criminal prosecution and loss of liberty. The "special need" beyond law enforcement that justifies relieving school administrators from the burden of obtaining warrants is the need to protect student safety.

Note the two-part analysis employed by the Supreme Court in *T.L.O.*:
1)   a search by school officials need only be reasonable at its inception, and
2)   its scope may not exceed what is necessary under the circumstances.

For example, a teacher who smells marijuana odor wafting from a student would be reasonable in believing that there was some rules violation, satisfying the first requirement that the search be "reasonable at its inception." After the student is sent to the assistant principal's office, an administrator or school liaison officer then asks the student if he has marijuana in his possession and asks him to turn out his pockets. This kind of search is regarded as "not intrusive" and satisfies the second part by "not exceeding what is necessary under the circumstances."

By contrast, a highly intrusive "strip search" would go beyond what was necessary in this case and would be unreasonable.

◆   In the *T.L.O.* case, a teacher at a New Jersey high school found two girls smoking in a school lavatory in violation of school rules. She brought them to the assistant vice principal's office, where one of the girls admitted to smoking in the lavatory. However, the other girl denied even being a smoker. The assistant vice principal then asked the latter girl to come to his private office, where he opened her purse and found a pack of cigarettes. As he reached for them, he noticed rolling papers and decided to thoroughly search the entire purse. He found marijuana, a pipe, empty plastic bags, a substantial number of one dollar bills and a list of "people who owe me money." The matter was then turned over to the police. A juvenile court hearing was held, and the girl was adjudicated delinquent. She appealed the juvenile court's determination, contending that her constitutional rights had been violated by the search of her purse. She argued that the evidence against her should have been excluded from the juvenile court proceeding.

The U.S. Supreme Court held that the search did not violate the Fourth Amendment's prohibition on unreasonable searches and seizures. Stated the Court: "The legality of a search of a student should depend simply on the reasonableness, under all the circumstances, of the search." Two considerations are relevant in determining the reasonableness of a search. First, **the search must be justified initially by reasonable suspicion of a violation**. Second, **the scope and conduct of the search must be reasonably related to the circumstances which gave rise to the search, and school officials must take into account the student's age, sex and the nature of the offense**. The Court upheld the search of the student in this case because the initial search for cigarettes was supported by reasonable suspicion. The discovery of rolling papers then justified the further searching of the purse, since such papers are commonly used to roll marijuana cigarettes. The Court affirmed the delinquency adjudication, ruling the "reasonableness" standard was met by school officials in these circumstances and the evidence was properly obtained. *New Jersey v. T.L.O.*, 469 U.S. 325, 105 S.Ct. 733, 83 L.Ed.2d 720 (1985).

◆   Based upon an anonymous tip that a student had a gun at school, a Florida assistant principal brought him to a conference room. A search of his book bag yielded a loaded semiautomatic handgun. In a juvenile court proceeding, the student sought to exclude the gun from evidence, arguing the search violated the Fourth Amendment. After a trial, the court imposed a 15-day detention and probation. Appeal reached a Florida District Court of Appeal, which held that generally, **an anonymous tip must have sufficient detail and information that could be independently verified by police to establish a level of reliability**. On the other hand, some circumstances justify protective searches based on a threat of extraordinary danger. Courts have recognized that schools are an area where a person's reasonable expectation of privacy is reduced. For this reason, public school officials are held to a standard of reasonable suspicion, rather than probable cause. In the court's view, the search in this case was reasonable. There were reasonable indicia of reliability to the tip, which accurately identified the student by name and his school. Given the student's reduced expectation of privacy, the moderate intrusiveness of the search, the gravity of the threat, and the reduced level of reliability necessary to justify a protective search, the court held the decision to search the book bag was reasonable. *K.P. v. State of Florida*, 129 So.3d 1121 (Fla. Dist. Ct. App. 2013).

◆   For years prior to 2011, Santa Fe, New Mexico Public Schools contracted with a private company for security at high school proms. According to four students, the private security guards subjected them to intrusive pat-down searches as they tried to enter the 2011 prom. Two of the girls said security guards pulled their dresses up and felt their bare legs. They also charged the security guards (all female) with placing their hands on their bras, running fingers down their dresses and patting down their back sides. In a federal court, the students' families sued the school district, its board, the principal and several others for violation of the students' Fourth Amendment rights. Evidence was produced that the principal did not pat down or assist the private security guards in patting down any students at the prom. While the searches had been performed within a few feet of the principal, she stated that did not see the guards touching students on their breasts or pulling on their bras. Finding the pat-down searches were likely unconstitutional, the court issued a temporary order prohibiting the school district from performing pat-down searches without reasonable suspicion. **Less intrusive searching, such as with visual inspection or the use of magnetic wands, was allowed.** The court ordered the company's guards to undergo instruction by the federal Transportation Safety Administration.

The court directed the school district to stop conducting pat-down searches of every student "as a first approach." **Security officers were to use a graduated approach similar to those used by airport security guards.** Only after such an approach, and when reasonable grounds existed, could security guards use pat-down searches. The court held the security officers could inspect phones and cameras and ask students to open them if necessary. After the students voluntarily dismissed most of their claims against the district and officials, the principal moved for judgment on the Fourth Amendment claim based on qualified immunity. In the court's opinion, no case law from the Supreme Court, the Tenth Circuit or elsewhere would have put the principal on notice that suspicionless, pat-down searches of students at a high school prom violated the Constitution. Even if the principal saw a guard order a student to lift her dress and expose her leg, the court held this did not violate a clearly established right at the time of the prom. It dismissed the claims against the principal. *Herrera v. Santa Fe Public Schools*, 956 F.Supp.2d 1191 (D.N.M. 2013).

Illinois' "Right to Privacy in the School Setting Act" will require schools to notify families that a school may require access to student social networking accounts, if there is a reasonable belief that the account has evidence of a school rule or policy violation. Under the 2014 law, public and nonpublic elementary and secondary schools must notify a student's parent or guardian that the school may request or require a student's social networking site password (or other account information) to gain access to an account or a student's profile on a social networking website. To obtain such access, the school must have reasonable cause to believe the student's account on the social networking website contains evidence that the student has violated a school disciplinary rule or policy. Notice of this access provision must be published in the school's disciplinary rules, policies, or handbook or communicated to families by similar means. Provisions of the law prohibit post-secondary schools from requiring students or parents to provide passwords or other account-related information to access a student's account on a social networking website. But the provision does not apply when a school has reason to believe the student's social networking website account contains evidence that the student has violated a school disciplinary rule. Ninety-Eighth Illinois General Assembly, P.A. 98-129, H.B. 64. Illinois Statutes Sections 105-75/1, 105-75/15, 105-75/20.

◆ An Oregon principal learned that a student had either called or texted a classmate that he would bring a gun to school and shoot her. Upon learning this, the principal called a deputy sheriff and the student's mother. While awaiting the deputy and mother, the principal searched the student's locker. After finding no gun there, he escorted the student to the office and confiscated his backpack. When the student denied making the threats, the principal continued to question him and searched his backpack, where a .45 caliber semi-automatic handgun and ammunition were found. The deputy confiscated the gun, placed the student in handcuffs and read him his criminal rights. In a juvenile court, the student sought to exclude the handgun and ammunition from the evidence. He argued the principal lacked reasonable suspicion to believe a weapon was in the backpack. In denying the student's motion, the court held the principal had relied on specific facts indicating a threat. It also held the search was not overly intrusive. On appeal, the court held a student can be searched without a warrant or probable cause when a school official reasonably suspects, based on specific and articulable facts, that the student possesses something that poses an immediate threat. In this case, the principal reasonably suspected the backpack could hold a weapon, and he did not know whether the student had the gun on his person, in the backpack, or at another place in school. The court held that **when school officials perceive an immediate threat to school safety, they must be able to take prompt, reasonable steps to address it**. As there was a real threat to safety in this case, the court held the search was reasonable. *State v. A.J.C.*, 254 Or. App. 717 (Or. Ct. App. 2013).

◆ Four California police officers learned from a high school principal that a student had told a classmate he would "shoot up" the school. He was said to be a victim of bullying and had been absent from school for two days. Concerned that the student was a threat, the police went to his house. When they arrived, they knocked on the door but received no response. Nobody answered the home telephone, and the student's mother hung up her cell phone after a police sergeant identified himself and said he was waiting outside. Soon, the student and his mother came outside and learned that the officers wanted to discuss the threats. The student responded, "I can't believe you're here for that." When the sergeant asked to come inside the house to talk, the mother refused. He asked her if there were any guns in the house, and she went inside. Fearing they were in danger, the officers entered the house. The student's father challenged their authority to be there, and they did not conduct any search. Ultimately, the officers concluded the report about the student was false. Later, the family sued the officers in a federal court for Fourth Amendment violations. Appeal reached the U.S. Supreme Court, which found none of its prior decisions had found a Fourth Amendment violation on facts comparable to those present in this case.

The Court held **a reasonable police officer could read the Court's prior decisions as allowing their entry into a residence if there was a reasonable basis to believe there was an imminent threat of violence**. As a result, the Court found a lower court had correctly held the officers had an objectively reasonable basis for their actions. This included the mother's initial failure to answer the door or the phone, hanging up the cell phone on the sergeant, refusing to answer questions, and running into the house. *Ryburn v. Huff*, 132 S.Ct. 987, 181 L.Ed.2d 966 (U.S. 2012).

B. Cell Phones and Other Electronic Devices

While it remains to be seen whether *Riley v. California*, below, will shape the law of school searches, the U.S. Supreme Court made plain that cell phones are unlike other items that may turn up in a police search. The Court found cell phones contain large amounts of personal data that would yield far more information than may be had in an extensive search of a home. The Court admonished police that, absent exigent circumstances, they must obtain a warrant to search the contents of a cell phone.

◆ A federal court held a Nevada student who made vulgar off-campus tweets about his high school basketball coaches lacked a privacy expectation in his social media comments. School administrators had accessed his tweets on the account of one of his "followers," so the court held the tweets were being disseminated to the public. While only Twitter "followers" could read private tweets, the court held a person who sent private tweets was still disseminating postings and information to the public. In fact, the court found the student's Twitter privacy settings were irrelevant to the case.

While only Twitter "followers" could read private tweets, **the court held a person who sent private tweets was still disseminating postings and information to the public**. A 1978 U.S. Supreme Court criminal case held that if a person shares information with a third party, he or she takes a risk that the third party may then provide it to the government. According to the court, **a person using Twitter takes the risk that friends will turn information over to the government**. Another federal court had held that when Facebook privacy settings allowed postings by friends, the government may access them through a cooperating "friend" without violating the Constitution. In addition to dismissing the student's Fourth Amendment claim, the court dismissed his equal protection and due process claims as meritless. *Roasio v. Clark County School Dist.*, No. 2:13-CV-362 JCM (PAL), 2013 WL 3679375 (D. Nev. 7/3/13).

◆ In separate criminal cases, two adult criminal suspects claimed their Fourth Amendment rights against unreasonable searches and seizure were violated when police officers examined the contents of their cell phones after their arrests. When their appeals reached the U.S. Supreme Court, it explained that police are typically required to obtain a warrant to meet the Constitutional "reasonableness" standard. Prior case law established that police may search a detainee for weapons that may be used to resist arrest. By contrast, a leading Supreme Court case held an extensive, warrantless search of a home was unnecessary to protect the safety of the police officers or to preserve evidence of a crime. In the Court's view, the risks identified in prior detention cases were not present when officers seized cell phones from criminal detainees. Cell phones held vast quantities of personal data. Searching them did not resemble the typically brief search of a suspect.

The Court refused to allow warrantless police searches of cell phones. It issued a sharp admonition to police seeking to view the contents of a suspect's cell phone: "Our answer to the question of what police must do before searching a cell phone seized incident to an arrest is accordingly simple – get a warrant." In ruling for both suspects, the Court held a cell phone search would typically reveal more than the search of a house. It recognized that "fact-specific threats may justify a warrantless search of cell phone data" if a specific risk of exigent circumstances was present. *Riley v. California*, 134 S.Ct. 2473, 189 L.Ed.2d 430 (U.S. 2014).

◆ A California campus safety officer entered a classroom to talk to a student about the theft of an iPod. After the suspect denied knowing of the theft, the officer searched the bags of all students present in the room. A small folding knife was found in a student's handbag. Although the student was suspended pending an expulsion, she later returned to school. She claimed the school retaliated against her for asserting her civil rights. In a federal court, she sued the security officer, principal, an assistant principal and the school district. In pretrial activity, the court found that government officials have qualified immunity from civil damage awards unless their conduct violates clearly established rights of which a reasonable person would have known at the time of the alleged violation. In this case, the court found **there was reasonable suspicion that the stolen Ipod was in the possession of a student in the classroom**. After the officer determined the original suspect did not have the item, the court held it was reasonable for him to conduct a limited search of the handbags of other students in the classroom. The search was not intrusive, as the officer did not touch the student. Since case law did not put him on notice that the search for the Ipod was prohibited, the court held he had qualified immunity. The court also found the other school officials did not violate constitutional rights by giving the knife to the police. *Gallardo v. Hanford Joint Union School Dist.*, No. 1:12-cv-01612 GSA, 2014 WL 792130 (E.D. Cal. 2/5/14).

◆ The U.S. Court of Appeals, Sixth Circuit, held "using a cell phone on school grounds does not automatically trigger an essentially unlimited right enabling a school official to search any content stored on the phone." The court stated that even if checking a student's messages on the cell phone was justified by a need to determine if he was contemplating harm to himself or others, any search was subject to the two-part analysis for all school searches. It had to be tailored to the nature of the violation and related to the objectives of the search. In the court's opinion, the viewing of the student's cell phone text messages was unreasonable. **General knowledge of drug abuse or depressive tendencies was not enough to enable such a search.**

Since the school district did not show that a search of the phone would reveal evidence of criminal activity, the court found the search was not justified at its inception and violated his rights. *G.C. v. Owensboro Public Schools*, 711 F.3d 623 (6th Cir. 2013).

◆ A federal court held a Mississippi student who used his cell phone in class had a "diminished expectation of privacy" in the phone because he violated a school rule by using it. Since the phone was contraband, the court held school officials did not violate the Fourth Amendment by viewing its contents. The court said when a staff member saw the student improperly using the phone, it was reasonable for him to find out why he was using it. He might have been using the phone to cheat or communicate with another student, who would also be subject to discipline for improperly using a cell phone at school. As the search was justified at its inception and reasonably related in scope to the circumstances which justified the phone confiscation, **the individual defendants were entitled to qualified immunity. The city was entitled to dismissal of a Fourth Amendment claim against it.**

But the court sent the matter of the student's one-year expulsion to a jury, as a district rule called for only a three-day suspension. While a police sergeant and principal had acted in good faith at the student's hearing, the court found no explanation for the hearing officer's finding that the student was a threat to the school. The sergeant did not reveal any basis for believing the cell phone pictures displayed gang signs. Yet the hearing officer decided the student should be expelled for a full year. For this reason, the court was "troubled" that the student "somehow found himself expelled for an entire school year when the only offense he committed was the minor offense of bringing a phone on school grounds." Since the most likely reason for expulsion was the testimony that the student was "a threat to school safety," **the court found it possible that the expulsion was based on subjective beliefs and not conduct**. Based on "serious concerns regarding the school district's actions," the court held that a jury would have to resolve the expulsion issue. *J.W. v. Desoto County School Dist.*, Civil Action No. 2:09-cv-00155-MPM-DAS, 2010 WL 4394059 (N.D. Miss. 11/1/10).

◆ A Georgia high school student violated a ban on electronic communication devices by bringing an iPod and cell phone to class. After confiscating the iPod and putting it in a drawer, the teacher left the room, and a classmate took it from the drawer. When the teacher returned, he found the iPod missing and asked who had taken it. After no student admitted having the iPod, all of them were told to open their book bags, turn out their pockets and untuck their shirts. A classmate later confided the identity of the iPod taker to the assistant principal. He avoided confronting the iPod taker to protect the identity of the informer. Although the identity of the iPod taker was already known, the secretary told a student to remove her pants and underwear. The student sued the teacher, district and others in a federal court. It held student searches must be "justified at its inception."

In *Thomas v. Roberts*, 261 F.3d 1160 (11th Cir. 2001), the Eleventh Circuit considered a strip search of Georgia fifth-graders for $26 in missing cash. **Roberts** **put schools on notice that a strip search for non-dangerous contraband violates the Fourth Amendment. Officials lacked individualized suspicion that the student had the iPod.** As the search was not based on individualized suspicion that the student had an iPod, a jury could find a Fourth Amendment violation. But as the assistant principal was not a "final policymaker" for the district, there could be no district liability. *Foster v. Raspberry*, 652 F.Supp.2d 1342 (M.D. Ga. 2009).

◆ A Pennsylvania student had his cell phone on, in violation of a school policy. When a teacher confiscated the phone, a text message appeared on its screen from another student requesting marijuana. The teacher and an assistant principal then called nine students listed in the cell phone's directory to see if their phones were turned on in violation of school policy. They accessed the student's text messages and voice mail and used the phone's instant messaging feature. The student stated the district superintendent later told the press that the student was a drug user or peddler, and the family sued the teacher, assistant principal, superintendent and school district in a federal district court. It held the superintendent could not assert absolute immunity for his statements to the press. The teacher and assistant principal also had no immunity for the invasion of privacy claims.

The court agreed with the family that **accessing the phone directory, voice mail and text messages, and use of the phone to call persons listed in the directory amounted to a "search or seizure" under the Fourth Amendment**. The court found no basis for the "search," as it was not done to find evidence of wrongdoing by the student, but instead to obtain evidence of possible misconduct by others. As a result, it held the Fourth Amendment claims would proceed. *Klump v. Nazareth Area School Dist.*, 425 F.Supp.2d 622 (E.D. Pa. 2006).

C. Strip Searches

◆ A Kansas student was accused by a classmate of placing marijuana in her bra while at school. After being brought to the school office, she consented to be patted down and to have her shoes and backpack searched. After the school resource officer found nothing, an assistant principal told her she would have to search her bra based on the classmate's report. Two female school officials then instructed the student to lift up her shirt and pull her bra from her body, exposing her breasts. No drugs or paraphernalia were found. Within a few weeks, the student "disenrolled from the school" and she later sued the school district. A federal court found no evidence of an unconstitutional policy or custom that would create district liability. The court expressed concern about the failure of school administrators to corroborate the classmate's tip as well as the manner of the search. But it held **the student did not identify any prior cases discussing whether a student informant's tip created "reasonable suspicion" for a school**

search. Federal case law did not clearly establish whether a student's tip created reasonable suspicion to search another student's bra. The Safford case did not establish that the conduct in this case violated the Fourth Amendment. Having dismissed the federal claims, the court held the state law claims should be heard by a state court. *S.S. v. Turner Unified School Dist. #202*, No. 12-CV-0246-CM, 2012 WL 6561525 (D. Kan. 12/14/12).

◆   An Arizona assistant middle school principal questioned a 13-year-old student about knives, lighters and a cigarette found in her planner. When the student denied owning any of the contraband, the assistant principal questioned her about prescription-strength ibuprofen pills and an over-the-counter painkiller. After the student denied knowing about the pills, the assistant principal told her he had received a report from a male student that she was giving pills to others at school. She denied this and allowed the assistant principal to search her belongings. He found no contraband there but told female staff members to further search the student in the nurse's office. An administrative assistant and school nurse asked the student to remove her jacket, socks, shoes, pants and T-shirt. They then instructed her to pull her bra to the side and shake it. Finally, the two staff members told the student to pull out the elastic of her underpants. No pills were found.

The student's mother sued the school district for Fourth Amendment violations. The case reached the U.S. Supreme Court, which held the male student's report created enough suspicion to justify searching the student's backpack and outer clothes. But asking her to pull away her underwear and expose her breasts and pelvic area made the search "categorically distinct, requiring distinct elements of justification on the part of school authorities for going beyond a search of outer clothing and belongings." Further, the "the suspicion failed to match the degree of intrusion." The Court stated "the *T.L.O.* concern to limit a school search to reasonable scope requires the support of reasonable suspicion of danger or of resort to underwear for hiding evidence of wrongdoing before a search can reasonably make the quantum leap from outer clothes and backpacks to exposure of intimate parts." **Despite the violation, this legal area was not so well established as to deprive school officials of immunity.** *Safford Unified School Dist. #1 v. Redding*, 557 U.S. 364, 129 S.Ct. 2633, 174 L.Ed.2d 354 (2009).

◆   Two students in an Ohio high school nursing class reported missing cash, a credit card and gift cards. The other 15 or 16 students in the class were taken to the first aid room, where their purses, books, shoes, socks and pockets were searched. After a search of each student's locker, staff members received a report that an unidentified student was hiding the missing items in her bra. The school director then instructed a female instructor to search the students in the lavatory. Eleven students sued the school district, instructors and other school officials in a federal district court for violating their Fourth Amendment rights. The court denied the officials' request for qualified immunity. On appeal, the U.S. Court of

Appeals, Sixth Circuit, affirmed the judgment, and the officials appealed to the U.S. Supreme Court. It returned the case to the Sixth Circuit in view of its decision in *Safford Unified School Dist. #1 v. Redding*, above.

The Sixth Circuit held there must be "reasonable grounds for suspecting that the search will turn up evidence that the student has violated or is violating either the law or the rules of the school." **A student handbook policy did not create mutual consent to conduct the strip searches, as the district argued.** There was no waiver of privacy expectations, as some students did not even know about the policy. The court held "students have a significant privacy interest in their unclothed bodies." The severity of the school's need in this case was held "slight." A search for money served a much less important interest than a search for drugs or weapons. The court found the search was unlikely to uncover any evidence and violated the students' rights. As a result, it again denied the officials immunity. *Knisley v. Pike County Joint Vocational School Dist.*, 604 F.3d 977 (6th Cir. 2010).

◆   A federal district court held Illinois charter school officials were immune to claims filed by a student who was strip-searched by a security guard and police officer. In *Safford Unified School Dist. #1 v. Redding*, this chapter, the Supreme Court held that a school official searching a student may claim qualified immunity where no clearly established law reveals a constitutional violation. The student could not show the law regarding school strip searches was "clearly established" at the time of the search. *Redding* was not released until after the search in this case. As for the other claims, the court rejected the student's argument that school and municipal officials placed her in a position of danger by allowing the search to go forward. **A single, isolated incident of wrongdoing by a non-policymaker was insufficient to establish municipal liability.** Rejecting other state law claims, the court disposed of many of the student's claims prior to any trial. *S.J. v. Perspectives Charter School*, 685 F.Supp.2d 847 (N.D. Ill. 2010).

◆   An Alabama seventh-grade teacher reported her $450 makeup bag and $12 in cash were missing. The principal, an assistant principal and a counselor told students to empty their book bags and purses, and take off their shoes and socks. Students were told to pull out their pants pockets, and the assistant principal and counselor patted down a few of them. The assistant principal stuck her hand into a student's pockets. The counselor reached into the pockets of male students and ran her hand down one student's thigh. The principal took some boys into the hallway for questioning. He then found the makeup bag in a trash can. The $12 was not in the bag, but the teacher said she was no longer concerned about it. Despite this response, the principal took the boys to the boys' lavatory, where he told them to drop their pants and raise their shirts. The counselor took the girls to the lavatory and asked most of them to do the same. A few of the girls were also told to pull up their bras. Parents of the students sued the school board, principal, assistant principal, and counselor for Fourth Amendment violations. The court found that the officials did not have any individualized suspicion that any student took the makeup bag. **The classroom searches which did not involve the touching of students were justified, but a strip search for the possible theft of $12 was unreasonable.** The strip searches were intrusive and violated the district's own policy. As the search was beyond the school officials' authority, they were not entitled to qualified immunity from the Fourth Amendment violation claims. *H.Y. v. Russell County Board of Educ.*, 490 F.Supp.2d 1174 (M.D. Ala. 2007).

D. Recent Search and Seizure Cases

◆   A young Florida student saw three older students in a school lavatory "examining" a handgun. He told his teacher that the student holding the gun was a tall, thin African-American with a dark complexion and a "low afro" haircut. He wore a red shirt and "skinny jeans," and was carrying a book bag with a cartoon character or "some type of bling" on it. The teacher advised the principal and school police officer of the description, and the principal emailed teachers to be on the lookout for someone with this description. The principal and officer then walked through the hallways to locate the student with the gun. The suspect student happened to be in the first classroom checked by the officer and principal. The student admitted having a gun and was charged with three offenses. In juvenile proceedings, he moved to suppress the gun and his statements from the evidence, claiming the school officials had no reasonable suspicion for the search. After denying the motion, the court found the suspect student delinquent on all three counts.

The student then appealed to a Florida District Court of Appeal. On appeal, the court explained that **a search may be unreasonable under the circumstances if it is based on a "generalized description" of a suspect that could apply to a large number of innocent people** in the area. But in this case, the court found the description given by the younger student was very specific. He provided details about height, weight, race and skin tone, and he described the approximate age, haircut, clothing and decorations on his book bag. Moreover, the informant was not anonymous. The court found school officials acted reasonably given the grave danger posed by an armed student on campus and the relaxed constitutional standards for school searches. As a result, the judgment was affirmed. *R.M. v. State of Florida*, 129 So.3d 1157 (Fla. Dist. Ct. App. 2014).

◆   In conjunction with law enforcement officials, a Missouri school district permitted police dogs to sniff student lockers, desks, backpacks and other items that were not in a student's possession. School personnel decided a drug detection search was necessary to address a drug problem in district schools. Searches were held in all of the district's high schools. A student claimed he fully zipped his backpack when he and others were told to leave the classroom for the search. He later said he "felt like the pockets of his backpack had been unzipped and stuff." On this basis, his parents sued the school district, along with school and sheriff's officials in a federal court.

During pretrial activity, the court held for the district and officials, finding their written procedures were reasonable and did not deprive students of any federal rights. On appeal, the Eighth Circuit noted that the Fourth Amendment demands that a seizure of property be reasonable. What is reasonable depends upon the context. In the court's opinion, the student was not harmed by being briefly separated from his possessions. **A drug dog search was found "minimally intrusive," and the court had previously found them to be an effective means to form individualized suspicion** for further, more intrusive searches. In addition, the court found the district showed an immediate need for a drug dog search based on substantial evidence of a drug problem in the school district. As the lower court had found, the claims against the school officials repeated the claims against the school district and had been properly dismissed as redundant. *Burlison v. Springfield Public Schools*, 708 F.3d 1034 (8th Cir. 2013).

◆ A California student who was searched because he was in a school hallway without a hall pass avoided a juvenile court sentence because the campus aide who detained him could not articulate a reason for performing the search. The Court of Appeal of California held that under ordinary circumstances, a search of a student by a school official must be justified at its inception, reasonably related to the objectives of the search, and not excessively intrusive. In a prior case, *In re Lisa G.*, 125 Cal.App.4th 801 (Cal. Ct. App. 2004), the court of appeal held that disruptive behavior alone did not justify the search of a student. In that case, a teacher failed to articulate a reasonable suspicion of misconduct by a student that was sufficient to justify searching the student's purse. Similarly, in this case, the aide was unable to explain a reasonable suspicion that searching the student would reveal evidence of a crime or violation of a school rule. In the court's view, **"a suspicion that a student was tardy or truant from class, without more, provides no reasonable basis for conducting a search of any kind."** As a result, it found the evidence seized in this case was inadmissible and should have been suppressed. The judgment was reversed. *In re Diego C.*, No. B232230, 2011 WL 6740151 (Cal. Ct. App. 12/29/11).

◆ A California student attended a class, left campus, and then returned to school. An assistant principal learned the student had left and called him to the office. There, the student was asked to empty his pockets based on a school policy subjecting students to searches when they returned to campus after being "out-of-bounds." A plastic bag containing 44 ecstasy pills was found, and a state juvenile court petition was filed against the student for possession of a controlled substance. He sought to suppress the pills from evidence on the theory that the policy of searching all students who leave and return to campus during the day was unlawful. After the court held the school's policy was constitutional, the student admitted possessing a controlled substance and was placed on probation. On appeal, the California Court of Appeal held the state constitution recognized rights of students and staff to attend safe, secure and peaceful campuses. School officials do not investigate violations of criminal law and "must be permitted to exercise their broad supervisory and disciplinary powers, without worrying that every encounter with a student will be converted into an opportunity for constitutional review." The policy supported safe schools. The search was done without touching the student, who was only asked to empty his pockets. **As the court found the search consistent with the special need to keep a safe school environment, it found no constitutional violation.** *In re Sean A.*, 191 Cal.App.4th 182 (Cal. Ct. App. 2010).

♦   A Minnesota special education cooperative provided federal Setting IV programs for students with disabilities from six different school districts. Many of the students had serious behavior problems. Each of the programs required the searching of students daily upon arrival. A federal district court held the daily searches of disabled students at these segregated facilities violated the Fourth Amendment's prohibition on unreasonable searches and seizures. The court found the cooperative's programs were educational and not punitive in nature. This distinguished the case from *C.N.H. v. Florida*, 927 So.2d 1 (Fla. Dist. Ct. App. 2006), where a Florida district court of appeal approved of daily pat-down searches at an alternative school where students attended by court order and in lieu of confinement. In the Minnesota case, the students did not attend school in lieu of detention. **A policy of daily, suspicionless searches was unconstitutional under the circumstances.** A jury would have to decide whether daily searches over a course of years was "highly offensive" under state law principles. *Hough v. Shakopee Public Schools*, 608 F.Supp.2d 1087 (D. Minn. 2009).

♦   A Minnesota student wrote an essay "detailing a fantasy murder-suicide inspired by the school shooting that took place at Columbine High School." He placed the essay in his folder, and his teacher read it a few weeks later. After the teacher reported the disturbing and graphic content of the essay, a child protection worker obtained an order to place the student in protective custody. The student was taken to a youth mental health facility, where he underwent a psychiatric evaluation. He was found not a threat to himself or others, and he was released after a total of 72 hours in custody. The family sued the school district, teacher, principal, and county law enforcement and child protection officials in a federal court for constitutional rights violations. Claims against the school district, teacher and principal were dismissed, but the family proceeded with speech and Fourth Amendment claims against law enforcement and child protection officials. The case reached the U.S. Court of Appeals, Eighth Circuit, which held **the student's essay was unprotected by the First Amendment, which does not protect a "true threat."** The essay was a serious threat, describing the student's "obsession with weapons and gore, a hatred for his English teacher," an attack at a high school, details of his teacher's murder and the narrator's suicide. *Riehm v. Engelking*, 538 F.3d 952 (8th Cir. 2008).

E. State Supreme Court Cases

In *J.P. v. Millard Public Schools*, below, the Supreme Court of Nebraska held school officials could not lawfully conduct an off-campus search of a student's vehicle. It rejected the argument that driving to and from school created "a nexus to the school" that justified the search. For a search to be reasonable, the court held the district needed the authority to perform a search in the first place. A Pennsylvania court had reached this conclusion in *Comwlth. v. Williams*, 749 A.2d 957 (Pa. Super. Ct. 2000).

◆   After arriving at his school, a Nebraska student left the building to retrieve items from his truck, which he had parked on a street off campus. When the student returned, an assistant principal told him to empty his backpack and pockets. Finding no contraband, the assistant principal told the student he would search the truck. In an off-campus search, drug pipes, papers, cigarettes and lighters were found in the truck. After a hearing and administrative appeals, the student was suspended for 19 days. A state trial court held the school board violated the Fourth Amendment and improperly charged him under a student handbook provision by searching his truck, since it had been parked off campus.

Appeal reached the Supreme Court of Nebraska. Noting school districts only have the powers granted to them by the legislature, the court found the Nebraska Student Discipline Act was limited to conduct "on school property, in school vehicles, or at school-sponsored activities." The court found no right of school officials to conduct off-campus searches that were unrelated to school-sponsored activities. Although the school board argued that driving to school is a school-sponsored activity that has a "nexus" to the school, the court found this claim of authority was too broad. Instead, the court held school authority "was not intended to overlap the authority of law enforcement officers to enforce order on the public streets." **A school district did not have implied authority to conduct an off-campus search of a student's vehicle.** In this case, school officials had all the information they needed to impose school discipline when the student returned to the building. The court commented that if they suspected there was contraband in the truck, they should have notified law enforcement authorities. *J.P. v. Millard Public Schools*, 285 Neb. 890, 830 N.W.2d 453 (Neb. 2013).

◆   A North Dakota school resource officer learned about possible drug use by students a short distance from school, and a security guard was assigned to patrol the area. Two students evaded the guard, who returned to campus and told the resource officer he had "smelled something funny." When the officer followed the students in a patrol car, they walked away. The officer told the principal of their evasive behavior and said he suspected drug activity. The principal questioned one student. He emptied his pockets, which contained a pipe and synthetic marijuana. In criminal proceedings, a state court convicted the student of felony charges. On appeal, the state supreme court held the "reasonable suspicion" standard applies when school officials initiate a search or when police involvement is minimal. **The reasonable suspicion standard applied when a school resource officer acted on his or her own initiative or at the direction of other school officials to further educational goals.** The court found the relevant factors supported applying the reasonable suspicion standard in this case. The resource officer did not initiate the investigation. He notified the principal of his observations and let him decide how to handle the situation. The officer had only a small role the questioning and worked with and at the direction of the principal. Applying the "reasonableness standard," the court held the search was justified at its inception and not excessively intrusive. It upheld the student's conviction. *State v. Alaniz*, 815 N.W.2d 234 (N.D. 2012).

◆ A New Hampshire school parking lot monitor observed a student walking away from the school. Three school employees caught up with the student as he crossed a field about 200 yards from the building. He said he did not feel well. The employees persuaded him to return to school, where they searched him under a policy applying to any student who returned to school after leaving an assigned area. An assistant principal asked the student if he "had anything on him that he shouldn't have on school property." The student handed over a small bag of marijuana he had hidden inside a sock. In juvenile proceedings, a New Hampshire family court denied his motion to exclude the marijuana from evidence. On appeal, the Supreme Court of New Hampshire found no distinction between a "search" and the treatment of the student in this case. According to the court, **courts and schools are to consider a child's age, school record, the extent of the problem to which the search was directed, the exigencies at the time, the probative value and reliability of information justifying the search, and prior experiences with the student**. Consideration of these factors did not support the state's claim that the search was "justified at its inception." There was no record of a drug problem at the school, and no administrator had any prior disciplinary experiences with the student. Since the search was not justified at its inception, it was held unreasonable under the state constitution. *In re Anthony F.*, 163 N.H. 163, 37 A.3d 429 (N.H. 2012).

◆ A Connecticut school policy allowed police to make unannounced searches on school property with drug-sniffing dogs even without warrants or suspicion of any crime. The policy recited that its inclusion in the student and/or parent handbook was the only notice required to advertise searches. A high school student was arrested as a result of contraband found during a sweep conducted according to the policy. His parents filed a state court lawsuit against the school board. After a hearing, the court found a policy of warrantless and suspicionless drug-dog sweeps on school property without notice to parents did not violate any constitutional rights. It held **the use of drug-sniffing dogs was not a "search" under the Fourth Amendment**, since "students do not have a reasonable expectation of privacy in the odor or 'aroma' emanating from their unattended lockers" and vehicles. Arguing that the trial court should have reviewed the case under the state constitution, the parents appealed. But when the case reached the Supreme Court of Connecticut, they acknowledged their son had graduated from high school. Since he was no longer subject to the policy, **the case was held moot, and the appeal was dismissed**. *Burbank v. Board of Educ. of Town of Canton*, 299 Conn. 833, 11 A.3d 658 (Conn. 2011).

◆   An Oregon student was called to the office and told that an anonymous witness saw him trying to sell drugs. After speaking to his mother, the student agreed to turn his pockets inside out. Marijuana, plastic bags and a pipe were found, and he admitted he had tried to sell marijuana. In juvenile court proceedings, the student claimed any evidence seized by school officials should be excluded from trial because there was no probable cause for a search. Finding probable cause was unnecessary, the juvenile court held the search was lawful. It also concluded that the student was delinquent. Appeal reached the Supreme Court of Oregon. It discussed Article I, Section 9, of the Oregon Constitution, which prohibits unreasonable searches or seizures. The court held school searches are different from law enforcement searches. Only searches involving safety concerns justify a departure from the "warrant and probable cause" requirement. When school officials perceive an immediate threat to safety, they need the ability to take prompt, reasonable steps.

   School officials have wide latitude to take safety precautions when they have reasonable suspicion based on specific and articulable facts that an individual poses a threat to safety or possesses an item posing such a threat. "Reasonable suspicion" applies to searches for drugs on school property. Since officials reasonably suspected that the student had illegal drugs at the time of the search and that he intended to sell them at school, the judgment was affirmed. *State ex rel. Juvenile Dep't of Clackamas County v. M.A.D.*, 348 Or. 381, 233 P.3d 437 (Or. 2010).

◆   A New Jersey assistant principal (AP) received a report that a high school student was under the influence of drugs. After being taken to the AP's office and interviewed, the student denied any wrongdoing. A search of his pockets yielded three white capsules. The AP searched his car and denied his request to call home. The search yielded contraband, including a bag containing what appeared to be illegal drugs. A school resource officer arrested the student, who waived his right to remain silent and admitted that the contraband was his. In juvenile court proceedings, he moved to suppress evidence seized from his car as a violation of his right to be free from unreasonable searches and seizures. Based on a finding that the AP's search of the car was reasonably related to a suspicion that the student had drugs and posed a danger to the school, the trial court denied the student's motion.

   Appeal reached the Supreme Court of New Jersey, which explained that under *New Jersey v. T.L.O.*, this chapter, the school setting required some easing of police search standards in view of the need to maintain school discipline and safety. The court found no reason to avoid the *T.L.O.* standard in vehicle cases, as "the school setting calls for protections geared toward the safety of students." **The court was not convinced by the student's claim to a greater expectation of privacy in his car than he might have in a locker or purse.** A "reasonable grounds" standard applied to the search of a student's car on school property by school authorities. Based on a classmate's statements, the student's apparent drug use, his statements and his possession of pills, it was reasonable for the AP to extend the search to the student's car. As a result, the court affirmed the judgment. *State v. Best*, 201 N.J. 100, 987 A.2d 605 (N.J. 2010).

◆   An Arkansas teacher confiscated a student's cell phone as he was using it in violation of a school rule. Although his parents demanded the return of the phone, it remained in the school office for two weeks, as required by a district policy. It was then returned, but the family sued the teacher and principal in a state court for trespass and taking property without due process of law. The court held for the district, and appeal reached the Supreme Court of Arkansas. On appeal, the parents claimed the Arkansas Code did not authorize the confiscation. The court explained that the section pertained only to the suspension or dismissal of students from public schools. **State law declared that school policies were to "prescribe minimum and maximum penalties, including students' suspension or dismissal from school."** Arkansas school boards have broad discretion to direct school operations, and "courts have no power to interfere with such boards in the exercise of that discretion unless there is a clear abuse of it." The court refused to interfere with the board's decision about the best way to enforce its policy. The family did not cite any authority defining a property right to have a cell phone at school. As a result, the judgment for school officials was affirmed. *Koch v. Adams*, 361 S.W.3d 817 (Ark. 2010).

F. Police Participation and *Miranda* Warnings

The Fifth Amendment prevents any person from being compelled to testify against him or herself in a criminal case. In *Miranda v. Arizona*, 384 U.S. 436 (1966), the U.S. Supreme Court announced the now familiar constitutional rights advisory known as the "Miranda" warning.

Under *Miranda*, a criminal suspect who is in police custody "must be warned that he has a right to remain silent, that any statement he does make may be used as evidence against him, and that he has a right to the presence of an attorney, either retained or appointed." Police must advise criminal suspects of their rights whenever there is a "custodial interrogation."

When police take a student into custody for questioning, the student must be advised of his or her Fifth and Sixth Amendment rights. However, courts have disagreed on what standard to apply to questioning done by school police. The Supreme Court of Pennsylvania has held school police officers are to be considered the same as municipal police. But courts in Texas, Rhode Island, New Jersey, Massachusetts, Florida and California have held school officials need not issue *Miranda* warnings when questioning students about rules violations.

In *Chavez v. Martinez*, 538 U.S. 760 (2003), the Supreme Court held courts cannot award damages against police investigators who wrongly induce suspects to provide incriminating information unless it is actually used in a criminal prosecution. Until compelled statements are used in a criminal case, there is no potential violation of the Fifth Amendment.

◆ An 11-year-old California student with disabilities forgot to take his attention deficit hyperactivity disorder medication. He had a "difficult day," and spent time in a "cool down" area designated in his Section 504 plan. Later, the student was unresponsive on the playground. A teacher went out to talk with him. When doing so, she recalled that when he was in grade four, he had run away from a class into the school parking lot. The student then told a staff member he wanted to go out into traffic and kill himself. Although the teacher invited the student to come back to her office, he did not respond. Recalling the prior incident, the teacher was concerned about the possibility that he would run from school grounds. After failing to persuade the student to return to the building, the teacher called the police.

The officers talked to the student, but he remained unresponsive. They handcuffed him, checking the cuffs to assure they were not too tight. After finding the student's guardian contact information, the police called his uncle to pick him up. As the uncle could not close his business, the officers brought the student there. In a federal district court action against the officers and their municipal employer, the student's parent alleged federal civil rights violations. When the case reached the U.S. Court of Appeals, Ninth Circuit, it found the district court judge had given the jury misleading instructions and then made attempts at clarification that were also potentially misleading. As a result, the court found there had to be a new trial. But **the Ninth Circuit found no clearly established law holding that police violate the Fourth Amendment by transporting a disruptive child from school** to a relative's home or business. When the case returned to the lower court, the officers would enjoy qualified immunity from the student's federal claims. *C.B. v. City of Sonora*, 730 F.3d 816 (9th Cir. 2013).

◆ A New Mexico seventh-grader was caught texting in a class. Her teacher told her to stop texting and turn over her phone as required by a school policy, but she refused to do so. An administrator brought the student to the office, where she ignored requests to give up her phone. The school resource officer (SRO) called for assistance, but the student continued to ignore requests to relinquish her phone. The SRO explained that she was also violating state law by texting in class and refusing to turn over her phone. Although the SRO told the student he would not arrest her if she agreed to give up her phone, she ignored this request. He then arrested and handcuffed her and brought her to a juvenile detention center. In a federal court, the student's parent sued the SRO and school district for civil rights violations.

During pretrial activity, the district moved for an order granting the SRO qualified immunity from any liability. The court explained that qualified immunity protects government officials "who are required to exercise their discretion by shielding them from liability for harm caused by reasonable mistakes." To show a Fourth Amendment violation, the student had to show a violation of a constitutional right that was clearly established at the time of the conduct. The court found her conduct was not clearly outside the conduct prohibited by a state law criminalizing acts that disrupted, impaired, interfered with, or obstructed school functions. Her refusal to follow instructions required the teacher to stop class and seek help. **The court found that "handcuffing is appropriate in nearly every situation where an arrest is authorized."** In any event, the court found the use of force was minimal. According to the student, the taking of her cell phone was an unlawful search. But the court held removing a cell phone that visibly protruded from a pocket was not unconstitutional under established law. Since nothing showed the SRO lacked probable cause to arrest the student, violated state law or used excessive force, the court held he was entitled to qualified immunity. *G.M. v. Casalduc*, 982 F.Supp.2d 1235 (D.N.M. 2013).

◆   A Delaware school resource officer (SRO) interrogated an eight-year-old student in a room with a classmate who was accused of bullying. The SRO used the student to elicit a confession of school misconduct from the classmate. The SRO carried a gun, handcuffs and other police equipment. After the incident, the student's parents sued the SRO and other officials. When the case reached the Supreme Court of Delaware, it held the Fourth Amendment was implicated because a reasonable eight-year-old in the student's position would not have felt free to leave the room. This was a "seizure" for Fourth Amendment purposes. Next, the court noted the SRO had said he was 99% sure the student was not involved in the reported bullying incident. He did not contact the student's mother or any school official for permission to question the student. The court found the SRO's reason for questioning was suspect. It was reasonable to infer that the SRO brought the student to the interview room to compel the bully's confession.

According to the court, **the fact that the SRO "shamed" the bully into confessing supported a finding that his seizure of the student was unreasonable**. There was evidence that the student was so upset that he could not return to school for the rest of the year. For this reason, the court held he could proceed with a claim for infliction of emotional distress. His false arrest claim was also viable. On the other hand, the court found no merit to a claim for battery. It returned the case to the lower court for further review of the Fourth Amendment, infliction of emotional distress and false imprisonment claims. *Hunt v. State of Delaware*, 69 A.3d 360 (Del. 2013).

◆   A Washington school resource officer arrested a student after he observed him with a bag of marijuana. The dean of students "took a passive role" during the arrest. As they waited for a patrol car, the officer noticed the student's backpack was padlocked. When the student refused to give him the key, the officer handcuffed and searched him. He found the key to the padlock, opened the backpack, and found a BB pistol inside. In juvenile court proceedings, the BB gun was used as evidence, and the student was convicted of carrying a gun and possessing marijuana at school. In ruling for the state, the juvenile court relied on the "reasonable suspicion" test from *New Jersey v. T.L.O.*, this chapter. On appeal, the Supreme Court of Washington found educators have a substantial interest in maintaining discipline that often requires swift action. At the time of the backpack search, the officer had already handcuffed the student. Because the student was under his control, there was no need for swift action. **There is a fundamental difference between a resource officer and a school administrator, based on the objectives of their searches.** As the officer's search did not further any educational goals, and he had already arrested and handcuffed the student, the court found no reason to apply *T.L.O.* Due to overwhelming indicia of police action, the court held the officer needed a warrant to search the backpack. Finding the search was unlawful, the court held the BB gun could not be used as evidence. *State v. Jamar Billy DeShawn Meneese*, 174 Wash.2d 937, 282 P.3d 83 (Wash. 2012).

◆ A uniformed school resource officer removed a 13-year-old North Carolina seventh-grader from class to question him about break-ins in his neighborhood. A police investigator, an assistant principal and a school intern were also present. Neither the officers nor any school administrators called the student's guardian prior to questioning the student, and nobody told him he was free to leave the room. After the student denied any wrongdoing, an assistant principal urged him to "do the right thing." The resource officer told the student "this thing is going to court," and threatened him with juvenile detention. The student then admitted he had committed the crimes. Only then did the officer inform him he could refuse to answer the questions and that he was free to leave the room. After offering further details, the student wrote a statement at the officer's request. After juvenile petitions were filed against the student, his public defender moved to exclude the statements and evidence obtained from the school interview. Finding the student was not "in custody" of the police at the time of the interrogation, the juvenile court found him delinquent.

Appeal reached the U.S. Supreme Court, which held that a duty to issue a *Miranda* warning arises if there has been such a restriction on a person's freedom as to render him or her in police "custody." Whether a suspect is in custody depends on the circumstances, and whether a reasonable person would feel at liberty to end the questioning and leave. According to the Supreme Court, a child's age and the school setting were relevant to the *Miranda* analysis. If the age of a child suspect was known to the officer at the time of questioning, or would have been objectively apparent to a reasonable officer, the Court held **consideration of age was consistent with the *Miranda* custody analysis.** The Court reversed the judgment and returned the case to a state court to determine if the student was in police custody at the time of the in-school police interrogation. *J.D.B. v. North Carolina*, 131 S.Ct. 2394, 180 L.Ed.2d 310 (U.S. 2011).

◆   An Oregon state child protective services worker and a deputy sheriff interviewed an elementary student at her school. They did so without a warrant or the consent of her parents, based on suspicion that her father had sexually abused her. At some point, the student said she had been abused, and her father was charged criminally. But a jury failed to reach a verdict, and the charges were dismissed. Years later, the student's mother sued the social worker and deputy sheriff in a federal court for failing to obtain a warrant in violation of the Fourth Amendment. The court held the officials violated the Constitution, but granted their request for qualified immunity, finding Fourth Amendment law on the issue was not clearly established.

Appeal reached the U.S. Supreme Court. It held **public officials had a right to appeal decisions that found their conduct violated the Constitution**, even if they were entitled to immunity and would not have to pay monetary damages. An official who was entitled to immunity still had an interest in appealing from an adverse decision in order to "gain clearance to engage in the conduct in the future." So the Court rejected the claim that the employees lacked standing. Fear of constitutional liability should not unduly inhibit officials in the discharge of their duties. But the student was now nearly 18 and had moved to Florida. As she would never again be interviewed by Oregon child protection officials, the Court held the case was moot. *Camreta v. Greene*, 131 S.Ct. 2020, 179 L.Ed.2d 1118 (U.S. 2011).

◆   An anonymous informant told Wisconsin school officials that a student had drugs at school. He consented to the search of his person, book bag and locker by a school liaison officer and a municipal police officer. When no drugs were found, an assistant principal searched the student's car and found marijuana, a pipe, Oxycontin and cash. She turned over these items to the police, who arrested the student and took him to the police station, where he received his criminal rights warnings, known as "*Miranda* rights." Prior to trial, the student sought to exclude evidence seized from his car and any statements he made during the investigation. He claimed he was "in custody" of the police at the time he was questioned in the parking lot. If this was the case, it was necessary to read him his *Miranda* rights at that time. The court denied the student's motions to suppress his statements and the evidence seized from his car. On appeal, the Court of Appeals of Wisconsin found *Miranda* **warnings are only required when a person is in police "custody."** Whether a person is in custody depends upon the circumstances. Formal arrest, restraint on freedom of movement, or interrogation that is likely to elicit an incriminating response are examples of "custody" for *Miranda* purposes. Here, while the student was "escorted" to his car by police, an assistant principal was still in control of the investigation, including the search of the car. As a reasonable person would not have considered himself to be in "custody" at the time, the student was not entitled to have his *Miranda* rights read to him in the parking lot. The court also found the search was reasonable under the circumstances. *State of Wisconsin v. Schloegel*, 769 N.W.2d 130 (Wis. Ct. App. 2009).

◆   A Tennessee student told a school resource officer that marijuana found in his truck belonged to him. As they returned to the school building, the student also admitted he had left school to smoke marijuana with a friend that morning. The resource officer took the student to juvenile court and charged him. The student later moved to suppress his statements on grounds that she did not inform him of his *Miranda* rights prior to questioning. The juvenile court denied the student's motion, finding the student was not in police custody at the time. On appeal, **the Supreme Court of Tennessee held that the student was not confined for questioning, and he was not in police "custody."** Thus, his incriminating statements had been properly admitted into evidence. However, since *New Jersey v. T.L.O.* was decided, there has been an increased presence of law enforcement officers in public schools. Municipalities have "blended" the traditional duties of school officials and law officers to protect the safety of students and teachers. Based on the resource officer's duties, a new trial would be held to find whether the search required probable cause or reasonable suspicion. *R.D.S. v. State of Tennessee*, 245 S.W.3d 356 (Tenn. 2008).

◆   A Boston middle school student showed a clear plastic bag containing over 50 bullets to other students. The school resource officer confiscated the bullets, and later conducted a pat-down search that yielded no further evidence. The officer then read the student his *Miranda* warnings and asked him to disclose the location of his gun. The student said he did not have a gun. His mother and grandmother arrived at school, and the officer continued questioning the student without informing the adults of the student's *Miranda* rights. After an expulsion hearing, the student led the officer to the gun. In juvenile delinquency proceedings, the judge found the resource officer had unlawfully failed to provide the student *Miranda* warnings in the presence of an interested adult, as required by state law.

The case reached the Supreme Judicial Court of Massachusetts, which noted that the juvenile court judge refused to apply the "limited public safety exception" to *Miranda* from *New York v. Quarles,* 467 U.S. 649 (1984). **Juvenile suspects under 14 may not waive their *Miranda* rights in the absence of an interested adult, such as a parent.** But the resource officer here was faced with an emergency situation that required him to protect 890 middle school students as well as area residents. Under the circumstances, he reasonably concluded that there was an immediate need to question the student. Possession of 50 bullets supported an inference that a gun was close by. Accordingly, the court reversed the juvenile court order. *Comwlth. v. Dillon D.*, 448 Mass. 793, 863 N.E.2d 1287 (Mass. 2007).

II. DISCIPLINE FOR DRUGS, WEAPONS AND ALCOHOL

A. Weapons Possession

This section considers recent case law on student discipline for school code violations and crimes. For new student discipline forms, please see Chapter Nine of this volume. See especially: Form IV-1: Sample Parent Letter Following Weapons Incident; and Form IV-2: Student Knife Contract.

◆   A Michigan high school freshman had conflicts with a classmate. On a school day, she tweeted "stab stab stab. Going to stab stab stab you today to see your insides, ya ya ya." The classmate told an assistant vice principal (AVP) about the tweets. After investigating, the AVP obtained a written statement from another student who said the student had told her she planned to stab the classmate with a knife she had in a binder. The AVP called the student's mother. The next day, the AVP met with the student and her family. She told them of the charges without revealing the statements. The AVP suspended the student, and the board later met to consider expulsion. The student requested a closed session where she answered the board's questions and submitted a statement from her psychologist. The board then voted for expulsion. The student sued the school district, board members and school administrators in a federal court. The court held for the district and officials, and the student appealed to the U.S. Court of Appeals, Sixth Circuit. According to the parent, the suspension exceeded 10 days because the AVP suspended her daughter during their phone conversation.

The court found that even if the AVP had suspended the student by phone, there was no due process violation. **Students who are a continuing danger may be immediately removed from school.** The court found there had been no due process violation, regardless of whether the student had received witness statements. She received an adequate explanation of their contents to prepare her defense. All told, the student had received three opportunities to tell her story, hear the charges against her and present evidence. Rejecting all her other arguments, the court held for the school district. *C.Y. v. Lakeview Public Schools*, 557 Fed.Appx. 426 (6th Cir. 2014).

◆   A 14-year-old California charter school student with attention deficit hyperactivity disorder (ADHD) brought a knife to his charter school and threatened others with it. He was dismissed from the school. In a state superior court, the student sought a special order (called a writ) declaring that the board did not provide him with a hearing as required by state Code of Civil Procedure Section 1094.5. He also said his knife did not meet applicable state education code definitions. The court denied the student's petition, finding the dismissal was proper based on his conduct. On appeal, the Court of Appeal of California rejected an argument that the knife was too short to meet a definition under state Education Code Section 48915.

According to the student, a "knife" had to meet each of the various descriptions in Section 48915. In the court's opinion, the characteristics described in Section 48915 were listed in the alternative. Proof of the court's interpretation could be found in the listing of both folding and fixed blades in the law. As the knife met Section 48915 definitions, the court held the student could not rely on the section to claim he was not in possession of a knife. Next, the court rejected the student's argument that the board order had to be set aside since it did not include any findings. Significantly, the court held the student was not entitled to an evidentiary hearing. There was a difference between a dismissal by a charter school and an expulsion under the education code. As charter schools were generally exempt from the laws governing school districts, **the court held state Education Code Section 48918 hearing requirements were inapplicable**. A charter school dismissal did not implicate the same concerns as a public school expulsion. A dismissed charter school student could immediately enroll in another school. In fact, a letter to the parent from the charter school had advised her to enroll him in another school and had attached his transcripts to facilitate this effort. As the student was not entitled to a hearing, the court affirmed the judgment. *Scott B. v. Board of Trustees of Orange County High School of Arts*, 217 Cal.App.4th 117, 158 Cal.Rptr.3d 173 (Cal. Ct. App. 2013).

◆ Illinois high school administrators received a bomb threat that later proved false. After an investigation, a student admitted that a friend had asked him to write the threatening note. Administrators suspended him for 10 days. At an expulsion hearing, the school relied on statements from other students that had been obtained by the principal during her investigation. As a result, the only testimony supporting the expulsion was hearsay. Over objection by the student's attorney, the board admitted the statements and expelled the student from school and school activities for two calendar years. The student's parent sued the school district and several officials for due process violations. A federal court held that to satisfy the Due Process Clause of the Fourteenth Amendment, **"the expulsion procedure must provide the student with a meaningful opportunity to be heard."** Expulsion procedures need not resemble a trial, as students need only have notice of the charges, the time of the hearing, and a full opportunity to be heard. In this case, the student was notified of the charges and informed of the time of his hearing. He did not present any witnesses and did not ask that any students attend. Under the circumstances, there was no due process violation. *Werner v. Board of Educ. of Pope County Community Unit School Dist. No. 1*, No. 11-cv-1095-JPG, 2012 WL 3562619 (S.D. Ill. 8/16/12).

◆ A Wisconsin student who was expelled for bringing a knife to school continued to use a weight room at the school and pick up friends in his car. A teacher saw him in the weight room and told him to leave. The student became confrontational, swore and punched a locker. School officials notified him that he could no longer enter school property. When the student later drove onto school grounds, a police officer cited him for trespassing. In a federal court, he asserted constitutional rights violations, including interference with his right to travel. The court held the student had no right to enter school property. On appeal to the U.S. Court of Appeals, Seventh Circuit, the student claimed the district violated his due process rights by banning him from school property without notice and an opportunity to be heard. But the court noted that when the ban was enacted, he was attending a private school. **A former student could be constitutionally banned from school property as a "non-student" without notice or a hearing.** The ban was indefinite and not permanent. In the court's view, a school district had discretion to bar members of the public from school property. The student was only a member of the general public without constitutional rights to access school property. As there was no violation of his right to intrastate travel, the court held for the district and officials. *Hannemann v. Southern Door County School Dist.*, 673 F.3d 746 (7th Cir. 2012).

◆ A South Dakota student fought with another student and brought a knife to school. An IEP team found his misconduct was not a manifestation of his learning disability. After missing four days of school, he was placed in an alternative educational setting. His grandmother asked for a board hearing but was told that was not possible because the student was no longer suspended. In his alternative placement, he received two hours of instruction four days a week instead of his usual 30 hours per week. An IDEA action was filed, which reached the U.S. Court of Appeals, Eighth Circuit.

In the court's view, the student had been suspended for four days. The assistant principal had explained the charges and given the student an opportunity to respond. **As suspensions of 10 days or less trigger only minimal due process protection, due process had been satisfied.** The IEP team could have placed the student in an interim alternative educational setting if it had chosen. A federal law provision allows an individualized education program (IEP) team to unilaterally remove a student to an interim alternative educational setting for up to 45 school days without holding a manifestation hearing based on weapons possession. The provision, found at 20 U.S.C. § 1415(k), also applies to the sale, use or possession of drugs at school, and to cases involving infliction of serious bodily injury while at school, on school grounds, or at a school event. The team could also place him in an alternative educational setting with parental consent. This is what occurred, as the grandmother agreed to the change. Federal law stated that IEP teams determine any interim alternative educational placement. Once the IEP team changed the student's placement with the grandmother's consent, the team, not the school board, "became the decision-maker authorized to change his placement" under 34 C.F.R. Part 300.530(d)(5). As the school district did not violate the student's rights, the judgment was reversed. *Doe v. Todd County School Dist.*, 625 F.3d 459 (8th Cir. 2010).

◆ After a Mississippi student reportedly sold drugs on campus, the school principal searched his backpack and found an item described as either a nail file or a knife. A school district appeals committee voted to expel the student after a hearing, and the school board later met to review the case. At his hearing, the student was permitted to argue that the item was a nail file. But since the item was unavailable for inspection, the board assigned to the superintendent the decision of determining whether it was a prohibited item. He decided it was a knife. The board upheld the expulsion, and the student was placed in an alternative school. Within weeks, he was accused of possessing marijuana. Another appeals committee accepted an expulsion recommendation and the student filed a lawsuit. A state chancery court reversed the board's decision, finding the expulsion was arbitrary and capricious, unsupported by substantial evidence and in violation of the student's due process rights. The student appealed, and the Supreme Court of Mississippi found a reasonable basis for the board to find that the item was a knife and not a nail file. The Mississippi Code did not require the school board to physically examine the weapon. **As the student was permitted to speak on his own behalf before the appeals committee, due process was satisfied.** The court reinstated the board's decision. *Hinds County School Dist. Board of Trustees v. D.L.B.*, 10 So.3d 387 (Miss. 2008).

◆ A Missouri high school student brought toy guns to school twice. The school superintendent issued an immediate 10-day suspension for the incidents, finding the student in possession of a "weapon" which he had used on school property. The school board voted in a closed session to exclude the student from school for one year. The student was provided a hearing where he was represented by an attorney, allowed to present evidence and to call and cross-examine witnesses. The board voted to uphold the 180-day suspension. The student appealed, arguing that the school handbook definition of "weapon" did not include toys and other look-alike items. On appeal, the Court of Appeals of Missouri found that superintendents may modify expulsion requirements on a case-by-case basis to comply with requirements of federal laws. The school board had adopted a weapons guide separate from the student handbook several years earlier. **The guide's definition of "weapon" included any object designed to look like or imitate a dangerous weapon.** While the guidelines were not personally handed to each student or parent, they were accessible through a district website and upon request. The guidelines were properly applied to the student. The toy guns were "dangerous instruments" that could cause an eye injury. The court upheld the suspension. *Moore v. Appleton City R-II School Dist.*, 232 S.W.3d 642 (Mo. Ct. App. 2007).

◆ A Pennsylvania student fired a soft pellet gun at his girlfriend from his car. He was suspended with a recommendation for a one-year expulsion. The superintendent agreed to modify an expulsion recommendation with several conditions, including 50 hours of community service, counseling, and compliance with behavior and academic requirements. The school board voted two weeks later in an open session to ratify the reduced sanctions. The student appealed, arguing that a soft pellet gun was not a "weapon" and that the shooting of a toy gun at a student was not a terroristic threat. He also claimed that the board violated the state Sunshine Act by taking official action in private. The Commonwealth Court of Pennsylvania noted that the state Public School Code defined "weapons" to include knives, guns and "any other tool, instrument or implement capable of inflicting serious bodily injury." Another court had applied the definition of "weapon" from the state Crimes Code to a student using a carbon dioxide-powered paintball. A pellet gun, like a paintball gun, could inflict serious injury to an eye. It was permissible to find it was a "weapon" under the code. **Even if the board had violated the Sunshine Act, its later vote in open session to modify the expulsion cured any violation.** *Picone v. Bangor Area School Dist.*, 936 A.2d 556 (Pa. Commw. Ct. 2007).

◆   A New York school board suspended a student for possessing a handgun off campus after learning he had talked about the gun while in the school cafeteria. The police decided to lock down the school, and the guns were found off school grounds. The student was suspended for the rest of the school year. The state education commissioner affirmed the suspension, but a state court vacated the discipline. The student sued the board and hearing officer in a federal district court for civil rights violations. The court dismissed the student's due process claim, since he already had received notice and a hearing to consider his suspension. This was all the process to which he was entitled under state law. The state court had vacated the discipline, curing any procedural defects. The court held that talking with students about handguns was a material and substantial disruption of the educational process. The suspension did not violate the student's due process rights. The court agreed with the board that public school students may be disciplined for conduct off school grounds. **It was within the board's discretion to punish conduct "outside the school situation, so long as there exists a nexus between the behavior and the school."**
The court refused to dismiss the student's speech rights claim. He raised a valid equal protection claim by asserting the other students implicated in the conversation were only suspended for three weeks, while he was suspended for the rest of the school year. The court refused to dismiss the equal protection claims against the board and hearing officer, and held they were not entitled to qualified immunity. The Second Circuit affirmed the decision in a brief memorandum. *Cohn v. New Paltz Cent. School Dist.*, 171 Fed.Appx. 877 (2d Cir. 2006).

B. Possession of Drugs and Alcohol

◆   A Massachusetts high school principal claimed a student was somehow involved in an on-campus marijuana sale. He did not disclose the informants to the student's parent. Claiming he had "direct evidence," the principal advised the father he "had no choice" but immediate expulsion. At a hearing, the student did not answer questions, and the superintendent did not present any witnesses or other evidence. She later upheld the expulsion.

In a state court action against the superintendent, a judge proposed allowing the student to return to school conditionally, with random drug testing at the family's expense and other conditions including completion of homework. He also required that the student eat together with his family at least three times per week. On appeal, the Supreme Judicial Court of Massachusetts held **the judge did not consider the proper standards for preliminary relief**. He failed to evaluate the facts and did not analyze the student's likelihood of success on his constitutional challenge. As the judge did not evaluate the superintendent's decision and had fashioned his own remedy, the preliminary order was vacated, and the case was returned to the trial court for reconsideration before a new judge. *Doe v. Superintendent of Schools of Weston*, 461 Mass. 159, 959 N.E.2d 403 (Mass. 2011).

When the case returned to the trial court, it held for the school system. **A state appeals court then held the student had no viable due process claims.** He did not contest statements by a school nurse and other students, and his silence justified a negative inference. After the court upheld the expulsion, the supreme judicial court refused to hear another appeal in the case. *Doe v. Superintendent of Schools of Weston*, 467 Mass. 1103, 3 N.E.3d 81 (Table) (Mass. appeal denied 1/14/14).

◆ An Ohio school resource officer reported drug activity at school that implicated a student. A search of the student's locker revealed nothing. The assistant principal (AP) questioned the student and she admitted she had received marijuana from another student at school. The AP notified the student of the school's intent to suspend her for a drug offense and general misconduct. When the student was interviewed, she was not accompanied by a counselor, teacher, parent or other individual, as required by a school handbook provision for questioning by school officials or staff "as part of a police investigation." A hearing was then held and she was notified that she was expelled for the remaining 55 days of the school year. Claiming that the lack of a representative during questioning was a due process violation, the student appealed to a state court. It noted that the assistant principal knew of a companion police investigation when he interviewed the student. As a result, the court agreed with the student that she had been denied her right to be accompanied during her interview as stated in the student handbook.

On appeal, the Court of Appeals of Ohio found the student was notified of the school's intention to suspend her and was provided with the reasons for this. When meeting with the AP, the student was provided with the constitutional minimum notice and opportunity to challenge the reasons for her suspension. It was clear to the court that the school had met the constitutional and statutory minimums for due process. In addition, the court found no violation of the handbook provision. **Although a school resource officer had turned over evidence to municipal police, the court found this did not convert the assistant principal's questioning into an interrogation done "as part of a police investigation."** As the handbook provision did not apply to the questioning in this case, the court held for the board of education. *Sellars v. Dublin City School Dist. Board of Educ.*, No. 12AP-1007, 2013 -Ohio- 3367 (Ohio Ct. App. 8/1/13).

◆   A New Jersey board of education approved a rule permitting revocation of student extracurricular participation rights based on off-campus misconduct. The rule encouraged students to maintain good grades and abide by all school rules. Extracurricular activities participants were required to refrain from using, possessing or distributing any alcoholic beverage or drugs both on and off school grounds during the season or activity in which the students participated. A student objected to the rule and filed a petition with the state commissioner of education to invalidate it. Appeal reached the New Jersey Superior Court, Appellate Division.

   The court found a board's authority to regulate off-campus student conduct is carefully circumscribed by state regulations. Section 6:A:16-7.6 of the state code permitted the discipline of students for off-campus conduct only when reasonably necessary for the safety, security and well-being of students and staff. To be subject to regulation, the off-campus conduct at issue has to materially and substantially interfere with the requirements of appropriate discipline in the operation of the school. The board's regulation exceeded its authority by encompassing too many potential conduct violations that did not meet the requirements of Section 6A:16-7.6. While the board cited the state's Anti-Bullying Bill of Rights Act as evidence of a legislative intent to allow school districts to regulate off-campus conduct, the court disagreed. **In defining harassment, intimidation or bullying, the act reaffirmed the requirement that there be a connection between the misconduct and school activities.** The court held for the student. *G.D.M. v. Board of Educ. of Ramapo Indian Hills Regional High School Dist.*, 427 N.J.Super. 246, 48 A.3d 378 (N.J. Super. Ct. App. Div. 2012).

◆   A whiskey bottle fell out of a Louisiana student's backpack and broke on the floor of his classroom. He told a disciplinary administrator he did not know the bottle was in his backpack and later gave the same account to the police. After the student was arrested for under-age alcohol possession, the school's student council president reported to the school that the whiskey bottle belonged to him and that he had put it in the student's backpack without telling him. The disciplinary administrator did not share this information with other school officials. After the student met informally with administrators, an expulsion and alternative placement for five months was recommended. At a hearing, the student called the student council president to give his account. A board member doubted this account, and the board voted 9-2 to expel the student. Instead of going to the alternative school assignment, he elected to obtain a GED. He sued the board in a state court for tort liability. The court found the disciplinary administrator's failure to tell other school officials the student council president's story tainted the disciplinary process. It held the board had a duty to ensure the correct application of its own policies, and it awarded the student $50,000.

On appeal to the Supreme Court of Louisiana, the board argued that, regardless of what administrators did, the board never deprived the student of due process. He received a hearing and was allowed to present evidence and argue on his own behalf. **While administrators did not properly review the evidence, the court found the student was not denied due process at the board hearing**, where his version of the facts was rejected. As the court held he did not show the board violated his due process rights, the judgment was reversed. *Christy v. McCalla*, 79 So.3d 293 (5th Cir. 2011).

◆ Texas school officials found a small amount of alcohol in a vehicle parked on school property. Under the school district's zero-tolerance policy, the student who had driven the vehicle to school had to be placed in an alternative school. After several hearings, an alternative school assignment was upheld. According to the district superintendent, the student would have been allowed to avoid the placement had he presented evidence to support his claim that he did not know there was any alcohol in his vehicle.

The student sued the school district and officials in a state court for due process violations. The case reached the Court of Appeals of Texas. It held the student did not show the zero-tolerance policy was unconstitutional as it was applied to him. It noted that zero-tolerance policies "have promoted consistency over rationality." Strict adherence to a zero-tolerance policy, without consideration of a student's state of mind, "would appear to run afoul of substantive due process notions." But **there was no due process violation in this case, because the superintendent offered the student a chance to show he did not know about the alcohol**. As the district provided him "an escape mechanism in lieu of strict application of the zero-tolerance policy," his challenge failed. *Hinterlong v. Arlington Independent School Dist.*, No. 2-09-050-CV, 2010 WL 522641 (Tex. Ct. App. 2/11/10).

◆ Several people told a Florida middle school principal that a student had been drinking alcohol with a friend at home the day before. Upon interviewing the student, the principal learned that the two girls drank alcohol before school. A sibling of the student had then taken them to school. A child study committee met and found the student was under the influence of alcohol at school. After a hearing, the school board expelled the student for substantially disrupting the orderly conduct of the school and for gross misconduct in violation of a school policy against drinking alcohol. On appeal, a Florida District Court of Appeal found **Florida law and the school's own policy limited the board's power to punish students to conduct occurring on school grounds or during school-provided transportation**. In this case, the consumption of alcohol occurred at the student's residence about 45 minutes before school began. As she argued, the board could not punish her for drinking alcohol at home.

There was no evidence that the student was under the influence of alcohol at school or that she behaved in an impaired manner. Since the court found no evidence that the student disrupted the learning environment despite her ingestion of alcohol, she could not be expelled under the school policy. As a result, the court vacated the school board's decision. *A.B.E. v. School Board of Brevard County*, 33 So.3d 795 (Fla. Dist. Ct. App. 2010).

◆   Alabama high school staff members noticed a student smelled of alcohol at a school prom. A Breathalyzer test showed his blood-alcohol level was between .001 and .006. A disciplinary committee held a hearing and found no evidence of alcohol possession at the prom. The student was also not "under the influence of alcohol to the extent that he would have been guilty of ... criminal offenses." Based on findings that he drank alcohol on the day of the prom, the board suspended him and sent him to an alternative school. The reason stated was being under the influence of alcohol at the prom in violation of a school handbook provision. In a juvenile court hearing, the court found the term "use" from the school policy meant "to ingest alcohol while on school property or at any other school function." As there was no evidence that the student had "used" alcohol on school property or at a school function, the court held he did not violate the policy. Appeal reached the Court of Civil Appeals of Alabama.

A 1985 state supreme court case held "a board of education must comply with the policies it adopts." **Rules governing student conduct had to be sufficiently definite to provide them reasonable notice that they must conform their conduct to the expected requirements.** In this case, the school had applied a student handbook provision to students who used alcohol shortly before going to the prom. A policy that did not notify the student of possible consequences for arriving at the prom after drinking alcohol deprived him of due process. The court affirmed the juvenile court's decision reinstating him to school. *Monroe County Board of Educ. v. K.B.*, 62 So.3d 513 (Ala. Civ. Ct. App. 2010).

◆   A Kentucky high school received a bomb threat. A private company under contract with the district to provide canine detection services found no explosives, but a dog alerted to a car parked in the school parking lot. The principal called the student from his class but did not accompany him to the parking lot, despite a board policy requiring principals or their designees to be present when any student search was conducted. A dog handler went with the student to the car and found marijuana inside it. The student was suspended pending an expulsion hearing, then expelled by the board. When the student sued the school board, the case reached the Court of Appeals of Kentucky. It found that the board's policy mandated that the school principal or designee be present during any student search. **Because the evidence for the expulsion was obtained in violation of the board's own policy, the decision to expel the student was arbitrarily based on incompetent evidence.** The board had to comply with its own policy. Since the only evidence used against the student was inadmissible, the expulsion was in error. *M.K.J. v. Bourbon County Board of Educ.*, No.2003-CA-0003520MN, 2004 WL 1948461 (Ky. Ct. App. 2004).

C. Employees

◆ A New York school bus driver tested positive for marijuana. She had no prior violations in 10 years with her school district. In disregard of a collective bargaining agreement (CBA) provision calling for progressive discipline, the school board decided to fire the driver. In an arbitration matter, the arbitrator found the board violated the CBA. He ordered her reinstated, although she would receive no back pay. This amounted to a six-month unpaid suspension. In addition, the award imposed follow-up drug and alcohol testing, evaluation by a substance professional and other conditions. The board appealed to the state court system, seeking to vacate the part of the arbitration award that reinstated the driver. When the case reached the state appellate division, the court found the CBA specified progressive discipline, except in the most serious cases. No "zero tolerance policy concerning positive drug tests" was referenced in the CBA, as the board maintained. Instead, the CBA controlled the relationship between the parties. The court held the arbitrator could have reasonably found the board violated the CBA by imposing discharge as if it were mandatory.

The court confirmed the arbitration award. Appeal then reached the New York Court of Appeals. It noted there were only three narrow grounds for vacating arbitration awards. A court could vacate an arbitration award if it violated a public policy, if it was irrational, or if it clearly exceeded a specifically enumerated limitation of the arbitrator's power. But the court found none of those conditions applied in this case. There was no abuse of arbitrator powers, as he determined that the agreement of the parties did not require termination in this case. In the court's opinion, **reinstatement under the conditions of the arbitration award was an appropriate outcome that did not violate public policy**. As a result, the judgment was affirmed. *Shenendehowa Cent. School Dist. Board of Educ. v. Civil Service Employees Ass'n*, 20 N.Y.3d 1026 (N.Y. 2013).

◆ The Urbana (Illinois) School District hired a teacher who had worked for McLean County (Illinois) schools. At an Urbana elementary school, he sexually abused two students. Parents of the victims sued the teacher, both districts and school officials. They said McLean administrators knew the teacher abused children after gaining their trust through "sexual grooming" behavior. McLean officials were accused of failing to record incidents, investigate reports or timely report abuse as mandated by law. The parents claimed the teacher left McLean under a severance agreement that intentionally concealed his abuses and falsely indicated he had worked a full school year. A court found no duty based on willful and wanton conduct and dismissed the case. Appeal reached the Supreme Court of Illinois.

In the court's opinion, a duty was owed to the parents based on McLean's misstatement about the teacher's work history on an employment verification form. Urbana officials were not told that the teacher was twice removed from his classroom for discipline and had left his job during the school year. **The**

court held misrepresentations of misconduct created a duty based on the relationship between the parties and supported the willful and wanton conduct claims. And the parents showed injury was reasonably foreseeable and likely. By falsely stating the teacher had taught for the full school year, McLean implied that his severance had been routine. Urbana officials had no reason to suspect he had left due to misconduct. Courts in California, New Mexico and Texas have found injuries were reasonably foreseeable based on similar facts. As injury was foreseeable and any "burden" of truthfully filling out employment forms was slight, the parents could pursue willful and wanton misconduct claims. *Doe-3 v. McLean County Unit Dist. No. 5 Board of Directors*, 973 N.E.2d 880 (Ill. 2012).

◆   A North Carolina high school student accused her band teacher of making many sexual advances and inducing her into having sex with him. He was eventually arrested and pleaded guilty to taking indecent liberties with a child. In a state court, the student sued the board of education for negligent hiring, supervision and retention. She added emotional distress and state constitutional violations claims. The court dismissed the negligence and emotional distress claims, but it refused to dismiss the constitutional claims. On appeal, the Court of Appeals of North Carolina noted the lower court had based its constitutional rulings on *Craig v. New Hanover City Board of Educ.*, 363 N.C. 334, 687 S.E.2d 351 (N.C. 2009). In *Craig*, the state supreme court had stated that the existence of common law claims that were barred by governmental immunity did not also bar a party from asserting any available constitutional claims. But **the court held there was no state constitutional right to recover damages from local boards for injuries based on negligent supervision of employees**. As the student did not state a viable claim under the state constitution, she could not recover damages, and the judgment was reversed. *Doe v. Charlotte-Mecklenburg Board of Educ.*, 731 S.E.2d 245 (N.C. Ct. App. 2012).

◆   An Alaska teacher arrived late to school and appeared intoxicated. Her principal sent her to an assessment program for alcohol testing. After her blood alcohol level was found to be 0.155, she was assigned to a treatment program. But the teacher violated program rules. She was allowed to sign a "last chance agreement," but she violated it as well. After the treatment program discharged the teacher, the district initiated termination proceedings. Upon the advice of a union representative, she resigned. The teacher secretly recorded a telephone conversation with a district human resources director in which the director said that the teacher would be ineligible for rehiring. But he added "you wouldn't have anything negative on your record if you were to apply somewhere else." The teacher resigned.

Later, the school district refused to provide a recommendation sought by the teacher for another district. In a state court, she sued the district for disability discrimination, breach of contract and related claims. A trial court held for the school district, and appeal reached the state supreme court. It found the director's promise in the resignation agreement "covered anything negative." As the teacher raised the possibility that the comments violated the agreement, the court reinstated the contract claim. But the court held **the district's refusal to provide a recommendation to other school districts did not violate the resignation agreement**. The trial court would have to reconsider whether the district had immunity. The director's statements could be an implied waiver of the district's right to disclose information about her. But the teacher could not prevail on her disability discrimination claim. The school district stated a legitimate, nondiscriminatory reason for discharging her. Upon learning that she had alcoholism, the district offered her rehabilitation assistance. She was threatened with firing only after she violated the last chance agreement. *Boyko v. Anchorage School Dist.*, 268 P.3d 1097 (Alaska 2012).

◆ Alabama's highest court refused to review a lower court decision allowing a school board to suspend a special education coordinator for possessing marijuana at school. Her daughter had placed the marijuana in her car without her knowledge. Although the employee was not charged with a crime, the board suspended her without pay for 90 days. She appealed, and a hearing officer found she did not intend to have an illegal substance at school. On appeal, the Court of Civil Appeals of Alabama held **the state's new Students First Act required the hearing officer to apply the board's zero tolerance policy against drug possession on campus**. Since he did not, the court reversed the judgment. *Chilton County Board of Educ. v. Cahalane*, 117 So.3d 363 (Ala. Civ. App. 2012).

◆ Mississippi first-grade students reported that their teacher was lying on her classroom floor with her eyes closed. An assistant superintendent instructed her to undergo a drug test pursuant to district policy. After initially refusing a test, she agreed to take one, and it indicated she had used opiates. She also admitted taking Xanax and Ambien, resulting in notice that she would be dismissed for refusing to take the drug test and for neglect of duty and insubordination. At a hearing, the school board voted for employment termination, based on the teacher's own testimony of a positive drug test and statements by other teachers. A state chancery court held the board action was arbitrary and capricious, and appeal reached the Supreme Court of Mississippi. A district policy defined "reasonable suspicion" as a belief that an employee was using or had used drugs or alcohol. Reasonable suspicion was based on "abnormal conduct or erratic behavior while at work, absenteeism, tardiness or deterioration in work performance." **The court held state law committed the entire matter to the discretion of the school board. Under this standard, the decision was not arbitrary and capricious.** District policy stated the consequences for those who refused to take a drug test upon request. The board had relied on the policy's clear language when it discharged the employee, and the court found its decision was well-reasoned. There was ample evidence that the teacher had refused to take the drug test. Since the board had the prerogative to select the appropriate punishment, the court upheld the decision. *Smith County School Dist. v. Barnes*, 90 So.3d 63 (Miss. 2012).

♦   A Texas teacher claimed her principal took her to a drug-testing facility because he believed she was under the influence of an illegal substance. Testing reflected no substance use, and she filed an incident report with the local police concerning the principal. When the district superintendent notified the teacher that her contract would not be renewed, she filed a grievance against the district. She later filed a lawsuit against the district, principal and other officials. A federal district court held the school officials were entitled to immunity for the teacher's state law false imprisonment claim. This was because she was also asserting the claim against the school district itself. Immunity applied to claims against the school district for punitive or exemplary damages. **A school district could only be liable for civil rights violations based on actions for which it was actually responsible.** The teacher claimed that an official district policy or custom was the moving force in the violation of her federally protected rights. If her claims were true, the teacher raised a valid question of her right to relief. As a result, the court denied the district's motion to dismiss the federal claims. *Catlett v. Duncanville Independent School Dist.*, No. 3:09-CV1245-K, 2010 WL 2217889 (N.D. Tex. 5/27/10).

♦   An Oregon teacher was afraid of a violent confrontation with her ex-spouse. Her school district banned possession of deadly weapons or firearms by all employees, contractors and volunteers on district property or at school-sponsored events. The teacher, who was licensed to carry a concealed handgun, filed a state court action against the school district, seeking an order that would allow her to carry a gun to her school. The teacher claimed the district's ban was preempted by a state law that gave the state legislature exclusive authority to regulate firearms possession. Appeal reached the Court of Appeals of Oregon. It noted that a violation of the policy called for sanctions or employee discipline, including dismissal and referral to law enforcement authorities. The district correctly argued that the state law did not preempt reasonable employee-related policies. An internal employment policy was not an "ordinance" under the state law. While the legislature had intended to enact a broad preemption statute when it passed the law, the court held the scope of that preemption did not extend to internal workplace policies. **As a school district employment policy was not an "ordinance" or an exercise of "authority to regulate firearms" that was prohibited by the state law, the court affirmed the judgment.** *Doe v. Medford School Dist. 549C*, 232 Or.App. 38, 221 P.3d 787 (Or. Ct. App. 2009).

♦   A West Virginia school board implemented a random, suspicionless drug-testing policy on employees in 47 "safety-sensitive positions," including teachers, coaches, cabinetmakers, handymen, plumbers and the district superintendent. Teachers and their employees' association sought to prevent implementation of the policy. A 19-year veteran teacher testified that he never witnessed a school employee coming to work in an impaired state. And the district superintendent admitted there had been no instances of any student injuries due to a drug- or alcohol-impaired teacher. A federal court found drug testing is a "seizure" under the Fourth Amendment. When a state agency conducts a search, there must ordinarily be individualized suspicion of wrongdoing. **The U.S. Supreme Court has found that special safety needs outweigh employee privacy interests where there are major safety concerns such as a risk of great harm to people and property.** But the teachers and other school employees in this case did not have a reduced privacy interest by virtue of their public employment. They were not in "safety-sensitive" positions. The risk of harm stated by the board was speculative, and it did not outweigh the employees' privacy interests. The court issued a preliminary order preventing implementation of the policy. *American Federation of Teachers - West Virginia, AFL-CIO v. Kanawha County Board of Educ.*, 592 F.Supp.2d 883 (S.D. W.Va. 2009).

◆ Pennsylvania's highest court reversed an appellate decision that would have reinstated an arbitration award for a maintenance employee who tested positive for use of marijuana shortly after sustaining a workplace injury. An arbitrator had interpreted the district's drug-free workplace policy to prohibit drug usage only on school grounds. He found the employee's off-school conduct was beyond the control of the school district. A trial court held the arbitrator exceeded his authority and that the award violated the state public school code. The state supreme court vacated an appeals court decision upholding the arbitration award. It ordered the trial court to reconsider the case in view of *Westmoreland Intermediate Unit #7 v. Westmoreland Intermediate Unit #7 Classroom Assistants Educ. Support Personnel Ass'n, PSEA/NEA*, this chapter. In *Westmoreland*, the court limited the power of state courts to reverse arbitration awards on public policy grounds. **Courts may only vacate an award that has no foundation or does not flow from a collective bargaining agreement.** *Loyalsock Township Area School Dist. v. Loyalsock Custodial Maintenance, Secretarial and Aide Ass'n*, 957 A.2d 231 (Pa. 2008).

III. TRUANCY AND JUVENILE JUSTICE

A. Truancy

◆ A Nebraska student missed 48.14 school days during a school year. A school guidance director sent her family letters explaining that state law banned more than five absences per quarter or 20 days in a school year for any reason. The school requested medical records to assess whether the absences were excused by a serious illness. Records showed the student had been sick, but two statements indicated she was to return to school. No meeting was ever held among the parents and school officials to discuss an attendance plan. But the school referred the case to the county attorney, who filed a petition for habitual truancy from school. A juvenile court found the student was habitually truant. On appeal, the Supreme Court of Nebraska noted that state law permitted a school attendance officer to make a report to the county attorney if a child was absent more than 20 days per year, even if the absences were excused. **Noncompliance with the compulsory education statutes without first being excused by a school established truancy and created juvenile court jurisdiction.** The student's noncompliance with the compulsory education statutes had been proven.

The court found evidence to overcome the student's claim that her due process rights had been violated. The school sent her family many letters before taking action, and the county attorney's office also wrote to the family regarding possible prosecution. Like the trial court, the supreme court rejected the student's argument that the school had to provide the services described in the compulsory education statutes before she could be found truant. **The court rejected the student's claim that juvenile court authority was premised on school compliance with Nebraska compulsory attendance statutes.** Since compulsory attendance laws imposed no preconditions on juvenile court jurisdiction, the district did not have to comply with the services described in the laws before the proceeding was initiated. As a result, the court held for the state. *In re Interest of Samantha C.*, 287 Neb. 644, 843 N.W.3d 665 (Neb. App. 2014).

◆   A Georgia school resource officer (SRO) confronted three students who were loitering in a school hallway and told them to come with him to the school office. A student became defiant and profane and shoved the SRO when he tried to handcuff him. Another SRO then arrived, and the officers took the student to the floor and handcuffed him. After being brought to the school office, the student continued his combative, loud, and profane behavior. He disparaged and threatened an SRO before being taken to a youth detention center for three days. A school administrator later advised the parents that the student was not suspended and could return to school after his release from juvenile detention. After the student returned to school, the board held an expulsion hearing. At his hearing, the student said he hit the SRO in self-defense. But the hearing officer found he violated the student code. Before the board of education, the student asserted violation of a state code provision requiring a school disciplinary hearing within 10 days of a suspension. Adopting the hearing officer's findings, the board modified the discipline by finding the disciplinary action "complete" as of the date of its decision. Appeal reached the Court of Appeals of Georgia.

The court noted that at the school disciplinary hearing, the student said he acted in self-defense. But he was not suspended before his disciplinary hearing. He was instead told he could return to school upon release from detention. **According to the court, law enforcement and juvenile officers could not cause a school "suspension."** This defeated the claim that his school hearing was not held within 10 days of a "suspension" and was untimely. There was "more than sufficient evidence" in this case that the student had cursed and repeatedly refused to follow the SRO's directions. As the evidence justified a suspension, the court held for the board. **State law permitted school administrators to report student criminal action to a law enforcement agency or officer for investigation.** *Fulton County Board of Educ. v. D.R.H.*, 325 Ga.App. 53, 752 S.E.2d 103 (Ga. 2013).

A California law was amended to allow school administrators discretion in determining a valid excuse for which a student may be absent from school under state truancy law. Under the amended law, when an initial truancy report is issued, a student and his or her parents may be requested to meet with a school counselor to discuss the root causes of attendance issues and develop a joint plan to improve attendance. If a second truancy report is issued in the same school year, the student may be given a written warning by a peace officer. If a fourth truancy report is issued in the same year, the student is classified as a truant and may come under the jurisdiction of a juvenile court. If a truant is found a ward of the court, the court may impose one or more sanctions. These include: (1) court-approved community services; (2) a fine of no more than $50 (for which the parent or guardian may be jointly liable); (3) suspension or revocation of driving privileges; and (4) attendance at a court-approved truancy prevention program. California 2011-12 Regular Session, Ch. 432, A.B. No. 2616. Education Code Sections 48260, 48264.5.

◆   Two male Mississippi students tried to sexually assault a female student when she left an after-school track practice to use a lavatory in the girls' locker room. On the next day, the school principal advised the parents of the offending students that each would be immediately suspended and that he would recommend their expulsion for a year. Prior to their disciplinary hearings before the school board, the male students obtained temporary restraining orders from a youth court to preclude the board from excluding them from school. The court ordered that they be re-enrolled in school.

At a hearing, the board expelled the male students for a calendar year. A week later, the youth court granted a motion by two of the students for re-enrollment. Relying on Section 43-21-621 of the code, the court held the actions did not fit any of the statutory categories permitting expulsion. Appeal reached the Supreme Court of Mississippi, which held the case was governed by Mississippi Code Section 43-21-621. This section permitted a youth court to order the enrollment or re-enrollment of any "compulsory-school-age child in schools, and further order appropriate educational services." But the students in this case were over 17, and thus not of "compulsory-school-age." In addition, the same code section forbade the reenrollment of a student who had been suspended or expelled by a public school for offenses including weapons possession or "involving a threat to the safety of other persons, or for the commission of a violent act." Moreover, the section authorized the superintendent of schools to assign students to alternative school programs. Ultimately, the court agreed with the school board that the youth court exceeded its authority by ordering the reenrollment of the students. **If the board had found evidence that a sexual assault had occurred, this was "without a doubt, a violent act."** In reversing the judgment, the court commented that the discretion in this situation lie with the school board. *Lauderdale County School Board v. Brown*, 106 So.3d 807 (Miss. 2013).

In 2012, **Washington** legislators amended state truancy laws to specify that truancy petitions will include information about the student's academic status at initial truancy status hearings. Mandatory truancy filing petition provisions are applicable to students under the age of 17. School districts shall periodically update courts regarding actions taken by the district and the child's academic status. Courts may not issue bench warrants against children who fail to appear at an initial truancy petition hearing. Sixty-Second Washington Legislature, 2012 Regular Session, Ch. 157. S.S.B. No. 6494, RCW Sections 28A.225.030, 28A.225.035.

◆ A group of Pennsylvania students who claimed their school district unlawfully sought and retained truancy fines could proceed with a federal court class action lawsuit against the district. According to the students, the district issued at least 1,489 truancy citations against more than 700 parents and students. While state law limited fines for truancy violations to $300 against the parents of a child violating the state compulsory attendance law, **the students claimed the district sought and retained at least $107,000 in illegal fines**. This included 340 fines greater than the statutory maximum, some of which exceeded $900. A federal court found the students satisfied all the requirements for representing all those in the school district whose rights might have been similarly violated. *Rivera v. Lebanon School Dist.*, No. 1:11-cv-147, 2012 WL 2504926 (M.D. Pa. 6/28/12).

Students have argued that failure by school officials to enforce truancy policies should result in school liability for off-campus injuries. But in *Collette v. Tolleson Unified School Dist. No. 214*, 203 Ariz. 359, 54 P.3d 828 (Ariz. Ct. App. 2002), the court held a school district had no duty to prevent students from leaving campus. Similarly, the Supreme Court of Florida has held that a school's general duty to supervise students does not create a duty to supervise the movements of all students at all times.

◆ A Washington school district notified a student's family that the student would be reported to a truancy court due to his poor school attendance. His father then participated in county court truancy review proceedings. At a hearing, the court ordered the student to attend school. In a separate action in federal district court, the family asserted civil rights violations as a result of the state truancy proceedings. In a federal suit against school and county officials, the family sought an order clearing the student's record of truancy and contempt findings, compensation of over $3 million, and other relief. In the court's opinion, there was an insufficient factual basis for any liability.

According to the court, a single instance or action by a municipal employee was insufficient to meet the liability standard for constitutional rights violations in cases filed under 42 U.S.C. § 1983. There could be no liability under Section 1983 based on an employment relationship. **Simple dissatisfaction with the truancy hearings and the "sentiment that constitutional violations occurred" were insufficient to support a Section 1983 claim.** As no municipal policy or custom was implicated in this case, the court held for the county and district. *Blevins v. County of Mason*, No. 3:12-cv-05451 RBL, 2012 WL 3815568 (W.D. Wash. 9/4/12).

◆ A Washington juvenile court found a middle school student truant. At her hearing, she was not represented by a lawyer. She kept missing school and at a contempt hearing held three weeks later, a court commissioner found her in contempt and ordered her to perform 10 hours of volunteer work. Over the next year, the student remained in contempt and appeared in juvenile court several times. Various orders were made requiring her to write papers, try an alternative school, spend time in detention at home with a monitor, or obtain therapy. Each of the orders failed to obtain the student's compliance. Over a year after the initial truancy hearing, her lawyer moved to set aside the finding of truancy, claiming she should have had an attorney appointed for her at the initial hearing. The case reached the Supreme Court of Washington, which found state law permitted initial truancy hearings without requiring the parties to be represented by legal counsel. It was significant that a contempt sanction could not be imposed at an initial truancy hearing. Only a contempt petition created the possibility that a juvenile court could deprive the student of her liberty.

As the truancy order issued at an initial hearing did not deprive the student of physical liberty, the court held she had no due process right to be represented by counsel at that point. The purpose of the compulsory school attendance and admission statute was to protect a child's right to an education. No private interest was affected by the initial truancy hearing that would trigger due process protection. While a child should be afforded an appointed counsel at a contempt hearing, the court held there was no such right at an initial truancy hearing. The court held the state law was not unconstitutional. *Bellevue School Dist. v. E.S.*, 171 Wash.2d 695, 257 P.3d 570 (Wash. 2011).

◆ A California student and three others walked out of their middle school with the intent of participating in protests against pending immigration reform measures. The middle school vice principal allegedly threatened them harshly with discipline upon their return, calling them "dumb, dumb and dumber" and warning them of the possible legal consequences of their truancy. He also allegedly threatened them with a $250 fine and juvenile sentencing, but this did not occur. After returning home on the day of the discipline, the student committed suicide, leaving a note that stated "I killed myself because I have too many problems. ... Tell my teachers they're the best and tell [the vice principal] he is a mother f#@(-)ker." The student's estate sued the school district, vice principal and others for constitutional and state law violations in a federal court. The case reached the U.S. Court of Appeals, Ninth Circuit. It held **no First Amendment retaliation claim could be based on threats of discipline if it was based on a lawful consequence that was never administered**. The policy of disciplining truancy violated no First Amendment rights, even if the students sought to leave for expressive purposes. Further, the vice principal's words were not a form of corporal punishment, and nothing indicated that he had a retaliatory or discriminatory motive. Finally, since the suicide was not foreseeable, the estate failed to show negligence. The court affirmed the judgment. *Corales v. Bennett*, 567 F.3d 554 (9th Cir. 2009).

◆   A Maryland student was absent 74 days during the 2006-07 school year. State prosecutors filed an adult truancy petition against her parent for violating the state compulsory attendance act. The parent claimed that the student usually arrived at school on a regular basis. But the student admitted that once at school, she often cut her classes and was "hanging out" in school hallways. The parent asserted that after her child was at school, she was in the care and custody of school officials. The trial judge expressed disbelief at the parent for failing to ask her child about missing classes and found her "involved in" the child's truancy. After the court upheld the petition and placed the parent on probation, she appealed to the Court of Appeals of Maryland, the state's highest court. The lower court had found the parent's testimony both "incomprehensible" and incredible. As it was error for the trial court judge to make an inference that the opposite of her testimony must be true, the parent was entitled to a new trial. Once the daughter entered the school building, her custody shifted to the school. **The compulsory attendance law did not make clear that criminal liability would be imposed on a parent whose child cut classes.** While children were at school, their parents transferred power to act as their guardians to school officials. In order to find that the parent violated the compulsory attendance law at a new trial, there had to be "proof beyond a reasonable doubt" that her child did not attend school. Evidence that the student was not in her homeroom when attendance was taken would be sufficient to establish that she did not attend school on that day. *In re Gloria H.*, 410 Md. 562, 979 A.2d 710 (Md. 2009).

◆   The parents of an Iowa student who was arrested and detained in a juvenile detention center could not claim any monetary damages from her school district. The state court of appeals affirmed a trial court decision ruling that **the district had no duty to notify parents that their daughter had been arrested**. There was no deprivation of any parental rights, and the parents had no standing to assert a claim based on their child's due process rights. Many attempts were made by staff to contact them after the student was detained. *Simmons v. Sioux City Community School Dist.*, 743 N.W.2d 872 (Table) (Iowa Ct. App. 2007).

B. Special Education Students

A federal regulation at 34 C.F.R. Part 300.535(a) explains that special education protections do not shield students who commit crimes or juvenile offenses from law enforcement efforts. No federal law prohibits an agency from reporting a crime committed by a child with a disability to appropriate authorities or prevents state law enforcement and judicial authorities from exercising their responsibilities with regard to the application of federal and state law to crimes committed by a child with a disability.

A federal court held New York school officials did not violate any constitutional provisions by calling law enforcement officers to investigate suspected child abuse without first calling a parent for her permission.

◆ A New York student with autism and other disabilities attended a public high school at age 19. A teacher asked her about a mark on her face. She said her brother had thrown something at her, and the teacher sent her to the school social worker. Police were called, and the student told a municipal officer that her brother had assaulted her. Although the brother was charged with third-degree assault, the charges were ultimately dismissed. Later, the parent sued the school district, teacher, social worker and others for constitutional and state law violations. A federal court dismissed the constitutional claims against the school district, since the case implicated no official policy or custom. There was no duty by school district officials to intercede to prevent an "unconstitutional seizure and interrogation."

The court found no authority to suggest that an interview of a possible child abuse victim at school violates the Fourth Amendment, at least where there was no removal of the child from the parents' custody. In any event, qualified immunity was available to school officials. There was no merit to the due process claims. The court held in-school interrogation of a child without parental consent did not infringe on the parent's rights to care, custody and control of her daughter. While the parent claimed school officials did not comply with state abuse reporting requirements, the court held them inapplicable, as the student was 19. Since the complaint did "not come close to stating a violation" of rights, the federal claims were dismissed. The family could refile the state claims in a state court. *K.D. v. White Plains School Dist.*, 921 F.Supp.2d 197 (S.D.N.Y. 2013).

◆ A Missouri student with a learning disability tried to bring a knife to his charter school. He was arrested and admitted to a psychiatric hospital. After the school expelled him, his mother enrolled him in a public school. The superintendent knew of the knife incident and his hospitalization, but didn't inform staff members, and the IEP did not refer to the knife incident. About a year later, the student attacked a classmate with a box cutter and sliced his neck open. The victim sued the superintendent for negligence, but the Supreme Court of Missouri granted him immunity under the Coverdell Act – a provision of NCLB. **The superintendent did not have to provide notice of the student's criminal conduct because the student was not attending district schools at the time of the incident.** Moreover, the student's IEP made no mention of potentially violent behavior. *Dydell v. Taylor*, 332 S.W.3d 848 (Mo. 2011).

◆   A Michigan student with Tourette's Disorder was suspended several times. School officials petitioned a county court to declare him guilty of school incorrigibility. After the court found him guilty, he appealed. The state court of appeals found the student engaged in repeated and escalating misconduct that disturbed others. Moreover, the educational agency did not have to provide his special education and disciplinary records prior to filing a juvenile petition. In a separate proceeding, **an administrative law judge had held the juvenile petition was not a "change in placement."** Since the student did not appeal from that finding, he could not attack it now. In any event, he was not removed from school for over 10 consecutive school days or a series of removals totaling more than 10 school days in one school year. So the court held that a manifestation determination hearing was unnecessary. State law did not require evidence of willful violations and did not exempt violations based on a juvenile's disability. **The IDEA does not prevent schools from reporting crimes by disabled students to appropriate officials.** As sufficient evidence supported an adjudication of guilt, the judgment was affirmed. *In re Nicholas Papadelis*, No. 291536, 2010 WL 3447892 (Mich. Ct. App. 9/2/10).

◆   A Kentucky middle school student accumulated 21 unexcused absences in a two-month period, and a family court complaint was filed against him. He argued that his school district should have determined if his truancy was a manifestation of a disability prior to filing the action. A school attendance coordinator testified that she made a home visit, mailed numerous letters and made many phone calls to gain compliance. Her intervention did not help, and the student only complained that "he did not like school." After a hearing, the court found the student habitually truant. While he could remain at home, he had to attend counseling and school, and cooperate with a state family services agency. On appeal, the Court of Appeals of Kentucky found that **prior to filing a truancy complaint, a school director of pupil personnel must determine the causes of a student's truancy, assess home conditions and conduct home visits**. All these requirements were met and ample evidence supported the finding of habitual truancy. Nothing in the Individuals with Disabilities Education Act required a manifestation determination to see if his truancy was related to a disability. The court affirmed the judgment. *R.B.J. v. Comwlth. of Kentucky*, No. 2008-CA-001349-ME, 2009 WL 1349219 (Ky. Ct. App. 5/15/09).

IV. GANGS AND CAMPUS INTRUDERS

A. Civil Cases

◆ After a Kentucky child was picked up from school by an unauthorized individual, the parent sued the education board and superintendent for negligence. The case reached the Court of Appeals of Kentucky, which stated that immunity applied to the board if it was performing a "governmental function." Here, the board's after-school pick-up and drop-off policy directly furthered the education of students, which was a governmental function. So the board was entitled to immunity. According to the parent, the superintendent did not investigate, take disciplinary action or enact policies to prevent future incidents. But the court held these alleged failures did not strip the superintendent of immunity. **Nothing in the complaint alleged any failure by the superintendent to exercise personal discretion, in good faith and within the scope of his authority.** Both the school board and superintendent were entitled to immunity. *Breathitt County Board of Educ. v. Combs*, No. 2009-CA-000607-MR, 2010 WL 3515747 (Ky. Ct. App. 9/10/10).

◆ A Minnesota kindergartner said that he did not want to go outside with his class for recess. He stayed in a supervised detention room in the school office, but an aide instructed him to use a lavatory down the hallway instead of the one in the detention area. While in the lavatory, the kindergartner was sexually assaulted by a recent high school graduate who had been inside the school several times in the days before the assault. He entered the school through a side door without signing in and obtaining a visitor badge. The kindergartner's mother sued the school district for negligent supervision and failure to have and enforce a specific policy on school security. A court denied pretrial judgment on the negligent supervision claim, and the Court of Appeals of Minnesota agreed that a trial was required on that issue. The aide had let the kindergartner go unaccompanied to a restroom outside a detention room equipped with its own lavatory, and the graduate somehow got in the school building without signing in and wearing a badge. But the school district was entitled to immunity for not having a specific policy to protect elementary children from intruders. **These decisions took place at the planning level and involved the evaluation of financial, political, economic and social factors.** *Doe v. Independent School Dist. No. 2154*, No. A09-2235, 2010 WL 3545585 (Minn. Ct. App. 9/14/10).

◆ Gang activities at a West Virginia high school escalated when a gang leader was arrested for shooting a police officer. Gang members verbally assaulted the faculty and staff at school, and fights and disturbances became prevalent. The principal advised staff members that the slogan "Free A-Train" was banned. A student wrote "Free A-Train" on his hands several times and was suspended for 10 days. He sued the school board in a federal district court for speech rights violations. The court held schools may ban gang-related clothing if evidence indicates a potentially disruptive gang presence and gang-related disturbances. Recent federal cases suggest schools may regulate expression if they can reasonably forecast material and substantial disruption at school. This defeated the student's claim that speech must lead to an actual disruption before school administrators may suppress it. As students and parents had expressed fear over the use of the slogan, administrators could reasonably forecast that allowing the student to keep displaying it may have exacerbated the tensions and increased these fears. **The court held the "distraction from classes or intimidation from passive displays of support may serve as the basis of a disruption,"** and found no speech rights violation. *Brown v. Cabell County Board of Educ.*, 714 F.Supp.2d 587 (S.D. W.Va. 2010).

◆   Nine North Carolina students sued the Durham Public School System, asserting a "wholesale challenge" to its disciplinary process. They claimed that they were disciplined more severely than white students for less serious offenses. In addition, the students claimed that the board's anti-gang policy was unconstitutionally vague. A state trial court dismissed the action, and the students appealed. The Court of Appeals of North Carolina held that most of the claims had been properly dismissed, as each individual student failed to allege a claim for relief against each individual official. But the lower court would have to reconsider a due process claim brought on behalf of a now-deceased student who had been suspended for 13 days. His mother claimed that the superintendent of schools misled her and backdated correspondence to make a long-term suspension appear to be a short-term suspension. The trial court was also to reconsider a challenge to the school board's anti-gang policy. On appeal, the Supreme Court of North Carolina held the student had an adequate remedy under state law. So he could not sue the board for due process violations. Here, two **North Carolina statutes allowed any student who was suspended in excess of 10 school days to appeal to the education board, and then to a state court**. The court did not consider the gang policy issue, which was to return to the trial court. *Copper v. Denlinger*, 688 S.E.2d 426 (N.C. 2010).

◆   A California student was attacked by eight males while he walked past the school gymnasium. A second student was assaulted by three others while approaching a school exit. Both students suffered substantial injuries, and their guardian sued the school district in a state court for negligence. She also asserted violation of a mandatory duty to supervise students found in California Government Code Section 815.6 and California Education Code Section 44807. The guardian claimed the officials were indifferent to reports of threats against the students, and that daily brawls and rampant gang activity were seen at the school. The court held for the district and officials.

The guardian appealed to the Court of Appeal of California. The court noted superior court findings that **the guardian did not show the assaults**

would not have occurred had the officials increased their security measures. In premises liability cases, the person seeking damages must produce "non-speculative evidence" and show a causal link between the injury and the failure to provide adequate security measures. The guardian failed to show the officials caused the injuries to the students arising from the third-party attacks. She did not show it was more probable than not that additional security precautions would have prevented the attacks. The court found this fatal to the negligence claims. Similarly, the guardian was unable to prove the breach of a mandatory duty to protect the students under Government Code Section 815.6 and Education Code Section 44807. The court affirmed the judgment for the district and officials. *Castaneda v. Inglewood Unified School Dist.*, No. B198829, 2008 WL 2720631 (Cal. Ct. App. 7/14/08) (Unpublished).

◆ An Illinois school disciplinary code defined "gang activity" as "prohibited student conduct." Gang activity included any act in furtherance of a gang, and use or possession of gang symbols, such as drawings, hand signs and attire. The code stated that gangs and their activities substantially disrupted school by their very nature. A student was suspended three times for drawing gang-related symbols, including an inverted pitchfork and crowns with five points. Each time, the student was informed about the code prohibition on gang symbols and warned of its disciplinary implications. After the third incident, the superintendent notified the student's mother of a proposed expulsion, the date of a hearing and the right of the student to counsel. A school resource officer testified at the hearing that the pitchfork and crowns were gang-related signs. The school board voted to expel the student for the second half of the school year, and his mother sued. **A federal court held that the student code sufficiently defined the term "gang symbol," using specific examples of prohibited conduct.** The court rejected all of the student's First Amendment arguments. Both he and his mother had been warned that his conduct was a violation before he was expelled. The decision to expel the student after documented violations of the student code was not contrary to the evidence or in conflict with board policy. *Kelly v. Board of Educ. of McHenry Community High School Dist. 156*, No. 06 C 1512, 2007 WL 114300 (N.D. Ill. 1/10/07).

B. Criminal Proceedings

◆ A Kansas municipal police officer confronted a jogger whose dog was running loose on school grounds. The jogger was placing items from the trunk of her parked car into an athletic bag on the ground next to her car at the time. When the officer looked down, he saw a handgun case in the athletic bag. After questioning the jogger, the officer recovered a 9 mm handgun from her and informed her that it was illegal to have a firearm on school property. The gun was not loaded, and the magazine clip was empty.

The jogger stated she did not have any ammunition in her possession. A state court considered a criminal charge of possessing a firearm on school property in violation of Kansas law. The court held that since school was not in session at the time of the offense, the jogger should be acquitted of the charge. The state appealed to the Court of Appeals of Kansas, which noted that trial courts are not permitted to inquire into legislative intent, unless there is ambiguity or lack of clarity. In this case, state law declared that possession of a firearm by any person (other than a law enforcement officer) on any school property or grounds was a criminal offense. No exception applied to this case. **The court held that whether school was in session was irrelevant to the outcome of this case.** If the jogger's argument was correct, a sniper arriving on school grounds would not violate state law until a student actually arrived on school property or if classes were in session. As a result, the court reversed the judgment. *State of Kansas v. Toler,* 41 Kan.App.2d 986, 206 P.3d 548 (Kan. Ct. App. 2009).

◆   An intruder entered an office at a Missouri university, saying he wanted to enroll. He acted strangely when he met with a professor. The next day, the intruder returned to the office. When the university president's assistant asked him to leave, he slammed the door to the office. The assistant hit a panic button to summon security, and the intruder ran out of the building. He went to the office of the psychology professor, apologized to her and left a written marriage proposal on her desk. When security personnel found the intruder, he told them he was from Homeland Security and said the university had failed a test because he was able to drive onto the campus. As he became more and more agitated, his comments became increasingly bizarre, and police arrested him for trespassing. The intruder told police he had explosives in his truck, which was parked on university property. The campus was evacuated, and a bomb squad was called. After a thorough search that included the use of a robot, no explosives were found.

The intruder was charged in a state court with making a terroristic threat. A jury found him guilty and sentenced him to three years in jail. The intruder appealed to the Court of Appeals of Missouri, claiming the evidence was insufficient to support the conviction. The court rejected the argument that the statute did not apply to false reports of explosives. **The threat involved a "condition involving danger to life," which is an element of the crime.** It would defy logic to hold that a failure to specify the type or amount of explosives made the situation less dangerous. As the evidence was sufficient to show the intruder consciously disregarded a substantial risk of causing the evacuation of the university, his conviction was affirmed. *State v. Tanis,* 247 S.W.3d 610 (Mo. Ct. App. 2008).

◆   Section 985.23(2)(a), Florida Statutes, allows courts to consider whether a juvenile is a member of a criminal street gang at the time of the commission of an offense when imposing a sentence in juvenile delinquency proceedings. At least two of eight statutory criteria must be proven in order to find a juvenile a "criminal street gang member." A student was charged with assaulting a law enforcement officer, resisting arrest and disruption of a school function. At his disposition hearing for juvenile delinquency, the state department of juvenile justice recommended probation. The state presented evidence that the student was a member of a gang called the "Weedside Boys." A school resource officer testified that the student was seen wearing homemade shirts and book bags identifying him as a gang member. The court adjudicated the student a delinquent, and deviated from the recommendation of probation by the department of juvenile justice. The court found the student was a criminal street gang member and placed him in a moderate-risk residential placement.

The student appealed to a Florida District Court of Appeal, which noted the resource officer's testimony that the student wore shirts and had a book bag decorated with gang symbols. However, there was no testimony that he frequented a particular street gang's area or associated with known criminal street gang members. Under the statute, it was necessary to establish that the student met at least one other criteria. **As there was no competent substantial evidence establishing the student met the definition of "criminal street gang member," the court held the trial court could not rely on alleged gang membership when imposing a sentence on him.** The case was reversed and remanded to the trial court. *R.C. v. State of Florida,* 948 So.2d 48 (Fla. Dist. Ct. App. 2007).

◆ A Miami-area high school student was spotted walking away from the campus of a school he did not attend. Police had twice warned him not to enter the school's safety zone, and they arrested him. Prosecutors filed a delinquency petition against the student, and he was charged with trespass in a school safety zone and resisting arrest. He moved to dismiss the petition, arguing that the law unconstitutionally restricted peaceful conduct and communication. The case reached the Florida District Court of Appeal, Third District, which noted that a Florida statute makes it unlawful for any person to enter a "school safety zone" without legitimate business or other authorization at the school from one hour prior to the start of school until one hour after the end of school. The statute allowed those with authorization or legitimate business at a school to remain in a school zone.

The student did not show that those seeking to engage in protected speech or assemblies could not receive "authorization." He did not show that persons who had received notices barring them from school safety zones have any First Amendment rights to return to a school safety zone. **The law was clearly intended to protect children, which is a compelling government interest.** The court affirmed the order declaring the student a juvenile delinquent. *J.L.S. v. State,* 947 So.2d 641 (Fla. Dist. Ct. App. 2007). The Supreme Court of Florida let the decision stand, refusing to review the case in *J.L.S. v. State,* 958 So.2d 919 (Fla. 2007).

◆ A California school security employee saw three teenagers sitting on the front lawn of a high school during school hours. Because the employee did not recognize any of them, he called a police officer. The officer approached the intruders and asked them for identification. One of them produced identification from another school. The officer decided to escort the three intruders to the office to verify their identities. For his own safety, he decided to pat them down. The officer discovered a knife with a locking blade on one intruder and confiscated it. The intruder was charged with unlawful possession of the knife on school property. He was charged with a crime, and his case reached the Court of Appeal of California. It held searches of students are justified if there is reasonable suspicion of a violation of a law, school rule or regulation. **Students may be detained without any particularized suspicion, so long as the detention is not arbitrary, capricious or for the purpose of harassment.** Here, the intruder did not attend the school. He had a lesser right of privacy than students who were properly on school grounds. The officer had ample cause to believe the intruder did not belong on campus. The state's interest in preventing violence on a campus outweighed the minimal invasion to the intruder's privacy rights. As the pat-down search was proper, the court affirmed the judgment. *In re Jose Y.*, 141 Cal.App.4th 748, 46 Cal.Rptr.3d 268 (Cal. Ct. App. 2006).

CHAPTER FIVE

Employment

I. HIRING PRACTICES

A huge part of school safety depends on having competent and trustworthy staff – and that starts with good hiring practices.

Among the most important of these are background checks. They are acknowledged to be so important that an increasing number of states and localities even require them for volunteers. Some have started running them for all visitors to a school.

Where job applicants are concerned, the background checks that are required may be out of your hands. You may simply have to follow the state laws, collective bargaining agreements, or other rules that dictate the procedure. But one area that may be within your discretion is checking an applicant's references.

Few people enjoy making the calls to check references, but it's an important step toward having a safe school. And like a failure to run background checks, a failure to check references for an employee that later goes south and hurts someone can come back to haunt a district, diocese, HR department, school or administrator by way of a lawsuit.

The injured parties may bring a negligent hiring suit to claim that running the background check or talking to references could have revealed an important reason not to hire the applicant.

◆ Just after his January hire, a new assistant principal pulled a 16- or 17-year-old special ed student out of class to talk to her about a bullying problem she'd reported. When he ran into her a few days later, they exchanged phone numbers. He texted her that day. That night, he picked her up at home and drove her to a hotel, where they had sex. The sexual relationship continued, and he sometimes pulled her out of class, prompting classmates to roll their eyes and call her a "whore" and a "home-wrecker." In April, teachers told the principal they suspected an improper relationship, but the student denied it, as did other students the principal questioned. But after a different student reported the relationship to a school resource officer in September, the police investigated and arrested the assistant principal. The student and her mother then sued the superintendent and principal for negligent hiring in violation of Pennsylvania law. They alleged school officials didn't adequately check his background so didn't discover he'd pled guilty to a disorderly conduct offense of inducing a minor to buy alcohol. While **that was a different offense, the court found "it does indicate a history of targeting minors"** so found it suggested the school defendants negligently hired him. However, the court dismissed the claim, finding the student and her mother didn't allege the malice or willful misconduct required to strip the defendants of their state-law immunity from negligence claims. *M.S. ex rel. Hall v. Susquehanna Township School Dist.*, No. 1:13–cv–2718, 2014 WL 4273300 (M.D. Pa. 8/29/14).

◆   The mother of an eight-year-old Louisiana student dropped her daughter off at around 7:20 a.m. for the school breakfast, which was to be served at 7:30. A janitor stopped the student on the way in and told her that a teacher wanted to see her. He led her to an upstairs classroom, put a towel over her head, told her to bare one foot and touched her with a part of his body that wasn't his hand. She reported the incident despite his warning not to, and her mother sued the school board for vicarious liability and negligence in its retention/supervision of the janitor. A court granted pretrial judgment to the school board, but the court of appeal reversed, finding issues of fact that required a trial. However, the court did state that **the board could not be liable for negligent hiring of the janitor because it performed a background check on him and found no criminal record**. *Booth v. Orleans Parish School Board*, 49 So.3d 919 (La. Ct. App. 2010).

◆   A high school teacher in Indiana had a sexual relationship with a student during the student's freshman and sophomore years. The student did not reveal the relationship until two years later during a therapy session. When the school discovered the relationship, it promptly suspended the teacher, who later pled guilty to sexual battery and resigned. The student's parents sued the district under Title IX and also asserted a claim for negligent hiring. A federal court ruled against them, and the Seventh Circuit affirmed. The Title IX claim could not survive because the school did not have actual knowledge of the teacher's misconduct. Further, there was no evidence that the school failed to exercise reasonable care when it hired the teacher. It had no way of knowing that the teacher was likely to abuse the student. Although the parents asserted that the teacher had engaged in inappropriate relationships with two former students prior to his hire – marrying one of them – the school never learned of those relationships. It received positive references from the teacher's previous employer and interviewed him several times. He also possessed a valid teaching license and was not on a list of known sex offenders. And there was no indication that the former student he married had been in a sexual relationship with him while he was her teacher. Thus, **the school's thorough hiring procedures protected it from the claim of negligent hiring**. *Hansen v. Board of Trustees of Hamilton Southeastern School Corp.*, 551 F.3d 599 (7th Cir. 2008).

◆ A Tennessee school district hired a school cafeteria worker as a cheerleading sponsor. Although she did not have a teaching certificate, she supervised the cheerleading squad for two and a half years without incident. She attended cheerleading camps, and she obtained training and assistance from a previous squad sponsor. One day, while the sponsor left to attend to other duties, the cheerleading squad warmed up for a pep rally. A cheerleader broke her arm when she landed on the ground while attempting to perform a "basket toss" maneuver. She sued the school board and the sponsor for negligent hiring and negligent supervision. The school board claimed immunity under the state's tort liability act. A trial court found that the board was not entitled to immunity, but it granted pretrial judgment to the defendants. The Tennessee Court of Appeals reversed in part. It held that **the school board could not be liable for negligent hiring because there was no causal connection between the sponsor's lack of experience and the injury**. The injured cheerleader failed to show that the sponsor's experience was inadequate or fell below an established standard of care. However, there was a question of fact regarding the negligent supervision issue. This required a trial. *Britt v. Maury County Board of Educ.*, No. M2006-01921-COA-R3-CV, 2008 WL 4427190 (Tenn. Ct. App. 9/29/08).

◆ A Florida teacher applied for a high school teaching job using the district's paper application process. He was offered a position even though he had disclosed two prior DUI convictions. He rejected the offer and taught elsewhere. Two years later, after his application with the district expired, he reapplied using the district's new electronic application process. This time he failed to disclose his DUIs. Again he was offered a job. However, when the district conducted a criminal background check, it discovered the teacher's criminal record. Without revealing any specifics, the district's human resources (HR) director notified the principal and a vice principal that the teacher's application was not accurate. The HR director disqualified the teacher and rescinded the job offer. A school district committee reconsidered hiring the teacher, but **required proof of treatment to fulfill obligations under its safe and drug-free workplace policy**. He submitted proof of treatment the day after another teacher was hired. When he sued for disability discrimination, the Florida District Court of Appeal ruled against him. It held that the district's policy was neutral and that he failed to prove discrimination. *St. Johns County School Dist. v. O'Brien*, 973 So.2d 535 (Fla. Dist. Ct. App. 2007).

◆ A freshman at a public school academy chartered by Central Michigan University claimed that the dean of students sexually assaulted her in an abandoned and unlit stairwell on school grounds and during school hours. She sued the school for negligence, vicarious liability, negligent hiring and violation of the Michigan Constitution. A state court granted pretrial judgment to the school, holding that the school was entitled to governmental immunity and that the dean's conduct was outside the scope of his employment. Therefore, the school was not vicariously liable.

The court of appeals affirmed. Here, the school procured a criminal background check of the dean before hiring him, which revealed that he had been arrested on one occasion for felony insurance fraud. However, he did not have any criminal convictions. More importantly, **the criminal background check did not reveal that he had ever been arrested for, or convicted of, criminal sexual conduct**. Because the student did not provide documentary evidence to support the conclusion that school officials were aware or should have been aware that the dean might sexually assault a student, the dean's conduct was not foreseeable and the ruling in the school's favor was proper. *Wilson ex rel. v. Detroit School of Industrial Arts*, No. 265508, 2006 WL 1237033 (Mich. Ct. App. 5/9/06).

II. POST-HIRING ISSUES

Liability for negligent supervision or retention occurs after employment begins, where the employer knows or should have known of an employee's unfitness and fails to take further action such as investigating the employee to determine potential unfitness, discharging the employee or reassignment.

Public entities generally can be held liable for the negligent acts or omissions of their employees acting within the scope of their employment except where either the employee or the public entity is immunized from liability by statute.

Where an employee is exercising discretion with respect to school safety and is not acting in bad faith, maliciously or with a conscious indifference to the rights of others, the employee probably will be entitled to immunity from suit.

A. Immunity

◆ An assistant principal found contraband, including knives and a cigarette, in an Arizona middle school student's day planner. The student denied that the contraband was hers and also denied distributing drugs to fellow students, but agreed to let him search her belongings. He searched her backpack and found nothing. He then had an administrative assistant take her to the nurse's office, where the nurse and administrative assistant made her strip to her underwear, then asked her to pull her bra out and shake it, and to pull out the elastic on her underpants, exposing her breasts and pelvic area to some degree. They found nothing. She and her mother sued for

Fourth Amendment violations, and the case reached the U.S. Supreme Court. The Court held that the strip search violated the Fourth Amendment because the assistant principal did not have sufficient suspicion to justify its extent. However, **the law was not clearly established at the time of the search**. Thus, the assistant principal, the administrative assistant and the nurse were entitled to qualified immunity. Only the district could be liable for the Fourth Amendment violation. *Safford Unified School Dist. No. 1 v. Redding*, 557 U.S. 364, 129 S.Ct. 2633, 174 L.Ed.2d 354 (2009).

◆ CJC, a 16-year-old special ed student, had a disciplinary record of sexually harassing girls. Rumors made high school administrators and teachers suspect he was asking girl students to have sex with him in a school bathroom. Principals investigated but couldn't substantiate the rumors. When 14-year-old BHJ told a teacher's aide that CJC had been propositioning her and had just asked her to have sex with him in a bathroom, the aide suggested BHJ go along with it just long enough for them to catch CJC in the act and put a stop to his harassment. They say they went to the office to run the plan past an assistant principal. She seemed "disinterested" and didn't give them the go-ahead or tell them not to do it. BHJ went into the bathroom with CJC. By the time the aide got two teachers to check the bathroom, CJC had pulled the girl's pants down and raped her. BHJ and her guardian sued the school board and the school's principals for claims that included negligent/wanton hiring, training and supervision. An Alabama federal judge granted most of the defendants – but not the assistant principal – judgment without a trial, finding they were protected by state law immunity. Alabama public employees are not entitled to immunity if they act beyond their authority. According to the student's story, the assistant principal arguably ratified the plan by hearing about it and not stopping it. If so, the regulations adopted by the board of education for dealing with students' sexual harassment complaints meant **it would have been beyond her authority "to use a female student as 'bait' to trap a male student suspected of sexual harassment."** *Hill v. Madison County School Board*, 957 F.Supp.2d 1320 (N.D. Ala. 2013).

◆ After a Delaware fourth-grade class watched a movie on a 32-inch screen TV perched atop a four-to-five-foot-tall rolling cart, the teacher told a student to move the cart to the back of the room. As she was pushing it, the TV's cord got tangled in the cart's wheels. The TV fell, striking the student's head and knocking her down. The student's mother sued district defendants, including the teacher, for personal injury. The trial court found the suit blocked by the state's immunity statute. The Delaware State Tort Claims Act provides all state political subdivisions, including school districts and their employees, immunity for discretionary acts performed in good faith and without gross negligence. The student's mother claimed the teacher was grossly negligent to have a student move the TV cart. Instead, the court found that allowing a student to assist in a classroom task does not constitute gross negligence: "a gross deviation from the standard of conduct that a reasonable person would observe." At most, the teacher was negligent. As **gross negligence was required to overcome the teacher's immunity to a personal injury claim**, the trial court granted the district's request to dismiss the case. *Morales v. Family Foundations Academy, Inc. School,* No. N12C-03-176 JRJ, 2013 WL 3337798 (Del. Super. Ct. 6/11/13).

◆ A North Carolina teacher was accused of allowing a teacher's aide to regularly force-feed and abuse a severely disabled student in her classroom. The aide allegedly yelled at the student, force-fed him to the point of choking, used abusive language, violently jerked his head and pulled his hair, and intimidated him with a stuffed toy because she knew it terrified him. After the student was hospitalized, his parents sued the teacher, the district and various officials. The teacher sought immunity, which a trial court denied. Subsequently, the North Carolina Court of Appeals affirmed that decision, noting that the teacher did not meet the test for public official immunity because her position was not "created by statute." Further, the complaint alleged that the teacher knew of and might have witnessed the abuse, and yet never intervened on the student's behalf. And the abuse violated clearly established constitutional rights of which the teacher should have known. *Farrell v. Transylvania County Board of Educ.*, 682 S.E.2d 224 (N.C. Ct. App. 2009).

◆ Over a 16-year period, an Alabama physical education teacher was accused of five incidents of inappropriate touching and comments. The district's personnel director investigated three of the incidents, which occurred at the high school. The teacher denied misconduct on each occasion and, after the investigations, written reports were placed in his personnel file. After the third incident, the teacher was transferred to an elementary school. The other two incidents did not involve physical contact but rather inappropriate comments.

An 11-year-old fifth-grader with speech and learning disabilities was then allegedly raped by the teacher, though she did not report it until after she transferred out of his class and to another school. When she finally told a school counselor, the personnel director placed the teacher on administrative leave and began investigating. The teacher retired before the board made a final employment decision. The student later sued the board and the personnel director for civil rights violations. The board and the director sought immunity. The Supreme Court of Alabama noted that **the board managed its own funds, established general policies and supervised education in county schools, which prevented it from being considered an "arm of the state" and also precluded it from asserting immunity**. However, the director was negligent at most in failing to recommend the teacher's termination and thus was entitled to immunity. It could not be shown that he acted with deliberate indifference to the student's civil rights. *Madison County Board of Educ. v. Reaves*, 1 So.3d 980 (Ala. 2008).

◆ A Tennessee high school principal decided to temporarily deny a female student access to a weightlifting class in the last semester before graduation. The class was scheduled to include about 30 males and one other female. Students were required to "spot" one another, requiring some physical contact. **The principal consulted with the weightlifting teacher and decided to remove the girls from the class for "safety and liability reasons," fearing a possible sexual assault.** A school official confirmed that the school would not permit enrollment of one or two girls in a class with all male students and a male teacher. After a state attorney notified the director of schools about a possible Title IX violation and informed the principal that the students could not be removed from class because of their gender, the principal allowed the students to return to class. The other student chose not to return, and the student who did return missed only three days of class and earned an A. However, she claimed that the incident caused her great stress and sued for constitutional rights violations.

A federal court granted the board's motion to dismiss the case, and the Sixth Circuit affirmed. Here, the principal was not executing an official board policy at the time he ordered the student's removal, and he was not acting as a board policymaker. The board had no role in the decision to remove the student from class, and it took immediate corrective action as soon as the director of schools learned about the incident. *Phillips v. Anderson County Board of Educ.*, 259 Fed.Appx. 842 (6th Cir. 2008).

◆ An adult former student of a Virginia elementary school claimed that a gym teacher improperly touched her when she was in grades four through six. She sued the school board and various administrators in a federal court for sexual harassment, claiming school officials were deliberately indifferent to his misconduct. She also asserted that the school principal investigated two similar incidents involving young girls who attended school at about the same time she did. In one case, the girl reported that she had sat on the teacher's lap and that he had picked her up so that her legs were straddling him. The principal's investigation determined that it was simply a matter of bad judgment, and she therefore did not report it to child protection authorities. Less than a week later, when the second girl reported that the teacher might have rubbed his private parts against her, the principal reported the allegations to her superiors and involved the school district's investigative specialist, who was a retired police officer. She set into place police and child protection investigations. The teacher denied improper conduct, and eventually it was concluded that the teacher's actions were unintentional. The principal determined that the teacher did not require any closer supervision or monitoring. Four years later, and two years after the adult former student advanced from elementary school, the teacher was fired for unprofessional conduct and insubordination.

When the adult former student sued the district, the court granted pretrial judgment to the principal, finding that even if she had been negligent, she did not demonstrate deliberate indifference to the adult former student. As such, she was entitled to immunity. On appeal, the Fourth Circuit affirmed. Here, **the principal responded reasonably to the risk that the gym teacher was sexually abusing female students**, immediately responding to both complaints she received, conducting her own investigation and reporting the allegations to her superiors. *Sanders v. Brown*, 257 Fed.Appx. 666 (4th Cir. 2007).

◆ An Ohio student attacked another student after gym class. The victim's parents sued the school district, claiming it knew of the attacker's history of assaulting students, yet did not take the necessary precautions to protect other students from him. **A trial court held that the district was immune, noting that it did not act with malice, in bad faith or recklessly.** It also found that **the teacher's supervision at the time of the attack was not even negligent**. The Ohio Court of Appeals affirmed. Although the student aggressor was disruptive at times, there were no indications that he was terrorizing other students. The fact that he had been in a juvenile detention center several times was not enough to put the school on notice that he was likely to attack another student. *Aratari v. Leetonia Exempt Village School Dist.*, No. 06 CO 11, 2007 WL 969402 (Ohio Ct. App. 3/26/07).

◆ On the last day of the school year for an Alabama elementary school, various teachers and coaches were called into the guidance counselor's office and asked to sit in the chair facing the guidance counselor's desk. As each teacher sat in the chair, the chair slowly reclined in the back, causing the front part to slant upward. As each teacher sat in this "sinking" chair, the guidance counselor and the other teachers present would laugh. The teachers would then summon another staff member on whom they could play the practical joke.

A coach who was summoned to the office and instructed to sit in the chair did so, at which point the chair reclined under her. She reinjured her back, upon which she had undergone several surgical procedures. She sued the principal (one of the first people duped by the "sinking chair"), the guidance counselor and others for negligence, wantonness, conspiracy, and failure to warn. A trial court granted judgment as a matter of law for the defendants, and the coach appealed.

The Court of Civil Appeals of Alabama noted that the principal was responsible for safety on the school campus. She knew of the condition of the chair, because she had sat in it earlier. She testified that she never viewed the chair as a safety problem. She left shortly after the joke was played on her and was absent from the school when the guidance counselor asked the coach to sit in the chair. The court determined that **the principal was exercising her judgment regarding school safety and concluded that she was entitled to state-agent immunity on the coach's claims of negligence and wantonness**. There was no evidence of a conspiracy, nor did the other teachers present have a duty to warn the coach about the sinking chair. The only person with potential liability to the coach was the guidance counselor, who brought the chair to school. *Bayles v. Marriott*, 816 So.2d 38 (Ala. Civ. App. 2001).

B. Safety Policies

◆ For more than two years, teachers picketed in front of a middle school at morning drop-off. They were protesting the district's failure to reach a contract with their union. When rain was forecast for a planned protest, teachers voted to park in front of the school that morning and display their picket signs in the car windows. They left room for dropped-off students to reach the sidewalk but not for parents to pull up to the curb as usual. Parents had to let children out in the middle of the street in the rain, and traffic backed up in both directions. Parents called the school about the traffic jam, and the principal called the police. The traffic snarl also made at least 16 teachers late that day. The picketing teachers were charged with misconduct. Two – one fined $500 and the other fined $1,000 – appealed to a court. Participating in a peaceful union protest is protected from retaliation under the First Amendment. The teachers alleged a violation of their speech rights. A trial court found the discipline was legal. The teachers appealed, and an appeals court reversed. The district appealed, and New York's highest court reversed again, upholding the discipline because the way the teachers engaged in their protected speech rights, "interfered with the safety of students[.]" The court found **the teachers' speech rights "were outweighed by the District's interests in maintaining an orderly, safe school[.]"** *Santer v. Board of Educ. of East Meadow Union Free School Dist.*, 13 N.E.3d 1028 (N.Y. 2014).

◆ A fired New Jersey school bus driver filed a bias charge with the state civil rights agency to allege his termination was discriminatory. The board of education agreed to settle his claim. As part of the settlement, the board agreed to reinstate him. He went back to work, Two months later, **the supervisor of security rode along on an afternoon run and heard a school bus full of students "shriek in fear"** because a railroad crossing gate had come down on top of the bus while its back end was still on the tracks. The driver ignored it when the vehicle ahead of him pulled up to give him room to clear the tracks. The bus remained on one set of tracks while a commuter train sped past on the next set, so close it made the bus rock. Something similar happened on the morning run five days later. Meanwhile, the board was getting calls and letters from parents complaining about the driver and worried about their children's safety. The board fired the bus driver for unsatisfactory performance, and the driver sued the board for breaching their settlement agreement. The court granted the board judgment. The bus driver appealed, but the appeals court affirmed, finding: **"[T]he Board's first responsibility was the safety and welfare of the children in the district,"** and it had reasonable grounds to question the driver's safety – including"uncontradicted evidence of two life-endangering incidents." The board didn't breach the settlement agreement by firing the bus driver under these circumstances. *Valos v. Garfield Board of Educ.*, No. A-3313-12T2, 2014 WL 4355637 (N.J. Super. Ct. App. Div. 4/9/14).

◆ A front office employee at a Georgia high school was approached by a man who claimed to be a student's uncle. She failed to ask for identification or verify that the man was allowed to check out the student. In fact, only the student's parents were allowed to check her out of class early. When the student arrived at the office, the man told her that her mother had sent him to pick her up. He then took her to his daughter's house and molested her. The student's parents sued the principal and the employee in their individual capacities. The defendants sought immunity, but the Georgia Court of Appeals granted it only to the principal. **The employee had a mandatory duty to verify that the man had the right to sign the student out of school and failed to do so.** As a result, the lawsuit against her could proceed. A jury would have to decide whether the molestation was a reasonably foreseeable consequence of her failure to follow the rules. *Cotton v. Smith*, 714 S.E.2d 55 (Ga. Ct. App. 2011).

◆ A social worker at a Florida middle school counseled a student who had been cutting herself after being ridiculed for texting a suggestive photo of herself to a boy. The social worker had the student sign a "no-harm contract," promising not to harm herself and to call the social worker if she thought about killing herself again. However, **the social worker failed to inform the student's parents about their daughter's risk of suicide**. The next day, the student killed herself at home. When the parents discovered the "no-harm contract," they sued the board, claiming that it improperly failed to train the social worker, resulting in their daughter's death. A federal court ruled that the parents had failed to prove deliberate indifference by the board – a necessary element to a claim brought under the Fourteenth Amendment. *Witsell v. School Board of Hillsborough County*, No. 8:11-cv-781-T-23AEP, 2011 WL 2457877 (M.D. Fla. 6/20/11).

◆ A Pennsylvania student was sexually assaulted by a driver's education teacher during a solo lesson. When she complained, the district suspended the teacher, but the principal sent out letters asking people to contribute to the teacher's defense and stating that he thought the student was lying. After the teacher was reinstated, the student left school and sued the district, claiming that it ignored the teacher's misbehavior for years before the incident, making it possible for him to assault her. She asserted that the teacher hadn't even been disciplined after asking a student if he could see her pierced nipple. The district sought to have the case dismissed, but a federal court allowed parts of the lawsuit to continue. The student had alleged a custom of inadequate training for employees who are likely to respond to incidents of sexual harassment. The district also allegedly had a custom of ignoring or downplaying reports of harassment, and had a custom of suppressing specific complaints of harassment against the teacher.

Finally, **the school district had a custom of allowing the teacher to take students out for driving lessons alone, in violation of official school district policy**. As a result, the student's lawsuit against the district could proceed with respect to those claims. *E.N. v. Susquehanna Township School Dist.*, No. 1:09-CV-1727, 2010 WL 4853700 (M.D. Pa. 11/23/10).

◆ A New York special education teacher noted a student's progressively disruptive behavior and aggression toward classmates, and initiated a "Type Three referral" to remove him from her classroom. This process could take as long as 60 days. Forty-one days later, the student attacked a classmate. The teacher intervened to protect the classmate, and she sustained injuries. She sued the city of New York for negligence. Although a jury awarded her $512,465 for her injuries, the Court of Appeals reversed the award. It found that **the district did not have a special relationship with the teacher such that it owed her an increased duty of care**. Her supervisors' vaguely worded assurances that they were working on removing the student from her class did not give rise to a reasonable reliance on her part that could result in liability. *Dinardo v. City of New York*, 921 N.E.2d 585 (N.Y. 2009).

◆ A Louisiana special education teacher noted that a student began making a sound he typically made before self-injurious episodes. When he starting hitting himself on the head, she called the PE coach, two paraprofessionals and the principal. She was pushed into a wall while trying to keep a mat under the 185-pound student to prevent injury. During the 45-minute struggle, she was twisting and sliding the entire time. However, she was not hit, knocked down or bitten by the student. When she sustained injuries to her hand, she nevertheless sought "assault pay" from the board. A court granted pretrial judgment to the board, but the court of appeal reversed, noting that there was a question of fact as to whether the teacher's injuries were a result of an assault by the student. **If the student intended to harm her during the episode, she would be entitled to assault pay.** The case required a trial. *Miller v. St. Tammany Parish School Board*, No. 2008 CA 2582, 2009 WL 3135208 (La. Ct. App. 9/11/09).

◆ In 2005, an Oregon school district adopted a policy that any employee having a firearm in school or at a school event would face discipline up to and including termination. A teacher in one of the district's schools had an ex-husband whom she feared might turn violent. She sought to bring a handgun to school, asserting that she was licensed to carry a concealed weapon and that she needed it for self-defense. The district's human resources department warned her that she could be fired for bringing the gun to school, and she sued. She claimed that the policy was illegal because Oregon law states that only the legislature can "regulate" firearms or pass ordinances concerning them. A court dismissed her claim, holding that the law didn't apply to workplace policies, and the Oregon Court of Appeals affirmed that decision. It noted that the state law was only intended to prevent cities and counties from creating a patchwork of conflicting laws concerning firearms, and that it wasn't intended to reach as far as internal employment policies. *Doe v. Medford School Dist. 549C*, 221 P.3d 787 (Or. Ct. App. 2009).

♦   A West Virginia county board of education implemented a random drug testing policy for all safety-sensitive employees, which included teachers. Three teachers and their union sued to block the new provisions from taking effect, claiming that the random testing would violate their Fourth Amendment right to be free of unreasonable search and seizure. A federal court granted a preliminary injunction prohibiting the board from enforcing the policy. **The board failed to show that there was a special need for the suspicionless searches.** In addition, the teachers did not hold safety-sensitive positions as that term has been defined by the Supreme Court. Thus, they did not have a reduced expectation of privacy. Finally, the risk of harm from not testing was more speculative than real. *American Federation of Teachers-West Virginia, AFL-CIO v. Kanawha County Board of Educ.*, 592 F.Supp.2d 883 (S.D. W. Va. 2009).

♦   A nine-year-old New Jersey student was dismissed from school on an early-dismissal day, walked off school grounds without an adult, and was struck by a car a few blocks from school over two hours later. The accident paralyzed him from the neck down.

The school district had a four-page policy memorandum titled "Pupil Safety" that addressed a wide range of student safety topics, including supervision of students at dismissal time. The memorandum stated that "[t]he chief school administrator shall seek the cooperation of parents/guardians to prevent any children [from] being unsupervised on school property during lunch hour and during morning arrival and afternoon dismissal times." The memorandum did not, however, outline how dismissal supervision would be administered by the schools.

Instead, the school adhered to a practice that all school personnel supervise dismissal. On a typical school day, the school's 500 students were dismissed at 2:50 p.m. Teachers escorted the students from their classrooms to designated exits at the sounding of the school bell, and the teachers remained at their designated duty stations to ensure that the children left the school premises. According to the principal, all school personnel – including teachers, teachers' aides, and security personnel – supervised dismissal to ensure that the children left school before the adults. The principal personally supervised early-dismissal days to "make sure that there were no children whose parents did not pick them up."

The student and his family sued, alleging that the school district and principal breached their duty of reasonable supervision. They also claimed they did not have advance notice of the early-dismissal day. The case reached the Supreme Court of New Jersey, which held that schools in New Jersey must exercise a duty of reasonable care for supervising students' safety at dismissal. **The duty requires school districts to create a reasonable dismissal supervision policy, provide suitable notice to parents of that policy, and effectively comply with the policy and subsequent and appropriate parental requests concerning dismissal.** The court remanded the matter to the trial court for further proceedings. *Jerkins v. Anderson*, 922 A.2d 1279 (N.J. 2007).

C. Fitness for Duty

◆   A high school physics teacher taught a math and physics class for struggling students. Many had behavioral issues or were diagnosed with attention deficit disorder or other learning-related conditions. To engage them, the teacher developed a less authoritarian, more collaborative teaching style. That meant students were more familiar with him than with other teachers. One day in class, a 17-year-old girl said she wasn't happy with her grade and asked if she could pay for a better grade. A male student responded, "You mean short of sexual favors?" The teacher joked, "Yes, that is the only thing that would be accepted." The students laughed. He added, "Don't be ridiculous," and said the only thing that would improve her grade was better work. He offered her extra help after school. When she arrived to take him up on the offer, he was helping another female student. **The student again asked to pay for a better grade. He replied she already knew "the only thing that I would accept is a sexual favor."** She laughed, but the other student reported the teacher's remark. He was put on administrative leave, investigated for sexual harassment, and ultimately fired for conduct unbecoming a teacher. The teacher appealed, and the matter went to arbitration. The arbitrator found that despite the teacher's intent, the remarks were objectively inappropriate and made a student uncomfortable enough to complain – so violated the school's sexual harassment policy and created a hostile educational environment. Even so, the arbitrator reinstated him, finding that was in the best interest of district students, given 11 years of strong performance weighed against a comparatively minor isolated incident. A court affirmed the arbitration award, but Massachusetts' highest court vacated it, finding the arbitrator didn't have the authority under the state's teacher's statute to reinstate the teacher. That law required the arbitrator to assess conduct that jeopardized students' safety or self-esteem primarily in light of the pupils' interest in a safe learning environment. **The arbitrator's error was in letting "pupils' interest in the academic success of their school to override their interest in a safe, supportive classroom environment."** The court found that ran contrary to the law's stated purpose "and the high standards of behavior the public expects from its teachers." *School Committee of Lexington v. Zagaeski*, 12 N.E.3d 384 (Mass. 2014).

◆   A Kentucky high school's SRO took two boys to the principal after classmates overheard them talking about a bomb and saw they had a map. The principal determined they had been discussing a video game. A few days later, on the same day as the school shooting in Newtown, Connecticut, the Spanish teacher dictated a letter to a student and told the student to sign his own name. It claimed a student had twice brought weapons to school and had "plotted a map of bomb and gun attack sites around the school area" but wasn't disciplined. **The letter asked if the superintendent was "afraid to enforce school rules[.]"** The superintendent met with police and then closed the high school and middle school to search for weapons. None were found. Final exams scheduled for that day were postponed. The lost day was made up on a day the rest of the district had off. After police discovered the Spanish teacher wrote the letter, **the superintendent fired her for insubordination and conduct unbecoming a teacher**. The teacher sued, alleging violation of her free speech rights. She asked for a court order to reinstate her employment pending the resolution of her lawsuit. The court refused, finding she wasn't likely to win her suit. Assuming the teacher was speaking as a private citizen on a matter of public concern, the district's interest in promoting the efficiency of its educational services outweighed any speech rights she had in the letter. She mailed the letter the day after Newtown shooting, and the day the school reopened, attendance was down by 10%. Also, closing the schools affected around 900 students and their families. This, plus the rescheduled exams and make-up day, meant she significantly impeded school operations. As the court found her speech wasn't protected, she wasn't likely to win her case. *Pacheco v. Waldrop*, No. 5:13-cv-00044-TBR, 2013 WL 2581016 (W.D. Ky. 6/11/13).

◆   A Kentucky teacher reprimanded a student for running in the hallway, but he told her she couldn't tell him what to do. He then began pulling a younger sibling's hair. The teacher grabbed him and started pulling him to the office. He complained that she was choking him. A school employee witnessed the event but didn't intervene. The teacher was suspended that day, then fired for conduct unbecoming a teacher. She challenged the termination and a tribunal changed her termination to a suspension. The case reached the Kentucky Court of Appeals, which reversed the suspension. **Here, the tribunal had concluded that the teacher didn't choke the student, but suspended her anyway.** Further, in prior disciplinary actions, conduct unbecoming a teacher always involved some sort of dishonest or corrupt behavior. That wasn't present here. *Board of Educ. of Fayette County v. Hurley-Richards*, No. 2010-CA-000840-MR, 2011 WL 3862217 (Ky. Ct. App. 9/2/11).

◆   A New York teacher exchanged emails and instant messages with a student, at one point telling him that the lines of their relationship were becoming blurred and that she was confused. The student reported the conversations to the principal, and the teacher entered therapy to cope with the situation. Later, the student found postings made by the teacher under an alias on a public website, in which she acknowledged her desire to be physically close to him and kiss him. She was suspended pending termination, but a hearing officer determined that **she had shown remorse and entered therapy, making termination too harsh a penalty**. Instead, she was suspended for 90 days and transferred to a different school. The New York Supreme Court, Appellate Division, upheld that decision. *City School Dist. of City of New York v. McGraham*, 905 N.Y.S.2d 86 (N.Y. App. Div. 2010).

◆ A Tennessee school district investigated a tenured teacher who was alleged to have kissed a student in class and written notes professing love for students. The district suspended the teacher (first with pay, then without pay), placed him on probation and forced him to take sensitivity training. Other students told investigators that the teacher had hugged them and told them that he loved them. He challenged the suspension, but the Tennessee Court of Appeals upheld it. While the teacher's unprofessional conduct was not a statutory ground for dismissal under the state's Tenured Teachers Act, **his unprofessional conduct was harmful to student learning and therefore justified the suspension**. *Taylor v. Clarksville Montgomery County School System*, No. M2009-02116-COA-R3-CV, 2010 WL 3245281 (Tenn. Ct. App. 8/17/10).

◆ A Delaware school district charged a teacher with four incidents of misconduct and/or immorality, including "selling" grades to students for cash, sleeping during the work day and swearing in front of students at a school football game. The most serious charge against the teacher was that he asked one of his students for a ride to a dangerous area to purchase drugs. At the time, the teacher's driving privileges were suspended due to a DUI conviction. A hearing officer found the teacher's statements inconsistent and incredible, while grade book evidence supported the charges that the teacher raised students' grades in exchange for amounts of $10 and $30. The hearing officer recommended discharge, and the Supreme Court of Delaware upheld the termination. The teacher's claim that the board had relied on "stale" evidence failed because the board was permitted to hear all evidence that could conceivably shed light on the controversy. And board procedures met minimum standards for due process. *Bethel v. Board of Educ. of Capital School Dist.*, 985 A.2d 389 (Table) (Del. 2009).

◆ A nontenured Connecticut teacher posted a profile on MySpace to keep in contact with students. A school counselor learned of the profile and was disturbed by what she saw – pictures of naked men and inappropriate comments posted near student pictures. She complained to the teacher, who took down the profile and created another one that was very similar. The district then notified the teacher that it would not be renewing his contract. It granted him a formal hearing, but affirmed its decision not to renew his contract. When he sued the district for violating his First and Fourteenth Amendment rights, he lost. A federal court held that his nonrenewal apparently resulted from his interactions with students. **His conduct as a whole was disruptive to school activities and indicated a potentially unprofessional rapport with students.** *Spanierman v. Hughes*, 576 F.Supp.2d 292 (D. Conn. 2008).

◆ A Maryland vice principal summoned a student to his office to discuss alleged harassment by the student. The vice principal claimed that he showed a knife to the student – a knife that a smaller student had brought to school after being picked on – and asked how he would feel if a student he had harassed brought a knife to school. However, **the student claimed that the vice principal brandished the knife directly in front of him**. He sued the vice principal for assault. The vice principal asked the school board to supply him with legal counsel, but the school board refused. The vice principal obtained an attorney under his insurance policy, and a jury ruled that he did not assault the student. His insurer then sought reimbursement for his defense costs. The Court of Appeals of Maryland held that the school board was required to provide legal counsel to the vice principal, and thus had to reimburse the insurer for the defense costs. Since the vice principal claimed that he acted in the scope of his employment and without malice, the school board had a duty to defend him. *Board of Educ. of Worcester County v. Horace Mann Insurance Co.*, 969 A.2d 305 (Md. 2009).

◆ A Pennsylvania classroom assistant worked with a special education teacher. One day, she did not feel well and left the classroom for about 45 minutes. She was discovered in a restroom stall, unconscious, choking and struggling to breathe. The police were called, and they found a Fentanyl patch on her back that had caused an overdose. She was charged with disorderly conduct and possession of a controlled substance. After she was suspended without pay and recommended for discharge, she filed a grievance. An arbitrator determined she could be fired only for just cause and that, **while her behavior had been foolish and irresponsible, it was not so grossly offensive to the morals of the community that it rose to the level of immorality**. It was the only incident of its kind in 23 years of service. A court and an appeals court overturned the arbitrator's decision, but the Pennsylvania Supreme Court held that the courts should have followed the deferential "essence test" to overturn arbitration awards only where there is no foundation for them or where they did not flow from a collective bargaining agreement. The court returned the case to the trial court for a determination of whether public policy precluded the award. *Westmoreland Intermediate Unit #7 v. Westmoreland Intermediate Unit #7 Classroom Assistants Educ. Support Personnel Ass'n PSEA/NEA*, 939 A.2d 855 (Pa. 2007).

◆ A West Virginia teacher, who was also the head football coach at his high school, beat his son with a belt after the son was disciplined for making inappropriate comments in front of his class. When staff members learned of the beating, they contacted the state department of health and human resources, which removed the son and two of his siblings from the house. The teacher was charged with felony child abuse and entered a plea of misdemeanor domestic battery. He also underwent counseling and a psychiatric evaluation, after which the school board rejected the superintendent's recommendation that the teacher be dismissed. A psychologist determined that the teacher presented no greater risk to his students than any other teacher, and he was allowed to return to the classroom. The state's Professional Practices Panel then determined the teacher's license should be suspended for four years. The teacher appealed to the Supreme Court of Appeals of West Virginia, which agreed with him that **the four-year suspension of his certificate was not based on unfitness to teach**. The state superintendent failed to show a nexus between the teacher's home conduct and the duties he had to perform as a teacher. He exhibited no cruel behavior to his students or the staff, and he was not unfit to teach. *Powell v. Paine*, 655 S.E.2d 204 (W. Va. 2007).

◆ A Mississippi high school teacher with no history of sexually harassing students began a sexually inappropriate relationship with a student, though both he and the student denied that sexual intercourse ever occurred. A rumor circulated about the relationship, but the principal detected no sign of it. He confronted the teacher, who vehemently denied there was any inappropriate relationship. However, the truth eventually came out in some discarded love letters and some impassioned emails. The student's family sued the school district for negligent hiring and retention, among other claims. A court ruled for the school district, and the Court of Appeals of Mississippi affirmed. Here, **the school district did not have either actual or constructive notice of the inappropriate relationship between the student and teacher, as required to establish a claim for negligent hiring or retention**. The teacher had no prior history of wrongdoing, and many of his contacts with the student were under the guise of innocence, such as his tutoring of the student and her babysitting of his child. *Doe v. Pontotoc County School Dist.*, 957 So.2d 410 (Miss. Ct. App. 2007).

◆ A tenured high school teacher in New York received several unsatisfactory evaluations and claimed that he was also denied certain benefits and opportunities. He sought an accommodation for dust and pollen allergies, which the school claimed it provided. He then sent letters to the assistant principal, calling her "Mein Fuhrer," and referring to her as a "snooperviser." He also referred to himself as "an indentured subject of her sick experiment." Fearing he represented a threat to the safety of staff and students, the school reassigned him to administrative work at another high school and required a psychological evaluation. Pending the results, his photograph was given to school safety officers and custodial staff who worked in his old high school building during evenings and weekends to ensure that he would not enter the building. He was determined to be fit for duty and was returned to the classroom without any loss of pay or benefits. He then sued for discrimination under state and federal law. A federal court granted pretrial judgment to the defendants. Here, the school provided an accommodation that met the requirements listed in the Board of Education Accommodation. He merely found them unsatisfactory. Further, **the reassignment was a temporary measure taken to ensure the safety of students and staff, and he was transferred back to a teaching position once the evaluation found him fit for duty.** *Krinsky v. Abrams*, No. 01 CV 5052(SLT)(LB), 2007 WL 1541369 (E.D.N.Y. 5/25/07).

D. Failure to Train

◆ A Washington special ed teacher had a closet-sized "safe room" to contain aggressive or "over stimulated" students. The parents of an autistic child in her class agreed to let her put their son in the room as long as the room wasn't used as a punishment, the door remained open and someone stayed inside with him. Instead, the parents claimed she locked him inside it alone to "break" him of bad behavior. They say that while in the room he urinated, defecated and took off his clothes. At home, his mother said he had night terrors. The parents began to homeschool him, but agreed to send him to a different district school the following year. They also sued district defendants, alleging violations of the child's Fourth and Fourteenth amendment rights. The court found the teacher was not entitled to qualified immunity on these claims, as it was established at the time of her alleged offenses that this level of confinement and use of force against a child violated the child's rights. **The parents also claimed the district breached the child's rights by failing to train the teacher on the use of aversive therapies.** The court allowed this claim to go forward, as a rational jury could find its failure to train her on these therapeutic techniques amounted to deliberate indifference and that it was a moving force behind the constitutional violations. *Payne v. Peninsula School Dist.*, No. 3:05-CV-05780, 2013 WL 4676041 (W.D. Wash. 8/30/13).

◆ A Florida teacher knew that other students had been taunting a 13-year-old girl who had texted sexually suggestive pictures of herself to a boy. The teacher saw what looked like self-inflicted cuts on the student's legs and sent her to the office. The school's social worker had the student sign a "no-harm contract," promising not to kill herself, but didn't notify the student's parents as required by school policy. **After the student killed herself at home the next day, the parents sued the school board for negligence, alleging that it failed to properly train the social worker.** The school board sought to have the case dismissed, but a judge refused to do so. Although the parents couldn't claim a constitutional violation, they could pursue their negligence claims. *Witsell v. School Board of Hillsborough County*, 2011 WL 2457877 (M.D. Fla. 6/20/11).

III. SCHOOL SECURITY OFFICERS

At schools in many states, school security officers are an integral component of an overall plan to maintain safety. Schools must ensure that these officers possess all required qualifications and/or certifications.

In Virginia, for example, state law requires that all school security officers are certified via a program administered by the state's department of criminal justice services. Training requirements for school security officers are established by regulation.

New school security officers in Virginia must complete the certification course, which is a 32-hour course, within 60 days from their date of hire. School security officers also are provided with opportunities to supplement their training. The state's department of criminal justice services also offers a course that school security officers can take to become certified school security officer instructors. Individuals who successfully complete this course can provide training to other school security officers. The state also has an online database of school security officers.

The certification program includes renewal requirements. Specifically, school security officers must complete 16 hours of in-service training during each two-year period after initial certification.

◆ Two New York high school students launched an unprovoked attack on a third student in a crowded school hallway. A security guard was only a few feet away at the time. The victim sued the school district for negligence, asserting that the guard had waited a few minutes for the attack to end before intervening. The guard maintained that the attack lasted only a few seconds and that he intervened immediately. The Supreme Court, Appellate Division, stated that the school district had no notice that the two assailants would attack the victim. However, **there was a question as to how quickly the security officer intervened**. That issue required a trial. The district might be liable for negligent supervision by security personnel. *Buchholz v. Patchogue-Medford School Dist.*, 88 A.D.3d 843 (N.Y. Sup. Ct. A.D. 2011).

◆ **A school security officer in Tennessee used gory photos in a scared-straight presentation to highlight the dangers of drunk driving.** He tried to ensure that none of the students would see pictures of dead relatives by checking names, asking teachers about students with potential issues, telling students they didn't have to look at the photos (which were placed in an envelope with the victims' names on the outside), and warning them about the nature of the accident and the names of the victims. Despite these precautions, a student saw a picture of her father. She didn't use her father's last name and knew him by his nickname rather than his given name. She and her mother sued the city for negligent infliction of emotional distress, and a judge awarded them nearly $67,000. However, the Tennessee Court of Appeals reversed, holding that the security officer didn't breach his duty to the students and that he'd taken reasonable steps to prevent such traumatic harm. *Marla H. v. Knox County*, 361 S.W.3d 518 (Tenn. Ct. App. 2011).

◆ A New Jersey man claimed that a former teacher had committed sex acts with him. To back up his claim, he agreed to phone the teacher and let police hear the call. However, the teacher had changed his number, so the police got his new number from the school resource officer, who obtained it with the permission of the principal. The number was also listed in the staff handbook/directory and school emergency plan. After the former student called the teacher and elicited information leading the police to believe that he had molested the former student, the police charged the teacher with sex crimes. He sought to have the evidence thrown out as an illegal search under the Fourth Amendment, but a trial court and an appellate court upheld the search as legal. **The teacher did not have a reasonable privacy interest in his phone number**, and even if he did, he waived that interest by disclosing the number to the school community. *State v. DeFranco*, 43 A.3d 1253 (N.J. Super. Ct. App. Div. 2012).

◆ The security department at a California high school received a call regarding vandalism on campus. Three campus security officers responded, while a peace officer with the unified school district drove his patrol car around the perimeter of the campus. The three campus security officers encountered a group of students, and one officer ordered a student with whom he'd had many conversations in the past to stop running. The student instead continued to flee, stopping only when the peace officer encountered him after he exited the campus. After the student was convicted of willfully resisting a public officer in the discharge of his duties, he appealed, asserting that campus security officers were not "public officers" under the law. A state court ruled that campus security officers are public officers, but the California Court of Appeal reversed the conviction, holding that campus security officers are not public officers. On further appeal, the California Supreme Court reversed the court of appeal, holding that **school security officers are "public officers."** A public officer is understood to include a variety of public officials and employees who perform law enforcement related duties in connection with their employment. *In re M.M.*, 278 P.3d 1221 (Cal. 2012).

◆ A security guard with a private company worked at a junior high school in New York. When a student fight broke out on campus, he intervened and ended up sustaining injuries. He brought a lawsuit against the school district, claiming negligent supervision, but a court ruled in favor of the district. An appellate division court affirmed, noting that **the district owed no legal duty of protection to the security guard**. The duty to supervise students was intended to prevent injuries to other students, not to adult security guards. *Stinson v. Roosevelt U.F.S.D.*, 877 N.Y.S.2d 400 (N.Y. App. Div. 2009).

◆ A high school safety officer's daughter, who attended the school where she worked, got into an altercation with another student outside the school.

The altercation resulted in the filing of charges against the safety officer's daughter. A day later, the safety officer called the other student's mother, claiming that she did so at the direction of the assistant principal for security. She asked the mother to come to the school to participate in a mediation. **The mother alleged that the safety officer threatened her on the phone, telling her that if she cared about her daughter's safety, she would drop the charges.** Based on the alleged threat, the safety officer was charged with aggravated harassment. After she was convicted, she appealed. A New York appellate division court upheld the conviction, noting that the lower court permissibly discredited her testimony that she never made the threat. *People v. Wilson*, 872 N.Y.S.2d 124 (N.Y. App. Div. 2009).

◆   A school security employee at an Idaho high school met with the principal to express concern over school safety and emergency policies, which he believed were inadequate. He also advised the principal of student drug and weapons violations. Around the same time, the principal took away the employee's responsibilities to perform police liaison work, enforce truancy policies, search students and investigate student misconduct. However, the employee retained the responsibilities of assisting with school security, preventing crime and supervising the school parking lot, grounds and hallways. **Although the principal instructed him to update a school emergency plan, his policy-making responsibilities were unclear.**

He later sent a letter to school district administrators complaining about the principal's handling of his earlier reports and expressing concern about specific district safety issues. At the end of that school year, his job was eliminated and his responsibilities were merged with those of three other positions. Another applicant was hired for that job. He filed a grievance, then sued under the First Amendment, claiming retaliation for his protected speech. A federal court granted pretrial judgment to the district, but the Ninth Circuit reversed, finding issues of fact that required a trial. There was a question about whether the employee's letter was part of his official duties. If it was, then according to the Supreme Court's ruling in *Garcetti v. Ceballos*, 547 U.S. 410 (2006), his speech would not be protected. *Posey v. Lake Pend Oreille School Dist. No. 84*, 546 F.3d 1121 (9th Cir. 2008).

◆   A Texas high school student traveled to a neighboring school to attend a basketball game. She had a ticket, but her sister did not, and the game was sold out. As she was bargaining with a ticket-taker to let her sister into the game with her, a district police officer approached her and asked whether she was "in or out." She told him she was "in" and tried to walk through the door. She claimed that he told her she was "out" and put her arm behind her back, throwing her face-first into a glass door. He then allegedly forced her to the ground, placed his knee on her back and handcuffed her. She was charged with criminal trespass and interference with public duties, but the charges were later dropped. She then sued the school district and the security officer, raising claims of excessive force and false arrest. The defendants sought pretrial judgment, but a magistrate judge determined that their request should be denied. The judge concluded that the claims against the officer should be allowed to proceed because **factual questions existed as to whether the officer used more force than was necessary**, and whether he had probable cause to arrest the student. However, the claims against the school district were to be dismissed, the judge ruled, because it was not shown to have a policy, practice or custom of engaging in the violations alleged by the student. *Cooper v. Killeen Independent School Dist.*, No. A-07-CA-082 LY, 2008 WL 194358 (W.D. Tex. 1/23/08).

◆ A New York school security officer became involved in an altercation with an honors student who entered the school before the start of scheduled classes. When the security officer asked the student to leave the building, the student refused to do so. The incident escalated, and the officer arrested the student. As the officer prepared to escort the student from the building, the principal asked the officer to take the student through a back entrance to save her the embarrassment of passing through the front entrance, where hundreds of students were waiting to enter. After the officer denied the principal's repeated requests to take the student out the back door, the principal physically blocked the main entrance to the school. **The security officer then attempted to arrest the principal, who flailed his arms and kicked the officer to avoid being handcuffed.** Eventually, the principal was charged with one count of resisting arrest and one count of obstruction of governmental administration. The principal asked to have the charges dismissed, and a court agreed to do so. The principal had a solid performance history, and his conduct did not threaten the safety of the officer or the school community. His request to take the student out the back entrance was reasonable. *People v. Federman*, 852 N.Y.S.2d 748 (N.Y. City Crim. Ct. 2008).

IV. EMPLOYEE PREPAREDNESS AND RESPONSE

Coordinating employee responsibilities with respect to crisis prevention and response is critical. One way to aid in forming an effective team among school employees is to conduct a staff skills inventory that matches individual employees with particular areas of experience and/or expertise. For a form that can be used to conduct such a skills inventory, see Form I-1 in Chapter Nine.

◆ A Pennsylvania teacher confiscated a student's knife. He informed the principal and his program's director, but he didn't think their response went far enough. He emailed them three days later to complain about their response. Shortly thereafter, he confiscated brass knuckles from a student.

After he became irate at a staff meeting and swore at another teacher, he was suspended for eight days, but a union arbitrator later overturned the discipline. He wrote to the state's school safety center to report unsafe classroom conditions, and later sued the principal and the program director for **violating his free speech rights by retaliating against him for speaking out about school safety**. A federal court granted pretrial judgment against him. Here, it was one of his duties to ensure school safety, so he wasn't speaking as a citizen when he complained, but rather as an employee. *Ankney v. Wakefield*, 2012 WL 2339683 (W.D. Pa. 6/19/12).

◆ An office assistant at a North Carolina school **claimed that the principal jokingly aimed a fire extinguisher at her and blasted her with powdery chemicals that damaged her lungs** and aggravated a neuromuscular disorder that had been in remission. She sued the principal to recover for her injuries. He claimed that he had only picked up the extinguisher to take it to his office for safety reasons and that it accidentally went off. Thus, the lawsuit should be dismissed and workers' compensation should be her exclusive remedy. The North Carolina Court of Appeals refused to dismiss the lawsuit, noting that state law allows employees to sue co-workers for injuries caused by recklessness. *Trivette v. Yount*, 720 S.E.2d 732 (N.C. Ct. App. 2011).

◆ An Alabama special education teacher sustained injuries when a student whom she had repeatedly reported as violent attacked the principal in the office and while doing so bit her, knocked her down and kicked her in the head. She sued the school district for violating her Fourteenth Amendment rights by failing to remove the student from school and by **failing to train her to handle him, despite knowing of his propensity for violence**. She claimed that this amounted to deliberate indifference to her safety. The district sought to have the case dismissed, and a federal court agreed that the case ought to be dismissed. The teacher failed to show that the district's policies amounted to deliberate indifference so as to reach the level of a constitutional violation. And this was not a case of a state actor inflicting injury on the teacher, but rather a private individual. As a result, the court dismissed the case. *May v. Mobile County Public School System*, No. 09-00625-NS-C, 2010 WL 3039181 (S.D. Ala. 7/13/10).

◆ On September 15, 1999, New Jersey's governor declared a state of emergency due to the approach of Hurricane Floyd. However, in Rutherford, New Jersey, less than an inch of rain fell that day, and school officials didn't cancel after-school football practice. After the practice, a 16-year-old student got a ride home from a teammate's sister. About a half-mile from the field, the driver lost control of the car on a curve and struck a tree. The student, who was sitting unrestrained in the rear passenger seat, suffered severe head injuries and sued the school district for negligence, asserting that it should have canceled the practice because of the hurricane warnings and that it shouldn't have let him go him with the teammate's sister, given the weather. A court ruled for the district, and the Superior Court of New Jersey, Appellate Division, affirmed. Here, most of the severe weather from the hurricane arrived the following day rather than the day in question. Because of the absence of extraordinary weather conditions, **the district's employees did not breach a duty of care to the student by not canceling the practice due to the impending hurricane**; nor did they breach a duty of care by allowing the teammate's sister to drive him home. *Pluchino v. Borough of Rutherford*, 2010 WL 335041 (N.J. Super. Ct. App. Div. 2/1/10).

◆ A custodian in Washington received a call from her supervisor asking her to report to work early to replace a distraught co-worker. The supervisor offered no further explanation. When the custodian arrived at school, the district superintendent repeatedly directed her to clean up the scene of a student's suicide. However, a law enforcement officer told her not to touch anything. She also learned of the possibility that the deceased student had left a bomb in the building. She was ordered to accompany the principal on a search for the bomb and was later given permission to clean up the suicide site. However, when she picked up a book bag, she was told to drop it. The book bag apparently contained a pipe bomb, which was detonated on a school field. The superintendent told her to make it look as though nothing had happened at the site. She finished her work at 4:15 a.m., at which point she was distraught and physically ill.

She had to return to the school by 8:00 a.m. to hand out cookies and coffee as counselors assisted students and staff. For the next several days, she had to clean up candles and cards left by students at the scene of the suicide. Later, she sued the school district and superintendent for infliction of emotional distress. A state court held that workers' compensation was her exclusive remedy, but the Washington Court of Appeals reversed. It held that **her post-traumatic stress disorder resulted from the performance of her duties over several days**. Thus, her injury was excluded from the workers' compensation act's definition of an occupational disease. Her lawsuit could continue. *Rothwell v. Nine Mile Falls School Dist.*, 206 P.3d 347 (Wash. Ct. App. 2009).

◆ An Ohio high school principal convened a meeting with senior staff members to discuss the subject of testing during a week when state educational tests were being administered at the school. While the meeting was in progress, the principal was informed that a female student had been assaulted and forced to perform sex acts on a number of male students. She was also told that another male student had videotaped part of the assault. She did not call the police or the department of children services. Instead, she set up a meeting for the following morning to discuss the assault. She also failed to report the sexual assault as her supervisor instructed her to do. She left at 4 p.m. to take care of some personal business without leaving anyone in charge. Nor did she assign anyone to meet with the police officers who had been summoned to the school by the victim's father. The board of education fired her, and she challenged the termination.

The Ohio Court of Appeals upheld the decision to fire her, noting that she violated state law by failing to report the sexual assault. Further, her failure to follow her supervisor's order to report the assault also justified her discharge. **She was not relieved of her duty to contact law enforcement just because the victim's father had called the police.** And her failure to handle the situation immediately was further evidence that she had been properly fired. *Crenshaw v. Columbus City School Dist. Board of Educ.*, No. 07AP-883, 2008 WL 802708 (Ohio Ct. App. 3/27/08).

CHAPTER SIX

Extracurricular Activities

I. AFTER-SCHOOL PROGRAMS

Schools can no longer throw open their doors so that neighborhood children can use their facilities after the school day ends. Nor can they rely on minimal supervision for after-school programs. Threats to security and student safety mean they must now devise plans for how to safely engage students after the school day ends.

Some well-recognized means of decreasing risk are:
- reducing the number of open doors
- concentrating after-school activities in limited areas

- assigning trained personnel to supervise activities rather than relying on custodians
- developing emergency/crisis preparedness training, and
- if contracting with an outside entity to run a program, building into the contract security requirements that must be followed.

A. Negligent Supervision

◆ Two ninth-graders slipped into a locker room during football practice and urinated all over a tenth-grader's gym locker. His father sued the school board, alleging negligent supervision. The Louisiana Court of Appeal upheld a judgment in favor of the school board, noting that there was no evidence that the coaches weren't properly supervising students at the time of the incident. **No one at the school had any notice that misbehavior might occur in the locker room because such an incident had never occurred before.** *Creekbaum v. Livingston Parish School Board*, 80 So.3d 771 (La. Ct. App. 2011).

◆ A California school district created an unstructured "open playground" for students who couldn't be picked up right away after school. Allegedly as few as two adults were responsible for overseeing up to 300 students. One seven-year-old student who stayed after school in the program was asked by another student to join a "kissing club" in an unlocked shed. She went to the shed, where a boy stuck his tongue in her mouth, which upset her so much that she left. Two days later, the student who had recruited her informed her that she had to come back to the club, which she did out of fear. At this meeting, the recruiter forced her to pull down her pants and the same boy then took off his pants and rubbed against her from behind. She later told a fifth-grader, who told the playground supervisor, who called the student's mother, who brought in the police.

In the lawsuit that followed, the school asserted that it didn't have a duty of care to children who participated in voluntary after-school programs. A court agreed, but the California Court of Appeal reversed, holding that a trial was needed to determine if the lack of supervision was responsible for the student's injury and if the injury was foreseeable. Here, **the after-school program, despite its voluntary nature, created a special relationship between the school district and the program participants**. And the student had a right to reasonable protection while in the program. *J.H. v. Los Angeles Unified School Dist.*, 107 Cal.Rptr.3d 182 (Cal. Ct. App. 2010).

◆ A Connecticut elementary student participated in an after-school program run by the town of New Milford. While hanging on a basketball rim installed seven feet above the ground, he fell onto the concrete surface below and sustained injuries. He sued the town and the employees who had been supervising the program for negligence. After examining the "imminent harm" exception to discretionary act immunity, the Superior

Court of Connecticut ruled in favor of the town. The imminent harm exception test requires three things: (1) an imminent harm; (2) an identifiable victim; and (3) a public official to whom it is apparent that his or her conduct is likely to subject that victim to that harm. Here, the supervisors testified that no one else had ever been hurt after dropping from the rim. Nor was hanging on the rim a prohibited activity. **Since there was no apparent risk of injury to the student, the town and employees were entitled to immunity.** *Zaborowski v. Town of New Milford*, No. LL1CV054002368S, 2007 WL 1413911 (Conn. Super. Ct. 4/24/07).

◆ The parents of a child injured on a school playground sued the after-school program providers, alleging negligent supervision. The child was injured when he slipped and fell while engaged in normal play on a "monkey-bars" apparatus in a schoolyard during an after-school program. Two supervisors employed by the defendants were approximately 15 feet away from the child when they saw him fall. At least one other supervisor was within the same complex of playground equipment, and two additional adult volunteers were assigned to supervise the group of 25 to 30 children of which the child was a member. The case reached the New York Supreme Court, Appellate Division, which noted that the child was not engaged in any rough or inappropriate play prior to the accident and that **the defendants were not on notice of any horseplay or defective condition so as to warrant closer supervision or intervention**. Accordingly, the degree of supervision afforded by the defendants was reasonable and adequate under the circumstances, and the child's injury was not proximately caused by a lack of supervision. The lawsuit was dismissed. *Berdecia v. City of New York*, 289 A.D.2d 354, 735 N.Y.S.2d 554 (N.Y. App. Div. 2001).

B. Duty to Protect Students

◆ A 14-year-old student injured his hand while playing basketball during an after-school program. **His hand hit a metal cage a foot away from the backboard, and the tip of a finger stuck there.** He sued the school to recover for his injuries. A court awarded him over $1 million in past and future damages (for the next 40 years). The Supreme Court, Appellate Division, upheld the finding of liability, noting that the student had not assumed the risk of such an injury. However, the damage award was excessive. The court offered the student $300,000 in damages or a new trial limited to determining an appropriate amount. *Robinson v. New York City Dep't of Educ.*, 94 A.D.3d 428 (N.Y. App. Div. 2012).

◆ The mother of an eight-year-old Louisiana student dropped her daughter off at around 7:20 a.m. for the school breakfast, which was to be served at 7:30. A janitor stopped the student on the way in and told her that a teacher wanted to see her. He led her to an upstairs classroom, put a towel over her head, told her to bare one foot and touched her with a part of his body that wasn't his hand. She reported the incident despite his warning not to, and her mother sued the school board for vicarious liability and failure to supervise. A court granted pretrial judgment to the school board, but the court of appeal reversed, finding issues of fact that required a trial. **It was reasonable to assume that the school board had a duty to supervise students and the janitor even though the breakfast hadn't officially started.** *Booth v. Orleans Parish School Board*, 49 So.3d 919 (La. Ct. App. 2010).

◆ A New York middle school student disobeyed his mother's instructions to attend an after-school program. Instead, he went to a park after school and fell from a swing, breaking his leg. He sued the after-school program, claiming a failure to adequately supervise. A trial court ruled against him, and the New York Supreme Court, Appellate Division, affirmed. A school's duty to supervise students is coextensive with its custody and control over them. Here, **the student got hurt while he was beyond the after-school program's authority.** Neither the program nor the school was responsible for his injuries. Even though the program failed to notify the student's mother that the student did not show up that day, that failure did not cause the child's injuries. *Fotiadis v. City of New York*, 853 N.Y.S.2d 591 (N.Y. App. Div. 2008).

◆ A California school opened its campus at 7:00 a.m., but trouble spots, such as restrooms, were unsupervised before 7:45 a.m. School administrators knew that one eighth-grade special education student was usually dropped off at 7:15 a.m. A classmate who also had disabilities teased and ridiculed the student daily before classes began. The student sometimes went to the office to escape this, and he complained to the staff. He was told to stay away from the classmate, even after he told the vice principal this did not work. The classmate twice isolated the student and sexually assaulted him. The district learned of the incidents and expelled the classmate, who was also arrested. The student was hospitalized with depression, and he attempted suicide. He sued the school district and the classmate's family. A jury trial resulted in a verdict of over $2.5 million for the student, and the district appealed.

The Court of Appeal of California observed that **school districts have a well-established duty to supervise students at all times while on school grounds. This duty included supervision during recess and before or after school.** The district was liable for injuries resulting from the failure of school staff to use ordinary care to protect students. The district unlocked its gates at 7:00 a.m. each day, but did not provide supervision until 7:45 a.m. It could have simply precluded students from arriving early or kept them in particular areas of the school. The district's claim to immunity failed because there was no exercise of discretion by the principal, and evidence that he knew of the classmate's violent behavior. The damage award was not excessive, and the court affirmed the judgment. *M.W. v. Panama Buena Union School Dist.*, 1 Cal. Rptr. 3d 673 (Cal. Ct. App. 2003).

◆ The family of a New York student brought a lawsuit against the board of education, seeking to recover damages for injuries the student allegedly sustained when, upon being pushed by a schoolmate, he fell down a staircase at a public school during an after-school program run by the YMCA of Greater New York. There was no handrail on the right side of the staircase where the student was walking. The supreme court denied the board's motion for pretrial judgment and the Supreme Court, Appellate Division, affirmed.

The testimony of the student at a hearing and at his deposition demonstrated that he tried to grab the handrail on the opposite side of the stairs to stop his fall, but could not reach it. The unchallenged statement of the family's expert **engineer demonstrated that the absence of a handrail on the right side of the staircase was a violation of the applicable building code**. Thus, there were triable issues of fact as to whether the absence of the handrail was a proximate cause of the student's injuries and whether the fact that he was pushed by a fellow student severed any nexus (connection) between the city's alleged negligence in the design of the staircase and his injuries. The case required a trial. *Ocasio v. Board of Educ. of City of New York*, 35 A.D.3d 825, 827 N.Y.S.2d 265 (N.Y. App. Div. 2006).

II. FIELD TRIPS AND OFF-CAMPUS ACTIVITIES

Field trips provide a dual challenge to schools. First, they must ensure the safety of their students off school grounds, in settings where outside influences are not as easily controllable.

Second, they must ensure the safety of the general public from reasonably foreseeable acts of violence or horseplay by students. This latter concern, while slight for many schools (especially elementary schools), can be a real problem for others.

Increased supervision presents the single easiest solution, especially the usage of parent volunteers to assist with oversight. But this also presents a problem: how to verify that parent volunteers are not a threat. Background checks are the best insurance policy against threats to students.

Some schools charge parents to conduct background checks; others impose a fee for all students for field trips, a part of which can be used to conduct the background checks. For a sample field trip permission slip, see Form VI-3 in Chapter Nine. A sample questionnaire for chaperones can be found at Form VI-1, and a sample of chaperone guidelines can be found at Form VI-2 in Chapter Nine.

◆   Graduates of a Washington high school arranged for kegs of beer for a party at an off-campus location and without adult supervision. During the party, three graduates confronted a junior, who was the only underclassman there. One of the graduates hit the junior on the forehead with a heavy beer mug. Although the wound appeared minor, the junior collapsed and fell into a coma four months later. Four years after that, the junior died, and **his estate sued the graduates who had purchased the beer** as well as the graduates who confronted the junior and the beer distributor who made the kegs available. The Court of Appeals of Washington ultimately ruled that only the junior's assailants could be liable for his death. It refused to recognize an inherent propensity for violence at teenage keg parties so as to broaden liability to others. *Cameron v. Murray*, 214 P.3d 150 (Wash. Ct. App. 2009).

◆ During a school-sponsored field trip, a Nevada student found a knife on the floor of the bus and turned it in to the bus driver. Another student admitted that the knife was his. He was allowed to participate in the field trip, but the next day, a school vice principal suspended him for 10 days pending expulsion. The vice principal drafted a letter to the student explaining the district's weapons policy and detailing the violation. A school district disciplinary panel conducted a hearing at which the charges against the student were read, and a school police liaison officer testified for the district. The student claimed that he brought the knife along accidentally, and his parents asserted that he was not a disciplinary problem. However, the panel recommended expulsion for the remaining weeks of the school year.

The school board met in a closed session, without the family, and accepted the recommendation for expulsion. Afterward, the family sued in a federal court, claiming that the district had not given the student adequate due process prior to expelling him. The court determined that **the disciplinary hearing met the heightened requirements for expulsion proceedings**. The school board did not need to conduct another hearing with the student. Accordingly, the student received all the due process to which he was entitled. And his admission that the knife was his also made another hearing unnecessary. *Hardie v. Churchill County School Dist.*, No. 3:07-CV-310-RAM, 2009 WL 875486 (D. Nev. 3/30/09).

A. Negligent Supervision

1. Duty of Care

◆ Staff at a private high school in Florida intercepted end-of-year party invitations with a faintly visible liquor bottle in the background. The principal announced that he intended to stop by the party and also talked with the host's parents to ensure that they would be home to chaperone. He arrived at the party around 4:00 p.m., confirmed that the host's mother was there, and left. About forty-five minutes later, two students who had gotten someone else to obtain alcohol for them left the party. They were drunk and crashed their car into a tree. One student died; the other became a quadriplegic. He and his parents sued the school and its archdiocese for negligence, **asserting that the principal, by undertaking to check on the party, had a duty to act with reasonable care**, and that he breached that duty. A jury found the school defendants 25% at fault, but the Florida

District Court of Appeal reversed. First, the private school's contract with students clearly stated that the school wasn't liable for events not officially sanctioned. Second, the accident occurred outside school hours at a non-school activity. The court refused to punish the school for the principal's good deed of checking up on the students. *Archbishop Coleman F. Carroll High School, Inc. v. Maynoldi*, 30 So.3d 533 (Fla. Dist. Ct. App. 2010).

◆   A California school organized an end-of-year field trip to a water park for its seventh-graders, to be supervised by the teaching staff as well as lifeguards at the park. Students who attended had to turn in permission slips signed by parents and/or guardians. After a student drowned, his family sued the water park, which then sued the school district, asserting that it failed to provide a minimum ratio of at least one adult chaperone for every 13 students, as its policies and regulations required. The water park also claimed the district should have determined the student's swimming ability, warned him of the risks at the park or watched him while he swam. A trial court dismissed the district from the lawsuit, and the California Court of Appeal affirmed. **Under state law, students who go on field trips waive their right to sue if they get hurt.** *Windsor R/V Waterworks Park Co. v. Santa Rosa City Schools*, No. A118090, 2008 WL 4601138 (Cal. Ct. App. 10/16/08) (Unpublished).

◆   During a field trip to an Ohio recreation center, a Kentucky special education student with profound mental disabilities broke his ankle. He had been fitted with a pair of roller skates, which were locked to prevent him from rolling. Peer tutors helped him while he wore the skates. An adult supervisor was on the floor taking pictures of students at the time of the accident. She approached the student and peer tutors to take their picture. **The student fell when he leaned over to kiss another student for the picture.** The teacher arrived after the student fell. She looked at his ankle after he indicated that it hurt, but she saw no obvious injuries. Later, the student's mother took him to a doctor, who discovered the broken ankle. The parents then sued the school board and the teacher to recover for his injuries. A trial court held that the board was entitled to governmental immunity and that the teacher had qualified immunity.

On appeal, the Court of Appeals of Kentucky noted that public employees have qualified immunity when they perform acts involving the exercise of discretion and judgment, if those acts are taken in good faith and within the scope of employment authority. On the other hand, employees have no immunity for ministerial acts, which involve imperative duties and do not require the exercise of discretion. Here, the teacher had to exercise discretion and personal judgment a number of times during the day, including on how to implement the student's IEP and how to supervise him. She also acted in good faith and within the course and scope of her employment. Both the teacher and the board were entitled to immunity. *Pennington v. Greenup County Board of Educ.*, No. 2006-CA-001942-MR, 2008 WL 1757209 (Ky. Ct. App. 4/18/08).

◆   After being released from school on a rainy day, a 12-year-old New York student used a cell phone to call his mother, who was parked across the street. Although there was a stop sign, crosswalk and crossing guard at one intersection and a stop light and crosswalk at the other, the student crossed in the middle of the street at his mother's direction. He was hit by a car and sustained injuries. His mother sued the school district for negligence in dismissing the student in an area it knew was hazardous. The New York Supreme Court, Appellate Division, dismissed the case, noting that schools are not insurers of student safety. **Schools' custodial duty of care for students ends when the students pass out of their "orbit of authority."** Here, the student was hurt while off school property and under the control of his mother, and there was no indication that the school had created a special hazard. *Vernali v. Harrison Cent. School Dist.*, 857 N.Y.S.2d 699 (N.Y. App. Div. 2008).

◆   An eleventh-grade Florida student left school without authorization along with four classmates after first period to go out for breakfast. She got into a classmate's car and was killed when he ran into a pair of trees at high speed. Her father sued the school board, claiming it could have prevented the accident by following its policy regarding habitual truancy. The policy required principals to report habitually truant students to the school board and state department of highway safety and motor vehicles. It also called for the filing of a truancy petition or a "child in need of services" petition. These steps were not taken for the student because she had not accumulated at least 15 absences in a 90-day period so as to be categorized as habitually truant. After the trial court ruled for the school board, the Florida District Court of Appeal affirmed. **The school was not obligated to supervise students while they were engaged in off-campus activities unrelated to school.** Further, the school could not be held liable for injuries suffered by students who violate school attendance policies. *Kazanjian v. School Board of Palm Beach County*, 967 So.2d 259 (Fla. Dist. Ct. App. 2007).

◆   Approximately 200 eighth-grade students from a middle school in Texas went on a field trip to an athletic club, where the activities included swimming. No lifeguards were hired. Sometime during the day, an eighth-grader drowned in the swimming pool. His family sued the district and various employees under 42 U.S.C. § 1983. The district employees sought pretrial judgment, asserting that they were entitled to immunity for their actions. The trial court disagreed, and the employees appealed to the Texas Court of Appeals.

The claims here included allegations that the school district employees committed constitutional violations because they failed to properly supervise and/or discipline the student on the field trip. The court held that the school district employees were acting within the scope of their discretionary authority at the time of the incident. Further, **there was no special relationship to create a constitutional duty on the part of the**

employees to safeguard the student against potential harm during the field trip. The employees should have been granted pretrial judgment. The appellate court reversed the lower court's decision. *Leo v. Trevino*, 285 S.W.3d 470 (Tex. Ct. App. 2006).

◆   An Arkansas student attended a band competition in Atlanta with his school band. He became ill after arriving and missed the entire competition while remaining in his hotel room. Shortly after the student returned home, his mother took him to a medical center. However, he suffered a cardiac arrest and died the next day. The death was attributed to undiagnosed diabetes. The mother sued the school district and officials in a federal district court for negligence and deliberate indifference to her son's medical needs. The court dismissed her federal constitutional claims. It held federal jurisdiction should be rejected in cases that involved common law torts incidentally involving action by a government employee. The mother appealed to the U.S. Court of Appeals, Eighth Circuit. The court echoed the district court's opinion, noting that "the Due Process Clause of the Fourteenth Amendment is not a 'font of tort law.'" Neither the text nor the history of the clause indicated state entities must guarantee minimal safety and security to individuals. The Due Process Clause generally does not confer affirmative rights to government aid, even if this may be necessary to secure individual life, liberty or property interests.

A state assumes a constitutional duty to protect an individual's safety only when it has restrained the individual's liberty through incarceration, institutionalization or some other form of restraint that renders the individual incapable of self-care. The district court had correctly dismissed the due process claim against the school district, because there was no district policy of violating student constitutional rights. There was also no evidence that the band director had restrained the student's ability to care for himself. **School officials have no duty to care for students who participate in voluntary school-related activities such as school band trips.** There was no claim that the student could not leave the band activity at any time, and his family was not prevented from arranging for him to leave Atlanta. The court found no evidence that the student's "voluntary participation evolved into an involuntary commitment" during the trip. While a tort remedy might still be available in the state courts, the judgment for the school district on the mother's federal claims was affirmed. *Lee v. Pine Bluff School Dist.*, 472 F.3d 1026 (8th Cir. 2007).

2. Harmful Acts of Others

◆   A student on a field trip to the National Zoo in Washington claimed that he was assaulted, kicked, and beaten by five male students who were on a school field trip with their private, non-profit school chartered under District of Columbia law for at-risk youths. **He alleged that at the time of the attack, the students were unsupervised.** He also alleged that he suffered a concussion and injuries to multiple areas of his body. He sued the school, alleging negligent supervision. The school sought to dismiss the case, arguing that it owed the victimized student no duty to provide a constant watch over its students during a school field trip in order to prevent an unforeseeable act of violence. The injured student argued that the school did owe him a duty of care and cited to the Restatement of Torts (2d) § 319:

> One who takes charge of a third person whom he knows or should know to be likely to cause bodily harm to others if not controlled is under a duty to exercise reasonable care to control the third person to prevent him from doing such harm.

The court permitted the injured student to maintain his negligence claim on the ground that the school had a duty to make reasonable efforts to protect members of the public from its students during the field trip. **A school's duty to supervise its students to guard against foreseeable harm does not disappear on field trips.** So if the injured student could show that the school should have known his attackers had a propensity for violence, the school could be liable. *Thomas v. City Lights School*, 124 F.Supp.2d 707 (D.D.C. 2000).

◆   A New York student's sixth-grade class, along with five other fifth- and sixth-grade classes, attended a drug awareness fair at a park near their school. Sponsored by the board of education and the police department, the fair permitted students to walk through the park on their own and participate in program activities that interested them. Seven teachers and four or five aides supervised the group. A student received permission to get lunch at a nearby pizzeria, but she did not return from lunch by the time her teacher decided to return to school. The teacher looked for her but did not inform any teachers or police officers providing security at the fair that he could not locate her. The student had left the park to walk home after she failed to find her classmates. On the way home, she was raped by a junior high school student and his friend. She sued the board of education for her injuries.

A jury ruled in her favor and awarded her $2,250,000 in damages, but the Supreme Court, Appellate Division, reversed. The case then reached the Court of Appeals, New York's highest court, which held that a rational jury could have determined, as the jury in this case did, that the foreseeable result of the danger created by the school's alleged lack of supervision was an injury such as occurred here. The jury permissibly determined that **the rape was the foreseeable result of a danger created by the school's failure to adequately supervise the student**. Thus, the board was liable for the student's injuries. *Bell v. Board of Educ. of the City of New York*, 687 N.E.2d 1325 (N.Y. 1997).

◆   A 16-year-old boy was shot and killed by another teen who had escaped 60 days earlier from a residential facility for troubled youth in the District of Columbia. The boy's mother sued the District, the Administrator of the D.C. Youth Services Administration (YSA), and the company that contracted with the YSA to run the facility. She claimed that the defendants knew the teen had absconded on two prior occasions and negligently failed to supervise him accordingly – a failure that caused her son's untimely death. A federal court ruled for the defendants, noting that **at the time of the shooting, the teen was far beyond the facility's custodial control**. Further, **the facility did not know of the teen's dangerous propensities**. Juveniles who are determined to pose a public danger are not assigned to group homes like the facility here. Thus, the defendants could not be held liable for the shooting of the boy. *Johnson v. District of Columbia*, No. 03-2548 (GK), 2006 WL 2521241 (D.D.C. 8/30/06).

◆ A Washington high school sponsored a "Workday" event, in which community members donated $15 for three hours of student work to raise funds for a student association. A student's mother agreed to let her daughter split and stack firewood with a classmate's father. She learned on the day of the event that the classmate's father planned to have the students split logs with a hydraulic log splitter. The mother cautioned the student, but apparently did not turn in a parental permission slip to perform the work. While the students were operating the log splitter, they were distracted by a car, and the student lost three fingers.

The student sued the school district and classmate's father for negligence. The court found the student's mother had consented to the activity and awarded judgment to the school district. The student appealed. The Court of Appeals of Washington stated that schools are not insurers of student safety, but are liable for foreseeable wrongful acts of third parties. **Liability may result if a school supervises and exercises control over extracurricular activities.** As the student was in the district's custody, it owed her a duty of reasonable care. A jury could have found the district should have taken appropriate steps to find out what was planned for each Workday location and identify any obvious safety problems. The student had presented enough evidence to receive a jury trial to decide whether her mother's consent superseded the district's duty. The court reversed and remanded the case for a trial. *Travis v. Bohannon*, 115 P.3d 342 (Wash. Ct. App. 2005).

B. School Policies – Permission

◆ The summer before her senior year, an Illinois student went on two school-sponsored trips to China. She was told repeatedly that alcohol was forbidden, and she signed a contract to that effect. She and other students were caught drinking during the second trip. When she returned home, her principal suspended her for 10 days. She sought a preliminary injunction to stop the suspension and only served three days because she graduated before the case came to trial. When her lawsuit challenging the suspension came before a judge, the court ruled that her procedural due process rights had been met because **she had been informed of the charges and given an opportunity to respond to them**. *Sabol v. Walter Payton College Preparatory High School*, 804 F.Supp.2d 747 (N.D. Ill. 2011).

◆ A sixth-grade student with asthma went on a field trip to a district-operated science camp. When she suffered an attack, camp counselors gave the student her inhaler and performed CPR on her until paramedics arrived. However, she died as she was being airlifted to a hospital. Her parents sued the district that operated the science camp for negligently failing to provide adequate medical staff and for misrepresenting the level of medical staffing that would be available. The case reached the California Court of Appeal, which held that the district was entitled to immunity under the state education code. **Any person on a school field trip or excursion is deemed to have waived all claims against the school district**, charter school or the state for injury, accident, illness or death occurring "during or by reason of the field trip or excursion." The parents' lawsuit failed. *Sanchez v. San Diego County Office of Educ.*, 182 Cal.App.4th 1580, 106 Cal.Rptr.3d 750 (Cal. Ct. App. 2010).

◆ A group of Ohio students attended a school-sponsored student exchange program in Germany. Before the trip, a teacher explained to students that they would stay with a "host family" for two weeks. They would have some supervised field trips, but would spend a great deal of time with host families without any direct supervision by school staff or the host school. While in Germany, a number of students drank alcohol with their "host parents." They were of legal drinking age in Germany and believed they were permitted to drink without supervision. Upon returning home, the school suspended the students for three to five days for violating student code prohibitions on consuming or possessing alcohol while in the school's control and custody. The students asked for a hearing before the school board, arguing the teacher had "verbally created an exception to the school's code of conduct regarding the consumption of alcohol." Students and parents understood the exception as allowing the parents and host parents to determine whether students could drink alcohol. The board overturned the suspensions but required the students to perform community service.

An Ohio trial court vacated the discipline, and the board appealed to the Court of Appeals of Ohio. The court stated that **Ohio law gives school districts the authority to devise codes of conduct, adopt a policy for suspension, expulsion and removal of students, and to specify the types of misconduct resulting in discipline**. There was undisputed evidence that the teacher had "engrafted an exception on the disciplinary code's provisions concerning alcohol consumption." Only the teacher and another employee had testified that the "exception" required direct supervision of host parents for any student drinking. The exception was not written. The students and parents had all stated their understanding of the policy allowed parents and host parents to determine the circumstances for alcohol consumption by students. The court upheld the trial court's decision to vacate any discipline. *Brosch v. Mariemont City School Dist. Board of Educ.*, No. C-050283, 2006 WL 250947 (Ohio Ct. App. 2/3/06).

◆   Minnesota students attending an auto shop class were bused to a body shop for class instruction. En route, the teacher observed a student holding a knife that was passed to him from a classmate. When the bus arrived at the body shop, the teacher called a school coordinator to report the knife. The coordinator and principal decided each student should be searched, and the principal called a school liaison officer. Before the search began, the classmate voluntarily handed over the knife. The liaison officer found a collapsible baton in the student's pocket, and he was charged with violating a state law prohibiting possession of a dangerous weapon on school property. The district brought an expulsion proceeding against the student, who sued for civil rights violations.

The case reached the Eighth Circuit, which stated that school and municipal officers are entitled to qualified immunity when their conduct does not violate clearly established federal statutory or constitutional rights of which a reasonable officer would have knowledge. While law officers are normally required to have probable cause of wrongdoing to support a search or seizure of persons or property, the more lenient standard of "reasonable suspicion" applies to searches and seizures in the context of public schools. School administrators initiated the search, and one of them played a substantial role in it. **The fact that the search took place off school grounds did not call for imposing the stricter probable cause standard.** The liaison officer's conduct was reasonable, as he did not know whether other students might also have weapons. He had reasonable grounds to believe that the student possessed a knife and was not required to use the least intrusive means of performing a search. As the search was justified and reasonable in scope, the officer was entitled to immunity. *Shade v. City of Farmington, Minnesota*, 309 F.3d 1054 (8th Cir. 2002).

◆   A teacher employed by the Kansas State School for the Deaf (KSSD) asked an assistant football coach to recruit players to help him improve property he owned. The project involved moving discarded railroad ties that weighed 150 pounds. The school's head teacher turned down a written request for a field trip to the property, but later signed the request form. Two students and the assistant football coach accompanied the teacher to the property. When the teacher left to prepare lunch, one of the students was struck and killed by a train. KSSD's board ruled the teacher's conduct did not reflect high standards of professional conduct, especially for the safety needs of deaf students. A KSSD investigation committee adopted a motion terminating the teacher's employment for jeopardizing the health and safety of students, failing to exercise appropriate professional judgment, failing to comply with school policies, and failing to conduct himself "in a manner reflecting positively on the school." However, a KSSD hearing committee held for the teacher, finding the board did not prove he displayed a lack of professional judgment.

The case reached the Kansas Supreme Court, which **upheld the hearing committee's finding that no school policy or student safety regulations applied to the case. The board showed no evidence of a loss**

of confidence in the teacher, as the testimony of members of the deaf community was "all to the contrary." While the teacher did not inform parents about the nature of the field trip, this was the head teacher's duty. There was evidence that the practice of taking railroad ties from railroad property was common and not inappropriate. The court refused to reweigh the evidence or substitute its judgment for that of the committee. *Kansas State Board of Educ. v. Marsh*, 50 P.3d 9 (Kan. 2002).

III. ATHLETIC EVENTS

Student-athletes assume the risks incidental to sports participation and, absent a showing of gross negligence or intentional conduct by a coach, league or school, may not recover damages for their injuries.

A. Participants

1. Duty of Care

State laws require a showing that the school or its staff acted recklessly or intentionally to overcome the defense of governmental immunity.

◆ New York City officials had no duty to protect a student at a game run by a local charity at his school. In 2010, Tottenville High School hosted a charity football game played by two other schools. A member of Tottenville's team attended the game as a spectator. During halftime, he went to the locker room to get gear from his locker. The locker room was being used by a Catholic school team playing in the charity game. In the locker room, the student got into a heated argument with the Catholic school's coach and head-butted him. Enraged, the team jumped the boy. His mother sued multiple parties for personal injury, including the City of New York and its department of education. The city defendants asked the judge to dismiss them from the case. The suit alleged the city defendants breached their duty to provide for students' safety, security, protection and well-being. The city provided security, but the family argued guards should have been posted at the gym entrance during halftime to prevent students from entering the locker room. But the judge agreed with the city defendants, **as public school officials have no duty to protect students from injury by third parties unless the school has a special relationship with the student**. That wasn't the case here, as the city defendants hadn't done anything to convey they would protect the student personally – and he hadn't relied on any such assurance. In addition, the school defendants weren't liable for the injury because they had no reasonable warning it might occur and the attack happened "in a matter of seconds" – too fast for an onlooker to step in. As the city defendants breached no duty to keep the student safe, the court dismissed them from his lawsuit. *Chavis v. City of New York*, 975 N.Y.S.2d 708 (N.Y. Sup. Ct. 2013).

◆ In New York, a cheerleader was injured while attempting a stunt at practice. The move required the girl to stand on another cheerleader's shoulders. But she fell during the stunt. She sued the district, claiming the school was negligent because it did not provide proper supervision while she attempted the stunt. The trial court refused to grant the school judgment without a trial, but on appeal, the appellate court reversed. Under New York law, **a student assumes the inherent risks of an extracurricular activity by participating**. And because falling is an obvious risk associated with cheerleading, the claim failed. *Kristina D. v. Nesaquake Middle School*, 98 A.D.3d 600 (N.Y. App. Div. 2012).

◆ A Florida student-athlete was left with permanent brain damage and will require 24-hour care for the rest of his life after he collapsed on the field during a soccer game. After the boy fell, the assistant coach called 911 while the school nurse performed CPR. The coach claimed he called for the automated external defibrillator (AED), as state law required the school to have one. But no one – not even the nurse – heard his request. Paramedics arrived on scene and used their AED without success. The boy's parents sued, claiming the school was negligent. They said it could have prevented their son's severe injuries if it had an AED as the law required. The court rejected the claim because the school had complied with state law. It had an AED at school, registered its location with local emergency responders and provided first aid. Further, the court explained the district's common-law duty in this state to take appropriate efforts to keep a student's injury from getting worse didn't include "a duty to maintain, make available or use an AED." **However, this is a developing area, and laws vary by state.** *Limones v. School Dist. of Lee County*, 111 So.3d 901 (Fla. Dist. Ct. App. 2013).

◆ An Iowa high school basketball player elbowed an opposing player in the head during a game and was immediately ejected. The other player went to the bench briefly, but then returned to the game, though he played poorly from that point on. His family sued the school district and the player, seeking damages of more than $1.5 million. The case reached the Iowa Supreme Court, which dismissed the claim against the district, noting that **the battery by the player was not reasonably foreseeable, as was required for the district to be held liable for breaching a duty of care**. The student's prior conduct, although aggressive, did not put the district on notice that he was a dangerous person. The court did uphold, however, a damage award against the student for $23,000. *Brokaw v. Winfield-Mt. Union Community School Dist.*, 788 N.W.2d 386 (Iowa 2010).

◆ A 13-year-old student on his junior high school basketball team blacked out at a Monday practice. His mother told the coach that he was only allowed to walk through plays – and could not do anything strenuous. But at the Wednesday practice, the coach made the whole team, including the student, perform a running drill. After the student collapsed and died, his parents sued the school district for wrongful death. The district asserted that the student knew better than to perform a running drill in his condition; thus, his contributory negligence prevented the parents from recovering money damages. However, the Supreme Court of Indiana disagreed. It noted that **children 7 to 14 years old are generally too young to be held responsible for their own injuries** because they lack the maturity to foresee harm and take steps to prevent it. The only way to rebut the presumption that a 7- to 14-year-old is not responsible for his injuries is to show that the child had the "mental capacity, intelligence and experience" to be accountable for himself. Since that was not the case here, the parents were entitled to recover from the district. *Clay City Consolidated School Dist. v. Timberman*, 918 N.E.2d 292 (Ind. 2009).

◆ A Louisiana cheerleader – the "flyer" on her squad – suffered injuries when she was lifted up by an untrained recruit who held onto her feet tightly even though he should have left her feet free in case she needed to jump. When she fell, she landed on her back and sustained herniated discs that left her with chronic pain. She sued the school district for her injuries, and **a jury found the district negligent for allowing the untrained recruit to participate in the difficult stunt**. It awarded her more than $274,000. However, the judge reduced the amount by one-fourth, ruling that she was a quarter to blame because she didn't fall the right way. The Louisiana Court of Appeal reversed the judge's decision and gave her the full jury award. She did not breach a duty to fall a certain way when the stunt went bad. *Comeaux v. Acadia Parish School Board*, 13 So.3d 252 (La. Ct. App. 2009).

◆ A member of a high school track team in Pennsylvania sustained injuries when a teammate hit her in the leg with a javelin during practice. She sued the district and the coaches for negligence, and she also asserted that her due process rights had been violated. The defendants sought to have the case dismissed, and a federal court agreed to do so. First, it found no due process violation because **the district had proper policies in place to deal with injuries**. And even if the district failed to comply with those policies, that was not sufficient to support a due process claim. Further, the district did not have a special relationship with her such that it owed her an increased duty of care. Finally, the district did not create the danger that resulted in her injuries. It was the teammate's decision to throw the javelin that caused the harm. *Leonard v. Owen J. Roberts School Dist.*, No. 08-2016, 2009 WL 603160 (E.D. Pa. 3/5/09).

◆ A junior high school wrestling coach in Pennsylvania instructed a 152-pound wrestler to grapple with a 240-pound teammate during a practice. They were to simulate competitive conditions, and the coach paired them up because there was no suitable partner for the heavier wrestler. The smaller wrestler injured his leg when his teammate fell on it. He sued the coach and his school district for violating his liberty interests under the Constitution. A federal court ruled against him, but the Third Circuit allowed his lawsuit against the coach to proceed. There was evidence that the coach acted with "deliberate indifference" to his constitutional rights. Under the state's interscholastic athletic association rules, students were not permitted to move more than one weight class from their own. Here, **the teammate who caused the injury was three weight classes above the injured student**. However, the lawsuit against the school district could not proceed because the coach did not make policy for the district, and the student failed to show that the district had a policy or custom of violating students' federal rights. *Patrick v. Great Valley School Dist.*, 296 Fed.Appx. 258 (3d Cir. 2008).

◆   A California community college student played on a visiting baseball team in a preseason game against a host college. The host team's pitcher hit him in the head with a pitch, cracking his batting helmet. The student claimed he was intentionally hit in retaliation for a pitch thrown by his teammate at a batter from the host team in the previous inning. After being hit, the student staggered, felt dizzy, and was in pain. His manager told him to go to first base. The student did so, but complained to his first-base coach, who told him to stay in the game. Soon after that, the student was told to sit on the bench. He claimed no one tended to his injuries. The student sued the host college for breaching its duty of care by failing to supervise or control its pitcher and failing to provide umpires or medical care. The court dismissed the case, but the state court of appeal reversed. The Supreme Court of California held that Section 831.7 of the California Government Code did not extend to injuries suffered during supervised school sports.

Section 831.7 was intended to be a premises liability provision for public entities. **In sports, the doctrine of assumption of risk precludes any liability for injuries deemed "inherent in a sport."** The college did not fail to adequately supervise and control the pitcher. Being hit by a pitch is an inherent risk of baseball. Colleges are not liable for the actions of their student-athletes during competition. The failure to provide umpires did not increase risks inherent in the game. The student's own coaches, not the host college, had the responsibility to remove him from the game for medical attention. *Avila v. Citrus Community College Dist.*, 38 Cal.4th 148, 41 Cal.Rptr. 299, 131 P.3d 383 (Cal. 2006).

◆   A Louisiana freshman football player injured his back in a weight training session. His physician diagnosed him with a lumbar strain and dehydrated disc, and gave him a medical excuse excluding him from football for one week with instructions for "no weightlifting, squats or power cleans." The coaching staff interpreted the weightlifting limitation to be for only one week, and a coach instructed the student to do a particular lift. He did the lift and suffered severe back pain. The student was diagnosed with a disc protrusion and a herniated disc. He lost interest in school, failed classes and transferred to an alternative school. The student sued the school board for personal injury. A state trial court awarded him less than $7,500 for medical expenses, but awarded him $275,500 for pain and suffering, future medical expenses and loss of enjoyment of life.

The school board appealed to a Louisiana Circuit Court of Appeal, which reviewed testimony that the student continued to experience severe back pain and often could not sleep. **The evidence supported the trial court's finding that he had been severely injured and would experience recurring pain that would limit his daily activities indefinitely.** The trial court did not commit error in awarding the student damages for pain and suffering. The court affirmed the damage award for loss of enjoyment of life, based on evidence that the student lost the opportunity to play varsity baseball and football. There was further evidence he suffered depression and emotional anguish. *Day v. Ouachita Parish School Board*, 823 So.2d 1039 (La. Ct. App. 2002).

◆   A Maryland high school junior was the first female football player in her county's history. She participated in weightlifting, strength-training exercises and contact drills. In the first scrimmage with another team, the student was tackled while carrying the football and suffered multiple internal injuries. Three years later, the student and her mother sued the school board, claiming it had a duty to warn them of the risk of serious, disabling and catastrophic injuries.

A Maryland trial court granted the board's motion for summary judgment, finding no such duty to warn of the risk of varsity football participation. The student and her mother appealed to the Court of Special Appeals of Maryland. There they argued the lower court had erroneously held the board had no duty to warn of catastrophic risks and that the student had assumed the risk of injury by participating. **The court found no case from any jurisdiction holding that a school board had a duty to warn varsity high school football players that severe injuries might result.** The dangers of varsity football participation were self-evident, and there was no duty to warn of such an obvious danger. The court therefore affirmed the order for summary judgment in favor of the school board. *Hammond v. Board of Educ. of Carroll County*, 639 A.2d 223 (Md. Ct. Spec. App. 1994).

2. Governmental Immunity

The doctrine of governmental immunity (sometimes called discretionary or official immunity) precludes school or individual liability when employees are performing "discretionary duties" within the scope of their employment. By contrast, employees performing "ministerial duties" are unprotected by immunity, as are those who do not act in the scope of their employment.

◆   The Third Circuit excused a Pennsylvania cheerleading coach from a lawsuit, finding she was entitled to immunity. After the squad saw the "twist down cradle" stunt at a competition, they wanted to learn it. The stunt called for four "base" cheerleaders to launch a "flyer" into the air, where she does a twist before landing in the bases' waiting arms. The coach waited seven months until she thought the squad was ready. Then she had another high school's cheerleader – an assistant coach for a middle school squad – demonstrate and help teach the stunt. The squad used a large room with a concrete floor for practice. Its carpeting had little if any padding. The day the squad started to learn the stunt, six to eight spotters plus four base cheerleaders were ready to catch the flyer. She overshot all of them. Landing badly, she struck her head on the floor and suffered a severe injury. The injured cheerleader sued the district and the coach, alleging they violated her substantive due process right to bodily integrity. A federal judge granted the district judgment without a trial. But it ruled the coach had to stand trial, as she wasn't immune to the claim. The coach appealed, and the Third Circuit reversed. School officials have qualified immunity if sued for violation of a constitutional right that wasn't clearly established at the time. The cheerleader argued that national cheering organizations' safety standards require padded floor mats, so the coach's "deliberate indifference" constituted a violation of her right to bodily integrity. But the Third Circuit found this wasn't clearly established, as **no court decisions would've informed "a reasonable person in [the coach's] position that failure to take certain precautions in a high school cheerleading practice** would amount to a constitutional violation" – so the court ruled the claim couldn't proceed. *Hinterberger v. Iroquois School Dist.*, 548 Fed.Appx. 50 (3d Cir. 2013).

◆   While lifting weights, two football teammates quarreled over the CD they were listening to. They started pushing each other, and teammates intervened to separate them. One began walking away, while teammates held the other one back. The coach then asked them if they wanted to settle it. The student being held back said he did, and the coach said, "OK." At that point, the formerly restrained student violently attacked the other one, causing injuries. When the student sued the coach for his injuries, the Michigan Court of Appeals ruled that **the coach was not the proximate cause of the injuries**, and thus he was entitled to immunity. He did not commit gross negligence, and the other student's assault was the most direct cause of the harm. *Gray v. Cry*, No. 07-717218-NO, 2011 WL 4375074 (Mich. Ct. App. 9/20/11).

◆   Two years after a highly publicized hazing incident involving football players at a New Mexico high school, a football player at another New Mexico high school was subjected to hazing by seniors. The seniors threw him to the floor, then physically and sexually battered him. He and his mother sued various officials, including the coaching staff, the principal and the superintendent, for negligence. The officials sought to have the case dismissed on immunity grounds, but a federal court allowed the lawsuit to proceed. Here, **they knew about the hazing at the other school and yet took no action to prevent hazing at the student's school**. *C.H. v. Los Lunas Schools Board of Educ.*, 852 F.Supp.2d 1344 (D.N.M. 2012).

◆   An Illinois school district operated a summer football camp. Coaches instructed camp participants to run from a locker room to the practice field. One student tripped over a grass-concealed shot-put bumper along the route and sustained injuries. His mother sued the school district for negligence, seeking $50,000. A state court granted recreational immunity to the district, but the Appellate Court of Illinois reversed. There was a question as to whether the camp was educational in nature, which would nullify the recreational immunity provisions of state law. The case required a trial. *Peters v. Herrin Community School Dist. No. 4*, 928 N.E.2d 1258 (Ill. App. Ct. 2010).

◆   A 17-year-old student suffered heatstroke during football practice at his Mississippi high school on a hot August day. After he collapsed, emergency responders were unable to revive him. Upon his death, his family sued the school district for negligence, and the case reached the Supreme Court of Mississippi, which ruled that **the district was entitled to immunity**. The Mississippi Tort Claims Act provides immunity to state and political subdivisions whose employees act in the course and scope of their employment and exercise discretion. Here, the coaches were exercising discretion in the way they conducted their practices. *Covington County School Dist. v. Magee*, 29 So.3d 1 (Miss. 2010).

◆   A Delaware school district agreed to let its facilities be used by a charitable organization that wanted to conduct a cheerleading competition. During the event, a man fell off the bleachers, which did not have guard rails installed. He sued the organization and the district for his injuries, and the school district asserted that it was entitled to immunity. The Superior Court of Delaware noted that the organization had agreed to indemnify the district for any damages resulting from a judgment against it. **The court then found some evidence that school employees, without justification, deliberately chose not to install safety devices** and thus created a known risk. As a result, an issue of fact remained that required a trial. If the district was grossly negligent in electing not to install guard rails, the organization would have to pay the man for his injuries. But the district would not have to pay. *Boyle v. Christiana School Dist. Board of Educ.*, No. 07C-07-248 JAP, 2009 WL 4653832 (Del. Super. Ct. 11/30/09).

◆   A Georgia high school student participated in a voluntary workout session for the football team. The next morning, he collapsed and died. His parents sued the school system, school officials and several coaches, asserting that their son had been subjected to an "intense and unreasonable practice." They claimed the coaches failed to give their son enough to drink and ignored signs that he was becoming dehydrated. They also stated that the coaches failed to attend to their son until after a team meeting, even though he had collapsed during drills. They maintained that the coaches violated their son's substantive due process rights. A federal court dismissed all the defendants except three coaches, who appealed. The Eleventh Circuit held that **the coaches were entitled to qualified immunity because their conduct did not rise to a "conscience-shocking" level**. The parents made no allegation that the coaches intended to harm their son. Thus, they failed to prove a constitutional violation. *Davis v. Carter*, 555 F.3d 979 (11th Cir. 2009).

◆ A 14-year-old Minnesota student participated in a community education gymnastics program sponsored by a local school district. She performed a difficult vault known as a Tsukahara vault, which she had performed many times previously. This time she under-rotated and landed on her knees. She told a coach she would try it again, but that she would need assistance. However, when she attempted it a second time, no assistance was provided. The second time, she also under-rotated and landed on her head. She sued the school district for negligence. The district sought to have the lawsuit dismissed on grounds of immunity, but a trial court refused to do so. The Minnesota Court of Appeals reversed the lower court and granted immunity to the district. **The state's recreational use statute generally bars claims based on injuries sustained on government property that is intended for recreational use.** And no exception applied to the statute in this case. *Goetz v. Independent School Dist. No. 625*, No. A08-0254, 2009 WL 22270 (Minn. Ct. App. 1/6/09).

◆ In an effort to improve security, a Tennessee school board approved the installation of video surveillance equipment throughout one of its middle schools. The assistant principal decided to place cameras in the boys' and girls' locker rooms. Images were displayed on a computer in the assistant principal's office. They could also be accessed through a remote Internet connection. **When the assistant principal learned that the cameras were videotaping areas where students routinely dressed, he recommended to the principal that the cameras be moved, but no changes were made.** After a visiting girls' basketball team noticed the camera and complained, the principal assured the coach that the camera was not operational, although in fact it was. The next day, the locker room cameras were removed. Thirty-four students then sued for a violation of their privacy rights. The principal, assistant principal, director of schools and school board members claimed immunity. The Sixth Circuit Court of Appeals held that the board members and the director were entitled to immunity because their roles in placing the cameras were too indirect to make them liable. However, the principal and assistant principal were not immune. They violated a clearly established constitutional right to privacy at the time of the videotaping. *Brannum v. Overton County School Board*, 516 F.3d 489 (6th Cir. 2008).

◆   An Ohio student injured his forehead and wrist during a pole vault at a high school track meet. He landed on improper padding near the landing pad. The padding was later identified as in violation of National Federation of State High School Associations rules. The student sued the school district, coach and other officials for negligence. The court awarded pretrial judgment to the district and school officials, but the Court of Appeals of Ohio held that the trial court had improperly granted immunity under the state recreational user statute. The student was not a "recreational user." The student did not assume the risk of being provided inadequate safety equipment for pole vaulting. The sponsor of a sporting event has a duty not to increase the risk of harm over and above any inherent risks of the sport.

While the Ohio Political Subdivision Tort Liability Act generally grants immunity to government entities, an exception applies when an injury was caused by employee negligence occurring on school grounds in connection with a governmental function. The court rejected the district's claim to immunity. The Tort Liability Act protects employees unless they act with a malicious purpose, in bad faith, or in a wanton or reckless manner. **The track coach was entitled to immunity, because there was no evidence he acted with malice, bad faith or reckless or wanton conduct.** The court affirmed the judgment in the coach's favor, but held the action could proceed against the school district. *Henney v. Shelby City School Dist.*, No. 2005 CA 0064, 2006 WL 747475 (Ohio Ct. App. 3/23/06).

◆   A Maine high school wrestling team ran timed drills in school hallways as part of its warm-up routine. A wrestler was seriously injured after being bumped into a window by a teammate during a drill. The school had no policy prohibiting athletic training in school hallways at the time. The student sued the school district in a state court for personal injury, asserting officials negligently allowed the team to competitively race through the hallways. The court held the district and officials were protected by discretionary immunity. The student appealed to the Maine Supreme Judicial Court, which stated that **governmental entities are generally entitled to absolute immunity from suit for any tort action for damages**. One of four state law exceptions to this rule imposes liability on government entities for the negligent operation of a public building.

The court held that allowing relay races in the school hallway was not the "operation of a public building." The focus of this case was the manner in which the team was required to run through the halls, not the operation of a high school building. To impose liability under the "public building" exception to immunity, the claim must implicate the physical structure of the building. Decisions such as wrestling team rules focused on the supervision of students, not the maintenance or operation of the building. **Since the failure to prohibit racing in the halls was not related to the operation of a public building, the district and officials were protected by discretionary immunity.** *Lightfoot v. School Administrative Dist. No. 35*, 816 A.2d 63 (Me. 2003).

◆   A Kansas school football team held its first practice on an August day
when the temperature reached 83 degrees by 8:00 a.m. Players practiced
from then until 12:50 p.m. with a 45-minute break at 10:15 and five-minute
water breaks every 20 minutes. The team then began circuit conditioning.
Players spent four minutes at various stations, then rested for two minutes
before rotating to another. A student reported feeling ill after completing
the first two stations. An assistant coach instructed him to drink some water,
which he did. He asked to sit out further drills and was told again to get
water. As the team left practice, the student collapsed and was taken to a
hospital, where he died the next day. His estate sued the school district and
head coach for negligence. A state court granted the estate's motion to
prevent the district and coach from relying on the "recreational use"
exception to the Kansas Tort Claims Act (KTCA), which precludes liability
for injury claims arising from the use of any public property used for
recreational purposes, except in cases of gross and wanton negligence.

The district and coach appealed to the state supreme court, which
observed the trial court did not take into account the KTCA's legitimate
purpose to encourage construction of public recreational facilities. The
court found a rational basis for distinguishing between injuries occurring
on public recreational property and those occurring elsewhere. The trial
court committed error by refusing to apply the discretionary function
exception to the KTCA. **The discretionary function exception protects
government entities and employees from claims based on the exercise
of discretion or the failure to exercise it.** The recreational use exception
eliminated any liability for ordinary negligence and barred all the claims.
The court reversed and remanded the case for a determination of whether
the district or coach acted with gross or wanton negligence. *Barrett v.
Unified School Dist. No. 259*, 32 P.3d 1156 (Kan. 2001).

3. Assumption of Risk and Waiver

Many courts have determined that when a participant has assumed the
risks of playing sports, a school district should not be held liable for
injuries. One way to guard against liability is through the use of releases.
Cases involving parental releases are uncommon, but the Supreme Judicial
Court of Massachusetts upheld the use of one in *Sharon v. City of Newton*,
below.

◆   **A New York wrestler contracted herpes simplex I and believed he
caught it from a wrestler at another school.** He sued his school, the other
school and the other student for personal injury. A state court refused to
dismiss the case, but the Supreme Court, Appellate Division, threw the case
out. It noted that communicable diseases are an inherent danger of the sport
and that students' participation is seen as an agreement to accept the
obvious risks associated with wrestling. Even the student's own expert
witness acknowledged that the possibility of contracting herpes and other

communicable diseases from wrestling was well known. *Farrell v. Hochhauser*, 65 A.D.3d 663 (N.Y. 2009).

◆ A Massachusetts school district required a signed parental release for all students seeking to participate in extracurricular activities. For four years, the father of a high school cheerleader signed a release form before each season. During her fourth year, she was injured during a practice. When the cheerleader reached age 18, she sued the city in a state superior court for negligence and negligent hiring, and retention of the cheerleading coach. The court awarded summary judgment to the city on the basis of the parental release, agreeing that **the father had forever released the city from any and all actions and claims**.

The cheerleader appealed to the Massachusetts Supreme Judicial Court, asserting the release was invalid. The court held the trial court properly allowed the city to amend its answer by asserting release. **Enforcement of a parental release was consistent with Massachusetts law and public policy.** There was undisputed evidence that the father read and understood the release before signing it, and that the form was not misleading, since it required two signatures and clearly ensured parental permission was granted. It was not contrary to public policy to require parents to sign releases as a condition for student participation in extracurricular activities. The father had signed the release because he wanted the student to benefit from cheerleading. The court found that to hold the release unenforceable would expose public schools to financial costs and risks that would lead to the reduction of extracurricular activities. *Sharon v. City of Newton*, 437 Mass. 99, 769 N.E.2d 738 (Mass. 2002).

◆ Indiana parents received a new trial in a lawsuit based on the death of their son from heatstroke after a school football practice. The release forms they signed did not specifically waive claims based on negligence. The student, who weighed over 250 pounds, had "dry heaves" early in a morning practice session. He stopped his activity for a minute, then told two coaches he felt better. The student ate lunch during a team rest period and kept it down. He spent time lying on the locker room floor. The head coach asked the student how he felt, and the student again said he was OK. Near the end of the afternoon session, the student told a coach he did not feel well. The coach told him to get water, but he soon collapsed. The coaches took him to the locker room and placed him in a cool shower. The student lost consciousness, and the coaches called for an ambulance. He died at a hospital the following day.

The student's parents sued the school district for negligence. A jury returned a verdict for the school district. The parents appealed to the Court of Appeals of Indiana, which noted that **the release forms signed by the parents and students did not refer to "negligence."** Thus, the district was not effectively released from negligence claims. The trial court should have granted the parents' request for a jury instruction stating they had not released the district from negligence. The court reversed and remanded the case for a new trial. *Stowers v. Clinton Cent. School Corp.*, 855 N.E.2d 739 (Ind. Ct. App. 2006).

◆ A New York student participated on his high school wrestling team and was instructed before a match to wrestle an opponent in the next higher weight class. The student agreed to do so and was injured when the opponent hit his jaw during a take-down maneuver. The student voluntarily continued participating in the match after a medical time-out. He later filed a personal injury lawsuit against the school district in a New York trial court, which denied the district's dismissal motion. On appeal, the New York Supreme Court, Appellate Division, stated that **the student had assumed the risk of incurring a blow to the jaw and the injury was reasonably foreseeable in a wrestling match**. There was evidence that the size of the opponent had not caused the injury and that the student was aware of the risks involved in wrestling. The district's duty of care was limited to protecting the student from unassumed, concealed or unreasonable risks. The trial court judgment was reversed. *Edelson v. Uniondale Union Free School Dist.*, 631 N.Y.S.2d 391 (N.Y. App. Div. 1995).

B. Spectators, Employees and Parents

◆ Having decided a federal claim could not proceed, a Georgia federal court refused to hear a coach's state-law claims and dismissed his suit. Georgia high schools Warren County and Hancock Central were football rivals. Early in the 2011 football season, Warren fired its head coach and Hancock hired the coach as an assistant. The coach said his new team saw that year's game against Warren as a chance to "get even" for the way he was treated by his former team. A week before the game, football players from both teams got into such a heated altercation that police put one boy in handcuffs. Over the next week, the players and other students exchanged taunting text messages. The matchup was Hancock's homecoming game. Twelve officers were scheduled for security, but only four officers were at the game. Hancock lost 21-2. After their loss, Hancock players taunted the Warren team. A fight broke out. Cops rushed forward with pepper spray, and the coach tried to stop a Hancock athlete from hitting a Warren player. The Hancock athlete turned and attacked, hitting the coach in the face and head with a helmet. He suffered a "blow out" of the bones around one eye, requiring multiple surgeries and metal plates. He also needed extensive treatment in a brain injury rehabilitation program. The injuries have permanently impaired his ability to work. He sued Hancock's school district in federal court. Along with state-law claims, the coach alleged a breach of his substantive Fourteenth Amendment right to bodily integrity by failing to protect him. He said the district hired only four off-duty deputy sheriffs and knew they had no crowd-control experience. The court dismissed the claim, finding **the acts didn't "shock the conscience" in the constitutional sense**. With no federal claims remaining, the federal court dismissed the suit. *Daniel v. Hancock County School Dist.*, No. 5:13-CV-390 (CAR), 2014 WL 1813712 (M.D. Ga. 5/7/14).

◆ A negligence claim filed by a student who was struck in the head by a discus during track practice could move forward, an Ohio appeals court decided. The student was standing in an area designated by school officials as a "safe zone" when a discus thrown by another student hit her in the head. She sued her school district, claiming it was negligent to tell her she was in a safe area when she was hit. She said there should've been a cage, fence or other safety device at the back of the discus circle. The district filed a motion to dismiss, arguing that the negligence claim was barred by political subdivision immunity as well as a recreational user statute. A trial court denied the motion, and it appealed. The state appeals court affirmed the trial court's ruling. Under state law, political subdivisions like the district are not liable for injuries caused by its employees and occurring on its premises unless the injury is caused by a "physical defect." The court said that **"the existence of an unsafe area that is supposed to be safe" can be a physical defect under the law. The issue required further development, the court explained.** The district separately argued that it was immune under a different state law that blocks claims by recreational users of public premises. But neither side had presented evidence relating to whether the practice area was open to the public. It was also too early to decide whether the student was a recreational user of the premises at the time of her injury. The decision to preserve the negligence claim was affirmed. *Roberts v. Switzerland of Ohio Local School Dist.*, No. 12 MO 8 (Ohio Ct. App. 1/7/14).

◆ A New York school hosted a charity football game played by two other schools. A student who was a member of the hosting school's football team attended the charity event as a spectator. During halftime, the student went into the locker room to get gear from his locker. The locker room was being used by one of the visiting teams playing in the charity game. There, the student got into an argument with the visiting team's coach and head-butted him. Defending their coach, the team jumped the student. He suffered injuries he claimed were permanent. The student sued multiple parties for personal injury, including the city of New York and its department of education. He claimed the defendants breached their duty to provide for students' safety. But the court ruled that the defendants have no duty to protect students from injuries by a third party unless the school had a special relationship with the student. **The school wasn't liable because it had no reasonable warning the attack might occur and the attack happened "in a matter of seconds" – too fast for an onlooker to step in.** So the claim failed. *Chavis v. City of New York*, No. 101909/11, 2013 WL 3388643 (N.Y. Sup. Ct. 6/28/13).

◆   The mother of a New Jersey high school football player claimed that she tripped in a hole by the football field while leaving a game. She injured her ankle and sued the school for her injuries. A court granted pretrial judgment to the school, and the superior court, appellate division, affirmed that decision. **The woman failed to prove that the hole existed.** The school's athletic director described the area where she fell as "grassy." And though she maintained that there was a hole and produced photos of the area, there was no definitive proof that the hole even existed. *Pazos v. Borough of Sayreville*, 2010 WL 3257800 (N.J. Super. Ct. App. Div. 8/17/10).

◆   An Illinois man took his son to the local high school's batting cage to throw batting practice for him. He sat on a bucket behind a screen to throw pitches. One ball hit back by his son struck the screen, passed through the mesh, and struck him in the face, causing injury. He sued the school, alleging that it was willful and wanton in providing defective equipment. However, the Appellate Court of Illinois ruled against him, noting that **no one had seen the defect in the screen, including the man himself**. Therefore, the school couldn't have been willful and wanton in providing defective equipment because no one saw a defect. *Vilardo v. Barrington Community School Dist. 220*, 941 N.E.2d 257 (Ill. App. Ct. 2010).

◆   A Louisiana child sustained injuries when she fell while on the bleachers at a high school football game. Her parents claimed the fall was caused by a lack of adequate traction guards on the bleachers, and they sued the school board. A school custodial supervisor, however, testified that he saw the child being chased just before she fell. He also testified that the girl's family did nothing to stop her while she ran along the bleachers. A court ruled for the school board, and the Louisiana Court of Appeal affirmed. **It found no evidence that the bleachers were defective** or that there had been prior similar incidents in the area where the fall had occurred. *Mason v. Monroe City School Board*, 996 So.2d 377 (La. Ct. App. 2008).

◆   A physical education teacher at a New York high school adjusted a volleyball net that had been set up improperly by another teacher. As she stepped back from the base that supported the net, the teacher fell and twisted her ankle. She sued the board of education to recover for her injuries, and the board sought pretrial judgment. The New York Supreme Court, Appellate Division, granted the motion. It noted that **the duty to provide a safe workplace does not obligate an employer to remove hazards that typically come with the job**. Nor are employers required to protect employees from conditions or defects that are open and obvious. The teacher was hurt while performing a task that was inherent in her employment. In addition, the condition that caused the fall was open and obvious. Accordingly, the teacher could not recover damages for her injuries. *Monahan v. New York City Dep't of Educ.*, 851 N.Y.S. 2d 586 (N.Y. App. Div. 2008).

◆ A West Virginia spectator slipped and fell on ice and snow on school grounds while going to a high school basketball game. On the day of the injury, the superintendent of schools cancelled all classes in county schools because of a major snow storm. But the high school principal and athletic director decided not to cancel the game. The spectator sued the board, arguing it was negligent to hold the basketball game on a day when the entire school system was closed. The school board claimed immunity under the state Governmental Tort Claims and Insurance Reform Act. The Supreme Court of Appeals of West Virginia ruled that the school board was entitled to immunity. **The court rejected the spectator's argument that the decision to hold the basketball game was an affirmative act that was not immunized.** While the act of holding the game may have encouraged her to venture out into the snow, it did not cause the conditions at the school. The Tort Claims and Insurance Reform Act provided immunity for losses or claims resulting from snow or ice on public ways caused by the weather. *Porter v. Grant County Board of Educ.*, 633 S.E.2d 38 (W.Va. 2006).

◆ A spectator at a high school football game in New York was stabbed during a fight that occurred on school grounds following the game. The spectator sued the school district and school officials in a New York trial court. The court held for the spectator, and the school appealed to a New York appellate division court. The spectator claimed the school was negligent when it failed to properly supervise the crowd. The court disagreed, holding **the district could not be found negligent because it did not have a duty to supervise non-student spectators at the game**. The court reversed the judgment and held for the district. *Jerideau v. Huntingdon Union Free School Dist.*, 21 A.D.3d 992, 801 N.Y.S.2d 394 (N.Y. App. Div. 2005).

IV. OTHER SCHOOL ACTIVITIES

Courts have held schools liable for injuries during school-sponsored events that resulted from the failure to provide a reasonably safe environment, failure to warn participants of known hazards (or to remove known dangers), failure to properly instruct participants in the activity, and failure to provide supervision adequate during age-appropriate school events, such as plays, dances, musicals and more. For a sample student behavior contract at school dances, see Form VI-11.

A. Physical Education Class Accidents

1. Duty of Care

Courts have held that schools and staff members are not liable for injuries that are unforeseeable. It has long been recognized that schools are not the insurers of student safety. The fact that each student is not personally supervised at all times does not itself constitute grounds for liability.

◆   A New York appeals court reversed a ruling to dismiss the suit of a student who was injured in gym class. The PE teacher told the class to walk backward fast. One girl asked to be excused from the exercise, saying her ankle hurt and felt unstable. The teacher denied her request to be excused. So the girl obeyed, but she fell while walking backward and was seriously hurt. Her family sued New York City's school district for personal injury, claiming the girl had been negligently supervised. The district asked the court to grant it judgment without a trial. It did and dismissed the lawsuit. But the family appealed, and the appeals court reversed. New York **schools have a duty to supervise students with the same degree of care as a "reasonably prudent parent."** Schools can be held liable for injuries that are foreseeably caused by their failure to do so. The appeals court decided a trial was needed to determine whether this school was negligent – as it's arguably foreseeable that a child with a weak and painful ankle could suffer a fall and an injury if forced to walk backward fast. The appeals court decided the trial court was wrong to dismiss the suit, so it sent the case back to the lower court for further proceedings. *Anastasiya M. v. New York City Board of Educ.*, 976 N.Y.S.2d 202 (N.Y. App. Div. 2013).

◆   An Illinois student was hurt while adjusting a volleyball net, presumably at her gym teacher's instruction. She did so by turning a crank attached to a "collar" wrapped around a pole. The collar bore the warning: "DO NOT OVERTIGHTEN – MAY CAUSE SERIOUS INJURIES[.]" As the student turned the crank, either it or the collar broke and struck her face. She sued the district for personal injury. But Illinois district are immune to injury claims related to recreational facilities unless staff caused the injury by "willful or wanton conduct" – meaning they meant to hurt the student or were deliberately indifferent to it. The student didn't make this showing, so the trial court dismissed her claim. She appealed, arguing the warning label proved that the school knew using the equipment was likely to hurt her – and was deliberately indifferent to the risk. The appellate court disagreed with her and affirmed the trial court ruling. **Warning labels make a product safer by telling the user how to avoid injury, the court explained.** *Leja v. Community Unit School Dist. 300*, 979 N.E.2d 573 (Ill. App. Ct. 2012).

◆   While in a required PE class, a 125-pound student wrestled a 220-pound classmate and wound up with injuries that included a dislocated elbow. He and his mother sued the district, which claimed that the student had assumed the risk of injury and that it couldn't be liable. Both sides sought pretrial judgment, which the court refused to grant. The New York Supreme Court, Appellate Division, then held that **assumption of the risk did not apply because the student was in a compulsory PE class and not involved in a voluntary sporting activity**. However, the student may have been partially at fault for choosing to wrestle against a classmate who outweighed him by almost 100 pounds. A trial was required. *Stoughtenger v. Hannibal Cent. School Dist.*, 90 A.D.3d 1696 (N.Y. App. Div. 2011).

◆   A New York fourth-grader fell off the balance bar during a physical education class. She climbed back on the bar, fell off again, climbed up again and fell a third time, injuring her ankle. A fellow student then ran over to the teacher to tell him about it. The student's parents sued the district for negligent supervision, and the district sought pretrial judgment. Both a trial court and the Supreme Court, Appellate Division, held that a trial was required. Here, the teacher admitted that both the balance beam station and the rope climbing station required extra supervision. Therefore, a question of fact existed as to whether the district was negligent in supervising the student and whether its alleged negligence caused the student's injury. **The student's three falls, plus the fact that a student had to run to get the teacher, suggested that the teacher failed to provide the extra supervision he knew was needed.** *Talyanna S. v. Mount Vernon City School Dist.*, 948 N.Y.S. 2d 103 (N.Y. App. Div. 2012).

◆   A 13-year-old student attending a charter school in New York sustained injuries during a PE class when a tennis ball rebounded off a gym wall and hit him in the eye. He sued the charter school as well as New York City's Board of Education and Department of Education, alleging negligent supervision. However, a state court granted pretrial judgment to all the defendants. First, **the board of education and the department of education couldn't be held liable because they didn't have custody over the charter school's students**. Nor did they have control of its classes. Also, the charter school wasn't liable because the accident was a spontaneous event that reasonable supervision could not have prevented. *Torres v. City of New York*, 910 N.Y.S.2d 409 (Table) (N.Y. Sup. Ct. 2010).

◆   New York high school students were playing floor hockey in a PE class when one student accidentally hurt another with his stick. The injured student sued the school district, alleging negligent supervision, and the district sought pretrial judgment. Although the trial court denied the motion, an appellate division court ruled that the district needn't go to trial on the student's claims. Here, **the injury wasn't foreseeable and it happened so fast that there was no way to avert it by closer supervision**. *Odekirk v. Bellmore-Merrick Cent. School Dist.*, 70 A.D.3d 910 (N.Y. 2010).

◆   A New Jersey PE student sustained injuries to her nose when a classmate hit her with a hockey stick during a floor hockey game. She required surgery, then sued the district, the gym teacher and the classmate to recover for her injuries. A court dismissed her claims, and the appellate division affirmed. It noted that even though gym class was mandatory and not voluntary, **she had to prove more than simple negligence by the classmate**; she had to show that he acted recklessly or intentionally when he hurt her. This she failed to do. Further, since she suffered no permanent injury, she could not pursue a claim for non-economic damages against the district. *Saracino v. Toms River Regional High School East*, 2009 WL 3460680 (N.J. Super. Ct. App. Div. 10/20/09).

◆   While playing freeze tag during a physical education class, a New York fourth-grader was knocked to the ground by a classmate. As he tried to get up, another classmate tripped over him and he fell, hitting his face on the floor. He suffered serious injuries to two permanent teeth. His father sued the school district for negligent supervision, claiming that the teacher and the teacher's aide were talking to each other when the accident happened. He asserted that the teachers should have intervened sooner and prevented the second child from tripping over his son. The New York Supreme Court, Appellate Division, ruled against him, noting that **school districts are not insurers of student safety**. The fact that the teacher and the aide did not see the accident happen failed to establish negligent supervision. The father could not show that more supervision would have prevented the injury, which appeared to result from a spontaneous and accidental collision. There was also no prior history of rough play, and the teacher-student ratio was adequate. *Doyle v. Binghamton City School Dist.*, 874 N.Y.S.2d 607 (N.Y. App. Div. 2009).

◆   A New York student, while participating in a game of dodgeball during gym class, stepped backward and tripped over a schoolmate's foot. The student and her mother sued the school district for her injuries, claiming the teacher failed to adequately supervise the class. The district sought pretrial judgment, which a trial court denied. An appellate division court, however, found for the district. **The accident happened so quickly that it could not have been avoided by even the most intense supervision.** Accordingly, the district was not liable. *Knightner v. William Floyd Union Free School Dist.*, 857 N.Y.S.2d 726 (N.Y. App. Div. 2008).

◆   Students in a gym class in New York were playing a baseball game with a foam-type ball and a bat that had a plastic handle as well as a foam head. Students waiting for their turn to bat stayed behind orange cones about 25 feet away. While batting, one student let go of the bat and it struck a classmate in the nose as he stood in the safety zone. His father sued the school district, seeking to recover for the student's injuries. The district sought to have the case dismissed. The New York Supreme Court ruled for the district, finding that it had met its duty of care to the student. The gym teachers had no notice of any special danger that might exist under the circumstances, and **they exercised reasonable care in setting up the safety zone 25 feet away from the batting area**. *Rosenthal v. Arlington Cent. School Dist.*, 867 N.Y.S.2d 378 (Table) (N.Y. Sup. Ct. 2008).

◆   A New York student was injured in phys ed class while participating in a game of "tape ball." The game was played in the school gymnasium and involved the use of bases that were placed on the floor. One of the bases slipped when the child stepped on it. He fell and sustained injuries. His mother sued the school district, claiming the student was hurt because it failed to adequately supervise the class and failed to provide proper equipment. A trial court denied the school district's motion for pretrial judgment, and the district appealed. The Supreme Court, Appellate Division, reversed. The parent failed to prove that the district was aware of a danger and breached its duty of care in a way that caused the injury. **The physical education teacher was present during the entire class period, and closer supervision would not have prevented the fall.** The school district only had to exercise the same degree of care "as a parent of ordinary prudence" in comparable circumstances, and it did so. *Milbrand v. Kenmore-Town of Tonawanda Union Free School Dist.*, 853 N.Y.S. 2d 809 (N.Y. App. Div. 2008).

◆ An autistic Kentucky student attended a gym class that was twice the size of a typical class and was staffed by two teachers. After the class began, the para-educator who was assigned to assist him and other special education students in the class lost sight of him and began to search the gym. She noticed an open door and searched the area outside the gym, but failed to spot the student. The student's mother and the police were notified, the search was expanded, and the student was eventually found three hours later about three blocks away. He was dirty and unclothed, but there were no signs he had been sexually assaulted. He was examined at a hospital and released. His father said the boy did not suffer any physical or emotional harm as a result of the incident, but his mother claimed she suffered an emotional injury. The family sued the school district for constitutional rights violations, but a federal court dismissed the case. **Public education is not a constitutionally protected right, and compulsory attendance laws do not create a constitutional obligation on the part of schools to maintain a safe environment.** Any claim for negligence would have to be made in state court. *A.P. v. Fayette County Public Schools*, No. 5:06-247-JMH, 2008 WL 215397 (E.D. Ky. 1/24/08).

◆ A New York student hurt his ankle during a soccer game in gym class when another student kicked him. He and his father sued the board of education and the city to recover for his injuries. They alleged that the injuries resulted from negligent supervision. A trial court refused to dismiss the case, but the New York Supreme Court, Appellate Division, did so. It explained that **the school could be held liable only if the injury was foreseeable and was caused by a lack of supervision**. Here, the student had admitted that the kick was an accident, and it happened so suddenly that it could not have been prevented by closer or increased supervision. Therefore, the school was not liable. *Paca v. City of New York*, 858 N.Y.S.2d 772 (N.Y. App. Div. 2008).

◆ A 14-year-old eighth-grader in Ohio obtained his gym teacher's permission to retrieve his prescription inhaler from his locker. Minutes later, another teacher found the student unconscious and not breathing on the locker room floor. Despite the administration of medical treatment, he died. The school board maintained a policy requiring parents or guardians to bring prescription medications to the school office. Students were not allowed to bring medicine to school themselves, but the school principal let students carry inhalers once they were at school. The student's estate sued the school board in the state court system for wrongful death. The jury found for the school board, and the estate appealed. The Court of Appeals of Ohio found that the district could not be liable because the student's death was not foreseeable. A physician had testified that the death of a student previously recognized as having only "mild asthma" was "one in a million." **According to the physician, not even medical professionals could have foreseen the death.** *Spencer v. Lakeview School Dist.*, No. 2005-T-0083, 2006 WL 1816452 (Ohio Ct. App. 6/30/06).

◆   A California school district was not liable for injuries to a student who was hit by a golf club swung by a classmate in their physical education class. The golf class teacher was relatively new. His only golf training was an hour-and-a-half seminar. During the sixth day of golf class, the teacher showed students how to do a full golf swing. Before students could try the full swings, he advised them of certain safety precautions. The teacher's practice was to whistle commands and signal when to hit balls and when to rotate positions. According to the student, the class was disorganized and the instructions confusing. She claimed at times students had to decide when to hit and when to change positions. A classmate who was in front of the student swung her club and hit the student in the mouth. According to the student, the teacher did not give a whistle command for the classmate to hit the ball. She sued the school district for negligence. The court found that the district did not breach its limited duty of care and awarded pretrial judgment to the district.

The student appealed to a California District Court of Appeal, which found that **the "prudent person" standard of care decides liability in cases of students injured during school hours. This simply required persons to avoid injuring others by using due care.** Applying the prudent person standard in this case would not deter vigorous athletic participation. As the superior court should have applied the prudent person standard of care, the court reversed the judgment. *Hemady v. Long Beach Unified School Dist.*, 143 Cal.App.4th 566, 49 Cal. Rptr.3d 464 (Cal. Ct. App. 2006).

◆   A 16-year-old Louisiana student who weighed 327 pounds collapsed and began having seizures during a physical education class. The class was conducted by a substitute art teacher in a gym that was not air-conditioned. The temperature was at least 90 degrees. The student collapsed after playing basketball for 20 minutes and died at a hospital. The substitute teacher had played in the game instead of monitoring students. The student's parent sued the board and its insurer in a state court for wrongful death, and the court awarded her $500,000.

The Court of Appeal of Louisiana found no error in trial court findings that the board breached its duty to exercise reasonable care and supervision. The lower court was also entitled to hear the testimony of a physical education professor and allow medical testimony as reliable. The court held teachers have a duty to exercise reasonable care and supervision over students in their custody, and to avoid exposing them to an unreasonable risk of injury. **As physical education classes may involve dangerous activities, due care must be used in them to minimize the risk of student injury.** *James v. Jackson*, 898 So.2d 596 (La. Ct. App. 2005). The state supreme court denied the board's appeal. *James v. Jackson*, 902 So.2d 1005 (La. 2005).

◆   A New York student was playing football in a physical education class when a classmate threw a football tee that hit her in the eye. A state trial court denied the school district's motion for summary judgment, and the district appealed. A state appellate division court held school districts have a duty to adequately supervise and instruct students, and are liable for foreseeable injuries proximately caused by their negligence. However, **school districts are not insurers of student safety and will not be held liable for every spontaneous, thoughtless or careless act by which one student injures another**. The degree of care required is what a reasonably prudent parent would exercise under similar circumstances. The court found the teacher had not instructed students on how to properly handle the tee and never told them not to throw it. The evidence differed as to whether the students had previously thrown the tee or had seen the teacher throw it. In affirming the judgment for the student, the court held a trial court must determine if the injury causing conduct was reasonably foreseeable and preventable. *Oakes v. Massena Cent. School Dist.*, 19 A.D.3d 981, 797 N.Y.S.2d 640 (N.Y. App. Div. 2005).

◆   Three Louisiana students assaulted a classmate in their locker room after a physical education class, causing serious injuries. The classmate sued the school board, the parents of the students and their insurers in a Louisiana court for personal injuries. A jury found the students were not at fault, and the court found the board 100% at fault. It held the coach caused the injuries by failing to supervise the students. According to the court, an atmosphere of roughhousing and lack of supervision invited the attack, and the board failed to conform to the required standard of care. On appeal, the state court of appeal apportioned 70% of the fault to the board and 30% to one of the students.

The state supreme court held school boards have a duty of reasonable supervision over students. Boards are not insurers of student safety, and constant supervision of all students is not required. **To hold a school board liable for negligence, it must be shown that a risk of unreasonable injury was foreseeable and could have been prevented with the required degree of supervision.** In this case, the attack happened suddenly and without warning. Because it was unforeseeable to the classmate himself, there was no way for the coach to foresee and prevent it. The trial court had erroneously imposed liability on the board independent of the students. As the incident could not have been prevented with a reasonable degree of supervision, the court reversed the judgment. *Wallmuth v. Rapides Parish School Board*, 813 So.2d 341 (La. 2002).

◆   Arkansas parents claimed their son's school district did not administer his Ritalin prescription for five consecutive school days, despite knowledge that failure to do so placed him in jeopardy of physical and psychological injury. The student fell from a slide on school grounds and fractured his right wrist. The parents sued the district in the state court system for outrageous conduct causing injury. The court dismissed the case, and the parents appealed.

The state court of appeals held the parents could not prevail unless they showed the district intended to inflict emotional distress on the student. They were further required to demonstrate extreme and outrageous conduct by the district, and to prove its conduct caused emotional distress so severe that no reasonable person could endure it. **The court found no evidence of knowledge by the district that failure to administer the student's medication would result in emotional distress.** The parents did not show his suffering was so great that no reasonable person could be expected to endure it. The court affirmed the judgment for the district. *Foote v. Pine Bluff School Dist.*, No. CA 02-806, 2003 WL 1827282 (Ark. Ct. App. 4/9/03).

2. Governmental Immunity

◆   An 11-year-old Missouri student, while skipping rope during PE class, fell and hit her head against a cinder block wall. She was taken to the nurse's office. The nurse gave her an ice pack for her head and made sure her pupils were dilating, then called her mother to pick her up and wrote a note explaining that she had suffered a minor head injury. The note instructed her mother to wake her at midnight, which the mother did. The next morning, the student stayed in bed. At 10:30, she was unresponsive. Paramedics failed to revive her. Her mother sued the district, the superintendent, the principal, the nurse and the teachers involved. A court dismissed the defendants, but the court of appeals reversed in part, finding that **the nurse was not entitled to official immunity, nor were the teachers**. Only if they had discretion in treating head injuries would they be entitled to immunity. A trial was required on that issue. *Nguyen v. Grain Valley R-5 School Dist.*, 353 S.W.3d 725 (Mo. Ct. App. 2011).

◆   An Ohio middle school included a weeklong roller-skating course in its PE program. It required students to bring signed permission slips to participate. A student who was inexperienced at roller skating grew tired of being the only student in the "safe zone" for beginners and moved to the general skating area. A classmate lost his balance and fell. His skate hit the student's leg, breaking it. When the student sued the school board and the teachers, the court ruled against him, holding that the defendants were immune to the lawsuit. **The student failed to show that the gym floor was too slippery for roller skating and thus defective.** *Simmons v. Yingling*, No. CA2010-11-117, 2011 WL 3567083 (Ohio Ct. App. 8/15/11).

◆ A Wisconsin student gashed his knee while diving after a volleyball in his freshman physical education class. He collided with the sharp metal edge of a volleyball net stand and had to undergo surgery. His family sued the school district in a state court for negligence, alleging other students had previously been injured when coming into contact with the net stand. The court held the district was entitled to state law immunity. The family appealed to the state court of appeals, arguing the district was liable under the "known danger" exception to the immunity rule, in view of the previous injuries involving the same equipment. **The court explained that immunity will not apply in a negligence case if it involves a ministerial duty and is the result of a known and compelling danger.** The known danger exception applied when a public officer's duty to act was absolute, certain and imperative. The court held the net stand was not so hazardous that the district was required to take some protective measure for students. As the danger was not so compelling that action was necessary, the known danger exception to immunity did not apply. The court affirmed the judgment for the school district. *Schilling v. Sheboygan Area School Dist.*, 705 N.W.2d 906 (Table) (Wis. Ct. App. 2005).

◆ A Wisconsin physical education teacher divided a class into two groups to practice golf. One group practiced driving while the other group practiced chipping. The teacher instructed the drivers to stand in line while waiting to hit and not to swing their clubs in the waiting area. While she was working with the chippers, the drivers practiced about 40 to 50 feet away. A student in the drivers' group was hit in the face by a club swung by a classmate. He sued the district in a state circuit court for personal injuries, but the case was dismissed.

The state court of appeals held Wis. Stat. § 893.80(4) bars actions against government entities and employees for acts done in the exercise of legislative, judicial and similar functions. The law allowed liability for the negligent performance of ministerial duties. Ministerial duties were "absolute, certain and imperative," leaving nothing for judgment or discretion. The teacher had a ministerial duty to conduct and supervise her class in a particular manner. **Her decision to provide students with safety instructions was discretionary and did not subject the district to liability.** The court affirmed the judgment, finding the danger created by swinging golf clubs was not so obvious and predictable as to be a compelling or known danger. *Livingston v. Wausau Underwriters Insurance Co.*, 260 Wis.2d 602, 658 N.W.2d 88 (Table) (Wis. Ct. App. 2003), review denied, 266 Wis.2d 62, 671 N.W.2d 849 (Table) (Wis. 2003).

◆   An Alabama purchasing foreman drafted bid specifications and made recommendations to his school board on bids for movable bleachers for a high school. After the board contracted for the bleachers, the foreman's office issued purchase orders, and the bleachers were installed. A student was severely injured when the bleachers collapsed on him as he and a classmate tried to close them at their teacher's request. The student sued the district and school officials, including the purchasing foreman, for negligent inspection and maintenance of the bleachers. The trial court entered pretrial judgment for all the officials except the foreman, and he appealed.

The Alabama Supreme Court considered the foreman's claim to state-agent immunity based on the discretionary nature of his activities. The student argued the foreman did not deserve immunity, as he was not engaged in discretionary functions. The court held the question of immunity was not properly addressed in the framework of discretionary or ministerial functions. Instead, it had devised an analysis based on categories of state-agent functions under which government employees are immune from liability in the exercise of judgment. One category was the negotiation of contracts, so the foreman was entitled to summary judgment for the claims that he had failed to properly evaluate bids for the bleachers and inspect them after installation. However, the court found **the act of passing along a maintenance brochure to other employees did not require judgment. The foreman was not entitled to state agent immunity** with respect to this claim, and the case was remanded for further proceedings. *Ex Parte Hudson*, 866 So.2d 1115 (Ala. 2003).

◆   Students in an Illinois physical education class had to run laps or rollerblade around a wooden gym floor. Rollerbladers paid a $7 fee to use rollerblades with "experimental" toe brakes, and they were not furnished with helmets, gloves or shin, elbow and knee guards. A student who chose to rollerblade fell and broke two bones in his right leg. He sued the school district in a state court for negligence, and willful and wanton failure to provide safety equipment. The court held the district was entitled to immunity under Sections 2-201 and 3-108(a) of the state governmental tort immunity act, which affords immunity to government entities and their employees for failing to supervise students except in cases of willful and wanton misconduct. The state appellate court reversed the judgment, and the district appealed to the Supreme Court of Illinois.

The supreme court observed that the immunity act did not create duties for government entities, but accorded them certain immunities based on specific government functions. The district's failure to provide necessary equipment did not involve supervision. The tort immunity act shielded any decision by district employees that involved a determination of policy or the exercise of discretion. **"Policy decisions" were those requiring the balancing of competing interests so that a government entity had to make a "judgment call." The court agreed with the school district that its decision not to provide safety equipment was discretionary and thus**

entitled to immunity. *Arteman v. Clinton Community Unit School Dist. No. 15*, 763 N.E.2d 756 (Ill. 2002).

B. Plays, Dances, Music and More

◆   The Fifth Circuit refused to find a school constitutionally liable for a student's drowning death on campus. A physics class went to the school pool to conduct buoyancy experiments. They made boats out of cardboard and duct tape and then sailed them in the shallow end of the pool. The teacher told them to stay out of the water when not testing their boats. But after the experiment, some kids jumped in and swam a lap. Minutes later, one student was spotted lying at the bottom of the pool. They pulled him out and called paramedics, but he died. His parents sued his principal and physics teacher, alleging they violated their son's Fourteenth Amendment right to life. A Texas federal judge granted the school defendants judgment without a trial. The parents appealed to the Fifth Circuit, but it affirmed. Public school officials have "qualified immunity" to such suits, meaning there is no liability unless they violated a clearly established federal legal right. The U.S. Supreme Court has explained that **the purpose of the immunity rule is to give government employees "breathing room to make reasonable but mistaken judgments about open legal questions."** The parents didn't show the school defendants violated a clearly established constitutional right. To do so, they would've had to show "reasonable teachers and school officials were on notice that designing and executing a high school science experiment involving a pool violated the constitutional right to life of any student that may drown." That wasn't the case, so school officials were immune to this suit – and the federal judge was right to dismiss it. *Estate of C.A. v. Castro*, 547 Fed.Appx. 621 (5th Cir. 2013).

◆   A Wisconsin student with brittle bone disease and poor balance attended class under an IEP that called for her to be released from class separately from other students so that she wouldn't have to be in the hallways with them between classes – thereby reducing her chance for injuries. Despite that, she fell in a school hallway walking between classes and sustained injuries. **Her parents sued the district for negligence, but the Wisconsin Court of Appeals ruled against them**, noting that the district was entitled to immunity. The IEP did not impose a ministerial duty (which would mean no immunity) on school employees because it did not eliminate discretion (which meant immunity was available). For example, the IEP didn't state whether the student should be released from class early or late. *Edwards v. Baraboo School Dist.*, 803 N.W.2d 868 (Table) (Wis. Ct. App. 2011).

◆   A 15-year-old North Dakota student got badly hurt practicing a bike stunt in the auditorium for a "Sixties day" event scheduled as part of a history class. He sued the district and the teacher to recover for his injuries, and a jury decided that **the district was 30% at fault, while the student was 70% at fault**. As a result, the student was not entitled to receive anything. On appeal, the Supreme Court of North Dakota upheld that determination. Neither the student nor his parents could recover 30% of his costs from the district. *M.M. v. Fargo Public School Dist. No. 1*, 815 N.W.2d 273 (N.D. 2012).

◆ During recess, a New York third-grader passed by a fire pole that students were sliding down while another student slid down the pole. The other student barreled into him and he sustained injuries. His father sued the district for negligent supervision, and the district sought pretrial judgment, asserting that it wasn't negligent and, even if it was, any negligence was incidental to the injury and not a cause. The Supreme Court, Appellate division, held that **there were questions about whether the district properly instructed students on how to use the playground equipment** and whether it provided a proper surface. Also, there was a question as to whether the student sliding down the pole was playing tag at the time in violation of school rules. A trial was required. *Dworzanski v. Niagara-Wheatfield Cent. School Dist.*, 89 A.D.3d 1378 (N.Y. Sup. Ct. A.D. 2011).

◆ A New York second-grader sustained injuries when he was pushed down a slide by a fellow student during lunch recess, who then slid down on top of him. He sued the school district for money damages, alleging negligent supervision. The case reached the Supreme Court, Appellate Division, which ruled against him. Here, **the school provided adequate playground supervision**, and that level of supervision had not caused the student's injuries. *Benavides v. Uniondale Union Free School Dist.*, 95 A.D.3d 809 (N.Y. Sup. Ct. App. Div. 2012).

◆ A Utah high school decided to perform the play "Oklahoma." The school's drama teacher wanted to enhance the sound effects during the performance by using a gun that would fire blanks. A vice principal approved the request provided that an adult brought the weapon, kept it under control at all times, and was the only person to fire it. However, the drama teacher did not ensure that the rules were followed, and a student fired the gun during rehearsals and the play's performances. The drama teacher apparently knew that the student was doing so. One day, prior to a performance, the student shot himself with a blank and died. His parents sued, alleging violations of the student's substantive and procedural due process rights. The school, the vice principal and the drama teacher sought to have the case dismissed, but a federal court dismissed only the school and the vice principal from the lawsuit. **The drama teacher may have acted in conscious disregard for the serious risks to the student, so the lawsuit against him was allowed to continue.** *Thayer v. Washington County School Dist.*, 781 F.Supp.2d 1264 (D. Utah 2011).

◆ A Connecticut student attended an eighth-grade graduation dance at a private facility. During the evening, a glass goblet fell to the floor and broke, leaving pieces of glass on the floor. A student shed her shoes while walking from her table to the dance floor and severely cut her foot on a shard of glass. She sued the school board and two teachers who chaperoned the event, alleging negligent supervision. A state court ruled that the school board was entitled to immunity, and the Supreme Court of Connecticut agreed. Here, **the school board's decision to sponsor the graduation dance was a discretionary decision that entitled it to immunity**. Further, the dance wasn't held at the school, attendance wasn't mandatory, and the student voluntarily took off her shoes. Thus, no extra duty of care was imposed on the school board to offset its claim to immunity. *Coe v. Board of Educ. of Town of Watertown*, 19 A.3d 640 (Conn. 2011).

◆ An Ohio student played in the marching band. One day, while they were practicing in a parking lot, a school maintenance employee asked the marching band director if he could mow the lawn in an area near where the marching band was practicing. School policy dictated that employees were not to mow in the vicinity of students, and when they mowed without a bag, they were supposed to use the manufacturer's discharge chute. The director told the maintenance employee he could mow near the marching band. However, the employee took the bag off the mower and did not install the discharge chute. A piece of metal ejected by the lawn mower struck a student in the head and cut an artery, causing him to lose consciousness and suffer some paralysis to his face. His family sued the school district, which sought immunity.

The Ohio Court of Appeals noted that school districts are generally entitled to immunity unless employees act in a "wanton or reckless" way. Here, the family alleged that the band director and the employee acted recklessly so as to disallow immunity. The court agreed that **the maintenance employee might have acted recklessly by failing to use the discharge chute**. However, the family failed to show that the band director acted recklessly or wantonly by allowing the employee to mow near the parking lot. Thus, the director was entitled to immunity, but the maintenance employee was not. *DeMartino v. Poland Local School Dist.*, No. 10 MA 19, 2011 WL 1118480 (Ohio Ct. App. 3/24/11).

V. TEACHER BEHAVIOR OUTSIDE OF SCHOOL

Although teachers have the freedom to do as they like off school grounds while not on duty, they cannot break the law or engage in behavior that could be construed as harmful to students.

A. Inappropriate Relations With Students

◆ A California teacher with a reputation as a hugger formed close friendships with four third-graders and their single mothers. The families of the students allowed the children to spend the night at his place, and he began molesting them. Eventually he was caught. When the families sued the school district for negligence and failure to report sexual abuse, a jury ruled against them. The court of appeal upheld the verdict for the district, noting that **it was unlikely the abuse could have been uncovered any earlier**. It also found no merit to the claims that district training on pedophiles would have led staff members to promptly recognize the teacher's "grooming" behavior prior to his abuse. *A.J. v. Victor Elementary School Dist.*, No. E049404, 2011 WL 1005009 (Cal. Ct. App. 3/22/11) (Unpublished).

◆   An Arkansas high school girls basketball coach sent inappropriate text messages to a number of students, including "are you drunk yet?" to a student who had obtained a public intoxication ticket, and "OMG you look good today" to another student. A school investigation found no other problems, but the school prepared to non-renew his contract at the end of the school year. Later, the coach entered into a sexual relationship with a ninth-grader. He was sentenced to 10 years in prison, with six years suspended. The ninth-grader's parents sued the principal and school officials under Title IX and 42 U.S.C. § 1983, asserting constitutional violations. The case reached the Eighth Circuit, which held that the principal and school officials were entitled to immunity because **the inappropriate text messages by the coach did not alert them to the sexual abuse that followed**. The principal and school officials had investigated following the text messages and found no evidence of improper physical contact. *Doe v. Flaherty*, 623 F.3d 577 (8th Cir. 2010).

◆   A Delaware elementary school teacher encountered a 17-year-old former student when she came to the school to pick up a younger sibling. The teacher later called her and offered to help her with her homework. After a time, **he became romantically involved, eventually engaging in a sexual relationship with the student**. The student told a friend, who told her parent, who reported it to the state police. The teacher was charged with fourth degree sexual rape because of the student's age and his position of trust, authority or supervision over her. However, the charge was later dropped. Shortly thereafter, the school board notified the teacher that it intended to fire him based on immorality and/or misconduct. After he was fired, the teacher appealed, asserting that he had not been criminally convicted, that the student no longer attended district schools, and that his positive employment evaluations indicated he was still able to teach. The Supreme Court of Delaware ruled against him, noting that he could be fired for immorality and that he had compromised his position of trust and his status as a role model. *Lehto v. Board of Educ. of Caesar Rodney School Dist.*, 962 A.2d 222 (Del. 2008).

◆   An Oklahoma student claimed that she was subjected to sexual harassment, advances and molestation by her music teacher when she was 15 years old. She claimed that he first kissed her in the school bus barn, and then began touching her inappropriately at least once a week, although the two never had sexual intercourse. When her parents learned of the inappropriate relationship, they contacted the school, which immediately suspended the teacher. He resigned shortly thereafter. The student sued the school district and the teacher under 42 U.S.C. § 1983 and Title IX. She asserted that the district had knowledge of the teacher's inappropriate behavior based on statements her boyfriend made to an assistant principal about the teacher and another student. The district moved for pretrial judgment, **claiming it never had actual notice that the teacher was acting inappropriately**. It showed that the boyfriend had admitted lying about the teacher having an inappropriate relationship with the other student. The court ruled for the school district, finding no evidence that it was deliberately indifferent to the inappropriate relationship between the teacher and the student. However, the student's lawsuit against the teacher under 42 U.S.C. § 1983 could proceed. *S.R. v. Hilldale Independent School Dist. No. I-29 of Muskogee County, Oklahoma*, No. CIV-07-335-RAW, 2008 WL 2185420 (E.D. Okla. 5/23/08).

◆ An 18-year-old Idaho student began flirting with a teacher. She confessed her feelings for him to another staff member, and the school conducted an investigation. Both the student and the teacher denied any impropriety. A month later, the teacher and student had sexual intercourse. She did not admit this until the end of the school year. The teacher resigned, and the student sued not only him but also the school district and various school officials, asserting claims of negligent supervision and violations of Title IX. Before a jury, the student presented evidence of post-traumatic stress disorder (PTSD) and other psychological harm. However, she offered no medical records, cost estimates or other statistics on damages. The school district offered testimony from a psychologist who stated that her emotional problems were triggered by the lawsuit itself and not by the sexual relationship.

The jury found that the school district was liable for negligent supervision, but that the student failed to prove she was entitled to damages. It therefore awarded her none. On appeal, the Supreme Court of Idaho held that a reasonable jury could have found **the student proved no damages. Even her own experts disagreed as to her condition**, with one finding she did not have PTSD. It seemed that the litigation brought about the psychological difficulties by focusing the student on her experience, memories and trauma. The district's expert also believed the student pursued the lawsuit to comply with her family's request. The district did not have to pay for the negligent supervision of the teacher. *Hei v. Holzer*, 181 P.3d 489 (Idaho 2008).

◆ A Maryland high school teacher gave a 14-year-old student who had a crush on him a ride home. On the way, he took her to his house to play pool and allegedly had consensual sexual intercourse with her. After he was convicted of child abuse and sexual offenses, he appealed. The Court of

Special Appeals of Maryland ruled that consensual sexual intercourse could constitute child abuse under Maryland law. The court stated that because a parent impliedly consents to a teacher taking all reasonable measures to assure the safe return of his or her child from school, including personally driving that child home; because the teacher assumed that responsibility when he agreed to drive the child home; because the events leading up to this unfortunate occurrence were set in motion on school property; and because, at the time of the offense, there had been no temporal break in the teacher and student relationship that existed between the teacher and the victim, the court would upheld his conviction.

The Court of Appeals of Maryland affirmed. It rejected the teacher's argument that once he was with a student off school grounds, for a non-school-related activity, the implied consent rationale was inapplicable and that once he was no longer acting as a teacher, he did not have a responsibility to supervise the student, so could not be convicted of child abuse.

It was uncontested that the act of sexual intercourse by an adult with a 14-year-old girl qualified as "abuse" under the statute. **Although the teacher was neither a parent nor household or family member of the victim, he had "responsibility for the supervision" of the victim at the time of the alleged misconduct.** The evidence was sufficient to support the conviction. *Anderson v. State*, 372 Md. 285, 812 A.2d 1016 (Md. 2002).

◆ A Michigan high school soccer coach addressed players with obscenities, engaged them in "flirtatious conversations," and made suggestive remarks. He called players and sent them emails at unusual hours. He told one student on the team that he had "a special interest" in a particular teammate. The student said that when she discouraged the coach from pursuing the teammate, he threatened the entire team with consequences. The assistant principal, principal and athletic director met with him to address complaints by parents about his late-evening communications. The administrators composed a memo prohibiting him from late calls and from emailing players unless he copied the assistant principal. The coach was prohibited from counseling players about personal matters, conducting activities off-campus without parents present, and from inappropriate relationships. The teammate later informed the student she had broken off her relationship with the coach. According to the student, the coach blamed her for this and threatened to "break her nose and take out her knees so she would never play soccer again." The coach then threatened suicide. Police arrived at his residence, recovered a pistol, and took him to a hospital.

The coach resigned and was prohibited from entering school property. The student transferred to a different school and sued the district, coach and school officials. The case reached the U.S. Court of Appeals, Sixth Circuit, which held that **the state civil rights act required her to show that she was subjected to unwelcome sexual advances, requests for sexual favors, or sexual conduct or communication**. The coach's threats to harm the student did not involve any sexual communication. While the threats were an abuse of authority, they did not pertain to sex. Liability can be imposed for creating hostile environment harassment only if there is reasonable notice and failure to take action by officials. The meeting with administrators and the subsequent memo were evidence of a prompt and reasonable response. The extent of the coach's misconduct did not become known until he resigned. The district and officials were not liable. *Henderson v. Walled Lake Consolidated Schools*, 469 F.3d 479 (6th Cir. 2006).

◆ A Georgia teacher socialized with a troubled student's family, befriending his mother and promising to "look after" both him and his sister. An assistant school superintendent received an anonymous email during the school year, accusing the teacher of having inappropriate relationships with a list of students who had graduated or dropped out of school. She learned of a similar complaint against the teacher three years earlier, but the student involved in that incident vehemently denied anything inappropriate. The assistant superintendent warned the teacher, both orally and in writing, to avoid any appearance of impropriety with students and situations where she would be alone with male students. Vehicles owned by the teacher and the troubled student were later seen parked together in some woods. The superintendent promptly notified the school board and the police, and asked the state Professional Standards Commission (PSC) to investigate the incident. She told the school principal to monitor the two, prevent unnecessary contact between them and to report suspicious behavior to her. The teacher resigned and surrendered her teaching certificate after a substitute teacher discovered a note written by the student that threatened to expose their relationship if she did not comply with certain demands. The parents sued the district in a federal court for Title IX and civil rights violations under 42 U.S.C. § 1983. The court awarded pretrial judgment to the district, and the parents appealed.

   The U.S. Court of Appeals, Eleventh Circuit, held that the parents could not demonstrate school officials acted with deliberate indifference at any time. They responded to each report of misconduct by investigating the charges and interviewing relevant persons. The officials consistently monitored the teacher and warned her about her interaction with students. They requested a PSC investigation after they received the first report specifically linking the teacher and student, monitored her and confronted her when the explicit note was discovered. In light of the many corrective measures taken by district officials, the court held they were not deliberately indifferent. **A district is not deliberately indifferent because the measures it takes are ultimately ineffective in stopping the harassment.** The court affirmed the judgment for the district. *Sauls v. Pierce County School Dist.*, 399 F.3d 1279 (11th Cir. 2005).

◆ New York twins claimed their history teacher sexually harassed them. One of them claimed the teacher confided to her about his personal life.

According to one of the twins, a school psychologist dismissed her report about the teacher and implied the relationship between her and the teacher was a good one. The psychologist later dismissed reports by the twins' mother and one of the twins. The psychologist did not investigate or report the teacher's conduct, which included improper touching and the giving of gifts and cards. Many incidents occurred before the principal met with the teacher and told him he was to have no more contact with the twins than he would with any other student. The following summer, the teacher spoke with one of the twins several times on her cell phone and left her a romantic message. Their parents gave the recorded message to the principal. The school reassigned the teacher the next day and told him not to report to the high school until further notice. The twins sued the school district in a federal district court for sexual harassment in violation of Title IX. The court held that even though the case did not involve allegations of an official policy of sex discrimination, there could be district liability for sexual harassment under Title IX. **The twins only had to show "an official of the school district – who at a minimum has authority to institute corrective measures on the district's behalf – had actual notice of, and was deliberately indifferent to, the teacher's misconduct."** The court rejected the district's claim that the principal had no actual notice that the teacher was harassing the twins until he heard the phone message. It denied the district's motion for summary judgment. *Tesoriero v. Syosset Cent. School Dist.*, 382 F.Supp.2d 387 (E.D.N.Y. 2005).

◆   The Court of Appeals of Florida held that a high school teacher accused of exchanging sexually explicit emails with students did not have to turn over all his home computers for inspection by his school board for use in his formal employment termination hearing. The board suspended the teacher for misconduct for exchanging emails and instant messages with students that were sexually explicit and made derogatory comments about staff members and school operations. An administrative law judge issued an order allowing a board expert to inspect the hard drives of the teacher's home computers to discover if they had relevant data for use against him in a formal termination hearing.

The teacher appealed, arguing production of the home computer records would violate his Fifth Amendment right against self-incrimination and his privacy rights. He argued the production of "every byte, every word, every sentence, every data fragment, and every document," including those that were privileged, substantially invaded his privacy and that of his family. The court noted that computers store bytes of information in an "electronic filing cabinet." It agreed with the teacher that **the request for wholesale access to his personal computers would expose confidential communications and extraneous personal information such as banking records**. There might also be privileged communications with his wife and his attorney. The only Florida decision discussing the production of electronic records in pretrial discovery held a request to examine a computer hard drive was permitted "in only limited or strictly controlled circumstances," such as where a party was suspected of trying to purge data. Other courts had permitted access to a computer when there was evidence of intentional deletion of data. There was no evidence that the teacher was attempting to thwart the production of evidence in this case. The court held the broad discovery request violated the teacher's Fifth Amendment rights and his personal privacy, as well as the privacy of his family. It reversed the administrative order allowing the board to have unlimited access to the teacher's home computers. *Menke v. Broward County School Board*, 916 So.2d 8 (Fla. Dist. Ct. App. 2005).

◆ A 14-year-old Illinois student gave birth to a child in 1986. Blood tests indicated a 99.99% probability that the assistant principal of her junior high school was the child's father. The school district dismissed him under Section 24-12 of the Illinois School Code. Almost two years later, the assistant principal was acquitted of aggravated criminal sexual assault. The student's paternity action was closed shortly after the acquittal based on "lack of activity." A hearing officer reversed the school board's action dismissing the assistant principal in 1991, finding the district did not prove he had sexual contact with the student. A state court affirmed the assistant principal's reinstatement, as did the Appellate Court of Illinois. In 1997, the paternity case was reopened and a court ordered him to pay child support. The state superintendent of education notified the assistant principal of an action to suspend his teaching and administrative certificates for immoral conduct. A hearing officer upheld the action under Section 21-23 of the state school code.

The case reached the Appellate Court of Illinois, which held that the action to suspend the assistant principal's certificates was not barred by the district's effort to dismiss him years earlier. The Section 24-12 employment dismissal and Section 21-23 certificate suspension proceedings were distinct and were brought by different entities. **The assistant principal's acquittal from criminal charges did not prevent the state superintendent from suspending his certificates. The code required the superintendent to suspend a holder's certificate for conviction of specified sex or narcotics offenses.** *Hayes v. State Teacher Certification Board*, 359 Ill.App.3d 1153, 835 N.E.2d 146 (Ill. App. Ct. 2005). The Supreme Court of Illinois denied further appeal.

B. Drugs and Alcohol

◆ A Tennessee county school board decided to conduct random drug screens after a second teacher in seven years was arrested on drug charges. The board hired a private company to perform the drug screens. Four teachers and their union sued, asserting that the random drug testing violated the Fourth Amendment, and a federal court agreed. **Although teachers are highly responsible for the safety of others, making random drug screening generally permissible, the way the policy was implemented**

violated the law. First, the policy didn't give teachers enough information about which drugs were being tested. It gave scientific names, but not brand names. And second, the way the policy was implemented allowed a company employee to separate out a sample into two containers (in case retesting was necessary) in front of other employees. This violated employees' privacy rights. *Smith County Educ. Ass'n v. Smith County Board of Educ.*, 781 F.Supp.2d 604 (M.D. Tenn. 2011).

◆ A California teacher received her third DUI and was placed on home detention for 30 days, but she was also allowed to teach her class during that time while wearing an ankle bracelet. Two years later, the state commission on teacher credentialing suspended her credential for 60 days. She challenged the suspension, but the state court of appeal upheld it, finding that **her drinking and driving, while off school grounds and away from children, provided enough evidence of her unfitness to teach** so as to justify the suspension. *Broney v. California Comm'n on Teacher Credentialing*, 108 Cal.Rptr.3d 832 (Cal. Ct. App. 2010).

◆ An Oregon teacher was dismissed by her school district for "immorality" and "neglect of duty" after a police search and ensuing events brought to light evidence that her husband had been using their jointly owned home to grow and sell marijuana and that the teacher was aware of that. The teacher appealed to the Fair Dismissal Appeals Board, which reversed the dismissal and ordered her reinstated. The district sought review before the Oregon Court of Appeals.

The court of appeals noted that the teacher's job responsibilities included instruction and extracurricular participation in the district's anti-drug program. Here, the teacher did essentially nothing to deter her husband's use of their home for illegal drug activities. Her workshop training gave clear notice that off-duty personal drug involvement was contrary to a teacher's role in connection with the anti-drug instructional program. **She had a duty to prevent her home from being used for marijuana sales regardless of how that act might upset her occasionally violent husband.** The appeals board should have focused on the propriety of her conduct in the light of her responsibilities to the district and her students. The court reversed and remanded the case to the appeals board for reconsideration. *Jefferson County School Dist. No. 509-J v. Fair Dismissal Appeals Board*, 102 Or. App. 83, 793 P.2d 888 (Or. Ct. App. 1990).

◆ A South Carolina teacher was arrested for possessing crack cocaine in 1988, but authorities dismissed his case. In 2000, the teacher was arrested "in his car in a well-known drug area" while his passenger attempted to buy crack. Charges against the teacher were dropped when the passenger pled guilty. After the 2000 incident, the teacher was placed on administrative leave, pending an investigation. The superintendent advised him by letter that his contract was being terminated. At his school board hearing, the superintendent said the termination was based solely on the teacher's unfitness and not on negative publicity. The board upheld the discharge. A state court held that being arrested but not convicted for two criminal charges was not substantial evidence of unfitness to teach. It reversed the board's decision, but the state court of appeals reinstated the board action. It found substantial evidence of the teacher's unfitness to teach, based on the arrests, his dishonesty, the publicity surrounding the 2000 arrest, and the negative response it caused in the community.

The Supreme Court of South Carolina held that the appeals court committed error by failing to confine its decision to the grounds stated in the order terminating his employment. **Two drug arrests, 12 years apart, neither resulting in charges, did not support a finding of unfitness to teach.** This was especially true when the district did not contend the teacher ever used, possessed or sold illegal drugs. The teacher was entitled to reinstatement with back pay and benefits from the date of his suspension. *Shell v. Richland County School Dist. One*, 362 S.C. 408, 608 S.E.2d 428 (S.C. 2005).

◆   About 48 hours after the adult son of a veteran Iowa teacher moved into her house, police officers executed a search warrant on the teacher's house. They found drugs and drug paraphernalia in five locations, including the teacher's bedroom. The district proposed terminating her teaching contract for reasons including drug possession, unprofessional conduct, poor role modeling and leadership, and failure to maintain a good reputation. The school board held a hearing and found that just cause existed to immediately terminate the teacher's employment contract. The teacher appealed to an administrative adjudicator, who found that the board's decision was not supported by the evidence.

A state trial court affirmed the decision, and the district appealed. The Court of Appeals of Iowa found "just cause" for teacher termination exists when the teacher has a significant and adverse effect on the high quality education of students. Just cause "relates to job performance, including leadership and role model effectiveness." **The board's findings did not show the teacher's conduct significantly and adversely affected her job performance. There was no evidence that she ever bought, sold or used marijuana** during her 15-year tenure in the district. The board found it likely she did not know that most of the evidence seized by police was in her house, since her son had returned there less than 48 hours before the search. Other items were kept as "mementos of her deceased husband" and as evidence of her son's marijuana use. The teacher presented evidence that she did not condone drug use and regularly instructed students to stay away from drugs. Since there was insufficient evidence of just cause to discharge the teacher, the judgment was affirmed. *Fielder v. Board of Directors of Carroll Community School Dist.*, 662 N.W.2d 371 (Table) (Iowa Ct. App. 2003).

◆   A Texas teacher checked out a district vehicle to drive to a soccer clinic. Before picking up a colleague who was going to the clinic, the teacher stopped at a dry cleaner and then a grocery store, where he purchased beer and other items. A witness reported seeing him leaving the store with beer and getting into the vehicle. The teacher admitted buying beer while using the vehicle when the school principal confronted him about it. He submitted his resignation after being formally reprimanded, but he later changed his mind and rescinded it. The superintendent recommended not renewing his contract, and the school board voted for non-renewal after a hearing. The state education commissioner affirmed the decision, finding substantial evidence that the teacher was "in the course and scope of his employment while he was in possession of alcohol."

A Texas district court affirmed the decision, and the teacher appealed to the state court of appeals, arguing he was on a personal side trip to run errands when he bought beer. The court held the commissioner's decision had to be affirmed unless it was arbitrary and capricious. **A court could not substitute its judgment for the commissioner's and could only review it to determine if it was supported by substantial evidence.** The teacher had admitted his error and stated buying beer "was a dumb thing to do." He also stated to the board he was acting within the scope of his duties to attend the soccer clinic. The teacher agreed it was reasonable to assume he was acting for the school when the school day began. As the commissioner's decision was supported by substantial evidence, the court affirmed it. *Simpson v. Alanis*, No. 08-03-00110-CV, 2004 WL 309297 (Tex. Ct. App. 2/19/04).

C. Assault

◆   After an Iowa student gave his football coach the finger, the coach put his hands on the student to escort him off the bus. The student said he was "thrown down the aisle." Seeing bruises on their son, his parents called the police, who charged the coach with assault. Then the state licensing board charged the coach with "student abuse." **At the hearing, the coach's previous written reprimands were examined. They included instances of the coach duct-taping droopy trousers to one student and grabbing another and ripping his shirt for calling the coach an "idiot."** The board revoked his teaching license for 90 days and his PE and coaching endorsements for good. The coach appealed to the state supreme court, which found the decision was supported by the evidence. *Christiansen v. Iowa Board of Educ. Examiners*, 831 N.W.2d 179 (Iowa 2013).

◆   First-graders in a California school sued their district and three others, alleging that they hired the substitute teacher who molested them even though they knew of his misconduct at prior schools. One of the prior hiring districts sought to be dismissed from the case, asserting that it could not be liable for the future molestation of the students in the current district. The court of appeal agreed with the district that **it could not be liable for future assaults at a different school district**. The reason there could be no liability was because the earlier district was never a "custodian" of the molested students in this case. So even if the district violated the state's Child Abuse and Neglect Reporting Act, it was not liable for the molestation. *P.S. v. San Bernardino City Unified School Dist.*, 94 Cal.Rptr.3d 788 (Cal. Ct. App. 2009).

◆   A Pennsylvania school district IT employee also served as an assistant coach for the girls' softball teams. He became friends with a student's family, but the mother grew suspicious when she noticed calls from her daughter to the employee at odd hours. She went to the head coach, who went to the principal who, along with the head coach, met with the parents and the student's sister. The family told the coach and principal that they suspected an inappropriate sexual relationship. **The principal told the employee to stay away from team members and that same day, the superintendent gave the employee the option of being fired or resigning.** He resigned. Ten months later, he was charged with sexual offenses against the student. The family then sued the district under 42 U.S.C. § 1983, alleging violations of the student's Fourteenth Amendment rights, but a federal court found no evidence that district officials knew about the sexual abuse or were deliberately indifferent to it. Here, the district conducted a background check on the employee before hiring him, had a written sexual harassment policy in place, and acted promptly to force the employee's resignation when confronted with evidence that he was behaving inappropriately with the student. *Maier v. Canon McMillan School Dist.*, No. 08-0154, 2009 WL 2591098 (W.D. Pa. 8/20/09).

◆   An Oregon teacher served a school district for 19 years with no disciplinary problems. Her husband left her, moved in with his girlfriend, and sought a divorce. The teacher drove to the girlfriend's house and had an argument with her husband. She attempted suicide by taking prescription medications, then rammed her vehicle into her husband's vehicle and damaged the house. She voluntarily committed herself for psychiatric treatment. The incident was reported in local newspapers. Law officials charged her with four crimes, three of which were dropped via plea bargain. She pleaded no contest to a criminal mischief charge, which provided for dismissal with no charges if she completed her term of probation. The school board voted to dismiss the teacher after a hearing, and she appealed to the Oregon Fair Dismissal Appeals Board (FDAB).

  An FDAB hearing panel heard testimony from a psychologist who said the teacher's conduct was isolated and unlikely to reoccur. The board had previously let two teachers return to work after suicide attempts, and another had returned after entering into a diversion agreement for domestic violence charges. The FDAB panel found the dismissal had been "unreasonable" under ORS § 342.905. The board overreacted to an isolated incident and had to reinstate the teacher. The Court of Appeals of Oregon reversed the panel's decision, and the teacher appealed. **The Supreme**

Court of Oregon stated that contract teachers may be dismissed only for immorality or neglect of duty. The FDAB was authorized to determine whether actions by school boards were "unreasonable" or "clearly an excessive remedy." In the context of the statute, "unreasonable" meant "acting without rational or logical justification" for an action. The FDAB panel failed to apply this interpretation, and its decision did not provide a rational connection between the facts and the conclusion. The court returned the case to the panel for further action. *Bergerson v. Salem-Keizer School Dist.*, 341 Or. 401, 144 P.3d 918 (Or. 2006).

◆   After a Pennsylvania teacher pled guilty to simple assault of his wife, the state education department filed a notice of charges and a motion with the state Professional Standards and Practices Commission to revoke his professional teaching certification. The notice informed the teacher that simple assault was a crime involving moral turpitude, requiring revocation. The teacher admitted the assault, but he contended he had pled guilty to avoid embarrassment to himself and his family. He asserted his actions were unrelated to moral turpitude but were the result of his wife's attempt to gain an advantage in divorce proceedings. The commission revoked the teacher's license without a hearing, finding that simple assault was within the state code's definition of "moral turpitude."

The teacher appealed to the Commonwealth Court of Pennsylvania, arguing that the commission denied him due process by refusing to give him a hearing. The court held that a teaching certificate is a property right entitled to due process protection. The court agreed with the teacher that **simple assault is not necessarily a crime involving moral turpitude**. It found the state code and cases defining the term "crime of moral turpitude" required the assailant to have a "reprehensible state of mind." At minimum, a crime of moral turpitude required knowledge of private impropriety or the potential for social disruption. Crimes involving dishonesty, such as fraud, theft by deception, and specific intent drug-trafficking offenses were crimes of moral turpitude. By contrast, the statutory definition of "simple assault" included negligence. A person could lack a "reprehensible state of mind" when engaged in a fight or scuffle by mutual consent. While many forms of simple assault, including spousal battery, were abhorrent, a simple assault was not always a crime of moral turpitude. The commission had erroneously revoked the teacher's certification without a hearing. The court reversed and remanded the case. *Bowalick v. Comwlth. of Pennsylvania*, 840 A.2d 519 (Pa. Commw. Ct. 2004).

D. Other Off-Duty Conduct

◆   A Michigan teacher attended a bachelor/bachelorette party and engaged in a simulated act of oral sex on a mannequin. Someone photographed her without her knowledge and posted the photos on a website without her consent. Two years later, students at her school accessed the photos until they were removed. The school board suspended and then fired the teacher for engaging in lewd behavior contrary to the moral values of the educational and school community. She appealed, and the state tenure commission found no professional misconduct and ordered her reinstatement. The Court of Appeals of Michigan upheld that decision, noting that **her conduct was not only off-duty, but lawful and not involving children**. And it did not have an adverse effect on the educational process. *Land v. L'Anse Creuse Public School Board of Educ.*, No. 288612, 2010 WL 2135356 (Mich. Ct. App. 5/27/10).

CHAPTER SEVEN

Health Issues

I. ALLERGIES

A. Food Allergies

1. Generally

All foods have the potential to cause an allergic reaction, and sometimes even a very small amount is all that is needed. Seven foods – peanuts, tree nuts, milk, egg, soy, wheat and fish – account for the vast majority of all food allergies. Of these, peanuts, tree nuts, eggs and milk most commonly cause problems for children, and the majority of severe and fatal reactions involve peanuts and tree nuts. Food allergies can be managed, but they are not curable.

Millions of Americans have food allergies, and food allergies in American children have increased significantly since 1997, according to a study by the Centers for Disease Control (CDC). In addition, the CDC reported a drastic increase in the number of hospital admissions related to children's food allergies, which indicates children's reactions to the allergens are becoming more severe.

Allergies are diseases that cause the immune systems of affected individuals to overreact to substances known as allergens. In people with food allergies, the immune system identifies a specific protein in a food as a potentially harmful substance. The immune system responds to the perceived threat by producing an allergic antibody to the food. This response triggers the release of what are known as chemical mediators, such as histamine. The release of the mediators can cause inflammatory reactions in the skin, the respiratory system, the gastrointestinal system, and the cardiovascular system. A potentially life-threatening condition called anaphylaxis occurs when these inflammatory reactions occur in more than one of these systems. Approximately 30,000 episodes of anaphylactic shock and an average of 200 deaths caused by the episodes occur in the U.S. each year – primarily in children, according to the National Institute of Allergy and Infectious Disease. Common symptoms of anaphylaxis include hives, vomiting, itching, swelling, coughing, dizziness, and difficulty swallowing.

Students who have food allergies should have an action plan to indicate how school officials should manage an allergic reaction that may progress to anaphylaxis. The action plan should indicate whether emergency treatment with an EpiPen or EpiPen Junior is required. EpiPen is an auto-injector that administers adrenaline and is available by prescription only. EpiPens should be stored properly and securely, but they should also be readily available. EpiPens should be accessible to school officials. Decisions regarding whether students should be allowed to carry their own EpiPens should be made on a case-by-case basis and according to the district's policies.

EpiPens should be stored in temperatures ranging from 68 degrees to 77 degrees. They should not be refrigerated, and they should not be exposed to light or extreme heat.

Two red flags indicate that an EpiPen should be replaced, even if it has not reached its expiration date. Specifically, an EpiPen should be discarded if it has solid particles in it or if it has a pink or brown tint.

In November of 2013, President Barack Obama signed into law the School Access to Emergency Epinephrine Act. This law encourages states to adopt laws that require schools to keep epinephrine auto-injectors on hand.

The law gives more grant preference to schools in states that:
- require schools to stock the auto-injectors
- allow students to self-administer medication for anaphylactic reactions (and asthmatic reactions), and
- submit a statement providing that the state's "Good Samaritan" laws adequately protect staffers who administer epinephrine to a student who is reasonably believed to be having an anaphylactic reaction.

Legislative action taken in Michigan was likely a response to the passage of this federal legislation. Effective on the first day of the 2014-15 school year, state law required all schools in the state to have at least two EpiPens in every school – and two staffers who know how to use them.

Children with food allergies present difficult challenges for school administrators and parents. Once a student is identified as having a food allergy, steps must be taken to ensure that the student can completely avoid the food while at school. Families, schools and students all have responsibilities when it comes to managing food allergies. See Form VII-18 in Chapter Nine for a Food Allergy Action Plan.
- It is the **family's** responsibility to notify the school of the existence of the student's food allergies and to work with the school to develop an effective management plan. It is also the responsibility of the family to teach the child to self-manage the food allergy to the maximum extent possible and to provide any required medications.
- **Schools** should form teams, consisting of the student's teacher, the school's principal, the school's nurse, food service personnel and other key personnel to work with the student and the family to develop an effective management plan. It is advisable to adopt and enforce a policy barring eating on school buses, except to accommodate legitimate special needs. Schools would also benefit by providing training and education to staff regarding food allergies and practicing emergency drill responses to food allergy reactions.

- **Students** with allergies should be instructed not to exchange food with others and not to eat anything with unknown ingredients. In addition, allergic students should be instructed to notify an adult immediately if they ingest something they believe might cause an allergic reaction.

Constant monitoring is crucial, as problems can arise in unforeseeable ways. Here's an example: High school student Joshua Hickson was charged with assault after he smeared peanut butter on the forehead of a student with a peanut allergy. Hickson was suspended from school and charged with misdemeanor assault, which is punishable by up to a year in jail and a $5,000 fine.

A multi-faceted approach to keeping allergic students safe is preferable. For example, Tim Henson, principal of a South Carolina elementary school, took all of the following steps:

- school sent letters to parents discussing food allergies and outlining what was permitted and what was not
- staffers talked to students about rules pertaining to nut-free tables that were set up in the cafeteria, and
- administrators talked to lunchroom employees, who completed special training regarding specifics such as cross-contamination and the proper way to clean nut-free tables.

In 2013, the Centers for Disease Control (CDC) issued guidelines for managing food allergies in schools. The CDC says schools should manage food allergies on a daily basis, prepare for food allergy emergencies and provide staff training on food allergies. The guidance is available online at *http://www.cdc.gov/healthyyouth/foodallergies/pdf/13_243135_A_Food_All ergy_Web_508.pdf.*

Harvard Medical School Professor Dr. Nicholas Christakis advises school officials not to overreact to food allergies by implementing a school-wide ban on nuts. The "disproportionate response" may contribute to an increased sensitization of children to nuts, he asserts, citing a study that reported children who were exposed to peanuts at a young age apparently had fewer allergies to peanuts than children who were exposed at a later age.

As in any other situation involving student safety, communication is a crucial element in keeping students with food allergies safe. Electronic media, such as a school's website, can be an effective communication tool. For example, in response to a student's allergy to AXE body spray, a high school principal in Pennsylvania posted a notice on his school's website. The notice appealed to students and parents to show concern for the student's health by refraining from using the spray at school.

For an example of a letter to parents explaining that a child in the class has a food allergy, see Form VII-1 in Chapter Nine. For a sample letter informing substitute teachers that a child in the class has a food allergy, see Form VII-2 in Chapter Nine.

2. Legal Decisions

◆ A school proposed to accommodate a student with a nut allergy by providing that he would eat only food brought from home and would sit at a nut-free table in the cafeteria. His parents objected because the student would be eating alone. The child's doctor asked the school to seat the child at a rectangular table with a two-foot buffer between him and classmates who also had nut-free lunches. However, the school only had round lunch tables. The parents withdrew the student from school and asked for a due process hearing. A hearing officer determined that the school met its obligation to accommodate the student, and a federal court agreed. **The proposed accommodations were reasonable**, and the parents did not show that the school officials were deliberately indifferent to the student's rights. *T.F. v. Fox Chapel Area School Dist.*, No. 12cv1666, 2013 WL 5936411 (W.D. Pa. 11/5/13).

◆ A nine-year-old student with allergies to many foods and substances began to have trouble breathing after finishing lunch at school. A school nurse injected the student with EpiPens, but he died two days later. His parents suspected that the student's reaction was triggered by his exposure to blueberries during a classroom lesson on the morning of the event. They sued the student's school, the city department of education and the school nurse, among others. They alleged that the defendants negligently allowed the student to be exposed to a substance to which he was allergic and then failed to properly respond to his symptoms. The court held that the department of education met its obligations by formulating a proper individualized education program for the student. In addition, the school provided adequate supervision; typically there were about 10 children in the student's class and four supervising adults. Further, **the nurse did not depart from good and accepted nursing and professional practice**, especially since blueberries were not included on the list of known allergens for the child and the parents never proved what triggered the student's reaction. *Begley v. City of New York*, 111 A.D.3d 5 (N.Y. App. Div. 2013).

◆ To accommodate a student's allergy to nuts, a school implemented a ban on nuts at school. The allergic child's Section 504 plan required a nut-free school. **A non-allergic student's mother sued, arguing that the ban could not be applied to her** because she and her daughter were not parties to the allergic child's Section 504 plan. The court rejected her claim. State law gave districts the authority to adopt policies for the health, safety and educational benefit of their students, and the general right of parents to be involved in the education of their children did not abridge "the school's authority to regulate what food items a child may bring to school in the exercise of its obligation to provide for the safety and welfare of other students." *Liebau v. Romeo Community Schools*, No. 306979, 2013 WL 660134 (Mich. Ct. App. 7/30/13).

◆   The parents of a child with an allergy to nuts sued an elementary school principal and others, claiming the defendants failed to consider the possibility of excluding nut products from the school and forced the child to eat his lunch in an office away from all the other children. The lawsuit accused the defendants of failing to make any reasonable accommodations for the child. **It also claimed the child's school served peanut butter cookies to all students and caused the child to suffer an allergic reaction, even though it knew he was allergic to peanuts.** The court dismissed the parents' claim for negligent infliction of emotional distress because they did not respond to the defendants' motion to dismiss it. The court also dismissed a claim for violation of 42 U.S.C. § 1983, a conspiracy claim under 42 U.S.C. § 1985, a claim under 42 U.S.C. § 1986, a claim of intentional infliction of emotional distress and a state civil rights claim with leave to amend. Finally, it denied a defense motion to dismiss a slander claim, which was based on the allegation that district defendants distributed false statements about the child to his classmates. *McCue v. South Fork Union School Dist.*, No. CV-F-10-233 OWW/DLB, 2010 WL 2089524 (E.D. Cal. 5/21/10).

◆   The parents of a kindergartner with an allergy to cheese sued a board of education and other defendants after the child allegedly was allowed to eat cheese at school. The parents claimed that as a result of a reaction to the cheese, the student wandered away from school. The trial court construed the parents' complaint to assert claims of assault, civil conspiracy, educational malpractice, reckless and/or negligent hiring and retention of services, and infliction of emotional distress. The trial court granted summary judgment in favor of the defendants, and the parents appealed. The appeals court affirmed the trial court's decision because the defendants were immune to the claims raised under state law. *Hopkins v. Columbus Board of Educ.*, No. 07AP-700, 2008 WL 852608 (Ohio Ct. App. 3/31/08).

◆   Residents of New York enrolled their child in a New Jersey nonprofit school that catered to developmentally atypical children. The child had severe food allergies and was accompanied by a private nurse at all times. He was instructed to eat only food that was supplied by his parents. The child died, allegedly after he was exposed to substances at the school and suffered an allergic reaction. The parents sued the school in a New York court, seeking monetary damages for personal injuries and wrongful death. The parents claimed that the school failed to exercise reasonable care of the child while the child was under its direction and control. The school filed a motion for summary judgment, arguing that it was immune from liability under a New Jersey statute that generally barred claims for damages against nonprofit corporations. The parents opposed the motion on the grounds that New York law did not recognize the principle of charitable immunity. The court held that the New Jersey law of charitable immunity did not apply because it offended the public policy of New York. The parents showed that sufficient contacts existed between them, the injury and New York, and they also showed that **application of the New Jersey charitable immunity statute would violate a "fundamental principle of justice."** The parents lived in New York, and the child's tuition at the New Jersey school was paid by the New York City Board of Education. Further, New York had an interest in protecting its citizens from "unfair and anachronistic foreign statutes," and the state of New York had first rejected the concept of charitable immunity nearly 50 years earlier. The school's motion for summary judgment was denied. *Begley v. City of New York*, 836 N.Y.S.2d 496 (N.Y. Sup. Ct. 2007).

◆   A child broke out in splotches and hives while at a day care facility. Following the incident, the child's doctor determined the child was allergic to peanuts and peanut derivatives. The child then suffered a second allergic reaction at the day care facility, after which the facility refused to provide further day care services to her. The child's mother then sued the facility under the Americans with Disabilities Act (ADA) and state law, claiming discrimination on the basis of disability. A district court granted summary judgment in favor of the day care facility, and the parent appealed. The appeals court upheld the district court's determination on the basis that the child did not have a "disability" as that term is defined in the ADA. Although the child's allergy was a physical impairment, it did not substantially limit her ability to eat or breathe. **The child's doctor stated that the child's allergy impacted her life only "a little bit," and the record did not show she was restricted from eating any other kind of food.** Nor did the parent show that the child was disabled under the ADA because she had a record of a disability or was regarded by the school as disabled. Finally, the court rejected the state-law claim because the child was not disabled under the state law. *Land v. Baptist Medical Center*, 164 F.3d 423 (8th Cir. 1999).

◆   A student with an allergy to peanuts went on a field trip with his elementary school class. The district's food staff, the boy's teacher, two school nurses and several parent volunteers all were aware that the child was allergic to peanuts. Nonetheless, the child was given a snack lunch that included peanut-based foods. The child reported feeling sick after he ate a peanut-based cookie. Trip chaperones did not want to curtail the activities of the other children on the trip, so they placed the student on the school bus to wait. His condition worsened, and he later died after being taken to a hospital by car. After the student's parents entered into a settlement agreement with the school district regarding the incident, a newspaper sought the release under a public disclosure act of an investigator's notes, an investigator's hand-drawn map, conference notes by counsel for the district, and counsel's report to an insurer. A trial court ruled that the records were not subject to disclosure because they were attorney work product and attorney-client privileged material. The newspaper appealed. The appeal court affirmed the determination that the records were not subject to disclosure. **The documents were attorney work product and were**

further protected by attorney-client privilege. The public disclosure act's provisions relating to open government did not outweigh the countervailing interest in insulating confidential pretrial communications from public inspection. Finally, the district did not waive its privilege to keep the information private when it made selected disclosures of information to the public and the student's family. The trial court's decision was affirmed. *Soter v. Cowles Publishing Co.*, 130 P.3d 840 (Wash. Ct. App. 2006). On appeal, the Supreme Court of Washington affirmed the appeals court's decision. *Soter v. Cowles Publishing Co.*, 174 P.3d 60 (Wash. 2007).

B. Other Allergies

1. Generally

School officials need to be aware that a range of allergies other than food-related allergies may affect the school environment, as shown by the following cases.

2. Legal Decisions

◆ A student with allergies to certain body sprays, perfumes, colognes, laundry detergents, fabric softeners and scented lotions alleged that his high school violated Title II of the Americans with Disabilities Act by refusing to implement a written policy against spraying perfumes at school. The student did not know which specific scents triggered reactions, how much of a particular fragrance was needed to trigger a reaction, or what the severity of any given reaction would be. The school offered several accommodations, including allowing the student to park in a different area and enter the school through a different door, allowing the student to leave class early, allowing the student to arrive at a different time, and exploring whether the student could wear a mask. **The court ruled for the school, finding it took sufficient steps to accommodate the student's condition.** Moreover, the student did not show that the written policy he sought would have been effective. *Zandi v. JVB Fort Wayne Community Schools*, No. 1:10-CV-395-JVB (N.D. Ind. 9/27/12).

◆ The parent of a two-year-old enrolled the child at a nursery school where teachers used powdered latex gloves to change children's diapers. The parent, who had an allergy to latex, asked the teachers at the school to use non-powdered latex gloves. She also asked her son's teacher to use non-latex gloves, and she offered to provide them. When the parent spoke to the head administrator at the school about switching to non-powdered gloves, the administrator initially told the parent he would look into it. The parent also had her physician send the administrator a letter explaining her allergy. Despite the request and the letter, the administrator allegedly later told the parent he was not willing to switch to another type of gloves. However, he did tell staff members not to use latex gloves when changing the diaper of the parent's child. After the parent provided the administrator with a letter discussing her rights under the law, the administrator asked the parent to withdraw the child from the school. The parent removed the child from the school and later sued it, claiming it violated a county human rights code by discriminating against her based on her latex allergy. A jury found in her favor and awarded $1,683 in economic damages and $5,000 in non-economic damages. It also awarded $22,800 in attorneys' fees. The trial court entered judgment on the verdict, and the school appealed. The appeals court reversed the lower court's judgment in favor of the parent because she did not show that her latex allergy was a disability under the law. However, the state's highest court reversed the appeals court's decision and held that **it was for a jury to decide whether the parent's latex allergy was a "handicap" within the meaning of the law** at issue. Since the evidence was sufficient for the jury to conclude the parent had a "handicap," the judgment favoring her was restored. *Meade v. Shangri-La Limited Partnership*, 36 A.3d 483 (Md. 2012).

◆   A parent of two students sued a city, a board of education and several individual defendants, claiming the defendants' failure to properly maintain public school buildings caused the students to become disabled. The parent asserted that the defendants' failure to properly maintain a middle school caused it to sustain water damage that led to mold and bacterial growth and high levels of moisture in the indoor air. She also claimed that the defendants' failure to properly maintain a high school resulted in asbestos problems, leaks and poor ventilation. **The parent said that conditions at the schools caused one of the students to suffer irreversible lung disease and the other to suffer allergies and asthma.** She claimed that the students were eligible for special education services and that the defendants wrongfully failed to provide them. The parent's suit against the defendants raised several claims, including federal claims under the Individuals with Disabilities Education Act, Section 504 of the Rehabilitation Act and the Americans with Disabilities Act. The parent also filed several state law claims. The defendants filed a motion to dismiss the case, and the parent filed a motion to remand the case to state court. The court granted the motion to dismiss several of the claims raised by the parent because the parent failed to exhaust her administrative remedies under the Individuals with Disabilities Education Act. It also declined to exercise supplemental jurisdiction over some remaining state law claims. The court remanded remaining state law claims to a state court. *Avoletta v. City of Torrington*, No. 3:07CV841 (AHN), 2008 WL 905882 (D. Conn. 3/31/08).

◆   A student with a latex allergy broke out in hives after he was given a latex ball to play with at school. His representatives sued the school district, accusing it of failing to prevent him from sustaining injury by failing to convey his special needs to teachers and aides. The representatives also raised claims under the Individuals with Disabilities Education Act and the Americans with Disabilities Act. After the school district removed the case to federal court, the representatives filed a motion to remand it back to state court. The court granted the motion to remand. **The theories of relief advanced by the student's representatives were based solely on state tort law.** Because no claim in the case arose under federal law, the court granted the motion to remand the case. *Reuther v. Shiloh School Dist. No. 85*, No. 07-cv-689-JPG, 2008 WL 191195 (S.D. Ill. 1/18/08).

◆   A village resident installed an outdoor wood-burning furnace adjacent to his garage and approximately 50 feet from the elementary wing of a local school. The resident used the furnace to provide heat for his home. Teachers, school employees and parents of students complained about the smell of smoke in the school cafeteria and some classrooms. After a school official advised the county department of health that teachers and students had allergies to wood smoke and were becoming ill from it, the health department ordered the resident to stop using the furnace. The resident sued the school district, the county and others, claiming they violated the Constitution by depriving him the right to use his property without due process of law. He also claimed an equal protection violation, alleging no enforcement actions were taken against others whose use of wood-burning furnaces caused smoke to enter the school. The court granted summary judgment against the resident. The resident failed to prove an equal protection violation because he did not identify any other resident who used wood for heating fuel. Even if he had, the equal protection claim would fail because the smoke created a respiratory hazard. The resident's due process claim failed as well, because **he did not have a constitutionally protected property interest in heating his home with wood**. The defendants' motions for summary judgment were granted. *Tallman v. County of Chautauqua*, No. 05-CV-02769A(Sr), 2007 WL 4276825 (W.D.N.Y. 12/3/07).

◆   A nine-year-old student was allergic to horse dander. The student's parents claimed that the school's assistant principal admitted that a new substitute teacher had not received training regarding the use of an EpiPen. The parents also alleged that school authorities suggested that the parents should transport the student to school. In addition, they claimed school authorities failed to respond to questions regarding teacher training relating to the student's condition. **The parents sought a preliminary injunction to bar school personnel and students from bringing horses or tack onto the school campus.** They also sought to require the school board to comply with an Individual Accommodation Plan that had been developed for the student. The court determined that the parents were not entitled to the requested injunction because they did not show they were likely to succeed on the merits of their claims under 42 U.S.C. § 1983 and Section 504 of the Rehabilitation Act. In addition, the parents did not show that the failure to grant the injunction would be likely to cause an irreparable injury. The parents had the option of keeping the child home or away from horses at school, and to provide alternative transportation. The request for an injunction was denied. *Smith v. Tangipahoa Parish School Board*, No. Civ.A. 05-6648, 2006 WL 16291 (E.D. La. 1/4/06).

◆   A high school student with a hearing impairment asked for permission to bring his service dog with him to school. At the time, the school was already providing other disability-related accommodations, including sign-language interpreter services for most classes, an FM transmitter, a student note taker, and extra test-taking time. The school denied the student's request, claiming that it already was accommodating the student's disability-related needs and that the dog would disrupt the school environment. The student and his parents sued the school district under the Americans with Disabilities Act, the Rehabilitation Act and state law, challenging the district's refusal to allow the dog in school. The student and his parents filed a motion for a preliminary injunction that would force the school district to allow the student to enter school facilities with the dog. The court determined that the school provided the student with reasonable accommodations. It denied the motion because the balance of hardships tipped in favor of the school district and school officials. **Although the dog would benefit the student, the school would be forced to endure hardships because two of the student's teachers and other students were allergic to dogs.** In addition, the dog would need to be confined to a particular area during gym class, and the student's schedule would need to be changed. The request for an injunction was denied. *Cave v. East Meadow Union Free School Dist.*, 480 F.Supp.2d 610 (E.D.N.Y. 2007). On appeal, the U.S. Court of Appeals for the Second Circuit held that the district court lacked subject-matter jurisdiction over the federal claims because the student and his parents failed to exhaust administrative remedies available to them under the Individuals with Disabilities Education Act (IDEA) and implementing state legislation. **Even though the complaint did not raise an IDEA claim, exhaustion under that statute was required because the complaint asserted claims for relief that was available under that statute.** The court also held that the exercise of supplemental jurisdiction over the state law claims was improper. The appeals court directed the lower court to dismiss the complaint without prejudice. *Cave v. East Meadow Union Free School Dist.*, 514 F.3d 240 (2d Cir. 2008).

◆   The parents of a sixth-grade student sued the student's school principal and others under the Americans with Disabilities Act, the Rehabilitation Act and state law, claiming they failed to accommodate the student's allergic reactions to environmental factors at her school. The parents claimed the student was hypersensitive to phenol, which can be present in vapors emitted by cleaning agents or paints. The defendants filed a motion to exclude the expert testimony of the student's primary treating physician, who concluded the student was hypersensitive to environmental phenol even though the student was unable to complete a test to determine whether the hypersensitivity existed. The court granted the motion to exclude the expert's testimony. **The expert's conclusion that the student was hypersensitive to phenol was an inference that was not based on adequate scientific data, testing or methodology.** As a result, it was unreliable and was not a proper subject for expert testimony. *Kropp v. Maine School Administrative Union #44*, 471 F.Supp.2d 175 (D. Me. 2007).

◆ The parents of an eighth-grade student with multiple chemical sensitivities protested a school board's plan to use pesticides on the playing fields at school district schools. The board approved the plan, and the parents asked the student's gym teacher to keep her inside while fields were sprayed. The student was assigned to begin ninth grade at a high school that was located across the street from a working farm. During the summer before the student's ninth-grade year, the student's parents asked the school district for a Section 504 Service Agreement that would permit the student to fulfill her gym requirement at a location away from the school. In addition, **they asked that the school not be sprayed with pesticides, and they asked for a transfer to a school that was located in a more urban area.** The school proposed a service agreement that excused the student from participating in outdoor physical education activities and offered a transfer to the urban high school. The parents objected to the proposed agreement for several reasons. Among other things, they wanted to substitute gym class with dance, and they stated there was no guarantee that balls used indoors had no pesticides on them. After the school proposed modified agreements, the parents withdrew their request for a service agreement but continued to seek accommodations for the student. The school district then submitted the matter for a due process hearing, and the hearing officer found the district had offered a reasonable agreement. The school district then informed the parents that the service agreement would be implemented and denied a request for a transfer to the other high school because a valid agreement was in place. The parents withdrew the student from school and sued the district and others under the Rehabilitation Act, the Americans with Disabilities Act, and 42 U.S.C. § 1983. **They claimed that the district's attempt to enter into a service agreement was an abuse of process and violated their due process rights.** The court granted the defendants' motion for summary judgment. There was no evidence that the district used process in any way not intended as proper use when it sought a due process hearing. In addition, the abuse of process claim was time-barred. The court also rejected the claim that the parents' civil rights were violated because they were forced into a Section 504 service agreement. To prove that the plan violated their due process rights, the parents were required to show actions on the part of the school district that "shocked the conscience." They failed to do so. The parents also failed to show that the district retaliated against them for exercising their First Amendment rights by intensifying the use of pesticides, forcing them into a service agreement or stigmatizing the student as disabled, and that claim was also time-barred. Finally, the court rejected claims of emotional distress and conspiracy. *Sutton v. West Chester Area School Dist.*, No. Civ.A. 03-3061, 2004 WL 999144 (E.D. Pa. 5/4/04).

◆   The parent of an 11-year-old sixth-grade student with an allergy to scents demanded that school officials provide the student a scent-free environment. In response to the demand, the school implemented a voluntary scent-free classroom for the student. The parent spoke to the student's teachers, classmates and their parents regarding the student's condition, and the teachers and classmates voluntarily refrained from wearing scents. However, the student was exposed to scents at school on three occasions. On one occasion, a school administrator who was wearing a scent left the student's classroom. On a second occasion, a substitute teacher wore a fragrance. The student was sent to the library. The student was also sent to the library on a third occasion when a classmate wore cologne. The parent continued to request a mandatory scent-free environment, but the school refused to provide one. School officials said a mandatory scent-free environment policy would be impossible to enforce and would conflict with the rights of other students and teachers. When the student's physician informed school officials that the student required a scent-free classroom, the school informed the parent that the student would no longer be allowed to attend because it could not provide a scent-free environment. **The parent then sued the school, claiming that it discriminated against the student on the basis of disability in violation of the Rehabilitation Act.** The parent filed a motion for injunctive relief. The court denied the motion and entered judgment for the school and other defendants. The school met its duty to provide the student with a minor adjustment when it provided a voluntary scent-free classroom. It would not be reasonable to require the school to enforce a mandatory scent-free policy. The student attended several different classrooms and also spent time in the school gymnasium and church, and **it would be unduly burdensome to require the school to implement a mandatory scent-free policy**. The court also found that the school was not required to provide a written contingency plan in the event the student was exposed to scents, and it rejected a claim of retaliation. *Hunt v. St. Peter School*, 963 F.Supp 843 (W.D. Mo. 1997).

II. DIABETES

A. Symptoms and Management

Diabetes is an incurable, chronic disease that is characterized by an inability to properly produce or use insulin, which is a hormone that converts food into energy. Lack of insulin causes blood glucose to rise to an abnormally high level, resulting in a condition called hyperglycemia. When this happens, the body may excrete blood glucose in the urine, causing it to lose its main fuel source.

There are two main types of diabetes. Individuals with Type 1 diabetes, which often afflicts school-age children, are unable to produce insulin and must receive insulin on a daily basis. Type 2 diabetes involves an inability to utilize insulin that the body produces. It can be controlled with insulin, oral medications or both.

Management of diabetes involves maintaining proper blood glucose control, a task which requires constant vigilance. Careful monitoring is imperative, and administration of insulin therapy is often required.

Controlling blood glucose levels is often a difficult balancing act. If not enough insulin is given, the individual's blood glucose level will rise to an unacceptable level. But administration of too much insulin can cause a dangerous condition called hypoglycemia, or low blood glucose. According to the U.S. Department of Health and Human Services, hypoglycemia presents a greater danger to school-age students than hyperglycemia. Some of the symptoms of hypoglycemia, as noted by the U.S. Department of Health and Human Services, include the following:

- shakiness
- sweating
- hunger
- pale appearance
- blurred vision
- sleepiness
- dizziness
- confusion
- disorientation
- lack of coordination
- irritability or nervousness
- change in personality
- inability to concentrate
- weakness
- lethargy
- changes in behavior

In severe cases, there may be an inability to swallow, seizure or convulsions, or loss of consciousness.

Because it is a relatively common disease among school-age children, many, if not most, schools will have a student or students with diabetes enrolled. School personnel play a key role in helping students manage the condition.

In New York, South Jefferson School District implemented on-site virtual clinics for students who have diabetes. Each school building in the district was equipped with a computer and a webcam. School nurses used the equipment to communicate with medical personnel at a diabetes center about students' blood glucose test results. School nurses could also download student data and coordinate meetings between students and the diabetes control center. The meetings took only 10 to 15 minutes, but they improved lab test results. In addition, the number of urgent calls relating to the diabetic students was significantly reduced.

For a sample diabetes management plan, see Form VII-3 in Chapter Nine.

B. Legal Decisions

◆   The parent of a seventh-grade student with Title I diabetes sued a city, city agencies and city officials. In the lawsuit, the parent accused the defendants of violating the Rehabilitation Act and the Americans with Disabilities Act by denying her request to heat the child's food at school. The parent claimed that the school was required to heat the child's food because the child would skip lunch if his food was not heated. The court rejected her claim, finding that **the child's school provided adequate accommodations by offering lunch menu options and monitoring the child's blood glucose level**. Heating the student's food may have helped him adjust to his disability, but the school was required to provide only meaningful access and not preferred arrangements. The laws relied upon by the parent did not require optimal accommodations, and it was undisputed that hot food is not essential to effective management of diabetes. *Moody v. NYC Dep't of Educ.*, 513 Fed. Appx. 95 (2d Cir. 2013).

◆   The Americans Nurses' Association and other trade organizations representing registered and school nurses sued to challenge a state department of education's decision to authorize public school employees other than nurses to administer insulin to students with diabetes. The plaintiffs in the case sought declaratory relief and a writ of mandate. A lower court ruled in favor of the associations, finding that state law did not authorize unlicensed school personnel to administer insulin. On appeal, the state's highest court reversed the lower court's decision. The appeals court determined that **state law did not ban school personnel other than licensed health care providers from administering insulin to students with diabetes**. In addition, it decided that advisory statements recommending administration only by licensed professionals were not entitled to deference. *American Nurses Ass'n v. Torlakson*, 304 P.3d 1038 (Cal. 2013).

◆   After a nine-year-old was diagnosed with Type I diabetes in March of a particular school year, her mother spent the rest of the school year arguing with a Kentucky school district over the best way to administer the child insulin injections at school. The mother ultimately sued the school district for disability discrimination. The court dismissed her complaint, finding the district did nothing wrong. The court determined that the district had tried to accommodate the child by offering multiple reasonable suggestions about how she could receive insulin injections at school, but the mother rejected all of them.

The child needed an insulin shot after every meal, and her elementary school didn't have a school nurse to administer a shot to her after lunch. The school principal told the child's mother a school around seven miles away did have a nurse, and the district had suggested transferring the child there. The mother refused because there was no bus service to that school. The district offered to transport the child there from her current drop-off point, but the mother found the suggestion unacceptable because it would mean the child would arrive a little late in the morning and have to leave a little early at the end of each day.

The mother also rejected the following suggestions:
- taking the child from school to a local doctor's office for her shot
- having EMTs from a nearby fire station come to the school to give her the shots
- letting the child administer her own shots
- having the mother come to school to administer them, and
- giving a local nurse, doctor and the mother shared responsibility to come to the school on different days to give the child her insulin injection.

The mother wanted the district to hire a nurse for the child's elementary school. The district refused because of the expense. Alternatively, the mother said the district could train one of its employees to administer the insulin injection, but the Kentucky Board of Nursing had a prohibition against training laypeople to administer injections. The district worried going against it would expose it to lawsuits.

By the end of the school year, the mother and the district hadn't reached a solution, but the child had always received her daily shot from one of four people: her mother, her grandmother, a local doctor or a local nurse.

The child's family moved over the summer, and the child entered a different school in the same district in the fall. The family was satisfied with the new school's procedure for giving the student her insulin shots. Even so, her mother sued the district, alleging it had violated Section 504 of the Rehabilitation Act, the Americans with Disabilities Act and the Kentucky Civil Rights Act by failing to accommodate the student's disability. The court dismissed the complaint, finding the school had fulfilled its duty.

All three laws prohibit discrimination on the basis of disability, and the failure to provide a reasonable accommodation can constitute disability discrimination. **But school districts don't have to provide accommodations that require them to make fundamental changes to their programs or impose an undue hardship on them.**

The court decided none of the three laws required the district to modify one school's program when the requested service (a school nurse) was available at another district school.

Also, since this discrimination allegation didn't involve the instruction the child was receiving, the mother had to show the district acted with "deliberate indifference" by showing a conscious disregard for the student's rights. She couldn't.

Instead, the district worked with the mother to try to find an accommodation they could agree on. It wasn't indifferent to the student's rights in refusing to hire a school nurse or train a staff member to give the injection

– it had genuine cost and legal-liability concerns. *B.M. v. Board of Educ. of Scott County*, No. 5:07-153-JMH, 2008 WL 4073855 (E.D. Ky. 8/29/08).

◆ A federal court in Minnesota refused to dismiss a disability discrimination case against a school district whose daycare program refused to train its staff to operate a diabetic child's blood-glucose meter and insulin pump.

A child was diagnosed with Type I diabetes when he was three years old, and he was fitted with an insulin pump when he was five.

An insulin pump is attached to a needle that remains inserted in the patient but is periodically moved to different places on the body. The patient wears the pump, which is an electronic device that can be programmed to dispense finely calibrated doses of insulin on a regular schedule as well as on demand – such as before or after eating.

To calculate the correct dose, blood sugar is checked by pricking the diabetic's finger and placing a drop of blood on a test strip which is then inserted into an electronic blood-glucose meter.

The student's parents wanted to enroll him in a summer daycare program. They notified its staff they would have to be trained to check the child's blood sugar with the electronic meter, work the child's insulin pump and administer a glucagon injection if he suffered severe hypoglycemia. The daycare refused to do so.

The parents enrolled the child in a private daycare instead, but hired a lawyer. The child was starting kindergarten at the district that fall, and the parents wanted to enroll him in the daycare's before- and after-school programs. But when the law office contacted the district's daycare, it said it wouldn't give the student glucagon injections and would only supervise the child's use of the pump and the glucose meter – such as by reminding him to check his blood sugar level – but not operate the equipment for him. The parents cancelled the child's enrollment in the daycare.

In September, the district initiated administrative proceedings to determine what accommodations it had to provide the student under Section 504 of the Rehabilitation Act. In March, it gave the parents a Section 504 plan for kindergarten and an inclusion plan for daycare.

The parents had no complaint with the Section 504 plan, but they objected to the inclusion plan. It provided that daycare staff would only supervise the child's use of the insulin pump. If he experienced severe hypoglycemia, the staff would kink the tube between the pump and the needle to stop the flow of insulin. The parents had their doctor write a letter stating the child needed a glucagon injection if he had a hypoglycemic emergency and that a trained adult should operate the child's insulin pump and blood-glucose meter.

The district asked the parents to put their requested changes to the inclusion plan in writing. They did, saying they wanted three-to-four staff members trained to:

• check the child's blood sugar level – as he sometimes needed help

when his blood sugar was low
- operate his insulin pump – so the flow of insulin could be shut off if his blood sugar became low, and
- give him a glucagon injection – because it would take an ambulance around six minutes to get to the school.

The parents also said that if it was district policy to allow only trained medical staff to do these things, the district should either change its policy or hire a school nurse.

The letter was delivered in early May. When the district had failed to respond by the end of the school year in June, the parents sued, alleging the district had violated the Americans with Disabilities Act (ADA), Section 504 of the Rehabilitation Act and the Minnesota Human Rights Act by refusing to grant the requested accommodations. The district asked for summary judgment, but the court refused to grant it, deciding a trial was needed to determine if the district had a duty to provide the requested accommodations or if they constituted an undue burden.

Several aspects of the ADA and its accompanying regulations made it clear that entities – like public school districts – covered under the act had to provide reasonable accommodations to people with disabilities. Also, U.S. Supreme Court decisions had clarified that failure to grant such accommodations constituted disability discrimination. There was no doubt the district had to make accommodations for the student's diabetes; the only question was whether the accommodations the parents requested were reasonable. **The court stated it believed the district would be unlikely to convince a jury that the requested accommodations were unreasonable.** To do so, the district would have to show providing the accommodations would require the daycare to fundamentally alter its program or place an undue burden on it.

As a trial was needed to determine that, the court refused to dismiss the case. *A.P. v. Anoka-Hennepin Independent School Dist. No. 11*, 538 F.Supp.2d 1125 (D. Minn. 2008).

◆   A seven-year-old second-grader with diabetes attended a parochial school. The student had Type I diabetes, which required that her blood sugar level be tested each day before lunch and before she participated in a weekly gym class. The board of education provided a nurse but limited her visits to just two per month. The school's principal asked the board to provide additional nursing services, but the board denied the request. As a result, the student's parents retained private nursing services, at a cost of $400 per week, to perform glucose testing and administer insulin injections to the child at school. The parents then filed a court petition to compel the board to provide additional nursing services. The trial court granted the petition and directed the board to provide the child with additional nursing services at her school. The trial court also ordered the board to reimburse the parents for the costs they incurred in retaining a private nursing service. On review, the court held that a provision of the state's education law required school boards to provide non-public school students within their districts with "all of the health and welfare services" that were provided to public school students. Those services were to be provided in the same manner and to the same extent as they were to public school students. In this case, there was no question that the daily nursing services required by the student were "health and welfare services" under the state law. As a result, the state law required the board to provide the student with the nursing services that would be available if she attended public school in the district. **The board employed a full-time nurse at a public school located within the district just two blocks away from the student's school.** The board conceded that the student's needs would be met if she attended the public school. Therefore, the court affirmed the trial court's decision. However, it modified the judgment to allow the board to determine the precise manner and location where the services would be provided. *Richard K. v. Petrone*, 31 A.D.3d 181 (N.Y. App. Div. 2006).

◆   The mother of a second-grade student became dissatisfied with the way her daughter's school was handling her diabetes. The mother informed the school nurse that she wanted the nurse to give the student insulin shots whenever her blood sugar tested higher than a specified level. The nurse told the mother that written authorization from a physician was required, but the mother never provided the authorization. The nurse later asked the student what she ate at home every day. She also called the student's doctor to ask what she should do if the student's blood sugar level showed a shot was needed and she could not reach the mother. Then, an anonymous caller filed a complaint against the mother with a governmental department of job and family services for medically neglecting the child. The mother later sued the school district and others, alleging that the district violated her right to privacy by asking the student what she ate at home and allegedly filing the anonymous complaint of alleged medical neglect. She also filed a retaliation claim against the school superintendent based on the superintendent's alleged role in filing the neglect complaint against her. The court granted summary judgment against the motion. It rejected her privacy claim because **she did not present authority to support the proposition that she had a fundamental liberty interest in information relating to her management of her child's diabetes**. In addition, the mother failed to produce evidence showing that the district or any of the other defendants had ever revealed the student's medical records to anyone. *Jenkins v. Board of Educ.*, 463 F.Supp.2d 747 (S.D. Ohio 2006). On appeal, the U.S. Court of Appeals for the Sixth Circuit reversed the lower court's ruling with respect to the retaliation claim because factual issues existed as to that claim. Otherwise, it affirmed the lower court's decision. *Jenkins v. Rock Hill Local School Dist.*, 513 F.3d 580 (6th Cir. 2008).

◆   The mother of a nine-year-old student with diabetes met with the student's school nurse at the start of the school year to discuss her daughter's diabetes-related needs. The mother provided the nurse, a teacher and the school principal with written materials describing her daughter's condition and the care she would need. She provided 12 copies of the materials so all of the student's teachers could be provided their own copy. Sometime after these materials were provided, the student asked a teacher for permission to leave a reading class to see the school nurse. The student informed the teacher that the student was having a hypoglycemic reaction. The teacher refused to allow the student to leave the class until 45 minutes later. By the time the student reached the nurse, the student was intermittently losing consciousness and could not inform the nurse that she needed medication. The student received no medical care for two hours and was eventually hospitalized for six days. The mother sued the school district, the nurse, the teacher and the principal under 42 U.S.C. § 1983 for alleged due process and equal protection violations. She also used Section 1983 as the basis for a claim under the Education of the Handicapped Act. **The court held that the mother did not state a Section 1983 claim against the school district because a single isolated incident did not prove the existence of an official policy or custom, as is required to establish a Section 1983 claim.** The equal protection claim against the individual defendants failed because children asserting disability discrimination by a public educator must proceed under the Education for the Handicapped Act and cannot assert a separate equal protection violation. The court dismissed the due process claims against the individual defendants because available common law remedies were available against them. Finally, the court rejected the claim related to the Education for the Handicapped Act because violations of the act cannot be redressed via Section 1983. *DeFalco v. Deer Lake School Dist.*, 663 F.Supp. 1108 (W.D. Pa. 1987).

◆ A child with Type I diabetes was accepted for admission into a preschool program. The child's status as a diabetic was disclosed at the time of the initial interview. A month before the child was to start attending the preschool, his mother informed the preschool's owner that the child had been fitted with an insulin pump. The mother then met with two teachers at the preschool to explain how the pump operated. She claimed that she offered to come to the school to train the teachers how to use the pump. The mother claimed that the owner withdrew the child's acceptance on the day of the meeting. She sued the preschool and the owner under a state law against discrimination. A trial court found that the school was a place of public accommodation under the state law and that the claim was not preempted by the Individuals with Disabilities Education Act. However, it ruled for the school because the law did not obligate the school to provide reasonable accommodations in connection with the child's care. Both sides appealed, and the appeals court affirmed in part and reversed in part. The appeals court affirmed the conclusions that the school was a place of public accommodation under the state law and that the claim was not preempted by the Individuals with Disabilities Education Act. **However, it held that the lower court erred**

when it concluded that the state law against discrimination did not obligate places of public accommodations to provide reasonable accommodations to individuals with disabilities. Regulations implementing the statute indicated that the provision of reasonable accommodations was required, and the law was to be construed broadly. In addition, federal precedent under the Americans with Disabilities Act, which requires places of public accommodation to provide reasonable accommodations, was relevant. The court was unable to determine whether the school had breached its duty to provide a reasonable accommodation. Therefore, it ordered further proceedings. *Ellison v. Creative Learning Center*, 893 A.2d 12 (N.J. Super. Ct. App. Div. 2006).

◆ A board of education posted a job opening for a classroom aide. State law defined the position as an aide who had completed a state-approved training program, held a high school diploma, or received a general educational development certificate. It did not include additional requirements. When the board posted the opening, it added the requirement that the successful candidate must be licensed as a practical nurse. The board added this requirement because the successful applicant would serve the needs of two diabetic students. Both students were considered "brittle" diabetics. One received insulin through an insulin pump, and the other received insulin injections. The board hired an individual who was licensed as a practical nurse. Two unsuccessful applicants, who were not licensed as practical nurses, filed grievances with a state grievance board. **They claimed that the board wrongfully expanded the statutory qualifications of the aide position by requiring the successful candidate to be licensed as a practical nurse.** The grievance board granted the grievances, finding that only a school nurse could administer the required care based on the students' specialized health needs. A lower court affirmed, and the board appealed. The appeals court held that the board of education permissibly added practical nurse licensure as a qualification for the position. It was within the discretion of the school board to hire an applicant who possessed the additional qualification of licensure as a practical nurse. The decision of the lower court was reversed. *Board of Educ. of the County of Randolph v. Scott*, 617 S.E.2d 478 (W. Va. 2005).

◆ The parents of a seventh-grade student with diabetes alleged that a school district and school officials violated the Individuals with Disabilities Education Act (IDEA) and Americans with Disabilities Act by failing to recognize that their daughter was a student with a disability and by failing to accommodate her condition. The parents claimed that the defendants denied the student extra time to complete assignments. They also alleged that they ridiculed her in front of other students based on her disability and displayed animosity toward her. The court ruled against the parents because they failed to exhaust administrative procedures and remedies under the IDEA. Exhaustion of administrative remedies is generally required before a party can proceed to court with an IDEA claim. Exhaustion is excused when it would be futile or fail to provide relief, or when an agency has adopted a policy or pursued a practice that violates the law. The parents argued that exhaustion was not required because the monetary relief they sought could not be granted at the administrative level. However, **a plaintiff seeking monetary damages must exhaust administrative remedies even though money damages may be unavailable under the IDEA or through the administrative process**. In this case, the plaintiffs alleged injuries that could be redressed, at least partially, via the IDEA's administrative procedures. Therefore, they were required to exhaust administrative remedies before filing a court claim. The court granted the defense motion for summary judgment. *Eads v. Unified School Dist. No. 289*, 184 F.Supp.2d 1122 (D. Kan. 2002).

◆   While a high school pep band was returning to school via bus following a basketball game, a student who was a pep band member asked the band instructor if the bus could stop so he could use a restroom. The student claimed the instructor failed to respond to his request. He also claimed that the instructor denied his request when he asked a second time and then ignored a third request. Other students began to tease the student, and the bus driver deliberately pumped the brakes to jar the bus and aid in the teasing of the student and other students who needed to use a restroom. The student then used a profanity while demanding that the instructor let him off the bus. Before he was able to get off, the student wet himself. The next day, the instructor told the student he would not be allowed to participate in the pep band for the next game and that he might be removed from the pep band. The student was given a one-day out-of-school suspension for using profanity on the bus, and the principal later ordered him to serve three days of detention. A short time later, the student was diagnosed as having diabetes and post-traumatic stress disorder (PTSD). His parents sued the instructor, the principal and the school district, claiming that they triggered or accelerated the student's development of diabetes and caused his PTSD. After the student's physician testified that the added stress created by the bus incident "could have" contributed to the student's development of diabetes, a trial court granted summary judgment against the parents on the ground that the harm to the student was not foreseeable. The parents appealed. **The appeals court affirmed the trial court's decision because the parents failed to present enough evidence of a causal connection between the actions of the defendants and the student's injuries.** The physician's testimony was admissible only if it was based on an opinion that it was more likely than not that the defendants' conduct caused the student's injuries. The physician's testimony that the stress of the bus incident could have caused the student's injuries did not meet this standard. Therefore, the parents failed to meet their duty to present expert testimony showing the requisite causal connection between the defendants' actions and the student's injuries. The trial court's decision was affirmed. *Hinkle v. Shepherd School Dist. #37*, 93 P.3d 1239 (Mont. 2004).

◆   While on a school field trip, a fourth-grade student informed her teacher that she felt sick. The school was aware that the child had diabetes, and the teacher instructed the student to eat a piece of fruit. A blood sugar reading showed that the student's blood sugar level rose after she ate the fruit. On the way back from the trip, the student threatened other students on the bus with an instrument that contained a nail file, a bottle opener and a one-half-inch knife. The next day, the principal suspended the student for five days and recommended that she be expelled. A hearing examiner, who was not notified that the student had diabetes, recommended expulsion, and the school superintendent concurred with the recommendation. The student's parents appealed the decision to the board of education, arguing that the student's diabetes caused her actions. They supported the appeal with a letter from the student's endocrinologist, who said the student could engage in belligerent behavior when her blood sugar fell below a certain level. The board of education upheld the expulsion, finding that the student violated the school code of conduct by possessing an object that could be considered a weapon and by using the object to intimidate other students. **The board of education also determined that the parents failed to prove the student's behavior was caused by low blood sugar.** The parents sued the school district, claiming violations of the Individuals with Disabilities Education Act (IDEA), the Rehabilitation Act and state law. They also filed a claim of negligence. The district filed a motion to dismiss or alternatively for summary judgment. The court rejected the IDEA and Rehabilitation Act claims because the parents failed to exhaust administrative remedies with respect to those claims. In addition, the district was not required to consider the effect of the student's diabetes on her actions because she had not been identified as a student with a disability at the time of the bus incident. In addition, the board did not violate state law because its decision to expel the student was not arbitrary and capricious. Finally, the parents' negligence claim failed because they did not allege that an alleged breach of duty by the district caused them harm. The district's motion was granted. *Brown v. Metropolitan School Dist. of Lawrence Township*, 945 F.Supp. 1202 (S.D. Ind. 1996).

IIII. ASTHMA

A. Symptoms and Management

Asthma is a chronic inflammation of the airways. It can leave students or teachers who suffer from it feeling tired, wheezing, suffering a persistent cough or even struggling to breathe.

Without asthma, our bodies do a very good job of filtering out things like smoke, dust and mold. They get stopped before they reach our lungs by getting trapped in phlegm so they can be coughed or sneezed away.

In people with asthma, the bronchial airways become inflamed by an over-reaction to irritants. The airways swell or become blocked, making it difficult for air to reach the lungs. This over-reaction could have several causes, but the overwhelming number of children with asthma – as many as 80% – also suffer from allergies. Other causes of asthma attacks include viruses and airborne irritants.

According to the Asthma and Allergy Foundation of America, 36,000 students miss school because of asthma – that's 36,000 students missing school because of asthma *every day*.

The American Lung Association says asthma comes first on the list of chronic illnesses that keep children out of school.

Asthma is also high on the list of things that send children to the hospital. In 2004, more than 640,000 children under age 15 visited emergency rooms because of their asthma.

Most serious of all, students occasionally die from asthma attacks – and the condition is affecting more students than ever.

The Centers for Disease Control and Prevention (CDC) has estimated 7 million children have asthma.

When it comes to treatment, the news is mixed. We're doing a good job of treating childhood asthma – when there's access to medicine. On the plus side, the CDC report, *The State of Childhood Asthma, United States, 1980 – 2005*, showed a direct correlation between the drop in death rates from juvenile asthma and increased medical treatment. But it also found a disproportionate number of African-American children dying from asthma. Experts say many of these deaths were avoidable. They were apparently caused by under-medication.

Which brings us to the most basic point about your school and asthma: Asthma can't be cured, but it can be controlled. And there are many things schools can do to help.

The American Lung Association defines controlling asthma as taking steps to reduce its frequency and severity in order to lessen its interference with asthmatics' everyday life. From your perspective, you not only want to keep all your students physically safe, you also want to do everything you can to make sure they're learning. A student who is worrying if the chest-tightness she's feeling is the first sign of an attack, or a student who is finding it hard to breathe, is too distracted to pay attention in class or concentrate on homework.

One crucial step in controlling asthma is to eliminate the common triggers for asthma attacks. In its publication *Asthma & Physical Activity in the School*, the National Heart, Lung and Blood Institute has identified the following as common triggers:
- exercise, especially in cold weather
- upper respiratory infections, such as head colds or the flu
- laughing or crying hard
- allergens, such as mold, dust and animal dander, and
- irritants, such as tobacco smoke, chemical fumes and chalk dust.

B. Controlling Asthma's Impact at School

There are many ways to make your school environment a place where asthmatics can breathe freely. These include:

- eliminating dust, dust mites and other allergens by keeping rugs, padded furniture, stuffed animals and cushions out of classrooms
- making sure classroom surfaces are kept clear so that janitors can wipe and mop them
- impressing on staff that using highly scented personal products – including laundry detergents and fabric softeners – could make it harder for some students to breathe
- keeping animals out of school
- maintaining a smoke-free environment, and
- having the right air filters – and keeping them clean.

There also are several things that staff should be on the alert for when it comes to students and asthma. For example:

- Persistent coughing. The American Lung Association has stated that coughing is the most common symptom of asthma. Coughing can be a sign that an asthmatic child may be in distress. In children not diagnosed with asthma, it could be a sign that they should be evaluated for it.
- Children who experience lots of respiratory infections also should be evaluated.
- Since exercise can be a trigger, gym teachers and playground monitors need to be especially vigilant – particularly when the air is cold.
- Emotion also can play a role in the onset and severity of asthma attacks. Adults can help by staying calm, themselves.

In the CDC's *Strategies for Addressing Asthma Within a Coordinated School Health Program*, a six-part plan of attack is suggested:

1. **Establish management and support systems for asthma-friendly schools.** These include identifying asthmatic students, setting up effective home-school-health provider communication, and assigning a person to coordinate asthma-control efforts.
2. **Provide appropriate school health and mental health services for students with asthma.** For example: following students' own asthma action plans or else a standard emergency protocol for students without individualized plans.
3. **Provide asthma education and awareness programs for students and school staff.** This could include teaching everyone asthma-control basics as well as providing quit-smoking support programs for staff.
4. **Provide a safe and healthy school environment to reduce asthma triggers.** In addition to strategies similar to those discussed above, the CDC encourages schools to use integrated pest management techniques.

5. **Provide safe, enjoyable physical education and activity opportunities for students with asthma.** Students should be encouraged to participate fully when well, but some asthmatics need preventative medication before participation. Immediate emergency access to medication also should be available.

6. **Coordinate school, family, and community efforts to better manage asthma symptoms and reduce school absences among students with asthma.** One thing schools can do is ask for parents' permission for the school health staff and the student's doctor to share health information. They also can get involved with asthma-control initiatives in the wider community.

Schools have been rising to the challenge to help control the impact of asthma on their students in other ways.

Some schools have obtained special equipment to make sure children can get necessary treatment at school.

One piece of equipment some schools consider vital is a peak-flow meter. This is a handheld device that measures how well people can move air out of their lungs.

Another piece of equipment is a nebulizer, a device that turns asthma medication into a fine mist that can be breathed in to penetrate deeply into the lungs. Some states have laws requiring nebulizers in schools.

Schools have also been educating themselves on the subject to better help their students. One excellent free resource you might want to check out is the American Lung Association's *Back to School with Asthma Toolkit*, available at *lung.org*.

In addition to learning about asthma, reducing triggers, training staff and having the right equipment, the following cases illustrate that a quick and appropriate response to a student asthma attack is absolutely necessary. See Forms VII-12 and VII-13 in Chapter Nine for parent and physician letters regarding asthma.

C. Legal Decisions

1. Asthma-Related Deaths

◆ Because the evidence supported the jury's verdict that a school district's negligence did not cause an asthmatic student's death, a Washington Appeals court affirmed the verdict for the school.

Elementary school student Mercedes Mears had both asthma and life-threatening allergies. The school had a doctor-prescribed inhaler on the premises for Mercedes in case of an asthma attack. It also had Mercedes' doctor-prescribed EpiPen for an allergic emergency.

One morning at school, Mercedes had trouble breathing and said she felt sick. The staff at the school's health room were familiar with her medical conditions. They decided she was having an asthma attack, so treated her with the inhaler. They tried it again when she didn't get better and then called 911.

Washington state law required an emergency health care plan for students like this so staff without medical training could respond if the child had a health emergency. The school nurse had prepared an emergency health care plan for Mercedes, but staff didn't look at it that morning. They also didn't call the school nurse. Mercedes lost consciousness before the ambulance arrived. Staff didn't perform CPR.

Mercedes died. The medical examiner who performed her autopsy attributed her death to asthma, but Mercedes' family sued the school district, its school health clerk, and the school nurse for wrongful death. The family argued at trial that Mercedes died of a severe allergic reaction. They claimed the district defendants were responsible for her death because they didn't administer the EpiPen or give her CPR.

At trial, expert testimony established Mercedes probably would have survived if staff had administered the EpiPen before she lost consciousness or administered CPR after she did. The epinephrine posed no real threat of side effects and an asthma attack could qualify as a medical emergency

The jury decided the school defendants were negligent but their negligence didn't cause Mercedes' death. The family appealed, but the appeals court affirmed.

To find against the school defendants, the jury had to decide their negligence proximately caused Mercedes' death. It didn't. And because the jury could have found staff might not have administered the EpiPen or performed CPR even if they consulted Mercedes' emergency plan or contacted a school nurse, the verdict didn't go against the evidence – so the appeals court affirmed it. *Mears v. Bethel School Dist.*, No. 403, No. 43121-1-II, 2014 WL 3933555 (Wash. Ct. App. 8/12/14).

◆   Based on finding a school nurse didn't negligently release an asthmatic student to his mother, a New York appeals court dismissed the parents' wrongful death suit against school defendant after he died later that day.

Eleven-year-old Shawn Martinez, **a lifelong asthmatic, arrived at the nurse's office coughing and wheezing**. He told the nurse his inhaler was out of medication, and his mother knew it was.

Shawn's mother picked him up. Neither she nor the nurse considered his condition an emergency, but the nurse said the mother should take him to the emergency room if she didn't have medication to treat him. The mother said she did and planned to treat him with a nebulizer at home.

But by the time Shawn walked up four flights of stairs to their apartment, he was in more distress. The nebulizer didn't relieve it. The mother called for emergency help, but Shawn was in cardiac arrest when it arrived. He was taken to the hospital, where he died.

Shawn's parents sued the city, the board of education and the school nurse for wrongful death. The school defendants asked for judgment without a trial. The judge denied the request. They appealed, and the appellate court reversed the judge as a matter of law.

A New York school **owes a student a duty of care until it relinquishes**

control of the student to a parent – unless it releases a child "without further supervision into a foreseeably hazardous setting it had a hand in creating."

That wasn't the case here. The student wasn't having an acute attack when the nurse released him, and she knew his mother had treated his asthma for 10 years, understood his condition, and planned to treat him with medication.

With no duty, there's no negligence. As the nurse wasn't negligent in releasing the student, the school defendants had no duty toward him once his mother resumed responsibility for him – so the appeals court dismissed the wrongful death claim against them. *Martinez v. City of New York*, 90 A.D.3d 718 (N.Y. App. Div. 2011).

◆ A California appeals court found the state's field-trip immunity law meant neither district could be sued over the death of one district's asthmatic student at another district's outdoor "camp."

The school district San Diego County Office of Education (SDCOE) owned and operated "Camp Fox" at the base of Palomar Mountain. The camp provided science-related programs to students. Its staff were all SDCOE employees.

Sixth-grader Virginia Sanchez from the McCabe Union School District went to Camp Fox for a voluntary five-day field trip with her class. While there, she had an asthma attack. Staff gave Virginia her inhaler and performed CPR until paramedics arrived, but she died.

Virginia's parents sued SDCOE for negligence. The trial court awarded SDCOE summary judgment, finding it immune under state law. The parents appealed, but the appellate court affirmed.

State law provided immunity to "the district, a charter school, or the State of California" for a student's "injury, accident, illness or death" while on a field trip. The parents claimed this immunity was only for the school district the student attended, so it could sue SDCOE. The court disagreed, finding the statute covered both districts – so blocked the parents' lawsuit entirely. *Sanchez v. San Diego County Office of Educ.*, 182 Cal.App.4th 1580 (Cal. Ct. App. 2010).

◆ At the start of an academic year, the mother of a five-year-old kindergarten student with asthma gave the school nurse asthma medication and an inhaler. She also provided an authorization and a pediatrician's directive regarding use of the inhaler, and she gave the nurse a separate authorization for an allergy medication.

The child began coughing in class, and the nurse gave him inhaler medication and determined he was breathing, alert and not in distress. The child's mother was notified, and she picked him up from the school. The nurse suggested the mother take the child to his pediatrician. But when the child became ill during the ride, she drove home and went inside to dial 911. The child died shortly after emergency personnel took him to the hospital.

The mother sued the school district and others, claiming the nurse was negligently hired and committed malpractice. The trial court denied a summary judgment motion filed by the district and nurse. They appealed. The appeals court reversed. **The child's mother did not show the defendants breached a legal duty owed to her or the child.** The mother removed the control of district employees. Also, she decided to take him home rather than to the doctor, as the nurse had suggested. *Williams v. Hempstead School Dist.*, 850 N.Y.S.2d 459 (N.Y. App. Div. 2007).

◆   The mother of a third-grader who died from an asthma attack at school could sue a teacher for violating his right not to be deprived of life without due process of law. There was evidence her actions led to his death.

When an asthmatic student started the third grade, his mother told the school he'd been treated in an emergency room at least 10 times and that not treating his symptoms immediately could put his life at risk.

The school developed an individualized education program that called for him to use his inhaler before exercise and when suffering symptoms; for his mother to be called promptly about any asthma-related incident; and for the school to perform CPR and call emergency services if he stopped breathing.

In late September, the student told his teacher he felt tired and was having trouble breathing. Instead of administering his inhaler, she told him to rest with his head on the desk. There was a phone in the room, but she didn't call for medical help or let him call his mother. About 15 minutes later, a classmate saw he wasn't breathing and had turned purple. His teacher sent a student to tell the office this. No school official tried to administer his inhaler or perform CPR, but someone did eventually call for emergency help. Medics weren't able to revive him, and he died in the hospital.

The mother sued the teacher, alleging she had violated the student's Fourteenth Amendment rights, and the court allowed the suit to go forward.

Under the state-created danger doctrine, a public school teacher can have a constitutional duty to protect a student if the court finds that:
- the harm was foreseeable
- the student was a foreseeable victim of it
- the teacher's actions were bad enough to "shock the conscience," and
- the teacher used classroom authority in a way that created the danger or made it worse.

Here, **the mother demonstrated that the school understood her son could die if his symptoms weren't promptly and properly treated** – so the harm and victim were both foreseeable. Also, the court said refusing to let an asthmatic child seek medical help was conscience-shocking. Finally, if the mother could show that the teacher refused to let her son call her for help, a Fourteenth Amendment violation could be shown. *Taylor v. Altoona Area School Dist.*, 513 F.Supp.2d 540 (W.D. Pa. 2007).

◆   An appeals court affirmed a verdict for a school district in a wrongful death suit brought by parents of a student found dead in a locker room shortly after his teacher gave him permission to go there to use his inhaler.

During gym class, a 14-year-old with a history of mild asthma asked his gym teacher for permission to go get his prescription inhaler from the locker room. The teacher said he could. Between five and 15 minutes later, the teacher found the student lying on the locker room floor with the inhaler in hand. The boy wasn't breathing and was later pronounced dead.

The boy's parents sued the school district for wrongful death. **The main issue at trial was if the school was negligent not to supervise the boy when he went to the locker room to get his inhaler.** If the court found it foreseeable the student was likely to die without supervision while he retrieved and used his inhaler, it would have found the school negligent.

But the Ohio trial court did not find the lack of supervision likely to lead to the student's death. First, the father testified it was normal for the boy to get and use his inhaler without adult supervision. Second, there was expert testimony the likelihood of this kind of death from only mild asthma was "one in a million." The parents appealed, but the appellate court affirmed the verdict for the school. *Spencer v. Lakeview School Dist.*, No. 2005-T-0083, 2006 WL 1816452 (Ohio App. Ct. 6/3006).

◆   The New Mexico Supreme Court decided parents could sue a school district for wrongful death after a substitute gym teacher ignored an asthmatic student's request to stop exercising and then administrators responded inadequately to her ensuing asthma attack.

A 14-year-old special ed student's individualized education program (IEP) said she was asthmatic. Her parents gave the school permission to get her emergency medical help without contacting them first. They also told her gym teacher exercise could trigger an attack. The gym teacher agreed to let her rest instead of participate if she felt an attack coming on.

The day the gym class had a substitute teacher, the student asked for permission to rest, but the sub said no. The student began to have trouble breathing. Others saw her face was red and she was crying as she struggled to keep up with the class.

The student used her inhaler after gym, but collapsed at her desk as her next class began. The teacher called the front office and then tried to administer the student's inhaler. A school secretary with some nursing training arrived, checked the student's vital signs and asked the office to call 911 – but the call wasn't made. Instead, staff put the student in a wheelchair and wheeled her into the hall. Seeing her there, a school police officer called 911. By that time, it was 15 minutes after the start of her asthma attack. When medical personnel arrived, the student had stopped breathing and couldn't be revived.

Her parents sued the school district for wrongful death, but a trial court and then an appeals court found the district was immune to the suit. The parents appealed to the New Mexico Supreme Court. It reversed, allowing the parents' wrongful death suit to go forward.

An exception to the state's immunity law OK'd school districts to be sued for negligence in operating or maintaining a building. The supreme court found **the school's failure to follow its safety procedures for a special needs student was similar to failing to follow procedures for a fire drill**. It failed to follow its procedures by ignoring the student's IEP, not administering CPR and not calling 911 immediately.

Immunity also wasn't proper here because the school knew the student was asthmatic, but an employee forced her to keep exercising in spite of her visible distress – so the school actively participated in causing the asthma attack. *Upton v. Clovis Municipal School Dist.*, 141 P.3d 1259 (N.M. 2006).

◆   An appeals court reapportioned the blame for a student's asthma-related death – finding a school counselor, not the principal, mainly responsible.

At a school event, a high school senior began to have an asthma attack. Her eighth-grade sister asked a security guard to call 911. Instead, he used a walkie-talkie to call the principal, who said to call the student's parents.

The walk to the office to use the phone aggravated the student's condition. When they got there, the guard and the sister were holding her up. The sister told a counselor to call 911 because the student was having an asthma attack. He told the sister to call her mother to ask if she would pay for the ambulance.

The sister had to wait for a phone and then couldn't reach her mother.

The student's condition deteriorated. The counselor fanned her and tried to help her use her medication and then tried taking her outside for fresh air. When the sister got back, the student told her, "I'm not going to make it." The sister called 911. About 10 minutes later, the counselor called 911, too. The student lost consciousness, and the school called 911 again.

The ambulance arrived around 50 minutes after the onset of the asthma attack. The student was pronounced dead at the hospital.

The student's sister and mother sued the school board, principal and counselor for negligence. The case was tried before a jury. **The court determined the failure to immediately call for emergency medical help was a cause-in-fact of the student's death.** It apportioned the blame for this as: 50% to the principal, 30% to the counselor and 20% to the school board. It awarded the family well over $1 million in damages. The school defendants appealed.

The appellate court affirmed the school's responsibility for the student's death, but reduced the damages by about $170,000 – leaving the award at just about $1 million.

The appellate court also determined the counselor bore the largest portion of the blame. Unlike the principal, he saw the seriousness of the student's condition. The court decided the principal was 30% to blame because he should have followed up on the report from the security guard and made sure someone called 911. The court found the counselor was 50% responsible. His failure to respond reasonably to a student in obvious distress created an immediate and fatal risk to her. *Declouet v. Orleans Parish School Board*, 715 So.2d 69 (La. Ct. App. 1998).

2. Other Asthma Cases

◆   A teacher who alleged school construction caused her asthma could bring disability bias claims against the school board, but not a claim of negligent failure to provide her a safe working environment.

A school board divided an elementary school art classroom in half by putting in a new wall. This left the room with poor ventilation, as there were no operable windows, exterior doors or air conditioning.

The art teacher complained about water damage to the ceiling tiles as well as strong construction odors from paints, sealants and adhesives. Ultimately, the students' art classes were moved elsewhere, but the teacher had to be in the room twice a day to load and unload art supplies. **She said the exposure to construction odors, dust and mold left her with asthma.**

The teacher went on medical leave in October. She filed a workers' comp claim in December – and says a school-board-requested medical exam confirmed conditions in the classroom caused her asthma.

The board installed an air filter, and she returned to work in January – but had a severe asthma attack after workers removed the skylight in the room while she was teaching, releasing dust and particles.

The teacher's doctor removed her from work for the rest of the year. She returned for the following school year, but discovered the air filter in her classroom had been recycled from a school since demolished due to mold problems. She says it was replaced by a poor-quality filter.

Her doctor removed her from work for the next school year, and she was diagnosed with multiple myeloma, an environmentally induced disease.

The teacher sued the board of education and others, alleging multiple claims. The school defendants asked the judge to dismiss her suit.

The judge found the defendants had state-law immunity with respect to the teacher's claim that the town and board negligently failed to provide her a safe working environment – so dismissed it.

But the judge found her claims under the Rehabilitation Act could go forward. They alleged the school board discriminated against her and retaliated against her by failing to accommodate her disability. *Gallagher v. Town of Fairfield*, No. 3:10-cv-1270 (CFD), 2011 WL 3563160 (D. Conn. 8/15/11).

◆   A school board was ordered to pay $130,000 to a disabled student who was hospitalized for six months after an asthma attack that could have been prevented if the school had followed policies it already had in place.

Under a middle school's policy, critical student health information was supposed to be collected from enrollment forms, entered into computer records, red-flagged and copied to the student's teachers.

School policy also required setting up individualized education program (IEP) meetings for transferring special ed students as soon as possible – preferably within two weeks. The student had mental retardation and qualified for special education, but a school social worker didn't come to his home to get his IEP information until mid-October.

The mother told the social worker the student had severe breathing problems and said the school should call 911 if he had trouble breathing at school. The student's enrollment forms clearly stated he had asthma, and his mother gave the school a doctor's note to allow him to use his inhaler at school. But the mother didn't include this information on the student's physical education (PE) health form or write any response to the form's request to list any reason the student should sit out PE or have a modified gym program.

In late October, a classmate who was also the student's next-door neighbor saw the student stop while doing laps in PE class. When he clutched his chest, she asked if he needed his inhaler. He nodded. She ran to tell the PE teacher, but the teacher dismissed her concern and told both children to keep running. The teacher later said he hadn't been told the student had asthma and mental retardation.

Later that day, the school called the student's mother to come pick him up because he was ill. When the breathing treatments his mother tried at home didn't work, she called an ambulance. The student spent the next six months in the hospital. At least one doctor stated his health crisis was caused by overexertion in PE class and failure to use his inhaler.

The student's mother sued the school board under the Tennessee Governmental Tort Liability Act. The court held for the student. The school board appealed, but the appellate court affirmed.

Under the act, governmental entities could be held liable for student injuries caused by staff members' "operational" acts – but not by their "discretionary" acts. Generally, "operational acts" are actions taken pursuant to an established order or policy, while "discretionary acts" are acts involving planning or policy-making.

On appeal, the school board argued that deciding how to gather student health information and distribute the information to staff fell into the "discretionary" category. The court disagreed. The board already had policies in place to notify teachers about a student's special ed status and health problems. **The judge found the board negligent for not following its own policies.**

The appellate court also upheld the lower court's apportionment of the blame and its damages award. The lower court judge decided the mother was 20% at fault – apparently because she didn't provide information on the PE health form that could have prevented the incident. The rest of the fault was apportioned to the school board. It was ordered to pay the student $130,000, the highest amount allowed under the act. *Small v. Shelby County Schools*, No. W2007-00045-COA-R3-CV, 2008 WL 360925 (Tenn. Ct. App. 2/12/08).

IV. MRSA INFECTION

A. Background

Methicillin-resistant staphylococcus aureus, more commonly referred to as MRSA, is a type of staph bacteria that is resistant to certain antibiotics. MRSA infection has been identified in hospital patients since the 1960s, and the overwhelming majority of cases continue to be associated with health care. However, MRSA infection has made its way into other community-based settings, including schools. Within the school setting, members of athletic teams are at a higher risk of contracting MRSA infection, especially if they participate in a contact sport such as wrestling or football. Despite the rise in incidence rates, MRSA infection is both preventable and treatable.

An October 2007 study released by the Centers for Disease Control and Prevention (CDC) reported the results of the agency's population-based surveillance for MRSA infection in nine geographic areas between July 2004 and December 2005. The study, which tracked nearly 9,000 cases, showed that MRSA infection affects particular populations disproportionately. Specifically, the study reported a significantly higher incidence rate among people age 65 or older. In addition, the incidence rate among African-Americans was about double the rate among others, and it was slightly higher among males.

The study also identified risk factors for MRSA infection. Among the most common were a history of hospitalization, a history of surgery, and long-term-care residence.

The CDC has identified the following five factors, which it refers to as the "5 C's," that increase the risk of the spread of MRSA infection:
- **Crowding**
- frequent skin-to-skin **Contact**
- **Compromised** skin (i.e., cuts or abrasions)
- **Contaminated** items and surfaces, and
- lack of **Cleanliness**.

B. Diagnosis and Treatment

MRSA infection occurs when staph bacteria, which sometimes are carried on the skin or in the nose of healthy people as well as in people who already are infected, enter a break in the skin of another person via skin-to-skin contact or a shared item such as a towel or piece of athletic equipment. The entry of the bacteria causes a skin infection that is characterized by symptoms such as pimples, rashes, boils, and impetigo. MRSA also can cause more serious infection, such as pneumonia and bloodstream infection. Symptoms of more serious infection include fever, swelling, headache and fatigue.

MRSA is definitively diagnosed via laboratory testing that specifically identifies the bacteria at the root of the infection. Laboratory testing helps healthcare professionals decide whether treatment with antibiotics will be required and, if so, which antibiotics to administer.

The specific course of treatment for MRSA infection varies depending on a number of factors, including the severity of the illness and the site of the infection. Treatment of MRSA infections typically includes keeping the infected area clean and dry. Infected individuals must also wash their hands after caring for the infected area and properly dispose of bandages. Treatment also may involve drainage of pus and the administration of antibiotics. If more severe infections occur, such as pneumonia or bloodstream infections, additional measures must be taken. However, such complications are rare in healthy people who contract MRSA infections.

MRSA can be difficult to treat, according to the CDC. Usually, it is resistant only to penicillin and other similar drugs. However, the CDC reported that of 824 samples, an alarming 10% were resistant to several stronger antibiotics.

C. Prevention

1. Generally

There are many steps schools should take to prevent the occurrence of MRSA infection among students. Perhaps the best way for schools to prevent MRSA infection is to encourage the practice of good hygiene. This involves frequent hand-washing with soap and water or use of an alcohol-based hand sanitizer. Encouraging good skin care is another way to prevent the spread of MRSA infection. Cuts, scrapes and other breaks in the skin must be kept clean and covered with a bandage, and contact with other people's bandages and wounds must be avoided. Students also should be instructed not to share personal items, such as towels, toothbrushes, razors or water bottles. Schools also should establish cleaning procedures for surfaces that regularly come into contact with people's skin, such as sinks, showers and toilets. These surfaces, which also include light switches, door handles, handrails, tables and desks, should be cleaned with a disinfectant on a routine basis. Access to sinks, soaps and clean towels should be ensured, and bar soaps should not be used. Gloves should be worn when handling dirty laundry or caring for wounds.

Schools now have the option of installing antimicrobial lockers, which are designed to minimize the spread of disease-causing microbes. These lockers feature a powder-coated finish that protects against bacteria, mold, yeast and mildew for up to 20 years. To see an example, visit *www.aPlusWhs.com*.

2. Athletic Programs

Because MRSA infection occurs more frequently in student-athletes than it does in other members of the student population, special additional steps should be taken with respect to school athletic programs. These include the following:

☑ CHECKLIST – *Avoiding MRSA Infection*

☐ Athletic equipment is disinfected between uses.

☐ Uniforms, towels and other items are laundered using hot water and detergent for washing and the hottest available setting for drying.

☐ Athletes shower with a non-hand soap and water immediately after participating in contact sports and use a dry clean towel.

☐ Athletic equipment and towels are not shared.

☐ Students avoid contact with other students' wounds or any items that have been in contact with the wounds.

☐ Antibiotics and ointments are not to be shared.

☐ Students avoid common hot tubs or whirlpools, especially if they have a break in the skin.

☐ Students do not share water bottles.

☐ Cuts and scrapes are kept clean and covered.

Sports equipment and athletic areas should be disinfected at least weekly. High-use equipment, such as wrestling mats, should be disinfected prior to each practice and several times a day during tournaments.

D. Response

1. Generally

In most cases, MRSA infection does not necessitate school closure. There are situations, such as the occurrence of an outbreak, where consultation with public health officials with respect to this issue would be appropriate. When a MRSA infection occurs, the school should disinfect surfaces that are likely to come into contact with infected areas of the skin that are not properly covered. MRSA can be removed from the school environment by cleaning facilities with disinfectants. The Environmental Protection Agency has compiled a 25-page list of cleaning products that are effective against MRSA. To view the list, go to *http://epa.gov/oppad001/chemregindex.htm.*

When a case of infection occurs, the school nurse and physician should decide whether students, parents and staff should be notified. The CDC advises that it usually is not necessary to inform the entire school community in the case of a single MRSA infection. A MRSA-infected student should not be barred from attending school unless exclusion is directed by a treating physician. Infected students should be instructed to cover the wound and clean their hands frequently. For a sample notice to parents regarding MRSA in general, see Form VII-4 in Chapter Nine.

2. Athletic Programs

Some additional specific measures can be taken when a student-athlete contracts a MRSA infection. It is not necessary to test all team members for

MRSA infection whenever a single student-athlete contracts a MRSA infection. However, it is helpful to take these steps:
- Prohibit student-athletes with MRSA infections from using whirlpools or hot tubs.
- Regularly clean all sports equipment and athletic areas that might come in contact with the wound.
- Place coverings over tables used to provide treatment.
- If disposable items come in contact with the infected site, dispose of them separately.
- Stress the importance of washing hands frequently.
- Make sure the student-athlete keeps the infected area covered at all times.
- Instruct the student-athlete to shower and wash clothes regularly.
- Use gloves to treat broken skin and discard them before treating another student-athlete.

E. Legal Decisions

◆ A 13-year-old student was admitted to a hospital for treatment of a MRSA infection. Over a period of 47 days, the student received treatment that included nine surgeries. The student's mother spoke to the principal of the school and other school officials about the possibility of home-schooling for the student. The mother was told that no teacher would go to the student's home for homeschooling because the student had MRSA. School officials also told the mother that the student's sister and two cousins, who attended a different school, needed to be picked up from school at once because they had been in close contact with the infected student. The school officials further informed the mother that none of the children would be permitted to return to school until they had received a "clean bill of health from a physician." The sister and cousins did not have any symptoms of MRSA, and they did not have a doctor. The student's doctor provided his school with informational literature about MRSA, including information indicating that children should not be excluded from school due to MRSA infection. School officials continued to ban the student, his sister and his cousins from school, and they were not provided any homeschooling services. The children's mothers sued the schools' principals and the district superintendent, claiming they violated the students' constitutional rights to due process and equal protection. The court denied a defense motion to dismiss the case. **Some process is required before a child is excluded from school, and the parents alleged that school officials banned their children from school without properly investigating whether allowing them to attend would pose an unreasonable risk of harm.** As to the substantive due process claims, which were based on the allegation that the school officials abused their power by arbitrarily banning the students from school, the court said the allegations supported an inference that the officials acted arbitrarily and irrationally. The equal protection claims, which were based on the charge that other students with contagious diseases were not banned from school, were not dismissed. It was too soon in the case to conclude that the parents would be unable to show that other students with contagious diseases were allowed to stay in school and that school officials lacked a good reason to make the distinction. *King-Cowser v. School Dist. 149*, No. 07 C 6551, 2008 WL 4104354 (N.D. Ill. 8/25/08).

V. MENTAL HEALTH

A. Emotional Problems vs. Mental Illness

The World Health Organization's definition of mental health is: "a state of well-being in which every individual realizes his or her own potential, can cope with the normal stresses of life, can work productively and fruitfully, and is able to make a contribution to her or his community."

At your school, students in this state of well-being are able to concentrate in class and while doing their homework. They get along well with others and are active members of your school community – whether that's singing in the choir, playing on the basketball team, painting scenery for the school play or attending Chess Club meetings.

The opposite is likely to be true for students with mental health issues. They might be having trouble keeping up scholastically. They also might be talking back to teachers or getting into fights with other students. Or – if they're depressed – it may be hard to get any response from them at all. Students with mental health issues also are more likely to hurt themselves with a weapon or by self-medicating with drugs, cigarettes, alcohol and other substances.

While there is a big difference between transitory emotional problems and serious mental illness, students need help with both.

You might find it easier to relate to the problems caused by transitory emotional problems because you've experienced them yourself. The capacity to cope with the big ups and downs of life increases with life experience – which is why young students need adults' help. This help could be anything from referring the matter to the school's counseling office to deciding a formal evaluation or an outside referral is required.

Alternatively, the best help available for a student struggling with a life issue might be an informal heart-to-heart with someone trusted – maybe the student's coach or music teacher.

The Centers for Disease Control and Prevention (CDC) has posted two online brochures that provide this kind of basic emotional guidance for students at *www.bt.cdc.gov/preparedness/mind*. One brochure is aimed at middle school students, and the other is intended for high school students. Titled, *Maintain a Healthy State of Mind*, the advice was compiled with the intention of helping children cope with disaster. But it's also useful for dealing with other emotional challenges – such as losing a pet or a loved one, or coping with serious illness.

This guidance doesn't wave any magic wands – there are some things only time can heal. But in the meantime, it can help students to know they are normal if they are reacting to a serious emotional blow by:

- feeling shock, numbness and disbelief
- having a hard time thinking clearly
- having trouble focusing on school, friends and family
- eating too much or too little
- having trouble sleeping
- experiencing bad dreams and nightmares
- crying more
- acting moodier, and
- wanting to either be alone or be surrounded by people more than usual.

If the problems connected to helping students with difficult (but transitory) emotional problems can seem daunting, the problems posed by students with mental illness might feel paralyzing.

One thing that helps is that there are mechanisms in place to deal with these serious conditions in the procedures related to the Individuals with Disabilities Education Act, Section 504 of the Rehabilitation Act, the Americans with Disabilities Act and state laws that address the rights of students with disabilities. For an emergency information form for students with autism, see Form VII-20 in Chapter Nine.

Because the Sandy Hook Elementary School intruder suffered from Asperger's syndrome, the tragedy opened up national conversations on the importance of students and mental health issues.

Due to the newfound interest in the topic, the CDC released the most comprehensive mental health study ever compiled. (The report is at *www.cdc.gov/mmwr/preview/mmwrhtml/su6202a1.htm?s_cid=su6202a1_w.*)

It outlines the number of U.S. children between the ages of three and 17 who have specific mental health disorders. To compile this comprehensive report, the CDC teamed up with three key federal partners:

- Substance Abuse and Mental Health Services Administration
- National Institute of Mental Health, and
- Health Resources and Services Administration.

In "Mental Health Surveillance Among Children – United States, 2005-2011," the data provides information on mental disorders, including:

- ADHD
- disruptive behavioral disorders (such as oppositional defiant disorder and conduct disorder)
- autism spectrum disorders, and
- mood and anxiety disorders (including depression, substance abuse disorders and Tourette syndrome).

The study found children between the ages of three and 17 had:

- ADHD (6.8%)

- Behavioral or conduct problems (3.5%)
- Anxiety (3%)
- Depression (2.1%)
- Autism spectrum disorders (1.1%), and
- Tourette syndrome (.02%).

The study also found:

- ADHD was the most prevalent current diagnosis among children between the ages of three and 17.
- Boys were more likely than girls to have ADHD, behavioral or conduct problems, autism spectrum disorders, Tourette syndrome and cigarette dependence.
- Adolescent boys between the ages of 12 and 17 are more likely than girls in the same age bracket to die from suicide.
- Adolescent girls between the ages of 12 and 17 are more likely than boys in the same age bracket to suffer from depression and/or abuse alcohol.

Since 2009, the United States Preventative Task Force has recommended a routine medical screening for depression for all teenagers. They said depression was too common – and too frequently undetected and untreated – to justify screening only kids in high-risk groups.

We know from the research that some groups of students are more at risk than others. Boys are more likely to have significant emotional or behavioral problems than girls, and students between the ages 15 and 17 represent the age group that is most at risk.

Not surprisingly, a 2009 survey of 5,000-plus children found a strong link between experiencing racism and having mental health problems. Compared to children who didn't report racism, Hispanic children who did were more than three times as likely to suffer depression. African-American children were twice as likely. There was also a heightened incidence of ADHD, oppositional disorder and conduct disorder among the children who'd experienced this discrimination.

Another common stressor is test anxiety – which some think has been kicked into overdrive by the No Child Left Behind Act requirements. The increase in standardized testing has caused stress and anxiety for many students – but there are some indications it's especially bad for first generation Asian-American students with parents who stress high academic achievement.

We also know poverty has a markedly negative impact on students' mental and emotional well-being. Only 4% of children from well-off households were found to have serious mental health issues, but this percentage rose to 5% in homes where money was tight, and then up to 7% for children from families that were living below the poverty line. These numbers have especially serious implications now, given the impact of the economic downturn on so many families.

Although most people associate student mental illness with school violence, this connection is not always present. As pointed out in the June 2007 Report to the President on Issues Raised by the Virginia Tech Tragedy, most people who are violent do not have a mental illness, and most people with a mental illness are not violent.

And as the CDC's Choose Respect initiative makes clear, violence is less likely to be a symptom of mental illness than it is to be rooted in denigrating attitudes caused by ignorance or a lack of empathy. Choose Respect is aimed at 11- to 14-year-olds. Its mission is to challenge harmful beliefs that lead to dating violence and thus eliminate the health problems that go with it, such as:

- injuries that send 8% of boys and 9% of girls to the emergency room after dates
- binge drinking
- suicide attempts
- unwanted pregnancies
- STDs and HIV infections, and
- poor self-esteem.

More information about this initiative is available at *cdc.gov/ chooserespect*.

Apart from the fact that the stereotypical connection between violence and mental illness is often absent, mental illness should be de-linked from school violence also because mental illness already bears enough of a social stigma – and too many students don't seek help for that reason.

B. Violent Students and Privacy Laws

While most people with mental illness aren't violent, the university student who committed the deadliest school shooting in U.S. history was. The young man who killed 32 people at Virginia Tech in April 2006 suffered from depression and an anxiety disorder called selective mutism.

In middle and high school, he received help under a special education plan. When his middle school teachers noticed he was writing about killing himself and other people in 1999 after the Columbine shootings, he was treated by a psychiatrist.

The fact that the student's university wasn't alerted to these red flags by his records led the governor-appointed Virginia Tech Review Panel to conclude that the state's mental health laws were flawed. Complicating the issue, the panel also found there was widespread confusion about sharing records among schools. Even when it came to students likely to harm themselves or others, schools weren't sure what information they could release to other schools without violating state and federal privacy laws.

Similarly, the Report to the President on Issues Raised by the Virginia Tech Tragedy found that schools were so worried about violating student privacy – or being sued for doing so – that they were likely to share less information about serious potential problems than the law actually allowed.

It is important to be aware of the fact that some state laws and regulations have stricter privacy requirements for student records than the federal Family Educational Rights and Privacy Act (FERPA) and the privacy rule of the Health Insurance Portability and Accountability Act. That said, one result of the Report to the President was the creation of new guides to help schools and parents better understand FERPA's requirements. They are available at *ed.gov/policy/gen/guid/fpco/ferpa/safeschools*.

This FERPA guidance for elementary and secondary schools specifies that:

- Schools don't need permission in an emergency to release "education records" to parties like law enforcement, public health officials or medical personnel if the release will protect anyone's health or safety.

- Guidance posted at *rems.ed.gov* in 2010 also reminds administrators who release info under this FERPA exception to make a note of the disclosure in the student's education records. The note should include: the info that was disclosed, the parties who received it and the threat that prompted the disclosure. The note should be made as soon as reasonably possible.

- The *ed.gov* guidance also spells it out that school officials don't need permission to pass along their personal observations about a student to the proper authorities. For example, if a teacher overhears a student making a threat, she can report it to the police.

- The school employees who serve as the school's "law enforcement unit" – responsible for calling the police when the school suspects a crime – might keep its own records, such as investigation logs. These are not "education records" subject to FERPA, so no permission is needed to disclose them. But the Department of Education suggests avoiding any confusion by keeping these documents separate from "education records."

- Tapes of students recorded by security cameras maintained by the "law enforcement unit" are also not "education records" subject to FERPA. Because of this, the Department of Education suggests schools that haven't designated a "law enforcement unit" should do so and assign the unit this responsibility.

- Schools have to notify parents every year about FERPA rights. In this notification, the school has to let parents know which office or school official serves as its "law enforcement unit." The Department of Education has suggested one way to go about this, which you can see if you turn to its Model Notification of FERPA Rights (Form VII-5 in Chapter Nine).

- In your notification to parents, you should list "law enforcement unit" personnel employed by the school as "school officials" with a "legitimate educational interest." This will mean they can access protected student records – but also that they are bound by the same FERPA restrictions as other school officials concerning "education records."

- You can send all "education records" to a transfer school or postsecondary institution a student plans to attend without parents' permission – so long as you have stated on your notification to parents that you make these disclosures to other schools. If you haven't stated this, you have to make a reasonable attempt to notify the parent of the disclosure (unless the parent asked you to send the records, of course). Also, if asked, you have to provide the parents a copy of the information you disclosed as well as provide them the opportunity for a hearing on the matter.

See Chapter Nine for a form explaining exactly what does – and does not – constitute an "education record."

Finally, although the responsibility for any judgment call remains yours, you can email the Department of Education's Family Policy Compliance Office at *FERPA@Ed.Gov* for a fast reply on a routine question. You can write to them for "a more formal response" at:

Family Policy Compliance Office
U.S. Department of Education
400 Maryland Avenue, SW
Washington, DC 20202-8520

Many perpetrators of school shootings, including the one whose attack prompted the FERPA guidance above, have ended the rampage by killing themselves.

The Bureau of Justice Statistics' *Indicators of School Crime and Safety 2010* points out "[v]iolent deaths at school are rare but tragic events" – with 15 homicides and 7 suicides at school for the year the report covered (July 1, 2008 to June 30, 2009). You can download this report at *nces.ed.gov/pubs2011/2011002.pdf.*

But while a violent death *at school* is a relatively rare occurrence, the numbers are much higher when it comes to off-campus suicides among those ages 10 to 24 – and this is of increasing concern not only to school officials but also to lawmakers because the evidence increasingly links young people's suicides to things that have happened at school.

C. Self-Injury

Self-injury habits start younger than most people might think, according to a 2012 study published in *Pediatrics.*

Researchers at the University of Denver and Rutgers University teamed up to conduct the study in Colorado and New Jersey.

Participating students in both locations shared similar reports about their behavior. Third-graders between the ages of seven and nine revealed:

- 8% admitted they'd intentionally hurt themselves by cutting, burning or poking their skin with sharp objects.
- Nearly two-thirds of those students said they'd intentionally hurt

themselves more than once.

Other findings include:

- 4% of sixth-graders self-injured their bodies, and
- about 13% of ninth-graders developed the habit.

Some students claim self-injuring helps them cope with emotional stressors, such as family issues, bullying and difficulty in school.

To reduce physical pain, the body releases endorphins, which are basically "feel-good hormones." Some researchers believe this naturally occurring endorphin release may explain why students "feel better" after hurting themselves.

Self-injury is often difficult to spot because most students keep wounds hidden, according to the Mayo Clinic. Warning signs that may indicate self-injury include students who:

- have fresh wounds or scars, such as from burns or cuts
- keep sharp objects on hand
- spend a lot of time alone
- wear long sleeves and pants – even in hot weather, and
- claim to have frequent accidents or mishaps.

The full study is available at *bit.ly/cutting555*.

D. Suicide Prevention

In 2010, the CDC reported a study by its scientists (published in the online edition of the *Journal of Pediatrics*) showed a connection between kids getting bullied and an increase in their suicidal thoughts and behaviors.

The CDC also reported suicide is the third leading cause of death for 10- to 24-year-olds, with boys overwhelmingly more at risk than girls. Boys account for 83% of the suicides for that age group.

But it was a girl's suicide after bullying that grabbed the most press attention in 2010 – partly because of the community's unusually legalistic response to the tragedy. First, in a highly unusual move, the district attorney filed criminal charges against the students who allegedly bullied Massachusetts student-suicide Phoebe Prince. Second, the state quickly enacted an anti-bullying law in response to two student suicides (one of them Prince's).

Many states have also decided they need to do more to prevent such tragedies. Colorado, Georgia, Mississippi and New Hampshire passed anti-bullying legislation in 2010, and Kentucky law began to require middle schools and high schools to provide suicide prevention information to students – and training on suicide prevention techniques to educators.

The suicide of college student Tyler Clementi prompted New Jersey to enact "The Anti-Bullying Bill of Rights" in 2011, amending its existing anti-bullying law. Now considered the toughest law in the country, it also contains a suicide-prevention component.

The federal government also provided some extra help to schools trying to put the pieces together after student suicides.

Grants awarded by the U.S. Department of Education's Office of Safe and Drug-Free Schools include Project School Emergency Response to Violence (SERV) awards. The funds they provide are intended to pay for resources districts need to recover from traumatic events and make affected schools safe places for students again.

In 2011, Project SERV awards included:

- $50,000 to Millard Public Schools in Omaha, Nebraska, to provide counseling and added security after a student shot and killed a vice principal who'd suspended him and then committed suicide after fleeing the school, and

- $46,484 to Vermont's Chittenden East Supervisory Union, which has 10 schools, following its fifth student suicide in a year; he shot himself in the head in a school bathroom. The area is extremely rural, and about a third of the population – less than 15,000 – are younger than 25. The money will be used for counseling as well as training to help parents and teachers recognize the signs of suicide.

If you're looking for ideas for suicide-prevention at your school, you might want to check out "The Youth Suicide Prevention School-Based Guide" at: *theguide.fmhi.usf.edu.*

Student suicides highlight the need for schools to help students with transitory emotional problems. Many students who consider suicide (or actually commit it) are suffering an "unbearable" problem that could be made bearable with the right kind of help from an adult. For suggestions about ways to deal with a student that you believe may be suicidal, see Form VII-6 in Chapter Nine.

Suicide risks for depressed students can start earlier than expected, according to a 2012 study published in the *Journal of Adolescent Health.* Collecting data on suicide attempts from 883 students who suffered from depression, researchers found:

- more than 40% of students who attempted to commit suicide first tried before high school, and

- the rate of suicide attempts rose sharply around the age of 12, or sixth grade, and continued to increase through the ninth grade.

Researchers concluded that mental health programs may need to start in elementary and middle school.

A student suicide is a traumatic event not only for the student's family but for his school community as well. For suggestions about how to announce a student suicide to the school, see Form VII-7 in Chapter Nine.

Whether or not the cause was suicide, any time a student dies it is a significant event in the life of the school that needs to be dealt with appropriately and with respect. For suggestions about making an announcement to let students know a classmate has died, see Form VII-8 in Chapter Nine. An alternate notification statement is available on Form VII-19. For model letters to provide more details to students or their parents after such an event, see Form VII-9 and Form VII-10 in Chapter Nine.

When a student does commit suicide, grieving parents may try to make sense of the tragedy by blaming the school for things the school did or did not do to prevent it. But as you will see from the cases summarized below, only very rarely will a court agree with the parents that the school had a duty to prevent the suicide.

In one of these decisions, the judge pointed out: "Attempted suicide by school-age children is no slight matter; but it has no single cause and no infallible solution [. ...] Different schools will react differently, depending upon resources, available information, and the judgment of school and public health authorities, who may fear making a bad situation worse. Absent a showing that the school affirmatively caused a suicide, the primary responsibility for safeguarding children from this danger, as from most others, is that of their parents; and even they, with direct control and intimate knowledge, are often helpless." *Hasenfus v. LaJeunesse*, 175 F.3d 68 (1st Cir. 1999).

E. Legal Decisions

1. Liability for Student Suicide

a. Constitutional Claims

◆   After a high school student with Asperger's Syndrome killed himself, his parents sued, alleging the district and principal violated his "liberty right to be free from psychological and bodily abuse" by not training staff to protect him from bullying – but a Georgia federal judge dismissed the case.

Seventeen-year-old Tyler Long hanged himself at home, leaving a note saying "This World [sic] will be a better place without me." He had Asperger's Syndrome, and Tyler's friends and parents said he'd been bullied at school because of it.

After his death, students wrote "we will not miss you" and "it was your own fault" on school walls – and some wore nooses at school.

Tyler's parents sued his principal and the district, alleging they breached Tyler's substantive due process right to be free from abuse.

The judge dismissed the case, finding **school defendants didn't have a constitutional duty to protect Tyler from other students**.

The Due Process Clause protects citizens from government officials' abuse of power. Apart from a few narrow exceptions, it *doesn't* require the government to protect citizens from each other.

Under Eleventh Circuit law binding on this Georgia federal court, the government had a duty to protect a citizen from other citizens if it had the victim in custody. Courts had found jail constituted custody, but not school.

A narrow exception existed when a government official caused harm by conduct that was "arbitrary or conscience shocking in a constitutional sense." That standard could be met by excessive corporal punishment at school. The parents claimed it was met by school defendants' failure to train staff to protect the student despite knowing he had a disability and was being bullied – but that was negligence or deliberate indifference at most.

As the parents' substantive due process claim didn't meet the required legal standard, the judge dismissed it. *Long v. Murray County School Dist.*, No. 4:10-CV-00015-HLM, 2012 WL 2277836 (N.D. Ga. 5/21/12).

◆ A Texas federal judge dismissed a suit brought by parents that alleged school officials breached the substantive-due-process and equal-protection rights of a student who committed suicide

Thirteen-year-old Jon Carmichael was bullied nearly every day at school. The day before he killed himself, students videotaped themselves stripping Jon naked, tying him up and then stuffing him into a trash can.

Jon's parents sued school officials, claiming they violated Jon's rights, but the judge dismissed their suit.

The parents claimed school officials breached Jon's substantive due process "right to life and bodily integrity" – but the judge dismissed the claim because Due Process Clause generally doesn't require the government to protect citizens from other citizens.

School officials hadn't "confined" Jon in a way that left him unable to protect himself, and the Fifth Circuit – with jurisdiction over this Texas federal court – hadn't adopted the state-created danger theory. Under it, a school can be held liable if it creates or increases the danger to a student.

The parents alleged officials discriminated against Jon as a male because they passed off the bullying by saying "boys will be boys " – but to state an equal protection claim, they had to show school officials applied policies differently when a girl was the victim or when the bully and victim weren't the same sex. As the parents' claims failed, the judge dismissed the case. *Estate of Carmichael v. Galbraith*, No. 3:11-CV-0622-D, 2012 WL 13568 (N.D. Tex. 1/4/12).

◆ A California federal judge refused to dismiss equal protection claims based on a principal's and assistant principal's failure to investigate and discipline the bullying of an openly gay student.

After Seth Walsh came out as gay in the sixth grade, classmates called him "pansy" and "sissy," pushed him into lockers and suggested he kill himself. His mother reported this. **The principal said classmates "in a perfect world" wouldn't harass Seth**, but these students were at a difficult age and the principal couldn't change attitudes they learned at home.

When Seth was in the seventh grade, the bullying became more widespread, sexually explicit and confrontational. The principal and vice principal saw it, and Seth's mother reported it, but the administrators took no steps to stop it. At some point, the vice principal suggested the solution to the problem was for Seth to leave school.

In September of Seth's eighth-grade year, the day after other students threatened and assaulted him, Seth hanged himself at home.

Seth's mother sued the district and district officials, alleging multiple claims. The school defendants asked the judge to dismiss her suit. The judge dismissed some claims, but not her equal protection claim against the principal and vice principal.

The principals argued the mother couldn't make this claim as she hadn't shown they responded differently to harassment claims made by non-homosexuals. The judge found she didn't have to at this stage of the case.

To make her equal protection claim at this stage, Seth's mother only had to show Seth was discriminated against due to his membership in an identifiable class. She did by showing Walsh suffered pervasive harassment as a homosexual and that neither administrator took disciplinary action – instead only saying he wouldn't be discriminated against in a perfect world or that the solution to a student being harassed at school was for the student to leave the school. *Walsh v. Tehachupi Unified School Dist.*, 827 F.Supp.2d 1107 (E.D. Cal. 2011).

◆ An Ohio federal judge found that "however tragic and unfair [it] may seem," a school had no constitutional duty to protect a student from student-on-student bullying – or from killing himself because of it.

Eric Mohat committed suicide at age 17. His parents claimed he was driven to it by constant bullying and harassment that school officials were aware of but did nothing about.

His parents sued the school district, alleging they were deprived of their substantive due process rights to familial association, a liberty interest under the Fourteenth Amendment's Due Process Clause.

Generally, the Constitution doesn't require public school officials to protect a citizen's life, liberty or property interests against "the invasions of private actors" – such as the students who harassed Eric.

One exception to this rule is the state-created danger exception, but the court found the exception didn't apply in this case because school officials didn't take *affirmative action* that increased the danger to the student.

The parents alleged the school's failure to step in when other students bullied Eric contributed to or caused his suicide. But this was an alleged failure to act rather than an affirmative act.

The court wrote that "although parents should be able to expect that their children will be kept reasonably safe when under the school's supervision, the school had no constitutional duty to take affirmative action to protect Eric from harm imposed by other students through bullying[.]" *Mohat v. Mentor Exempted Village School Dist. Board of Educ.*, No. 1:09 CV 688, 2011 WL 2174671 (N.D. Ohio 6/1/11).

◆ A Texas federal judge dismissed a suit that claimed a school district violated a student's rights by not doing more to prevent her suicide attempt.

High school staff confiscated a note from the student that prompted the principal to call her mother to advise she get counseling for the girl.

A year later, the student spent a week at a psychiatric treatment facility. Not long after her release, she was arrested for shoplifting.

The day after her arrest, her mother went to school. She told the school secretary about the arrest and asked to be called if "anything happened[.]"

In English class, the student told a friend she was going to kill

herself. The friend told the teacher, and the teacher sent the student to a counselor. The mother later claimed the counselor was so busy she simply sent the student to her next class without telling anyone else about her suicide threat.

The student was excused from her next class to go to the bathroom. There, she tried to kill herself. The attempt was unsuccessful but allegedly left her with a permanent injury.

Her mother sued the district and several individuals under Section 1983 of the U.S. Code. She alleged they violated the student's rights by not adopting a suicide prevention program and not taking steps to prevent her suicide attempt.

The school defendants asked the judge to dismiss the suit. He did.

To violate Section 1983, either a school official must commit "deliberate conduct" that makes the official "the 'moving force' behind the injury" or else the district must create a "special relationship" with the student – such as by making a specific promise to keep him or her safe.

Unlike most jurisdictions, the Fifth Circuit doesn't recognize a "state-created danger" ground for liability – which can make a district liable if it increased the danger to the student.

The court found **this suit only alleged negligence** – not a valid claim of a constitutional violation under Section 1983. So the court dismissed it. *Hejny v. Grand Saline Independent School Dist.*, No. 2-10-cv-50-TJW, 2010 WL 2521007 (E.D. Tex. 6/17/10).

◆ The mother of a boy who committed suicide after his guidance counselor determined he was not suicidal could not hold the counselor or the school district responsible for his death.

A 16-year-old boy passed a note to his ex-girlfriend after he found out she was dating someone new. He wrote the news "almost made me want to go kill myself," which worried her, so she took the note to a counselor.

The boy's guidance counselor called him into her office. The counselor told him his friends were worried about him and asked if he was having girl trouble. He said he'd been upset about a girl two months ago but was no longer upset. Asked if he had plans to hurt himself or would ever do so, he said, "definitely not." The counselor also asked him "forward thinking" questions and heard he had future plans. She asked if anything else was upsetting him and he said no.

Believing he was not at risk, the counselor did not contact the school psychologist or the boy's mother.

A few days later, the student returned to ask the counselor if a blond girl had given her a note he'd written. The counselor said she couldn't tell him that. The boy said he'd thought she'd say that and didn't seem upset.

That night, the boy and his mother had an argument. Later that night, he hanged himself.

The deceased student's mother sued the district and the counselor, **arguing they violated his constitutional right not to be deprived of life**

without due process of law because the counselor did not prevent his death by reporting he was suicidal.

Generally, public schools cannot be held responsible for acts of violence committed by non-school-personnel. But there is an exception to that rule if the school created the danger that harmed the student.

The mother could not succeed on her state-created danger claim because she could not show:

- it was foreseeable the student would kill himself if the counselor didn't report she'd screened him for suicidal ideation
- the counselor's behavior was bad enough to shock the conscience
- the student was a member of a group likely to commit suicide because of this behavior, and
- the counselor used her authority in a way that put the student in danger or put him at more risk than if she hadn't acted at all.

When the case reached the Third U.S. Circuit Court of Appeals, it found no one – including the student's mother – had considered him suicidal. It also did not consider the language in the note to be a clear cry for help and found the counselor had responded to the situation quickly and appropriately. *Sanford v. Stiles*, 456 F.3d 298 (3d Cir. 2006).

◆   A school did not have the responsibility to protect a student from committing suicide even though the student could be considered emotionally fragile and there had been a rash of suicides at the school in previous months.

A female student was raped when she was 13 years old and then had the trauma of testifying against her rapist in court. Less than a year later, the student was out on the school softball field with her gym class when several of her classmates began harassing her about the rape and her decision to testify. The student became upset. She shouted obscenities and threatened to hurt them. The gym teacher broke this up and told the student to go back to the locker room. There, the student tried to hang herself.

Classmates found her and called for emergency help. The student did not die, but she went into a coma. She ultimately emerged from the coma but was left with permanent impairments.

In the three months before this incident, seven students at that middle school had attempted suicide. Several of the attempts had happened at school or school events, and the student knew at least two of the students.

The student's parents sued the board of education and the gym teacher, alleging they violated the student's right to substantive due process. The trial court dismissed the case. The parents appealed, but the First U.S. Circuit Court of Appeals affirmed.

The parents argued the school had a duty to protect the student because it knew she'd been raped the year before and other students had attempted suicide. But this was not enough for the school to recognize her as part of an identifiable group of students at risk for committing suicide. Also, the gym teacher's actions were not bad enough to shock the conscience, another prerequisite to a finding of a constitutional violation.

He only reprimanded a 14-year-old for misbehavior and sent her out of class. *Hasenfus v. LaJeunesse*, 175 F.3d 68 (1st Cir. 1999).

◆ A principal and a school counselor could be sued under the state-created danger theory for the suicide of a special education student with known emotional problems.

A learning-disabled 16-year-old special ed student had psychological and emotional problems including depression and impulsivity.

When the principal reprimanded him for harassing an elementary student, he threatened the teacher who'd reported it. The principal suspended him and told a counselor to drive him home. The principal also called the police to report the suspension and tell them to detain the student if they saw him on school property.

The counselor knew the student had access to guns at home and also saw the student was very angry. Earlier that year, the student had told a school aide he might be better off dead and had threatened to shoot himself.

Contrary to school policy, the principal didn't tell the counselor to make sure the parents were home and bring the student back to school if they weren't. Also, instead of following policy by talking to the parents, the counselor simply dropped off the student. When his parents got home, they discovered he'd shot himself. He died.

The parents sued the principal and the counselor, arguing they violated the student's constitutional right to due process. The school defendants asked for summary judgment. The court refused, finding a trial was needed to determine if their acts fell under an exception to the general rule that public schools aren't constitutionally responsible for non-school-personnel's acts of violence.

The school defendants appealed. The Tenth U.S. Circuit Court of Appeals upheld the need for a trial on the state-created danger claims against the principal and counselor. **A trial was needed to determine if the principal and counselor increased the risk the student would kill himself** because:

- he was a member of a limited and definable group: special education students who had threatened to commit suicide, and
- the principal and counselor suspended him – making him so distraught he threatened violence – then took him home and left him there alone, knowing he had access to guns.

Armijo v. Wagon Mound Public Schools, 159 F.3d 1253 (10th Cir. 1998).

b. Negligence Issues

◆ Montana's highest court affirmed a ruling that a school wasn't liable for a student-athlete's suicide. The 17-year-old senior had racked up a long disciplinary record for things like talking back, theft, fighting and skipping school. After a school counselor saw him "putting a can of chew in his pocket," the principal, superintendent, and athletic director explained to the teen that having tobacco at school had triggered a school suspension – plus a 60-day suspension from sports under the athletic department's policy. The student was on the varsity wrestling team. He became very upset when he realized the sports suspension meant he would miss the state tournament. Later that day, he committed suicide while at home. His mother sued the town, the school and the superintendent, saying her son died due to their negligence. The trial court granted the school defendants judgment without a trial. His mother appealed to the state supreme court, but it affirmed. The rule in Montana is: No one but the suicide victim is responsible for his or her death. The court was willing to consider an exception based on foreseeability, but it found the exception didn't apply. In this case, **the student didn't tell anyone he felt suicidal or react to prior disciplinary punishments by threatening or attempting suicide**. The court said that if a student responds to discipline by getting suicidal – but the school has no reason to know about it – the school is not liable for an ensuing tragedy. *Gourneau v. Hamill*, No. DA 13-0210, 2013 WL 5634125 (Mont. 10/15/13).

◆   Delaware's highest court found school officials may be liable for failing to warn a suicidal student's family – even though the student killed himself at home. The court held that the school's inaction could be "negligence per se" – a legal doctrine that deems conduct negligent because it violated a law or regulation. The doctrine was relevant in this case because a state regulation requires schools to try to contact parents or guardians immediately if students are "clearly dangerous to themselves." A student told his school's behavior interventionist (BI) that his friend had tried to kill himself. The BI called the suicidal student into her office, where the boy admitted he had tried to take his own life. They talked for about four hours before the BI felt the student was OK. Then the boy was sent to class. The BI was a contract employee, so she emailed school staff to explain how she'd handled the incident and asked if she needed to do anything else. No one called the boy's family. That night, the student hanged himself at home. **The boy's family sued, claiming the school was negligent.** The court granted the school judgment without a trial. But the high court reversed, finding more info was needed with respect to the negligence per se claim. It wrote the family can base this claim on "violations of the State Department of Education and the School District's mandatory requirements to notify a parent or guardian" if a student is suicidal. So the case was sent back to the trial court for further development. *Rogers v. Christina School Dist.*, No. 45, 2013, 2013 WL 3722554 (Del. 7/16/13).

◆   A Michigan appeals court held a principal was immune to a father's suit claiming his son committed suicide due to a principal's gross negligence in being unduly harsh when disciplining him.

The court also said the proximate cause of 16-year-old Stan Burland's death "was his decision to take his own life and not defendant's conduct earlier in the day."

According to the principal, another student's mother showed him text messages that implicated Stan in a drug deal. After investigating, the principal called Stan's father. The principal said he read Stan and his father some of the text messages, suspended Stan for 10 days, and said Stan could be expelled if he discovered Stan was involved in drug dealing.

In Stan's father's version – which the principal denied – the father said he arrived to find Stan crying. He claimed the principal behaved in a physically intimidating manner and said: Stan would be expelled, the police would be involved, and "[t]his is going to be big[.]"

Later that day, Stan committed suicide.

The father sued, alleging the principal's gross negligence was the proximate cause of the student's suicide. The judge granted the principal judgment without a trial, finding him immune to the suit. The father appealed, but the appellate court affirmed.

Under Michigan law, the principal had legal immunity to this suit because the alleged conduct the father objected to occurred when the principal was performing employment duties as a principal. Also, he acted within the scope of his authority, there was no evidence he acted maliciously or for an improper purpose, and his acts were "discretionary" (that is, requiring him to use his own judgment") rather than "ministerial" (that is, simply following the rules).

The appeals court affirmed summary judgment for the principal because he met the test for state law immunity and because the judge found the proximate cause of the student's death was the student's decision to commit suicide – not the principal's discipline *Burland v. French*, No. 305652, 2012 WL 2362442 (Mich. Ct. App. 6/21/12).

◆ A Connecticut judge found school staff's alleged failure to follow a suicide-prevention policy may have made a student's suicide foreseeable – so he refused to dismiss negligence claims against them.

The school system was required by state law to have a suicide-prevention policy. The policy required any "school employee who may have knowledge of a suicide threat" to report it to the principal. It also required them to immediately refer an at-risk student to emergency medical personnel, a school psychologist or a school social worker. The policy specifically said the student was not to be left alone or allowed to go home alone. Instead, he could only be released to a responsible adult.

Student Michael Girard was allegedly despondent over a breakup.

His mother and stepfather – the Caseys – alleged high school staff heard Michael say he was going to hurt or kill himself. They also said a counselor knew Michael was suicidal, but let him go home alone one morning.

He died at home that day of a methadone overdose at around 10:30 a.m.

The Caseys brought a negligence suit against the board of education plus the superintendent, the principal and the counselor in their official capacities. The school defendants asked the judge to strike the negligence claims against them. He refused.

The general rule in Connecticut is that only the person who commits suicide can be held legally responsible for it. This is partly based on the theory that the act can't be predicted. The court found that rule may not apply in this case because Michael's suicide may have been foreseeable.

The judge concluded "a student's suicide could be a foreseeable result of school staff's failure to follow the suicide prevention policy" – so he refused to dismiss the negligence claims. *Girard v. Putnam*, No. CV085002754-S, 2011 WL 783599 (Conn. Super. Ct. 1/28/11).

◆   The Ninth Circuit affirmed parents couldn't hold a school responsible for their son's suicide because they couldn't show a harsh lecture he got at school was the proximate cause of his decision to shoot himself.

Three California students left their middle school without permission to attend public protests against a law that would have made it illegal to help undocumented immigrants.

One of them was on juvenile court probation for bringing a knife to school. His mother later said he could have been sent to prison for three years for violating probation.

Back at school, the students were called to a vice principal's office. According to one of them, he pointed to the students, saying, "You guys are all dumb, dumb, and dumber." He lectured them about the possible consequences of truancy – including police involvement, a $250 fine and a juvenile hall sentence. He also said they couldn't participate in a year-end trip to Disneyland.

After school, the boy on probation told a classmate he was afraid his mother would be mad at him and worried about the fine and juvenile hall.

The mother was running errands that day, but called home. The boy told her what had happened, but not in a way that made her fear for his safety. When she got home, however, she found he'd shot himself.

The student left a suicide note telling his family he loved them and saying: "Tell my teachers [they're] the best" and tell the vice principal "he is a motherf#@ker."

The boy's parents sued the school district, the principal and the vice principal, arguing they'd negligently caused the boy's death. A California federal court found they hadn't. The parents appealed to the Ninth U.S. Circuit Court of Appeals, but it affirmed the judgment.

To make their case, **the parents had to show the vice principal's harsh lecture was the proximate cause of the boy's suicide**. They couldn't.

Between hearing the lecture and killing himself, the boy went to classes and then spoke with a classmate and his mother. He also wrote a detailed suicide note. The court said: "The record seems to show he had the opportunity to appreciate the nature of his actions."

Because the parents couldn't show a reasonably close connection between the harsh lecture and the boy's suicide, judgment for the school defendants was proper. *Corales v. Bennett*, 567 F.3d 554 (9th Cir. 2009).

◆   A student's bereaved family failed to establish that a teacher's negative remarks to the student, apparently echoed in his suicide note, were a substantial factor in causing his death – because there wasn't reliable evidence the teacher actually said them.

A 13-year-old eighth-grade boy struggled with his grades. His family made it a rule he couldn't go hunting if he didn't pass his classes.

When the boy got his fall mid-term grades, he saw he had failed every class except gym. He complained to his science teacher that this meant he wouldn't be able to go deer hunting.

The teacher said he told the boy he wouldn't be going anywhere – meaning he wouldn't be going hunting. But according to the family, another student later told them the teacher actually said, "Your life is going nowhere" and called the student one of the dumbest people he had ever taught. But the family couldn't identify the student they said told them this.

The next day, the boy shot himself after the rest of his family left the house. He left a note saying, "I relize (sic) my life is going noware (sic) fast so I decided that i don't need to live anymore."

A trustee acting on behalf of the boy's family brought a wrongful death suit against the school, arguing school staff had caused the boy's suicide. The court held **the school didn't have a legal duty to prevent the suicide because the school could not have foreseen it**. The trustee also argued the boy used the same words in his note that his science teacher allegedly spoke to him, which meant these spoken words were a substantial factor in causing the suicide. However, the evidence that the teacher actually said those words wasn't reliable. The trustee appealed, but the appellate court affirmed. *Jasperson v. Anoka-Hennepin Independent School Dist. No. 11*, 2007 WL 3153456 (Minn. Ct. App. 10/30/07).

◆   An English teacher didn't violate a state duty to report a student was suicidal – even though the student killed himself six months after turning in an essay about overcoming suicidal tendencies – because the essay discussed past (not present) suicidal ideation.

For the student's junior-year high school English class, he wrote an essay in April called "My Most Difficult Decision." In it, he stated he had overcome the urge to kill himself and that the trigger for that urge was gone and he could enjoy life now. His teacher wrote him a note on the essay saying he was glad he was no longer suicidal, but to come talk to him if the urge to kill himself ever came back.

The student's family moved to another state for the student's senior year. That November, his mother told police the student was missing, she'd found a note in his room saying "I'm sorry," and he'd written "Goodbye" on his calendar over the day he'd disappeared. The family was also missing a rifle, but the student's mother told police she had no reason to believe he was suicidal.

Not long after, his body was found in the state his family had moved from. The deceased student's family sued the school district and his former

English teacher, arguing they had failed to comply with their state law duty to warn if a teacher had direct knowledge a student had suicidal tendencies. The case reached the state supreme court, which found **there was no violation of the duty to warn because a student's suicidal tendencies had to be present rather than past in order to trigger it – and the student's essay discussed overcoming an urge to kill himself in the past.** *Carrier v. Lake Pend Oreille School Dist. No. 84*, 134 P.3d 655 (Idaho 2006).

c. Sexting-Related Cases

◆ An Ohio federal judge refused to dismiss Title IX and equal protection claims brought against a school board based on its response to students circulating a nude photo of a student who later killed herself.

In May of Jessica Logan's senior year, a counselor sent her to the school resource officer (SRO) after she reported her nude photo was being texted around the school. (A proceeding dismissing a claim against the SRO in this suit is reported later in this section.)

Jessica went on to appear on a TV show about sexting. Her identity was disguised, but her parents claimed people saw through the disguise. On the show, Jessica cried over harassment she was experiencing at school – which her parents say got even worse after the TV appearance.

Jessica killed herself that summer.

Her parents sued the school board and several school officials. The school defendants asked the court to grant them summary judgment. **The judge could decide the case without a trial only if the parties agreed on all the facts that could affect the legal outcome.** They didn't when it came to the Title IX and equal protection claims.

To make their Title IX sexual harassment claim, the parents had to show the harassment was severe enough to deprive Jessica of access to educational benefits or opportunities, district officials knew about the harassment, and the officials were deliberately indifferent to the harassment.

The parties disagreed about whether the school defendants knew the nude image of Jessica was circulating and students were harassing her because of it.

To win their equal protection challenge, the parents had to show a key policymaker for implementing the school's sexual harassment policy, such as the principal, treated Jessica's report of harassment differently than other students' reports of harassment. Again, the parties disagreed whether administrators knew Jessica was being harassed. As the parents and school defendants disagreed about key facts that could change the legal outcome of these claims, the judge refused to grant school defendants judgment without a trial. *Logan v. Sycamore Community School Board of Educ.*, No. 1:09-cv-00885, 2012 WL 2011037 (S.D. Ohio 6/5/12).

◆ A Florida federal judge held a school board wasn't constitutionally liable for a 13-year-old's suicide following a sexting incident. Though tragic, an isolated incident of a staff member failing to follow the suicide-prevention policy didn't rise to a constitutional offense.

Thirteen-year-old H.S.W. had texted a suggestive photo of herself to a boy, and other students were harassing her about it. A teacher noticed shallow cuts on H.S.W.'s thigh and sent her to the office to talk to a counselor.

The school board had a written policy on suicide prevention. It required staff members to notify a student's parents if the student appeared to be at risk of suicide.

In the office, a school social worker counseled H.S.W. and then signed a "no-harm contract" with her. In it, H.S.W. agreed not to "attempt suicide or die by suicide" and to call the social worker if she had suicidal thoughts again. **The counselor didn't notify the student's parents that their child was at risk of suicide.**

The next day, H.S.W. killed herself at home. Her parents found the no-harm contract H.S.W. had signed with the social worker. They sued the school board, alleging it had violated their and their daughter's Fourteenth Amendment substantive due process rights by failing to train the social worker in the suicide prevention policy.

A municipality could be liable for a constitutional violations if it failed to properly train staff and knew the failure to train amounted to a deliberate indifference to constitutional rights. However, a single incident of a breached right wasn't enough to support this claim.

The court found the parents couldn't hold the school board liable, while noting that the parents had alleged "an admittedly tragic but isolated incident in which a social worker failed to follow established protocol." *Witsell v. School Board of Hillsborough County*, No. 8:11-cv-781-T-23AEP, 2011 WL 2457877 (M.D. Fla. 6/20/11).

◆   A Kentucky federal judge dismissed a claim against a principal, finding she couldn't have prevented a student's suicide attempt. The male student attempted suicide after his girlfriend discovered he'd texted nude photos of himself to a male teacher.

A high school student sent nude photos to a math teacher who'd been tutoring him – and giving him backrubs, touching his legs, and exposing himself to the student at a YMCA.

One Saturday morning, **the student's girlfriend found the nude photos and texts on the student's phone**. They quarreled. He went home around 11:00 a.m. and attempted suicide.

Meanwhile, the girlfriend called a different teacher to report what she'd discovered. The teacher passed the information along to the principal via a voicemail he left on her home phone. She got the message late Saturday or early Sunday.

On Monday morning, the principal spoke to the girlfriend and then suspended the math teacher and called the police. The math teacher was later arrested and fired.

The student sued the principal. Among his charges, he alleged the

principal committed the tort of outrage by not investigating and calling the
police as soon as she got the voicemail. He said a call to his mother could
have prevented his suicide attempt.

The judge dismissed this claim. The principal got the voicemail hours
after the student's suicide attempt, so an immediate investigation couldn't
have prevented it.

In addition, Kentucky cases didn't allow an outrage claim alongside a
negligence claim based on the same allegations – unless the allegedly
outrageous conduct was intended "to cause extreme emotional distress in
the victim[.]" The student had brought negligence claims against the
principal based on the same allegations and didn't show she was trying to
cause him extreme emotional distress. *Cole v. Shadoan*, 782 F.Supp.2d 428
(E.D. Ky. 2011).

◆   Parents of a student who committed suicide didn't convince an Ohio
federal judge that a school resource officer (SRO) increased the risk to their
daughter's life by mishandling a sexting incident. Therefore, the judge
dismissed the SRO from the lawsuit.

High school senior Jessica Logan texted a nude photo of herself to a
male classmate. It wound up on several classmates' phones. They harassed
her, and she went to the SRO.

**The SRO confronted Logan's classmates, telling them to delete the
photo and stop harassing her.** He also asked a prosecutor if Logan could
take legal action, but was told she had no case as she wasn't a minor.

The SRO told Logan a television reporter had contacted him, hoping to
create awareness about the consequences of sexting by telling students'
stories. With her parents' approval, Logan agreed to a televised interview,
hoping to influence other girls not to sext. It aired with her appearance and
identity concealed and her voice altered.

Logan's parents said she was subjected to increased harassment at
school after the interview. Logan then killed herself.

Her parents sued the SRO, saying he increased the risk to Logan's life
by encouraging her to be interviewed. The judge disagreed and dismissed
the SRO from their lawsuit.

Government officials like police officers are immune from federal
claims unless they violate clearly established rights a reasonable person
could be expected to know about.

The SRO had no general constitutional duty to protect Logan's life. But
her parents argued the state-created danger exception applied, saying he had
a duty to protect her because he'd increased the risk to her life.

The judge disagreed, finding the claims weren't credible. The parents
alleged the SRO encouraged Logan to be interviewed on TV – but the court
found he only gave her the reporter's phone number. They also claimed the
interview intensified her harassment at school – but no evidence supported
that allegation. Though they claimed the SRO was deliberately indifferent
to the danger he'd caused Logan, **the judge found the SRO acted in good**

faith to try to help the student.

Finding the SRO was entitled to qualified immunity, the judge dismissed him from the case. *Logan v. Sycamore Community School Board of Educ.*, 780 F.Supp.2d 594 (S.D. Ohio 2011).

2. Other Mental Health Issues

◆ A North Carolina court ruled against a student who was sentenced to life without parole following a shooting. The student unsuccessfully argued that the jury wasn't properly instructed on the insanity defense.

On August 30, 2006, high school student Rafael Castillo shot and killed his father at home. He then drove to school, where he set off smoke bombs and shot two students.

When Castillo's gun jammed, **the school's resource officer (SRO) and a teacher told Castillo to put down his weapons**. He did, and the SRO arrested him.

Charges against Castillo included first-degree murder, discharging a gun on school property, and assault with a deadly weapon with intent to kill.

At trial, the jury considered whether he was not guilty by reason of insanity. Under North Carolina law, a jury could reach this conclusion if it determined Castillo had a "disease or deficiency of the mind" that so impaired him that he didn't know "the nature or quality of his act" or wasn't capable of knowing if it was right or wrong.

Castillo's defense attorney argued the boy believed God wanted him to "sacrifice" his father. He'd also written in his diary, "I might save some children from sin" – and told officers immediately after the shootings that he'd tried "to save those kids from sex, drugs, pornography, and abusive people" like his father. When his mother later visited him at a mental institution, he told her that he "did the right thing."

But there was also evidence Castillo had idolized the Columbine shooters. He'd visited Columbine with his mother and bought himself a black trench coat during the trip. He'd also tried to kill himself on the anniversary of the Columbine shootings.

Several experts testified Castillo couldn't tell right from wrong and that he thought he was getting messages from God. But a hospital psychiatrist testified Castillo was severely mentally ill but could tell right from wrong. **She testified that he'd idolized the Columbine shooters and wanted to share their notoriety.**

The jury found Castillo didn't qualify for the insanity defense. He was sentenced to life without possibility of parole.

Castillo appealed, arguing he was entitled to the defense. He claimed the judge had improperly instructed the jury. But the appeals court found no error. The judge's instructions tracked the language in the state's Pattern Jury Instructions. Also, if the judge had agreed to use the instructions requested by Castillo's attorney, it wouldn't have affected the outcome because it wouldn't have changed the question the jury had to answer: whether Castillo was "under a delusion that God commanded him to kill his father and carry out a school shooting[.]" *State v. Castillo*, 713 S.E.2d 190 (N.C. Ct. App. 2011).

◆   Parents couldn't simply sue a district over its refusal to decide a student with depression and anxiety qualified for special education. Before suing, they first had to "exhaust administrative remedies" via hearings.

An Ohio elementary school student's academic performance deteriorated. He began to have anger issues and exhibit "demonstrated explosive behavior." He also began to refuse to go to school and to make comments about committing suicide.

In March, his mother asked the district to conduct a Multi-Factored Evaluation (MFE) to assess the student for special education eligibility. She said the principal told her it was too late in the year to conduct an MFE.

Two months later, his mother gave the school guidance counselor a copy of a psychiatrist's report diagnosing the student with ADHD, Asperger's Disorder, anxiety disorder and severe depression. She again asked for an MFE. Administrators again denied her request.

The parents and the district continued to discussed the matter over the summer. **Less than a week before the start of the new school year, the school district refused to concede the student had a disability.**

The parents sued the district under the Individuals with Disabilities Education Act (IDEA), Section 504 of the Rehabilitation Act and the Americans with Disabilities Act. The district asked the federal judge to dismiss the suit because the parents couldn't sue over an IDEA issue under any law without first exhausting administrative remedies, as required under the IDEA, by completing every hearing and appeal required by the state's special education law.

The judge agreed with the district that the parents had to exhaust administrative remedies before going to court. He dismissed the case. *Doe v. Dublin City School Dist.*, No. 2:09-cv-738, 2010 WL 1434318 (S.D. Ohio 2010).

◆   The Seventh U.S. Circuit Court of Appeals reversed the dismissal of a teacher's claim that a school violated the Americans with Disabilities Act (ADA) by refusing to accommodate her seasonal affective disorder by giving her a classroom with natural light.

After five successful years teaching kindergarten at a Wisconsin elementary school, a teacher asked to teach a first-grade class. The school agreed, but it assigned her to a classroom with no windows.

The teacher told the principal she had seasonal affective disorder, a form of depression. The teacher said she would have trouble functioning in a room with no natural light.

The district worked with the teacher to resolve her other complaints about the room, but it refused to move her to a room with windows – even though another first-grade teacher was willing to swap rooms with her and another classroom was empty.

When the school year began, the teacher began experiencing fatigue, anxiety, hypervigilance, tearfulness, racing thoughts and trouble organizing her thoughts. By late September, she was having panic attacks, uncontrollable crying jags and trouble eating. She began thinking about suicide, and she had serious trouble focusing on her job and her students. On Oct. 17, her doctors put her on medication and suggested she take a leave of absence for the remaining three months of the semester.

She was granted leave. In late November, she sent the district's workers' compensation claims representative a letter from her doctor. It clarified "the importance of natural light for individuals with a history of this disorder" and said the teacher's "current episode of depression was most likely directly related" to being assigned to a classroom with no windows.

The district didn't reassign the teacher to a different room, and she never returned to the elementary school. She started teaching at a university the next year.

The teacher sued the district in federal court, alleging it violated the ADA by failing to accommodate her disability. The judge dismissed the case, finding the district had met its accommodation duty by engaging in an interactive process with the teacher and "making changes aimed at reducing her stress." She appealed to the Seventh Circuit. It reversed.

The teacher's case had to go forward because she presented enough evidence for a judge or jury to find she was a qualified person with a disability and the district knew of her disability but didn't accommodate it.

The Seventh Circuit said cases involving accommodation requests for a mental disability require extra information "because any necessary accommodation is often nonobvious to the employer. Thus our cases have consistently held that **disabled employees must make their employers aware of any nonobvious, medically necessary accommodations with corroborating evidence" from a doctor before the employer is required to provide it**. Here, the teacher provided such information when her doctor wrote to the workers' compensation representative to explain her condition.

Because the teacher provided the evidence needed for a judge or jury to find she was legally entitled to the accommodation she'd requested, the lower court was wrong to dismiss her case. *Ekstrand v. School Dist. of Somerset*, 583 F.3d 972 (7th Cir. 2009). On remand to the lower federal court, the district again asked for judgment without a trial. The judge found the Seventh Circuit had considered the same facts and arguments the district was making but found a trial was needed as the parties genuinely disagreed about facts that could affect the legal decision about whether:

- she had a disability under the ADA
- the district was aware of her disability, and
- it failed to accommodate the disability.

So the judge denied the district's request for judgment. *Ekstrand v. School Dist. of Somerset*, No. 08-cv-193-bbc, 2010 WL 3123143 (W.D. Wis. 8/6/10).

◆   Discovering a student had been admitted to a mental hospital triggered a school district's child find duty under the Individuals with Disabilities Education Act to determine if she qualified for special education. Its failure to do so entitled the student to tuition reimbursement.

The student had been attending a private school, but her parents enrolled her in the local public school in Connecticut the summer before her eleventh-grade year. The public school didn't know she'd been admitted to a hospital after the private school's psychologist told her parents the student was bulimic and suicidal.

Then, just before the school year began, the student overdosed and was admitted to a psychiatric hospital. A few days later, her mother gave the public school's nurse the health assessment record the state required for public school enrollment. It reported the student was taking antidepressants. Not long after, the mother told the school the student was in a psychiatric hospital and wouldn't be able to attend her first day of school. A few days later, her parents enrolled her in an intensive therapeutic program in Utah.

The public school apparently didn't notice her absence. Her parents received a mid-quarter progress report in October saying the student was making good progress in Algebra and was a pleasure to have in class. In November, the parents enrolled her in a therapeutic boarding school in Massachusetts.

In December, the public school in Connecticut wrote to tell her parents their daughter – who had never attended the school – was making good progress in U.S. history class. Later that month the student was admitted to another hospital. In January, her parents enrolled her in another program in Utah. Their attorney wrote to the school to ask it to evaluate the student for special education.

The district convened a "planning and placement team" (PPT) meeting. At it, one of the student's doctors said he believed she met the criteria for special education under the emotional disturbance category and thought she needed to be educated in a therapeutic boarding school.

The PPT refused to find she qualified for special ed. It also refused to reimburse the parents for her therapeutic school tuition.

The parents requested a due process hearing. The hearing officer found the district had violated its child find duty – and had sufficient information by the PPT meeting to have determined she was eligible for special ed under the emotional disturbance category. It ordered the district to reimburse the parents for her therapeutic school costs starting with the date the parents had notified the district of their intent to enroll the student there.

The district appealed, but the court affirmed.

To find a procedural violation of a district's child find obligation, the court had to find school officials "overlooked clear signs of a disability" or were "negligent in failing to order testing" or had "no rational justification for not deciding to evaluate." It did.

The court agreed **the district ignored a clear sign of a disability when the student's mother informed it that the student couldn't come to**

school because she'd been admitted to a psychiatric hospital – especially coupled with the info provided on the health assessment form.

Because the district's "disregard of its Child Find obligations constituted a gross procedural violation," the court affirmed the hearing officer's decision to award the student compensatory education by ordering the district to pay for her tuition at a therapeutic private school. *Regional School Dist. No. 9 Board of Educ. v. Mr. and Mrs. M.*, No. 3:07-CV-01484 (WWE), 2009 WL 2514064 (D. Conn. 8/7/09).

◆ A school custodian diagnosed with post-traumatic stress syndrome caused by events surrounding a student's gruesome suicide at school was allowed to sue the school district for damages – her remedy wasn't limited to workers' comp.

A school custodian was called in to work early because a student had shot himself in the head in the main entrance of the high school. After the school superintendent ordered her to clean up the site, she overheard a police detective say the dead student's name. She'd known the boy and was so upset she had to take half an hour to compose herself.

When she returned, the police told her not to touch the site. Instead, the principal told her to go through the classrooms where the boy had attended classes that day to look for any bombs he might have left. She found none.

When she returned, she got the OK to clean the site. She found a bookbag in the corner and was carrying it away when she was told to leave it, so she dropped it. Later, she found out a robot had carried it out of the building and watched as a bomb squad detonated a pipe bomb that had been in the bookbag.

This shocked and frightened her, as no one had warned her the bag had belonged to the suicide victim – and she'd dropped it, not suspecting it might contain a bomb.

The superintendent told her to make it look like the suicide hadn't happened. **She was there cleaning – including soot from the bomb detonation as well as brain matter, bone bits and blood – until after 4:00 a.m.** She was told to come back by 8:00 a.m. She spent the day handing out cookies and coffee to students, staff and parents there for grief counseling as well as guarding the school gates. The custodian was also ordered to clean up the suicide site every night because other people left candles and cards there to honor the boy who'd died. She found removing these items extremely upsetting. Over the next few weeks, she experienced anxiety, sleeplessness, recurring nightmares and frequent crying. She was diagnosed with post-traumatic stress syndrome.

The custodian sued the school district alleging intentional and negligent infliction of emotional distress. The trial court dismissed the suit, deciding her only remedy was to file a claim under the state's worker's comp statute. She appealed, and the appellate court reversed.

Washington's Industrial Insurance Act provided the exclusive remedy for workers injured in the course of their employment – but the appellate court found it didn't apply here because the custodian's injuries didn't fit the act's definition for "injury."

The act defined an "injury" as "a sudden and tangible happening, of a traumatic nature, producing an immediate or prompt result[.]" That wasn't the case here, as the emotionally traumatic events the custodian suffered did not occur suddenly or have an immediate result. Also, her mental injury wasn't the result of any one or identifiable task ordered by the district.

Since her injury didn't fall under the definition of the state's worker's comp statute, she wasn't limited to that remedy. The appellate court found her emotional distress suit could go forward. *Rothwell v. Nine Mile Falls School Dist.*, 206 P.3d 347 (Wash. Ct. App. 2009).

◆ Citing constitutional rights to privacy and childrearing, parents were allowed a trial against their daughter's school corporation after it gave her an intrusive mental health screening without their permission.

In 2003, an Indiana high school student killed himself. In response to the tragedy, the community formed a task force to look into ways to prevent teen suicides. These included TeenScreen, a test developed by Columbia University to identify mental health problems. It was only to be administered on a voluntary basis.

The task force asked the school if the local mental health center could administer the test at the school. The school agreed and mailed a letter to parents about TeenScreen, asking them to sign and return the enclosed consent forms.

When only nine parents signed and returned the forms, **the task force suggested using a "passive consent" form for the 2004 test. This meant parents only signed and returned a form to block the school from testing their children.** The school agreed to this with the added requirement that each student also had to sign a form before the test stating they were voluntarily taking the test.

When the November issue of the school newsletter was mailed to parents, it included an opt-out form that explained TeenScreen would be administered to students unless parents signed and returned the form within the next few weeks.

The school received 23 opt-out forms, but some families treated the school newsletter as junk mail. A 15-year-old student's parents later said they never saw any notice about TeenScreen from the school.

According to the student, the day she was administered TeenScreen, her homeroom teacher told students they would be taking a test that day, but she didn't know what it was. The school had sent teachers a memo asking them not to explain the test, saying students would receive a letter about it – presumably the opt-out letter. When the student reached the test room, she said a woman told students to sign the forms waiting on desks as quickly as possible because many other students needed to take the test. The student said the woman didn't tell them they could refuse to take it. The student said she thought she had to take the test and also had to sign the form, which she thought was just an acknowledgment that she was there to take it.

After she followed directions by signing on to a computer and honestly answering the questions on the screen, she was taken aside and told she had "Obsessive Compulsive Disorder for cleaning and social anxiety disorder." She was told she could talk to a counselor or have her mother call the mental health center to arrange for treatment.

The student was upset and confused by this and became more so as the day continued. When she got home, she asked her mother to explain what Obsessive Compulsive Disorder and social anxiety disorder were.

The student's parents sued the school corporation as well as high school staff including the principal, associate principals and guidance counselors. The parents argued that giving the student the test without their written permission violated their constitutional rights to privacy and to direct their child's upbringing. The school defendants asked for summary judgment, but the court refused to grant it, deciding instead that a trial was needed on the parents' claims.

As an earlier decision had held, **school-sponsored counseling and psychological testing that pry into private family activities can overstep a school's authority and usurp parents' constitutional rights to raise their children**. Also, while the right to privacy has never been concretely defined, the court stated that the U.S. Supreme Court has apparently recognized a right not to disclose personal matters. The parents argued administering TeenScreen to the student without their consent violated this right because the test extracted highly personal and private information from her. Also, given the circumstances under which the student signed the assent form, the court found it doubtful her participation in the test was voluntary. *Rhoades v. Penn-Harris-Madison School Corp.*, 574 F.Supp.2d 888 (N.D. Ind. 2008).

◆ A school district violated the Individuals with Disabilities Education Act (IDEA) by failing to identify a student as eligible for special education and provide her services despite clear evidence of her severe and persistent depression.

The student began to exhibit behavioral and emotional problems at school in the eighth grade. The next year, she tried to kill herself by swallowing a bottle of aspirin. After a hospital pumped her stomach, it admitted her to the pediatric mental health unit for five days, ultimately diagnosing her with clinical depression. The students' parents informed the school of this.

The next year, when the first report cards were issued, the student's parents discovered her grades had nosedived and she'd been skipping a lot of school. Her mother contacted her daughter's teachers to ask for help, but most didn't respond.

The student's parents had her tested by a psychologist, then forwarded his report to the school. He suggested ADHD might be an issue, so the parents had the student tested by an expert in that field, who diagnosed her with ADHD and major depression.

A few months after the student's parents arranged for her to start therapy, she was hospitalized for 11 days. During this stay, staff determined the student had suffered from a major depressive disorder since she was 12.

The parents contacted the school to ask it to assess her for services under Section 504 of the Rehabilitation Act. They provided doctors' diagnoses and other information. But when school staff met with the parents, they only seemed interested in making sure the student passed into the next grade, not in addressing the problems behind her poor grades.

Ultimately, the school's failure to respond to what the parents saw as their child's real needs prompted them to enroll her in a private school. There, her mood and performance improved. A year later, they approached the school about special education, but had such a hard time getting answers that they hired an attorney. When a school team finally assessed the student, it determined she wasn't entitled to special ed services.

The parents asked for a due process hearing, but the hearing officer upheld the ineligibility determination and also ruled against the parents on their charge that the district had violated its child find duty by not identifying their daughter for a special ed assessment based on what it knew about her mental health diagnoses and school performance.

The parents appealed, and a federal court reversed. It held that the student was eligible for special ed on the basis of **an emotional disturbance, defined under the IDEA's regulations as "a condition exhibiting one or more of the following characteristics over a long period of time and to a marked degree that adversely affects a child's educational performance."** The listed characteristics include:

- being unable to learn
- difficulty forming or maintaining school relationships
- having inappropriate emotional responses
- being pervasively depressed, or
- having physical symptoms or fears associated with personal or school problems.

The hearing officer wrongfully found the student's emotional disturbance didn't impact her education enough to create a duty on the part of the school to evaluate her for special ed. The school was aware of her suicide attempt, treatment for depression, the diagnoses by mental health professionals and the student's deteriorating academic performance. The district violated its child find duty by not assessing her for services. It also incorrectly determined she wasn't eligible for services once it did perform an assessment. The court ordered the district to reimburse the parents for the student's private school tuition. *N.G. v. District of Columbia*, 556 F.Supp.2d 11 (D.D.C. 2008).

◆ A student wasn't eligible for special education on the basis of emotional disturbance because his depression wasn't pervasive and didn't adversely impact his academic performance.

The student made two suicide attempts as a high school freshman and was admitted twice to a facility that provided psychiatric treatment.

As a sophomore, he turned in homework to his teacher Mr. Kieffer in which he wrote that he was planning to take over the world and then "kill ... or something that won't get me in trouble ... all the teachers that gave me F's," adding: "fair warning, Mr. Keefer [*sic*]."

The district expelled the student for threatening a teacher and paid for him to attend an alternative school for students with behavioral problems.

The student's mother asked the district to assess him for special ed. At a meeting to discuss this, she said the school should have determined the student had a mental illness disability based on his suicide attempts and psychiatric treatments as a freshman.

But after evaluating him, the school determined he wasn't eligible for special ed. The mother asked for a due process hearing. The hearing centered on whether the student's condition was an emotional disturbance that adversely affected his academic performance as defined by the IDEA's regulations. The hearing officer decided it was and that the school had to provide him services.

The district appealed in federal court. By this time, the student was a junior, not receiving special ed, successfully carrying a full class load, no longer depressed and enjoying playing on a football team. The district asked for summary judgment, and the court granted it.

The evidence showed the student didn't have an "emotional disturbance" under the IDEA. His inappropriate behavior and emotional responses were isolated incidents, not exhibited over a long period of time and to a marked degree. Also, the fact that he'd received passing grades – two As, a B and a C – at the end of his freshman year indicated his problems hadn't adversely impacted his academic performance to the degree required for him to be eligible to receive services under the IDEA. *St. Joseph-Ogden Community High School Dist. No. 305 v. Janet W.*, No. 07-CV-2079, 2008 WL 170693 (C.D. Ill. 1/17/08).

VI. WEIGHT-RELATED ISSUES

A. Weight Management

To maintain a healthy weight, students need to balance the number of calories they consume with the number they burn. To create this balance, which fosters a healthy lifestyle, students need to engage in regular physical activity and make healthy food choices, advises the Centers for Disease Control and Prevention (CDC).

The body mass index (BMI) method is a typical way to screen children and adolescents for excess weight and obesity. BMI assesses weight in relation to height. More information about BMI – plus charts – is available at *www.cdc.gov/growthcharts*.

One touted advantage of using BMI to determine whether students are at a healthy weight is that the method is minimally invasive – which is important when dealing with a vulnerable population such as children. But while asking for students' weights or having them get on a scale does not physically invade their bodies, it might trigger a big emotional reaction.

School officials might want to remember how touchy the subject of personal body weight is in this culture.

Because of the possibility of an overwhelming emotional reaction (which can be closely followed by hurtful teasing as other students pick up on it) some sensitivity on the school's part might be called for when personal body weight is discussed.

Schools – and state legislatures – are getting more involved in health initiatives to combat the problem. This is because an unhealthy body weight poses serious health issues.

1. Obesity

"Obesity" means a person's body weight is much higher than considered healthy for a person of that height.

Children whose weight is above what is deemed a healthy range have been shown to be at greater risk of developing – or suffering more from – certain diseases and other health problems. These include:

- diabetes
- asthma
- liver problems
- gall stones
- acid reflux
- sleep apnea
- hypertension
- high blood pressure
- high cholesterol levels, and
- depression linked to self-esteem.

In addition to health problems, students who are overweight or consider themselves to be overweight are more likely to attempt suicide, according to a 2009 survey conducted by the *Journal of Adolescent Health*.

More than 14,000 high school students participated in the study, which examined the links between teen suicide attempts and body mass indexes. With results equal in boys and girls, the study determined suicide risk is higher for students who:

- are obese
- are overweight, and
- have perceived notions of being too heavy.

The number of overweight students between the ages of 12 and 19 has tripled in the previous two decades, according to the CDC. The percentage of overweight children jumped from between 5% and 6% to its current percentage of around 17% – more than one obese child among every six.

The leap is even greater in some individual groups. In the early 1970s, 4% of 6- to 11-year-old children were overweight. By the early 2000s, that percentage had more than quadrupled to 18%.

The Federal Interagency Forum on Child and Family Statistics also tracked the trend. Although its numbers are slightly different, it found that among children ages 6 to 17:

- 6% were overweight in 1976-1980
- 11% were overweight in 1988-1994, and
- 18% were overweight in 2003-2004.

The good news is the 2008 CDC announcement that this upward spiral seemed to have stopped in recent years, with the percentage holding steady at around 17%. The bad news is that this is an incredibly high number.

In practical terms, this percentage means that one in six students is at risk for other health problems.

The CDC has come up with tactics to make important changes in things schools can control, such as its curriculum and policies. A 10-point plan is available at *http://www.cdc.gov/healthyyouth/keystrategies/pdf/make-a-difference.pdf.*

Schools officials are coming up with their own strategies, too. For example, more and more elementary schools are deciding to eliminate birthday "treats" – if the treat is food. There are lots of creative ways to celebrate a child's birthday at school that have nothing to do with cupcakes, such as letting the student pick a story to read to the class.

A big concern is using food as a reward, according to a 2010 report, *Bridging the Gap.* In it, school administrators were asked, "Are teachers allowed to use food as a reward for good behavior?" They answered:

- Yes (30%)
- Yes, but it is discouraged (31%)
- No (39%).

Nearly one-third of teachers are free to use food as a reward without any resistance from school administrators, according to this survey. Physical activity, such as extra recess or a game, would be a better reward for good behavior, according to First Lady Michelle Obama's "Let's Move!" plan.

A disturbing trend reported by the CDC is that Type II diabetes – formerly called "adult onset diabetes," because that was typically when it started – has begun showing up in children and adolescents.

When onset occurs this early, the complications that go with the disease (such as kidney failure and cardiovascular disease) also set in much earlier.

Schools can help students lower this risk, according to a 2010 HEALTHY national study. More than 4,600 middle school students who were overweight participated in the study and took Type II diabetes "intervention" steps at school, such as:

- going to longer gym classes
- eating more nutritious lunches
- getting classroom education on signs and symptoms, and
- engaging in other school activities that promote a healthy lifestyle.

By the end of the study, the group had a 21% lower obesity rate than their non-participating counterparts.

And according to a 2008 *New York Times* investigation, children are also increasingly being prescribed medications for other obesity-related conditions – such as acid reflux, high blood pressure, high cholesterol – that, like Type II diabetes, were virtually unseen in children 20 years ago.

Another worrying finding is that, according to 2009 research, obese adolescents have the arteries you'd expect to find in people in their forties.

Even when obesity is not linked to a serious illness, overweight children are missing more days of school, according to a study published in a 2007 issue of the journal *Obesity*. Among the 1,000 fourth- and fifth-graders the study followed, the overweight children missed two days more of school a year than the average-weight students.

Another problem related to overweight students that virtually every school has to deal with is teasing and bullying. A 2004 study showed that overweight children are more likely to be bullied than normal-weight children. There is a huge social stigma attached to obesity in this country.

State legislatures are well aware of the problems. Recent laws include policies to make sure schools provide healthier food options for students – and restrict or keep trans fat out of school food.

Published in *Pediatrics*, a 2012 study found that laws restricting the sale of sugary snacks and drinks at school help students avoid excessive weight gain. Conducted over a three-year period, the study tracked weight changes of 6,300 students. It found that students living in states with laws restricting the availability of sugar gained 2.25 fewer pounds than their peers who were able to purchase sugary snacks and drinks at school.

When it comes to wider social problems that drive up the incidence of obesity – and over which schools obviously have no control – the Department of Agriculture offers help through the National School Lunch Program and the School Breakfast Program.

Obesity is obviously caused by too many calories in and not enough burned off. But other influences significantly impact students' body weight, including their physical environments, their cultures, their personal attitudes, whether their parents are immigrants and whether their families are prosperous or struggling financially.

There is a direct correlation between poverty and obesity. Fresh fruits and vegetables cost a lot more than fast food and are not nearly as filling. The original reason behind the South's tradition of fried foods was that adding fat was a way the poor could make a limited amount of food go farther. Deep frying makes food more filling so it can feed more people. A speaker at the 2007 Childhood Obesity Conference in Oklahoma put it this way: With a dollar, you can buy either 200 nutritious calories or 800 calories of junk. Given the soaring price of produce since then, a dollar is buying even fewer nutritious calories now.

Where children live can also have a huge impact on their weight. It is almost universally true that poor areas of towns are short on two health basics: stores that stock affordable fresh food, and safe outdoor places where children can ride bikes or run around and play.

One reason behind rising obesity rates for children could be an increase in poverty.

Catholic Charities, for example, reported in late 2007 that they had experienced a 60% rise in people receiving their food services between 2002 and 2006. These services include food banks, soup kitchens and congregate meals.

And a Department of Agriculture study released in November 2007 found that more than 35.5 million Americans – or 12% of the population, more than one in every nine people – reported having to go hungry in 2006 because they didn't have enough money to meet their basic needs. Of these 35.5 million people, 12.6 million were children. Since then, of course, we've experienced a worldwide recession and soaring unemployment numbers in the United States.

Schools cannot be expected to solve the problem of poverty, but they can help to fight off its nutritional impact on their students by making sure children participate in PE classes and by making sure eligible students take advantage of the U.S. Department of Agriculture's School Breakfast Program and National School Lunch Program.

But due to the social stigma associated with poverty, the very students who most need it may not want to be seen getting a free-or-reduced meal. Depending on how things are set up at your school – or ways you can change them – it may be possible to protect students' dignity *and* get healthy food into their bodies.

The U.S. Department of Agriculture chose Michigan for a pilot program that will provide free breakfast, lunch and snacks to all students in eligible schools.

If at least 40% of students' families qualify for public assistance, schools can participate in the program, which aims to reduce the negative stigma associated with getting free lunches.

Starting in the fall of 2011, all students in Detroit Public Schools will "walk through a lunch line and not have to pay. Low-income students will not be easily identifiable and will be less likely to skip meals," a school official pointed out.

Part of the Healthy, Hunger-Free Kids Act of 2010, the free lunch program will be available to schools in additional states in coming years, with the long-term goal of being nationwide in the 2014-15 school year.

A 2010 report from the Food Research and Action Center found that many students don't take advantage of breakfasts offered at school.

So California school officials considered why students would want to skip breakfast. They identified two key problems:

- some students preferred to spend free time in the mornings with their friends, and
- some students don't arrive at school early enough to wait in line and eat.

The schools started offering more than just the typical breakfast options. Cafeteria staff still served traditional breakfasts, but also started:

- serving breakfasts in classes
- making cart rounds in the halls, where students could grab a bagged morning meal, and
- offering "second-chance" breakfasts served to students during mid-morning study halls.

2. Eating Disorders

The National Eating Disorders Screening Program (NDESP) coordinated the first nationwide screening initiative for U.S. high school students in 2000. With more than 35,000 participants, the study revealed that 25% of girls and 11% of boys reported "disordered eating and weight control symptoms severe enough to warrant clinical evaluation," according to researchers.

The study concluded that screening high school students for potential eating disorders may identify at-risk students. These students may benefit from early intervention, which would help prevent long-term health complications associated with anorexia and other eating disorders.

The NDESP is held annually during National Eating Disorders Awareness Week. More information about the program is available online at *www.mentalhealthscreenings.org*.

Students who have eating disorders usually have unrealistic fears about gaining weight and distorted perceptions about their bodies. They also tend to deny the seriousness of their illness.

Eating disorders are commonly divided into two categories: anorexia nervosa and bulimia nervosa. Many individuals exhibit symptoms from both anorexia and bulimia. The disorders can be overcome, but doing so is extremely difficult for students for two reasons:

1. Anorexia and bulimia aren't really about food. The disorders stem from a negative self-image. While onset can occur at any age, eating disorders are commonly triggered just before or during puberty. In practical terms, students are most likely to develop eating disorders during puberty because that's a time when their bodies are changing, which can lead to self-doubt. Reflecting today's extreme "societal pressure to be thin," advertising and the media only make students' self-image problems worse, according to the National Alliance on Mental Illness (NAMI).

2. In previous years, more students who suffered from anorexia and bulimia often felt alone and isolated. But technology has enabled students from around the world to interact with others who also suffer from eating disorders. The Internet has thousands of underground websites dedicated to promoting and maintaining anorexic and bulimic lifestyles. Sufferers have personified the disorders, commonly calling anorexia "Ana" and bulimia "Mia."

Some students with eating disorders even refer to "Ana" or "Mia" as their best friend. Because students communicate primarily via technology, this online support system to perpetuate the disorders makes intervention and treatment more challenging than ever. On the websites, sufferers share tips on how to trick others into thinking they are eating and how to avoid giving in to hunger pains. The pro-ana/pro-mia online community glorifies anorexia and bulimia, calling them lifestyle choices rather than disorders.

It is difficult to do so, but students can overcome their eating disorders. The following resources are available to schools to help educate students:

- Entering Adulthood: Looking at Body Image and Eating Disorders is age-appropriate material for high school students. It's available in a pdf file at *www.eric.ed.gov/PDFS/ED329840.pdf.*
- Dying to be Thin: PBS Video and Teaching Resources are available from the PBS at *www.pbs.org/wgbh/nova/thin/.*

People who suffer from anorexia refuse to eat enough to maintain a healthy minimum body weight, which is generally accepted to be within 15% of an individual's recommended body weight. Students who have anorexia:

- are often preoccupied with food and dieting
- refuse to maintain a healthy body weight, and
- believe they look fat when they're actually very thin.

In addition, anorexic females experience amenorrhea, which is the absence of three consecutive menstrual cycles due to extreme weight loss.

They also complain about feeling cold when others are comfortable. This is a sign of hypothermia, which is caused by a drop in body temperature caused by excessive weight loss. Lanugo (very fine hair, such as on newborns) may grow on the face or body. Other visible body changes include brittle nails, thin hair and dry, yellow skin.

Anorexia is potentially life-threatening. Seriously underweight students who refuse to eat have been shown to be at greater risk of developing – or suffering more from – certain diseases and other health problems, such as:

- damage to vital organs (heart, kidneys, brain)
- low heart rate
- mild anemia
- low blood pressure
- irregular heart rhythms
- heart failure
- osteoporosis, and
- death by starvation.

A 2010 research study conducted by the National Alliance on Mental Illnesses (NAMI) found that anorexia nervosa has the highest mortality rate of all psychiatric illnesses. The majority who suffer from anorexia are female adolescents between the ages of 15 and 24. However, anorexia has also been diagnosed in girls as young as seven and boys.

When people suffer from anorexia, they often develop eating rituals. For example, they may cut food into tiny pieces or refuse to eat in front of others. Common excuses for not eating include:
- "I already ate."
- "I had a big breakfast/lunch."
- "I just brushed my teeth."

Having college-educated parents may increase high school girls' risks of developing eating disorders, according to a 2009 study published in the *American Journal of Epidemiology.*

Researchers tracked more than 13,000 girls and found several links between higher education, academic excellence and eating disorders.

Having college-educated parents doubles girls' risks of developing eating disorders. Additionally, the risk is increased six-fold among girls whose maternal grandmothers have college educations. And those rates go up even more if the girl is also a good student.

For example, 15-year-old students who earned the highest grades in the class were twice as likely to require hospitalization due to an eating disorder than the 15-year-old students with the lowest scores.

This study does not indicate that education leads to eating disorders, researchers say. Instead, the findings point to a group of students who may be at higher risk than their peers.

School officials and parents can watch for warning signs that students may need help. Potential signs of an eating disorder include:
- feeling an unattainable pressure to succeed
- ongoing, unexplained weight loss, and
- going to the restroom immediately after meals.

Teachers and school officials should be aware of red flags at school that might indicate anorexia. They should watch for students who:
- have lost a significant amount of weight
- become extraordinarily reclusive
- wear very baggy clothing (to hide excessive weight loss)
- wear lots of layers (to add bulk as well as to keep warm)
- huddle around near heat vents or radiators (to keep warm)
- skip meals or bring their own low calorie food, and
- exercise during lunchtime instead of eating.

Anorexic students have specific challenges at school. Teachers and school officials can help students by:
- allowing severely malnourished students to opt out of physical activity until health improves
- remembering that lunchtime and meals are stressful for students who have eating disorders, and
- offering alternative meal locations other than the cafeteria, if the student desires.

Anorexia can be triggered by internal factors. For example, anorexic behaviors might be triggered by a personality trait. One of the most common personality traits of anorexics is perfectionism. Because of this, it may take an anorexic student longer to complete tests. Teachers can help anorexic students perform to their academic potential by allowing them to have a warm drink or a blanket to reduce chills (a common side effect), which often cause students to be distracted from their assignments.

The disorder can also be triggered by external challenges, such as peer bullying – and that can cause legal hassles for school officials.

For example, a mother in Pennsylvania filed a lawsuit against Pittsburgh Public Schools, claiming school officials failed to stop five male classmates from bullying her daughter about her weight.

The victim and the bullies were sent to the guidance counselor's office and the principal's office at least three times, according to the suit. The victim alleged that the bullying was "open and apparent."

The suit claimed the ongoing bullying the girl suffered triggered an eating disorder – which eventually required her to leave school to enter an inpatient anorexia nervosa program.

Filed under Title IX, the lawsuit didn't have to prove bullying *caused* the student's anorexia. Instead, the girl's mother only had to show the school failed to protect her daughter, which caused her to miss school.

School officials asked for dismissal, but the court refused to grant it because the U.S. Supreme Court has already ruled that peer-on-peer harassment violates Title IX if the school doesn't stop the abuse, and as a result, the victim loses educational opportunities. *Mary V. v. Pittsburgh Public Schools*, No. CA 9-1082, 2010 WL 562909 (W.D. Pa. 2/17/10).

Rather than face a costly trial, the district paid $55,000 to settle the claim.

People who suffer from bulimia binge and purge. Sufferers frequently eat unusually large amounts of food and immediately try to remove the ingested calories by inducing vomiting, taking laxatives and exercising excessively. Students with bulimia often:

- feel as if they can't control their eating behavior
- refuse to eat in public, but binge in private
- eat to the point of discomfort during binges
- use or abuse laxatives, dietary supplements and herbal remedies
- exercise obsessively, and
- worry and complain they are fat.

Most students who are bulimic maintain normal body weight or are slightly overweight, which makes it harder for school officials and parents to detect the problem. This is extremely dangerous because bulimic students face health risks including:

- amenorrhea
- abnormal bowel functioning
- damaged teeth and gums
- dehydration
- gastroesophageal reflux disorder

- irregular heart rhythms
- chronically inflamed or sore throat
- kidney problems from diuretic abuse
- swollen salivary glands in the cheeks
- sores, scar or calluses on knuckles or hands (from forced vomiting)
- depression, and
- anxiety.

The majority who suffer from bulimia are female adolescents and young adults who have been subjected to "teasing" about their appearance from family members and/or peers.

Binging and purging is done in secret, so many students who have bulimia successfully hide their disorder. Red flags that might indicate students are bulimic include:

- wearing very baggy clothing to hide weight fluctuation
- following erratic diets, such as eating only a certain color food
- making frequent trips to the restroom – especially after eating
- talking about food constantly
- bringing their own food in a purse or bookbag, and
- avoiding the cafeteria (or other social eating environments).

Eating disorders are common among student-athletes. A recent study conducted by the ERCI found that more than one-third of female athletes reported attitudes and behaviors that put them in the "at risk" category for eating disorders.

Sports that require athletes to weigh in or maintain a certain size to stay competitive further increase students' risks. Examples include gymnastics, bodybuilding, diving, wrestling, track and field, figure skating and dance.

Paying attention to warning signs is the most important thing coaches can do to help students, according to Karin Kratina of the National Eating Disorders Association. The leading causes of death for students with eating disorders are suicide and cardiac arrest. School officials and coaches can help reduce athletes' vulnerability to eating disorders by:

- adopting a positive coaching style in favor of an authoritative one
- influencing and supporting teammates by displaying health attitudes about athletes' sizes and shapes, and
- emphasizing contribution and teamwork more than a win-at-all-cost competitive mind-set.

Female student-athletes who have eating disorders have additional health risks, such as the loss of menses – which leads to calcium and bone loss. This means female athletes are more prone to stress fractures of the bones, according to a study relating to the impact of eating disorders on women's health and athletic activity conducted by the University of Minnesota Tucker Center.

The U.S. Department of Health and Human Services compiled the following list of recommendations school officials can follow to promote healthy weight control for student-athletes:

1. Nutritional needs for growth and development must be placed above athletic considerations. Fluid or food deprivation should never be allowed. There is no substitute for a healthy diet consisting of a variety of foods from all food groups with enough energy (calories) to support growth, daily physical activities, and sports activities. Daily caloric intake for most athletes should consist of a minimum of 2000 calories. Athletes need to consume enough fluids to maintain proper hydration levels.

2. In sports for which weigh-ins are required, athletes' weights and body composition should be assessed once or twice per year. The most important assessment is obtained before the beginning of the sport season. This should include a determination of body fat and minimal allowable weight when the athlete is adequately hydrated. Weigh-ins for competition should be performed immediately before competition. Athletes should be permitted to compete in championship tournaments only at the weight class in which they have competed for most other athletic events that year.

3. Male high school athletes should not have less than 7% body fat. This minimal allowable body fat may be too low for some athletes and result in sub-optimal performance. Female athletes should consume enough energy (calories) and nutrients to meet their energy requirements and experience normal menses. There are no recommendations on body-fat percentages for female athletes.

4. A program for the purpose of gaining or losing weight should (a) be started early to permit a gradual weight gain or loss over a realistic time period, (b) permit a change of 1.5% or less of one's body weight per week, (c) permit the loss of weight to be fat loss and the gain of weight to be muscle mass, (d) be coupled with an appropriate training program (both strength and conditioning), and (e) incorporate a well-balanced diet with adequate energy (calories), carbohydrates, protein, and fat. After athletes obtain their desired weight, they should be encouraged to maintain a constant weight and avoid fluctuations. A weight-loss plan for athletic purposes should never be instituted before the ninth grade.

5. Any athlete who loses a significant amount of fluid during sports participation should weigh in before and after practices, games, meets, and competitions. Each pound of weight loss should be replaced with one pint of fluid containing carbohydrates and electrolytes before the next practice or competition. Fluids should be available, and the drinking of fluids should be encouraged at all practices and competitions.

6. Weight loss accomplished by over-exercising; using rubber suits, steam baths, or saunas; prolonged fasting; fluid reduction; vomiting; or using anorexic drugs, laxatives, diuretics, diet pills, insulin, stimulants, nutritional supplements, or other legal or illegal drugs and/or nicotine should be prohibited at all ages.

7. Athletes who need to gain weight should consult their physician for resources on healthy weight gain and referral to a registered dietitian. They should be discouraged from gaining excessive weight, which may impair performance, increase the likelihood of heat illness, and increase the risk of developing complications from obesity.

8. Ergogenic aids and non-therapeutic use of supplements for weight management should be prohibited.

9. Young athletes should be involved in a total athletic program that includes acquisition of athletic skills and improvement in speed, flexibility, strength, and physical conditioning while maintaining good nutrition and normal hydration. This should be done under the supervision of a coach who stresses a positive attitude, character building, teamwork, and safety.

B. Nutrition

1. School Meals

The U.S. Department of Agriculture's School Breakfast Program and National School Lunch Program require schools to serve meals that are low in fat and provide a certain percentage of the Recommended Dietary Allowances of protein, Vitamin A, Vitamin C, iron, calcium and calories – one-third for school lunches and one-quarter for school breakfasts.

Poor nutrition, from which many children suffer, has a negative impact on brain development and school performance. The National PTA's website notes that children who eat meals served by the school meal programs:
- get more nutritious meals than children who do not, and
- show improved standardized test scores, attendance and class participation.

Another advantage of school meal programs is that they are based on parental income, so they are either free or available at a greatly reduced cost to children that really need them.

The CDC has announced a four-part plan intended to help schools teach students that wellness is a lifestyle. It suggests that schools:
1. establish a coordinated school health program that includes these eight components:
   - health education
   - physical education
   - counseling, psychological and social services
   - health services
   - nutrition services
   - healthy school environment
   - parent/community involvement, and
   - staff wellness
2. establish a school health council to promote healthy eating and exercise
   - Since 2004, federal law has required all school districts

participating in federally funded school meal programs to establish a local school wellness policy through a process that involves parents, students, school representatives, and the public. A school health council can meet that requirement.

3. assess existing health programs and suggest improvements
    *   To help, the CDC provides a self-assessment and planning tool at *apps.nccd.cdc.gov/shi.*
4. improve the school's food and exercise policies
    *   For example, schools can find ways to make cafeteria food both healthy and tasty and come up with ways to incorporate exercise into the school day.

One concern is that some schools promote unhealthy lifestyles by offering too many sugar-sweetened soft drinks in school vending machines. However, a 2006 CDC study of school health policies found that many schools had replaced soda with bottled water in vending machines. In 2000, only about 29% of schools offered bottled water. In 2006, the percentage was up to 46%.

In spite of the continued push to provide healthier school meals, about half of elementary students could still buy whole milk, sodas, sports drinks and sugary fruit drinks during the 2009-10 and 2010-11 school years, according to a study published online in the *Archives of Pediatrics & Adolescent Medicine.*

You might be wondering: How is that possible?

Students purchased the sugary drinks and whole milk at school in *a la carte* lines, snack bars and vending machines. Because healthy beverages are an essential part of a healthy diet, the Institute of Medicine recommends that – if schools have *a la carte* lines and vending machines – they should offer the following beverages only:

*   100% fruit or vegetable juice
*   non-fat or 1% milk, and
*   water.

In 2010, former governor of California Arnold Schwarzenegger signed SB 1413 into law. The legislation requires public schools in the state to provide students with access to fresh, free drinking water in food service areas during meal times at schools. The law took effect on Jan. 1, 2011.

To meet the new legal requirement, schools:

*   gave students 8-ounce bottles of water with their meals, and
*   supplied 5-gallon containers of bottled water and paper cups for students in the lunchroom.

And that's not the only change in California. Jamie Oliver's Food Revolution convinced the Los Angeles Unified School District (LAUSD) to remove strawberry- and chocolate-flavored milk from school menus.

When students returned to school in the fall of 2011, they had "wholesome plain white milk with their meals instead of liquid candy," according to the Food Revolution website.

Oliver's battle with LAUSD was televised on the ABC show, *Jamie Oliver's Food Revolution*. On the show, Oliver orchestrated stunts, such as filling school buses with sugar to help viewers visualize unhealthy choices. But behind the scenes, Oliver worked with schools and parents to help share nutritional information about flavored milk. A downloadable Sweetened Milk Calculator and nutritional milk fact sheet is at *http://sn.im/milk444*.

While that's good news, other studies show there's still room for improvement in school nutrition. For example, in 2010, the Physicians Committee for Responsible Medicine (PCRM) analyzed lunch menus from 18 schools across the country.

The result? Schools are still serving meals that are too high in saturated fat and sodium, according to PCRM nutritionist Kathryn Strong.

After the analysis was complete, PCRM identified what it called the worst lunches to serve to students. Here are the top five worst school lunches:

- Beef and cheese nachos. Topping the list, this meal has too much sodium (1,500 mg) and fat (24 g).
- Meatloaf and potatoes packs unhealthy calories (472) and cholesterol (78 mg).
- Cheeseburgers, which often have more saturated fat than students should have in an entire meal.
- Grilled cheese sandwiches and cheese quesadillas (tied) are loaded with saturated fat (7 g) and sodium (nearly 1,000 mg).
- Pepperoni pizza. The average slice contains saturated fat (6 g) and its processed meat has also been shown to increase cancer risk.

Schools can help children develop healthier eating habits by offering:

- more fruits, vegetables, lean meats and whole grains
- less fat, and
- appropriate portion sizes.

Students may balk at the options, but schools can take steps to encourage students to eat healthier foods, according to research conducted at Cornell University.

Smarter Lunchroom researchers found that students are more likely to choose healthy meals when schools:

- provide healthy "grab and go" options in the lunchroom
- offer fruits and veggies as "default" sides
- make a gradual switch to whole grains, and
- sell suggestively at the register, as in "Would you like to add an apple?"

Be prepared to think creatively, too. For example, school officials in Minnesota looked for ways to get students to at least try healthy options instead of just grabbing the typical go-to favorites, such as the ones listed above. But students weren't interested, so the staff stirred up some intrigue by holding a "coolest veggie" contest.

Cafeteria staffers passed out sample cups of veggies to students who were waiting in the lunch line. Four veggies were in the running: jicama sticks, portabella mushrooms, red peppers and pickled beets. After lunch, students filled out a survey to vote for their favorite. When the votes were tallied, jicama sticks was named the coolest veggie.

Getting students' input helped the school find out which healthy options students would eat. Jicama sticks remained one of the students' favorite veggies on the lunch menu for years.

School officials can do other things to promote healthy lunch choices – and doing so doesn't have to break the budget. In 2010, Smarter Lunchrooms suggested the following well-planned tweaks to the layout of school cafeterias to improve students' lunch choices:

- The cash register. Remember – convenience is key! Students stand in line waiting. What last-minute items of convenience will they add to their trays? Replace chips and other pre-packaged goodies with fresh fruit or 100% fruit juice.
- The menu. What's in a name? Turns out, plenty when it comes to food. One cafeteria reported a 28% increase in sales after "vegetable soup" was renamed "rich vegetable medley soup." Smarter Lunchrooms recommends three specific food labels: nostalgic, regional and descriptive. For example: Grandma's chicken noodle soup, real Boston baked beans and creamy corn chowder.
- Walls and tables. Get creative by adding brightly colored posters of healthy fruits and veggies – and nutritional info – on cafeteria walls. Add a "try it table" – use table tents to invite students who are waiting in line to sample healthy options.
- Display cases. Lighting affects the way students view their choices. Make sure healthy lunch options are visually appealing by using well-lit display cases. Place the healthiest options at students' eye levels.
- The web. More and more cafeterias are putting their menus on school websites. Students who plan their meals based on online menus usually stick to healthier food choices than students who make decisions on a whim – while they're waiting in line and starving. If you haven't posted your menu on the web yet, it might be a good time to consider going online.

A 2010 investigation published in *USA Today* uncovered problems with food contamination in schools.

In response, USDA Secretary Tom Vilsak pledged the government will increase efforts to communicate with schools regarding potential food contaminations, according to a *Reuters* report. School nutrition programs are expected to undergo a complete overhaul in the next couple of years, the report said.

The Healthy School Meals Act of 2010 is one of the catalysts behind school lunch reform. The legislation required key changes to be tested in a pilot program, which was an overwhelming success in Berkeley, California schools.

President Obama signed the Healthy, Hunger Free Act of 2010 on

Dec. 13, 2010. The new legislation:

- improves access to federally funded school meals by using Medicaid data to automatically determine eligibility for students
- increases focus on nutrition and health by improving the quality of school meals, removing junk food from schools and strengthening wellness policies
- improves school lunch program management by providing training for school food service providers and improving recall procedures in school settings, and
- saves taxpayer money by eliminating a Supplemental Nutrition Assistance Program (SNAP) benefit.

Key provisions included a pilot program conducted by the USDA to improve students' nutrition and eating habits to the National School Lunch and Breakfast Programs. The pilot program included free daily breakfasts for all students and organic lunch options. Changes included:

- incorporating more plant-based products into school cafeterias. The USDA also provides training to employees about nutritional information and food preparation
- offering incentives for schools to provide healthy plant-based meals. If districts offer at least two-thirds of students plant-based entrees on the daily lunch menu, those schools will receive additional USDA funding – 25% of the districts' total commodity assistance. The additional funding can be used to purchase additional plant-based food, such as fresh or frozen produce, legumes and whole grains.
- removing non-dairy milk substitution restrictions. Due to an increase in the number of students who have food allergies and suffer from lactose intolerance, the School Lunch program will be permitted to offer a milk substitute, such as soy- , almond- or rice-based fluids. One key requirement to note: The substitute must meet USDA nutritional standards. Additionally, students are no longer required to have written permission to choose milk alternatives, and schools will be reimbursed for meals that include healthy milk substitutions.

In response to the Healthy, Hunger-Free Kids Act of 2010, the U.S. Department of Agriculture (USDA) proposed and finalized rules on school nutrition standards, which took effect at the start of the 2012-13 school year.

Under the new standards, school meals must:

- provide students with twice the amount of fruits and veggies as previously offered
- contain only whole grains
- include only low-fat or fat-free milk
- stay with sodium limits, and
- fall between minimum and maximum calorie requirements.

The USDA provided schools with a sample "Before and After" lunch menu, available at *http://sn.im/usda551*.

In 2011, the USDA also replaced the familiar food pyramid. On the new website, recommendations are now illustrated on a dinner plate in an attempt to help students visualize portion sizes of a healthy meal.

ChooseMyPlate.gov includes:

* nutrition information
* interactive games for students
* lesson plans for teachers, and
* poster displays for classrooms.

Visit *http://choosemyplate.gov/kids/index.html* to access these free resources.

In 2010, First Lady Michelle Obama introduced "Let's Move!" an all-encompassing initiative designed to improve student health. The USDA's voluntary HealthierUS School Challenge was incorporated into "Let's Move!" and a monetary award was added to encourage school officials to create healthier environments by promoting healthy nutrition and physical activity.

The financial incentive improved participation, as 809 awards were doled out to schools in 37 states within the first seven months of incorporation into "Let's Move!" In 2011, the program met its goal to expand, reaching 1273 certified schools in 43 states.

For more information on participating in the HealthierUS School Challenge, go to *www.fns.usda.gov/tn/healthierus/index.html.*

2. Education

Wellness initiatives are designed to foster healthy food choices at a young age and to create habits that last a lifetime. Doing so helps students reduce health risks and increase their quality of life. Also, as opposed to going on and off reduced-calorie diets, developing good eating and exercise habits helps students maintain a healthy weight while ensuring their bodies have the nutrients to grow into healthy adults.

A key element is educating students on the benefits of healthy choices. Talk about it. Promote it at your school.

For example, remind students that being healthy is a lifestyle. Every healthy thing they do today – such as eating an apple instead of a candy bar or taking the stairs instead of the elevator – will pay off tomorrow. Getting into healthy habits has a cumulative effect.

Many school districts are finding ways to incorporate healthy, hands-on lessons into the school curriculum. For example, middle school students in Missouri are learning how to grow their own herb and vegetable gardens during science classes.

School officials in Maine have taken a light-hearted approach to encourage young students to make healthy choices. Each March during National Nutrition Month, teachers dress up as fruits and vegetables. But they don't stop there. Dressed in rented watermelon, banana, broccoli and carrot costumes, teachers march in a special parade in the hallway while students cheer as their favorites march by.

School officials noted that the parade helps remove some of the students' negative ideas associated with fruits and vegetables. The annual event has encouraged more students to eat – or at least try – fruits and vegetables. When financial constraints threatened the parade, school officials found a way to save the program from the budget ax. They found they could borrow costumes for free from their state department of education, as long as they made reservations in advance.

School officials should also consider the products promoted when students participate in school fundraising efforts. Do students sell candy bars? Are other options available? In 2000, almost 70% of schools sold cookies, candy and other baked goods to raise money. That number dropped to just over 50% in 2006, according to a study conducted by the Department of Health for the City of Saint Louis. While the reduction is good, there's always room to improve on showing students how school lessons should be applied in real-life settings. Non-food items that can be sold during school fundraisers or used as rewards include:

- special school supplies
- homemade crafts
- gift certificates to local gyms or mini-golf courses, and
- discount coupons to local sporting goods stores.

C. Physical Activity

There are six national standards for physical education (PE) in U.S. schools.
1. development of motor/movement skills
2. knowledge and application of movement concepts
3. personal/social responsibility
4. regular participation in physical activity
5. development and maintenance of physical fitness, and
6. valuing physical activity.

Every student in the U.S. needs physical activity, whether it's in a formal PE program or free play at recess – and more students are getting it at school. According to a 2010 study conducted by the National Association for Sport and Physical Education (NASPE) most states mandate PE. Here's the breakdown:

- 43 states mandate PE in elementary schools (up from 36 in 2006)
- 40 states mandate PE in middle schools (up from 33 in 2006), and
- 46 states mandate it for high school students (up from 42 in 2006).

While that's an improvement, the study noted that most states still do not specify minimum requirements. The NASPE recommends that schools provide at least 150 minutes of PE instruction each week to elementary school students. Middle and high school students need more PE – at least 225 minutes per week, according to recommendations.

The study also found about half of schools allow PE exemptions and/or substitutions, which the NASPE calls loopholes that reduce the effectiveness of the mandates.

In 2010, 32 states let students substitute other physical activities for their required PE credits, up from 27 states in 2006. Common allowed substitutions include:

- JROTC (18 states)
- interscholastic sports (15 states)
- marching band (10 states), and
- cheerleading (10 states).

In 2010, 30 states allowed schools or districts to grant waivers or exemptions from PE requirements. That's up from 18 states in 2006. Common reasons schools grant PE exemptions for students include:

- health issues
- physical disabilities
- religious beliefs, and
- early graduation.

Here's proof that technology's everywhere: Currently 22 states allow students to earn required PE credits online. But fewer than half of those states (only 10) require online PE classes to be taught by state-certified physical education teachers.

Five states – Illinois, Iowa, Massachusetts, New Mexico and Vermont – were recognized as the most consistent because every K-12 student was required to take PE classes in 2010. Two – New Jersey and Rhode Island – required students in grades one through twelve to take PE classes in 2010.

First Lady Michelle Obama's "Let's Move!" is one of the latest initiatives to increase students' activity. The program challenges all students to earn a Presidential Active Lifestyle Award (PALA). To earn a PALA, students must document their active exercise – at least 60 minutes per day, five days a week, for six weeks. Students can register at *www.fitness.gov* and log their daily activity. At the end of six weeks, students will receive a certificate of recognition from the President. More importantly, they'll be building healthy habits and feeling better with a more active lifestyle.

CHAPTER EIGHT

Statutes and Regulations

The following federal statutes and regulations address school safety and security issues.

I. SAFE AND DRUG-FREE SCHOOLS AND COMMUNITIES ACT

20 USC § 7101 et seq.

SUBCHAPTER IV - 21ST CENTURY SCHOOLS

PART A - SAFE AND DRUG-FREE SCHOOLS AND COMMUNITIES
7101. Short title.
7102. Purpose.
7103. Authorization of appropriations.

SUBPART 1 - STATE GRANTS
7111. Reservations and allotments.
    (a) Reservations.
    (b) State allotments.
    (c) Limitation.
7112. Reservation of State funds for safe and drug-free schools.
    (a) State reservation for the chief executive officer of a State.
    (b) In State distribution.
    (c) State activities.
7113. State application.
    (a) In general.
    (b) Interim application.
    (c) Approval process.
7114. Local educational agency program.
    (a) In general.
    (b) Eligibility.
    (c) Development.
    (d) Contents of applications.

PART A - SAFE AND DRUG-FREE SCHOOLS AND COMMUNITIES

Sec. 7101. Short title

This part may be cited as the "Safe and Drug-Free Schools and Communities Act."

Sec. 7102. Purpose

The purpose of this part is to support programs that prevent violence in and around schools; that prevent the illegal use of alcohol, tobacco, and drugs; that involve parents and communities; and that are coordinated with related Federal, State, school, and community efforts and resources to foster a safe and drug-free learning environment that supports student academic achievement, through the provision of Federal assistance to -

(1) States for grants to local educational agencies and consortia of such agencies to establish, operate, and improve local programs of school drug

and violence prevention and early intervention;

(2) States for grants to, and contracts with, community-based organizations and public and private entities for programs of drug and violence prevention and early intervention, including community-wide drug and violence prevention planning and organizing activities;

(3) States for development, training, technical assistance, and coordination activities; and

(4) public and private entities to provide technical assistance; conduct training, demonstrations, and evaluation; and to provide supplementary services and community-wide drug and violence prevention planning and organizing activities for the prevention of drug use and violence among students and youth.

Sec. 7103. Authorization of appropriations

There are authorized to be appropriated -

(1) $650,000,000 for fiscal year 2002, and such sums as may be necessary for each of the 5 succeeding fiscal years, for State grants under subpart 1 of this part; and

(2) such sums for fiscal year 2002, and for each of the 5 succeeding fiscal years, for national programs under subpart 2 of this part.

SUBPART 1 - STATE GRANTS

Sec. 7111. Reservations and allotments

(a) Reservations

(1) In general

From the amount made available under section 7103(1) of this title to carry out this subpart for each fiscal year, the Secretary -

(A) shall reserve 1 percent or $4,750,000 (whichever is greater) of such amount for grants to Guam, American Samoa, the United States Virgin Islands, and the Commonwealth of the Northern Mariana Islands, to be allotted in accordance with the Secretary's determination of their respective needs and to carry out programs described in this subpart;

(B) shall reserve 1 percent or $4,750,000 (whichever is greater) of such amount for the Secretary of the Interior to carry out programs described in this subpart for Indian youth; and

(C) shall reserve 0.2 percent of such amount for Native Hawaiians to be used under section 7117 of this title to carry out programs described in this subpart.

(2) Other reservations

From the amount made available under section 7103(2) of this title to carry out subpart 2 of this part for each fiscal year, the Secretary -

(A) may reserve not more than $2,000,000 for the national impact evaluation required by section 7132(a) of this title;

(B) notwithstanding section 3 of the No Child Left Behind Act of 2001, shall reserve an amount necessary to make continuation grants to grantees under the Safe Schools/Healthy Students initiative (under the same terms and conditions as provided for in the grants involved).

(b) State allotments

(1) In general

Except as provided in paragraph (2), the Secretary shall, for each fiscal year, allot among the States -

(A) one-half of the remainder not reserved under subsection (a) of this section according to the ratio between the school-aged population of each State and the school-aged population of all the States; and

(B) one-half of such remainder according to the ratio between the amount each State received under section 6334 of this title for the preceding year and the sum of such amounts received by all the States.

(2) Minimum

For any fiscal year, no State shall be allotted under this subsection an amount that is less than the greater of -

(A) one-half of 1 percent of the total amount allotted to all the States under this subsection; or

(B) the amount such State received for fiscal year 2001 under section 4111 as such section was in effect the day preceding January 8, 2002.

(3) Reallotment

(A) Reallotment for failure to apply

If any State does not apply for an allotment under this subpart for a fiscal year, the Secretary shall reallot the amount of the State's allotment to the remaining States in accordance with this section.

(B) Reallotment of unused funds

The Secretary may reallot any amount of any allotment to a State if the Secretary determines that the State will be unable to use such amount within 2 years of such allotment. Such reallotments shall be made on the same basis as allotments are made under paragraph (1).

(4) Definition

In this section the term "State" means each of the 50 States, the District of Columbia, and the Commonwealth of Puerto Rico.

(c) Limitation

Amounts appropriated under section 7103(2) of this title for a fiscal year may not be increased above the amounts appropriated under such section for the previous fiscal year unless the amount appropriated under section 7103(1) of this title for the fiscal year involved are at least 10 percent greater that (!2) the amounts appropriated under such section 7103(1) of this title for the previous fiscal year.

Sec. 7112. Reservation of State funds for safe and drug-free schools

(a) State reservation for the chief executive officer of a State

(1) In general

The chief executive officer of a State may reserve not more than 20 percent of the total amount allocated to a State under section 7111(b) of this title for each fiscal year to award competitive grants and contracts to local educational agencies, community-based organizations (including community anti-drug coalitions) other public entities and private organizations, and consortia thereof. Such grants and contracts shall be used to carry out the comprehensive State plan described in section 7113(a) of this title through programs or activities that complement and support activities of local educational agencies described in section 7115(b) of this title. Such officer shall award grants based on -

(A) the quality of the program or activity proposed; and

(B) how the program or activity meets the principles of effectiveness described in section 7115(a) of this title.

(2) Priority

In making such grants and contracts under this section, a chief executive officer shall give priority to programs and activities that prevent illegal drug use and violence for -

(A) children and youth who are not normally served by State educational agencies or local educational agencies; or

(B) populations that need special services or additional resources (such as youth in juvenile detention facilities, runaway or homeless children and youth, pregnant and parenting teenagers, and school dropouts).

(3) Special consideration

In awarding funds under paragraph (1), a chief executive officer shall give special consideration to grantees that pursue a comprehensive approach to drug and violence prevention that includes providing and incorporating mental health services related to drug and violence prevention in their program.

(4) Peer review

Grants or contracts awarded under this section shall be subject to a peer review process.

(5) Use of funds

Grants and contracts under this section shall be used to implement drug and violence prevention activities, including -

(A) activities that complement and support local educational agency activities under section 7115 of this title, including developing and implementing activities to prevent and reduce violence associated with prejudice and intolerance;

(B) dissemination of information about drug and violence prevention; and

(C) development and implementation of community-wide drug and violence prevention planning and organizing.

(6) Administrative costs

The chief executive officer of a State may use not more than 3 percent of the amount described in paragraph (1) for the administrative costs incurred in carrying out the duties of such officer under this section.

(b) In State distribution

(1) In general

A State educational agency shall distribute not less than 93 percent of the amount made available to the State under section 7111(b) of this title, less the amount reserved under subsection (a) of this section, to its local educational agencies.

(2) State administration costs

(A) In general

A State educational agency may use not more than 3 percent of the amount made available to the State under section 7111(b) of this title for each fiscal year less the amount reserved under subsection (a) of this section, for State educational agency administrative costs, including the implementation of the uniform management information and reporting system as provided for under subsection (c)(3) of this section.

(B) Additional amounts for the uniform management information system

In the case of fiscal year 2002, a State educational agency may, in addition to amounts provided for in subparagraph (A), use 1 percent of the amount made available to the State educational agency under section 7111(b) of this title for each fiscal year less the amount reserved under subsection (a) of this section, for implementation of the uniform management information and reporting system as provided for under subsection (c)(3) of this section.

(c) State activities

(1) In general

A State educational agency may use not more than 5 percent of the amount made available to the State under section 7111(b) of this title for each fiscal year less the amount reserved under subsection (a) of this section, for activities described in this subsection.

(2) Activities

A State educational agency shall use the amounts described in paragraph (1), either directly, or through grants and contracts, to plan, develop, and implement capacity building, technical assistance and training, evaluation, program improvement services, and coordination activities for local educational agencies, community-based organizations, and other public and private entities. Such uses -

(A) shall meet the principles of effectiveness described in section 7115(a) of this title;

(B) shall complement and support local uses of funds under section 7115(b) of this title;

(C) shall be in accordance with the purposes of this part; and

(D) may include, among others activities -

(i) identification, development, evaluation, and dissemination of drug and violence prevention strategies, programs, activities, and other information;

(ii) training, technical assistance, and demonstration projects to address violence that is associated with prejudice and intolerance; and

(iii) financial assistance to enhance drug and violence

prevention resources available in areas that serve large numbers of low-income children, are sparsely populated, or have other special needs.

(3) Uniform management information and reporting system

(A) Information and statistics

A State shall establish a uniform management information and reporting system.

(B) Uses of funds

A State may use funds described in subparagraphs (A) and (B) of subsection (b)(2) of this section, either directly or through grants and contracts, to implement the uniform management information and reporting system described in subparagraph (A), for the collection of information on -

(i) truancy rates;

(ii) the frequency, seriousness, and incidence of violence and drug-related offenses resulting in suspensions and expulsions in elementary schools and secondary schools in the State;

(iii) the types of curricula, programs, and services provided by the chief executive officer, the State educational agency, local educational agencies, and other recipients of funds under this subpart; and

(iv) the incidence and prevalence, age of onset, perception of health risk, and perception of social disapproval of drug use and violence by youth in schools and communities.

(C) Compilation of statistics

In compiling the statistics required for the uniform management information and reporting system, the offenses described in subparagraph (B)(ii) shall be defined pursuant to the State's criminal code, but shall not identify victims of crimes or persons accused of crimes. The collected data shall include incident reports by school officials, anonymous student surveys, and anonymous teacher surveys.

(D) Reporting

The information described under subparagraph (B) shall be reported to the public and the data referenced in clauses (i) and (ii) of such subparagraph shall be reported to the State on a school-by-school basis.

(E) Limitation

Nothing in this subsection shall be construed to authorize the Secretary to require particular policies, procedures, or practices with respect to crimes committed on school property or school security.

Sec. 7113. State application

(a) In general

In order to receive an allotment under section 7111(b) of this title for any fiscal year, a State shall submit to the Secretary, at such time as the Secretary may require, an application that -

(1) contains a comprehensive plan for the use of funds by the State educational agency and the chief executive officer of the State to provide safe, orderly, and drug-free schools and communities through programs and

activities that complement and support activities of local educational agencies under section 7115(b) of this title, that comply with the principles of effectiveness under section 7115(a) of this title, and that otherwise are in accordance with the purpose of this part;

(2) describes how activities funded under this subpart will foster a safe and drug-free learning environment that supports academic achievement;

(3) provides an assurance that the application was developed in consultation and coordination with appropriate State officials and others, including the chief executive officer, the chief State school officer, the head of the State alcohol and drug abuse agency, the heads of the State health and mental health agencies, the head of the State criminal justice planning agency, the head of the State child welfare agency, the head of the State board of education, or their designees, and representatives of parents, students, and community-based organizations;

(4) describes how the State educational agency will coordinate such agency's activities under this subpart with the chief executive officer's drug and violence prevention programs under this subpart and with the prevention efforts of other State agencies and other programs, as appropriate, in accordance with (5) provides an assurance that funds reserved under section 7112(a) of this title will not duplicate the efforts of the State educational agency and local educational agencies with regard to the provision of school-based drug and violence prevention activities and that those funds will be used to serve populations not normally served by the State educational agencies and local educational agencies and populations that need special services, such as school dropouts, suspended and expelled students, youth in detention centers, runaway or homeless children and youth, and pregnant and parenting youth;

(6) provides an assurance that the State will cooperate with, and assist, the Secretary in conducting data collection as required by section 7132 of this title;

(7) provides an assurance that the local educational agencies in the State will comply with the provisions of section 7881 of this title pertaining to the participation of private school children and teachers in the programs and activities under this subpart;

(8) provides an assurance that funds under this subpart will be used to increase the level of State, local, and other non-Federal funds that would, in the absence of funds under this subpart, be made available for programs and activities authorized under this subpart, and in no case supplant such State, local, and other non-Federal funds;

(9) contains the results of a needs assessment conducted by the State for drug and violence prevention programs, which shall be based on ongoing State evaluation activities, including data on -

(A) the incidence and prevalence of illegal drug use and violence among youth in schools and communities, including the age of onset, the perception of health risks, and the perception of social disapproval among such youth;

(B) the prevalence of risk factors, including high or increasing rates of reported cases of child abuse or domestic violence;

(C) the prevalence of protective factors, buffers, or assets; and

(D) other variables in the school and community identified through scientifically based research;

(10) provides a statement of the State's performance measures for drug and violence prevention programs and activities to be funded under this subpart that will be focused on student behavior and attitudes, derived from the needs assessment described in paragraph (9), and be developed in consultation between the State and local officials, and that consist of -

(A) performance indicators for drug and violence prevention programs and activities; and

(B) levels of performance for each performance indicator;

(11) describes the procedures the State will use for assessing and publicly reporting progress toward meeting the performance measures described in paragraph (10);

(12) provides an assurance that the State application will be available for public review after submission of the application;

(13) describes the special outreach activities that will be carried out by the State educational agency and the chief executive officer of the State to maximize the participation of community-based organizations of demonstrated effectiveness that provide services such as mentoring programs in low-income communities;

(14) describes how funds will be used by the State educational agency and the chief executive officer of the State to support, develop, and implement community-wide comprehensive drug and violence prevention planning and organizing activities;

(15) describes how input from parents will be sought regarding the use of funds by the State educational agency and the chief executive officer of the State;

(16) describes how the State educational agency will review applications from local educational agencies, including how the agency will receive input from parents in such review;

(17) describes how the State educational agency will monitor the implementation of activities under this subpart, and provide technical assistance for local educational agencies, community-based organizations, other public entities, and private organizations;

(18) describes how the chief executive officer of the State will award funds under section 7112(a) of this title and implement a plan for monitoring the performance of, and providing technical assistance to, recipients of such funds; and

(19) includes any other information the Secretary may require.

(b) Interim application

(1) Authority

Notwithstanding any other provision of this section, a State may submit for fiscal year 2002 a 1-year interim application and plan for the use of funds under this subpart that is consistent with the requirements of this section and contains such information as the Secretary may specify in regulations.

(2) Purpose

The purpose of such interim application and plan shall be to afford the State the opportunity to fully develop and review such State's application and comprehensive plan otherwise required by this section.

(3) Exception

A State may not receive a grant under this subpart for a fiscal year after fiscal year 2002 unless the Secretary has approved such State's application and comprehensive plan as described in subsection (a) of this section.

(c) Approval process

(1) Deemed approval

An application submitted by a State pursuant to this section shall undergo peer review by the Secretary and shall be deemed to be approved by the Secretary unless the Secretary makes a written determination, prior to the expiration of the 120-day period beginning on the date on which the Secretary received the application, that the application is not in compliance with this subpart.

(2) Disapproval

The Secretary shall not finally disapprove the application, except after giving the State educational agency and the chief executive officer of the State notice and an opportunity for a hearing.

(3) Notification

If the Secretary finds that the application is not in compliance, in whole or in part, with this subpart, the Secretary shall -

(A) give the State educational agency and the chief executive officer of the State notice and an opportunity for a hearing; and

(B) notify the State educational agency and the chief executive officer of the State of the finding of noncompliance, and in such notification, shall -

(i) cite the specific provisions in the application that are not in compliance; and

(ii) request additional information, only as to the noncompliant provisions, needed to make the application compliant.

(4) Response

If the State educational agency and the chief executive officer of the State respond to the Secretary's notification described in paragraph (3)(B) during the 45-day period beginning on the date on which the agency received the notification, and resubmit the application with the requested information described in paragraph (3)(B)(ii), the Secretary shall approve or disapprove such application prior to the later of -

(A) the expiration of the 45-day period beginning on the date on which the application is resubmitted; or

(B) the expiration of the 120-day period described in paragraph (1).

(5) Failure to respond

If the State educational agency and the chief executive officer of the

State do not respond to the Secretary's notification described in paragraph (3)(B) during the 45-day period beginning on the date on which the agency received the notification, such application shall be deemed to be disapproved.

Sec. 7114. Local educational agency program
(a) In general

(1) Funds to local educational agencies

A State shall provide the amount made available to the State under this subpart, less the amounts reserved under section 7112 of this title to local educational agencies for drug and violence prevention and education programs and activities as follows:

(A) 60 percent of such amount based on the relative amount such agencies received under part A of subchapter I of this chapter for the preceding fiscal year.

(B) 40 percent of such amount based on the relative enrollments in public and private nonprofit elementary schools and secondary schools within the boundaries of such agencies.

(2) Administrative costs

Of the amount received under paragraph (1), a local educational agency may use not more than 2 percent for the administrative costs of carrying out its responsibilities under this subpart.

(3) Return of funds to State; reallocation

(A) Return

Except as provided in subparagraph (B), upon the expiration of the 1-year period beginning on the date on which a local educational agency receives its allocation under this subpart -

(i) such agency shall return to the State educational agency any funds from such allocation that remain unobligated; and

(ii) the State educational agency shall reallocate any such amount to local educational agencies that have submitted plans for using such amount for programs or activities on a timely basis.

(B) Carryover

In any fiscal year, a local educational agency, may retain for obligation in the succeeding fiscal year -

(i) an amount equal to not more than 25 percent of the allocation it received under this subpart for such fiscal year; or

(ii) upon a demonstration of good cause by such agency and approval by the State educational agency, an amount that exceeds 25 percent of such allocation.

(C) Reallocation

If a local educational agency chooses not to apply to receive the amount allocated to such agency under this subsection, or if such agency's application under subsection (d) of this section is disapproved by the State educational agency, the State educational agency shall reallocate such amount to one or more of its other local educational agencies.

(b) Eligibility

To be eligible to receive a subgrant under this subpart, a local educational agency desiring a subgrant shall submit an application to the State educational agency in accordance with subsection (d) of this section. Such an application shall be amended, as necessary, to reflect changes in the activities and programs of the local educational agency.

(c) Development

(1) Consultation

(A) In general

A local educational agency shall develop its application through timely and meaningful consultation with State and local government representatives, representatives of schools to be served (including private schools), teachers and other staff, parents, students, community-based organizations, and others with relevant and demonstrated expertise in drug and violence prevention activities (such as medical, mental health, and law enforcement professionals).

(B) Continued consultation

On an ongoing basis, the local educational agency shall consult with such representatives and organizations in order to seek advice regarding how best to coordinate such agency's activities under this subpart with other related strategies, programs, and activities being conducted in the community.

(2) Design and development

To ensure timely and meaningful consultation under paragraph (1), a local educational agency at the initial stages of design and development of a program or activity shall consult, in accordance with this subsection, with appropriate entities and persons on issues regarding the design and development of the program or activity, including efforts to meet the principles of effectiveness described in section 7115(a) of this title.

(d) Contents of applications

An application submitted by a local educational agency under this section shall contain -

(1) an assurance that the activities or programs to be funded comply with the principles of effectiveness described in section 7115(a) of this title and foster a safe and drug-free learning environment that supports academic achievement;

(2) a detailed explanation of the local educational agency's comprehensive plan for drug and violence prevention, including a description of -

(A) how the plan will be coordinated with programs under this chapter, and other Federal, State, and local programs for drug and violence prevention, in accordance with section 7846 of this title;

(B) the local educational agency's performance measures for drug and violence prevention programs and activities, that shall consist of -

(i) performance indicators for drug and violence prevention programs and activities; including -

(I) specific reductions in the prevalence of identified risk factors; and

(II) specific increases in the prevalence of protective factors, buffers, or assets if any have been identified; and

(ii) levels of performance for each performance indicator;

(C) how such agency will assess and publicly report progress toward attaining its performance measures;

(D) the drug and violence prevention activity or program to be funded, including how the activity or program will meet the principles of effectiveness described in section 7115(a) of this title, and the means of evaluating such activity or program; and

(E) how the services will be targeted to schools and students with the greatest need;

(3) a description for how the results of the evaluations of the effectiveness of the program will be used to refine, improve, and strengthen the program;

(4) an assurance that funds under this subpart will be used to increase the level of State, local, and other non-Federal funds that would, in the absence of funds under this subpart, be made available for programs and activities authorized under this subpart, and in no case supplant such State, local, and other non-Federal funds;

(5) a description of the mechanisms used to provide effective notice to the community of an intention to submit an application under this subpart;

(6) an assurance that drug and violence prevention programs supported under this subpart convey a clear and consistent message that acts of violence and the illegal use of drugs are wrong and harmful;

(7) an assurance that the applicant has, or the schools to be served have, a plan for keeping schools safe and drug-free that includes -

(A) appropriate and effective school discipline policies that prohibit disorderly conduct, the illegal possession of weapons, and the illegal use, possession, distribution, and sale of tobacco, alcohol, and other drugs by students;

(B) security procedures at school and while students are on the way to and from school;

(C) prevention activities that are designed to create and maintain safe, disciplined, and drug-free environments;

(D) a crisis management plan for responding to violent or traumatic incidents on school grounds; and

(E) a code of conduct policy for all students that clearly states the responsibilities of students, teachers, and administrators in maintaining a classroom environment that -

(i) allows a teacher to communicate effectively with all students in the class;

(ii) allows all students in the class to learn;

(iii) has consequences that are fair, and developmentally appropriate;

(iv) considers the student and the circumstances of the situation; and

(v) is enforced accordingly;

(8) an assurance that the application and any waiver request under section 7115(a)(3) of this title will be available for public review after submission of the application; and

(9) such other assurances, goals, and objectives identified through scientifically based research that the State may reasonably require in accordance with the purpose of this part.

(e) Review of application

(1) In general

In reviewing local applications under this section, a State educational agency shall use a peer review process or other methods of assuring the quality of such applications.

(2) Considerations

In determining whether to approve the application of a local educational agency under this section, a State educational agency shall consider the quality of application and the extent to which the application meets the principles of effectiveness described in section 7115(a) of this title.

(f) Approval process

(1) Deemed approval

An application submitted by a local educational agency pursuant to this section shall be deemed to be approved by the State educational agency unless the State educational agency makes a written determination, prior to the expiration of the 120-day period beginning on the date on which the State educational agency received the application, that the application is not in compliance with this subpart.

(2) Disapproval

The State educational agency shall not finally disapprove the application, except after giving the local educational agency notice and opportunity for a hearing.

(3) Notification

If the State educational agency finds that the application is not in compliance, in whole or in part, with this subpart, the State educational agency shall -

(A) give the local educational agency notice and an opportunity for a hearing; and

(B) notify the local educational agency of the finding of noncompliance, and in such notification, shall -

(i) cite the specific provisions in the application that are not in compliance; and

(ii) request additional information, only as to the noncompliant provisions, needed to make the application compliant.

(4) Response

If the local educational agency responds to the State educational agency's notification described in paragraph (3)(B) during the 45-day period beginning on the date on which the agency received the notification, and resubmits the application with the requested information described in paragraph (3)(B)(ii), the State educational agency shall approve or disapprove such application prior to the later of -

(A) the expiration of the 45-day period beginning on the date on which the application is resubmitted; or

(B) the expiration of the 120-day period described in paragraph (1).

(5) Failure to respond

If the local educational agency does not respond to the State educational agency's notification described in paragraph (3)(B) during the 45-day period beginning on the date on which the agency received the notification, such application shall be deemed to be disapproved.

Sec. 7115. Authorized activities

(a) Principles of effectiveness

(1) In general

For a program or activity developed pursuant to this subpart to meet the principles of effectiveness, such program or activity shall -

(A) be based on an assessment of objective data regarding the incidence of violence and illegal drug use in the elementary schools and secondary schools and communities to be served, including an objective analysis of the current conditions and consequences regarding violence and illegal drug use, including delinquency and serious discipline problems, among students who attend such schools (including private school students who participate in the drug and violence prevention program) that is based on ongoing local assessment or evaluation activities;

(B) be based on an established set of performance measures aimed at ensuring that the elementary schools and secondary schools and communities to be served by the program have a safe, orderly, and drug-free learning environment;

(C) be based on scientifically based research that provides evidence that the program to be used will reduce violence and illegal drug use;

(D) be based on an analysis of the data reasonably available at the time, of the prevalence of risk factors, including high or increasing rates of reported cases of child abuse and domestic violence; protective factors, buffers, assets; or other variables in schools and communities in the State identified through scientifically based research; and

(E) include meaningful and ongoing consultation with and input from parents in the development of the application and administration of the program or activity.

(2) Periodic evaluation

(A) Requirement

The program or activity shall undergo a periodic evaluation to assess its progress toward reducing violence and illegal drug use in schools to be served based on performance measures described in section 7114(d)(2)(B) of this title.

(B) Use of results

The results shall be used to refine, improve, and strengthen the program, and to refine the performance measures, and shall also be made available to the public upon request, with public notice of such availability provided.

(3) Waiver

A local educational agency may apply to the State for a waiver of the requirement of subsection (a)(1)(C) of this section to allow innovative activities or programs that demonstrate substantial likelihood of success.

(b) Local educational agency activities

(1) Program requirements

A local educational agency shall use funds made available under section 7114 of this title to develop, implement, and evaluate comprehensive programs and activities, which are coordinated with other school and community-based services and programs, that shall -

(A) foster a safe and drug-free learning environment that supports academic achievement;

(B) be consistent with the principles of effectiveness described in subsection (a)(1) of this section;

(C) be designed to -

(i) prevent or reduce violence; the use, possession and distribution of illegal drugs; and delinquency; and

(ii) create a well-disciplined environment conducive to learning, which includes consultation between teachers, principals, and other school personnel to identify early warning signs of drug use and violence and to provide behavioral interventions as part of classroom management efforts; and

(D) include activities to -

(i) promote the involvement of parents in the activity or program;

(ii) promote coordination with community groups and coalitions, and government agencies; and

(iii) distribute information about the local educational agency's needs, goals, and programs under this subpart.

(2) Authorized activities

Each local educational agency, or consortium of such agencies, that receives a subgrant under this subpart may use such funds to carry out activities that comply with the principles of effectiveness described in subsection (a) of this section, such as the following:

(A) Age appropriate and developmentally based activities that -

(i) address the consequences of violence and the illegal use of drugs, as appropriate;

(ii) promote a sense of individual responsibility;

(iii) teach students that most people do not illegally use drugs;

(iv) teach students to recognize social and peer pressure to use drugs illegally and the skills for resisting illegal drug use;

(v) teach students about the dangers of emerging drugs;

(vi) engage students in the learning process; and

(vii) incorporate activities in secondary schools that reinforce prevention activities implemented in elementary schools.

(B) Activities that involve families, community sectors (which may include appropriately trained seniors), and a variety of drug and violence prevention providers in setting clear expectations against violence and illegal use of drugs and appropriate consequences for violence and illegal use of drugs.

(C) Dissemination of drug and violence prevention information to schools and the community.

(D) Professional development and training for, and involvement of, school personnel, pupil services personnel, parents, and interested community members in prevention, education, early identification and intervention, mentoring, or rehabilitation referral, as related to drug and violence prevention.

(E) Drug and violence prevention activities that may include the following:

(i) Community-wide planning and organizing activities to reduce violence and illegal drug use, which may include gang activity prevention.

(ii) Acquiring and installing metal detectors, electronic locks, surveillance cameras, or other related equipment and technologies.

(iii) Reporting criminal offenses committed on school property.

(iv) Developing and implementing comprehensive school security plans or obtaining technical assistance concerning such plans, which may include obtaining a security assessment or assistance from the School Security and Technology Resource Center at the Sandia National Laboratory located in Albuquerque, New Mexico.

(v) Supporting safe zones of passage activities that ensure that students travel safely to and from school, which may include bicycle and pedestrian safety programs.

(vi) The hiring and mandatory training, based on scientific research, of school security personnel (including school resource officers) who interact with students in support of youth drug and violence prevention activities under this part that are implemented in the school.

(vii) Expanded and improved school-based mental health services related to illegal drug use and violence, including early identification of violence and illegal drug use, assessment, and direct or group counseling services provided to students, parents, families, and school personnel by qualified school-based mental health service providers.

(viii) Conflict resolution programs, including peer mediation programs that educate and train peer mediators and a designated faculty supervisor, and youth anti-crime and anti-drug councils and activities.

(ix) Alternative education programs or services for violent or drug abusing students that reduce the need for suspension or expulsion or that serve students who have been suspended or expelled from the regular educational settings, including programs or services to assist students to make continued progress toward meeting the State academic achievement standards and to reenter the regular education setting.

(x) Counseling, mentoring, referral services, and other student assistance practices and programs, including assistance provided by qualified school-based mental health services providers and the training of teachers by school-based mental health services providers in appropriate identification and intervention techniques for students at risk of violent behavior and illegal use of drugs.

(xi) Programs that encourage students to seek advice from, and to confide in, a trusted adult regarding concerns about violence and illegal drug use.

(xii) Drug and violence prevention activities designed to reduce truancy.

(xiii) Age-appropriate, developmentally-based violence prevention and education programs that address victimization associated with prejudice and intolerance, and that include activities designed to help students develop a sense of individual responsibility and respect for the rights of others, and to resolve conflicts without violence.

(xiv) Consistent with the fourth amendment to the Constitution of the United States, the testing of a student for illegal drug use or the inspecting of a student's locker for weapons or illegal drugs or drug paraphernalia, including at the request of or with the consent of a parent or legal guardian of the student, if the local educational agency elects to so test or inspect.

(xv) Emergency intervention services following traumatic crisis events, such as a shooting, major accident, or a drug-related incident that have disrupted the learning environment.

(xvi) Establishing or implementing a system for transferring suspension and expulsion records, consistent with section 1232g of this title, by a local educational agency to any public or private elementary school or secondary school.

(xvii) Developing and implementing character education programs, as a component of drug and violence prevention programs, that take into account the views of parents of the students for whom the program is intended and such students, such as a program described in subpart 3 of part D of subchapter V of this chapter.

(xviii) Establishing and maintaining a school safety hotline.

(xix) Community service, including community service performed by expelled students, and service-learning projects.

(xx) Conducting a nationwide background check of each local educational agency employee, regardless of when hired, and prospective employees for the purpose of determining whether the employee or prospective employee has been convicted of a crime that bears upon the employee's fitness -

(I) to be responsible for the safety or well-being of children;

(II) to serve in the particular capacity in which the employee or prospective employee is or will be employed; or

(III) to otherwise be employed by the local educational agency.

(xxi) Programs to train school personnel to identify warning signs of youth suicide and to create an action plan to help youth at risk of suicide.

(xxii) Programs that respond to the needs of students who are faced with domestic violence or child abuse.

(F) The evaluation of any of the activities authorized under this subsection and the collection of objective data used to assess program needs, program implementation, or program success in achieving program goals and objectives.

(c) Limitation

(1) In general

Except as provided in paragraph (2), not more than 40 percent of the funds available to a local educational agency under this subpart may be used to carry out the activities described in clauses (ii) through (vi) of subsection (b)(2)(E) of this section, of which not more than 50 percent of such amount may be used to carry out the activities described in clauses (ii) through (v) of such subsection.

(2) Exception

A local educational agency may use funds under this subpart for activities described in clauses (ii) through (v) of subsection (b)(2)(E) of this section only if funding for these activities is not received from other Federal agencies.

(d) Rule of construction

Nothing in this section shall be construed to prohibit the use of funds under this subpart by any local educational agency or school for the establishment or implementation of a school uniform policy if such policy is part of the overall comprehensive drug and violence prevention plan of the State involved and is supported by the State's needs assessment and other scientifically based research information.

Sec. 7116. Reporting

(a) State report

(1) In general

By December 1, 2003, and every 2 years thereafter, the chief executive officer of the State, in cooperation with the State educational agency, shall submit to the Secretary a report -

(A) on the implementation and outcomes of State programs under section 7112(a)(1) of this title and section 7112(c) of this title and local educational agency programs under section 7115(b) of this title, as well as an assessment of their effectiveness;

(B) on the State's progress toward attaining its performance measures for drug and violence prevention under section 7113(a)(10) of this title; and

(C) on the State's efforts to inform parents of, and include parents in, violence and drug prevention efforts.

(2) Special rule

The report required by this subsection shall be -

(A) in the form specified by the Secretary;

(B) based on the State's ongoing evaluation activities, and shall include data on the incidence and prevalence, age of onset, perception of health risk, and perception of social disapproval of drug use and violence by youth in schools and communities; and

(C) made readily available to the public.

(b) Local educational agency report

(1) In general

Each local educational agency receiving funds under this subpart shall submit to the State educational agency such information that the State requires to complete the State report required by subsection (a) of this section, including a description of how parents were informed of, and participated in, violence and drug prevention efforts.

(2) Availability

Information under paragraph (1) shall be made readily available to the public.

(3) Provision of documentation

Not later than January 1 of each year that a State is required to report under subsection (a) of this section, the Secretary shall provide to the State educational agency all of the necessary documentation required for compliance with this section.

Sec. 7117. Programs for Native Hawaiians

(a) General authority

From the funds made available pursuant to section 7111(a)(1)(C) of this title to carry out this section, the Secretary shall make grants to or enter into cooperative agreements or contracts with organizations primarily serving and representing Native Hawaiians for the benefit of Native Hawaiians to plan, conduct, and administer programs, or portions thereof, that are authorized by and consistent with the provisions of this subpart.

(b) Definition of Native Hawaiian

For the purposes of this section, the term "Native Hawaiian" means any individual any of whose ancestors were natives, prior to 1778, of the area which now comprises the State of Hawaii.

SUBPART 2 - NATIONAL PROGRAMS

Sec. 7131. Federal activities

(a) Program authorized

From funds made available to carry out this subpart under section 7103(2) of this title, the Secretary, in consultation with the Secretary of Health and Human Services, the Director of the Office of National Drug

Control Policy, and the Attorney General, shall carry out programs to prevent the illegal use of drugs and violence among, and promote safety and discipline for, students. The Secretary shall carry out such programs directly, or through grants, contracts, or cooperative agreements with public and private entities and individuals, or through agreements with other Federal agencies, and shall coordinate such programs with other appropriate Federal activities. Such programs may include -

(1) the development and demonstration of innovative strategies for the training of school personnel, parents, and members of the community for drug and violence prevention activities based on State and local needs;

(2) the development, demonstration, scientifically based evaluation, and dissemination of innovative and high quality drug and violence prevention programs and activities, based on State and local needs, which may include -

(A) alternative education models, either established within a school or separate and apart from an existing school, that are designed to promote drug and violence prevention, reduce disruptive behavior, reduce the need for repeat suspensions and expulsions, enable students to meet challenging State academic standards, and enable students to return to the regular classroom as soon as possible;

(B) community service and service-learning projects, designed to rebuild safe and healthy neighborhoods and increase students' sense of individual responsibility;

(C) video-based projects developed by noncommercial telecommunications entities that provide young people with models for conflict resolution and responsible decisionmaking; and

(D) child abuse education and prevention programs for elementary and secondary students;

(3) the provision of information on drug abuse education and prevention to the Secretary of Health and Human Services for dissemination;

(4) the provision of information on violence prevention and education and school safety to the Department of Justice for dissemination;

(5) technical assistance to chief executive officers, State agencies, local educational agencies, and other recipients of funding under this part to build capacity to develop and implement high-quality, effective drug and violence prevention programs consistent with the principles of effectiveness in section 7115(a) of this title;

(6) assistance to school systems that have particularly severe drug and violence problems, including hiring drug prevention and school safety coordinators, or assistance to support appropriate response efforts to crisis situations;

(7) the development of education and training programs, curricula, instructional materials, and professional training and development for preventing and reducing the incidence of crimes and conflicts motivated by hate in localities most directly affected by hate crimes;

(8) activities in communities designated as empowerment zones or enterprise communities that will connect schools to community-wide efforts

to reduce drug and violence problems; and

(9) other activities in accordance with the purpose of this part, based on State and local needs.

(b) Peer review

The Secretary shall use a peer review process in reviewing applications for funds under this section.

Sec. 7132. Impact evaluation

(a) Biennial evaluation

The Secretary, in consultation with the Safe and Drug-Free Schools and Communities Advisory Committee described in section 7134 of this title, shall conduct an independent biennial evaluation of the impact of programs assisted under this subpart and of other recent and new initiatives to combat violence and illegal drug use in schools. The evaluation shall report on whether community and local educational agency programs funded under this subpart -

(1) comply with the principles of effectiveness described in section 7115(a) of this title;

(2) have appreciably reduced the level of illegal drug, alcohol, and tobacco use, and school violence and the illegal presence of weapons at schools; and

(3) have conducted effective parent involvement and training programs.

(b) Data collection

The National Center for Education Statistics shall collect data, that is subject to independent review, to determine the incidence and prevalence of illegal drug use and violence in elementary schools and secondary schools in the States. The collected data shall include incident reports by schools officials, anonymous student surveys, and anonymous teacher surveys.

(c) Biennial report

Not later than January 1, 2003, and every 2 years thereafter, the Secretary shall submit to the President and Congress a report on the findings of the evaluation conducted under subsection (a) of this section together with the data collected under subsection (b) of this section and data available from other sources on the incidence and prevalence, age of onset, perception of health risk, and perception of social disapproval of drug use and violence in elementary schools and secondary schools in the States. The Secretary shall include data submitted by the States pursuant to subsection 7116(a) of this title.

Sec. 7133. Hate crime prevention

(a) Grant authorization

From funds made available to carry out this subpart under section 7103(2) of this title the Secretary may make grants to local educational agencies and community-based organizations for the purpose of providing assistance to localities most directly affected by hate crimes.

(b) Use of funds

(1) Program development

Grants under this section may be used to improve elementary and secondary educational efforts, including -

(A) development of education and training programs designed to prevent and to reduce the incidence of crimes and conflicts motivated by hate;

(B) development of curricula for the purpose of improving conflict or dispute resolution skills of students, teachers, and administrators;

(C) development and acquisition of equipment and instructional materials to meet the needs of, or otherwise be part of, hate crime or conflict programs; and

(D) professional training and development for teachers and administrators on the causes, effects, and resolutions of hate crimes or hate-based conflicts.

(2) Application

In order to be eligible to receive a grant under this section for any fiscal year, a local educational agency, or a local educational agency in conjunction with a community-based organization, shall submit an application to the Secretary in such form and containing such information as the Secretary may reasonably require.

(3) Requirements

Each application under paragraph (2) shall include -

(A) a request for funds for the purpose described in this section;

(B) a description of the schools and communities to be served by the grants; and

(C) assurances that Federal funds received under this section shall be used to supplement, and not supplant, non-Federal funds.

(4) Comprehensive plan

Each application shall include a comprehensive plan that contains -

(A) a description of the hate crime or conflict problems within the schools or the community targeted for assistance;

(B) a description of the program to be developed or augmented by such Federal and matching funds;

(C) assurances that such program or activity shall be administered by or under the supervision of the applicant;

(D) procedures for the proper and efficient administration of such program; and

(E) fiscal control and fund accounting procedures as may be necessary to ensure prudent use, proper disbursement, and accurate accounting of funds received under this section.

(c) Award of grants

(1) Selection of recipients

The Secretary shall consider the incidence of crimes and conflicts motivated by bias in the targeted schools and communities in awarding grants under this section.

(2) Geographic distribution

The Secretary shall attempt, to the extent practicable, to achieve an equitable geographic distribution of grant awards.

(3) Dissemination of information

The Secretary shall attempt, to the extent practicable, to make available information regarding successful hate crime prevention programs, including programs established or expanded with grants under this section.

(d) Reports

The Secretary shall submit to Congress a report every 2 years that shall contain a detailed statement regarding grants and awards, activities of grant recipients, and an evaluation of programs established under this section.

Sec. 7134. Safe and Drug-Free Schools and Communities Advisory Committee

(a) Establishment

(1) In general

There is hereby established an advisory committee to be known as the "Safe and Drug Free Schools and Communities Advisory Committee" (referred to in this section as the "Advisory Committee") to -

(A) consult with the Secretary under subsection (b) of this section;

(B) coordinate Federal school- and community-based substance abuse and violence prevention programs and reduce duplicative research or services;

(C) develop core data sets and evaluation protocols for safe and drug-free school- and community-based programs;

(D) provide technical assistance and training for safe and drug-free school- and community-based programs;

(E) provide for the diffusion of scientifically based research to safe and drug-free school- and community-based programs; and

(F) review other regulations and standards developed under this subchapter.

(2) Composition

The Advisory Committee shall be composed of representatives from -

(A) the Department of Education;

(B) the Centers for Disease Control and Prevention;

(C) the National Institute on Drug Abuse;

(D) the National Institute on Alcoholism and Alcohol Abuse;

(E) the Center for Substance Abuse Prevention;

(F) the Center for Mental Health Services;

(G) the Office of Juvenile Justice and Delinquency Prevention;

(H) the Office of National Drug Control Policy;

(I) State and local governments, including education agencies; and

(J) researchers and expert practitioners.

(3) Consultation

In carrying out its duties under this section, the Advisory Committee shall annually consult with interested State and local coordinators of school- and community-based substance abuse and violence prevention programs and other interested groups.

(b) Programs

(1) In general

From amounts made available under section 7103(2) of this title to carry out this subpart, the Secretary, in consultation with the Advisory Committee, shall carry out scientifically based research programs to strengthen the accountability and effectiveness of the State, chief executive officer's, and national programs under this part.

(2) Grants, contracts or cooperative agreements

The Secretary shall carry out paragraph (1) directly or through grants, contracts, or cooperative agreements with public and private entities and individuals or through agreements with other Federal agencies.

(3) Coordination

The Secretary shall coordinate programs under this section with other appropriate Federal activities.

(4) Activities

Activities that may be carried out under programs funded under this section may include -

(A) the provision of technical assistance and training, in collaboration with other Federal agencies utilizing their expertise and national and regional training systems, for Governors, State educational agencies and local educational agencies to support high quality, effective programs that -

(i) provide a thorough assessment of the substance abuse and violence problem;

(ii) utilize objective data and the knowledge of a wide range of community members;

(iii) develop measurable goals and objectives; and

(iv) implement scientifically based research activities that have been shown to be effective and that meet identified needs;

(B) the provision of technical assistance and training to foster program accountability;

(C) the diffusion and dissemination of best practices and programs;

(D) the development of core data sets and evaluation tools;

(E) program evaluations;

(F) the provision of information on drug abuse education and prevention to the Secretary of Health and Human Services for dissemination by the clearinghouse for alcohol and drug abuse information established under section 290aa(d)(16) of title 42; and

(G) other activities that meet unmet needs related to the purpose of this part and that are undertaken in consultation with the Advisory Committee.

Sec. 7135. National Coordinator Program

(a) In general

From funds made available to carry out this subpart under section 7103(2) of this title, the Secretary may provide for the establishment of a

National Coordinator Program under which the Secretary shall award grants to local educational agencies for the hiring of drug prevention and school safety program coordinators.

(b) Use of funds

Amounts received under a grant under subsection (a) of this section shall be used by local educational agencies to recruit, hire, and train individuals to serve as drug prevention and school safety program coordinators in schools with significant drug and school safety problems. Such coordinators shall be responsible for developing, conducting, and analyzing assessments of drug and crime problems at their schools, and administering the safe and drug-free grant program at such schools.

Sec. 7136. Community service grant program

(a) In general

From funds made available to carry out this subpart under section 7103(2) of this title, the Secretary may make grants to States to carry out programs under which students expelled or suspended from school are required to perform community service.

(b) Allocation

From the amount described in subsection (a) of this section, the Secretary shall allocate among the States -

(1) one-half according to the ratio between the school-aged population of each State and the school-aged population of all the States; and

(2) one-half according to the ratio between the amount each State received under section 6334 of this title for the preceding year and the sum of such amounts received by all the States.

(c) Minimum

For any fiscal year, no State shall be allotted under this section an amount that is less than one-half of 1 percent of the total amount allotted to all the States under this section.

(d) Reallotment

The Secretary may reallot any amount of any allotment to a State if the Secretary determines that the State will be unable to use such amount within 2 years of such allotment. Such reallotments shall be made on the same basis as allotments are made under subsection (b) of this section.

(e) Definition

In this section, the term "State" means each of the 50 States, the District of Columbia, and the Commonwealth of Puerto Rico.

Sec. 7137. School Security Technology and Resource Center

(a) Center

From funds made available to carry out this subpart under section 7103(2) of this title, the Secretary, the Attorney General, and the Secretary of Energy may enter into an agreement for the establishment at the Sandia National Laboratories, in partnership with the National Law Enforcement and Corrections Technology Center - Southeast and the National Center for

Rural Law Enforcement in Little Rock, Arkansas, of a center to be known as the "School Security Technology and Resource Center" (hereafter in this section "the Center").

(b) Administration

The Center established under subsection (a) of this section shall be administered by the Attorney General.

(c) Functions

The center established under subsection (a) of this section shall be a resource to local educational agencies for school security assessments, security technology development, evaluation and implementation, and technical assistance relating to improving school security. The Center will also conduct and publish school violence research, coalesce data from victim communities, and monitor and report on schools that implement school security strategies.

Sec. 7138. National Center for School and Youth Safety

(a) Establishment

From funds made available to carry out this subpart under section 7103(2) of this title, the Secretary of Education and the Attorney General may jointly establish a National Center for School and Youth Safety (in this section referred to as the "Center"). The Secretary of Education and the Attorney General may establish the Center at an existing facility, if the facility has a history of performing two or more of the duties described in subsection (b) of this section. The Secretary of Education and the Attorney General shall jointly appoint a Director of the Center to oversee the operation of the Center.

(b) Duties

The Center shall carry out emergency response, anonymous student hotline, consultation, and information and outreach activities with respect to elementary and secondary school safety, including the following:

(1) Emergency response

The staff of the Center, and such temporary contract employees as the Director of the Center shall determine necessary, shall offer emergency assistance to local communities to respond to school safety crises. Such assistance shall include counseling for victims and the community, assistance to law enforcement to address short-term security concerns, and advice on how to enhance school safety, prevent future incidents, and respond to future incidents.

(2) Anonymous student hotline

The Center shall establish a toll-free telephone number for students to report criminal activity, threats of criminal activity, and other high-risk behaviors such as substance abuse, gang or cult affiliation, depression, or other warning signs of potentially violent behavior. The Center shall relay the reports, without attribution, to local law enforcement or appropriate school hotlines. The Director of the Center shall work with the Attorney General to establish guidelines for Center staff to work with law enforcement around the Nation to relay information reported through the hotline.

(3) Consultation

The Center shall establish a toll-free number for the public to contact staff of the Center for consultation regarding school safety. The Director of the Center shall hire administrative staff and individuals with expertise in enhancing school safety, including individuals with backgrounds in counseling and psychology, education, law enforcement and criminal justice, and community development to assist in the consultation.

(4) Information and outreach

The Center shall compile information about the best practices in school violence prevention, intervention, and crisis management, and shall serve as a clearinghouse for model school safety program information. The staff of the Center shall work to ensure local governments, school officials, parents, students, and law enforcement officials and agencies are aware of the resources, grants, and expertise available to enhance school safety and prevent school crime. The staff of the Center shall give special attention to providing outreach to rural and impoverished communities.

Sec. 7139. Grants to reduce alcohol abuse

(a) In general

The Secretary, in consultation with the Administrator of the Substance Abuse and Mental Health Services Administration, may award grants from funds made available to carry out this subpart under section 7103(2) of this title, on a competitive basis, to local educational agencies to enable such agencies to develop and implement innovative and effective programs to reduce alcohol abuse in secondary schools.

(b) Eligibility

To be eligible to receive a grant under subsection (a) of this section, a local educational agency shall prepare and submit to the Secretary an application at such time, in such manner, and containing such information as the Secretary may require, including -

(1) a description of the activities to be carried out under the grant;

(2) an assurance that such activities will include one or more of the proven strategies for reducing underage alcohol abuse as determined by the Substance Abuse and Mental Health Services Administration;

(3) an explanation of how activities to be carried out under the grant that are not described in paragraph (2) will be effective in reducing underage alcohol abuse, including references to the past effectiveness of such activities;

(4) an assurance that the applicant will submit to the Secretary an annual report concerning the effectiveness of the programs and activities funded under the grant; and

(5) such other information as the Secretary determines appropriate.

(c) Streamlining of process for low-income and rural LEAs The Secretary, in consultation with the Administrator of the Substance Abuse and Mental Health Services Administration, shall develop procedures to make the application process for grants under this section more user-friendly, particularly for low-income and rural local educational agencies.

(d) Reservations

(1) SAMHSA

The Secretary may reserve 20 percent of any amount used to carry out this section to enable the Administrator of the Substance Abuse and Mental Health Services Administration to provide alcohol abuse resources and start-up assistance to local educational agencies receiving grants under this section.

(2) Low-income and rural areas

The Secretary may reserve 25 percent of any amount used to carry out this section to award grants to low-income and rural local educational agencies.

Sec. 7140. Mentoring programs

(a) Purpose; definitions

(1) Purpose

The purpose of this section is to make assistance available to promote mentoring programs for children with greatest need -

(A) to assist such children in receiving support and guidance from a mentor;

(B) to improve the academic achievement of such children;

(C) to improve interpersonal relationships between such children and their peers, teachers, other adults, and family members;

(D) to reduce the dropout rate of such children; and

(E) to reduce juvenile delinquency and involvement in gangs by such children.

(2) Definitions

In this part:

(A) Child with greatest need

The term "child with greatest need" means a child who is at risk of educational failure, dropping out of school, or involvement in criminal or delinquent activities, or who lacks strong positive role models.

(B) Eligible entity

The term "eligible entity" means -

(i) a local educational agency;

(ii) a nonprofit, community-based organization; or

(iii) a partnership between a local educational agency and a nonprofit, community-based organization.

(C) Mentor

The term "mentor" means a responsible adult, a postsecondary school student, or a secondary school student who works with a child -

(i) to provide a positive role model for the child;

(ii) to establish a supportive relationship with the child; and

(iii) to provide the child with academic assistance and exposure to new experiences and examples of opportunity that enhance the ability of the child to become a responsible adult.

(D) State

The term "State" means each of the several States, the District of Columbia, the Commonwealth of Puerto Rico, the United States Virgin Islands, Guam, American Samoa, and the Commonwealth of the Northern Mariana Islands.

(b) Grant program

(1) In general

The Secretary may award grants from funds made available to carry out this subpart under section 7103(2) of this title to eligible entities to assist such entities in establishing and supporting mentoring programs and activities for children with greatest need that -

(A) are designed to link such children (particularly children living in rural areas, high-crime areas, or troubled home environments, or children experiencing educational failure) with mentors who -

(i) have received training and support in mentoring;

(ii) have been screened using appropriate reference checks, child and domestic abuse record checks, and criminal background checks; and

(iii) are interested in working with children with greatest need; and

(B) are intended to achieve one or more of the following goals with respect to children with greatest need:

(i) Provide general guidance.

(ii) Promote personal and social responsibility.

(iii) Increase participation in, and enhance the ability to benefit from, elementary and secondary education.

(iv) Discourage illegal use of drugs and alcohol, violence, use of dangerous weapons, promiscuous behavior, and other criminal, harmful, or potentially harmful activity.

(v) Encourage participation in community service and community activities.

(vi) Encourage setting goals and planning for the future, including encouragement of graduation from secondary school and planning for postsecondary education or training.

(viii) Discourage involvement in gangs.

(2) Use of funds

(A) In general

Each eligible entity awarded a grant under this subsection shall use the grant funds for activities that establish or implement a mentoring program, that may include -

(i) hiring of mentoring coordinators and support staff;

(ii) providing for the professional development of mentoring coordinators and support staff;

(iii) recruitment, screening, and training of mentors;

(iv) reimbursement to schools, if appropriate, for the use of school materials or supplies in carrying out the mentoring program;

(v) dissemination of outreach materials;

(vi) evaluation of the mentoring program using scientifically based methods; and

(vii) such other activities as the Secretary may reasonably prescribe by rule.

(B) Prohibited uses

Notwithstanding subparagraph (A), an eligible entity awarded a grant under this section may not use the grant funds -

(i) to directly compensate mentors;

(ii) to obtain educational or other materials or equipment that would otherwise be used in the ordinary course of the eligible entity's operations;

(iii) to support litigation of any kind; or

(iv) for any other purpose reasonably prohibited by the Secretary by rule.

(3) Availability of funds

Funds made available through a grant under this section shall be available for obligation for a period not to exceed 3 years.

(4) Application

Each eligible entity seeking a grant under this section shall submit to the Secretary an application that includes -

(A) a description of the plan for the mentoring program the eligible entity proposes to carry out with such grant;

(B) information on the children expected to be served by the mentoring program for which such grant is sought;

(C) a description of the mechanism the eligible entity will use to match children with mentors based on the needs of the children;

(D) an assurance that no mentor will be assigned to mentor so many children that the assignment will undermine the mentor's ability to be an effective mentor or the mentor's ability to establish a close relationship (a one-to-one relationship, where practicable) with each mentored child;

(E) an assurance that the mentoring program will provide children with a variety of experiences and support, including -

(i) emotional support;

(ii) academic assistance; and

(iii) exposure to experiences that the children might not otherwise encounter on their own;

(F) an assurance that the mentoring program will be monitored to ensure that each child assigned a mentor benefits from that assignment and that the child will be assigned a new mentor if the relationship between the original mentor and the child is not beneficial to the child;

(G) information regarding how mentors and children will be recruited to the mentoring program;

(H) information regarding how prospective mentors will be screened;

(I) information on the training that will be provided to mentors; and

(J) information on the system that the eligible entity will use to manage and monitor information relating to the mentoring program's -

(i) reference checks;

(ii) child and domestic abuse record checks;

(iii) criminal background checks; and

(iv) procedure for matching children with mentors.

(5) Selection

(A) Competitive basis

In accordance with this subsection, the Secretary shall award grants to eligible entities on a competitive basis.

(B) Priority

In awarding grants under subparagraph (A), the Secretary shall give priority to each eligible entity that -

(i) serves children with greatest need living in rural areas, high-crime areas, or troubled home environments, or who attend schools with violence problems;

(ii) provides high quality background screening of mentors training of mentors, and technical assistance in carrying out mentoring programs; or

(iii) proposes a school-based mentoring program.

(C) Other considerations

In awarding grants under subparagraph (A), the Secretary shall also consider -

(i) the degree to which the location of the mentoring program proposed by each eligible entity contributes to a fair distribution of mentoring programs with respect to urban and rural locations;

(ii) the quality of the mentoring program proposed by each eligible entity, including -

(I) the resources, if any, the eligible entity will dedicate to providing children with opportunities for job training or postsecondary education;

(II) the degree to which parents, teachers, community-based organizations, and the local community have participated, or will participate, in the design and implementation of the proposed mentoring program;

(III) the degree to which the eligible entity can ensure that mentors will develop longstanding relationships with the children they mentor;

(IV) the degree to which the mentoring program will serve children with greatest need in the 4th through 8th grades; and

(V) the degree to which the mentoring program will

continue to serve children from the 9th grade through graduation from secondary school, as needed; and

(iii) the capability of each eligible entity to effectively implement its mentoring program.

(D) Grant to each State

Notwithstanding any other provision of this subsection, in awarding grants under subparagraph (A), the Secretary shall select not less than one grant recipient from each State for which there is an eligible entity that submits an application of sufficient quality pursuant to paragraph (4).

(6) Model screening guidelines

(A) In general

Based on model screening guidelines developed by the Office of Juvenile Programs of the Department of Justice, the Secretary shall develop and distribute to each eligible entity awarded a grant under this section specific model guidelines for the screening of mentors who seek to participate in mentoring programs assisted under this section.

(B) Background checks

The guidelines developed under this subsection shall include, at a minimum, a requirement that potential mentors be subject to reference checks, child and domestic abuse record checks, and criminal background checks.

SUBPART 3 - GUN POSSESSION

Sec. 7151. Gun-free requirements

(a) Short title
This subpart may be cited as the "Gun-Free Schools Act."
(b) Requirements
(1) In general
Each State receiving Federal funds under any subchapter of this chapter shall have in effect a State law requiring local educational agencies to expel from school for a period of not less than 1 year a student who is determined to have brought a firearm to a school, or to have possessed a firearm at a school, under the jurisdiction of local educational agencies in that State, except that such State law shall allow the chief administering officer of a local educational agency to modify such expulsion requirement for a student on a case-by-case basis if such modification is in writing.

(2) Construction
Nothing in this subpart shall be construed to prevent a State from allowing a local educational agency that has expelled a student from such a student's regular school setting from providing educational services to such student in an alternative setting.

(3) Definition
For the purpose of this section, the term "firearm" has the same meaning given such term in section 921(a) of title 18.

(c) Special rule

The provisions of this section shall be construed in a manner consistent with the Individuals with Disabilities Education Act [20 U.S.C. 1400 et seq.].

(d) Report to State

Each local educational agency requesting assistance from the State educational agency that is to be provided from funds made available to the State under any subchapter of this chapter shall provide to the State, in the application requesting such assistance -

(1) an assurance that such local educational agency is in compliance with the State law required by subsection (b) of this section; and

(2) a description of the circumstances surrounding any expulsions imposed under the State law required by subsection (b) of this section, including -

(A) the name of the school concerned;

(B) the number of students expelled from such school; and

(C) the type of firearms concerned.

(e) Reporting

Each State shall report the information described in subsection (d) of this section to the Secretary on an annual basis.

(f) Definition

For the purpose of subsection (d) of this section, the term "school" means any setting that is under the control and supervision of the local educational agency for the purpose of student activities approved and authorized by the local educational agency.

(g) Exception

Nothing in this section shall apply to a firearm that is lawfully stored inside a locked vehicle on school property, or if it is for activities approved and authorized by the local educational agency and the local educational agency adopts appropriate safeguards to ensure student safety.

(h) Policy regarding criminal justice system referral

(1) In general

No funds shall be made available under any subchapter of this chapter to any local educational agency unless such agency has a policy requiring referral to the criminal justice or juvenile delinquency system of any student who brings a firearm or weapon to a school served by such agency.

(2) Definition

For the purpose of this subsection, the term "school" has the same meaning given to such term by section 921(a) of title 18.

SUBPART 4 - GENERAL PROVISIONS

Sec. 7161. Definitions

In this part:

(1) Controlled substance

The term "controlled substance" means a drug or other substance identified under Schedule I, II, III, IV, or V in section 812(c) of title 21.

(2) Drug

The term "drug" includes controlled substances; the illegal use of alcohol and tobacco; and the harmful, abusive, or addictive use of substances, including inhalants and anabolic steroids.

(3) Drug and violence prevention

The term "drug and violence prevention" means -

(A) with respect to drugs, prevention, early intervention, rehabilitation referral, or education related to the illegal use of drugs;

(B) with respect to violence, the promotion of school safety, such that students and school personnel are free from violent and disruptive acts, including sexual harassment and abuse, and victimization associated with prejudice and intolerance, on school premises, going to and from school, and at school- sponsored activities, through the creation and maintenance of a school environment that is free of weapons and fosters individual responsibility and respect for the rights of others.

(4) Hate crime

The term "hate crime" means a crime as described in section 1(b) of the Hate Crime Statistics Act of 1990.

(5) Nonprofit

The term "nonprofit," as applied to a school, agency, organization, or institution means a school, agency, organization, or institution owned and operated by one or more nonprofit corporations or associations, no part of the net earnings of which inures, or may lawfully inure, to the benefit of any private shareholder or individual.

(6) Protective factor, buffer, or asset

The terms "protective factor," "buffer," and "asset" mean any one of a number of the community, school, family, or peer individual domains that are known, through prospective, longitudinal research efforts, or which are grounded in a well- established theoretical model of prevention, and have been shown to prevent alcohol, tobacco, or illegal drug use, as well as violent behavior, by youth in the community, and which promote positive youth development.

(7) Risk factor

The term "risk factor" means any one of a number of characteristics of the community, school, family, or peer- individual domains that are known, through prospective, longitudinal research efforts, to be predictive of alcohol, tobacco, and illegal drug use, as well as violent behavior, by youth in the school and community.

(8) School-aged population

The term "school-aged population" means the population aged five through 17, as determined by the Secretary on the basis of the most recent satisfactory data available from the Department of Commerce.

(9) School based mental health services provider

The term "school based mental health services provider" includes a State-licensed or State-certified school counselor, school psychologist, school social worker, or other State-licensed or -certified mental health professional qualified under State law to provide such services to children and adolescents.

(10) School personnel

The term "school personnel" includes teachers, principals, administrators, counselors, social workers, psychologists, nurses, librarians, and other support staff who are employed by a school or who perform services for the school on a contractual basis.

(11) School resource officer

The term "school resource officer" means a career law enforcement officer, with sworn authority, deployed in community oriented policing, and assigned by the employing police department to a local educational agency to work in collaboration with schools and community based organizations to -

(A) educate students in crime and illegal drug use prevention and safety;

(B) develop or expand community justice initiatives for students; and

(C) train students in conflict resolution, restorative justice, and crime and illegal drug use awareness.

Sec. 7162. Message and materials

(a) "Wrong and harmful" message

Drug and violence prevention programs supported under this part shall convey a clear and consistent message that the illegal use of drugs and acts of violence are wrong and harmful.

(b) Curriculum

The Secretary shall not prescribe the use of specific curricula for programs supported under this part.

Sec. 7163. Parental consent

Upon receipt of written notification from the parents or legal guardians of a student, the local educational agency shall withdraw such student from any program or activity funded under this part. The local educational agency shall make reasonable efforts to inform parents or legal guardians of the content of such programs or activities funded under this part, other than classroom instruction.

Sec. 7164. Prohibited uses of funds

No funds under this part may be used for -

(1) construction (except for minor remodeling needed to accomplish the purposes of this part); or

(2) medical services, drug treatment or rehabilitation, except for pupil services or referral to treatment for students who are victims of, or witnesses to, crime or who illegally use drugs.

Sec. 7165. Transfer of school disciplinary records

(a) Nonapplication of provisions

This section shall not apply to any disciplinary records with respect to a suspension or expulsion that are transferred from a private, parochial or other nonpublic school, person, institution, or other entity, that provides education below the college level.

(b) Disciplinary records

In accordance with the Family Educational Rights and Privacy Act of 1974 (20 U.S.C. 1232g), not later than 2 years after January 8 2002, each State receiving Federal funds under this chapter shall provide an assurance to the Secretary that the State has a procedure in place to facilitate the transfer of disciplinary records, with respect to a suspension or expulsion, by local educational agencies to any private or public elementary school or secondary school for any student who is enrolled or seeks, intends, or is instructed to enroll, on a full- or part-time basis, in the school.

II. GUN-FREE SCHOOL ZONES ACT

18 U.S.C. § 922(q)

(q)(1) The Congress finds and declares that –

(A) crime, particularly crime involving drugs and guns, is a pervasive, nationwide problem;

(B) crime at the local level is exacerbated by the interstate movement of drugs, guns, and criminal gangs;

(C) firearms and ammunition move easily in interstate commerce and have been found in increasing numbers in and around schools, as documented in numerous hearings in both the Committee on the Judiciary of the House of Representatives and the Committee on the Judiciary of the Senate;

(D) in fact, even before the sale of a firearm, the gun, its component parts, ammunition, and the raw materials from which they are made have considerably moved in interstate commerce;

(E) while criminals freely move from State to State, ordinary citizens and foreign visitors may fear to travel to or through certain parts of the country due to concern about violent crime and gun violence, and parents may decline to send their children to school for the same reason;

(F) the occurrence of violent crime in school zones has resulted in a decline in the quality of education in our country;

(G) this decline in the quality of education has an adverse impact on interstate commerce and the foreign commerce of the United States;

(H) States, localities, and school systems find it almost impossible to handle gun-related crime by themselves – even States, localities, and school systems that have made strong efforts to prevent, detect, and punish gun-related crime find their efforts unavailing due in part to the failure or inability of other States or localities to take strong measures; and

(I) the Congress has the power, under the interstate commerce clause and other provisions of the Constitution, to enact measures to ensure the integrity and safety of the Nation's schools by enactment of this subsection.

(2)(A) It shall be unlawful for any individual knowingly to possess a firearm that has moved in or that otherwise affects interstate or foreign commerce at a place that the individual knows, or has reasonable cause to believe, is a school zone.

(B) Subparagraph (A) does not apply to the possession of a firearm –

(i) on private property not part of school grounds;

(ii) if the individual possessing the firearm is licensed to do so by the State in which the school zone is located or a political subdivision of the State, and the law of the State or political subdivision requires that, before an individual obtains such a license, the law enforcement authorities of the State or political subdivision verify that the individual is qualified under law to receive the license;

(iii) that is –

(I) not loaded; and

(II) in a locked container, or a locked firearms rack that is on a motor vehicle;

(iv) by an individual for use in a program approved by a school in the school zone;

(v) by an individual in accordance with a contract entered into between a school in the school zone and the individual or an employer of the individual;

(vi) by a law enforcement officer acting in his or her official capacity; or

(vii) that is unloaded and is possessed by an individual while traversing school premises for the purpose of gaining access to public or private lands open to hunting, if the entry on school premises is authorized by school authorities.

(3)(A) Except as provided in subparagraph (B), it shall be unlawful for any person, knowingly or with reckless disregard for the safety of another, to discharge or attempt to discharge a firearm that has moved in or that otherwise affects interstate or foreign commerce at a place that the person knows is a school zone.

(B) Subparagraph (A) does not apply to the discharge of a firearm –

(i) on private property not part of school grounds;

(ii) as part of a program approved by a school in the school zone, by an individual who is participating in the program;

(iii) by an individual in accordance with a contract entered into between a school in a school zone and the individual or an employer of the individual; or

(iv) by a law enforcement officer acting in his or her official capacity.

(4) Nothing in this subsection shall be construed as preempting or preventing a State or local government from enacting a statute establishing gun free school zones as provided in this subsection.

CHAPTER NINE

Forms

Form I-1: Staff Skills Inventory

(To be conducted annually)

Name: _____   Room #: _____

Please check any of the following areas in which you have expertise or training:

Emergency Response:

__ First Aid   __ Search and Rescue   __ Emergency Management

__ CPR   __ Law Enforcement   __ CISD (Critical Incident
                                                   Stress Debriefing)

__ EMT   __ CB Radio   __ Other (Specify)

__ Firefighting   __ Ham Radio   _____

Mobile/cellular phone to be used in emergency:

_____

____ I speak the following foreign languages:

_____

_____

_____

_____

Source: Virginia Department of Education

Form I-2: Crisis Team Member List

Position/Name	Work Phone	Cell Phone
Principal _____	_____	_____
Ass't Principal_____	_____	_____
Guidance Director _____	_____	_____
School Nurse _____	_____	_____
Resource Officer _____	_____	_____
School Psychologist _____	_____	_____
Social Worker _____	_____	_____
Secretary _____	_____	_____
Teacher _____	_____	_____
Administrator _____	_____	_____
Counselor _____	_____	_____
Custodian _____	_____	_____

Source: Virginia Department of Education

Form I-3: Authorization to Release Children in Emergency

Dear Parents/Guardians:

Our school has developed an emergency business plan for use in the event of a disaster. The emergency plan is devoted to the welfare and safety of your child during school hours. It is available for inspection in the school office.

We are requesting your assistance at this time:
Should there be an emergency, such as a major fire, tornado or explosion, your child may be required to remain in the care of the school until it is deemed safe by an Emergency Services authority that the child can be released. At that point, children may be released only to properly authorized parents/guardians and/or designees. Therefore, please list as many names (with local telephone numbers and addresses) as possible, of those persons to whom you would allow your child's release in the event of an emergency. Be sure to notify those persons listed that you have authorized their supervision in case of an emergency.

If you are unable to come to school, it is essential that others be designated to care for your child. No child will be released to the care of unauthorized persons.

We appreciate your cooperation in this important matter.

CHILD: _____ **TEACHER:** _____ **GRADE:**_____

You may release my child to any of the persons listed below:

Name	*Phone*	*Address*	*Relationship*
_____	_____	_____	_____
_____	_____	_____	_____
_____	_____	_____	_____
_____	_____	_____	_____
_____	_____	_____	_____

Parent/Guardian: _____ Date:_____
                        Signature

Home Phone: _____ Cell/Work Phone: _____

Source: Virginia Department of Education

Form I-4: Situation Involving Weapon

These are steps for key personnel to take in situations involving a weapon at school.

Staff:
1. Notify principal or other designated individual.

2. Remain calm.

3. Avoid heroics.

4. Don't threaten.

5. Keep a safe, non-intimidating distance.

6. Avoid abrupt, sporadic movements.

7. Look to see whether there is a place you can dive or jump to.

8. Negotiate minimally until the principal, a designee or law enforcement personnel arrive.

Administrator or Designee:

1. Assess the situation and decide whether to call a lockdown or to handle the situation on a need-to-know basis.

2. Call 911.

3. Contact the superintendent at telephone number _____.

4. Inform another administrator or designee of the threat, ensuring classes do not change until an "all clear" has been issued.

5. Provide as much information as possible.

   • Be prepared to act as a resource and liaison between school and police.

   • Have a map of the school and grounds available for police.

6. Gather as much detailed information as possible and try to determine:

   • Location, identity and detailed description of individual.

Situation Involving Weapon *(continued)*

- Location and description of weapon.

- Any pertinent background information regarding the individual, including possible reason for carrying a weapon.

7. Isolate the individual. If the location of the weapon is known, prevent access to it.

8. Remain calm. Try not to raise your voice. If raising your voice becomes necessary, speak decisively and with clarity. Your tone and demeanor will strongly influence the outcome of the crisis.

9. Avoid heroics. Look for a place where you can dive or jump to, and keep a safe, non-intimidating distance.

10. Do not use force or touch the person or weapon. Avoid sudden moves or gestures.

11. Negotiate minimally until law enforcement arrives.

12. Meet with police when they arrive and follow their instructions.

Source: University of Arkansas System, Criminal Justice Institute, School Violence Resource Center

Form I-5: Violent Situations

These are general guidelines to follow when dealing with a violent or potentially violent individual at school.

Staff:
1. Notify principal or other designated individual.

2. Follow the following guidelines:

- Be empathetic. Try not to be judgmental regarding the person's feelings. They are real and must be attended, even if they are not based on reality.

- Clarify messages. Listen to what is really being said. Ask reflective questions. Use both silence and restatements.

- Respect personal space. Stand at least 1.5 to 3 feet away from the person who is acting out. Encroaching on personal space tends to escalate the situation.

- Be aware of your body position. Standing eye to eye and toe to toe sends a message of challenge. Standing one-leg length away and at an angle off to the side makes it less likely that the situation will escalate.

- Permit verbal venting if possible. Allow the individual to release as much energy as possible by venting verbally. If this cannot be allowed, state directives and reasonable limits during lulls in the venting process.

- Set and enforce reasonable limits. If the individual becomes belligerent, defensive or disruptive, state limits and directives clearly and concisely.

- Remain calm, rational and professional. How you respond will directly affect the individual's conduct.

- Use physical techniques only as a last resort. Use the least restrictive effective method. Using physical techniques on someone who is only acting out verbally can escalate the situation.

- Ignore challenge questions, as answering them can fuel a power struggle. When the individual challenges your

Violent Situations *(continued)*

position, training, etc., redirect the individual's attention to the issue at hand.

- Keep your nonverbal cues non-threatening. Be aware of your body language, movement and tone of voice. The more an individual loses control, the less he listens to your actual words. More attention is paid to nonverbal cues.

-From the National Crisis Prevention Institute

Administrator or Designee:

1. Follow the same above guidelines.

Source: University of Arkansas System, Criminal Justice Institute, School Violence Resource Center

Form I-6: Parent Letter Regarding Weapon at School

Dear Parent,

During third period today a student reported that another student had a hand gun in his backpack. The backpack was secured by administration, and the local police department was immediately notified. The police quickly responded, and the student and backpack were detained by police. The administration is working with the police department in an ongoing investigation.

I want to assure you that the safety of our students and staff is our top priority. The confiscation of the backpack and the detention of the student is due to the efforts of our staff and the local police department. Our administration and the local police department will continue to work together to make sure that all parties involved are held accountable.

Our school's staff and your school district are committed to keeping our campus safe. There are no additional safety issues related to this incident. We will continue to be diligent in the enforcement of our rules and will work in conjunction with law enforcement to keep our campus a safe place to learn.

Respectfully,

Principal

Source: John Speer, Principal, Millenium High School, Goodyear, AZ

Form II-1: Situation Involving Severe Weather

These are steps for key personnel to take in situations involving severe weather.

Tornadoes, Hurricanes and Thunderstorms

If a tornado watch or severe thunderstorm warning is received during school hours:

1. The principal or a designee should notify all school staff.

2. Teachers continue regular classroom activities.

3. School will dismiss at the normal hour in the regular manner. Drivers will follow regular routes using extra caution.

4. Review school procedures for establishing safe areas.

If there has been a tornado warning stating that a tornado has actually been sighted:

1. The principal or designee will receive the warning by way of radio tuned to a weather channel, a call from the superintendent or a designated representative, or the civil defense office.

2. The principal will inform the staff.

3. Staff and students will immediately proceed to an area predetermined by the school and assume a position protecting the face and head.

4. Teacher will take attendance and notify the principal or a designated representative if anyone is missing.

5. The school secretary or other designated individual will close all vaults and secure important records.

6. All qualified personnel will render first aid if necessary.

7. Staff and students will not return to their classrooms until the principal or a designated representative declares an "all clear."

If no warning has been issued, but a tornado has been sighted and is approaching the school, the principal or a designated representative will direct all individuals to proceed as follows:

Situation Involving Severe Weather *(continued)*

Plan 1 - If time permits, take classes to designated areas.

Plan 2 - If time does not permit removal to designated areas:

- Go to the nearest enclosed hallway, not to open corridors.

- Avoid open spaces and outside hallways.

- Avoid areas with large roof expanse such as the gymnasium, cafeteria or auditorium.

Take Cover Procedures

For the protection of all building occupants, it is important that everyone is informed and understands what to do in the event of severe weather that makes it necessary for the school population to take cover. The following take-cover procedures should be taught in each class:

1. Discuss the take-cover warning.

2. Practice the take-cover position.

3. Encourage students to remain calm and not to panic in the event of a crisis situation.

4. Discuss the "all clear" code.

Staff:

1. Take students to a hallway or other approved location. Seat them on the floor in the hall with their backs against the lockers/walls. If necessary, double up against the lockers/walls. If there is no time to move the students, have them get on the floor away from glass.

2. Instruct students to put their heads down against their knees, cover their necks with their hands and their faces with their arms.

TORNADO WATCH OR SEVERE THUNDERSTORMS

Administrators or designee:

1. The superintendent or a designee will decide whether to close the schools based on current weather information.

Situation Involving Severe Weather *(continued)*

2. If the schools close early, all procedures for the emergency closing of schools will be in effect.

If the weather becomes severe enough during the night or on the weekends to close the schools, all procedures for the emergency closing of schools will be put into effect.

Source: University of Arkansas System, Criminal Justice Institute, School Violence Resource Center

Form II-2: Sample Notice to Parents
Regarding Lockdown Drill

Date

Dear Parents/Guardians:

In keeping with our ongoing efforts to maintain a safe school, we will be conducting a lockdown drill on _____ (DATE) at _____ (TIME). Your child's teacher will prepare each class for this drill by discussing its specifics with the class ahead of time.

Please talk to your child about this drill.

- Calmly explain that a lockdown is something that the school does to keep students safe when a danger is present, such as when someone gains unauthorized access into the building.

- Assure your child that we hope a lockdown is never needed but that practicing the drill will help keep him or her safe.

- Compare the drill to a school drill they already are familiar with, such as a fire drill or a weather emergency drill.

- Remind your child that by practicing the drill we are better prepared to stay safe.

Form II-3: Gas Leak Response

Gas leaks are often identified by an odor similar to the odor of rotten eggs. If a gas leak is suspected, key personnel should take these steps:

Staff:
1. Notify principal or other designated individual.

2. If you are instructed to evacuate:

- Leave lights on.

- Do not lock doors.

- Instruct students to take with them any items that are easily accessible.

Administrator or Designee:
1. Determine whether you need to evacuate or shelter in place.

2. If evacuation is required:

- Assign staff members to check halls, restrooms, locker rooms and other areas for students.

- If inside, allow fresh air ventilation, if possible.

- If outside, move upwind from any odor.

3. Contact appropriate administrator at telephone number _____.

4. Contact insurance representative at telephone number _____.

5. Determine whether first aid is needed.

6. Establish safe places for classes to reconvene.

Source: University of Arkansas System, Criminal Justice Institute, School Violence Resource Center

Form II-4: Hazardous Spill Response

In the event of a hazardous spill, key personnel should take these steps.

Staff:
1. Notify principal or other designated individual.
2. Avoid direct or indirect contact with material spill.
3. Remove any contaminated clothing.
4. If you are instructed to evacuate:

- Leave lights on.

- Do not lock doors.

- Instruct students to take with them any items that are easily accessible.

Administrator or Designee:
1. Determine whether you need to evacuate or shelter in place.
2. Evacuate the area:

- If spill is outside, move students inside.

- If spill is inside, move students to location with different ventilation system.

- Assign staff members to check halls, restrooms, locker rooms and other areas for students.

- Avoid direct or indirect contact with material spill.

- Remove contaminated clothing.

3. Contact appropriate administrator at telephone number _____.
4. Contact insurance representative at telephone number _____.
5. Determine whether first aid is needed.
6. Establish safe places for classes to reconvene.

Source: University of Arkansas System, Criminal Justice Institute, School Violence Resource Center

Form II-5: Crisis Kit Checklist

Use this checklist to help make sure you have the materials you need to respond to a crisis. Gather and store crisis kit items at strategic locations inside and outside the school. Store the items in a large bag, plastic garbage bag or barrel. Possible storage areas include principals' offices, local fire and police departments, police car trunks, and designated school locations. Update the information in the kits as needed, and make sure you have enough supplies based on your school's size.

- Emergency response telephone numbers

- Placards with directional words like PARENTS, COUNSELORS, MEDIA, CLERGY, VOLUNTEERS and KEEP OUT

- Color-coded name tags and sign-in sheets for service personnel

- Blank white poster board for signs and duct tape to attach signs to tables

- Notebooks, pens and markers

- Preprinted referral pads to be given to counselors and clergy indicating name of counselor/clergy, name of person to be referred for follow-up, concerns and date

- Walkie-talkies to communicate with members of the crisis response team and other emergency personnel. Include extra batteries

- Ankle bands or wrist bands to identify victims

- First aid supplies

- Blankets

- School site layout, floor plans and aerial maps

- Current roster of student and staff with pictures, addresses, phone numbers, emergency contacts and medical information

- Attendance rosters

- Brief summary of school history, number of teachers and staff, and name of principal

Crisis Kit Checklist *(continued)*

- District fact sheet with enrollment, number of schools, etc.

- County map with school district bus routes marked

- Bus rosters and routes

- Resources list of support personnel, such as a contact person for the local phone company

- Caution tape

- Telephone directory for school system

Source: U.S. Department of Education

Form II-6: Emergency Telephone Numbers

Call 911 in any situation that presents an immediate danger to life and property. In addition, the following is a list of other important numbers.

	PHONE	FAX
Poison Control Center	_____	_____
Police	_____	_____
Sheriff's Office	_____	_____
Superintendent	_____	_____
Assistant Superintendent	_____	_____
Director of Transportation	_____	_____
Bus Transportation	_____	_____
Insurance	_____	_____

Source: University of Arkansas System, Criminal Justice Institute, School Violence Resource Center

Form II-7: Sample Letter Home Following Crisis Event

Date

Dear Parents/Guardians,

We regret to inform you about an unfortunate event affecting our school. Yesterday [provide a brief factual statement regarding the event]. An investigation is under way. Until it is complete, we will not have all the details about this tragedy.

The school's crisis team has begun meeting with students and staff. We anticipate that some may need continuing support for awhile to help them deal with the emotional upset that such an event produces. Enclosed are some materials that you may find helpful in talking about the matter at home.

If you have any questions or concerns that you think we can help address, please feel free to call the school at [phone number] and ask for any of the following staff members: [identify staff members].

The following community agencies are ready to help anyone who is feeling overwhelmed by their emotions:

• [Provide name and number of community health center].

• [Provide name and number of other available services provider].

We know events such as this are stressful. We are taking every step we can to be responsive to the needs of our students and their families.

Sincerely,

Principal

Source: U.S. Department of Education

Form II-8: Initial Announcement of Crisis Event

TO:
FROM:

We have just been advised of a tragedy involving a member of our school. I am sad to announce that _____
has died/has been in a serious accident. As soon as we have more information, we will pass it on to you. People will be available in the building to help those of you who need extra support in dealing with this situation. Your teachers will advise you of the location and times available for this support.

As soon as we know the family's/families' wishes regarding _____ we will share that information with you. We ask that all students remain in their classrooms and adhere to their regular schedules.

Source: Virginia Department of Education

Form II-9: Parent Information Sheet - Post-Disaster

Helping Your Child After a Disaster

Children may be especially upset and express feelings about the disaster. These reactions are normal and usually will not last long. Listed below are some problems you may see in your child:

- Excessive fear of darkness, separation, or being alone

- Clinging to parents, fear of strangers

- Worry

- Increase in immature behaviors

- Not wanting to go to school

- Changes in eating/sleeping behaviors

- Increase in either aggressive behavior or shyness

- Bed-wetting or thumb-sucking

- Persistent nightmares; and/or

- Headaches or other physical complaints.

The following will help your child:

- Talk with your child about his/her feelings about the disaster. Share your feelings, too.

- Talk about what happened. Give your child information he/she can understand.

- Reassure your child that you are safe and together. You may need to repeat this reassurance often.

- Hold and touch your child often.

- Spend extra time with your child at bedtime.

- Allow your child to mourn or grieve over a lost toy, a lost blanket, a lost home.

Parent Information Sheet - Post-Disaster *(continued)*

- If you feel your child is having problems at school, talk to his/her teacher so you can work together to help your child.

Please reread this sheet from time to time in the coming months. Usually a child's emotional response to a disaster will not last long, but some problems may be present or recur for many months afterward.

Your community mental health center is staffed by professionals skilled in talking with people experiencing disaster-related problems.

Source: Virginia Department of Education

Form II-10: Thank You Letter - Faculty/Staff

SCHOOL LETTERHEAD

Dear Faculty and Staff Members:

We would like to thank you for your support during the recent crisis at our school. Your professionalism and dedication were evident as we all worked to quiet and soothe scared students and allay their fears while still tending to instructional responsibilities.

We know that this has been an extremely difficult time for you as well as the students. Without your courage and concern, our school could not possibly have come through this crisis as well as we did.

Thank you once again. Your expertise and commitment have enabled all of us to work together as a team and overcome this tragic situation.

Sincerely,

Principal

Guidance Chair

Source: Virginia Department of Education

Form II-11: Bomb Threat Report Form

Make numerous copies and keep them at the main telephone or switchboard for immediate use.

Questions to Ask

1. When is bomb going to explode?
2. Where is it right now?
3. What does it look like?
4. What kind of bomb is it?
5. What will cause it to explode?
6. Did you place the bomb?
7. Why?
8. What is your address?
9. What is your name?

Caller's Voice

____	Calm	____	Nasal
____	Angry	____	Stutter
____	Excited	____	Lisp
____	Slow	____	Raspy
____	Rapid	____	Deep
____	Soft	____	Ragged
____	Loud	____	Clearing Throat
____	Laughter	____	Deep Breathing
____	Crying	____	Cracking Voice
____	Normal	____	Disguised
____	Distinct	____	Accent
____	Slurred	____	Familiar
____	Whispered		

Exact Wording of Threat

_____

_____

_____

Time:_____ Date: _____
Sex of caller: ____ Culture: ____
Age: _____ Length of call: ____

Number at which call was received:

_____

If voice was familiar, who did it sound
like? _____

Background Sounds

_____	Street	____	Animal Noises
_____	PA System	____	Static
_____	Voices	____	Music
_____	Motor	____	House Noises
_____	Local	____	Office Machines
_____	Booth	____	Long Distance

Remarks:

_____

_____

_____

Threat Language

____ Well-spoken
____ Foul language
____ Taped
____ Incoherent
____ Message read

Source: Virginia Department of Education

Form II-12: Intruder Response

In the event that an intruder gains unauthorized access to school premises, key personnel should take these steps.

Staff:
1. Notify principal or other designated individual.

2. Take attendance and remain with students.

3. Wait for instructions.

Administrator or Designee:
1. Assess situation and determine threat level.

2. Call 911 if danger is indicated.

3. Contact appropriate administrator at telephone number _____.

4. If lockdown is needed, notify teachers.

5. Keep telephone lines open for emergency use.

6. Provide police with maps of building and grounds.

Source: University of Arkansas System, Criminal Justice Institute, School Violence Resource Center

Form II-13: Students/Staff Needing Special Assistance for Evacuation

Name	Grade/Homeroom	Assistance Needed/Assister

Main Building

_____	_____	_____
_____	_____	_____
_____	_____	_____
_____	_____	_____
_____	_____	_____
_____	_____	_____
_____	_____	_____
_____	_____	_____
_____	_____	_____
_____	_____	_____

Annex A

_____	_____	_____
_____	_____	_____
_____	_____	_____
_____	_____	_____
_____	_____	_____
_____	_____	_____
_____	_____	_____
_____	_____	_____

Source: Virginia Department of Education

Form II-14: 911 Script and Phone List – Cheerleader Injury

(Post by phones)

In case of emergency, call: _____

When the call is answered, talk slowly and clearly and say:

"We are located at (school or name of location). Our address is (street address, city, state and zip code). Our phone number is (a number that can be called back). One of our cheerleaders has injured her (describe nature of injury) and needs an ambulance. Please come to (provide the specific location at the site, such as "Main Gym" or "Tyler Field") located at (provide specifics of the location, such as "on the corner of Main Street and Tiger Drive"). We will have someone there to direct you."

Stay on the line until the dispatcher says you can hang up!

Additional Numbers:

Training Room Number: (_____) _____ - _____

Campus Security Number: (_____) _____ - _____

Other Numbers: (Principal, etc.)

_____ (_____) _____ - _____

_____ (_____) _____ - _____

_____ (_____) _____ - _____

Source: American Association of Cheerleading Coaches and Administrators

Form II-15: Parental Consent Form for Mercury Testing

Parents,

Please fill out the information below for your child (one for each student) and sign.

Student's name _____

SSN _____

Address _____

Sex (Circle one):   M   F

Date of birth _____

Phone number _____

Race (Circle one):
    American Indian   Alaska Native   Asian
    Black/African American   Native Hawaiian
    Other Pacific Islander   Underreported/Refuse to report

Ethnicity (Circle one):
    Hispanic/Latino   Non-Hispanic/Latino
    Underreported/Refuse to report

I give CONSENT to the LOCAL health department and its staff for my child named at the top of this form to have mercury levels checked with a urine test. (If this consent form is not signed and dated, then your child will not be tested.)

Signature of parent/legal guardian _____

Date (mm/dd/yy) _____

Source: Birmingham City Schools

Form II-16: Crisis Procedure Checklist

A crisis plan must address many complex contingencies. There should be a step-by-step procedure to use when a crisis occurs. For example:

____Assess life/safety issues immediately.

____Provide immediate emergency medical care.

____Call 911 and notify police/rescue first. Call the superintendent second.

____Convene the crisis team to assess the situation and implement the crisis response procedures.

____Evaluate available and needed resources.

____Alert school staff to the situation.

____Secure all areas.

____Implement evacuation and other procedures to protect students and staff from harm. Avoid dismissing students to unknown care.

____Adjust the bell schedule to ensure safety during the crisis.

____Alert person in charge of various information systems to prevent confusion and misinformation. Notify parents.

____Contact appropriate community agencies and the school district's public information office, if appropriate.

____Implement post-crisis procedures.

Source: U.S. Department of Education

Form II-17: What Are "Education Records"?

When you can – and can't – release information can be tricky business, thanks to the Family Educational Rights and Privacy Act (FERPA). As a general rule, FERPA requires schools to protect students' privacy. However, exceptions to FERPA confidentiality requirements apply in emergency situations.

Led by the Federal Bureau of Investigation and the Federal Emergency Management System, several government agencies – the Departments of Education, Homeland Security, Justice, Health and Human Services – completed the "Guide for Developing High-Quality School Emergency Operations Plans."

This guide provides examples of emergency-related exceptions to FERPA confidentiality rules.

Before we discuss the exceptions, we need to know what an "education record" is.

These types of records generally are considered to be education records, meaning they are protected under FERPA:

1. Transcripts

2. Disciplinary records

3. Standardized test results

4. Health (including mental health) and family history records

5. Records on services provided to students under the IDEA

6. Records on services and accommodations provided to students under Section 504 and Title II of the ADA

These types of records generally are not considered to be education records, meaning they are not protected by FERPA:

1. Records that are kept in the sole possession of the maker and used only as personal memory aids

What Are "Education Records"? *(continued)*

2. Law enforcement unit records

3. Grades on peer-graded papers before they are collected and recorded by a teacher

4. Records created or received by a school after an individual is no longer in attendance and that are not directly related to the individual's attendance at the school

5. Employee records that relate exclusively to an individual in that individual's capacity as an employee

6. Information obtained through a school official's personal knowledge or observation rather than from the student's education records

Source: Guide for Developing High-Quality School Emergency Operations Plans, http://rems.ed.gov/docs/REMS_K-12_Guide_508.pdf

Form II-18: Threat and Hazard Types and Examples

Planning teams must consider the probability, magnitude, warning time and duration of each possible threat or hazard. Some threat and hazard examples to consider include:

<u>Natural Hazards</u>

- Earthquakes

- Tornadoes

- Lightning

- Severe wind

- Hurricanes

- Floods

- Wildfires

- Extreme temperatures

- Landslides or mudslides

- Tsunamis

- Volcanic eruptions

- Winter precipitation

<u>Technological Hazards</u>

- Explosions or accidental release of toxins
  from industrial plants

- Accidental release of hazardous materials
  from within the school, such as gas leaks or laboratory spills

- Hazardous material releases from major highways
  or railroads

- Radiological releases from nuclear power stations

- Dam failure

Threat and Hazard Types and Examples *(continued)*

- Power failure

- Water failure

<u>Biological Hazards</u>

- Infectious diseases, such as pandemic influenza, extensively drug-resistant tuberculosis, *Staphylococcus aureus* and meningitis

- Contaminated food outbreaks, including Salmonella, botulism and *E.coli*

- Toxic materials present in school laboratories

<u>Adversarial, Incidental and Human-caused Threats</u>

- Fire

- Active shooters

- Criminal threats or actions

- Gang violence

- Bomb threats

- Domestic violence and abuse

- Cyber attacks

- Suicide

(Source: Guide for Developing High-Quality School Emergency Plans, www.dhs.gov/sites/default/files/publications/REMS%20K-12%20Guide%20508_0.pdf)

Form II-19: FEMA's Earthquake Preparedness Checklist

To keep students and staff safe in an earthquake, prepare them by conducting safety drills.

If students are <u>inside the school</u>, they should:

- Drop to the ground, take cover under a sturdy table or desk and hold on until the shaking stops.

- Cover their faces and heads in their arms and crouch in a corner if sturdy desks or tables aren't available for shelter.

- Stay away from glass, windows or anything that might fall, such as light fixtures.

- Stay inside until the shaking stops.

- Avoid the elevators.

If students are <u>outside</u>, they should:

- Stay outside.

- Get away from utility wires, buildings, streetlights and other structures. (Most earthquake-related deaths occur from flying debris, collapsing buildings and falling objects.)

If students are on the school bus, drivers should be trained to:

- Stop as quickly as safety permits.

- Avoid stopping near or under buildings, trees, overpasses, underpasses or utility wires.

- Keep students on the bus.

- Proceed with caution after the quake has stopped.

- Avoid roads, bridges or ramps that may have been structurally damaged.

- Contact the school if possible.

Source: http://www.ready.gov/earthquakes

Form II-20: Checklist: Reunification After a Crisis

When the feds updated their guidance to help school officials align their emergency planning practices with new national safety and security standards, they included plans to reunite families after a crisis.

As part of the "Family Reunification Annex," the emergency planning team must contemplate the best ways for school officials to:

- Protect parents' and students' privacy

- Verify that an adult has the authority to take custody of a student

- Facilitate communication between the parent check-in area and the student assembly area

- Ensure students do not leave on their own

- Address language barriers that may exist, and

- Keep families updated.

Source: Guide For Developing High-Quality School EmergencyOperations Plans

Form III-1: Bus Transportation Accident Response

Steps for key personnel to take in the event of a bus transportation accident:

Bus Driver:
1. Notify dispatch using proper procedures.
2. Secure the bus, making sure no passengers leave and no one boards the bus.
3. Set out warning devices such as triangle or cones.
4. Determine whether anyone has been injured.
5. Move the bus to a safer location on the side of the road, if possible.
6. Passenger safety is the most important thing to keep in mind. If the bus is not badly damaged and is not in danger of being struck, keep the passengers on the bus until help arrives.
7. Refer media to administration.

Dispatch:
1. Take control. Remain calm and help the driver make proper decisions.
2. Call designated management staff.
3. Call appropriate law enforcement agency or 911.

Transportation Personnel:
1. Upon arrival, assess for immediate safety concerns.
2. Complete accident reports and take pictures.
3. Refer media to administration.

Schools:
1. Contact parents and relay necessary information.
2. Conduct follow-up on any student who received medical treatment within three days of accident.

Source: University of Arkansas System, Criminal Justice Institute, School Violence Resource Center

Form III-2: Parent Letter - Notice of Bus Accident

Dear Parents,

This morning, prior to school, there was an accident involving a school bus and an automobile. There were known injuries to the passengers of the car. The children on Bus # _____ witnessed the aftermath of the accident but were not involved in it.

The children from the bus involved in the accident were taken to the library by the guidance counselors and administration. The children were asked if they were injured in any way and their parents were then contacted. Because your child was on Bus # ____ he or she may show delayed reaction to the accident. Please be alert over the next several days to symptoms of delayed reaction, including:

- a desire to be alone, unusually quiet

- loss of appetite

- problems with sleeping, nightmares

- difficulty with concentration

- crying

- angry outburst, short temper

- headaches, upset stomach

- depressed, sad

Your child may also exhibit some physical complaints. Please contact (principal's name) to fill out an accident report. The school will be offered support services for students needing help dealing with the accident. We will also provide counseling services to parents in helping their children to cope. Please don't hesitate to call if you have any questions or concerns.

Sincerely,

Principal of School

Source: Virginia Department of Education

Form III-3: Policy Regarding Social Networking Websites

All employees, faculty and staff of the _____ school district who participate in social networking websites (such as MySpace or Facebook) shall not post any data, documents, photographs or inappropriate information on any website that might result in a disruption of classroom activity. This determination will be made by the Superintendent. Employees, faculty and staff should not give social networking website passwords to students. Fraternization via the Internet between employees, faculty or staff and students is prohibited, and violation of any of these policies may result in disciplinary action, up to and including termination. Nothing in this policy prohibits employees, faculty, staff or students from using educational websites such as _____, since these sites are used solely for educational purposes. Access of social networking websites for individual use during school hours is prohibited.

Source: Lamar County (Mississippi) School District

Form III-4: Letter to Parents Regarding Sexting

Dear Parents and Guardians,

Today, our staff spoke with students in their first-period classes about some troubling behavior in which teens are engaging and which has occurred at the national, state and local levels. The behavior is commonly referred to as "sexting" (the act of sending sexually explicit material via cell phone). This week, we learned that this behavior is occurring at our school and at other schools in our district.

In an effort to better educate our students about this topic, teachers at our school were directed to read the following to students at the conclusion of morning announcements:

Some students at our school and other schools in our district have been sending and receiving inappropriate pictures on their cell phones. The pictures have been sexually explicit in nature. This practice is commonly referred to as "sexting." This is a particularly dangerous behavior for middle school students to engage in because they are minors.

If you or anyone you know has engaged in this activity, you must remove those pictures from your phone or any other place they may be (computer, etc.) and not engage in this behavior in the future. It is important for you to know that engaging in this behavior is a serious offense.

Our intent is to educate you about this matter and to help protect you from the serious social and criminal consequences that can occur if you engage in this behavior. Our overall goal is to keep you safe and to provide a safe and supportive learning environment here at our school.

Teachers were also instructed to remind students that electronic communications can spread rapidly anywhere in the world and can be tracked.

We care deeply about the students and the community we serve, and we appreciate your support as we educate our students about this issue. Please use this as an opportunity to talk to your child about proper cell phone use and the potential consequences of misuse. If you have any questions on the matter, please contact me at [PHONE].

Sincerely,

Principal

Source: Kristen Rae, Principal, Chinook Middle School, Lacey, WA

Form III-5: Harassment/Bullying Incident Report Form

Date: _____ Time: _____ Room/Location: _____

□ Staff □ Student(s) Accused of Bullying/Harassment:

_____ Grade: ____ Class: _____

_____ Grade: ____ Class: _____

□ Staff □ Student(s) Affected:

_____ Grade: ____ Class: _____

_____ Grade: ____ Class: _____

Inappropriate behaviors observed by adult(s) (check all that apply):

□	Name calling	□	Spitting
□	Stalking	□	Demeaning Comments
□	Inappropriate Gesturing	□	Stealing
□	Staring/Leering	□	Damaging Property
□	Writing/Graffiti	□	Shoving/Pushing
□	Threatening	□	Hitting/Kicking
□	Taunting/Ridiculing	□	Flashing a Weapon
□	Inappropriate Touching	□	Intimidation/Extortion
□	Cyberbullying	□	Other _____

Harassment/Bullying Incident Report Form *(continued)*

Describe the incident:

_____

_____

Did the injury involve physical injury?

☐   Yes   ☐   No

Names of witnesses:

_____

_____

_____

Physical Evidence:

☐ Graffiti   ☐ Notes   ☐ E-Mail   ☐ Websites _____

☐ Videotape ☐ Audiotape ☐ Other _____

Staff signature: _____ Title: _____

Parent(s) contacted: Date: _____   Time: _____

                         Date: _____   Time: _____

Administrative action taken:

_____

_____

Source: Oklahoma State Department of Education

Form III-6: Student Pledge for iPad Use

1. I will take good care of my iPad.

2. I will never leave the iPad unattended. Unattended iPads will be taken to the office.

3. I will never loan out my iPad to other individuals.

4. I will know where my iPad is at all times.

5. I will charge my iPad completely before the beginning of the school day.

6. I will keep food and beverages away from my iPad since they may damage the device.

7. I will not disassemble any part of my iPad or attempt any repairs or jailbreak my iPad.

8. I will protect my iPad by keeping it in the school-provided protective case.

9. I will use my iPad in ways that are appropriate, meet district expectations and are educational in nature.

10. I will not deface or place decorations (stickers or markers, etc.) on the iPad. I will not deface the serial number.

11. I understand that my iPad is subject to inspection at any time without notice and remains property of the school district. I will not put a security code on my iPad.

12. I will follow the policies outlined in the district's iPad Handbook at all times.

13. I will file a police report in case of theft, vandalism and other acts covered by insurance.

14. I will be responsible for all damage or loss caused by neglect or abuse.

Student Pledge for iPad Use *(continued)*

15. I agree to return the district iPad and power cords in good
    working condition.

16. I will not utilize unauthorized photos, videos and/or audio recordings
    of myself or any other person in an inappropriate manner.

I agree to the stipulations set forth in the Student Pledge for iPad Use.

Student's name (Please Print): _____

Grade: _____

Student signature: _____

Date: _____

Parent/guardian name (Please Print): _____

Parent/guardian signature: _____

School iPads and accessories must be returned to _____
at the end of each school year. Students who graduate early, withdraw, are
suspended or expelled, or terminate enrollment at _____ for
any other reason must return their iPad on the date of termination.

Source: Oakley High School, Oakley, Kansas

Form IV-1: Sample Parent Letter Following
Weapons Incident

Dear Parents and Guardians,

I am writing as a follow-up to my previous phone message regarding the student who carried disassembled pieces of a gun onto a (school name) bus today, and the subsequent steps taken to ensure student safety.

As explained in my message, the disassembled parts could not be discharged. Still, the pieces were quickly confiscated thanks to the responsible actions of another student who promptly reported their presence. This eliminated any possible danger to students and staff. We then contacted police, who are investigating the incident.

Please tell your children that the very presence of any weapon, even in pieces, poses serious potential threat. That is why the weapons are strictly prohibited in school and there are serious consequences for violators.

In today's situation, students were never in immediate danger. Continued safety was assured because a student did the right thing by reporting the matter to an adult.

Please discuss what happened with students who are old enough to understand. Reassure them that they are safe at school, but let them know they play an important role in maintaining that safety.

I will continue to keep you informed of all situations that affect our commitment to student safety. Working together, we can all keep (school name) a safe place to learn and grow.

Thank you for your understanding and support.

Sincerely,

Source: Ellis Elementary School,
Prince William County Schools, Virginia

Form IV-2: Student Knife Contract

We can work together to keep knives out of school. At [*school name*], every student has the right to feel safe and be safe at school.

- There is no reason for a student to have a knife at school

- No knives are allowed to be taken to school by students

- It is against the law for a student to have a knife at school

- A student who has a knife at school may receive serious consequences

What kinds of knives are banned?

You are not allowed to have any type of knife at school, including:

- Flick knives, ballistic knives, sheath knives, push daggers, trench knives, butterfly knives, star knives, butter knives, fruit knives or craft knives

- Any item that can be used as a weapon, for example, a chisel

What will happen if I bring a knife to school?

If you have a knife at school:

- The principal may call the police

- Police may search you and your property

- You may be disciplined, such as [include specific examples according to school policy]

- You may face criminal charges

How can I help to keep [school name] safe?

- Make sure you know the laws and rules about knives

- Ask your parents not to put knives or knife tools in your lunch box, pencil case or craft kit

Student Knife Contract *(continued)*

- Contact your teacher immediately if you are being bullied or threatened at school

- Immediately tell your teacher or another adult if you think someone had a knife at school, or if someone mentioned bringing a knife to school

- Immediately tell a teacher if a student is threatening anyone with an object that could cause injuries.

Source: Adapted from Queensland Government, Australia

Form VI-1: Questionnaire for Chaperones

Thank you for volunteering to serve as a chaperone for the following field trip: [INSERT TRIP DESCRIPTION AND DATE OF TRIP]. We value your willingness to help our school and our students.

Please complete, sign and date this form and return it to _____ no later than _____. Once we review the completed form, we will notify you whether you have been selected to serve as a chaperone on this trip. If the answer to any question below is "Yes," please explain in the space provided.

1. ___ Yes ___ No   Have you ever been disciplined for any type of misconduct in connection with your employment?

2. ___ Yes ___ No   Have you ever been convicted of a criminal offense?

3. ___ Yes ___ No   Are you on probation in any state?

4. ___ Yes ___ No   Have you ever been acquitted or found not guilty of any criminal offense for reasons related to insanity or diminished mental capacity?

5. ___ Yes ___ No   Are any criminal charges currently pending against you?

I certify that I am at least 21 years of age and have completed this form truthfully and to the best of my knowledge.

PRINT NAME: _____ SIGNATURE: _____

DATE: _____

ADDRESS: _____

PHONE: _____

Form VI-2: Guidelines for Chaperones

Thank you for agreeing to serve as a chaperone for the following field trip: [INSERT TRIP DESCRIPTION AND DATE OF TRIP].

As a chaperone, you serve as a role model and help students learn. The following guidelines for chaperones apply to this trip. Please review them carefully. Please sign and date this form and return it to _____ no later than _____. Once again, thank you for your assistance.

1. Chaperones are required to remain with their assigned group at all times, until chaperoning duties are finished.

2. Chaperones agree to continuously monitor their group's activities.

3. Chaperones will not use any alcohol or tobacco products during the trip at any time.

4. Chaperones will refrain from using profane or inappropriate language at any time during the trip.

5. Chaperones are NEVER to touch a child unless the child is presenting an immediate threat to the health or safety of himself or others.

6. Chaperones are not to administer medications to students.

7. Chaperones may not bring along non-student siblings or other children on the trip.

8. Chaperones will report any safety or health concerns to a teacher immediately.

I have read the above guidelines and agree to abide by them.

NAME: _____

SIGNATURE: _____

DATE: _____

Form VI-3: Field Trip Permission Slip

On _____, your child's class will be taking a field trip to _____.
We will be leaving the school at _____
and returning at _____. The cost of this trip is _____.

If cost is a concern, please contact the school principal.

Please complete and return the bottom portion of this form no later than
_____. Your child will not be permitted to attend if this slip is not
completed and returned.

I give permission for my child, _____, of room ____,
to attend the field trip to _____ on _____
I am enclosing a check or money order in the amount of _____
made payable to _____, to cover the cost of this trip.

I hereby grant permission for school personnel to arrange for the provision
of medical treatment to _____ in the event of a medical
emergency. If such an emergency occurs, please contact
_____ at phone number _____ or
_____ at phone number _____

If your child is allergic to any medications, please list them here (if none,
write "none"): _____.

NAME: _____

SIGNATURE _____

PHONE: _____

RELATIONSHIP TO STUDENT_____

Form VI-4: Mentor Contract

Name: _____   Date: _____

By choosing to participate in this mentoring program, I agree to:
- Follow all rules and guidelines as outlined by the program coordinator, mentor training, program policies, and this contract
- Provide the support and advice to help my mentee succeed
- Make a one-year commitment to being matched with my mentee
- Meet at least eight hours per month with my mentee
- Make at least weekly contact with my mentee
- Obtain parent/guardian permission for all meeting times at least three days in advance, if possible
- Be on time for scheduled meetings or call my mentee at least 24 hours beforehand if I am unable to make a meeting
- Submit monthly meeting times and activities to the program coordinator, and regularly and openly communicate with the program coordinator as requested
- Inform the program coordinator of any difficulties or areas of concern that may arise in the relationship
- Keep any information that my mentee tells me confidential except as may cause him or others harm
- Always obey traffic laws when in the presence of my mentee and keep a copy of his/her health insurance coverage in the automobile at all times when traveling together
- Never be in the presence of my mentee when I have or am consuming alcohol, tobacco, or controlled substances
- Participate in a closure process when that time comes
- Notify the program coordinator if I have any changes in address, phone number, or employment status
- Attend in-service mentor training sessions twice per year

_____ (please initial) I understand that upon match closure, future contact with my mentee is beyond the scope of this program and may happen only by the mutual consensus of the mentor, the mentee, and parent/guardian.

I agree to follow all the above stipulations of this program as well as any other conditions as instructed by the program coordinator.

_____   _____
(Signature)   (Date)

Source: U.S. Department of Education

Form VI-5: Mentor Acceptance Letter

Date

Mr. John Doe
123 Main Street
Anytown, USA

Dear Mr. Doe,

Congratulations!

On behalf of our mentoring program, we are happy to inform you of
your acceptance as a mentor. Without the enthusiasm of volunteers like
you, we would not be able to accomplish our mission.

We thank you for taking the time and effort to join our program and
look forward to continuing to support you and assist you as a mentor.
At this time, we are working in finding you a suitable match and will
contact you when we have found you a mentee.

Sincerely,

Principal/Program Coordinator

Source: U.S. Department of Education

Form VI-6: Mentor Rejection Letter

Date

Mr. John Doe
123 Main Street
Anytown, USA

Dear Mr. Doe,

On behalf of our mentoring program, I wanted to express my sincere
thanks for your interest in our program. I understand that you have
given a considerable amount of time to this process and we greatly
appreciate your effort. Unfortunately, we are unable to accept your
application to be a mentor for our program.

Thank you again for your time and interest in our program.

Sincerely,

Principal/Program Coordinator

Source: U.S. Department of Education

Form VI-7: Parent/Guardian Mentoring Contract

Name: _____   Date: _____

By allowing my son/daughter to participate in the mentoring program, I agree to:

- Allow my child to participate in the program and to be matched with a mentor
- Follow and encourage my child to follow all rules and guidelines as outlined by the program coordinator, mentee training, program policies, and this contract
- Support my child in this match by allowing him to meet with his mentor at least eight hours per month and have weekly contact with him/her for a year
- Support my child being on time for scheduled meetings or have him/her call the mentor at least 24 hours beforehand if unable to make a meeting
- Regularly and openly communicate with the program coordinator as requested
- Inform the program coordinator if I observe any difficulties or have areas of concern that may arise in the match relationship
- Participate in a closure process when that time comes
- Notify the program coordinator if I have any changes in address or phone number
- Provide the program coordinator and the mentor with any updated health insurance information for my child

_____ (please initial) I understand that upon match closure, future contact between my child and his/her mentor is beyond the scope of this mentoring program, and can happen only by the mutual consensus of the mentor, the mentee, and their parent/guardian.

I agree to follow all the above stipulations of this program as well as any other conditions as instructed by the program coordinator.

_____   _____
(Signature)   (Date)

Source: U.S. Department of Education

Form VI-8: Mentor Contact and Information Release Form

Youth's Name: _____ Date: _____

School: _____

I hereby grant permission for the mentoring program to make contact with my child and conduct a personal interview for the purpose of applying to be a mentee. The program may also make contact with my child on school premises for the purpose of screening and interviewing as well as ongoing support of his/her participation in the mentoring program.

I authorize the program to obtain any needed information regarding my child from his/her school's staff, including academic and behavioral records and conversations with teachers, counselors, and other administrative staff.

Further, I understand that basic information about my child will be anonymously (without names) shared with a prospective mentor(s) to aid in determining a suitable match. Once a mentor/mentee match is determined, my child's identity and other relevant information will be shared with the mentor to the extent it aids in facilitating a successful match.

_____   _____
Parent/Guardian Signature   Date

Parent/Guardian Name: _____

Street Address: _____

City: _____ State: _____ Zip: _____

Source: U.S. Department of Education

Form VI-9: Playground Safety Checklist

Use this checklist to make sure your playground area is a safe place to play.

1. Make sure the surfaces surrounding playground equipment either have at least 12 inches of wood chips, mulch, sand, or pea gravel, or are mats made of safety-tested rubber or rubber-like materials.

2. Check that protective surfacing extends at least six feet in all directions from play equipment. For swings, be sure surfacing extends, in front and back, twice the height of the suspending bar.

3. Make sure play structures more than 30 inches high are spaced at least nine feet apart.

4. Check for dangerous hardware, such as open "S" hooks or protruding bolt ends.

5. Make sure spaces that could trap children, such as openings in guardrails or between ladder rungs, measure less than 3.5 inches or more than nine inches.

6. Check for sharp points or edges in equipment.

7. Make sure there are no tripping hazards, such as exposed concrete footings, tree stumps and rocks.

8. Make sure elevated surfaces such as platforms and ramps have guardrails to prevent falls.

9. Regularly check to ensure that equipment and surfacing are in good condition.

10. Carefully supervise children at all times.

Source: U.S. Consumer Product Safety Commission

Form VI-10: Concussion Quiz for Coaches, Athletes and Parents

Mark each of the following statements as True (T) or False (F).

1. A concussion is a brain injury.

2. Concussions can occur in any organized or unorganized recreational sport or activity.

3. You can't see a concussion and some athletes may not experience and/or report symptoms until hours or days after the injury.

4. Following a coach's rules for safety and the rules of the sport, practicing good sportsmanship at all times, and using the proper sports equipment are all ways that athletes can prevent a concussion.

5. Concussions can be caused by a fall or by a bump or blow to the head or body.

6. Concussions can happen even if the athlete hasn't been knocked out or lost consciousness.

7. Nausea, headaches, sensitivity to light or noise, and difficulty concentrating are some of the symptoms of concussion.

8. Athletes who have a concussion should not return to play until they are symptom-free and have received approval from a doctor or health care professional.

9. A repeat concussion that occurs before the brain recovers from the first can slow recovery or increase the likelihood of having long-term problems.

ANSWER KEY: 1. True. 2. True. 3. True. 4. True. 5.True.
6. True. 7. True. 8. True. 9. True.

Source: Centers for Disease Control and Prevention

Form VI-11: Behavior Contract/Prom Permission Slip

Student's Name _____

Guest's Name _____

Student Release Information

I have read the rules on this form, the Behavior Contract/Prom Permission Slip, and agree to abide by them. I understand the consequences for any inappropriate behavior. I understand the dance is a school event, and like all school events, is TOBACCO, DRUG AND ALCOHOL FREE. **MY DATE AND I AGREE TO REMAIN DRUG AND ALCOHOL FREE FOR THIS EVENT!**

Student signature _____

Printed name _____Date _____

I understand that I may be called if my child has a problem at this event. The phone numbers where I may be reached are

(home) _____ and (cell) _____

Parent/Guardian signature _____

Relationship to student _____Date _____

Guest Release Information

I have read the rules on this form, the Behavior Contract/Prom Permission Slip, and agree to abide by them. I understand the consequences for any inappropriate behavior. I understand the dance is a school event, and like all school events, is TOBACCO, DRUG AND ALCOHOL FREE. MY DATE AND I AGREE TO REMAIN DRUG AND ALCOHOL FREE FOR THIS EVENT!

Guest signature _____

Printed name _____Date _____

Grade ____Age ____ School attending _____

I understand that I may be called if my child has a problem at this event. The phone numbers where I may be reached are

(home) _____ and (cell) _____

Parent/Guardian signature _____

Relationship to student _____Date _____

Please have an administrator from the guest's school sign below and include the administrator's business card. **NOTE: Please do not sign if guest has been suspended or expelled.**

Administrator's signature_____

Administrator's printed name _____

Phone number _____

Behavior Contract/Prom Permission Slip *(continued)*

The prom will be held on _____, beginning at ___ and ending at ___
at _____ _____. Students who
purchase tickets are required to inform their guests of all contract rules.
Students and guests are required to abide by all school rules and terms
of this contract. Any student or guest exhibiting disruptive behavior will
be removed from the dance, and the student/guest will be released to
a chaperone or police if parents cannot be reached. Students will be
held accountable for the behavior of their guest. No reimbursement or
refund will be given if students and guests are asked to leave for not
following this agreement.

Tickets
Tickets will be on sale beginning _____. They will be
available at _____.
Ticket prices are $_____. Accepted forms of payment include ____
_____.

Refunds will be considered up until 48 hours before the dance.
Absolutely no refunds after that point. Students who are removed
or denied entry will not receive refunds.

Students must bring a clear copy of their student ID. Guests must
bring a clear photocopy of a current high school photo ID card or a
government-issued photo ID that shows date of birth. Copies must be
legible to be accepted.
We do not make copies – bring your own.

Admittance
Admittance is subject to administrator's approval. **Admittance is
a privilege, not a right**, which may be revoked for a lack of
responsibility at the school, including but not limited to: unpaid fines,
unfulfilled detentions, serious (suspensions or expulsions) or chronic
discipline issues, unsatisfactory attendance or failing grades.

All attendees must present valid picture identification at the registration
table at the dance to be admitted.
NO VALID ID, NO ENTRANCE!

All attendees must be willing to submit to alcohol/drug testing. All
students and their guests may be searched for weapons and illegal
substances prior to entry of the dance.

No one will be admitted after _____ without prior written
consent from _____. Attendees are
required to stay until _____ before they are released from the
dance. Students and guests who leave the prom will not be readmitted.

Behavior Contract/Prom Permission Slip *(continued)*

All students and guests must be picked up by _____.

Rules
All school rules and regulations are enforced at any school event.
Any student or guest suspected of using alcohol or any controlled or
illegal substance will be removed from the dance. Parents will be called
to escort the student home. Smoking tobacco at school events is
prohibited. Any student who is under the influence of any substance
is subject to suspension.

Students who purchase tickets are required to inform their guests about
the contract rules. Guests are required to abide by the rules and the
terms of this contract. Any student or guest exhibiting disruptive
behavior will be removed from the dance, and the student/guest will
be released to a chaperone or police if parents cannot be reached.
Students will be held accountable for the behavior of their guest. No
reimbursement or refund will be given if students and guests are asked
to leave for not following this agreement.

Students who violate any school rule or the terms of this contract will
face disciplinary action.

Conduct
No dancing such as freaking, moshing or slamming will be permitted.
No back-to-front dancing, bending over, no leg or hip riding, both feet
must be on the floor and any other dancing deemed inappropriate by
administration. **NOTE: Violation of the dancing policy will consist
of removal from the dance floor and forfeit attendance at the next
school sponsored formal dance.** No reimbursement will be given to
attendees who are asked to leave for violating the dance policy.

Dress Code
Formal attire is required for prom. The following dress code restrictions
will be in effect. Violations may result in non-admittance. If dress code
violations occur after admittance, students and/or guests may be
removed from the dance. If anyone has specific questions regarding
the appropriateness of their dress, please consult with
_____ or _____
prior to the event.

Females: Dresses that expose skin in the midriff area are not
acceptable, including revealing sides and low-cut backs.

Bandeau/tube/scarf tops and excessively low cut or plunging
necklines are prohibited.

Behavior Contract/Prom Permission Slip *(continued)*

Dresses must be an appropriate length, which is _____.

Any other clothing deemed inappropriate by the school dress code is prohibited.

Males: Collared shirts, slacks, ties required.

No jeans or shorts are permitted.

Undershirts may not be worn in place of collared shirt.

Bare chest may not be exposed.

Any other clothing deemed inappropriate by the school dress code is prohibited.

Checklist to include with completed form:

_____ Photocopies of all attendees' IDs (attach to form).

_____ Payment for tickets.

_____ Permission slip signed by all parties and filled out completely.

_____ Administrator's signature for guest admittance.

Source: Mission Viejo High School

Form VII-1: Parent Letter Regarding Child with Allergy

Dear Parents,

This letter is to inform you that a student in your child's classroom has a severe peanut/nut allergy. Strict avoidance of peanut/nut products is the only way to prevent a life-threatening allergic reaction. We are asking your assistance in providing the student with a safe learning environment.

If exposed to peanuts/nuts the student may develop a life-threatening allergic reaction that requires emergency medical treatment. The greatest potential for exposure at school is to peanut products and nut products. To reduce the risk of exposure, the classroom will be peanut/nut free. Please do not send any peanut- or nut-containing products for your child to eat during snack-time in the classroom. Any exposure to peanuts or nuts through contact or ingestion can cause a severe reaction. If your child has eaten peanuts or nuts prior to coming to school, please be sure your child's hands have been thoroughly washed prior to entering the school.

Since lunch is eaten in the cafeteria, your child may bring peanut butter, peanut or nut products for lunch. In the cafeteria there will be a designated peanut-free table where any classmate without peanut or nut products can sit. If your child sits at this table with a peanut or nut product, s/he will be asked to move to another table. This plan will help to maintain safety in the classroom while allowing non-allergic classmates to enjoy peanut/nut products in a controlled environment. Following lunch, the children will wash their hands prior to going to recess or returning to the class. The tables will be cleaned with soap, water and paper towels after each lunch.

We appreciate your support of these procedures. Please complete and return this form so that we are certain that every family has received this information. If you have any questions, please contact me.

x _____
Signature of Principal/Teacher/Nurse

I have read and understand the peanut/nut-free classroom procedures. I agree to do my part in keeping the classroom peanut and nut free.

Child's name:_____

Parent's signature: _____

Date: _____

Source: Massachusetts Department of Education

Form VII-2: Substitute Teacher Letter
Regarding Child with Allergy

Dear Substitute Teacher,

The students listed below in this class have life-threatening food allergies.

Please maintain the food allergy avoidance strategies that we have developed to protect these students.

Should a student ingest, touch or inhale the substance to which they are allergic (the allergen), a severe reaction (anaphylaxis) may follow requiring the administration of epinephrine (Epi-pen$^{®}$).

The Allergy Action Plan, which states who has been trained to administer epinephrine, is located _____.
Epinephrine is a life-preserving medication and should be given in the first minutes of a reaction.

Student	Allergies

Please treat this information confidentially to protect the privacy of the students. Your cooperation is essential to ensure their safety. Should you have any questions please contact the school nurse _____ or the principal _____.

_____
Classroom teacher

Source: Massachusetts Department of Education

Form VII-3: Sample Diabetes Management Plan

Effective Dates: _____

This plan should be completed by the student's personal health care team and parents/guardian. It should be reviewed with relevant school staff and copies should be kept in a place that is easily accessed by the school nurse, trained diabetes personnel, and other authorized personnel.

Student's Name: _____

Date of Birth: _____ Date of Diagnosis: _____

Grade: _____ Homeroom Teacher: _____

Physical Condition: _____ Type 1 Diabetes _____ Type 2 Diabetes _____

Contact Information

Mother/Guardian: _____

Address: _____

Telephone: Home: _____ Work: _____ Cell: _____

Father/Guardian: _____

Address: _____

Telephone: Home: _____ Work: _____ Cell: _____

Other Emergency Contacts:

Name: _____

Relationship: _____

Telephone: Home: _____ Work: _____ Cell: _____

Notify parents/guardian or emergency contact in the following situations:

_____

_____

Sample Diabetes Management Plan *(continued)*

Blood Glucose Monitoring

Target range for blood glucose: ____ 70-150 ____ 70-180 ____ Other: ____

Usual times to check blood glucose:_____

Times to do extra blood glucose checks (*check all that apply*):

____ before exercise

____ after exercise

____ when student shows signs of hyperglycemia

____ when student shows signs of hypoglycemia

____ other (explain): _____

Can student perform own blood glucose checks? ____ Yes ____ No

Type of blood glucose meter student uses: _____

Insulin

Usual Lunchtime Dose

Base dose of Humalog/Novolog/Regular insulin at lunch (circle type of rapid-/short-acting insulin used) is ____ units or does flexible dosing using ____ units/ ____ grams carbohydrate. Use of other insulin at lunch: (circle type of insulin used): intermediate/NPH/lente ____ units or basal/Lantus/Ultralente ____ units.

Insulin Correction Doses

Parental authorization should be obtained before administering a correction dose for high blood glucose levels. ____ Yes ____ No

____ units if blood pressure is ____ to ____ mg/dl

____ units if blood pressure is ____ to ____ mg/dl

____ units if blood pressure is ____ to ____ mg/dl

____ units if blood pressure is ____ to ____ mg/dl

____ units if blood pressure is ____ to ____ mg/dl

Can student give own injections? ____ Yes ____ No

Can student determine correct amount of insulin? ____ Yes ____ No

Can student draw correct dose of insulin? ____ Yes ____ No

____ Parents are authorized to adjust the insulin dosage under the following circumstances: _____

Sample Diabetes Management Plan *(continued)*

For Students with Insulin Pumps

Type of pump: _____ Basal rates: _____ 12 am to _____

_____ _____ to _____

_____ _____ to _____

Type of insulin in pump: _____

Type of infusion set: _____

Insulin/carbohydrate ratio: _____ Correction factor: _____

Student Pump Abilities/Skills	*Needs Assistance*	
Count carbohydrates	____ Yes	____ No
Bolus correct amount for carbohydrates consumed	____ Yes	____ No
Calculate and administer corrective bolus	____ Yes	____ No
Calculate and set basal profiles	____ Yes	____ No
Calculate and set temporary basal rate	____ Yes	____ No
Disconnect pump	____ Yes	____ No
Reconnect pump at infusion set	____ Yes	____ No
Prepare reservoir and tubing	____ Yes	____ No
Insert infusion set	____ Yes	____ No
Troubleshoot alarms and malfunctions	____ Yes	____ No

For Students Taking Oral Diabetes Medications

Type of medication: _____ Timing: _____

Other medications: _____ Timing: _____

Meals and Snacks Eaten at School

Is student independent in carbohydrate calculations and management? ___ Yes ___ No

Meal/Snack	*Time*	*Food content/amount*
Breakfast	_____	_____
Mid-morning snack	_____	_____
Lunch	_____	_____
Mid-afternoon snack	_____	_____
Dinner	_____	_____

Sample Diabetes Management Plan *(continued)*

Snack before exercise? _____ Yes _____ No

Snack after exercise? _____ Yes _____ No

Other times to give snacks and correct amount: _____

Preferred food snacks: _____

Foods to avoid, if any: _____

Instructions for when food is provided to the class (e.g., as part of a class party or food sampling event):

_____

_____

Exercise and Sports

A fast-acting carbohydrate such as _____ should be available at the site of exercise or sports.

Restrictions on activity, if any: _____

Student should not exercise if blood-glucose level is below _____ mg/dl or above _____ mg/dl or if moderate to large urine ketones are present.

Hypoglycemia (Low Blood Sugar)

Usual symptoms of hypoglycemia: _____

_____

Treatment of hypoglycemia: _____

_____

Urine should be checked for ketones when blood-glucose levels are above _____ mg/dl.

Treatment for ketones: _____

Supplies to Be Kept at School

_____ Blood-glucose meter, test strips, batteries   _____ Insulin pump and supplies

_____ Lancet device, lancets, gloves, etc.   _____ Insulin pen, needles cartridges

_____ Urine ketone strips   _____ Carbohydrate containing snack

_____ Insulin vials and syringes   _____ Glucagon emergency kit

Sample Diabetes Management Plan *(continued)*

Signatures

This Diabetes Medical Management Plan has been approved by:

_____   _____
Student's Physician/Health Care Provider   Date

I give permission to the school nurse, trained diabetes personnel, and other
designated staff members of _____ school to perform
and carry out the diabetes care tasks as outlined by _____'s
Diabetes Medical Management Plan. I also consent to the release of the information
contained in this Diabetes Medical Management Plan to all staff members and other
adults who have custodial care of my child and who may need to know this
information to maintain my child's health and safety.

Acknowledged and received by:

_____   _____
Student's Parent/Guardian   Date

_____   _____
Student's Parent/Guardian   Date

Source: U.S. Department of Health and Human Services

Form VII-4: Parent Letter Regarding MRSA

Dear Parents,

This letter is being sent to provide information regarding Methicillin-Resistant Staphlylococcus Aureus (MRSA) infections in schools.

MRSA infection is a type of staph infection that is resistant to some antibiotics. It has existed for decades but has just recently begun to become more prevalent in non-health care settings, including schools. Although MRSA infection is a cause for some concern, it is completely preventable and completely curable.

Our school district has posted information about MRSA infection and precautions that your child can take on our Web site at _____. Further information is available from the Centers for Disease Control and Prevention at www.cdc.gov. We are providing additional information in this letter to tell you what we are doing at our schools to guard against an outbreak. We are also offering suggestions you can follow at home.

Steps Being Taken at Our Schools:

School restrooms, locker rooms and team rooms are being disinfected on a daily basis, and the artificial turf on our athletic playing field is being disinfected once per week. We have placed spray bottles with disinfectant and gel disinfectant dispensers in all weight rooms. Supervisory personnel are instructing all students who use the weight room to disinfect weight room equipment before and after use. These students are also being instructed to use the gel disinfectant on their hands when they leave the weight room.

Steps to Take at Home:

The best way to prevent MRSA infection is to practice good hygiene habits. Keeping hands clean with soap and water or an alcohol-based hand soap is very important. Students should take a shower after engaging in sports activity. Cuts and scrapes must be kept clean and completely covered until they are completely healed. Contact with other people's wounds and bandages is to be avoided, as is the sharing of personal items, such as towels, toothbrushes and razors.

Thank you for your assistance.

Sincerely,

Superintendent

Form VII-5: Model Notification of FERPA Rights

The Family Educational Rights and Privacy Act (FERPA) affords parents and students over 18 years of age ("eligible students") certain rights with respect to the student's education records. These rights are:

1. The right to inspect and review the student's education records within 45 days of the day the School receives a request for access. Parents or eligible students should submit to the School principal [or appropriate school official] a written request that identifies the record(s) they wish to inspect. The School official will make arrangements for access and notify the parent or eligible student of the time and place where the records may be inspected.

2. The right to request the amendment of the student's education records that the parent or eligible student believes are inaccurate or misleading. Parents or eligible students may ask the School to amend a record that they believe is inaccurate or misleading. They should write the School principal [or appropriate official], clearly identify the part of the record they want changed, and specify why it is inaccurate or misleading. If the School decides not to amend the record as requested by the parent or eligible student, the School will notify the parent or eligible student of the decision and advise them of their right to a hearing regarding the request for amendment. Additional information regarding the hearing procedures will be provided to the parent or eligible student when notified of the right to a hearing.

3. The right to consent to disclosures of personally identifiable information contained in the student's education records, except to the extent that FERPA authorizes disclosure without consent. One exception, which permits disclosure without consent, is disclosure to school officials with legitimate educational interests. A school official is a person employed by the School as an administrator, supervisor, instructor, or support staff member (including health or medical staff and law enforcement unit personnel); a person serving on the School Board; a person or company with whom the School has contracted to perform a special task (such as an attorney, auditor, medical consultant, or therapist); or a parent or student serving on an official committee, such as a disciplinary or grievance committee, or assisting another school official in performing his or her tasks. A school official has a legitimate educational interest if the official needs to review an education record in order to fulfill his or her professional responsibility.

[Optional] Upon request, the School discloses education records without consent to officials of another school district in which a student seeks or intends to enroll.

Model Notification of FERPA Rights *(continued)*

[NOTE: FERPA requires a school district to make a reasonable attempt to notify the parent or eligible student of the records request unless it states in its annual notification that it intends to forward records on request.]

4. The right to file a complaint with the U.S. Department of Education concerning alleged failures by the School to comply with the requirements of FERPA. The name and address of the Office that administers FERPA are:

Family Policy Compliance Office

U.S. Department of Education

400 Maryland Avenue, SW

Washington, DC 20202-5901

[NOTE: In addition, an institution may want to include its directory information public notice, as required by Section 99.37 of the regulations, with its annual notification of rights under FERPA.]

Source: U.S. Department of Education

Form VII-6: Dealing with Suicidal Students

These are steps for key personnel to take when it appears that a student is at risk for committing suicide.

Staff:
1. Notify principal or other designated individual.

2. Respond by listening empathetically and gathering information.

3. Refer the student to a guidance counselor.

Guidance:
1. Gather information and check for lethality indicators.

2. Contact the student's parents or guardians.

3. If your assessment indicates the student is currently a suicidal risk, keep the student with you until a parent/guardian arrives for pickup.

4. Contact the school resource officer.

5. Provide the parents/guardians with a list of agencies for referral.

6. If the parents/guardians refuse to accept/seek help, contact the appropriate children and families services agency at phone _____.

7. Document all actions taken by school personnel.

8. Complete these follow-up steps:

   • Try to have the student commit to contact you or another adult if suicidal feelings return.

   • Make guidance appointments for the student on a continuing basis and monitor how the student is coping.

   • Contact parents/guardians to check on progress with referral agencies and to make them aware of student's behavior at school.

   • Keep the principal, other administrators and the student's teachers apprised of the student's situation.

Dealing with Suicidal Students *(continued)*

Social Worker:

1. May assist by contacting parents/guardians who cannot be reached by school personnel.

Administrator or Designee:

1. If suicide is attempted at school, contact superintendent or designee at telephone number _____.

2. If suicide is attempted at school, contact insurance representative at telephone number _____.

3. Provide support as needed.

4. Follow up with guidance department.

Source: University of Arkansas System, Criminal Justice Institute, School Violence Resource Center

Form VII-7: Announcement of Student Suicide

(To be read to students by the classroom teacher.)

TO: School Faculty
FROM: Principal
SUBJECT: (Crisis)
DATE:

John Doe committed suicide early Saturday morning. As a faculty, we extend our sympathy to John's family and friends.

We encourage all students to consider the tragic nature of this death and to realize that death is final. John's death is a reminder to us all that the act of taking one's own life is not an appropriate solution to any of life's problems nor is it an act of courage. Please let your teachers know if you would like to talk to a counselor or other staff member.

Funeral services for John will be held in _____
and there will not be a memorial service in this area. Expressions of sympathy may be sent to _____.

Source: Virginia Department of Education

Form VII-8: Announcement - Student Death
From Accident or Illness

As many of you are aware, we were sorry to hear that _____, a student in the _____ grade of our school, died on _____ from injuries in a car crash. As soon as we learn the funeral plans, we will announce them. Those of you who want to discuss your feelings about _____'s death should obtain a hall pass from your teacher to go to the library. This help will be available throughout the school day. Let us have a moment of silence. Thank you for your cooperation today.

Source: Virginia Department of Education

Form VII-9: Parent Letter: Unexpected Student Death

Dear Parents,

Yesterday, we learned that one of our first graders, _____, died while in the hospital. _____ had his tonsils removed over the past weekend. Complications set in after his parents took him home where he died yesterday afternoon.

Today, at school, each teacher read a short message about _____ to his/her class. We discussed what happened and how _____ died. We also stressed that many people have their tonsils out every day and have no problems with it. Our guidance counselor and our school psychologist were available throughout the day to talk with any student that may have had a particularly difficult time dealing with the news.

Any death is difficult for children to understand. _____'s death is particularly difficult due to his young age and its unexpectedness. The fact that _____ died while at the hospital and the fact that it was related to having his tonsils out may also be frightening for children, especially those who may need to have their own tonsils out in the future.

We recommend that you take some time to discuss death with your child. We suggest allowing your child to talk about how he/she feels and any fears or concerns he/she may have as a result of hearing this news. We are enclosing a list of suggestions to help you talk with your child about _____'s death and/or the death of any loved one.

If you feel that your child would benefit from talking with our guidance counselor or our school psychologist, please call us at the school and share your concerns.

The faculty, staff and students extend our heartfelt sympathies to the family and to all their friends. We, at the school, will miss _____ very much. He was our friend and we loved him.

Sincerely,

School Principal

Source: Virginia Department of Education

Form VII-10: Student/Parent Letter - Sudden Student Death

SCHOOL LETTERHEAD

Date

Dear Students and Parents:

On Friday, John Doe, a fifth-grade student at [School] was in a terrible accident. Apparently, John was hit by a car that was speeding and had crossed over the median strip to the wrong side of the road. John died instantly.

John's death is a tragic, emotional loss for the entire [School] family. I am sure all of us will make every effort to comfort and support John's family as they attempt to deal with this traumatic loss. There are no adequate words to express our sense of grief and sympathy for the family.

Because John's death is felt so deeply by so many, on Monday and thereafter as needed, we will bring in our crisis team to discuss this accident and loss with students and faculty.

We encourage each of you to discuss this loss with your child. In order to help you do so we are holding a parent meeting on [date], and [time], in the cafeteria of [School]. The topic will be ways to help children cope with loss and will be presented by
_____ , a local mental health professional.

John's family, friends, and the school are suffering deeply. Please join us in supporting John's family.

Sincerely,

Principal

(School)

Source: Virginia Department of Education

Form VII-11: Parent Letter Regarding Nutrition Habits

Dear Parent:

Children who learn to live healthy, live longer. By establishing healthy habits early in life, children can dramatically reduce their health risks and increase their chances for longer, more productive lives. We all want the best for our children. Here's how you can help.

The Brentwood Middle School Health Council encourages you to support our efforts to create a healthy school nutrition environment. We are promoting healthy food choices throughout our school – in the school meal programs, in vending machines, and at school-sponsored events. We are also supporting nutrition education and physical activity. You can help your children lead the healthiest lives possible by supporting our efforts to create a healthy school nutrition environment, and by reinforcing healthy habits at home.

Please join us and other parents on Tuesday, October 17 at 7:00 p.m. in the school auditorium for a meeting to learn more about the healthy school nutrition environment project and how you can get involved. Our keynote speaker, Dr. Roger Peterson, a national expert on education, will talk about the importance of nutrition to good health and academic performance.

Please call me at (827) 339-2525 if you have questions. Hope to see you on October 17.

Sincerely,

David Dewhurst, PhD

Principal

Source: United States Department of Agriculture

Form VII-12: Parent Letter Regarding Asthma

Dear Parent:

The school team at _____ school is looking forward to an excellent year for your child, _____.

Our School Asthma Management Program will provide the following health services:

- Access to the school nurse

- Help for students with asthma in following their asthma action plans

- Asthma education for all students in grade(s) _____

- Asthma in-service training for all school staff

- Indoor Air Quality (IAQ) Tools for Schools to promote a healthy environment

In order to provide the best possible school asthma management for your child, we request your assistance with the following:

Please

- Obtain an asthma action plan (a statement of your child's treatment goals, medication and peak flow plan, and environmental risk reduction measures) from your physician. Please be sure guidelines are included for managing symptoms during special school or off-site events (recess, gym, outdoor play, field trips, parties, art class, etc.). You may use the attached form.

- Meet with the school nurse – before school entry and as needed – to explain your child's condition, medication, devices, and environmental triggers.

- Submit a Medication Administration form for any medication that is administered in school. Please provide pharmacy-labeled medications, personally bring them to school, and keep them refilled as needed.

Parent Letter Regarding Asthma *(continued)*

- Meet with teachers to setup expectations for maintaining communication and continuity during absences.

- Prepare your child. Discuss and rehearse the medication plan; discuss how to handle symptoms, triggers, food restrictions, and school policies.

- Keep the school staff up to date on any changes in your child's asthma action plan.

- Keep your physician up to date on school services and supports for helping your child manage his or her asthma.

Thank you for working with us to assist your child.

Sincerely,

Principal (signature)

School Nurse (signature)

Source: U.S. Department of Education, U.S. Department of Health and Human Services

Form VII-13: Physician Letter Regarding Asthma

Dear _____:

The school team at _____ school is looking forward to an excellent year for your patient, _____.

Our School Asthma Management Program will provide the following health services:

- Access to the school nurse

- Help for students with asthma in following their asthma action plans

- Asthma education for all students in grade(s) _____

- Asthma in-service training for all school staff

- Indoor Air Quality (IAQ) Tools for Schools to promote a healthy environment

In order to provide the best possible school asthma management for your patient, we request your assistance with the following:

- Complete an asthma action plan or provide comparable information on another form and return to us at school.

- Complete a medication administration form for any medications that may need to be administered in school and return it to us at school. (Students may self-carry and administer their quick relief medications if you and the parents or guardians indicate approval on the form.)

- Inform us of additional patient needs.

- Assist us in supporting family priorities. Connect parents or guardians with each other, support groups, and resources such as the Allergy and Asthma Network/Mothers of Asthmatics (AAN/MA), the American Lung Association (ALA), and the Asthma and Allergy Foundation of America (AAFA).

Physician Letter Regarding Asthma *(continued)*

Let us know if you need information on educational rights and responsibilities (Individuals with Disabilities Education Act [IDEA] and Section 504 of the Rehabilitation Act of 1973) for your patients.

We look forward to working with you. Thank you for your help.

Sincerely,

Principal (signature)

School Nurse (signature)

Source: U.S. Department of Education, U.S. Department of Health and Human Services

Form VII-14: Parent Letter Regarding Flu

Dear Parent,

As you may know, flu can be easily spread from person to person. Therefore, we are taking steps to reduce the spread of flu in [School name]. We want to keep the school open to students and functioning in a normal manner during this flu season. **But, we need your help to do this.**

We are working closely with the [county/state education agency] and the [county/state] health department to monitor flu conditions and make decisions about the best steps to take concerning schools. We will keep you updated with new information as it becomes available.

If the flu becomes more severe, we may take additional steps to prevent the spread such as:

- conducting active fever and flu symptom screening of students and staff as they arrive at school

- making changes to increase the space between people such as moving desks farther apart and postponing class trips, and

- dismissing students from school for at least 7 days if they become sick.

For now we are doing everything we can to keep our school functioning as usual. Here are a few things you can do to help.

- **Teach your children to wash their hands** often with soap and water or an alcohol-based hand rub. You can set a good example by doing this yourself.

- **Teach your children not to share personal items** like drinks, food or unwashed utensils, and to cover their coughs and sneezes with tissues. Covering up their coughs or sneezes using the elbow, arm or sleeve instead of the hand when a tissue is unavailable.

- **Know the signs and symptoms of the flu.** Symptoms of the flu include fever (100 degrees Fahrenheit, 37.8 degrees Celsius or greater), cough, sore throat, a runny or stuffy

Parent Letter Regarding Flu *(continued)*

nose, body aches, headache, and feeling very tired. Some people may also vomit or have diarrhea.

- **Keep sick children at home** for at least 24 hours after they no longer have fever or do not have signs of fever, without using fever-reducing drugs. Keeping children with a fever at home will reduce the number of people who may get infected.

- **Do not send children to school if they are sick.** Any children who are determined to be sick while at school will be sent home.

For more information, [see the attached flyer/additional information and] and visit www.flu.gov, or call 1-800-CDC-INFO for the most current information about the flu. For more information about flu in our community and what our school is doing, visit [school/health department Web site] or call [appropriate phone number]. We will notify you of any additional changes to our school's strategy to prevent the spread of flu.

Sincerely,

[School administrator's name and signature]

Source: Centers for Disease Control

Form VII-15: Parent Letter Regarding Severe Flu

Dear Parent,

As you may know flu is spreading easily from person to person and school-age children are among the groups most affected. We are taking steps to prevent the spread of flu in [School name]. Currently, flu conditions in [name of county or area or in the United States] have become more severe. We want to keep the school open and functioning as normal for as long as possible. **We need your help to do this.**

We are working closely with the [county/state education agency] and the [county/state] health department to monitor flu conditions and make decisions about the best steps to take. Since flu conditions have become more severe, we are now implementing the following steps to prevent the spread of flu within our school.

- **Extending the time sick students or staff stay home** for at least 7 days, even if they feel better sooner. People who are still sick after 7 days should continue to stay home until at least 24 hours after their symptoms have gone away.

- **Allowing high risk students and staff to stay home.** Certain groups are at higher risk of developing serious complications from flu. These groups include children under the age of 5 years, pregnant women, people of any age who have chronic medical conditions (such as asthma, diabetes, or heart disease), and people age 65 years and older. These students and staff should consult their doctor to make the decision to stay home.

- **Conducting active fever and symptom screening** of students and staff upon arrival at school. School staff will ask students about symptoms suggestive of a respiratory infection such as fever, cough, sore throat, runny or stuffy nose, body aches and fatigue. Any student who has at least 2 of these symptoms will be separated from others, offered a surgical mask, and sent home as soon as possible.

- **Increasing social distances** (the space between people) at school. We will be rotating teachers between classrooms while keeping the same group of students in one classroom, canceling classes that bring students together from multiple

Parent Letter Regarding Severe Flu *(continued)*

classrooms, holding classes outdoors when possible, moving desks farther apart, dividing classes into smaller groups, discouraging use of school buses and public transit, moving classes to larger spaces to allow more space between students, and postponing class trips.

- **Dismissing students.** We will keep students home for [5-7] days and then reassess with the [county/state education agency] and the [county/state] health department. We will keep you informed of when students may return to school. During dismissal we will continue school work from home through [homework packets, web-based lessons, phone calls, etc.]. Staff will remain at school to develop and deliver lessons and materials and continue to provide [important services, school lunches, etc.]. We will also be [canceling, postponing] all school-related mass gatherings. This includes [sporting events, school dances, performances, rallies, commencement ceremonies, etc.].

Here are a few things you can do to help since flu conditions are now more severe.

- **Teach your children to wash their hands** often with soap and water. You can set a good example by doing this yourself.

- **Teach your children not to share personal items** like drinks, food or unwashed utensils, and to cover their coughs and sneezes with tissues. If they don't have a tissue, they should cough or sneeze into their upper sleeve, not their hands.

- **Know the signs and symptoms of the flu.** Symptoms of the flu include fever (100 degrees Fahrenheit, 37.8 degrees Celsius or greater), cough, sore throat, a runny or stuffy nose, body aches, headache, and feeling very tired. Some people may also vomit or have diarrhea.

- **Extend the time sick children stay home** for at least 7 days, even if they feel better sooner. People who are still sick after 7 days should continue to stay home until at least 24 hours after symptoms have gone away.

- **If a household member is sick, keep any school-age brothers or sisters home for 5 days** from the time the

Parent Letter Regarding Severe Flu *(continued)*

household member became sick. Parents should monitor
their health and the health of other school-age children for
fever and other symptoms of the flu.

- **Don't send children to school if they are sick.** Any
  children who are sick at school will be sent home. Staying
  home when sick will allow your children to rest and allows
  you to monitor their health closely. Keeping your sick child
  home is the responsible thing to do. It protects fellow
  students and school staff, especially those who are at higher
  risk of severe illness from the flu.

For more information, [see the attached flyer/additional information
and] visit www.flu.gov, or call 1-800-CDC-INFO for the most current
information about the flu. For more information about flu in our
community and what our school is doing, visit [school/health
department Web site] or call [appropriate phone number]. We will
notify you of any additional changes to our school's strategy to prevent
the spread of flu.

Sincerely,

[School administrator's name and signature]

Source: Centers for Disease Control

Form VII-16: Eating and Feeding Evaluation
Children with Special Needs

PART A			
Student's Name		Age	
Name of school	Grade Level	Classroom	
Does the child have a disability? If Yes, describe the major life activities affected.		Yes	No
Does the child have special nutritional feeding needs? If yes, complete Part B of this form and have it signed by a licensed physician.		Yes	No
If the child is not disabled, does the child have special nutritional or feeding needs? If Yes, complete Part B and have it signed by a recognized medical authority.		Yes	No
If the child does not require special meals, the parent can sign at the bottom and return the form to the school food service.			
PART B			
List any dietary restrictions or special diet.			
List any allergies or food intolerances to avoid.			
List foods to be substituted.			
List foods that need the following change in texture. If all foods need to be prepared in this manner, indicate "All." Cut up or chopped into bite-size pieces: Finely ground: Pureed:			
List any special equipment or utensils that are needed.			
Indicate any other comments about the child's eating or feeding patterns.			
Parent's Signature		Date:	
Physician or Medical Authority's Signature		Date:	

Source: U.S. Department of Agriculture

Form VII-17: Information Card Regarding Students with Special Dietary Needs (For Food Service Staff)

Student's Name	Teacher's Name

Special Diet or Dietary Restrictions

Food Allergies or Intolerances

Food Substitutions

Foods Requiring Texture Modifications:

Chopped:

Finely Ground:

Pureed or Blended:

Other Diet Modifications:

Feeding Techniques

Supplemental Feedings

Physician or Medical Authority:

Name:
Telephone:
Fax:

Additional Contact: Name: Telephone: Fax:	Additional Contact: Name: Telephone: Fax:

School Food Service Representative/Person Completing Form:
Title:

Signature:

Source: U.S. Department of Agriculture

Form VII-18: Food Allergy Action Plan

Name: _____

DOB: _____ Weight: _____

Allergy: _____

Asthma: Yes _____ (if yes, higher risk for a severe reaction) No _____

| Place student's photo here |

Extremely reactive to the following foods: _____

Therefore:

_____If checked, give epinephrine immediately for ANY symptoms if allergen was *likely* eaten.

_____If checked, give epinephrine immediately if allergen was *definitely* eaten, even if no symptoms are noted.

Any **SEVERE SYMPTOMS** after suspected or known ingestion:

One or more of the following:

LUNG: Short of breath, wheeze, repetitive cough

HEART: Pale, blue, faint, weak pulse, dizzy, confused

THROAT: Tight, hoarse, trouble breathing/swallowing

MOUTH: Obstructive swelling (tongue and/or lips)

SKIN: Many hives over body

Or **combination** of symptoms from different body areas:

SKIN: Hives, itchy rashes, swelling (e.g., eyes, lips)

GUT: Vomiting, diarrhea, crampy pain

→

1. **INJECT EPINEPHRINE IMMEDIATELY**
2. Call 911
3. Begin monitoring (see box below)
4. Give additional medications*
   a. Antihistamine
   b. Inhaler (bronchodilator) if asthma

*Antihistamines & inhalers/bronchodilators are not to be depended upon to treat a severe reaction (anaphylaxis). USE EPINEPHRINE.

MILD SYMPTOMS ONLY:

MOUTH: Itchy mouth

SKIN: A few hives around mouth/face, mild itch

GUT: Mild nausea/discomfort

→

1. **GIVE ANTIHISTAMINE**
2. Stay with student; alert healthcare professionals and parents
3. If symptoms progress (see above), USE EPINEPHRINE
4. Begin monitoring (see box below)

Medication/Doses

Epinephrine (brand and dose): _____

Antihistamine (brand and dose):_____

Other (e.g., inhaler-bronchodilator if asthmatic):_____

Food Allergy Action Plan *(continued)*

Monitoring

Stay with student; alert healthcare professionals and parents. Tell rescue squad epinephrine was given; request an ambulance with epinephrine. Note time when epinephrine was administered. A second dose of epinephrine can be given 5 minutes or more after the first if symptoms persist or recur. For a severe reaction, consider keeping student lying on back with legs raised. Treat student even if parents cannot be reached.

_____ _____   _____ _____
Parent/Guardian signature   Date   Physician/Healthcare Provider signature   Date

Source: Centers for Disease Control

Form VII-19: Suicide Notification Statement for Students

It is with great sadness that I have to tell you that one of our students, _____, has taken [his, her] own life. All of us want you to know that we are here to help you in any way we can.

A suicide death presents us with many questions that we may not be able to answer right away. Rumors may begin to circulate, and we ask that you not spread rumors you may hear. We'll do our best to give you accurate information as it becomes known to us.

Suicide is a complicated act. It is usually caused by a mental disorder such as depression, which prevents a person from thinking clearly about his or her problems and how to solve them. Sometimes these disorders are not identified or noticed; in other cases, a person with a disorder will show obvious symptoms or signs. One thing is certain: There are treatments that can help. Suicide should never, ever be an option.

Each of us will react to _____'s death in our own way, and we need to be respectful of each other. Feeling sad is a normal response to any loss. Some of you may not have known _____ very well and may not be as affected, while others may experience a great deal of sadness. Some of you may find you're having difficulty concentrating on your schoolwork, and others may find that diving into your work is a good distraction.

We have counselors available to help our school community deal with this sad loss and to enable us to understand more about suicide.

If you'd like to talk to a counselor, just let your teachers know.

Please remember that we are here to help you.

Respectfully,

Principal

Source: American Foundation for Suicide Prevention and Suicide Prevention Resource Center. 2011. After a suicide: A Toolkit for Schools. Newton, MA: Education Development Center, Inc

Form VII-20: Emergency Information for Individuals with Autism

Legal Name _____ Nickname _____

Parent/Guardian _____

Siblings _____

Signature consent (to release form to emergency responders)

_____

Address _____

City_____ State _____ Zip _____

Home phone _____ Cell phone _____

Work phone _____

Date of Birth _____ Age _____ Gender _____ Height _____ Weight _____

Eye color _____ Hair color _____

Scars (other identifying marks) _____

Medical Diagnosis _____

Special Diet or Diet Restrictions _____

_____

_____

_____

Medications (List name, dose and time to be taken) _____

_____

_____

_____

_____

Medication allergies _____

Other allergies _____

Health Insurance _____ Plan _____

Policy _____

Pharmacy _____ Phone number _____

Primary Care Physician _____ Phone number _____

Specialist _____ Phone number _____

Emergency Information for Individuals with Autism *(continued)*

Emergency Contacts

Name _____

Address _____

City_____ State _____ Zip _____

Home phone _____ Cell phone _____

Work phone _____

Name _____

Address _____

City_____ State _____ Zip _____

Home phone _____ Cell phone _____

Work phone _____

Name _____

Address _____

City_____ State _____ Zip _____

Home phone _____ Cell phone _____

Work phone _____

Common problems for the individual _____

_____

_____

Things to avoid _____

_____

Favorite places _____

_____

Source: Autism Safety Project, www.autismsafetyproject.org

Form VII-21: Food Allergy Policy Checklist

A comprehensive policy for the management of life-threatening food allergies in school and school-associated settings should be developed by school boards in partnership with school personnel (school administrators, 504 coordinators, licensed healthcare providers [e.g., registered nurse, physician], school health advisory council members, teachers, school nutrition staff, bus companies/drivers, after-school program personnel, etc.), students, families, and others particularly affected by, or involved in, the implementation of the policy.

A comprehensive policy addresses all of the following essential components:

1. Identification of students with food allergies and provision of school health services

2. Individual written management plans

3. Medication protocols: storage, access and administration

4. Healthy school environment: comprehensive and coordinated approach

5. Communication and confidentiality

6. Emergency response

7. Professional development and training for school personnel

8. Awareness education for students

9. Awareness education and resources for parents/guardians

10. Monitoring and evaluation

Source: The National School Boards Association, www.nsba.org/Board-Leadership/SchoolHealth/SelectedNSBAPublications/Food-Allergy/Safe-at-School-and-Ready-to-Learn.pdf

Form VII-22: Sample Response to Anaphylactic Shock

The purpose of this posting is to make all parents, staff and students aware of a medical issue involving a (school name) student having an extreme allergy to Axe Body Spray.

This allergy is potentially life-threatening for this student.

Most recently this student has been transported to the hospital by ambulance for emergency medical treatment due to this student being exposed to Axe Body Spray while attending school.

My request to all (school name) members is that we take into consideration this student's allergy to Axe Body Spray and refrain from using it as your cologne or fragrance of choice while attending (school name).

On behalf of this student's family and myself, thank you for your consideration.

Source: Freedom High School, Bethlehem, Pennsylvania, posted on the school's website.

**Form VII-23: Checklist: Steps to Take Within
24 Hours of a Nonfatal Food Allergy Reaction**

- Call parent or guardian to follow up on student's
  condition

- Review anaphylactic or allergic episode with parent
  or guardian and student:

  — identify allergen and route of exposure

  — discuss signs and symptoms with parent
    or guardian

  — review action steps taken

  — discuss positive and negative outcomes

  — discuss any needed revision to care plan based
    on the experience or outcome

- Discuss family's role with parent or guardian to
  improve outcomes

- Discuss school and home concerns to improve
  prevention, response and student outcomes

- Ask parent or guardian to replace epinephrine dose
  that was administered, if necessary

- Ask parent or guardian to follow up with health
  care provider

Source: Centers for Disease Control

Form VII-24: Sample Letter to Parents About Student Vaccinations

We all need shots (also called vaccinations or immunizations) to help protect us from serious diseases.

To help keep our community safe, [*your school name*] is proudly participating in National Immunization Awareness Month.

Shots can prevent serious diseases like the flu, measles and tuberculosis (TB). It's important to know which shots you need and when to get them.

- **[Add details about your local activities.]**

- **[Include quote from your organization.]**

Everyone age 6 months and older needs to get a flu shot every year. Other shots work best when they are given at certain ages.

Talk to your doctor or nurse to make sure that everyone in your family gets the shots they need.

Also, talk to school officials about required vaccinations – or required waivers – for student enrollment.

For more information, contact [*insert your school's point of contact.*].

Source: U.S. Department of Health and Human Services, www.healthfinder.gov

Form VII-25: Parent Letter Regarding Flu Prevention

Dear students, faculty, staff and parents,

As you may know, flu can be spread easily from person to person. Therefore, we are taking steps to prevent the spread of flu at [*name of institution*] for as long as possible, **but we need your help to accomplish this**.

We are working closely with the [*County/State*] health department to monitor flu conditions and make decisions about the best steps to take concerning our institution. We will keep you updated with new information as it becomes available to us.

For now, we are doing everything we can to keep our institution operating as usual. Here are a few things you can do to help:

- **Practice good hand hygiene** by washing your hands with soap and water, especially after coughing or sneezing. Alcohol-based hand cleaners also are effective.

- **Practice respiratory etiquette** by covering your mouth and nose with a tissue when you cough or sneeze. If you don't have a tissue, cough or sneeze into your elbow or shoulder, not into your hands. Avoid touching your eyes, nose, or mouth; germs are spread this way.

- **Know the signs and symptoms of the flu.** A fever is a temperature taken with a thermometer that is equal to or greater than 100 degrees Fahrenheit or 38 degrees Celsius. Look for possible signs of fever: if the person feels very warm, has a flushed appearance, or is sweating or shivering.

- **Stay home if you have flu or flu-like illness for at least 24 hours after you no longer have a fever** (100 degrees Fahrenheit or 38 degrees Celsius) or signs of a fever (have chills, feel very warm, have a flushed appearance, or are sweating). This should be determined without the use of fever-reducing medications (any medicine that contains ibuprofen or acetaminophen). Don't go to class or work.

- **Talk with your health care providers about whether you should be vaccinated for seasonal flu.** Also if you are at higher risk for flu complications from 2009 H1N1 flu, you should consider getting the H1N1 vaccine when it becomes available. People at higher risk for 2009 H1N1 flu complications include pregnant women and people with

Parent Letter Regarding Flu Prevention *(continued)*

chronic medical conditions (such as asthma, heart disease, or diabetes). For more information about priority groups for vaccination, visit *www.cdc.gov/h1n1flu/vaccination/acip.htm.*

If this year's flu season becomes more severe, we may take the following additional steps to prevent the spread of the virus:

- **Allow students, faculty, and staff at higher risk for complications to stay home.** These students, faculty, and staff should make this decision in consultation with their health care provider.

- **Find ways to increase social distances** (the space between people) in classrooms such as moving desks farther apart, leaving empty seats between students, holding outdoor classes and using distance learning methods.

- **Extend the time sick students, faculty, or staff stay home or in their residence.** During severe flu conditions sick people should stay home for at least 7 days, even if they feel better sooner. Those who are still sick after 7 days should continue to stay home until at least 24 hours after symptoms have gone away. Symptoms of flu include fever or chills *and* cough or sore throat. In addition, symptoms can include runny nose, body aches, headache, tiredness, diarrhea or vomiting.

- **Suspend classes.** This decision will be made together with local and state public health officials. The length of time classes should be suspended will depend on the goal of suspending classes as well as the severity and extent of illness.

For more information about flu in our community and what our institution is doing, visit [*institution's website*] or call [*appropriate phone number*].

For the most up-to-date information on flu, visit *www.flu.gov*, or call 1-800-CDC-INFO (232-4636). We will notify you by [*e-mail, institution's website, text message, Facebook, Twitter, etc.*] of any additional changes to our school's strategy to prevent the spread of flu on our campus.

Sincerely,

[*Institution administrator's name and signature*]

Source: www.flu.gov

Form VII-26: Restraint and Seclusion Checklist: 15 Principles

The ED, in collaboration with SAMHSA, has identified 15 principles that should be considered when developing and implementing policies and procedures to ensure that any use of restraint or seclusion in school does not occur, except when there is a threat of imminent danger of serious physical harm to the student or others, and occurs in a manner that protects the safety of all children and adults at the school.

1. Every effort should be made to prevent the need for the use of restraint and for the use of seclusion.

2. Schools should never use mechanical restraints to restrict a child's freedom of movement, and schools should never use a drug or medication to control behavior or restrict freedom of movement (except as authorized by a licensed physician or other qualified health professional).

3. Physical restraint or seclusion should not be used except in situations where the child's behavior poses imminent danger of serious physical harm to self or others and other interventions are ineffective and should be discontinued as soon as imminent danger of serious physical harm to self or others has dissipated.

4. Policies restricting the use of restraint and seclusion should apply to all children, not just children with disabilities.

5. Any behavioral intervention must be consistent with the child's rights to be treated with dignity and to be free from abuse.

6. Restraint or seclusion should never be used as punishment or discipline (e.g., placing in seclusion for out-of-seat behavior), as a means of coercion or retaliation, or as a convenience.

7. Restraint or seclusion should never be used in a manner that restricts a child's breathing or harms the child.

8. The use of restraint or seclusion, particularly when there is repeated use for an individual child, multiple uses within the same classroom, or multiple uses by the same individual, should trigger a review. And, if appropriate, revision of strategies currently in place to address dangerous behavior,

Restraint and Seclusion Checklist: 15 Principles *(continued)*

if positive behavioral strategies are not in place, staff should consider developing them.

9. Behavioral strategies to address dangerous behavior that results in the use of restraint or seclusion should address the underlying cause or purpose of the dangerous behavior.

10. Teachers and other personnel should be trained regularly on the appropriate use of effective alternatives to physical restraint and seclusion, such as positive behavioral interventions and supports, and only for cases involving imminent danger of serious physical harm, on the safe use of physical restraint and seclusion.

11. Every instance in which restraint or seclusion is used should be carefully and continuously and visually monitored to ensure the appropriateness of its use and safety of the child, other children, teachers and other personnel.

12. Parents should be informed of the policies on restraint and seclusion at their child's school or other educational setting, as well as applicable Federal, State or local laws.

13. Parents should be notified as soon as possible following each instance in which restraint or seclusion is used with their child.

14. Policies regarding the use of restraint and seclusion should be reviewed regularly and updated as appropriate.

15. Policies regarding the use of restraint and seclusion should provide that each incident involving the use of restraint or seclusion should be documented in writing and provide for the collection of specific data that would enable teachers, staff and other personnel to understand and implement the preceding principles.

Source: The U.S. Department of Education

Form VII-27: Seclusion/Restraint Documentation

Student's name: _____

School: _____

DOB: _____ Grade: _____

Student ID: _____

Person completing form: _____

Date of incident: _____ Time of incident: _____

Circle those that apply

- IEP

- Behavior Intervention Plan (BIP)

- 504 plan

Description of the incident leading up to seclusion, isolation and/or physical restraint: _____

_____

_____

_____

_____

_____

Please indicate and describe any of the following interventions that were used

Seclusion: confinement of a student alone in an enclosed space from which the student is physically prevented from leaving by locking hardware. Seclusion is allowed in emergency situations while awaiting the arrival of law enforcement personnel.

Description and duration: _____

_____

_____

_____

_____

_____

Seclusion/Restraint Documentation *(continued)*

<u>Seclusion</u>: confinement of a student alone in an enclosed space from which the student is physically prevented from leaving by locking hardware. Seclusion is allowed in emergency situations while awaiting the arrival of law enforcement personnel.

Description and duration: _____

_____

_____

_____

_____

<u>Isolation</u>: the confinement of a student alone in an enclosed space without locking hardware. Isolation is allowed after de-escalating procedures have failed, student's behavior poses a serious, probable threat of imminent physical harm to self or others, with parental approval as specified in the student's IEP, 504 plan or BIP.

Description and duration: _____

_____

_____

_____

_____

<u>Physical restraint</u>: the use of person-to-person physical contact to restrict the free movement of all or a portion of a student's body. It includes briefly holding a student without undue force for instruction or other purposes, briefly holding a student to calm them, taking a student's hand to transport them for safety purposes, physical escort or intervening in a fight. Physical restraint is allowed when less restrictive measures have not effectively de-escalated the situation, or with parental approval as specified in a student's IEP, 504 plan or BIP.

Description and duration: _____

_____

_____

_____

_____

Seclusion/Restraint Documentation *(continued)*

<u>Mechanical restraint</u>: Only as specified in the student's IEP, 504 plan or BIP with two exceptions: a. vehicle safety restraints shall be used according to state and federal regulations and b. mechanical restraints employed by law enforcement officers in school settings should be used in accordance with their policies and appropriate professional standards.

Description and duration: _____

_____

_____

_____

_____

Staff involved in the incident

Name and title _____

Name and title _____

Name and title _____

Name and title _____

Name and title _____

Was the student injured?   Yes   No

Description of injury, if applicable: _____

_____

_____

_____

Was any staff injured?   Yes   No

Description of injury, if applicable: _____

_____

_____

_____

Nurse Observation

Date: _____ Time: _____

Observations: _____

_____

_____

_____

Seclusion/Restraint Documentation *(continued)*

Parent/Guardian notification

Name and title: _____

Date: _____ Time: _____

Email or phone number: _____

_____

A student's parent or guardian shall be notified through verbal or electronic means of the emergency situation involving the use of seclusion, isolation or restraint as soon as possible, but no later than the end of the day of the incident. A student's parent or guardian shall also receive a written report of the emergency situation within 5 school days of the incident. The report shall include all of the following:

- Date, time of day, location, duration and description of the incident and interventions

- Events that led up to the incident

- Nature and extent of any injury to the student

- Name of district employee the parent or guardian can contact regarding the incident

- Plan to prevent the need for future use of seclusion, isolation or restraint

- Documentation that a nurse observed the student following the restraint

Description of consequences or discipline (if any) as a result of the incident: _____

_____

_____

_____

Signature of person completing this form   _____

Source: Rockwood School District, Missouri

THE JUDICIAL SYSTEM

In order to allow you to determine the relative importance of a judicial decision, the cases included in *Keeping Your School Safe & Secure: A Practical Guide* identify the particular court from which a decision has been issued. For example, a case decided by a state supreme court generally will be of greater significance than a state circuit court case. Hence a basic knowledge of the structure of our judicial system is important to an understanding of school law.

Almost all the reports in this volume are taken from appellate court decisions. Although most education law decisions occur at trial court and administrative levels, appellate court decisions have the effect of binding lower courts and administrators so that appellate court decisions have the effect of law within their court systems.

State and federal court systems generally function independently of each other. Each court system applies its own law according to statutes and the determinations of its highest court. However, judges at all levels often consider opinions from other court systems to settle issues which are new or arise under unique fact situations. Similarly, lawyers look at the opinions of many courts to locate authority which supports their clients' cases.

Once a lawsuit is filed in a particular court system, that system retains the matter until its conclusion. Unsuccessful parties at the administrative or trial court level generally have the right to appeal unfavorable determinations of law to appellate courts within the system. When federal law issues or constitutional grounds are present, lawsuits may be appropriately filed in the federal court system. In those cases, the lawsuit is filed initially in the federal district court for that area.

On rare occasions, the U.S. Supreme Court considers appeals from the highest courts of the states if a distinct federal question exists and at least four justices agree on the question's importance. The federal courts occasionally send cases to state courts for application of state law. These situations are infrequent and, in general, the state and federal court systems should be considered separate from each other.

The most common system, used by nearly all states and also the federal judiciary, is as follows: a legal action is commenced in district court (sometimes called trial court, county court, common pleas court or superior court) where a decision is initially reached. The case may then be appealed to the court of appeals (or appellate court), and, in turn, this decision may be appealed to the supreme court.

Several states, however, do not have a court of appeals; lower court decisions are appealed directly to the state's supreme court. Additionally, some states have labeled their courts in a nonstandard fashion.

In Maryland, the highest state court is called the Court of Appeals. In the state of New York, the trial court is called the Supreme Court. Decisions of this court may be appealed to the Supreme Court, Appellate Division. The highest court in New York is the Court of Appeals. Pennsylvania has perhaps the most complex court system. The lowest state court is the Court of Common Pleas. Depending on the circumstances of the case, appeals may be taken to either the Commonwealth Court or the Superior Court. In certain instances the Commonwealth Court functions as a trial court as well as an appellate court. The Superior Court, however, is strictly an intermediate appellate court. The highest court in Pennsylvania is the Supreme Court.

While supreme court decisions are generally regarded as the last word in legal matters, it is important to remember that trial and appeals court decisions also create important legal precedents. For the hierarchy of typical state and federal court systems, please see the diagram below.

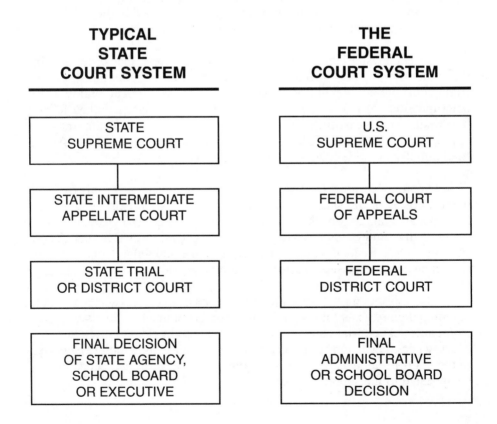

TYPICAL STATE COURT SYSTEM

- STATE SUPREME COURT
- STATE INTERMEDIATE APPELLATE COURT
- STATE TRIAL OR DISTRICT COURT
- FINAL DECISION OF STATE AGENCY, SCHOOL BOARD OR EXECUTIVE

THE FEDERAL COURT SYSTEM

- U.S. SUPREME COURT
- FEDERAL COURT OF APPEALS
- FEDERAL DISTRICT COURT
- FINAL ADMINISTRATIVE OR SCHOOL BOARD DECISION

Federal courts of appeals hear appeals from the district courts which are located in their circuits. Below is a list of states matched to the federal circuits in which they are located.

First Circuit	— Maine, Massachusetts, New Hampshire, Puerto Rico, Rhode Island
Second Circuit	— Connecticut, New York, Vermont
Third Circuit	— Delaware, New Jersey, Pennsylvania, Virgin Islands
Fourth Circuit	— Maryland, North Carolina, South Carolina, Virginia, West Virginia
Fifth Circuit	— Louisiana, Mississippi, Texas
Sixth Circuit	— Ohio, Kentucky, Michigan, Tennessee
Seventh Circuit	— Illinois, Indiana, Wisconsin
Eighth Circuit	— Arkansas, Iowa, Minnesota, Missouri, Nebraska, North Dakota, South Dakota
Ninth Circuit	— Alaska, Arizona, California, Guam, Hawaii, Idaho, Montana, Nevada, Northern Mariana Islands, Oregon, Washington
Tenth Circuit	— Colorado, Kansas, Oklahoma, New Mexico, Utah, Wyoming
Eleventh Circuit	— Alabama, Florida, Georgia
District of Columbia Circuit	— Hears cases from the U.S. District Court for the District of Columbia
Federal Circuit Appeals	— Sitting in Washington, D.C., the U.S. Court of Federal Circuit, hears patent and trade appeals and certain appeals on claims brought against the federal government and its agencies.

HOW TO READ A CASE CITATION

Generally, court decisions can be located in case reporters at law school or governmental law libraries. Some cases can also be located on the Internet through legal websites or official court websites.

Each case summary contains the citation, or legal reference, to the full text of the case. The diagram below illustrates how to read a case citation.

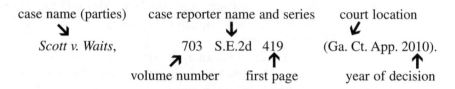

Some cases may have two or three reporter names such as U.S. Supreme Court cases and cases reported in regional case reporters as well as state case reporters. For example, a U.S. Supreme Court case usually contains three case reporter citations.

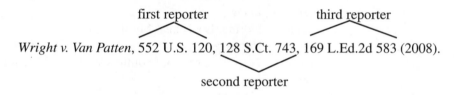

The citations are still read in the same manner as if only one citation has been listed.

Occasionally, a case may contain a citation which does not reference a case reporter. For example, a citation may contain a reference such as:

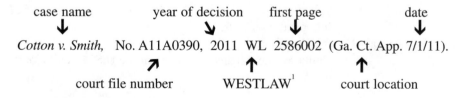

The court file number indicates the specific number assigned to a case by the particular court system deciding the case. In our example, the Georgia Court of Appeals has assigned the case of *Cotton v. Smith* the case number of "No.

[1]WESTLAW® is a computerized database of court cases available for a fee.

A11A0390" which will serve as the reference number for the case and any matter relating to the case. Locating a case on the Internet generally requires either the case name and date of the decision, and/or the court file number.

Below, we have listed the full names of the regional reporters. As mentioned previously, many states have individual state reporters. The names of those reporters may be obtained from a reference law librarian.

P.	**Pacific Reporter**	
	Alaska, Arizona, California, Colorado, Hawaii, Idaho, Kansas, Montana, Nevada, New Mexico, Oklahoma, Oregon, Utah, Washington, Wyoming	
A.	**Atlantic Reporter**	
	Connecticut, Delaware, District of Columbia, Maine, Maryland, New Hampshire, New Jersey, Pennsylvania, Rhode Island, Vermont	
N.E.	**Northeastern Reporter**	
	Illinois, Indiana, Massachusetts, New York, Ohio	
N.W.	**Northwestern Reporter**	
	Iowa, Michigan, Minnesota, Nebraska, North Dakota, South Dakota, Wisconsin	
So.	**Southern Reporter**	
	Alabama, Florida, Louisiana, Mississippi	
S.E.	**Southeastern Reporter**	
	Georgia, North Carolina, South Carolina, Virginia, West Virginia	
S.W.	**Southwestern Reporter**	
	Arkansas, Kentucky, Missouri, Tennessee, Texas	

F.	**Federal Reporter**	
	Decisions from the thirteen federal courts of appeals.	
F.Supp.	**Federal Supplement**	
	Decisions from federal district courts within the thirteen federal judicial circuits. *See The Judicial System, p. 521* for specific circuits.	
Fed.Appx.	**Federal Appendix**	
	Contains unpublished decisions of the U.S. Circuit Courts of Appeal.	

U.S.	**United States Reports**	
S.Ct.	**Supreme Court Reporter**	U.S. Supreme Court Decisions
L.Ed.	**Lawyers' Edition**	

GLOSSARY

Americans with Disabilities Act (ADA) - The ADA is a federal law that bars discrimination on the basis of disability in several contexts, including employment, access to programs and services provided by public entities, and access to places of public accommodation.

Assumption of Risk - A defense to a claim of negligence, in which the defendant asserts that the injured plaintiff is barred from recovery because he knowingly and voluntarily exposed himself to the hazard that caused his injury.

Biometrics - Methods and techniques used to identify individuals on the basis of a behavioral or physical characteristic or trait.

Class Action Suit - Federal Rule of Civil Procedure 23 allows members of a class to sue as representatives on behalf of the whole class provided that the class is so large that joinder of all parties is impractical, there are questions of law or fact common to the class, the claims or defenses of the representatives are typical of the claims or defenses of the class, and the representative parties will adequately protect the interests of the class. In addition, there must be some danger of inconsistent verdicts or adjudications if the class action were prosecuted as separate actions. Most states also allow class actions under the same or similar circumstances.

Clery Act - see Jeanne Clery Disclosure of Campus Security Policy and Campus Crime Statistics Act.

Crime Prevention Through Environmental Design (CPTED) - An approach to increasing safety in a variety of contexts, including the school context, that recognizes the important role that the design of the built environment can play in reducing the risk of criminal activity.

Cyberbullying - Student bullying that is perpetrated via the Internet, mobile phone or other electronic technology.

Due Process Clause - The clauses of the Fifth and Fourteenth Amendments to the Constitution which guarantee the citizens of the United States "due process of law" (see below). The Fifth Amendment's Due Process Clause applies to the federal government, and the Fourteenth Amendment's Due Process Clause applies to the states.

Due Process of Law - The idea of "fair play" in the government's application of law to its citizens, guaranteed by the Fifth and Fourteenth Amendments. Substantive due process is just plain *fairness*, and procedural due process is accorded when the government utilizes adequate procedural safeguards for the protection of an individual's liberty or property interests.

Enjoin - see Injunction.

Equal Protection Clause - The clause of the Fourteenth Amendment which prohibits a state from denying any person within its jurisdiction equal protection of its laws. Also, the Due Process Clause of the Fifth Amendment which pertains to the federal government. This has been interpreted by the Supreme Court to grant equal protection even though there is no explicit grant in the Constitution.

Establishment Clause - The clause of the First Amendment which prohibits Congress from making "any law respecting an establishment of religion." This clause has been interpreted as creating a "wall of separation" between church and state. The test frequently used to determine whether government action violates the Establishment Clause, referred to as the *Lemon* test, asks whether the action has a secular purpose, whether its primary effect promotes or inhibits religion, and whether it requires excessive entanglement between church and state.

Exclusionary Rule - A rule that allows criminal suspects to have excluded from consideration any evidence that is seized in violation of the Fourth Amendment.

42 U.S.C. §§ 1981, 1983 - Section 1983 of the federal Civil Rights Act prohibits any person acting under color of state law from depriving any other person of rights protected by the Constitution or by federal laws. A vast majority of lawsuits claiming constitutional violations are brought under § 1983. Section 1981 provides that all persons enjoy the same right to make and enforce contracts as "white citizens." Section 1981 applies to employment contracts. Further, unlike § 1983, § 1981 applies even to private actors. It is not limited to those acting under color of state law. These sections do not apply to the federal government, though the government may be sued directly under the Constitution for any violations.

Family Educational Rights and Privacy Act (FERPA) - A federal law that protects the privacy of student education records.

Fourth Amendment - Federal constitutional amendment that protects individuals from unreasonable searches and seizures.

Free Exercise Clause - The clause of the First Amendment which prohibits Congress from interfering with citizens' rights to the free exercise of their religion. Through the Fourteenth Amendment, it has also been made applicable to the states and their sub-entities. The Supreme Court has held that laws of general applicability which have an incidental effect on persons' free exercise rights are not violative of the Free Exercise Clause.

Government Accountability Office (GAO) - A federal agency that acts as the investigative arm of Congress. The GAO examines matters relating to the receipt and payment of public funds.

H1N1 Flu – Also referred to as swine flu based on early indications that it resembled influenza viruses that normally occur in pigs, 2009 H1N1 is an influenza virus that was first detected in humans in the United States in April 2009. In June 2009, the World Health Organization (WHO) declared that a pandemic of this flu had begun. Typically, those who contracted the virus recovered without the need for specialized medical treatment. But certain people, including people age 65 or older, people younger than five, pregnant women, and people with certain preexisting medical conditions, were at high risk of developing severe complications. In August 2010, the WHO announced that the virus had "largely run its course" but also noted the likelihood of continued localized outbreaks.

Incorporation Doctrine - By its own terms, the Bill of Rights applies only to the federal government. The Incorporation Doctrine states that the Fourteenth Amendment makes the Bill of Rights applicable to the states.

Individualized Educational Program (IEP) - The IEP is designed to give children with disabilities a free, appropriate education. It is updated annually, with the participation of the child's parents or guardian.

Individuals with Disabilities Education Act (IDEA) - Also known as the Education of the Handicapped Act (EHA), the Education for All Handicapped Children Act (EAHCA), and the Handicapped Children's Protection Act (HPCA). Originally enacted as the EHA, the IDEA is the federal legislation which provides for the free, appropriate education of all children with disabilities.

Injunction - An equitable remedy (see Remedies) wherein a court orders a party to do or refrain from doing some particular action.

Jeanne Clery Disclosure of Campus Security Policy and Campus Crime Statistics Act - A federal law requiring colleges and universities to disclose information regarding crime on and around campus.

Jurisdiction - The power of a court to determine cases and controversies. The Supreme Court's jurisdiction extends to cases arising under the Constitution and under federal law. Federal courts have the power to hear cases where there is diversity of citizenship or where a federal question is involved.

***Miranda* Warning** - Warning that police must provide to an individual in police custody before proceeding with questioning.

MRSA - MRSA, which stands for Methicillin-resistant staphylococcus aureus, is a type of staph bacteria that is resistant to certain antibiotics.

National Incident Management System (NIMS) - a system developed by the Secretary of Homeland Security to provide a national template that helps government, private, and nongovernmental organizations effectively coordinate efforts during crisis events.

Negligence per se - Negligence on its face. Usually, the violation of an ordinance or statute will be treated as negligence per se because no careful person would have been guilty of it.

Overbroad - A government action is overbroad if, in an attempt to alleviate a specific evil, it impermissibly prohibits or chills a protected action. For example, a law attempting to deal with street litter by prohibiting the distribution of leaflets or handbills could be challenged as overbroad.

Rehabilitation Act - Section 504 of the Rehabilitation Act prohibits employers who receive federal financial assistance from discriminating against otherwise qualified individuals solely on the basis of disability.

Remand - The act of an appellate court in returning a case to the court from which it came for further action.

Remedies - There are two general categories of remedies, or relief: legal remedies, which consist of money damages, and equitable remedies, which consist of a court mandate that a specific action be prohibited or required. For example, a claim for compensatory and punitive damages seeks a legal remedy; a claim for an injunction seeks an equitable remedy. Equitable remedies are generally unavailable unless legal remedies are inadequate to address the harm.

Res Judicata - The judicial notion that a claim or action may not be tried twice or re-litigated, or that all causes of action arising out of the same set of operative facts should be tried at one time. Also known as claim preclusion.

Safe and Drug-Free Schools and Communities Act - Federal law supporting programs that prevent violence in and around schools, prevent illegal alcohol, tobacco and drug use, and foster a safe and drug-free school environment.

Section 1981 & Section 1983 - see 42 U.S.C. §§ 1981, 1983.

Sheltering-in-place - A planned response to the danger presented by the possible release of environmental contaminants that calls for students and personnel to take refuge in a safe interior location.

Sovereign Immunity - The idea that the government cannot be sued without its consent. It stems from the English notion that the "King can do no wrong." This immunity from suit has been abrogated in most states and by the federal government through legislative acts known as "tort claims acts."

Special Relationship Doctrine - A legal doctrine by which a state defendant can be held liable for a person's injury if the state defendant took actions that created a legal duty to protect the person from injury.

Standing - The judicial doctrine which states that in order to maintain a lawsuit a party must have some real interest at stake in the outcome of the trial.

State-Created Danger Doctrine - A legal doctrine by which a state defendant can be held liable for a person's injury if the state's actions either created or significantly increased the danger that caused the injury.

Statute of Limitations - A statute of limitation provides the time period in which a specific cause of action may be brought.

Swine Flu - see H1N1 flu.

Summary Judgment - Also referred to as pretrial judgment. Similar to a dismissal. Where there is no genuine issue as to any material fact and all that remains is a question of law, a judge can rule in favor of one party or the other. In general, summary judgment is used to dispose of claims which do not support a legally recognized claim.

Supremacy Clause - Clause in Article VI of the Constitution which states that federal legislation is the supreme law of the land.

Title IX - Federal law barring discrimination on the basis of sex under any educational program or activity that receives federal financial assistance.

Title VI - A part of the Civil Rights Act of 1964 that prohibits discrimination based on race, color or national origin in programs or activities that receive federal financial assistance.

Title VII of the Civil Rights Act of 1964 (Title VII) - Title VII prohibits discrimination in employment based upon race, color, sex, national origin, or religion. It applies to any employer having fifteen or more employees. Under Title VII, where an employer intentionally discriminates, employees may obtain money damages unless the claim is for race discrimination. For those claims, monetary relief is available under 42 U.S.C. § 1981.

Vacate - The act of annulling the judgment of a court either by an appellate court or by the court itself. The Supreme Court will generally vacate a lower court's judgment without deciding the case itself, and remand the case to the lower court for further consideration in light of some recent controlling decision.

Writ of Certiorari - The device used by the Supreme Court to transfer cases from the appellate court's docket to its own. Since the Supreme Court's appellate jurisdiction is largely discretionary, it need only issue such a writ when it desires to rule in the case.

INDEX